# DICTIONARY OF ALTERNATIVE MEDICINE

Notice: The author and the publisher of this volume have taken care to make certain that the doses of drugs and schedules of treatment are correct and compatible with the standards generally accepted at the time of publication. Nevertheless, as new information becomes available, changes in treatment and in the use of drugs becomes necessary. The reader is advised to carefully consult the instruction and information material included in the package insert of each drug or therapeutic agent before administration. This advice is especially important when using, administering, or recommending new or infrequently used drugs. The author and publisher disclaim all responsibility for any liability, loss, injury, or damage incurred as a consequence, directly or indirectly, of the use and application of any of the contents of this volume.

98 99 00 01 02 / 10 9 8 7 6 5 4 3 2 1

Prentice Hall International (UK) Limited, *London*
Prentice Hall of Australia Pty. Limited, *Sydney*
Prentice Hall Canada, Inc., *Toronto*
Prentice Hall Hispanoamericana, S.A., *Mexico*
Prentice Hall of India Private Limited, *New Delhi*
Prentice Hall of Japan, Inc., *Tokyo*
Simon & Schuster Asia Pte. Ltd., *Singapore*
Editoria Prentice Hall do Brasil Ltda., *Rio de Janeiro*
Prentice Hall, *Upper Saddle River, New Jersey*

ISBN 0-8385-1620-3

9 780838 516201 90000

Editor-in-Chief: Cheryl L. Mehalik
Cover Designer: Mary Skudlarek

PRINTED IN THE UNITED STATES OF AMERICA

# Dedication

For my wife, Susan, who has tolerated more than her share

For my in-laws, Pete and Connie, my eternal lifeline

For my children, Joseph, Monica, and David, who've given me purpose

For my few friends, Harry M, MD, Myles K, MD, Rafael C, MD, and David Good

who believed, when I no longer could

In Memory of Jim McCusker (1939-1997)

Gilberto Beltran Garcia, MD (1951-1988)

# Introduction

Alternative medicine is defined as:

> '...*a heterogeneous set of practices that are offered as an alternative to conventional medicine, for the preservation of health and the diagnosis and treatment of health-related problems; its practitioners are often called healers'* [1]; these practices or alternative health care systems constitute a vast array of treatments and ideologies, which may be well-known, exotic, mysterious, or even dangerous, and are based on no common or consistent philosophy; the practitioners range from being sincere, well-educated, and committed to their form of healing, to charlatans, deprecatingly known as 'quacks.'

Alternative or complementary medicine has been an area of explosive growth in the health care industry[2]. The heightened interest in alternative approaches to treating disease by mainstream medical practitioners[3] is coupled with the recognition that more data is required before such therapies can be either sanctioned for broader use, or be limited by caveats.[4]

Therapies and management philosophies designated as 'alternative' fall into three groups:

**Formal therapeutic systems** Such systems have been developed over the course of hundreds to thousands of years and require formal training by their practitioners. Formal therapeutic systems include the 5000-year-old ayurvedic medicine, the 3000-year-old traditional Chinese medicine (acupuncture and Chinese herbal medicine), chiropractic, herbal medicine, homeopathy, naturopathy, and osteopathy. In the present work, many of the entries related to formal therapeutic systems carry the adjectival modifier, 'alternative.'

**Informal therapeutic systems** Such systems often developed by a well-intentioned individual who creates a 'school' dedicated to teaching the technique or system, the scientific foundation of which might be regarded as weak, often due to the sporadic and anecdotal nature of the claimed cures. Informal therapeutic systems include aromatherapy, biofeedback training, color therapy, energy medicine, hydrotherapy, iridology, light therapy, massage therapy, mind/body medicine, music therapy, sound therapy, and others. In the present work, many of the entries related to informal therapeutic systems carry the adjectival modifier, 'fringe.'

**Quackery** Such methods range from those that are harmless, but driven by a profit motive, to those that ruthlessly prey on victims of dread diseases, eg AIDS, cancer, and other terminal illnesses, for which the prognosis is poor and the likelihood of dying from the disease is very high. Unproven therapies and devices include laetrile, snake oil treatments, and radionic devices. In the present work, the entries related to potentially predatory practices carry an adjectival modifier, 'unproven' or, if the product, device, or its developer has been found guilty of a crime, 'fraud.'

Included in this work are terms that range from those with known therapeutic efficacy, to those in which the efficacy is uncertain at best, and possibly dangerous at worse. No judgment is made as to claims of efficacy. Inclusion of a therapeutic modality or substance is not to be construed as an endorsement of its efficacy. Whether a person believes that a particular therapy is effective or not is in part an act of faith, which must be validated by clinical observation of patients with similar conditions.

Also included in this work are modalities that are not specifically the domain of alternative therapies for physical, but rather for mental conditions. They are included in this work, as they are referred to in general texts of alternative medicine. Terminology from areas that have been associated with the alternative health care movement such as human (eg Amnesty International, Medecins sans Frontiers) and animal (eg Animal Liberation Front) rights were not included as inclusion of such material was both impractical and distracting.

This collection is derived in part from *The Dictionary of Modern Medicine* (Parthenon Publishing Group, Carnforth, UK, 1992) and the related *Current MedTalk* (Appleton & Lange, Stamford, CT, 1995), which were compiled because of a personal conviction that the language of the world in general, and of medicine specifically, had undergone drastic changes which were not being appropriately documented in the currently available lexicons. Sources used for compiling this collection are listed in the bibliography.

Joseph C Segen, MD
Lexicographer
Manhasset, NY
May, 1997

---

[1]New England Journal of Medicine 1992; 326:61.

[2]As evidenced by the changing in reimbursement policies by the governmental agencies and insurance carriers.

[3]As indicated by the recent conference given at Harvard Medical School (March 4-8, 1997).

[4]Alternative health care has been legitimitized in part by the opening of the Office of Alternative Medicine, which functions under the National Institutes of Health. The Office's role is to fund projects that would provide data on the efficacy or inefficacy of alternative therapies.

**A.A.A.O.M.** American Association of Acupuncture and Oriental Medicine, see there

**A.A.M.A.** American Academy of Medical Acupuncture, see there

**A.A.N.P.** American Association of Naturopathic Physicians, see there

**A.A.O.** American Academy of Osteopathy, see there

**Aaron's rod** 1. Goldenrod, see there, *Solidago canadensis* 2. Mullein, see there, *Verbascum thapsus*

**abdomen** see *Hara*

**abdominal breath** AYURVEDIC MEDICINE A type of breathing taught in yoga, in which the practitioner breathes through the nose, inhaling and expanding only the abdominal muscles; this is followed by the diaphragm breath, and the upper breath, which are linked in a wavelike movement; the three comprise the so-called 'complete breath of yoga'. See Complete breath, Diaphragm breath, Upper breath, Yoga

**abdominal segment** ALTERNATIVE PSYCHOLOGY The sixth (of seven) segment of the body according to Reich, which may express latent sexual repression through muscular armoring; this defense may be resolved by massage and deep breathing. See Armoring, Body armor, Reich, Reichian therapy

***abhyanga*** Ayurvedic massage, see there

***Abies balsamea*** Popularly known as balsam fir, see there

**Dr Albert Abrams** An American physician (1863-1924) who was dubbed the '*Dean of the 20th Century Charlatans*;' Abrams earned a medical degree at Heidelberg, and another at what is now Stanford University Medical School; his books and writing were well-received and he served as Vice President of the California Medical Society; he abruptly switched to quack methods in the early 1900s; he died shortly before the onset of the legal backlash of his unusual practices (*Armstrong, 1991*). See Oscilloscope, Radionics

**Abrams box** Abrams' generator, see there

**Abrams generator** Abrams' box HEALTH FRAUD A device invented by Dr Albert Abrams, which he claimed measured biocurrents through fluctuation in electrical resistance in a wire, which could be used to assess disharmonies or distortions in an individual's energy patterns that translate into disease; the generator and Abrams' theories of radionics were discredited. See Radionics; Cf De la Warr box, Drown box, Emanometer

**abreaction** PSYCHOLOGY A general term for emotional release associated with remembering and resolving mentally traumatic experiences that were repressed in childhood

**absent healing** PARANORMAL PHENOMENA 1. Prayer for the sick, see there 2. Absentee healing, distant healing, distance healing, remote healing, teletherapeutics The alleged treatment of a patient through various techniques, including meditation, prayer, magic, spirit mediums or doctors, or telepathy, which are believed to be judgement transmitted to a distantly located patient; it is a permutation of faith healing, in which the healer projects positive healing energy. See Faith healing, Psychic healing

**absentee healing** 1. Prayer for the sick, see there 2. Absent healing, see there

**absinthe** Wormwood, see there, *Artemisia absinthium*

**absinthium** Wormwood, see there, *Artemisia absinthium*

**absolute oil** FRINGE MEDICINE-AROMATHERAPY An essential oil used in aromatherapy that is prepared by enfleurage, which is more concentrated than oils prepared by steam distillation. See Aromatherapy, Enfleurage, Essential oil

**accommodation** Near and far focusing ALTERNATIVE OPHTHALMOLOGY One of the exercises used in the Bates method of vision training, which consists of changing the point of focus from near to far distances 10 to 20 times. See Bates vision training

**Accutane baby syndrome** Vitamin A embryopathy, see there

**acemannin** ALTERNATIVE PHARMACOLOGY A complex sugar obtained from *Aloe vera*, which is administered as a concentrate or injected; it has been anecdotally reported to have antiretroviral activity (*Am Med News 21 Nov 1994 p13*); Cf AIDS fraud

***Aceranthus sagittatum*** Horny goat weed, see there, *Epimedium sagittatum*

**ACES** ALTERNATIVE PHARMACOLOGY A regionally popular acronyn for the major antioxidants in the diet–vitamin A and beta carotene, vitamin C, vitamin E, and selenium; increased consumption of the ACES group is believed to reduce the effects of aging and stimulate the immune system

**acetyl L-carnitine** ALTERNATIVE PHARMACOLOGY A form of carnitine, an amino acid with antioxidant activity, which is thought to metabolize lipofuscin and age-related pigment accumulations; it is believed to be of use in attenuating age-associated memory impairment and Alzheimer's disease, and may increase longevity; acetyl-L-carnitine is present in meats (beef, chicken, pork), dairy products, fruits, vegetables, and grains

***Achillea millefolium*** Popularly known as yarrow, see there

***Achyranthes bidentata*** *Niou hsi* CHINESE MEDICINE A perennial herb, the root of which is used in Chinese medicine as a diuretic, cardiotonic, for pain in the lower back and knees, epistaxis, and menstrual disorders. See Chinese herbal medicine

**acid aerosol** PUBLIC HEALTH Colloidal suspensions of hydrogen ion-containing particles that form the so-called 'summer haze' generated by sulfur dioxide ($SO_2$) and nitrogen dioxide emissions from coal-burning electrical power plants; acid aerosols are transformed into ammonium bisulfate, sulfuric and nitric acids and coupled to low level ozone, where they are inculpated in pulmonary dysfunction in those who exercise during the warm weather. See Acid haze, Acid rain, Air pollution, Environmental disease

Note: Acid 'rain' derives from the same sources

**acid haze** PUBLIC HEALTH Air laden with sulfur dioxide, which causes a haziness in otherwise clear air. See Acid aerosols, Acid rain, Air pollution, Environmental disease

**acid rain** ENVIRONMENT Precipitation laced with air pollutants, produced predominantly by power plants that burn coal of variable purity, generating sulfur dioxide and nitrous oxide, lowering the pH of precipitation. See Acid aerosols, Acid haze, Air pollution, Environmental disease

**acidophilus** see *Lactobacillus acidophilus*

**aconite** *Aconitum napellus*, friar's cap, monkshood, wolfsbane HERBAL MEDICINE Given aconite's toxicity, it is not used in herbal medicine; in homeopathy, the concentration of aconite is extremely low TOXICITY Anxiety, blurred vision, burning, cardiac arrhythmias, chest pain, diaphoresis, dyspnea, impaired

**aconite** *Aconitum napellus*

speech, muscular weakness, nausea, paresthesias, vertigo, vomiting, and possibly death due to respiratory failure or ventricular fibrillation. See Botanical toxicity, Poisonous plants HOMEOPATHY *Aconite* A homeopathic remedy for treating swelling, fever, infections, restlessness, anxiety and panic attacks, and paresthesias; it has also been used for anginal pain, arrhythmias, arthritis, asthma, bronchitis, respiratory infections, laryngitis, sore throat, and toothaches. See Homeopathy

***Acorus calamus*** Popularly known as sweet flag, see there

**ACPS-R** ALTERNATIVE ONCOLOGY A polysaccharide identified in the root of the Chinese herb, *Actinidia chinensis*, which is said to normalize the immune system and may be of use as an adjuvant antitumor therapy (*Moss, 1992*). See Unproven methods for cancer management

***Actaea racemosa*** HERBAL MEDICINE Black cohosh, see there, *Cimicifuga racemosa* HOMEOPATHY See *Cimic*

**actinidia** See ACPS-R

**activated charcoal** Medicinal charcoal A substance that is the residue of the destructive distillation of organic materials, resulting in carbonaceous granules (charcoal); activated charcoal has been heated to 200ºC to remove volatile gases, and is effective in removing various substances from a fluid or gas of interest ALTERNATIVE PHARMACOLOGY Acti-vated charcoal has been used in an oral capsule form to reduce low density lipoprotein-cholesterol and raise high-density lipoprotein-cholesterol (*Fox, 1996*) CLINICAL TOXICOLOGY Activated charcoal is used for early management of oral intoxications and is effective against most toxic substances except mercury, iron, lithium, and cyanide; if the drug has an enterohepatic cycle, as do barbiturates, glutethimide, morphine and other narcotics and tricyclic antidepressants, activated charcoal may be repeated for up to 24 hours; adult dose 50–100 g INDUSTRIAL HYGIENE Activated charcoal can be used to purify gases, as a deodorant, decolorant, and filtering agent

**active muscle relaxation technique** ALTERNATIVE MEDICINE A type of bodywork that is used to relax overly active muscles and manage soft tissue pain; the technique requires isometric contractions of either the overactive muscle, or its antagonist(s) against resistance; once the patient learns the technique, he becomes quasi-independent of the therapist and performs it on his own; the method is complementary to, but not a substitute for, passive muscle massage and chiropractice techniques. See Bodywork

**actualism** *Agni* yoga, fire yoga, light work A modern form of yoga that is intended to integrate the mind, body, personality, and spirit, which is believed to 'awaken' and 'empower' the individual. See Bodywork

**actualism bodywork** ALTERNATIVE MEDICINE A system of bodywork practiced at the New York Actualism Center, which is believed to awaken a person to his inner consciousness of the 'indwelling Creator' and His love; the system has 14 patterns of bodywork, each of which is designed to increase sensory awareness and increase a person's sense of self-fulfillment. See Bodywork

**acupoint** CHINESE MEDICINE An acupressure point that is believed to be a relay station for the flow of energy (*chi* or *qi*) through the meridians and collateral neural pathways. See Acupuncture, Meridian

**acuball technique** A permutation of acupressure that is performed by a person on himself, using soft rubber or other balls to increase local pressure. See Chinese reflex balls; Cf Gold ball technique

**acupressure** Acupressure massage, G-jo, jin shin do, shin tao ALTERNATIVE MEDICINE A 4000-year-old Oriental technique that combines massage and features of acupuncture; in the usual format, the practitioner uses the fingers, knuckles, and thumbs, less commonly the palms, elbows, and feet, to apply pressure for a period of 3 to 10 seconds on the same points that are used in acupuncture; the pressure points are specific for each meridian or energy channel; acupressure is believed to balance the natural flow of energy through the body and enhance natural vital forces; anecdotal reports suggest that acupressure may be effective in treating such diverse conditions as arthritis, bruxism, claustrophobia, common cold, gastrointestinal tract problems including nausea, vomiting, and irritable bowl syndrome, gout, gynecologic complaints, insomnia, laryngitis, migraines, painful conditions (eg myalgia, neuralgia, sciatica, slipped or prolapsed vertebral disks), renal disease, sports injuries, stuttering, sweating, tinnitus, and vertigo; acupressure therapists undergo 150-hour basic to 850-hour advanced training programs. See Acupuncture, Barefoot shiatsu, Bodywork, Acu-yoga, Do-in, Jin Shin Do® Bodymind Acupressure™, Jin Shin Jyutsu, Massage, Shiatsu, Tui-na, Zen shiatsu *RESOURCE: Acupressure Institute, 1533 Shatttuck Ave, Berkeley, CA 94709 ☎ 1.510.845.1059*

**acupressure massage** Acupressure, see there

**acupuncture** Needle treatment CHINESE MEDICINE A system of health care that has been practiced in China for more than 4000 years; acupuncture balances the body's 'life force' by inserting fine needles in or beneath the skin at one of 365 to 2000 (depending on the acupuncturist) where horizontal and vertical 'energy' lines meet along the 12 (or 14) major meridians; these lines and points are said to represent various internal organs or tissues; while acupuncture can relieve pain and to produce surgical anesthesia, the data supporting its use is weak

▶ **HYPOTHESES, MECHANISM OF ACUPUNCTURE'S ANESTHETIC EFFECT**

- Release of endogenous endorphins and enkephalins
- Placebo response
- Autosuggestive phenomena
- Alteration of the flow of body energy or electricity
- Gate theory, in which the acupuncture needles may block the flow of pain along a neural pathway other than that which is normal for painful sensations

Reports (anecdotal and otherwise) suggest that acupuncture may be effective in treating such diverse conditions as addiction disorders, agoraphobia, allergies, angina pectoris, anorexia, anxiety, arthritis, bronchitis, bruxism, bunions, the common cold, dry mouth, dysmenorrhea, eczema, emphysema, fatigue, fluid retention, gastrointestinal tract problems including nausea, vomiting, and irritable bowl syndrome, hay fever, headaches, hypo- and hypertension, infertility, insomnia, mental depression, migraines, various painful conditions including neuralgia, mood swings, obesity, panic attacks, periodontal disease, post-partum depression, premenstrual syndrome, prostate disease, sciatica, slipped or prolapsed vertebral disks, renal disease, sexual problems, sinusitis, sports injuries, stasis (decubitus) ulcers, stress, thyroid disease, tinnitus, tooth extraction, vertigo, warts, weight increase or loss. See Akabane test, Auricular therapy, Five element acupuncture, Meridians, Moxibustion, Tongue diagnosis; Cf Acupressure, Bodywork, Massage, Osteopuncture *RESOURCE: American Association of Acupuncture and Oriental Medicine, 433 Front St, Catasauqua, PA 18032 ☎ 1.610.433.1433*

Note: When genuine acupuncture is compared to sham acupuncture to control moderate stable angina, there is no significant difference (*J Intern Med 1990; 227:25*)

**acupuncture therapy** Acupuncture, see there

**acupuncturist** A practitioner of acupuncture; to be formally designated as an acupuncturist, the practitioner must be certified by the National Commission for Acupuncturists; there are currently approximately 5000 acupuncture practitioners in the US, and 30 schools that offer training in acupuncture; the curriculum consists of 2400 hours of instruction taken over 3 to 4 years; some acupuncturists are medical doctors (MDs), many of whom belong to the American Academy of Medical Acupuncture *RESOURCE: American Academy of Medical Acupuncture, 5820 Wilshire Blvd, Suite 500, Los Angeles, CA 90036 ☎ 1.213.937.5514*

**acuscope** Electro-Acuscope™, see there

**Acu-Stop 2000** A proprietary device worn on the ear, which is claimed to act on the acupoints that suppress the appetite, and obviate the need for dieting in the obese; see Auricular acupuncture

**acu-yoga** A form of acupressure in which yogic positions are used to press on acupressure points with the whole body rather than with just the hands; acu-yoga is believed by its advocates to be of particular use in treating menstrual dysfunction, premenstrual syndrome, and in stimulating the immune system. See Acupressure, Shiatsu, Yoga

**adaptation energy** *Courage–Lord Moran (quoted in D Watson, 1995)*; adaptation energy is that which a person expends when subjected to a severe emotional or physical trauma; according to H Selye, there is a limited amount of adaptation energy which, once it is exhausted, leads to burnout; see Burnout

**adaptation response** ALTERNATIVE PSYCHOLOGY A response to stress, in which an organism, eg animal, sentient being, or human prepares to resist a stressful mental situation by repressing emotions, or physical situation (eg trauma or war) by stiffening joints and other flight-or-fight responses; according to H Selye, the adaptation response is preceded by an alarm stage, and followed by a burnout stage. See Flight-or-fight response; Cf Alarm stage, Burnout

**adaptogen** A generic term for a family of natural substances, which are believed to compensate for fluctuations in homeostasis; adaptogens are believed to act on serum glucose, white blood cells, temperature, blood pressure, and pulse, by increasing or decreasing the substance of interest; ginseng is regarded by some as the prototypic adaptogen

**adaptogenic effect** See Adaptogen

**adderwort** Bistort, see there

**additives** Food additives, see there

***Adhayatma* yoga** *Adhyata* yoga FRINGE MEDICINE The form of yoga that seeks the pathway to transcendental wisdom by overcoming identification with the body and mind. See Ayurvedic medicine, Yoga

***Adhyatma* yoga** *Adhayata* yoga, see there

**adjustment** CHIROPRACTIC A general term for any of a number of manipulations used by chiropractors to reposition misaligned vertebrae and other joints; see Chiropractic

**adrenal type** FRINGE NUTRITION An endocrine profile based on a hypothesis advanced by E Abravanel, MD, that each person has a dominant endocrine organ; according to Abravanel, each type of person craves and overeats certain foods in an effort to stimulate that organ; adrenal types are believed to crave cholesterol-rich and salty foods, both of which stimulate the adrenal glands; adrenal type men tend to be large and strong; adrenal type women gain weight in the waist and breasts; adrenal types are advised to consume a vegetarian diet and parsley tea. See Body type, Diet

**adrenochrome** A term coined by Drs Hoffer and Osmond for a metabolic product of adrenaline, which they believed to be responsible for schizophrenia (*Kastner, 1993*)

***Aegle sepiaria*** Trifoliate orange, see there, *Poncircus trifoliata*

**aerion therapy** Air ionization therapy, see there

**Aerobic Dance™** A proprietary form of aerobic exercise developed in 1969 by an American, Jacki Sorensen; a complete Aerobic Dance™ routine consists of a flexibility routine, designed to increase the elasticity of the muscles, a warm-up routine, which incorporates stretching into a dance, which slowly accelerates the heart rate and increases the muscle temperature, followed by the dance routines themselves, which last from 20 to 30 minutes, and ending with a cool-down routine with stretching. See Aerobic exercise

**aerobic exercise** A generic term for cardiorespiratory exercises (eg rapid walking, jogging, bicycling, swimming, and dancing) that are performed at 60 to 70% of the maximum heart rate for a period of 20 to 30 minutes; intense aerobic exercise results in the re-synthesis of high energy compounds in the presence of oxygen, and improves circulation, controls weight, and glucose levels; the energy expenditure is maximized when performing rhythmic contractions of large muscles over distance (eg jogging) or against gravity (eg jazz-dancing); both of the above are types of 'endurance' training, and cause physiologic cardiac hypertrophy and with time, a desirable bradycardia; some experts recommend at least 3 sessions of aerobic exercise/week; see Aerobic dancing, Exercise, Vigorous exercise; Cf Anaerobic exercise

Note: Aerobic exercise can be initiated as early as 6-8 weeks pospartum and has no adverse effect on lactation (*N Engl J Med 1994; 330:449OA*)

***Aesculus hippocastanum*** Popularly known as horse chestnut, see there

***Aesclepias tuberosa*** Popularly known as pleurisy root, see there

**affirmation** ALTERNATIVE PSYCHOLOGY A statement of intention that is made as if it were a fact; affirmations are elements central to positive thinking, a concept championed by Emile Coué, the creator of autosuggestion therapy, and subsequently by Normal Vincent Peale; Coué suggested that his clients repeat affirmative 'mantras,' eg '*...every day, in every way, I am getting better and better...*'. See Autosuggestion therapy, Pealeism

**affluent diet** Western diet CLINICAL NUTRITION A diet characterized by a marked increase in fat, saturated fat, cholesterol, and calories, which is commonly consumed in wealthier nations; this regimen is believed to be responsible for the marked increase in cardiovascular disease typical of North Americans and northern Europeans (*N Engl J Med 1992; 327:52c*); Cf Mediterranean diet

**African holistic health** ETHNOMEDICINE A general term for any of a number of healing systems indigenous to Africa; in contrast to Western medicine–which is based on diagnosing and treating one part of a person, African health systems address the physical, mental and spiritual causes of disease, which affect the the entire person. See Ethnomedicine

**agape-eros center** ALTERNATIVE PSYCHIATRY One of four 'ontological being centers' defined in the construct of organismic psychotherapy, a form of Reichian therapy; the agape-eros center is located in the chest and mediates open interactions with others. See Ontological being centers, Organismic psychotherapy

**agar** *Gelidium cartilagineum*, red seaweed HERBAL MEDICINE A highly hydrophilic seaweed used as a bulk laxative. See Bulk laxative, Herbal medicine, Laxative

**agastache** *Agastache rugosa*, patchouli, pogostemon CHINESE MEDICINE An aromatic herb, the root of which is used for gastrointestinal complaints (bloating, diarrhea, nausea, vomiting), morning sickness, poor appetite, and afebrile colds. See Chinese herbal medicine

***Agastache rugosa*** Popular known as agastache, see there

**agila wood** Eagle wood, see there, *Aquilaria agallocha*

**aging** The multifaceted process in which bodily structures and functions undergo a negative deviation from the optimum; aging phenomena include decline in memory, muscular strength, manual dexterity, cardiac output, auditory and visual acuity, loss or thinning of hair, decreased muscle mass, increased body fat, increased risk of cancer, diabetes mellitus, infections, osteoarthritis, and osteoporosis with accompanying decrease in height related to a decrease in the intervertebral space. See Life-extending diet

***agni dhatu*** *Agni dhatu* therapy, *samadhi* therapy AYURVEDIC MEDICINE A spiritual or 'higher power'-related form of bodywork believed to '*...tranquilize the subconscious and cause core tissues to "bloom"*' (*Raso, 1994*)

***agni dhatu* therapy** *Agni dhatu*, see there

***agni* yoga** Actualism, see there

***Agrimonia eupatoria*** Popularly known as agrimony, see there

**agrimony** *Agrimonia eupatoria*, church steeples, cocklebur, cockleburr, philanthropos, stickwort HERBAL MEDICINE An herb with a high content of tannin which is anti-inflammatory, anti-microbial, astringent, hemostatic, and an intestinal tonic; it is used to treat athlete's foot, diarrhea, gastric ulcers, colitis, gallstones, cirrhosis, renal disease, and to lower uric acid levels in gout. See Herbal medicine, Musket-shot water

***Agropyron repens*** Popularly known as couch grass, see there

**ague grass** Colicroot, see there, *Aletris farinosa*

**ague root** Colicroot, see there, *Aletris farinosa*

**ague tree** Sassafras, see there, *Sassafras albidum*

**agueweed** Boneset, see there, *Eupatorium perfoliatum*

**aguru** Eagle wood, see there, *Aquilaria agallocha*

***Ah shi* point** Alarm point, see there

**AIDS fraud** AIDS quackery HEALTH FRAUD A general term for any form of health care fraud committed against patients with AIDS, which is estimated to have been perpetrated against 10% or more of those with AIDS; AIDS fraud is committed almost invariably for financial gain on the part of the perpetrator; it is similar to many unproven methods for cancer management and differs only in the agents being used; AIDS therapies identified by the FDA as frankly fraudulent are CanCell, hydrogen peroxide therapy, and ozone treatment; herb-based therapies that have been anecdotally reported to be of some benefit in treating AIDS include acemannan, bitter melon and its protein extract, curcumin, glycyrrhizin, MAP-30, megadoses of vitamins, and Chinese herbal formulae (*Am Med News 21 Nov 1994 p13*). See Acemannin, Bitter melon, CanCell, Curcumin, Glycyrrhizin, Hydrogen peroxide therapy, MAP-30, Ozone treatment

**AIDS quackery** AIDS fraud, see there

**AIDS therapy** Various therapeutic modalities have been used for HIV-positive individuals; some delay the progression of AIDS

▶ **EFFECTIVE** Approved-Zidovudine (AZT), ddC (dideoxycytidine), ddI (dideoxyionsine)

▶ **EXPERIMENTAL SUBSTANCES**

- DAB/486IL-2 An interleukin-2 (IL-2) receptor-specific 'fusion' cytotoxin that selectively eliminates HIV-infected cells
- PE40 A 40 kD *Pseudomonas* exotoxin linked to either IL-2 or the CD4 determinant with varying efficacy in vitro
- Ro24-7429 Targets *tat* gene product
- U-81749 A synthetic substance that blocks HIV-1's protease

▶ **INEFFECTIVE SUBSTANCES** Compound Q, dextran sulfate, isoprinosine, lentinan, peptide T, TIBO derivatives, viroxan.

See AIDS fraud

**aikido** A Japanese martial art, the modern form of which was developed by M Uyeshiba; aikido is believed by its advocates to have health-enhancing effects; the aim of aikido is promote harmony and love on a universal basis; unlike many forms of weaponless combat, aikido recognizes that there is a balance between winning and losing, and thus the goal is to learn to cooperate with opponents, with oneself, and eventually, with the universe; the physical activity of aikido consists of a series of fluid, circular movements in which the partners divert the direction and impetus of each others' attacks through centrifugal and centripetal forces; *'There is no dualistic opposition, but the partner's body, while under control of one's own, is in complete unity with it. . . .the continuity of . . .circular or spherical motion is maintained, the grace and rhythm unique to aikido appears.'* (*British Aikido Federation*, in *Inglis, West, 1983*). See Irimi-nage, Martial arts; Cf T'ai chi ch'uan

**air ionization therapy** Aerion therapy, ionization therapy UNPROVEN THERAPIES The use of a special device (eg that produced by the Alpha-Omega Company) to artificially produce negatively charged particles (ions) in the air; advocates of air ionization therapy believe that an increase in positively charged particles in the environment, largely due to air pollution, is responsible for various diseases; air ionizers have been approved by the FDA (*Inglis, West, 1983*) for treating allergies, hay fever, and other respiratory diseases, but not other conditions

**air pollution** PUBLIC HEALTH The presence of substances (carbon monoxide, nitrogen dioxide, ozone, particulate matter, and sulfur dioxide, figure, below) in the air that are byproducts of human activities, which have an adverse effect on human health. See Acid aerosols, Acid haze, Acid rain, Environmental disease, Sick building syndrome

Note: In the South Coast Air Basin (Los Angeles) daily emissions are 1375 tons of hydrocarbons, 1208 tons of nitrogen oxides, 4987 tons of carbon monoxide, 134 tons of sulfur oxides, and 1075 tons of particulate matter (Sci Am 1993; 269/4:24); it is estimated that if the residents of Los Angeles (population 14 million, registered motor vehicles 10.6 million) were able to achieve the US federal standard for ozone and

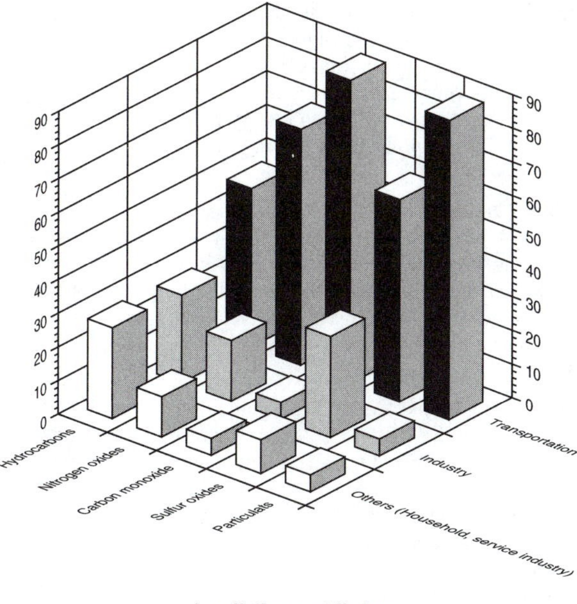


**air pollution-contributers**

particulates, there would be an estimated $9.4 billion gain in health benefits, eliminating 1600 premature deaths in those with chronic respiratory diseases, 15 million workdays in those with respiratory disease, 18 million days of restricted activity, 65 million days of chest discomfort, 180 million days of sore throats, 190 million days of eye irritation

**A.I.R.A.** American International Reiki Association One of two organizations that are dedicated to the practice of Reiki, see there

**Paavo Airola** A deceased, self-proclaimed nutritionist, whose 14 books and pamphlets continue to be widely read and sold despite containing what are regarded as major scientific flaws; Airola believed in fasting and enemas for acne, alcoholism, jaundice, multiple sclerosis, Parkinson's disease, and others; adrenal cortical extract for hypoglycemia, lactovegetarian diet for diabetes mellitus; magnesium for diarrhea; garlic for hemorrhoids; raw milk and eggs for jaundice, gerovital (procaine) for impotence and aging, and many others *(Butler, 1992)*

**ajoene** An antithrombotic principle found in garlic oils, which is formed from allicin in a 4:1 ratio; it has been used to 'thin' the blood, lower cholesterol, and prevent heart attacks and strokes; it is synergistic with other antiplatelet compounds. See Allicin, Garlic

**akabane test** ORIENTAL MEDICINE A clinical test that consists of repeatedly bringing glowing incense near the endpoint of any of the 12 acupuncture meridians; the test is used to determine a person's energy levels, as (in theory) those with high energy levels tolerate fewer applications. See Acupuncture; Cf Moxibustion

***Akebia quinata*** *Mu tong, mu tung, tung tsao* CHINESE MEDICINE A potassium salt-rich climbing vine, the stem of which is analgesic, anti-inflammatory, diuretic; it is used to treat dry mouth, laryngitis, and sinusitis, to promote secretion, and to ease childbirth. See Chinese herbal medicine

**Alar** Daminozide ENVIRONMENT A pesticide used for apples in the US that has the advantage of imparting a 'natural' red color and increasing shelf life; one of Alar's metabolic products, UDMH, is carcinogenic with an estimated increased cancer risk of 1-4/$10^6$ individuals exposed (*Science 1989; 244:755c*)

The Natural Resources Defense Council estimated the cancer risk in children at 24 cancer deaths/$10^5$, resulting in a public outcry that forced a temporary ban on Alar's use, as 20-50% of apples tested were contaminated; in subsequent re-evaluation of Alar, the EPA concluded that the carcinogenic effect is ± $\frac{1}{2}$ of its first estimate (*Science 1991; 254:20n&v*)

**alarm point** *Ah shi* point ACUPUNCTURE A pressure point (acupoint) in acupuncture that is characterized by increased sensitivity due to an acute illness; alarm points located on the front (anterior) of the body are called *mu* points; those on the back (posterior) are known as *shu* points; each of the alarm points is believed to correspond to a particular organ or body site. See Acupoint, Acupressure, Acupuncture

**alarm stage** ALTERNATIVE PSYCHOLOGY The first response to stress, in which an organism suffers physical injury and pain or emotional trauma in the form of shock; according to H Selye, the alarm stage is followed by an adaptation response which, if prolonged or repeated multiple times, leads to apathy and burnout. See Flight-or-fight response; Cf Adaptation response, Burnout

**alchemical hypnotherapy** Alchemical work FRINGE PSYCHOLOGY A type of hynotherapy developed by a Californian, D Quigley, that combines Jungian and transpersonal psychology, neurolinguistic programming, past-life/lives therapy, psychosynthesis, and shamanism; Quigley believes the technique helps the client work with 'Inner Guides' to change his life (*Raso, 1994*). See Hypnotherapy

**alchemical work** Alchemical hypnotherapy, see there

***Alchemilla vulgaris*** Popularly known as lady's mantle, see there

**alchemy** MEDICAL HISTORY-FRINGE MEDICINE A pseudoscience of the Middle Ages, the intent of which was to use the laboratory to understand the secrets of nature and the universe; some alchemists attempted to turn base metals into gold

**alder buckthorn** *Rhamnus frangula, R alnifolia, R purshiana*, alder-leafed buckthorn, arrowwood, black dogwood, buckthorn, glossy buckthorn HERBAL MEDICINE A deciduous shrub, the bark of which contains anthraquinones; it is laxative and has been used internally to treat constipation, and topically for minor cuts TOXICITY Alder buckthorn should not be used for prolonged periods, as it may evoke a 'lazy bowel' syndrome, nor should it be used in those with colitis, hemorrhoids, or gastric ulcers; it should not be used in pregnancy or while nursing. See Herbal medicine

**alehoof** Ground ivy, see there, *Glechoma hederacea*

**aletris** Colicroot, *Aletris farinosa*

**alder buckthorn**
*Rhamnus frangula*

***Aletris farinosa*** Popularly known as colicroot, see there

**Frederick Mathis Alexander** An Australian-British (1869-1956) Shakespearean actor, who developed his posture-correction technique in 1904 after periodically losing his voice on the stage; see Alexander technique, Alexander therapist

**Gerda Alexander method** Eotony (therapy), see there

**Alexander technique** BODYWORK A bodywork technique developed in London in 1904 by an Australian actor FM Alexander; the method consists of improving posture in all physical activities, including standing sitting, walking, and working in various positions; central to success in the method is achieving 'primary control' over the posture and movement of the vertebral column

▶ **ALEXANDER TECHNIQUE IS USEFUL FOR**

- **CHRONIC CONDITIONS** Asthma, depression, headaches, low back pain, irritable bowel syndrome, and ulcers
- **SKILL DEVELOPMENT** Improving the performance of athletes, in sprinting and in tennis, and of those in the performing arts, eg actors, dancers, and musicians
- **PERSONAL DEVELOPMENT** Improving the self-image. sense of self-worth, and instilling a sense of self-responsibility

Accompanied by breathing exercises, the technique is believed by its advocates to alleviate anxiety, arthritis, asthma, chronic fatigue syndrome, depression, dyspnea, exhaustion, headaches, hypertension, irritable bowel syndrome, low back pain, menstrual disorders, muscle tension, neuralgia, osteoarthritis, panic attacks, postpartum depression, premenstrual syndrome, respiratory disease, rheumatoid arthritis, sciatica, snoring, sports injuries, stress, ulcers, and varicose veins. See Bodywork, Structural integration; Cf Aston patterning, Feldenkreis method, Hellerwork®, Massage, Ortho-bionomy, Rolfing®, Rosen method, Tragerwork® RESOURCE: *North American Society of Teachers of the Alexander Technique, PO Box 517, Urbana, IL 61801 ☎ 1.800.473.0620*

Among those who have undergone Alexander therapy are John Cleese–of Monty Python, John Dewey–of the Dewey decimal system, Aldous Huxley, Lily Langtree, Paul Newman, George Bernard Shaw, and Nobel laureat Tinbergen; the Alexander technique is part of the curriculum of the Julliard School, The Royal Academy of Music, and other performing arts institutions

**Alexander therapist** A person trained in the Alexander technique; therapists undergo 1600 hours of training and education over a period of 3 years; there are an estimated 3000 Alexander therapists in the world. See Alexander, Alexander technique

**alfalfa** *Medicago sativa*, buffalo herb, lucerne, purple medic HERBAL MEDICINE A bushy perennial that contains canavanine and saponins and is a rich source of vitamins C, D, E, and K, which is regarded as animal fodder '*health food advocates have made many extravagant claims for its use, even cancer.*' (*Magic & Medicine of Plants, 1986*); alfalfa has been used internally for alcoholism, caries, diabetes, bladder inflammation, gastrointestinal complaints (bloating, constipation, indigestion) and halitosis TOXOCITY Pancytopenia due to canavanine, and saponins. See Herbal medicine

**alga** Any plant of the Group Alga including virtually all seaweeds, eg rockweed, sea lettuce, sea moss, and freshwater forms; alga range in size from single-celled organisms to large seaweeds measuring up to 200 meters in length ALTERNATIVE ONCOLOGY A number of algae produce chemicals that may have anticarcinogenic effects; clinical data on their efficacy is limited *(Moss, 1992)*. See Spirulina (blue-green) algae

Note: In medicine, the term alga often is understood to mean single-celled organisms, while the term seaweed is used for larger plants

**alisma** *Alisma plantago-aquatica*, water plantain CHINESE MEDICINE A perennial herb, the rhizome of which is used for bloating, fluid retention, and urinary tract dysfunction TOXICITY Gastroenteritis. See Chinese herbal medicine; Cf Plantain

***Alisma plantago-aquatica*** Popular known as alisma, see there

**Alivizatos, Hariton** see Greek cancer cure

**alkaloid** HERBAL MEDICINE Any of a number of medicinally active compounds produced by plants; alkaloids are often active in small amounts, and toxic in large amounts; well known alkaloids produced by plants include caffeine, codeine, morphine, nicotine, quinine, and strychnine. See Herbal medicine

**alkanet** *Anchusa officinalis*, bugloss, common alkanet HERBAL MEDICINE A biennial herb that is antidepressive, antipyretic, antitussive, astringent, diuretic, emollient, and expectorant; it has been promoted as a blood purifier. See Herbal medicine

**alkylglycerol** ALTERNATIVE ONCOLOGY Any of a number of compounds which, in nature, are esterified with fatty acids; the most abundant source of alkylglycerols is shark oil; they are present in red blood cells, bone marrow, liver, spleen, and breast milk; alkylglycerols, in particular batyl alcohol, increases hematopoiesis, and stimulates the immune system and is said to be of use for treating leukemias and other malignancies (*Pelton, Overholser, 1994*). See Shark cartilage, Unproven methods for cancer management

**all-heal** 1. Heal-all, see there, *Prunella vulgaris* 2. Valerian, see there, *Valeriana officinalis*

**allicin** A low-molecular-weight phytochemical with antibacterial and antifungal activity, which is present in garlic oil. See Garlic

***Allium cepa*** Red onion HOMEOPATHY A remedy that has been used for neuralgia, colds, hay fever, watery nasal discharge, conjunctivitis, laryngitis, toothaches. See Homeopathy, Onion

***Allium sativum*** Garlic, see there

**allopathic medicine** Mainstream medicine, see there

**allopathy** Mainstream medicine, see there

***Aloe barbadensis*** *Aloe vera*, see there

**aloeroot** Colicroot, see there, *Aletris farinosa*

***Aloe vera*** *Aloe barbadensis, Aloe vulgaris*, Barbados aloe, Curaçao aloe, elephant's gall, first aid plant, *hsiang dan, lu hui* CHINESE MEDICINE A stemless plant with succulent leaves that is found in subtropical and tropical zones, the juice of which is rich in aloin has a wide range of therapeutic uses; extract of *Aloe vera* has been administered internally (see below, toxicity) for constipation, dermatitis, gastritis, headaches, hepatitis, hypertension, hypotension, intestinal parasites, and vertigo; *Aloe vera* is used topically for acne, athlete's foot, burns, hemorrhoids, insect bites, premature balding, psoriasis, and sunburns TOXICITY Aloe should not be taken internally as it is a potent laxative. See Chinese herbal medicine; Cf Botanical toxicity FRINGE MEDICINE-FLOWER ESSENCE THERAPY *Aloe vera* essence is said to balance and center the creative activities in vital life energy. See Flower essence therapy HERBAL MEDICINE *Aloe vera* is used in Western herbal medicine for indications similar to that of Chinese herbal medicine; it has been used in mainstream medicine for radiation therapy-induced burns. See Herbal medicine

***Aloe vulgaris*** *Aloe barbadensis*, *A vera*, see there

***Aloe barbadensis*** *Aloe vera*

**aloes wood** Eagle wood, see there, *Aquilaria agallocha*

**alpha-lipoic acid** Alpha-lipotene, pyruvate oxidation factor, thioctic acid ALTERNATIVE PHARMACOLOGY A substance that is regarded by some as a 'conditionally essential nutrient' (*Fox, 1996*); it is an antioxidant, and appears to have several roles in the body, including the chelation of metals (cadmium, copper, iron, lead, mercury, and others) and extraction of energy from food; supplementation with alpha-lipoic acid is believed to be effective in treating cardiovascular disease, diabetes mellitus (by preventing glycation), strokes, gangrene, Alzheimer's disease, Parkinson's disease, and retinal degeneration

**alpha-lipoic acid**

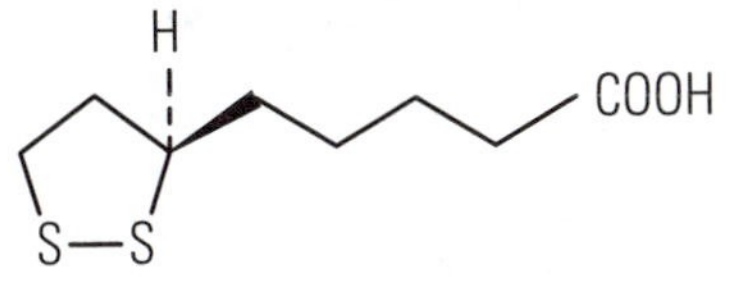

**alpha waves** NEUROLOGY 'Superficial' brain

H COOH S—S

waves that occur at 8 to 12 cycles/second (Hz), with an amplitude of 50 μV; alpha waves are normally present in the occipital and parietal lobes, and are intentionally induced in Silva mind control, an alternative form of psychological therapy, as Silva believed that the alpha pattern is typical of daydreaming. See Brain waves, Silva mind control; Cf Mantra, Meditation, Theta waves, Yoga

***Alpina oxyphylla*** Cardamom, see there

**Alpine scurvy** Pellagra, see there

**alterative** HERBAL MEDICINE An herb that positively influences (alters) the course of a disease, which is believed to purify the blood, increase appetite, improve digestion, and eliminate toxins; alteratives include barberry (*Berberis vulgaris*), burdock (*Artium lappa*), chaparral (*Larrea tridentata*), figwort (*Scrophularia nodosa*), prickly ash (*Xanthoxylum americanum*), red clover (*Trifolium pratense*) sassafras (*Sassafras officinale*), and wild indigo (*Baptista tinctoria*) (*Trattler, 1985*). See Herbal medicine

**alternating sitz bath** Contrast sitz bath NATUROPATHY A sitz bath in which the tub water is maintained at high temperatures at one end, and at low temperatures at the other end; the individual switches back and forth several times (ie bottom hot-feet cold, followed by bottom cold-feet hot). See Hydrotherapy, Sitz bath

**alternative** *adjective* Pertaining or referring to that which is not conventional, mainstream, or traditional; other adjectives, eg 'biological' and 'holistic' are preferred by some authors; given that certain activities are not, per se 'biological', eg replacing dental amalgams with inert materials, or 'holistic', in that only a part of the patient is treated, the adjective 'alternative' appears more appropriate for such areas as nursing or dentistry; Cf Fringe, Integrative, Mainstream

**alternative birthing center** ALTERNATIVE OBSTETRICS An obstetrics unit or facility that provides a pleasant, 'friendly' atmosphere for women who are expected to have an uncomplicated vaginal delivery; these centers are staffed by obstetricians or midwives, and are located either within a hospital or may be free-standing units. See Alternative obstetrics, Doula, Lamaze, Midwife, Natural childbirth, Natural family planning

**alternative dentistry** Biological dentistry, Holistic dentistry ALTERNATIVE MEDICINE A field that '*...treats the teeth, jaw, and related strutures with specific regard to how the therapy will affect the entire body*.' alternative dentistry addresses a wide range of dental problems, including problems with specific teeth related to acupuncture meridians, and the autonomic nervous system, toxicity and/or toxicity from dental restoration materials, electrogalvanism and ion migration, and temporomandibular joint dysfunction (*Alternative Medicine, Future Med Pub, 1994*); alternative dentists may use acupuncture, biofeedback, craniosacral therapy, herbal medicine, homeopathy, and other techniques. See Alternative, Alternative medicine, Amalgam toxicity, Amalgameter, Bass method, Dental amalgams, Flossing, Fluoridation; Cf Psychic dentistry

**alternative healing** Natural healing A philosophical stance based on the principles of alternative medicine, in which a person is brought back to a state of well-being through a therapy that is not 'mainstream' in nature. See Alternative medicine

**alternative health care** Alternative medicine, see there

**alternative gynecology** Holistic gynecology ALTERNATIVE MEDICINE The practice of gynecology in a non-traditional fashion; integral to the philosophy of alternative gynecology is the use of herbs and vitamins to address a woman's gynecologic needs, an increased ratio of vaginal to cesarean deliveries, the use of imagery and visualization for reducing pain and the need for anesthetics, bodywork and massage for recuperation from delivery, and other alternative methods. See Alternative birthing center, Alternative, Alternative medicine, Doula, Lamaze technique, Naturopathic obstetrics; Cf Menstrual extraction

**alternative medicine** '...*a heterogeneous set of practices*[1] *that are offered as an alternative to conventional medicine, for the preservation of health and the diagnosis and treatment of health-related problems; its practitioners are often called healers'* (*N Engl J Med 1992; 326:61*); alternative health care practices constitute a vast array of treatments and ideologies, which may be well-known, exotic, mysterious, or even dangerous, and are based on no common or consistent philosophy; the practitioners range from being sincere, well-educated, and committed to their form of healing, to charlatans

▶ **ALTERNATIVE THERAPIES, TYPES OF**

- **ALTERNATIVE (FORMAL) SYSTEMS** Acupuncture, ayurvedic medicine, Chinese herbal medicine, homeopathy, osteopathy
- **BODY AWARENESS** Exercise and movement therapies, eg Dance therapy, martial arts, yoga
- **MANIPULATIVE THERAPIES** Chiropractic, Hellerwork, Rolfing®
- **MENTAL THERAPIES** Humanistic psychology, hypnosis
- **NATURAL REMEDIES** Diet, eg macrobiotics, naturopathy
- **SENSORY THERAPIES** Art, color, and music therapy

STATISTICS Estimated expenditures for alternative medicine (1990) \$13.7 x $10^9$ (\$10.3 x $10^9$ out-of-pocket); one-third of US citizens had used at least one form of alternative therapy in the previous year; one-third had made an average of 19 visits to alternative health care providers; the highest users of alternative medicine were upper-income whites, 25-49 years of age; 72% did not tell their physicians; most had sought relief from chronic, non-life-threatening conditions, eg allergies, arthralgias, back pain, insomnia, and other conditions; by US congressional edict, the US National Institutes of Health established the Office of Alternative Medicine; alternative medicine claims a 'whole body' approach to healing, and health maintenance, which entails the integration of the body, mind, and spirit, based on the holistic doctrine, which holds that the entire organism cannot be understood merely by studying lower levels of organization, eg the organ system approach (which is the philosophy of 'mainstream' medical practice); alternative medicine disciplines include acupuncture[2], aural analysis, biofeedback, chiropractic[2], clairvoyant diagnosis, homeopathy, hypnosis, iridology, organicism, naturopathy, psychic healing, rolfing, t'ai chi ch'uan, and zone therapy. See Fringe medicine, Holistic medicine, Integrative medicine, Office of Alternative Medicine; Cf Unproven methods for cancer management

[1]Alternative terms for alternative therapies include adjunctive medicine (German term), alternative healing (discussed separately elsewhere), alternative health care, alternative therapy, complementary medicine, extentional medicine, fringe medicine, gentle medicine (French term), holistic (see below) medicine, innovative medicine, integrative medicine, irregular medicine, mind/body medicine, natural healing, natural medicine, New Age medicine, nontraditional medicine, sectarian medicine, soft medicine (German term), 'traditional' medicine, unconventional medicine, and unorthodox medicine [2]Acupuncture and chiropractic medicine are also 'holistic', but are generally regarded with less suspicion by mainstream medical practitioners as some data suggest they may be effective in certain types of diseases; alternative medicine is criticized as being more 'mystical' or magical than scientific in its approach to understanding disease; it has been noted (*GottschalkOlsen, 1989*) that not all alternative methods of medical therapy are by definition, 'holistic'

**alternative nursing** Holistic nursing, see there

**alternative therapy** Alternative medicine, see there

**alternative 12 steps** Non-theistic twelve-step program, see Twelve step program

**althea** Popularly known as marshmallow, see there, *Althea officinalis*

***Althea officinalis*** Popularly known as marshmallow, see there

**aluminum** A metallic element (atomic number 13; atomic weight 26.98) that may be toxic; manifestations of aluminum toxicity include vitamin D-refractory osteodystrophy with impaired mineralization and decreased bone formation, hypercalcemia, anemia, severe progressive encephalopathy and dementia

**alumroot** Cranesbill, see there, *Geranium maculatum*

***ama*** AYURVEDIC MEDICINE A general term for a physiologic impurity, as used in the context of ayurvedic medicine. See Ayurvedic medicine, *Panchakarma*, *Prana*

**amalgam** Dental amalgam, see there

**amalgam toxicity** ALTERNATIVE DENTISTRY An increase of mercury that is believed to be caused by the leaching of mercury from dental amalgams, which are up to 50% mercury by weight; although scientific data does not support the existence of this condition, some practitioners of alternative medicine and dentistry recommend treating amalgam toxicity with chelation, detoxifying supplements (eg EDTA), enemas, and herbs. See Alternative dentistry, Amalgameter, Dental amalgam

**Amalgameter** ALTERNATIVE DENTISTRY A device with an incorporated mercury vaporizer that has been claimed to indicate the presence of a significant release of mercury from dental amalgams by chewing; almalgameters are regarded as having no legitimate role in detecting toxic levels of mercury, which are quantified in the laboratory by atomic absorption spectrophotometry using blood and urine. See Alternative dentistry, Amalgam toxicity, Dental amalgam

***amaroli*** Urine therapy, see there

**amber** *Pinites succinifer, hu bo, hu buo*, tiger's soul CHINESE MEDICINE A yellowish resin that contains intact bodies of various insects; amber has been used medicinally as a diuretic, nerve tonic, sedative, and to dissolve blood clots, as well as for amenorrhea, cataracts, convulsions, hysteria, and nocturnal emissions. See Chinese herbal medicine

**amber touch-and-heal** Saint John's wort, see there, *Hypericum perforatum*

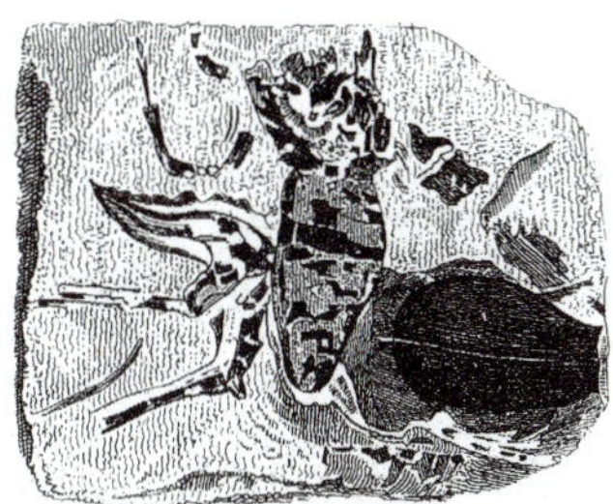

**amber**

**Ambrosia™** M5 See Maharishi Amrit Kalash™

**American Academy of Medical Acupuncture** An organization for physician practitioners of acupuncture, which promotes education about acupuncture and acts in the interests of physicians (MDs and DOs) who practice acupuncture; the AAMA has two categories of members: full members have had at least 220 hours of formal training or apprenticeship, two years of experience, and an endorsement from another member of the academy; associate members have not fulfilled these requirements. See Acupunc-ture, Chinese medicine, Traditional Chinese medicine

**American Academy of Osteopathy** The professional organization for osteopathic physicians, who actively use manipulation in their practice, and adhere to a philosophy that is in keeping with the original precepts of osteopathy, as espoused by Andrew Taylor Still. See Osteopathy, Still; Cf American Osteopathic Association RESOURCE: *American Academy of Osteopathy, 3500 DePauw Blvd, Suite 1080, Indianapolis IN 46268 ☎ 1.317.879.1881*

**American aspen** White poplar, see there, *Populus tremuloides*

**American Association of Acupuncture and Oriental Medicine** An organization for the practitioners of acupuncture, which promotes education about acupuncture and acts as its advocate in public. See Acupuncture, American Academy of Medical Acupuncture, Chinese medicine, Traditional Chinese medicine

**American Association of Naturopathic Physicians** A professional organization for naturopaths, most of whom have completed a period of formal training in one of the three schools of naturopathy in North America; the AANP promotes education about naturopathy and acts in the interests of naturopaths, of which there are approximately 750 in the US and Canada. See Naturopathy

**American Biologics Hospital** FRINGE ONCOLOGY A health care center located in Tijuana, Mexico, which offers various alternative cancer therapies, including laetrile, nutritional supplements, and megadoses of vitamin C and other antioxidants, DHEA, tissue extracts (glandulars), and detoxification in the form of colon therapy (*Alternative Medicine. Future Med Pub, 1994*). See Tijuana, Unproven methods for cancer management

**American cedar** Thuja, see there, *Thuja occidentalis*

**American ginseng** *Panax quinquefolius*, five fingers, tartar root HERBAL MEDICINE A perennial herb, the root of which has been used by Native Americans, Chinese, and Indians as a general and immune tonic, and a cure-all for anemia, asthma, common cold, depression, fatigue, flu, low back pain, stress, and other conditions; as with Oriental ginseng, American ginseng is believed to be an aphrodisiac TOXICITY American ginseng has been associated with asthmatiform episodes, arrhythmias and palpitations, hypertension, and postmenopausal bleeding. See Herbal medicine; Cf Ginseng, Siberian ginseng

**American indigo** Wild indigo, see there, *Baptista tinctoria*

**American mandrake** Mayapple, see there, *Podophyllum peltatum*

**American mistletoe** *Phoradendron flavescens, P serotinum*, golden bough, mistletoe HERBAL MEDICINE A parasitic evergreen shrub that is a sedative and has been used to treat hypertension, menstrual disorders, paralysis, seizures, strokes, tuberculosis, and intoxications TOXICITY American mistletoe is listed by the FDA as 'unsafe'. See Herbal medicine, Iscador, Poisonous plants

**American nervousness** Neurasthenia, see there

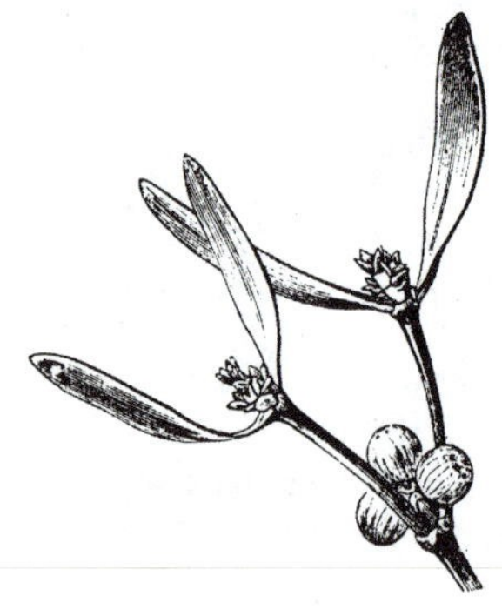

**American mistletoe**
*Phoradendron flavescens*

**American Osteopathic Association** The primary professional organization for osteopathic physicians, which promotes education about osteopathy, and acts in the interests of its practitioners. See Osteopathy; Cf American

**American ginseng**
*Panax quinquefolius*

Academy of Osteopathy *RESOURCE: AOA, 142 E Ontario St, Chicago IL 60611 ☎ 1.312.280.5800*

**American sloe** Black haw, see there, *Viburnum prunifolium*

**American valerian** Lady's slipper, see there, *Cypripedium calceolus*

**americanitis** Neurasthenia, see there

**Ames test** TOXICOLOGY An assay that detects mutagenesis, which is used to screen for compounds with carcinogenic potential TECHNIQUE A strain (TA100) of *Salmonella typhimurium* that cannot synthesize histidine (and therefore requires histidine) is incubated in a histidine-poor growth medium with the compound of interest; if the chemical is mutagenic, then TA100 reverts to a form that can synthesize its own histidine (*New York Times 5 July 1994; C1*)

**amino acid drink** Protein drink, see there

**amino acid therapy** ALTERNATIVE PHARMACOLOGY The use of free-form (pure) amino acids in powder, capsules, or pills for various therapeutic purposes; mainstream medical practitioners generally do not recommend the use of free-form amino acids, as they are abundantly present in high protein foods, including dairy products, eggs, legumes, fish, meats, nuts, poultry, and soybeans; naturopaths may prescribe, or health 'buffs' may self-administer, certain amino acids for specific 'indications'; as examples, L-lysine may be used to control herpetic lesions, DL-phenylalanine to control pain and suppress the appetite, L-tyrosine may be used in combination with phenylalanine to combat depression, and L-glutamine may be used to curb cravings for sugary foods or alcohol; L-tryptophan was transiently popular as a therapy for depression, but was removed from the marketplace, when one poorly manufactured lot was linked to the eosinophilia-myalgia syndrome. See L-Tryptophan

Note: The use of single amino acid supplements is a questionable practice, given that amino acids compete with each other for absorption in the gastrointestinal tract; an excess of one may lead to a deficiency of one or more of the others; in absence of a defect in the metabolism of a specific, there are no valid indications for use of single amino acid supplements

***amma*** Chinese massage, see there

**Amma therapy®** A proprietary healing system developed in the 1960s by a Korean-American, T Sohn, that incorporates bodywork, diet, herbs, and vitamin supplements; Amma therapy® is based in part on the massage of energic points identified by Sohn and her husband, R Sohn. See Wholistic Health Center

***Ammi visnaga*** *Khella*, see there

***Amomum amarum*** Cardamom, see there, *Alpina oxyphylla*

***Amomum xanthoides*** Popularly known as grains of paradise, see there

**Amrit** Maharishi Amrit Kalash™, see there

**Amrit Nectar™** M4 See Maharishi Amrit Kalash™

**A.M.T.A.** American Massage Therapy Association

**amygdalin** A β-cyanogenic glycoside that is structurally related to the semisynthetic laetrile, which is derived from the pits of certain fruits. See Laetrile

**'anabolic enhancer'** see Invalid claims of efficacy

**anaclitic depression** NEONATOLOGY A response seen in infants who have been separated from their mothers for prolonged periods of time, resulting in a disruption of the mother-child dyad; by six months, infants are strongly attached to a mother figure; when they are separated from that person after 6 months, by the mother's death, incarceration, or other force and a substitute mother figure is provided, the initial panic and searching reactions give way to anxiety, ending with apathy and withdrawal, accompanied by hypotonia and inactivity, a saddened facial expression, loss of appetite, weight loss, profound disturbances in motor, social, and language development and, when the reaction is extreme, death. See Genie, Holtism, Social isolation; Cf Bonding, Companionship, Infant massage

**anaerobic exercise** A general term for a form of exercise that consists of slow rhythmic movements, eg calisthenics (push-ups, sit-ups) and weight lifting, which result in a minimal increase in heart rate; anaerobic exercise strengthens muscles, increases joint mobility, and decreases the risk of injury to the musculoskeletal apparatus; Cf Aerobic exercise

**analgesic** Anodyne HERBAL MEDICINE An herb that is believed to reduce nerve excitability; herbal analgesics include catnip (*Nepeta cataria*), chamomile (*Anthemis nobilis*), hops (*Humulus lupulus*), mistletoe (*Viscum album*), skullcap (*Scutellaria lateriflora*), white bryony (*Bryonia alba*), wild yam (*Dioscorea villosa*), and wintergreen (*Gaultheria procumbens*) (*Trattler, 1985*). See Herbal medicine

**analysand** PSYCHIATRY A person being analyzed

***Ananas comosus*** Pineapple, see there

***Anchusa officinalis*** Popularly known as alkanet, see there

**android obesity** Upper body obesity, see there

**'anecdotal'** Unsubstantiated, as in an anecdotal patient response to an unproven method for cancer management, or anecdotal cause-and-effect relationship between a noxious environmental element and clinical disease. See Fringe, Unproven; Cf Blinding

***Anemarrhena asphodeloides*** *Jih mu*, *Zhi mu* CHINESE MEDICINE A lily-like plant that is rich in saponins, asphonin, and mucilage, the stems and rhizomes of which are anti-inflammatory, antipyretic, diuretic, and emollient for the intestine; it is used for high fever, bleeding gums, bronchitis, constipation, coughs with increased mucus production, hypersexuality, impotence, insomnia, night sweats, nocturnal emissions, pneumonia, vertigo. See Chinese herbal medicine

***Anemone pratensis*** HOMEOPATHY *Pulsatilla*, see there

***Anemone pulsatilla*** HOMEOPATHY *Pulsatilla*, see there

***Anethum graveolens*** Popularly known as dill, see there

**aneurine** Thiamin, see there

***angakok*** An Alaskan Eskimo native healer or shaman. See Healer, Shamanism

**angelic healing** PARANORMAL PHENOMENA A type of healing in which a person supplicates to a higher power through meditation, so that angels (or spirits) can be called upon guide, protect, and heal a person through radiant energy; components of angelic healing include auric massage technique, channeling, guided imagery and visualization, laying on of hands, and prayer. See Absent healing, Auric massage technique, Channeling, Guided imagery, Laying on of hands, Miracle, Prayer, Psychic healing, Spirit healing

**angelica** *Angelica archangelica*, garden angelica, root of the Holy Ghost A perennial herb that contains volatile oils, eg caryophyllene, linalool, limonene, phellandrene, pinene, and others, as well as coumarins, eg bergapten, umbelliferone, xanthotoxol FRINGE MEDICINE-FLOWER ESSENCE THERAPY Angelica essence is believed to provide protection and guidance from spiritual beings at the time of birth and death; see Flower essence therapy HERBAL MEDICINE Angelica is antimicrobial, antispasmodic, diuretic, and expectorant, and has been used to treat asthma, bronchitis, colds, gastrointestinal complaints, and urinary tract infections. See Herbal medicine; Cf *Angelica anomala*, *A pubescens*-purple, *A pubescens*-yellow, *A sinensis*

***Angelica anomala*** *Bai jih, bai zhi, fang-hsiang*, floral fragrance CHINESE MEDICINE A perennial herb, the root of which is an analgesic, antidote, aromatic, circulatory stimulant, and sedative; it has been used to treat dermatitis, headaches, nasal congestion, purulent discharges, snakebites, toothaches, and vertigo. See Chinese herbal medicine

***Angelica archangelica*** Angelica, see there

***Angelica grosserrata*** *Angelica pubescens*-yellow, see there

***Angelica polymorpha*** *Angelica sinensis*, see there

***Angelica pubescens*-purple** *Chiang huo* CHINESE MEDICINE A perennial herb, closely related to *Angelica pubescens*-yellow, the root of which is analgesic, antirheumatic, and diaphoretic; it has been used to treat arthritis, headaches, low back pain, loss of vision, stokes, and vertigo. See Chinese herbal medicine; Cf *Angelica pubescens*-yellow

***Angelica pubescens*-yellow** *Angelica grosserrata, du huo* CHINESE MEDICINE A perennial herb, closely related to *Angelica pubescens*-purple, the root of which is analgesic, antirheumatic, and diaphoretic; it has been used to treat arthritis, cold-temperature-related paresthesias, headaches, low back pain, loss of vision, and vertigo. See Chinese herbal medicine; Cf *Angelica pubescens*-purple

***Angelica sinensis*** *Angelica polymorpha*, Chinese angelica root, *dan gui, dong quai*, honeywort, mountain celery, *shan chin* CHINESE MEDICINE A fragrant peren-

**angelica** *Angelica archangelica*

nial herb, the root of which is analgesic, sedative, and an immune stimulant; angelica has been used for abscesses and sores, anemia, arrhythmias, cancer, dysmenorrhea, headaches, loss of appetite, menstrual dysfunction, premenstrual syndrome, post-traumatic and post-surgical pain, and blurred vision TOXICITY *Angelica* should not be used in early pregnancy. See Chinese herbal medicine

**angelica tree** Northern prickly ash, see there, *Zanthoxylum americanum*

**anima** See Animus

**animal fat** A general term for saturated fatty acids of animal (beef, pork, lamb) origin, which are associated with an increased risk of colorectal carcinoma (*N Engl J Med 1990; 323:1664OA*). See Fatty acid, Saturated fatty acid; Cf Unsaturated fatty acid

**animal magnetism** Mesmerism, see there

**animal protein factor** Vitamin $B_{12}$, see there

**animus** PSYCHIATRY A term coined by Carl Jung for a masculine image that women carry with them–anima is the term used for the feminine image that men carry; according to Jung, children incorporate the characteristics of their phenotypic sex in their conscious personality, which the opposite sexual characteristics reman latent in the unconscious; it is believed that people fall in love and often marry those who are positive versions of the unconscious image; as the partners evolve past the stage of infatuation with their 'complementary opposite,' they learn to appreciate each other as individuals, a process that Jung calls individualization (*Watson, 1995*). See Individualization, Jungian psychoanalysis

**anise** *Pimpinella anisum*, aniseed, sweet cumin HERBAL MEDICINE An annual herb that contains volatile oils, eg coumarins, glycosides, and anethole; anise seeds are carminative, expectorant, and insecticidal and have been used for coughs, indigestion, nausea, and to stimulate breast milk; anise is believed by some to be an aphrodisiac. See Herbal medicine

**aniseed** Anise, see there, *Pimpinella anisum*

***anma*** 1. Chinese massage, see there 2. A form of traditional Japanese massage that was intended to increase circulation; *anma* has been incorporated into shiatsu; see Shiatsu

***anmo*** Massage, see there

**Annette Martin method** PARANORMAL PHENOMENA A health system based on clairvoyant diagnosis and the Edgar Cayce method(s) of therapy. See Cayce

**anodyne** See Analgesic-Herbal medicine

**anodyne imagery** ALTERNATIVE MEDICINE A '*...technique of conditioned relaxation, induction of a trance-like state, and guided processing of internal imagery...* (which) *allows patients to confront their fear and develop ways to overcome their anxiety during interventional procedures, eliminating the need for intravenous sedation*' (*RT Image, 30 Jan, 1995*); anodyne imagery is believed by some radiologists to offer an alternative to sedation during radiologic procedures, which may depress cardiorespiratory function. See Imagery and visualization

**Antahkarana Master Frequency Unit** FRINGE MEDICINE A device that operates on uncertain scientific principles, which is marketed by Reverend AL Robertson of the American Reiki Master Association; it is claimed to be a perpetual self-empowered broadcaster;

**anise** *Pimpinella anisum*

the use of these devices is claimed to cause remission in AIDS in less than 2 hours, and relieve Alzheimer's disease, cancer, multiple sclerosis, and other conditions; Cf Health fraud, Quackery

**anthelmintic** HERBAL MEDICINE An herb that is believed to either kill (vermicidal) or evoke the expulsion (vermifugal) of intestinal worms; herbal anthelmintics include aloe (*Aloe vera*), bitterwood (*Picraena excelsa*), butternut (*Juglas cinerea*), garlic (*Allium sativum*), papaya (*Carica papaya*), pomegranate (*Puncia granatum*), worm grass (*Spigelia marilandica*), wormseed (*Chenopodium anthelminticum*), and wormwood (*Artemisia absinthium) (Trattler, 1985*). See Herbal medicine

***Anthemis nobilis*** Roman chamomile, see there

**anthroposophical medicine** ALTERNATIVE MEDICINE A philosphical vision of health and disease, which is based on the writings of an Austrian philosopher Rudolph Steiner (1861-1925); like many before and after him, he believed that *prana* (the energy of life according to the ayurvedic construct) was the source of good health, and that the goal of the medical practitioner is to free the mind and body from anything that obstructed the flow of living energy; Steiner viewed a person as having four 'bodies': The physical body, the 'etheric' body–which is based on formative forces, the 'astral' body-which reflects a person's emotions and inner drives, and a conscious body-which is the domain of the ego and self; anthroposophical medicine partially overlaps the philosophies of homeopathy and the Alexander technique, the latter through the use of eurhythmic dancing; in the mid-1970s, there were an estimated 1000 practitioners of 'anthroposophically-extended' medicine in Europe (*Inglis, West, 1983*). See Alexander technique, Homeopathy

**anthroposophically-extended medicine** Anthroposophical medicine, see there

**antiachromotrichia factor** Pantothenic acid, see there

**anti-aging diet** Life-extending diet, see there

**antianemic factor** Vitamin $B_{12}$, see there

**'anti-arthritis diet'** see Arthritis diet

**antiberiberi factor** Thiamin, see there

**antiberiberi vitamin** Thiamin, see there

**antibiotic** HERBAL MEDICINE An herb that kills or inhibits bacterial growth; herbal antibiotics include bitter orange (*Citrus aurantium*), coneflower (*Echinacea augustifolia*), eucalyptus (*Eucalyptus globulus*), garlic (*Allium sativum*), goldenseal (*Hydrastris canadensis*), horseradish (*Cochlearia armoracia*), onion (*Allium cepa*), Peruvian bark (*Cinchona ledgeriana*), and watercress (*Nasturtium officinale*) (*Trattler, 1985*). See Herbal medicine

**'anti-cancer diet'** CLINICAL NUTRITION A series of dietetic guidelines (table, below) promulgated by the American Cancer Society, the National Cancer Institute, and the American Institute for Cancer Research. that are intended to reduce a person's risk of cancer. See Folk cures for cancer, Unproven methods for cancer management

**anticanites factor** Pantothenic acid, see there

**DIETARY GUIDELINES FOR REDUCING CANCER RISK**

Reduce fat consumption, in particular of saturated fats

Reduce consumption of smoked, salt-cured, and nitrate-cured foods, eg bacon, ham, cheese, corned beef and luncheon meats

Reduce consumption of alcohol

Eat high fiber foods, eg whole grains, legumes, fruits, and vegetables

Eat foods rich in vitamins A and C, and beta-carotene, eg leafy green vegetables, citrus fruits, and red, orange, and yellow fruits and vegetables

Eat cruciferous vegetables, eg broccoli and cabbage

**OTHER RECOMMENDATIONS**

Avoid tobacco

Avoid refined sugar and salty foods

Avoid obesity

Exercise regularly and vigorously

**anticoagulant** A general term for any substance that prevents the coagulation of blood ALTERNATIVE ONCOLOGY It has been proposed that anticoagulants may be of use in treating cancer, by inhibiting the growth and spread of cancer *(Moss, 1992)*. See Unproven methods for cancer management

**antidermatitis factor** Pantothenic acid, see there

**antidermatitis factor of chicks** Pantothenic acid, see there

**antidote** HOMEOPATHY A general term for any substance that may inhibit or destroy the beneficial effect of a homeopathic remedy; antidotes can be chemical (eg coffee, camphor, mint, strong tastes, recreational drugs, or mainstream medicines) or physical (eg electrical blankets, dental drilling or other dental work, strong smells, MRI-magnetic resonance imaging) in nature; antidotes are also unique to the individual–while coffee is considered the most important antidote, and is believed to reverse the therapeutic effect of many remedies, this effect is not universal. See Homeopathy, Proving, Remedy, Vital force

**antidoting** HOMEOPATHY The negation of the effect of a homeopathic remedy by another substance or factor. See Antidote, Homeopathy, Proving, Remedy, Vital force

**anti-egg-white factor** Biotin, see there

**antifluoridation campaign** see Fluoridation

**anti-foaming agents** FOOD INDUSTRY A substance added to canned liquids, which allows the container to be completely filled with a liquid, without the liquid bubbling or foaming. See Food additives; Cf Anti-foaming agent

**anti-gray hair factor** Pantothenic acid, see there

**antihemorrhagic factor** Vitamin K, see there

**antihemorrhagic vitamin** Vitamin K, see there

**antineoplaston** FRINGE ONCOLOGY Any of a number of peptides isolated from urine that are said to have antineoplastic activity and inhibit the growth of osteosarcoma, myeloblastic leukemia, lymphoma, breast cancer, astrocytomas (brain tumors) in children, and other cancers. See Unproven methods for cancer management; Cf Health fraud, Quackery

Note: Data on the claimed efficacy of antineoplaston has been distributed by Stanislaw R Burzynski, MD, PhD; some data was published between 1973 and 1979; the FDA has received no IND (investigational new drug) applications from Dr Burzynski, nor has it received information on the safety or efficacy of antineoplaston A or other related products in treating cancer; interstate shipment of these products is illegal; as of 4/24/90, the American Cancer Society considers antineoplaston therapy to be unproven, and recommends that patients do not participate in its routine use (*American Cancer Society-data sheets*); the National Cancer Institute (US) has concluded that these agents have no effect in treating malignancy; the reader interested in evaluating the Burzynski controversy is referred to his sympathizers *(Moss, 1992)* and detractors *(JAMA 1992; 267:2924)*

**antineuritic factor** Thiamin, see there

**antineuritic vitamin** Thiamin, see there

**antioxidant** CLINICAL NUTRITION Any agent, eg vitamins A, C, and E, selenium, and others, that can reduce highly histotoxic oxygen reduction products and reactive oxygen species (eg hydroxyl radical), derived from superoxide anion ($O_2^{\cdot -}$) and $H_2O_2$—the univalent and bivalent reduction products of oxygen, generated during the normal intermediary metabolism of the respiratory chain; other antixodants include glutathione, α-tocopherol (vitamin E), bilirubin. See Free radical, Superoxide dismutase

**antioxidant therapy** A general term for the use of any agent (eg antioxidant vitamins, glutathione reductase, superoxide dismutase) to 'scavenge' oxygen free radicals (OFRs) or excited oxygen molecules, which are by-products of normal metabolic reactions); excess OFRs have been linked to cancer secondary to OFR-induced DNA damage, and to cardiovascular disease secondary to OFR-induced oxidation of low-density lipoprotein (LDL)-cholesterol to a more atherogenic form; in cardiology, antioxidant therapy attempts to block the oxidative modification of LDL, which is thought to be an early step in fatty streak development, atherogenesis and atherosclerosis-related pathologies, including coronary artery disease, and cerebrovascular accidents. See Antioxidant, Antioxidant vitamin

*Notes: The jury is still out as to whether antioxidant therapy is effective in preventing cancer, and as of 1994, skepticism about such claims appears to be appropriate (*N Engl J Med 1994; 330:1080ed*); while antioxidant therapy has yet to be implemented, there is evidence in experimental animals that the antioxidant probucol may have an atheroreductive effect, and epidemiological evidence points to an inverse relation between coronary artery disease and increased levels of vitamin E and selenium, both of which are antioxidants

**antioxidant vitamin** A general term for any vitamin, eg beta carotene (provitamin A), ascorbic acid (vitamin C), and alpha-tocopherol (vitamin E) with antioxidant activity. See Antioxidant, Antixoxidant therapy

Note: It is unclear whether antioxidant vitamins are effective in reducing the risk of cancer; some recent data suggest they are not (*N Engl J Med 1994; 330:1029oa*)

**antipernicious anemia factor** Vitamin $B_{12}$, see there

**antiscorbutic factor** Vitamin C, see there

**antiscorbutic vitamin** Vitamin C, see there

**antiseptic** HERBAL MEDICINE An herb that is used internally or externally to either prevent the breakdown of tissues by microorganisms or inhibit their growth; herbal antiseptics include barberry (*Berberis vulgaris*), coneflower (*Echinacea augustifolia*), eucalyptus (*Eucalyptus globulus*), garlic (*Allium sativum*), goldenseal (*Hydrastris canadensis*), horseradish (*Cochlearia armoracia*), myrrh (*Commiphora myrrha*), St John's wort (*Hypericum perforatum*), and white pond lily (*Nymphaea odorata*) (*Trattler, 1985*). See Antibiotic, Herbal medicine

**antispasmodic** HERBAL MEDICINE An herb used to prevent or inhibit muscles spasms; herbal antispasmodics include black cohosh (*Cimicifuga racemosa*), blue cohosh (*Caulophyllum thalictroides*), chamomile (*Anthemis nobilis*), lady's slipper (*Cypripedium pubescens*), lobelia (*Lobelia inflata*), mistletoe (*Viscum album*), passion flower (*Passiflora incarnata*), skullcap (*Scutellaria lateriflora*), and wild yam root (*Dioscora villosa*) (*Trattler, 1985*). See Herbal medicine, Nervine

**antistatin** ALTERNATIVE ONCOLOGY A protein produced by the salivary glands of the Mexican leech (*Haementaria officinalis*), which inhibits coagulation and metastases in malignancy (*J Biol Chem 1987; 262:9718*). See Unproven methods for cancer management

**antisterility factor** Vitamin E see there

**antisterility vitamin** Vitamin E, see there

**antitumor B** FRINGE ONCOLOGY A formulation of Chinese herbs that is said to reduce the incidence of esophageal cancer (*Moss, 1992*). See Unproven methods for cancer management

**AOA** American Osteopathic Association, see there

***Apis mellifera*** Honeybee HOMEOPATHY A major homeopathic remedy obtained from bees, that is used to treat bee stings and other insect bites, edema, and other causes of burning and swelling including cystitis, allegies, and sore throat, *Apis* is also used for arthritis, mumps, peritonitis, and pleuritis. See Bee venom therapy, Homeopathy

**apple** ALTERNATIVE NUTRITION The fruit of the tree *Malus sylvestris*, which has a long tradi-

***Apis mellifera*** Honeybee

tion as a 'healthy food'*; the component held responsible for the apple's effect is its high content of pectin, a soluble fiber, as well as polyphenols; apples are believed to be useful in preventing cancer, controlling diabetes mellitus, defects in gastrointestinal transit—both constipation and diarrhea, and for cardiovascular disease, as pectin reduces cholesterol levels. See Healthy foods

**To eat an apple before going to bed, will make the doctor beg for his bread*, attributed to 10th century England (*M Castleman, 1996*), which is now expressed as '*an apple a day keeps the doctor away*'

**apple cider vinegar** Vinegar made from fermented apple cider; Dr DC Jarvis (*Folk Medicine, 1958; Arthritis and Folk Medicine, 1960, Holt, Rinehart & Winston, New York*) believes that apple cider vinegar is virtually a cure-all and should be ingested with all meals, in particular to maintain the urine acidic and prevent kidney stones; this recommendation has been questioned by others in health care (*Bricklin, 1976, 1983*); apple cider vinegar may be used topically for sunburns, dandruff, and oily skin

**apple mono diet** ALTERNATIVE NUTRITION An alkaline diet in which the person ingests only apples, apple juice, and water, but no solid foods; it is recommended for gout or other inflammatory conditions. See Fasting

**apple-of-Peru** Jimsonweed, see there, *Datura stramonium*

**applied kinesiology** Kinesiology FRINGE MEDICINE A system of pseudodiagnosis and pseudotherapy developed by an American chiropractor, George Goodheart, Jr, that is based on the posit that disease is caused by the accumulation of toxins around major muscle groups, which translates into weaknesses of specific muscle groups; stimulation or relaxation of these muscle groups is believed to reduce the 'health imbalances' in the body's organs and glands; once such imbalances are identified, the therapist applies various kinesiology techniques to restore balance and posture; applied kinesiology is said to be useful in determining a person's health status, restoring posture, improving gait, and range of motion, and normalizing digestive, endocrine, immune, neural, and other systems (*Alternative Medicine, Future Med Pub, 1994*); kinesiologists believe their tests can identify food allergies, mineral and vitamin deficiencies, and slowed peripheral and lymphatic circulation; kinesiology is delivered by the fingertips at appropriate pressure points; anecdotal data suggest that kinesiology may be effective in treating allergies, back and/or neck pain, common cold, depression, fatigue, headache, indigestion, mineral and vitamin deficiencies, muscular weakness, sciatica, tension, and other conditions. See Alternative medicine, Innate intelligence, Muscle reflex testing; Cf Applied Physiology *RESOURCE: International College of Applied Kinesiology, PO Box 905, Lawrence, Kansas 66044-0905 ☎ 1.913.542.1801*

**applied nutrition** ALTERNATIVE MEDICINE An ad hoc term coined to emphasize the role that diet has in both promoting health, and as a therapy. See Diet

**Applied Physiology** ALTERNATIVE MEDICINE A '...*system of stress management procedures using muscle monitoring and biofeedback, which allows the body to communicate what is out of balance and what it requires to correct each stress condition*.' (*Kastner, Burroughs, 1993*); Applied Physiology was developed in the early 1980s by R Utt, who had initially undergone an apprenticeship in applied kinesiology; the state of the muscles is monitored using an indicator muscle–defined as one that is neither overstressed nor understressed; the indicator muscle communicates with what Utt terms the body's own 'biocomputer'–the innate intelligence that coordinates the activity of the parasympathetic nervous system; this in turn controls blood pressure, digestion, respiration, and other involuntary physiologic activities; once the imbalances are evaluated (based on the indicator muscle), '...*important information is learned about the state of stress in tissues, organs, meridians, and emotions related to these points*.' (*ibid*) ; therapy is effected by acupressure; Applied Physiology is believed by its advocates to be useful in rehabilitating patients with accidents, muscular dystrophy, polio and trauma, and in treating skin conditions, environmental and food-related 'stress', and dyslexia; Applied Physiologists undergo a 500-hour training course

**apricot seed** Bitter almond CHINESE MEDICINE The inner kernel of apricots (*Prunus armeniaca*) which are antitussive, expectorant and laxative TOXICITY Apricot seeds are poisonous, and contain prussic acid; 50 seeds are fatal in adults, 10 are fatal in children; see Chinese herbal medicine FRINGE ONCOLOGY Apricot seeds or pits (*Prunus armeniaca*) are a source of amygdalin or Laetrile. See Laetrile

**apricot vine** Passionflower, see there, *Passiflora incarnata*

**A.P.R.T.** Association for Past-Life Research and Therapy, see Past life/lives therapy

***Aquilaria agallocha*** Popularly known as eagle wood, see there

**arachidonic acid-rich proteins** CLINICAL NUTRITION A general term that encompasses egg yolks, fatty red meat, and organ meats, foods that are viewed as 'unhealthy foods'. See Bad eicosanoids, Zone-favorable diet; Cf Good eicosanoids

**arbor vitae** Thuja, see there, *Thuja occidentalis*

**archetype** PSYCHIATRY A term coined by Carl Jung as hypothetical patterns of behavior and thought that constitute a collective unconsciousness (*D Watson, 1995*). See Animus, Archetypal psychology, Jungian psychoanalysis

**archetypal psychology** ALTERNATIVE PSYCHOLOGY A system of mental therapy that was developed by JS Bolen, which analyses myths as the keys to self-knowlege. See Archetype, Jungian psychoanalysis, Spiritual psychology

***Arctium lappa*** Popularly known as burdock, see there

***Arctostaphylos uva-ursi*** Popularly known as bearberry, see there

**A.R.E.** Association for Research and Enlightment, see there

***Argentum nitriticum*** *Argent nit*, devil's stone, hellstone, lunar caustic HOMEOPATHY A homeopathic remedy formulated from acanthite, a silver nitrate-based mineral; *Argent nit* is used for fear and anxiety linked to an overactive imagination, which results in sweating and palpitations; it may be used for a 'nervous bowel,' pulsating headaches, uterine prolapse, menstrual dysfunction, and conjunctivitis. See *Argent nit* type, Homeopathy

***Argent nit* type** HOMEOPATHY A constitutional type of person who is generally happy and extroverted, but emotionally volatile and often in a state of constant anxiety, resulting in insomnia, irrational fears and phobias; *Argent nit* types prefer fresh air, cool temperatures, salty or sweet foods, and may appear prematurely aged WORSE Warmth, night, emotional stress, menstruation FEARS Failure, lateness, loneliness, loss of self-control, dread disease WEAKEST BODY REGIONS Nerves, mucosal membranes, left side of body. See *Argentum nitricum*, Constitutional type, Homeopathy

**arginine** FRINGE ONCOLOGY An amino acid that is believed to be of use in reducing the risk of cancer, administered as a nutritional supplement (*Moss, 1992*). See Unproven methods for cancer management

**Ze Arigo** see Psychic surgery

**arm absolute yin meridian** Heart constrictor meridian, see there

**arm greater yang meridian** Small intestine meridian, see there

**arm greater yin meridian** Lung meridian, see there

**arm lesser yang meridian** Triple warmer meridian, see there

**arm lesser yin meridian** Heart meridian, see there

**arm sunlight yang meridian** Large intestine meridian, see there

**A.R.M.A.** American Reiki Masters Association A 500-member organization that promotes Reiki, as well as supplementary therapies, including aromatherapy, chakra balancing, crystal therapy, imagery and visualization, kofutu, nutritional supplements, reflexology, shiatsu, and others. See Reiki

**armor** Body armor, see there

***Armoracia rusticana*** Horseradish, see there, *Cochlearia armoracia*

**armoring** ALTERNATIVE MEDICINE An ad hoc term used in some forms of Oriental massage for muscle tension of physical or emotional origin. See Jin Shin Do® Bodymind Acupressure™, Massage therapy; Cf Body armor

**arnica** *Arnica montana,* leopard's bane, mountain daisy, mountain tobacco, sneezewort, wolf's bane FRINGE MEDICINE-FLOWER ESSENCE THERAPY Arnica essence is believed to aid in recuperation from shock and trauma; See Flower essence therapy HERBAL MEDICINE An annual, the flower and extracts of which contain thymol, resins, arnicin, carotenoids, and flavonoids; it is antibacterial, anti-inflammatory, an immune stimulant, and cardiotonic; it should not be used internally at full strength TOXICITY Diarrhea, muscle weakness, nausea, vomiting, cardiovascular collapse, coma, and possibly death. See Botanical toxicity HOMEOPATHY *Arnica* is a major homeopathic remedy used for bruises, concussions, emotional and physical shock, eyestrain, fractures, groin strain pain, joint and muscle pain, recuperation from surgery or dental work; in children, *Arnica* is used for whooping cough, and nightmares. See Homeopathy

***Arnica montana*** Arnica, see there

**aroma behavioral conditioning** Neurolinguistic programming (behavioral conditioning) through aromatherapy. See Aromatherapy, Neurolinguistic programming

**aroma-marketing** PSYCHOLOGY The use of various fragrances and volatile oils to increase a consumer's willingness to purchase a product; examples of aroma-marketing include baking foods in a house being sold and use of floral fragrances when selling articles of clothing. See Aromatherapy

**aromatherapy** FRINGE MEDICINE The use of concentrated essential oils* extracted from herbs, flowers, and other plant parts to treat various diseases; modern aromatherapy was developed in the 1930s by a French chemist, RM Gattefossé; the field was changed somewhat through the efforts of Dr Maury

**arnica** *Arnica montana*

in the 1960s, who incorporated the doctrine of signatures as the basis for selecting flowers and scents; more than 100 oils are used by aromatherapists, which are divided into those that invigorate (eg rosemary), those that tone the body (eg lemon grass oil), and those that relax the body (eg orange blossom); other oils used include basil, bergamot, black pepper, camphor, cedar, chamomile, fennel, frankincense, hyssop, jasmine, lavender, melissa, patchouli, and rose; various scents, eg lemonapple-cinnamon have been shown to improve performance of mental tasks, and reduce clerical error rates (*Castleman, 1996*) MECHANISM FOR ALLEGED BENEFICIAL EFFECT Aromatic molecules are thought to interact with appropriate receptors at the cribriform plate at the base of the skull, and stimulate the limbic system OILS USED: Eucalyptus (*Eucalyptus radiata*), lavender (*Lavendula angustifolia*), peppermint (*Mentha piperita*), lemon oil, and others ROUTES OF ADMINISTRATION: Vapor (steam inhalation), topical (baths, lotions), or internally; anecdotal reports suggest that aromatherapy may be useful in treating such diverse conditions as abscesses, agoraphobia, allergies, anal disorders, anemia, anxiety, arthritis, asthma, bipolar (manic-depressive) disorder, bronchitis, bruises, bunions, burns, bursitis, candidiasis, common cold, chickenpox, chronic fatigue syndrome, circulatory defects, colds, colic, compulsive eating, coughing, croup, dandruff, dry skin, depression, diarrhea, eczema, emphysema, fatigue, fear of flying, flatulence, fluid retention, foot problems, frozen shoulder, bacterial, viral, and fungal infections, genital herpes, gastrointestinal tract problems, eg indigestion, hay fever, headaches, insomnia, menstrual disorders, mood swings, muscle cramps, nausea, various painful conditions including neuralgias, nose and throat complaints, panic attacks, periodontal disease, phobias, postpartum depression, premenstral syndrome, prostate disease, psoriasis, sciatica, slipped or prolapsed vertebral disks, renal disease, sexual problems, sinusitis, skin disease, sleep disorders, sports injuries, stings, stress, sweating, tinnitus, toothaches, travel sickness, urinary tract disorders, warts, and wounds (*Alternative Medicine, Future Med Pub, 1994*). See Bach's flower remedies, Carrier oil, Diffusor, Distillation, Doctrine of signatures, Hydrosol *RESOURCE: National Association for Holistic Aromatherapy, PO Box 17622, Boulder, CO 80308-7622 ☎ 1.303.444.0533*

**aromatic** *adjective* Pertaining or referring to a substance that has a fragrant (usually understood to be pleasant) odor due to the presence of volatile oils *noun* A general term for any of a number of herbal medicines that have a fragrant odor, many of which are believed to be mild stimulants. See Aromatics®, Aromatherapy, Herbal medicine

**aromatic oil** See Aromatherapy

**Aromatics®** A proprietary permutation of aroma behavior conditioning, which combines neurolinguistic programming (behavioral conditioning) with aromatherapy, through the use of video and audiotapes; Aromatics® is believed by its proponents to be of use in reducing weight, stress, nicotine addiction, and to help an individual become more energetic or enthusiastic. See Aromatherapy, Neurolinguistic programming

**arousal disorder** A general term for any condition that is attributed to frequent and/or prolonged stress that is not resolved by a flight-or-fight reaction or relaxation. See Adaptation response, Flight-or-fight response; Cf Relaxation response

**arrowwood** Alder buckthorn, see there, *Rhamnus frangula*

**arsenic** A metallic element (atomic number 33, atomic weight 74.92) that has been linked to deficiency states in some plants and animals; arsenic has no known physiological role in humans, and in large amounts, is extremely toxic. See *Arsenicum album*, Trace element; Cf Trace mineral

**arsenic intoxication** Arsenic is a key component of herbicides, insecticides, rodenticides, wood preservatives, and used in manufacturing glass, and paints; the usual fatal dose is 100–200 mg; there are ± 1900 arsenic intoxications/year (US), 85% of which are accidental by children under age 6, with the remainder being suicidal in adults CLINICAL Vague gastrointestinal and neurologic symptoms, and the classic sign of 'garlic' breath, followed by dysphagia, severe abdominal pain and bloody diarrhea, then by renal and cardiac failure and circulatory collapse. See Heavy metals

***Arsenicum album*** HOMEOPATHY Arsenic oxide A homeopathic remedy prepared from arsenopyrite, an arsenic-based mineral; it is used for fear and anxiety linked to insecurity and oversensitivity; it has been used for food poisoning, overconsumption of food or alcohol, diarrhea-related dehydration, angina, asthma, anxiety, burns, colitis, dyspepsia, dyspnea, fatigue, flu, fluid retention, hay fever, high fever with chills, hacking coughs, insomnia, migraines with vertigo, watery nasal discharge, skin problems, and vomiting. See *Arsen alb* type, Homeopathy

***Arsen alb* type** HOMEOPATHY A constitutional type of person who is meticulous, perfectionistic, opinionated, and intolerant of others' opinions; *Arsen alb* types prefer warmth, movement, lying down with head elevated; they tend to have an aristocratic mien, tire easily, and like alcohol as well as warm, sweet, sour, and fat-rich foods WORSE Cold, dry, cold drinks, after midnight FEARS Poverty, loneliness, dread disease, food poisoning WEAKEST BODY REGIONS Gastrointestinal and respiratory tracts, mucosal membranes, liver, heart, skin. See *Arsenicum album*, Constitutional type, Homeopathy

**art therapy** ALTERNATIVE PSYCHOLOGY A rehabilitation technique that was developed in Britain after World War II as an extension or replacement for traditional psychotherapy, which is of greatest use in depression, stress, and tension; it is thought that by losing the inhibitions related to free expression, an individual can overcome repressed and suppressed emotions; art therapy is believed by its advocates to be beneficial in anorexia nervosa, bereavement, learning disabilities, low self-esteem, mental depression, physical disabilities, stress, and tension, and help in personal development; art therapists have a master's degree or equivalent, 600 hours of supervised training, and are registered by the American Art Therapy Association, as Art Therapists, Registered. See Sensory therapy; Cf Color therapy, Dance therapy, Music therapy, Poetry therapy, Recreational therapy *RESOURCE: American Art Therapy Association, 1202 Allanson Rd, Mundelein, IL 60060 ☎ 1.708.949.6064*

***Artemisia absinthium*** Popularly known as wormwood, see there

***Artemisia dracunculis*** Popularly known as tarragon, see there

***Artemisia vulgaris*** Popularly known as mugwort, see there

**'arthritis diet'** Arthritis diet CLINICAL NUTRITION A series of dietetic guidelines promulgated by the Arthritis Foundation that are intended to reduce a person's risk of suffering arthritic complaints, which is accompanied by an Arthritis Foundation policy statement, '*There are some scientific reasons to think that diet affects arthritis*'; these recommendations include the eating of a variety of foods, maintaining an optimal weight, avoidance of excess cholesterol, fat, sugar, sodium, reduction of alcohol consumption, accompanied by consumption of adequate starch and fiber. See Diet, Dong diet, No-nightshade diet; Cf 'Anticancer diet'

**arthritis types** CHINESE MEDICINE Arthritis is divided according to ancient Chinese medical tradition into four different types

▶ **TYPES OF ARTHRITIS** (PER CHINESE MEDICAL CONSTRUCT)

- ***RE BI*** Hot arthritis, with pain and swelling in one or more joints; the pulse is fast and slippery; the tongue is usually covered by a dry yellow coating
- ***TONG BI*** Arthritis characterized by severe pain that lingers for days in one or more joints; it is caused by excessive cold,

which slows the flow of *chi* and blood; it is worsened by cold and inactivity, improved by heat; the joints are not usually inflammed

- ***XING BI*** Migratory arthritis, with the pain moving around the body; it is caused by wind, dampness, and cold, which obstructs the flow of *chi* and circulation; the patients are thin, dislike the wind, and may have a white coating on the tongue
- ***ZUO BI*** Fixed arthritis, characterized by dampness and stagnation of the flow of *chi* and circulation; the affected joints become heavy and numb, there is a greasy white coating on the tongue; the pain is worse on rainy and cloudy days

**articulatory technique** High velocity-low amplitude technique OSTEOPATHY An osteopathic technique in which the joints are adjusted rapidly, often accompanied by a popping or snapping sound; the technique results in a transient stretching of joint capsules, and is believed to reset the position of the spinal cord and nerves, allowing the nervous system to function optimally and improve the body's biomechanical efficiency. See Osteopathy

**artificial color** Artificial dye, see there

**artificial colorant** Artificial dye, see there

**artificial coloring** Artificial dye, see there

**artificial dye** Artificial color, artificial colorant, artificial coloring, synthetic coloring principle, synthetic dye FOOD INDUSTRY A synthetic substance that imparts a desired color to a food, drug, or cosmetic; the early dyes were prepared from aniline and coal-tar, and were used without discrimination between those that were harmless and those that were toxic; artificial dyes are now certified by the FDA and classified into 3 groups: FD&C dyes, which can legally be used in foods, drugs, and cosmetics; D&C dyes that can be used in drugs and cosmetics, and external D&C dyes that are allowed only for externally applied medicines and cosmetics that are not intended for contact with mucosal surfaces, including the lips; most dyes are relatively unstable chemicals due to their unsaturated structures, and are subject to fading due to light, metals, heat, microorganisms, oxidizing and reducing agents, as well as strong acids and bases (*AR Gennaro, Ed, Remington's Pharmaceutical Sciences, 18th ed, Mack Publishing Co, Easton, PA, 1990*). See FD&C Red No. 3, FD&C Yellow No. 5, FD&C Yellow No. 6, Food additives

**artificial flavor** Synthetic flavor FOOD INDUSTRY A synthetic substance that imparts a desired flavor to a food or drug, which often possess the same delicate flavor and aroma of the natural products, are chemically stable and relatively inexpensive; use of artificial flavors (eg benzaldehyde) increased during World War II because of a shortage of the natural oil; there is a close relationship between the chemical structure of flavorings and their taste; taste is influenced by solubility, degree of ionization, and types of ions produced in the saliva, which affects how the sensation is interpreted by the brain; artificial flavorings include anethole (anise flavor), benzaldehyde (almond), ethyl acetate (fruit), and methyl salicylate (wintergreen). See Food additives

**artificial sweetener** Any of a group of substances with a taste similar to the usual dietary sugars, glucose and sucrose, which are metabolized incompletely or not at all, resulting in a minimal gain of calories; given the known, albeit minimal, risk of bladder cancer and unknown teratogenic potential of saccharine and cyclamates, aspartame is the regarded as the best artificial sweetener to use in pregnancy. See Aspartame, Cyclamates, Sugar substitutes, Sweet proteins

**artistic temperament** PERFORMING ARTS MEDICINE, PSYCHOLOGY A personality 'profile' that is well-described in creative writers, artists, and composers, which in the extreme case borders on a mental illness

> *'Men have called me mad, but the question is not yet settled, whether madness is or is not the loftiest intelligence-whether much that is glorious-whether all that is profound-does not spring from disease of thought-from moods of mind exalted at the expense of the general intellect.'*–Edgar Allen Poe

many artists have been afflicted by major depression[1], bipolar disorder[2], cyclothymia; and die by their own hand[3]; episodes of hypomania or mania (which are characterized by expansive moods, increased self-esteem, insomnia, abundant energy, irritability, rapid movement of thought and fluid movement from one subject to another) may form the 'substrate' for the creative bursts[4] (*Sci Am 1995; 272/2:63*)

[1]Characterized by apathy, lethargy, hopelessness, insomnia, slowed movement and thought, and total anhedonia (lack of pleasure for otherwise enjoyable life events) [2]Manic-depressive disease which, with cyclothymia, is thought to be 10 to 20 times more common among artists than in the general population [3]The suicide rate among artists is up to 18 times greater than the general population [4]Robert Schumann, the composer, produced the majority of his musical works in 1840 and 1849, both were years in which he was described as hypomanic (ie, 'nuts')

**AS-101** ALTERNATIVE ONCOLOGY A synthetic organotellurium that boosts the immune system by increasing the production of interleukin-2 and colony-stimulating factor, which may be of use in stimulating the immune system of cancer patients TOXICITY Anorexia, bone marrow suppression, cardiotoxicity, and liver damage (*Moss, 1992*). See Organotellurium, Unproven methods for cancer management

***asana*** AYURVEDIC MEDICINE Any of a number of poses used in the practice of yoga, usually performed in the context of a routine of exercises, which are practiced daily for 10 to 20 minutes; the *asana* aid in neuromuscular integration, or are intended to specifically stimulate the activity of certain organs

▶ **THERAPEUTIC *ASANAS***

- **BOAT POSE** A pose that strengthens the back muscles, and vertebral column, and helps in digestion
- **COBRA POSE** A serpentine pose that improves digestion
- **CORPSE POSE** A pose of complete relaxation, which is believed to be effective in treating back pain, stress, and hypertension
- **DANCER POSE** A pose that improves balance, opens nasal passages, strengthen hips and thighs, and combats fatigue
- **EASY BRIDGE POSE** A pose that reduces back pain and fatigue, hypertension, improves the circulation to the head, and stimulates the endocrine system
- **HALF BOAT POSE** A less strenuous form of the boat pose
- **LION POSE** A breathing pose that relaxes facial muscles and eases tension
- **MOUNTAIN POSE** A pose that is the basis for all other poses; it teaches correct posture, and is believed to slow the progression of osteoporosis
- **STANDING SUN POSE** A pose believed to improve neural function, constipation, bladder problems, and loosen the hips and shoulders
- **SEATED SUN POSE** A pose that is believed to help in digestion and impotence, and strengthen leg muscles
- **TREE POSE** A pose that tones the legs, improves balance, concentration, and breathing
- **WINDMILL POSE** A pose that loosens the hips, lower back, and improves breathing

See Ayurvedic medicine, *Prana*, *Rasayana*

***Asarum heterotropoides*** *Asarum sieboldi*, see there

***Asarum sieboldi*** *Asarum heterotropoides*, *hsi hsin*, *xi xin* CHINESE MEDICINE A perennial herb, the rootlets of which are analgesic, diaphoretic, expectorant, secretory, and sedative; it is used to treat arthritis, earaches, headaches, sinusitis, and toothaches. See Chinese herbal medicine

***Asclepias syriaca*** Popularly known as milkweed, see there

**ascorbic acid** Vitamin C, see there

***ashtanga* yoga** 1. *Raja* yoga, see there 2. A form of yoga based on *raja* yoga that was developed by Pathabi Jois that has 8 limbs, which includes ethical precepts (*yama* and *niyama*), physical practices (*hatha* and *pranayama*), inner-directed practices (*pratyahara* and *dharana*), meditation (*dhyana*) and absorption (*samadhi*). See Yoga

**ashwaganda** *Withania somnifera* AYURVEDIC HERBAL MEDICINE A shrub from India which is regarded as a tonic for bone marrow, muscles, and other tissues; it is used internally for fatigue, heart disease, hay fever, indigestion, infertility, loss of libido, multiple sclerosis, rheumatic complaints, and topically for skin conditions including abscesses, cuts, and ringworm; it is believed to be an aphrodisiac and prevent male sterility. See Herbal medicine

**Asian ginseng** Ginseng, see there, *Panax ginseng*

***Asparagus falcatus*** Shiny asparagus, see there, formally known as *Asparagus lucidus*

***Asparagus lucidus*** Popularly known as shiny asparagus, see there

**aspartame** Nutrasweet® An artificial sweetener that is a dipeptide ester of aspartic acid and phenylalanine which was discovered in 1965, approved by the FDA in 1983; it is believed to be safer than saccharin (with the notable exception of patients with phenylketonuria); some 'soft' experimental data suggests it is associated with brain tumors ADVERSE REACTIONS Excess consumption of aspartame may cause mild depression, headaches, insomnia, loss of

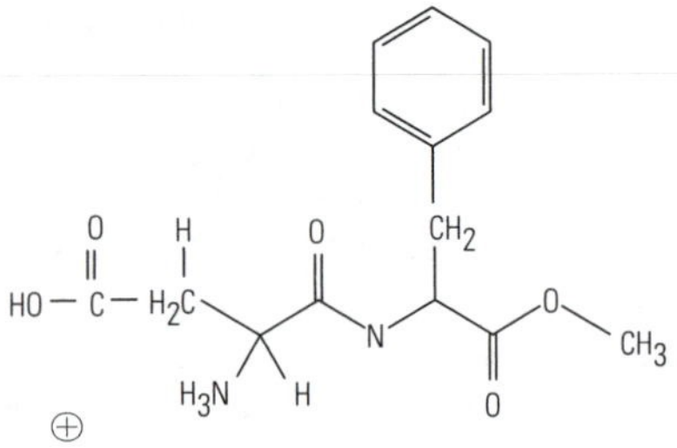

**aspartame**

motor control, nausea, seizures, and tinnitus (*Quarterly report on Adverse Reactions Associated with Aspartame; FDA, April 1988*). See Artificial sweeteners

***Asperula odorata*** Popularly known as sweet woodruff, see there

***Aspidium falcatum*** see Fern-Chinese medicine

**ass-ear** Comfrey, see there, *Symphytum officinale*

**ass's foot** Colt's foot, see there, *Tussilago farfara*

**assertiveness training** ALTERNATIVE PSYCHOLOGY A type of behavior modification in which a person is trained to distinguish between aggressiveness, a behavior often rooted in anger and/or meanness, and assertiveness, in which an individual learns to stand up for his rights; assertiveness training is intended to convert anxiety, panic, fear of failure, and low self-esteem into positive interactions with others (*Watson, 1995*). See Est, Humanistic psychology

**assist** PARANORMAL PHENOMENA A term used in Scientology® for any action that is intended to help an individual overcome the effects of past mental trauma. See Scientology®

**Association for Research and Enlightenment** PARANORMAL PHENOMENA An organization located in Virginia Beach, VA that is centered around the life scripts and therapies of Edgar Cayce (1877-1945), a clairvoyant healer. See Cayce

***astana* yoga** AYURVEDIC MEDICINE A permutation of hatha yoga, which incorporates lifestyle manipulation and *ujaya* breathing, the latter of which is believed to purify cells and tissues. See Yoga

***astanga* yoga** 1. *Ashtanga* yoga, see there 2. *Raja* yoga, see there

**Astara** PARANORMAL PHENOMENA A New Age church of mystic Christianity, which follows Jesus Christ, and honors the saints and prophets of other religions; it offers correspondence courses in paranormal phenomena, and is the home base for Astara healing science (*Raso, 1994*). See Astara healing science

**Astara healing science** PARANORMAL PHENOMENA A spiritual healing philosophy that involves the use of crystals, etheric contacts, scientific prayer, imagery and visualization, and tapping the magnetic energies of the 'White Light' (*Raso, 1994*). See Astara

**asthma weed** Lobelia, see there, *Lobelia inflata*

**Aston patterning** A form of structural integration (bodywork) developed in the mid-1970s by a dancer, Jane Aston, initially under Ida Rolf, and subsequently as a movement therapy a sui generis; in contrast to Rolf's model, which assumes that a state of health requires alignment and symmetry, Aston believes that all movement of the body is by nature asymmetrical; Aston's work has four components: massage, movement reeducation, fitness training, and environmental (ie workplace) design; Aston patterning is believed to address poor posture, and neck and back pain, and sports injuries; Aston patterning certification requires a 16-week training program over a 15-month period. See Structural integration; Cf Alexander technique, Feldenkreis method, Hellerwork™, Massage, Ortho-bionomy, Rolfing®, Rosen method, Tragerwork

**ASTRA 8 formula** CHINESE MEDICINE A combination of herbs (astragalus, atractylodes, codonopsis, eluthero, ganoderma, ginseng, licorice, and schizardra) that is used as an energy tonic; ASTRA 8 has been used in patients with AIDS-related complex, and is believed to improve appetite, digestion, and sleep. See Astragalus 10 plus, Chinese herbal medicine, Power mushroom formula

**Astragalus 10 plus** CHINESE MEDICINE A combination of herb and fruits (astrogalus, cistanche, eluthero, ganoderma, ginseng, licorice, ligustrum, lycium fruit, morus fruit, and ophiopogan) that is used as an energy tonic and immune enhancer. See ASTRA 8 formula, Chinese herbal medicine, Power mushroom formula

**astragalus** *Astragalus membranaceus, Astragalus hoantchy, huang chi, huang qi,* milk-vetch root An herb that contains betaine, choline, essential fatty oils, glycosides, saponins, and vitamin A CHINESE MEDICINE In Chinese herbal medicine, the root is cardiotonic and diuretic; it is used to treat adrenal insufficiency, anorexia, bronchitis, cancer, colds, chronic fatigue, diabetes, diarrhea, hepatitis, hypertension, immune deficiency, organ prolapse, profuse sweating, and weakness of extremities. See Chinese herbal medicine FRINGE ONCOLOGY Astragalus is believed to be a cancer therapy as it boosts the immune system (*Moss, 1992*). See Unproven methods for cancer management WESTERN HERBAL MEDICINE In Western herbal medicine, astragalus has been used as a digestive tonic, to enhance the immune system, and for AIDS, cancer, chronic fatigue, and the common cold. See Herbal medicine

***Astragalus hoantchy*** Astralagus, see there, *Astragalus membranaceus*

***Astragalus membranaceus*** Popularly known as astragalus, see there

**'astral' body** see Anthroposophical medicine

**astral healing** Medical astrology, see there

**astringent** HERBAL MEDICINE An herb that causes a hardening and contraction of tissues due to its high tannin content, and serves to prevent bacterial penetration, inhibit discharges, diarrhea, and hemorrhage; astringents include bayberry (*Myrica cerifera*), blackberry (*Rubus* species), calendula (*Calendula officinalis*), cranesbill (*Geranium maculatum*), myrrh (*Commiphora myrrha*), pinus bark (*Tsuga canadensis*), tormentil (*Potentilla tormentilla*), white oak (*Quercus alba*), and witch hazel (*Hamamelis virginiana*) (*Trattler, 1985*). See Herbal medicine

**astrologic medicine** Medical astrology, see there

**astrological healing** Medical astrology, see there

**astrology** '*Astrology, when it is concerned with health, derives from the belief that there is a correspondence between the positions of the sun, moon, and planets in the twelve Zodiac signs and physical, mental, spiritual, and emotional well-being.*' (*Inglis, West, 1983*). See Medical astrology

Further discussion of this occult art is beyond the intent of the present work—Author's note

**astromedicine** Medical astrology, see there

**astronaut diet** SPACE MEDICINE A fiber-free food fare that was designed to reduce stool bulk and minimize or eliminate the problems inherent in use of a solid waste management system in zero gravity. See Diet

**atavistic regression** PSYCHIATRY A term used by Australian psychotherapist Ainsley Meares for a return to a mental state in which an individual's instinct is allowed a freer reign than is otherwise normal in the current consciousness-oriented society; some workers believe hypnotherapy acts by evoking atavistic regression. See Hypnotherapy

**Atkins' diet** CLINICAL NUTRITION A carbohydrate-poor, fat-rich 'fad' diet developed by Dr Robert Atkins in which 73% of the caloric content is fat; the basis of the diet is the deliberate induction of ketosis, in which stored fat is burned for energy; foods permitted without restriction in the Atkins' diet are high-fat, high-protein animal foods, eggs, and dairy products, vegetable oils, fats, and butter, and vegetables; the regimen severely limits fruits, sweeteners including dextrose, fructose, honey, lactose, maltose, sorbitol, and sucrose, and alcohol. See Diet

**A.T.R.** Art therapist, registered, see Art therapy

***Atractylodes chinensis*** Popularly known as thistle, see there

***Atractylodes lancea*** see Thistle

***Atractylodes lyrata*** see Thistle

***Atractylodes macrocephala*** see Thistle

***Atractylodes ovata*** see Thistle

***Atropa belladonna*** Belladonna, see there

**attar** Essential oil, usually used specifically in reference to the essential oil of roses, as in attar of roses

**attenuation** HOMEOPATHY The reduction of the absolute concentration of a homeopathic remedy by serial dilution; according to the law of the infinitesimal dose, the more the substance is attenuated (diluted), the greater is the effect. See Homeopathic remedy, Homeopathy, Potentization

**attunement** FRINGE MEDICINE A general term for the interaction of lifestyle manipulation and vibrational healing arts; attunements are believed to link the student with the universal life-force energy. See Reiki

**aucklandia** *Aucklandia lappa*, costus root, saussurea CHINESE MEDICINE An herb, the root of which is used in Chinese medicine for gastrointestinal complaints including anorexia, bloating, diarrhea, nausea, pain, and vomiting. See Chinese herbal medicine

**auditing** PARANORMAL PHENOMENA A term used in Scientology® for the erasing of the painful effects of traumatic memories (engrams); an individual who has successfully audited himself is known as a 'clear'. See Scientology®

**aura** PARANORMAL PHENOMENA A subtle energy field that is believed to envelop the human body, and correspond to the soul; many names have been given to the aura, see table; according to some, the aura can be analyzed by a number of techniques, and the information obtained therefrom provides the basis for diagnosing and monitoring disease; Cf Vital force NEUROLOGY A subjective (illusionary or hallucinatory) or objective (motor) event marking the onset of an epileptic attack or a migraine headache. See Seizure

**aura analysis** Aura reading, auric diagnosis PARANORMAL PHENOMENA The analysis of an 'etheric band' of energy (aura) that is believed by some to surround every living being; according to its proponents, the aura which reflects a person's state of health, emotions, internal conflicts, and vulnerabilities; although the aura is invisible to the naked eye of normal individuals, aura therapists claim to be able to 'see' nine different colors (white, red, orange, yellow, green, blue, indigo, violet, and black) in a person's aura; aura therapists have no formal training, and generally are regarded as psychics or faith healers. See Aura analysis; Cf Aurasomatherapy, Faith healing

There is little data in peer-reviewed literature to verify these claims; aura therapy is the most peripheral of alternative therapies; its effect, if any, may reflect a person's beliefs–Author's note

**AURA-SYNONYMS**

Astral body, auric field, bioenergy field, biofield, bioplasmic body, bioplasmic force field, doppelgänger, dream body, etheric body, etheric double, hakra, human atmosphere, human energy field, sidereal body, spiritual body, spiritual skin, star body, subtle body, subtle organizing energy field, vital body

can be analyzed either directly (if the person is clairvoyant–or more correctly, clairsentient), or indirectly by examination of the effects of the energy field, by means of Kirlian photography or a Kilner screen; according to aura analysts, the colors seen indicate personality traits, a person's state of mind, and whether a particular organ is improperly functioning. See Kilner screen, Kirlian photography

**aura balancing** Aura cleansing, aura clearing, aura healing, auric healing, aura therapy PARANORMAL PHENOMENA The process of harmonizing the aura (energy field) around a person's head or body; aura balancing is based on the belief that each living life form is surrounded by an electromagnetic field (or aura),

**aura cleansing** Aura balancing, see there

**aura clearing** Aura balancing, see there

**aura healing** Aura balancing, see there

**aura reading** Aura analysis, see there

**aura therapy** Aura balancing, see there

**aurasomatherapy** PARANORMAL PHENOMENA A system developed by British clairvoyant, Vicky Wall, which combines color therapy and chakra healing; the system is used to diagnose various conditions; these conditions are then 'treated' using 'color bottles' that contain essential and volatile oils and herbal extracts, which are purported to help revitalize and balance the aura. See Aura, Aura balancing

**auric diagnosis** Aura analysis, see there

**auric massage** PARANORMAL PHENOMENA A permutation of angelic healing, in which the aura is rebalanced by moving the practitioner's hands above the surface of the body; see Angelic healing, Aura, Aura balancing

**auricular acupuncture** Auriculotherapy, auricular therapy, ear acupuncture ALTERNATIVE MEDICINE A permutation of acupuncture that was practiced in ancient China and has recently been revitalized; acupuncture needles are inserted in various highly specific sites in the auricle (external ear); according to its advocates, there are over 200 acupuncture points on the auricle that are believed to affect any diseased part of the body; anecdotal reports suggest that auricular acupuncture may be effective in such diverse conditions as addiction disorders, anorexia, arthritis, asthma, dyspnea, gastrointestinal problems (eg indigestion), gout, migraines, pain including post-operative and childbirth-related pain, panic attacks, and urinary tract disease. See Acupressure, Acupuncture; Cf Auricular reflexology, Shiatsu

A controlled study of 36 patients with chronic pain undergoing auriculotherapy–reported in 1984 in the Journal of the American Medical Association concluded that any relief produced by auriculotherapy was attributed to a placebo effect (*Raso, 1994*)

**auricular medicine** Auricular reflexology, see there

**auricular reflexology** Auricular medicine A permutation of auricular acupuncture reported in 1967 by a Frenchman, Dr PFM Nogier; the 'Nogier' variant differs in theory from that of Chinese auricular therapy, as he believed the effect to be neuroendocrine in nature; Cf Auricular acupuncture

**auricular therapy** 1. Auricular acupuncture, see there 2. Auricular reflexology, see there

**auriculotherapy** 1. Auricular acupuncture, see there 2. Auricular reflexology, see there

***Aurum metallicum*** Gold HOMEOPATHY A remedy that has been used for bone pain, mental disorders (eg depression and suicidal ideation), headache, jaundice, retrosternal pain, sinusitis, and undescended testicles; see Homeopathy

**'authentic self'** True self, see there

**autocontractile pain response** See SHEN therapy

**autogenic discharge** ALTERNATIVE MEDICINE An abrupt sensation of fear or pain that is experienced by a person undergoing autogenic feedback training, which is believed to occur with the release of suppressed physical or emotional energy. See Autogenic feedback training

**autogenic feedback training** Autogenic therapy ALTERNATIVE PSYCHOLOGY A hypnosis-based healing method that was developed in the 1920s by a German neurologist, Johannes Schultz; the technique consists of 6 mental exercises for relaxing the individual, and relieving suppressed anger, emotion, and tension; the exercises are intended to evoke deep relaxation, and consist of controlling breathing and heart rate, and in visualizing warmth and heaviness of the abdomen, arms and legs, and cooling of the head; it is claimed that these exercises result in self-healing, and may enhance the performance of athletes and performing artists including dancers WARNING Autogenic feedback training is not well-suited for those with alcoholism or other addiction disorders, insulin-dependent diabetes mellitus, mental disorders including schizophrenia, and seizures, and should only be carried out under traditional (mainstream) medical supervision; anecdotal reports suggest that autogenic feedback training may be beneficial in addiction disorders, AIDS, allergies, angina pain, anxiety, cancer, cardiovascular disease, chronic fatigue syndrome, circulatory problems, depression, eczema, gastrointestinal tract problems (eg colitis, constipation, indigestion, and irritable bowel syndrome), depression, hemorrhoids, hostility, hypercholesterolemia, hypertension, infertility, jet lag, low self-esteem, low back pain, menstrual disorders, migraines, mood swings, multiple sclerosis, neck pain, neuralgia, obesity, panic attacks, postpartum depression, premenstrual syndrome, sciatica, sexual problems, shock, skin disease, speech disorders, sports injuries, stage fright, stress, (nervous) sweating, tension, ulcers, urinary tract disease, and writer's cramp. See Autosuggestion therapy, Biofeedback, Biopsychosocial model, Breath therapy, Flight-or-fight response, Healing visualization, Hypnosis, Meditation, Mind/body medicine, Mindfulness Psychoneuroimmunology, Stressor Visualization therapy *RESOURCE: International Committee for Autogenic Training, 101 Harley St, London, W1N 1DF, England* PHYSIOLOGY A self-healing method that has been studied as a means of controlling certain physiologic responses, eg to motion sickness, hypertension, and others; in autogenic feedback training, the individual's heart rate, respiration, perspiration, and blood flow to a finger are displayed on digital and oscilloscope readouts; the individual is placed in a device (eg, Stille-Werner rotating chair) that evokes the response (eg, motion sickness), and learns to conquer the response through breath and muscle control, and autosuggestion, while watching the displays of his/her physiologic responses to the induced effect (eg, rotation); autogenic feedback training has been used to to control motion sickness in astronauts (*Discover 5/90, p 74*). See Biofeedback training

**autogenic therapy** Autogenic feedback training, see there

**autogenics** Autogenic feedback training, see there

**autohypnosis** see Autosuggestion, autosuggestion therapy

**autointoxication** ALTERNATIVE MEDICINE A questionable theory advanced by VE Irons and others, that many diseases are caused by chronic poisoning due to intestinal stasis, putrefaction within the intestine, and absorption of toxins; the theory of autointoxication was popular at the turn of the 20th century, but was abandoned by the scientific community in the 1930s, given that healthy individuals have a wide range of bowel habits; the theory periodically resurfaces in various forms, in particular to justify colon therapy. See Colon therapy, High colonic

**autolymphocyte therapy** A form of immunotherapy for treating metastatic renal carcinoma, in which a patient's white blood cells are removed and stimulated by monoclonal antibodies, which causes the white cells to produce and secrete cytokines; the cytokine supernatant is then removed and readministered with some of the patient's own white cells; Cf Immunoaugmentive therapy

**autosuggestion** Autohypnosis, self-hypnosis ALTERNATIVE PSYCHOLOGY The use of the principles of hypnosis on oneself; autosuggestion requires complete relaxation, slow deep breathing, and repetition of the same phrases used in hypnosis, eg '*my eyelids are getting heavy…Very heavy…I am getting sleepy*'. See Hypnosis, Hypnotherapy

**autosuggestion therapy** Couéism ALTERNATIVE MEDICINE A hypnosis-based healing method that was developed in the 1890s by a French apothecary, Emile Coué, which is based on the belief that a person is able to 'will' himself back to a state of health; Coué advocated yoga to improve the ability to concentrate; the individual is taught to free his mind of all distractions and then to repeat, throughout the course of the day, various mantra-like 'positive' phrases; autosuggestion therapy is complemented by autogenic feedback training, healing visualization, and meditation; the technique is intended to relax the individual, relieve anger, emotion, tension, and evoke deep relaxation; anecdotal reports suggest that autosuggestion therapy may be effective in treating such diverse conditions as addiction disorders, allergies, asthma, chronic fatigue syndrome, low back pain, migraines, mood swings, neuralgia, panic attacks, phobias, postpartum depression, sciatica, shock, sports injuries, stress, tension, and trauma. See Affirmation, Autogenic feedback training, Healing visualization, Hypnosis, Imagery and visualization, Mantra, Meditation, Pealeism, Yoga

**auto-urine therapy** Urine therapy, see there

**autumn crocus** *Colchicum autumnale*, colchicum, meadow saffron, naked ladies HERBAL MEDICINE A perennial herb that is the primary source of colchicine, an alkaloid used for treating gout in mainstream medicine

**AVATAR** PSYCHOLOGY A belief management seminar developed in 1987 that may be applicable to a range of problems including health, education, and occupation; central to the concept of AVATAR is the belief that a person has the natural ability to create or

**autumn crocus** *Colchicum autumnale*

'discreate' a reality at will; this ability is believed to be part of the consciousness that is termed 'source' (*J Raso, 1994*). See Assertiveness training, Behavior modification, Est

***Avena sativa*** Oats, see there

**aversion therapy** PSYCHOLOGY A form of

behavioral therapy, in which adverse or negative behaviors or habits, eg alcohol, drug, or tobacco abuse, are unlearned, through punishment or negative reinforcement of the undesired behavior; an example of aversion therapy is the use of disulfiram for alcoholics; because disulfiram inhibits alcohol dehydrogenase, alcohol consumption results in an increase in acetaldehyde in the blood, which evokes tremor, hypo- or hypertension, nausea, and possibly vomiting. See Behavioral therapy, Encounter group therapy, Flooding, Image aversion therapy, Systematic desensitization

**Avogadro limit** HOMEOPATHY A point, based on Avogadro's number ($6.02 \times 10^{23}$, which represents the number of molecules in a gram molecule), at which a homeopathic remedy has been diluted (attenuated) to the point where it is unlikely that any molecules of the remedy are present; the Avogadro limit is passed 23 × ($10^{23}$ or 23D); a major obstacle for accepting homeopathic principles by mainstream scientists is that many of the homeopathic remedies prescribed are believed to be effective at dilutions of 30 × ($10^{30}$), 200 × ($10^{200}$), and higher. See Homeopathic remedy, Homeopathy, Potentization

**'Awakened for Life' program** PSYCHOLOGY An audiocassette program developed by an American psychotherapist, Dr WW Dyer; the program teaches the client to attune himself to a 'Higher Power' (God, nature, life force); once the consumer is 'awakened', he is equipped with tool for combating cancer, addictions (eg to alcohol, drugs, and tobacco), and other conditions

**awareness-oriented structural therapy** Structural bodywork BODYWORK A psychological approach to mind/body medicine, which combines various structural bodywork techniques with 'natural psychotherapy'; awareness-oriented structural therapy borrows components of various forms of bodywork, including connective tissue therapy, deep tissue massage, neuromuscular therapy, polarity therapy, and structural integration; its psychological aspects are borrowed from Gestalt therapy, Hakomi therapy, meditation, present-centered awareness and therapy, psychosynthesis, and sensory awareness; structural bodywork is believed by its advocates to increase balance, vitality, movement, dynamic interaction with gravity, improve metabolism, relieve pain, enhance mental clarity, release emotions, and ultimately lead to personal growth and transformation; therapists certified in this form of bodywork have completed a 500-hour course. See Bodywork

**awareness through movement** see Feldenkreis method

**ayurveda** 1. The Indian philosophy that forms the basis for ayurvedic medicine; although the terms ayurveda and ayurvedic medicine are often used interchangeably, the former is more global and includes both the ayurvedic philosophy and those components of ayurveda that are rarely applied in modern ayurvedic medicine; the major branches of ayurveda incorporated into current ayurvedic medicine are internal medicine, geriatrics, aphrodisiac medicine, and *panchakarma*; the other branches of ayuveda—ophthalmology, otorhinolaryngology, psychiatry, psychotherapy, pediatrics, surgery, and toxicology, have been largely abandoned in favor of the Western versions of these fields 2. Ayurvedic medicine, see there

**ayurvedic healing** Ayurvedic medicine, see there

**ayurvedic herbal medicine** AYURVEDIC MEDICINE A therapeutic system based on the classification of foods and herbs into four groups: Energy–*virya*, taste–*rasa*, post-digestive effect–*vipaka*, and potency–*vipaka*; specific herbs are used to increase or decrease the *doshas* (*kapha*, *pitta*, and *vata*). See Ayurvedic medicine, *Dosha*, *Kapha*, *Pitta*, *Vata*; Cf Chinese herbal medicine, Herbal medicine

**ayurvedic lymphatic massage** Ayurvedic massage, see there

**ayurvedic massage** *Abhyanga*, ayurvedic lymphatic massage, marma therapy AYURVEDIC MEDICINE A form of massage, that stimulates specific *marma* points, which are invisible but palpable junction points between mind and matter, analogous to the pressure points in acupuncture; *abhyanga* is performed by touch and using special oils and transcendental meditation. See Ayurvedic medicine, *Marma*, *Prana*, *Rasayana*

**ayurvedic medicine** Ayerveda, ayurvedic healing,

ayurvedism, vedic healing, vedic medicine ALTERNATIVE MEDICINE Sanskrit, *ayur*–Life, *veda*–knowledge The oldest existing medical system in the world, which is practiced by approximately 300 000 physicians, primarily in the subcontinent of India; ayurvedic medicine encompasses aromatherapy, diet and nutrition, herbal medicine, massage, and vedic astrology; ayurvedic philosophy holds that disease is caused by an imbalance of homeostatic and immune mechanisms related to three physiological principles or '*doshas*'

► ***DOSHAS***

- ***VATA DOSHA*** Wind force *Vata* represents fluid and motion, and corresponds to the Western concepts of circulation and neuromuscular activity
- ***PITTA DOSHA*** Sun force *Pitta* directs all metabolic activities, energy exchange, and digestion
- ***KAPHA DOSHA*** Moon force *Kapha* represents structure, cohesion and fluid balance and, when deranged, predisposes toward respiratory disease, diabetes, atherosclerosis, and tumors

According to the ayurvedic construct, there are four categories of diseases

► **AYURVEDIC DISEASES**

- **ACCIDENTAL**, eg typhoon, elephant trampling
- **MENTAL**, eg loss of mental harmony
- **NATURAL**, eg aging, childbirth
- **EXTERNAL**, eg weather, foods, and others

► **AYURVEDIC APPROACHES TO THERAPY**

- **DIET**–Foods should be consumed slowly, in their natural season in a tranquil surrounding; occasional fasting is thought to promote health
- **MEDICINE**–The primary therapeutic and preventative arsenal is based in herbal remedies, which may be supplemented by homeopathy and conventional (western or orthodox) drugs
- **PRACTICAL**–Behavior modification, breathing exercises, mental counseling, enemas, transcendental meditation, yoga, and a 'healthy' life style (*JAMA 1991; 265:2633*)

► **AYURVEDIC REMEDIES**

- **CONSTITUTIONAL REMEDIES**–Diet, mild herbs, mineral preparations, and lifestyle adjustments, which are intended to balance life forces, and return the body to its normal state of harmony
- **CLINICAL REMEDIES**–Medication and strong herbs, coupled with purification practices, which include purgation, medicated enemas, therapeutic vomiting, nasal medication, and therapeutic bloodletting *RESOURCE: Ayurvedic Institute, 1311 Menaul NE, Suite A, Albuquerque, NM 87112* ☎ *1.505.291.9698*. See *Asanas*, *Doshas*

**ayurvedism** Ayurvedic medicine, see there

**azelaic acid** FRINGE ONCOLOGY A substance first identified in rancid oleic acid that interferes with anerobic glycolysis and mitochondrial activity, which may have some efficacy in treating melanomas (*Moss, 1992*). See Unproven methods for cancer management

**B need** Self-actualization need, see there

**B value** Self-actualization need, see there

**babunah** Chamomile, see there

**baby blue eyes** *Nemophila menziesii* FRINGE MEDICINE—FLOWER ESSENCE THERAPY A flower essence that is believed to provide childlike innocence, trust, feelings of love and support, and a connection with the spiritual world. See Flower essence therapy

**baby B.E.S.T.** A permutation of the bio-energetic synchronization technique (BEST) of massage applied to infants, which was developed in 1991 by an American chiropractor, MT Morter; the objective of baby BEST is to remove the segmentation imbalances and restore symmetry to the child, and 'update' the afferent and efferent responses to and from the brain. See Bio-energetic synchronization technique; Morter HealthSystem

**Bach, Dr Edward** An English physician and homeopath (1886-1930) who abandoned a career in mainstream medicine to study the effects of various flowers on human disease, and developed the field of flower essence therapy. See Bach flower remedy

**Bach flower remedy** Flower remedy FRINGE MEDICINE—FLOWER ESSENCE THERAPY A form of alternative health care delineated by a British physician, Edward Bach; in Bach therapy, flowers are used to '...*directly address a person's emotional state to...facilitate both psychological and physiological well-being...balancing negative feelings and stress, flower remedies can...remove the emotional barriers to health and recovery.*' (*Alternative Medicine, Future Med, 1994*); Bach descibed 38 concoctions, which consist of infusions prepared from freshly-picked, sun-exposed flowers placed in spring water and brandy, which form a so-called 'Mother Essence'; Bach identified 38 wild flowers, which he believed had therapeutic value, and divided them into 7 groups based on the type of negative state of mind that each addressed

► **BACH'S THERAPEUTIC GROUPS**

- **DEPRESSION** Crabapple, elm, larch, oak, pine, Star-of-Bethlehem, sweet chestnut, willow
- **FEAR** Aspen, cherry plum, mimulus, red chestnut, rock rose
- **LACK OF INTEREST IN THE PRESENT** Clematis, honeysuckle, wild rose
- **LONELINESS** Heather, impatiens, water violet
- **OVERCONCERN FOR WELFARE OF OTHERS** Beech, chestnut bud, chicory, mustard, olive, rock water, vervain, vine, white chestnut
- **OVERSENSITIVITY** Agrimony, centaury, holly, walnut
- **UNCERTAINTY** Cerato, gentian, gorse, hornbeam, scleranthus, wild oat

Anecdotal reports suggest that Bach flower remedies may be effective in treating as addiction disorders, agoraphobia, allergies, amnesia, anxiety, asthma, bites and stings, bronchitis, bruxism, bruises, bunions, burns, chronic fatigue syndrome, claustrophobia, common cold, depression, eczema, fatigue, fluid retention, hay fever, headaches, hypotension, hypertension, infertility, insomnia, migraines, various painful conditions including neuralgia, mood swings, panic attacks, post-partum depression, premenstral syndrome, psoriasis, sciatica, slipped or prolapsed vertebral disks, renal disease, sexual dysfunction, stress, and tension. See Alternative medicine, Dr Bach's Emergency Stress Formula, Flower essence therapy *RESOURCE: Ellon, USA, Lynbrook, NY 11563 ☎ 1.516.593.2206*

**Dr Bach's Emergency Stress Formula** Rescue remedy, emergency stress relief formula, Calming Essence™, five-flower formula FRINGE MEDICINE—FLOWER ESSENCE THERAPY The most widely used of the Bach flower remedies[1], which is composed of clematis, impatiens, rock rose, cherry plum[2], Star-of-Bethlehem[2]; it is recommended by its enthusiasts following physical or mental trauma; the 'Formula' is believed by its users to have a tranquilizing effect in acute situations including anxiety, asthma, bereavement, hysteria, labor pains, migraines, physical trauma and, when applied topically, is believed to be useful for bruises, burns, cuts, animal or insect bites. See Bach's flower remedy

[1]Legend has it that Dr Bach discovered the formula while treating a shipwrecked sailor, who had washed up on the beach near his laboratory; [2]Bach's original formula contained the first three herbs; the last two were added by his followers

**bacquet** MEDICAL HISTORY—FRINGE MEDICINE An iron rod filled with healer-treated water that was used to treat Anton Mesmer's patients. See Mesmerism

**'bad blood'** MEDICAL HISTORY A popular term for unknown factors that were said to be present in the blood of those with various illnesses—most of which were probably infections; in the heroic age of medicine, 'bad blood' was treated by bleeding the patient with leeches or lancets, often resulting in the loss of one-half or more of the person's blood volume (*Armstrong, 1991*); the demise of the concept of 'bad blood' coincided with Pasteur's germ theory

**'bad' cholesterol** LDL-cholesterol Cholesterol that is carried in the circulation by low-density lipoprotein, the elevation of which is directly related to the risk of coronary artery disease and cholesterol-related morbidity (*New York Times, 8 Feb 1994; C1*). See LDL-cholesterol; Cf Good cholesterol

**bad eicosanoid** A colloquial term for eicosanoid that arises from the metabolism of dihomogamma-linolenic acid by the enzyme delta-5-desaturase into arachidonic acid, which in turn is converted into thromboxane $A_2$ (which increases platelet aggregation), $PGE_2$ (which promotes pain and depresses the immune system), and leukotrienes (which are associated with allergic responses and skin disease); bad eicosanoids' adverse effects include increased coagulation (platelet aggregation), vasoconstriction causing hypertension, increased cell proliferation, depressed immune system, increased inflammation, and increased sensitivity to pain (*B Sears. The Zone, Harper-Collins, New York, 1995*). See Zone-favorable diet; Cf Good eicosanoid

**bad habit** CLINICAL MEDICINE Unhealthy habit A general term for any behavior that is considered to be detrimental to one's physical or mental health, which is often linked to a lack of self-control; bad habits include alcohol or drug abuse, consumption of tobacco in any form, overeating, regular 'junk food' consumption, late-night 'partying,' and compulsive activities including gambling, shopping, sexual addiction, and others; Cf Good habit

**Baggie™ therapy** A colloquial term coined by PD Utsinger, MD for the use of ice-water placed in a plastic bag (Baggie™) as a means of providing transient pain relief in patients with rheumatoid arthritis (*Bricklin, 1976, 1983*). See RICE

***baguazhang*** *Pa kua chang,* circle walking An exercise system developed in the 19th century by Dong Hai Chuan, which has been likened to internal kung fu; the practitioner uses various stepping techniques, that mimic the ambulation of chickens, elephants, snakes, and other animals; it is believed by its practitioners to enhance health, prolong life, and strengthen *qi* forces

***bai guo*** *Gingko biloba*, see there

***bai ji*** *Bletilla striata*, see there

***bai jih*** *Angelica anomala*, see there

***bai liang jin*** Tree peony, see there, *Paeonia moutan*

***bai shao*** White peony, see there, *Paeonia albiflora*

***bai zhi*** *Angelica anomala*, see there

**Mary Ellen Baker** The founder (1821-1910) of Christian Science; she changed her name to Mary Baker Eddy in 1873 at the time of her third marriage to Asa Eddy. See Christian Science

**balanced diet** CLINICAL NUTRITION A general term for a diet containing proportionate amounts of those food groups that are considered to be optimal for good health; a properly balanced diet should be highest in fruits and vegetables, have a moderate amount of refined carbohydrates (eg breads and cereals), fish, and dairy products, lesser amounts of meat, and minimal amounts of fats (eg butter); the food pyramid promulgated by the US Department of Agriculture is an attempt to simplify the planning of a balanced diet. See Food groups, Food pyramid

**balance therapy** A health system developed by A Beliavstev, which includes 'diagnostic' acupressure, herbal medicine, and homeopathy

**balloon flower** *Platycodon grandiflorum*, also known as *Campanula grandiflora, jie geng, Platycodon chinensis* CHINESE MEDICINE A perennial herb containing saponins, the root of which is used as a bronchodilator and expectorant; it is used for abdominal pain, bronchitis, chest pain, colds, cough, diarrhea, oral abscesses, respiratory tract infections, sore throat, and tonsillitis. See Chinese herbal medicine

**balm** Lemon balm, see there, *Melissa officinalis*

**balm of Gilead** *Populus* spp (*P canadensis, P nigra, P balsamifera*), balsam poplar, black poplar, poplar buds HERBAL MEDICINE A deciduous tree, the leaf buds of which contain volatile oils (eg bisabolol, cineole, humulene), palicin, phenolic acids, and salicin; balm of Gilead has a long history of use as a medicinal herb; it is analgesic (due to its high content of salicin), antibacterial, anti-inflammatory, antiseptic, and expectorant, and has been used topically to treat abscesses, burns, hemorrhoids, and rheumatic complaints. See Herbal medicine

**balm of Gilead** *Populus* spp

**balm of Gilead fir** Balsam fir, see there, *Abies balsamea*

**balsam fir** *Abies balsamea*, balm of Gilead fir, fir balsam, fir pine, sapin, silver fir, silver pine HERBAL MEDICINE An evergreen, the root and needles of which once had currency as aromatic adjuncts in the sweat lodges of Native Americans, for whom it was used to treat asthma, colds, cough, and as a laxative. See Herbal medicine

**balsam fir** *Abies balsamea*

**balsam of Peru** *Myroxylon balsamum* HERBAL MEDICINE An evergreen tree, the resin of which is anthelmintic, antifungal, astringent, and diuretic; it has been used internally and externally for hemorrhoids and skin infections. See Herbal medicine

***ban hsia*** *Pinellia ternata*, see there

***ban xia*** *Pinellia ternata*, see there

**bancha** A type of green tea that is thought to have a higher concentration of EGCG (epigallocatechin gallate), a carcinoprotective chemical, than is found in other green teas (*Moss, 1992*). See Epigallocatechin gallate, Green tea

**banting** Dieting MEDICAL HISTORY–CLINICAL NUTRITION An ad hoc term coined after William Banting, a corpulent Britton who in 1861, at the age of 65, was placed on a diet of lean meat, toast, and vegetables by his surgeon; within 2 years he had lost 50 pounds; he then wrote the popular *Letter on Corpulence*, which advocated consumption of vegetables and loss of weight, at a time when vegetables were not a dietary staple, meat was the centerpiece of a proper meal, and obesity was not considered a disease, but rather a mark of social status. See Diet

***bao chiang wei*** Multiflowered rose, see there, *Rosa multiflora*

**baptista** Wild indigo, see there

***Baptista tinctoria*** Popularly known as wild indigo, see there

**Barbados aloe** *Aloe vera*, see there

**barberry** *Berberis vulgaris*, berberry, common barberry, European barberry, jaundice berry, pepperidge bush HERBAL MEDICINE A deciduous shrub, the bark and fruit of which contain alkaloids (berberine, columbamine, oxyacanthine, palmatine, and others), resin, starch, and tannins; it is antibacterial, anticonvulsant, antiviral, and vasodilatory, and has been used internally for anemia, cholera, constipation, diarrhea, gallstones, hangover, heartburn, hepatitis, hypertension, menstrual pains, and splenomegaly, and topically for conjunctivitis, skin infections, and sore throats TOXICITY Berberine should not be used in pregnancy as it stimulates uterine contractions. See Berberine, Botanical toxicity, Herbal medicine

***bardos*** Plane of existence after death, see there, spirit world

**barefoot shiatsu** A form of shiatsu in which the feet are used instead of the hands; this allows the practitioner to exert greater force on the acupressure points by standing on certain parts of the patient's body. See Acupressure, Shiatsu

**barium carbonate** *Baryta carbonica*, see there

**bark** 1. *China*, see there 2. Cinchona, see there, *Cinchona* species

**barley green** FRINGE NUTRITION A powder made from the squeezed juice of fresh barley leaves that has been allowed to evaporate; barley green has been sold as a health-promoting 'miracle food' that increases longevity and vitality; pamphlets used to market barley green have made exaggerated claims as to both its high concentration (in fact they are relatively low) of vitamins, minerals, and amino acids, and its efficacy in treating arthritis, cancer, and other conditions

**Bartenieff fundamentals system** A system of body re-education (bodywork) developed in the 1960s by a physical therapist, I Bartenieff. See Bodywork

***Baryta carbonica*** Barium carbonate, witherite HOMEOPATHY A minor homeopathic remedy that is believed to enhance growth and development in those are physically or mentally challenged; it is used primarily in children (eg with Downs' syndrome) and the elderly (eg with senile dementia). See Homeopathy

**baseline health** A person's state of health when first seen by a physician

**Basic Four Food Groups** Four food groups, see there

**basic health diet** CLINICAL NUTRITION A core dietary regimen that incorporates sound eating habits (eg eating when one is relaxed, chewing thoroughly, and drinking adequate water during the day) and consumption of the 'right' foods; the basic health diet is primarily vegetarian, with most of the protein being provided by grains, beans, and nuts, fish, low-fat dairy products, and lean meats, ideally grown without adding hormones or antibiotics to the feed; frying is discouraged, as is serving the foods either too hot or too cold; the basic health diet is supplemented by vitamins, minerals, and digestive aids, including betaine, bromelain, lecithin, ox bile, pancrelipase, and papain. See Diet

**basic need** Physiologic need PSYCHOLOGY A term coined by Abraham Maslow for a physiologic requirement without which a person becomes sick; basic needs include oxygen, food, drink, shelter, sleep, and sex, and are usually prioritized over other needs of the individual including the needs for safety, love and belongingness, self-esteem and respect from others, and the need for self-actualization; Cf Self-actualization need

**basil** *Ocimum basilicum*, basilisk, herbe royale, sweet basil HERBAL MEDICINE A bushy annual culinary and medicinal herb (see page 38) that contains camphor, estragol, eugenol, linalol, lineol, tannins, and thymol; basil is grown indoors in southern Europe as a fly repellant; it is antipyretic and carminative, and has been used for abdominal bloating, cramps, diarrhea, and nausea. See Herbal medicine

**Basilica of Our Lady of Guadelupe** see Healing shrine

**basilisk** Basil, see there, *Ocimum basilicum*

***basti*** AYURVEDIC MEDICINE An herbal enema used in ayurvedic medicine to eliminate *ama* (physiologic impurities). See Ayurvedic medicine, *Panchakarma*, *Prana*

**basil** *Ocimum basilicum*

**Bass brushing** PREVENTIVE DENTISTRY A technique for brushing teeth developed by CC Bass, MD, that is intended to dislodge accumulated foods and plaque from the crevices between the gums and teeth; in the Bass method, the toothbrush is inserted into the crevice at a 45° angle to the vertical length of the teeth, and the brush is wiggled back and forth in short strokes; the tips of the brush remain virtually stationary; the bleeding that is associated with the Bass technique usually disappears in a few days (*M Bricklin, 1976, 1983*); the benefits of the Bass method are enhanced by regular flossing. See Alternative dentistry, Flossing

**bastard cardamom** Grains of paradise, see there, *Amomum xanthiodes*

**bastard ginseng** *Codonopsis pilosula*, see there

**Bates-Corbett method of vision training** Bates vision training, see there

**Bates vision training** Bates-Corbett method of vision training ALTERNATIVE OPHTHALMOLOGY A method for improving a person's eyesight that was developed in the 1920s by an American ophthalmologist, WH Bates, and extended by MD Corbett; in contrast to mainstream ophthalmologic thought, which assumes that vision is genetically determined and fails with age, the Bates method is based on the belief that eyesight can be improved through various maneuvers described below

▶ **BATES MANEUVERS**

- **BLINKING** Lubricating the eye, ideally while taking a breath, or reading
- **NEAR AND FAR FOCUSING** Holding a pencil or other object at 15 cm, then at arm's length, repeating the exercise 10-12 times
- **PALMING** Using the palms to shut out all light to closed eyelids, for 5-10 minute periods, two to three times per day; at the same time the individual should remember and imagine colors and scenes
- **SHIFTING** Shifting the visual focus rather than stare at the same spot on an object
- **SPLASHING** Splashing the eyes directly with warm and cold water, about 10 times twice per day
- **SUNNING** Facing the sun with closed eyes
- **SWINGING** Swaying side to side about 100 times while staring at an object in middle distance

Cf Eye-Robics™, Vision training

**Battle Creek** MEDICAL HISTORY-NUTRITION A city in Michigan that is the birthplace of cold breakfast cereals, first produced by the Kellogg brothers and CW Post (*Armstrong, 1991*); Cf Graham cracker

**batyl alcohol** see Alkylglycerol

**bayberry** *Myrica cerifera*, candleberry, wax myrtle, waxberry HERBAL MEDICINE A shrub, the root bark of which contains myricadiol–a triterpene, myricitrin–a flavonoid glycoside,. tannins, resin, and gum; it is anti-inflammatory, antipyretic, and astringent, and has been used internally for diarrhea, fever, menstrual disorders, postpartum hemorrhage, gastroenteritis, and sore throat, and topically for poor circulation, hemorrhoids, and varicose veins TOXICITY Electrolyte derangements, with retention of sodium and loss of potassium; those with edema, hypertension, congestive heart failure, and renal disease should be evaluated by a mainstream health care professional before using bayberry; it should not be used by those with malignancies, as it is positive by the Ames test. See Ames test, Herbal medicine

**bCG** bacille Calmette-Guerin ALTERNATIVE ONCOLOGY A strain of *Mycobacterium bovis* that has been grown multiple generations on potato, bile glycerine agar to a point where it has retained its immunogenicity, but lost its virulence; bcg is an effective vaccine for tuberculosis and has been used to non-specifically stimulate the immune response in patients with certain malignancies, eg melanoma. See Immune booster; Cf Coley's toxin, Ubenimex

Because of its long-term persistence in the body, bCG has potential use as a vector for genes encoding HIV proteins including Gag, Pol, Env, reverse transcriptase, gp20, gp40 and tetanus toxin (*Nature 1991; 351:479, 442*); extrachromosomal and integrative expression vectors carrying the regulatory sequences for major bcg heat-shock proteins (hsp60 and hsp70) allow the expression of foreign antigens present in BCG (*Nature 1991; 351:456*), and may be used as a live recombinant vaccine vehicle to induce immune response to the pathogen's protein

**Beano™** A commercial product added to beans deemed extremely flatulogenic; Beano™ contains an enzyme that digests raffinose and stachyose, two carbohydrates for which humans have no enzymes. See Beans

**beans** ALTERNATIVE NUTRITION Any of a number of protein-rich foods including garbanzos, baked, black, kidney, lentil, navy, pinto, red, soy, and white beans; beans are high in folic acid, manganese, and soluble fiber, and are believed to be useful in reducing the risk of cancer of the lung and pancreas, neural tube defects, osteoporosis, and cardiovascular disease, and in controlling diabetes mellitus; one cup of beans/day reduces serum cholesterol an average of 10%; beans' well-known flatulogenic effect can be reduced by soaking them in water overnight, and pouring off the water or by using a commercial product, Beano™. See Beano™, Healthy foods

**bearberry** *Arctostaphylos uva-ursi*, beargrape, bear's grape, crowberry, foxberry, hog cranberry, hogberry, kinnikinnick, mealberry, mountain cranberry, rockberry, uva ursi HERBAL MEDICINE An evergreen shrub, the leaves of which contain allantoin, arbutin, flavonoids, hydroquinone, phenolic acid, and tannins; it is diuretic and tonic, and has been used topically for cuts, and internally for hypertension, low back pain, menstrual dysfunction, and urinary tract infections TOXOCITY It should not be used in pregnancy, as it stimulates uterine contractions; in extremely high doses, bearberry may cause nausea, tinnitus, and convulsions. See Herbal medicine

**beargrape** Bearberry, see there, *Arctostaphylos uva-ursi*

**bear's grape** Bearberry, see there, *Arctostaphylos uva-ursi*

**bear's foot** Lady's mantle, see there, *Alchemilla vulgaris*

**Beard Anthrone Test** Chorionic Gonadotropin Quan-titative Test FRINGE DIAGNOSTICS A test developed by HH Beard, PhD of Fort Worth, Texas, that was based on measuring chorionic gonadotropin in urine, and claimed to be highly accurate in both diagnosing cancer, and monitoring its progress*; after 1967, the test was available through Dr Ernesto Contreras Rodriquez (*Am Can Soc, Files on 'Unproven Methods of Cancer Management,' 1971*); see Contreras method, Hemacytology Index, Laetrile, Unproven methods for cancer management

*The high accuracy claimed for this test in diagnosing and managing cancer has not been confirmed

**bedstraw** Cleavers, see there, *Galium aparine*

**bee balm** 1. Bergamot, see there, *Monarda didyma* 2. Lemon balm, see there, *Melissa officinalis*

**bee bread** 1. Borage, see there, *Borago officinalis* 2. Red clover, see there, *Trifolium pratense*

**bearberry** *Arctostaphylos uva-ursi*

**bee's nest** Queen Anne's lace, see there, *Daucus carota*

**bee pollen** FRINGE NUTRITION A substance that contains sugar (50% by weight), as well as protein, fat, minerals, vitamins, and water; bee pollen is said to be effective in treating allergies and anaphylactic shock in those allergic to bees; if the bee pollen contains bee parts, it could evoke an anaphylactic reaction; bee pollen has been promoted as a 'superfood' and claimed to enhance athletic performance and be an effective therapy for alcoholism, balding, diabetes, defects in vision, loss of memory, and other conditions. See *Apis*, Honey, Mad honey, Royal jelly

**bee venom therapy** FRINGE MEDICINE The use of honeybee (*Apis mellifora*) venom to treat arthritic complaints, including bursitis, neuritis, osteoarthritis, rheumatoid arthritis, and tendinitis; the venom is delivered by local injection of a rehyrdated lyophilized concentrate of venom, or less commonly, by allowing the patient to be stung by a bee; the effect of bee venom therapy (if any), is attributed to nonspecific stimulation of the immune system, as the venom contains formic acid, histamine, magnesium phosphate, and alkaloids. See *Apis*

**'beer gut' obesity** Upper body obesity, see there

**beggar's basket** Lungwort, see there, *Pulmonaria officinalis*

**beggar's buttons** Burdock, see there, *Arctium lappa*

**behavioral intervention** Behavior modification, behavior 'mod', behavioral therapy, behaviorism PSYCHOLOGY The use of operant conditioning models, ie positive and negative reinforcement, to modify behavior; BI was first studied by Ivan P Pavlov (1849-1936), using the technique of conditioning; his findings were expounded upon by BF Skinner (1902-1990), who championed the natural extension of operant conditioning, the concept of reinforcement; behavioral intervention is also a general term that refers to any of a number of psychological maneuvers (eg attentional distraction, hypnosis, relaxation training, systematic desensitization, and others), which are intended to help a person control responses to unpleasant situations or events; behavioral intervention has been used for patients with cancer as means of controlling their response to pain, and anticipatory reactions–as occurs in chemotherapy-related nausea. See Aversion therapy Encounter group therapy, Flooding, Imaging aversion therapy, Systematic desensitization

**behavioral kinesiology** Life energy analysis, life energy technique BODYWORK A form of applied kinesiology developed by an American psychiatrist, Dr John Diamond, as a means of helping patients cope with external stress and lifestyle changes that affect a person's stamina; behavioral kinesiology combines applied kinesiology testing with preventive medicine, psychiatry, psychosomatic medicine, and the humanities. See Applied kinesiology, Bodywork

**behavioral medicine** A relatively new medical discipline (the Society of behavioral medicine was founded in 1978) that integrates behavioral, psychosocial, and biomedical approaches to health and illness (*JAMA 1996; 275:1144MN&P*); a major thrust of behavioral medicine is lifestyle intervention, eg smoking cessation and dietary intervention, and increases the emphasis in health care on prevention, which is recognized as being less expensive, rather than on curing disease; the advantages of behavioral medicine's approach is recognized by health maintenance organizations as a way of improving the quality of health care while reducing costs. See Mind/body medicine

For some, the terms behavioral medicine and mind/body medicine are synonymous; because the term behavioral medicine appears to be more acceptable, and possibly embraced by more mainstream medical practitioners, while the term mind/body medicine may be more accepted to advocates of alternative health care they are, in this work, listed as separate entries–Author's note

**behavioral optometrist** ALTERNATIVE OPHTHALMOLOGY A person who practices Skeffington's vision training. See Vision therapy

**behavioral therapy** Behavioral intervention, see there

**behaviorism** Behavioral intervention, see there

***bei dzao*** Northern jujube, Chinese jujube, see there

**belladonna** *Atropa belladonna*, deadly nightshade, dwale, fair lady HERBAL MEDICINE A perennial herb that is extremely toxic when taken internally at its full concentration (see below, homeopathy); belladonna contains scopolamine and hyoscyamine, which are used as antispasmodics in mainstream medicine; belladonna has been used topically in herbal medicine to treat gout and rheumatic complaints TOXICITY Diarrhea, dilated pupils, dry mouth, flushing, hallucinations, hypertension, incoordination, nausea, speech impairment, tachycardia, vision impairment, vomiting, coma, and possibly death. See Botanical toxicity, Herbal medicine, Poisonous plants HOMEOPATHY A homeopathic remedy that is used for conditions of abrupt onset as well as acute infections; it has been used to treat cough, earache, fever, pounding headaches, seizures, sore throat, teething in children,

**belladonna** *Atropa belladonna*

and urinary tract infection. See Homeopathy

***Bellis*** *Bellis perennis*, bruisewort, European daisy, garden daisy HOMEOPATHY A minor homeopathic remedy used for trauma, aches, chills, lymph node swelling, and pregnancy-related uterine pain. See Homeopathy

**Belvedere cypress** *Kochia scoparia*, broom grass, *Chenopodium scoparia, di fu dze, di fu zi, sao jou tsao* CHINESE MEDICINE A saponin-rich plant native to Asia, the seeds of which are anti-inflammatory, astringent, diuretic, and tonic; it is used in traditional Chinese medicine for hemorrhoids, impotence, inflammation, urinary incontinence, and urinary tract infections; the shoots and stems are used in Western herbal medicine for gastrointestinal complaints. See Chinese herbal medicine, Herbal medicine

**Benjamin system of muscular therapy** ALTERNATIVE MEDICINE A system of muscle therapy, exercise, and education, that was developed in 1967 by BE Benjamin to reduce chronic muscle tension and promote health; the therapy combines the deep massage therapy of Dr A Kagan, the Alexander Technique for posture and movement training, injury evaluation and deep transverse friction of Dr J Cyriax, and the Reichian theory that disease is a physical manifestation of emotional distress; Benjamin believes that muscle tension has a mechanical and an emotional substrate, the latter being termed armor by Reichian therapists; Benjamin system practitioners receive 1200 hours of instruction with a 500-hour externship in the two-year curriculum

**benzaldehyde** FRINGE ONCOLOGY An essential oil present in bitter almond oil, which is used as a flavoring agent, and thought to have anticarcinogenic activity (*Moss, 1992*). See Unproven methods for cancer management

While some advanced cancers (eg, gastrointestinal, liver, lung, pancreas, and prostate) show partial response, research activity has waned, and most workers abandoned investigation of benzaldehyde's effects on malignancy in the mid-1980s–Author's note

**benzoin tree** *Styrax benzoin* HERBAL MEDICINE An African tree, the resin of which is antimicrobial, astringent, and expectorant; it is applied externally for skin cuts, dryness, and infections including shingles, ringworm, and other conditions but, given its bitterness, is rarely used internally, and then only as a steam inhalation to loosen mucus and phlegm, eg in children with croup. See Herbal medicine

**berberine** PHARMACOGNOSY A bitter alkaloid (figure, page 42) abundant in the rhizomes and roots of goldenseal (*Hydrastis canadensis*); it is antibacterial, antimalarial, antipyretic, sedative, a gastric tonic, and possibly antihypertensive. See Goldenseal, Herbal medicine

***Berberis vulgaris*** Popularly known as barberry, see there

**berberry** Barberry, see there, *Berberis vulgaris*

**bereavement** PSYCHOLOGY The act of bereaving or mourning the loss of a 'significant other' or other loved one; berereavement is generally accompanied by a transient (usually less than several months) period of depression; it may become the focus of clinical attention and be misdiagnosed as a mental disease including depression

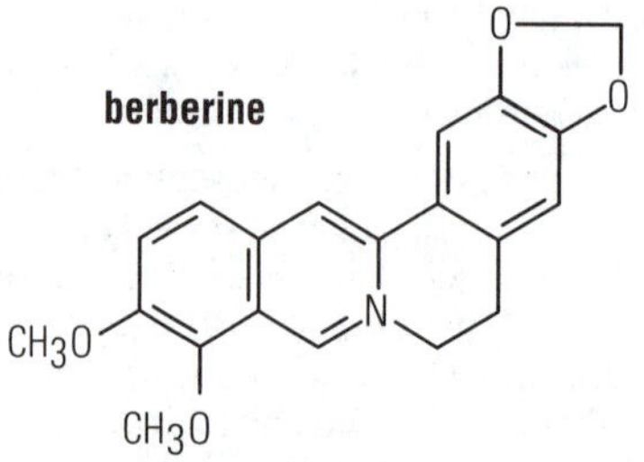

**Beres Drops® Plus** ALTERNATIVE NUTRITION A mineral supplement or 'paramedicine'(a term used by the Hungarian Institute of Pharmacy) formulated by Dr Josef Beres that contains boron, cobalt, copper, fluorine, iron, magnesium, manganese, molybdenum, nickel, potassium, sodium, vanadium, and zinc (*Moss, 1992*).

**bergamot** *Monarda didyma*, bee balm, Indian plume, Oswego tea, scarlet bergamot FRINGE MEDICINE—FLOWER ESSENCE THERAPY An essence that is believed to have an antidepressant effect, and possibly stimulate the immune system to ward off infections. See Flower essence therapy HERBAL MEDICINE A perennial herb that contains volatile oil and tannic acid, which is highly aromatic, but little used in modern herbal medicine. See Herbal medicine

**Bernadette** see Saint Bernadette

**B.E.S.T.** Bio Energetic Synchronization Technique, see there

**Bestatin®** Ubenimex, see there

**beta carotene** CLINICAL NUTRITION A fat-soluble retinoid provitamin that is metabolized to vitamin A, which is an antioxidant and free radical scavenger; it is present in fresh fruit (cantaloupe) and vegetables (broccoli and carrots), and has immunostimulatory activity; increased beta carotene consumption is associated with a decreased risk of bladder, breast, cervix, colon and rectum, esophagus, lung, oral cavity, stomach, and skin cancer, and cancer cell growth in vitro (*New York Times 21 Feb 1995; C1*)*; beta carotene also guards against heart disease, strokes, and aging. See Carotenoid, Vitamin A; Cf Cruciferous vegetables, Indoles

*A large randomized, double blinded, placebo-controlled trial involving 22 071 physicians with 12 years of supplemental beta carotene, revealed no positive or negative effects on the incidence of malignancy, cardiovascular disease, or death from all causes (*N Engl J Med 1996; 334:1145OA*); another study examining the effect of dietary supplementation with beta caotene and retinol (vitamin A) on 18 314 smokers, former smokers, and asbestos workers found no benefit and, if anything, a slight increase in cardiovascular and/or pulmonary mortality and morbidity (*N Engl J Med 1996; 334:1150OA*)

**betel palm** *Areca catchu* HERBAL MEDICINE A palm native to tropical Asia, the nuts of which contain alkaloids (eg arecholine) and tannins; betel nuts are astringent, teniacidal (ie kill tapeworms), and mildly stimulating. See Herbal medicine

**bethroot** Birthroot, see there, *Trillium erectum*

**betula** White birch, see there, *Betula alba*

***Betula alba*** Popularly known as white birch, see there

**betulinic acid** AIDS A triterpene extracted from bark of the plane tree that was reported to block HIV-1 infection at a post-binding step, specifically after HIV's gp120 binds to the host cell CD4 molecule, possibly due to conformational changes in the gp120-gp41 complex (*Proc Nat Acad Sci (US) 1994; 91:3564OA*). See AIDS therapy

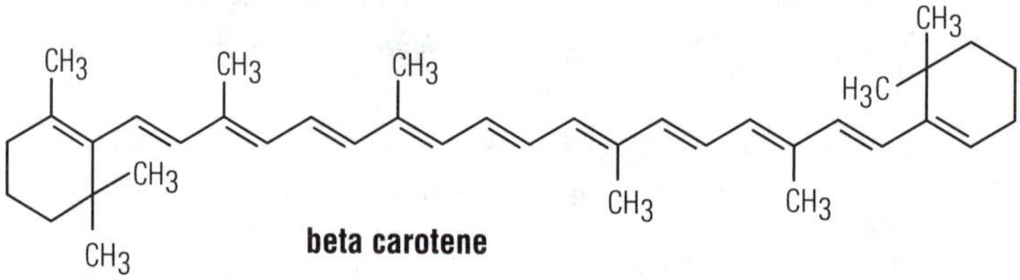

**Beverly Hills diet** FRINGE NUTRITION A fruit-based 'fad' diet of uncertain benefit published by Judy Mazel (*Macmillan, New York, 1979*); the diet was criticized for ignoring sound nutritional principles (*JAMA 1981; 246:2235-2237*); criticisms include the questionable admonition that fruits be consumed on separate days, eg papaya on one day, pineapple on the next, and so on; in addition to its low amount of protein (6% of the calories are protein), the Beverly Hills diet supplies no vitamin $B_{12}$, one-third the recommended daily allowances (RDAs) for calcium, and one-half or less of five essential nutrients. See Diet, Fad diet

**BHA** Butylated hydroxyanisole FOOD INDUSTRY A food preservative that may cause cardiac palpitations, headaches, nausea, and nerve damage. See BHT

***bhakti yoga*** A form of yoga that seeks the pathway to a higher spiritual power through devotion and love. See Yoga

**bhang** Marijuana, see there, *Cannabis sativa*

**BHT** Butylated hydroxytoluene FOOD INDUSTRY A food preservative used to prevent fats and oils in packaged foods from becoming rancid; BHT is believed to be teratogenic in mice, and cause a significant decrease in cholin-esterase activity, aggressiveness, sleep disturbances, and weight loss (*Alternative Medicine, Future Med Pub, 1994*); both BHA and BHT increase the levels of UDP-glucuronosyltransferase, the enzyme thought to be responsible for the anticancer effects of the cruciferous vegetables. See BHA, Unproven methods for cancer management FRINGE NUTRITION BHT has been recommended* for aging, hangovers, and herpes, reducing sleep SIDE EFFECTS Excess consumption has been associated with abdominal cramping, confusion, nausea, liver toxicity, vertigo, vomiting, and loss of consciousness. See BHA

*By nutrition advocates D Pearson and S Shaw, who recommend the consumption of 2 grams/day; one gram/day is lethal in rabbits

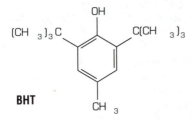

OH

$(CH_3)_3C$ $C(CH_3)_3$

$CH_3$

**BHT**

**bian** MEDICAL HISTORY–ACUPUNCTURE A tool found in Stone Age archeologic 'digs' in China that are believed to correspond to early acupuncture needles. See Acupuncture

**biblical counseling** Nouthetic counseling ALTERNATIVE PSYCHOLOGY The use of devotional phrases and/or biblical scripture to address spiritual (and by extension, psychological) problems. See Bibliotherapy, Poetry therapy

**bibliotherapy** ALTERNATIVE PSYCHOLOGY A general term for the use of books and literature as a means of helping an individual identify and transcend emotional problems (*Bricklin, 1976*). See Poetry therapy; Cf Drama therapy

**Bier's hyperemic treatment** NATUROPATHY A therapeutic modality developed by a German physician, August Bier (1861-1949), which increases the flow of blood to a specific part of the body by surrounding the region with hot air; Bier's therapy was used for arthritis, low back pain, and varicose veins. See Naturopathy

Regional hyperthermia is more efficiently evoked by using hot water–Author's note

**bilateral nasal specific** FRINGE CHIROPRACTIC A permutation of the cranial adjustment technique developed by an American chiropractor, J Richard Stober; the technique consists of the insertion of balloons into the nasal cavity, as a means of realigning the bones of the skull*; the bilateral nasal specific technique is believed by its practitioners to be effective in treating blindness, deafness, paralysis, mental retardation, and other conditions. See Chiropractic malpractice

*These bones are fused at birth; the efficacy of this therapy is, therefore, uncertain

**bilberry** *Vaccinium myrtilloides*, Canada blueberry HERBAL MEDICINE A shrub, the berries of which contain anthocyanosides; it is believed to prevent atherosclerosis, and may be used internally for eye problems (cataracts, glaucoma, macular degeneration, myopia, and night blindness), diabetes, gastrointestinal complaints including colic, constipation,

**bilberry** *Vaccinium myrtilloides*

and diarrhea, and hypertension, externally for burns, hemorrhoids, skin conditions, spider nevi, and varicose veins. See Herbal medicine

**biliary constitution** Mixed constitution FRINGE MEDICINE-IRIDOLOGY A hazel iris which, according to the construct of iridology, is owned by a person who is prone to hepatobiliary and pancreatic disease; this partially overlaps conditions believed to be more common in those with a hematogenic constitution (ie those with brown eyes); individuals with biliary constitutions are said to be prone to gastrointestinal and hematologic disease, gallstones, and diabetes. See Iridology, Iris constitution; Cf Hematogenic constitution

**bindegewebsmassage** Connective tissue massage, see there

**bindweed** *Convolvulus sepium*, *Calystegia sepium*, hedge bindweed HERBAL MEDICINE A perennial vine that is a laxative, and used as a folk remedy for jaundice, gallbladder disease, and to increase the flow of bile. See Herbal medicine

**bindweed** *Calystegia sepium*

**binge** PSYCHIATRY A component of bulimia nervosa that consists of an episode of hyperpolyphagia, in which up to 15 000 calories may be consumed in one hour; binges are commonly followed by self-induced emesis or 'purging' COMPLICATIONS Gastric rupture (Mallory-Weiss syndrome), vascular compression, pancreatitis, aspiration pneumonia, ipecac-induced myocarditis, cardiac failure, refeeding edema, hypokalemia, hypochloremia, and metabolic alkalosis

**biochemic (system of) medicine** Schüssler's biochemic system of medicine, see there

**biochemic tissue salts** Schüssler's tissue salts, see there

**biochemical approach** NATUROPATHY A philosophical stance that is adopted by some naturopaths, in which patients are treated with herbs and diet as a first-line approach to disease, which is closer to mainstream medicine, as it is less mystical than the vitalistic approach; mainstream medical practitioners, and the scientists who study biological phenomena, have difficulty with a vitalistic approach that seeks to allow natural healing forces–which are difficult to measure and study–to act in the most optimal fashion. See Biochemical technique, Naturopathy; Cf Vitalistic approach

**biochemical technique** ALTERNATIVE MEDICINE A general term for any form of alternative health care that incorporates the use of food, herbs, and essences as means of optimizing health through natural chemicals, which can be ingested, inhaled, or absorbed through the skin or mucosa; biochemical techniques include aromatherapy, ayurvedic medicine, Chinese herbal medicine, diet and nutrition therapy, herbal medicine, homeopathy, polarity therapy, and others, discussed elsewhere in this work. See Biochemical approach

**biochemistry** ALTERNATIVE MEDICINE A term used by a German homeopath, WH Schüssler, for the use of 'tissue salts' to treat patients with alleged mineral deficiencies. See Schüssler's tissue salts

**bio-chromatic chakra alignment** PARANORMAL PHENOMENA The balancing of the *chakras* (energy centers) of the body using devices known as 'visionary tools'. See Bio-Chromatic Integration Device, *Chakra*, *Chakra* balancing, Visionary tool

**Bio-Chromatic Integration Device** PARANORMAL PHENOMENA A 'visionary tool' that is believed by its proponents to be of use in balancing the chakras (energy centers); it is purported to convert deep space energy into 'human frequencies'. See *Chakra*, *Chakra* balancing, Visionary tool; Cf Starchamber™

**biocomputer** ALTERNATIVE MEDICINE A term coined by R Utt, developer of the technique of Applied Physiology, for the 'innate intelligence' that coordinates the activity of the parasympathetic nervous system, which in turn controls blood pressure, digestion, respiration, and other involuntary physiologic activities. See Applied Physiology

**biocurrent** HEALTH FRAUD A term coined by Albert Abrams for what he considered to be a form of bioenergy. See Abrams, Abrams' generator, Radionics

**biocurve** Biorhythm, see there

**biocycle** Biorhythm, see there

**biodynamic massage** BODYWORK A form of bodywork developed by a Norwegian psychologist, Gerda Boyeson, which incorporates Reichian therapy, deep breathing, and relaxation; according to Boyeson, the flow of energy through the body can become blocked by the accumulation of fluids between muscles and nerves, which can be dispersed by biodynamic massage

**biodynamic psychology** 1. Body-oriented psychology, see there 2. Biodynamic psychotherapy, see there

**biodynamic psychotherapy** Biodynamic psychology A permutation of Reichian therapy developed by a Norwegian psychologist and physical therapist, Gerda Boyeson; massage and breathing methods are used to increase the client's awareness of emotions; the client's body armoring is addressed through Boyeson's concept of psycho-peristalsis-emotional release through the machinations of the gastrointestinal tract. See Body armoring; Cf Body-oriented psychotherapy

**biodynamometer** Abrams' generator, see there

**bioelectric testing** Electrodiagnosis, see there

**bioelectromagnetics** FRINGE MEDICINE A field of pseudodiagnostics that is based on the belief that distant electromagnetic activity, eg from geomagnetic movement, seismic acitivity, solar wind, sunspots, and changes in the weather, affect an individual's electrostatic aura–the existence of which is unproven, which in turn affects the individual's behavior

**Bio Energetic Synchronization Technique** Bio energetics, B.E.S.T., Morter B.E.S.T. CHIROPRACTIC A non-forceful, self-healing permutation of chiropractic and polarity balacing developed in 1974 by an American chiropractor, MT Morter; according to Morter, the body '*...does not know how to be sick.*' (*Raso, 1994*), and has an 'innate intelligence' that regulates health. See Baby B.E.S.T, Morter HealthSystem; Cf Bioenergetics

**bio energetics** 1. Bio Energetic Synchronization Technique, see there 2. Bioenergetics, see there

**bioenergetics** ALTERNATIVE PSYCHOLOGY A therapeutic technique that was developed by an American psychoanalyst, Alexander Lowen; Dr Lowen viewed disease as a defect in the flow of the body's life energy (bioenergy), which is most often due to chronic muscle tension; bioenergetics helps the individual integrate his mind, through verbal expression of emotional conflicts with his body in terms of breathing, moving, self-expression, and sexuality; anecdotal reports suggest that bioenergenics may be effective in treating asthma, dyspnea, headache, stress-related disease, and post-shock syndrome. See Biofeedback, Reichian therapy; Cf Bio Energetic Synchronization Technique (B.E.S.T.)

**bioenergy** 1. Life energy, also known as *chi* (Chinese traditional medicine), *prana* (Ayurvedic medicine), vital force (homeopathy). See Vital force 2. Bioenergetics, see there 3. Bioenergy healing, see there 4. Orgone energy, see there

**bioenergy healing** PARANORMAL PHENOMENA Bioenergy The balancing of a person's aura by acting on the magnetic field. See Aura balancing

**bioentrainment** The process by which living beings become locked onto cycles, rhythms, or waves from outside of their body limits (*Playfair, quoted in Watson, 1995*); bioentrainment is linked to circadian rhythms, the menstrual cycle and is believed to be linked to the lunar cycle, and seizures evoked by strobe lights. See Biorhythm, Circadian rhythm

**biofeedback** A method of controlling a living system by reinserting into it the results of previous performance. See Biofeedback device,

Biofeedback training

**biofeedback device** A general term for any instrument that measures physiologic parameters including electromyographic activity, galvanic (electrodermal) skin resistance, muscle tension, blood pressure, and others; there is an interest among mainstream medical practitioners that such devices may be useful in controlling tachycardia, hypertension, fecal incontinence, and other conditions. See Biofeedback training, Electromyograph feedback, Galvanic skin response

**biofeedback training** A form of operant conditioning in which a patient learns to control certain deranged physiologic functions; components of the dysfunction may be 'translated' into perceivable stimuli, such that the patient is made aware of the nature of the dysfunction by watching or listening to an instrument (eg electrocardiograph, electromyogram) that records or measures the deranged process; biorhythms that may be monitored in biofeedback training include brain waves, breathing, galvanic skin response, muscle tension, pulse, and body temperature; as examples, control of fecal incontinence may be increased by watching the recorder of a balloon manometer, control of constipation in the elderly may be increased by watching an anal-plug electrode, and the pulse rate can be reduced by listening to amplified pulse sounds; success in biofeedback training hinges on motivation, (reasonable) expectations of success, and the competence and training of the trainer; anecdotal evidence suggests that biofeedback training may be useful in controlling anxiety, asthma, bruxism, cardiac arrythmias, chronic pain, constipation, diabetes mellitus, fecal incontinence, headaches, hypertension, low back and other pain, Raynaud's phenomenon, seizures, strokes, and neuromuscular dysfunction–including Bell's palsy, paralysis, cerebral palsy, peripheral nerve and spinal cord injuries, and TMJ (temporomandibular joint) syndrome; it may also be useful for stress-related disorders, including ulcers, angina pectoris, and migraines; Cf Behavioral intervention *RESOURCE: Association for Applied Psycho-physiology and Biofeedback, 10200 W 44th Ave, Suite 304, Wheatridge CO 80033 ☎ 1.303.422.8436*

**bioflavonoids** Flavonoids, see there

**biokinesiology** A system of pseudodiagnosis that is based on the belief that a person's internal state can be evaluated by testing the resistance of muscles to external pressure exerted by an examiner. See Applied kinesiology

**biological dentistry** Alternative dentistry, see there

**biological thyroid hormone** Any of a number of thyroid hormone preparations obtained from slaughterhouse animals; these extracts contain thyroxine ($T_4$) and triiodothyronine ($T_3$), in proportions that differ according to the animal species, iodine content in the animal's diet, season, and other factors; it is available as either crude desiccated thyroid or thyroglobulin; mainstream endocrinologists do not use these preparations as their potency and bioavailability is uncertain, making them difficult to measure and to consistently titrate a patient's dose. See endogenous endocrinotherapy, Glandular

Note: biological thyroid hormone continues to have currency for self-proclaimed nutritionists and holistic health practitioners who reason that the more 'natural' the product, the safer it is (*JAMA 1989; 261:2694ed*)

**biomagnetic medicine** 1. Biomagnetics, see there 2. Biomagnetism, see there 3. Magnet therapy, see there 4. Magnetic healing, see there 5. *Mana*, see there

**biomagnetic therapy** 1. Biomagnetics, see there 2. Biomagnetism, see there 3. Magnet therapy, see there 4. Magnetic healing, see there 5. *Mana*, see there

**biomagnetics** 1. Biomagnetics PARANORMAL PHENOMENA Biomagnetic medicine A system of vibrational bioenergetics medicine, in which a diagnosis is made through a device that is said to detect audio frequency electromagnetic waves produced by organs and tissues in the body, and therapy administered based on the diagnosis. See Pseudodiagnosis 2. Biomagnetism, see there 3. Magnet therapy, see there 4. Magnetic healing, see there 5. *Mana*, see there

**biomagnetism** 1. Biomagnetics, see there 2. Biomagnetism AYUERVEDIC MEDICINE *Mana*, see there MAINSTREAM MEDICINE Biomagnetic therapy The formal study of magnetic fields associated with life activities; biomagnetism is a new 'discipline' of biomedicine, the boundaries of which are not yet delineated; it potentially offers a new tool for localizing electrical activity seen in normal and abnormal cortical and cardiac functions; the EEG and EKG 'average' the impulse throughout large regions of measured organ's electrical activity, magnetocardiogram and magnetoencephalogram sample the magnetic field produced by the ion flow inside the cell; biomagnetism is an intradisciplinary hybrid with roots in quantum mechanics, superconductivity, and bioelectricity PARANORMAL PHENOMENA Biomagnetics, see there 3. Magnet therapy, see there 4. Magnetic healing, see there 5. *Mana*, see there

Note: Biomagnetism and magnetic resonance imaging are among the legitimate uses of magnetic fields in medicine; practitioners of alternative medicine may use magnetism for that which is less scientific and more speculative; frankly fraudulent references to some form of magnetic effect may be made by purveyors of various devices that may be found in the offices of some practitioners of alternative medicine

**Biomate** A proprietary device marketed in the UK that is said to allow the calculation of biorhythms. See Biorhythm

**biometer** A permutation of the pendulum developed in the early 20th century by Dr Oscar Brunler and M Bovis; the biometer was used in psychometric analysis to detect energy waves believed to be emitted from all living beings. See Pendular diagnosis, Psychometric analysis, Radiesthesia

**biopsychosocial model** ALTERNATIVE MEDICINE A theoretical framework that seeks to integrate psychological interactions when studying the pathogenesis of a particular disease; these interactions can be genetic, environmental (eg pathogens, physical agents, pollution), psychological (eg attitudes, behaviors, levels of stress, lifestyle), and socioeconomic (eg relationships with family, coworkers, the community), financial well-being, access to health care, and others. See Mind/body medicine, Flight-or-fight response, Psychoneuroimmunology

**biorhythm** Biocurve, biocycle ALTERNATIVE MEDICINE A hypothetical triphasic rhythm that is 'set' at the time of a person's birth; the biorhythm theory was first proposed by H Swoboda and W Fleiß, the latter of whom was a contemporary and colleague of Sigmund Freud; while there is no definitive proof for the existence of biorhythms, its proponents believe that there are three distinct cycles: A physical cycle of 23 days (which corresponds to coordination, immunity, self-confidence, and strength), an emotional cycle of 28 days, and an intellectual cycle of 33 days, all of which are defined by a sine wave; 'critical periods' are believed to exist as an individual crosses the middle of a cycle, either from a high to a low or a low to a high. See Biomate, Chronobiology, Circadian rhythm, Critical period, Kosmos

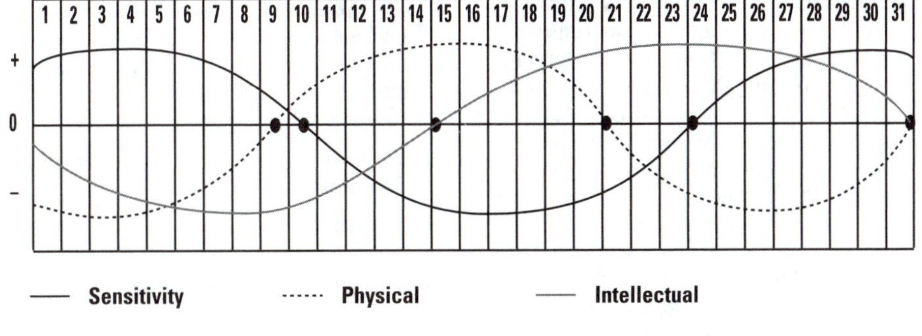


**biorhythm**

**bioplasmic energy** Vital force, see there

**bioplasmic healing** ALTERNATIVE MEDICINE 1. A permutation of magnetic healing that involves manipulation of the vital force (bioplasmic energy). See Magnetic healing 2. Pranic healing, see there

**biosonics** PARANORMAL PHENOMENA A 'mystical' permutation of sound therapy, which incorporates astrology, color breathing, crystal therapy, mantras, massage, music, and tuning forks. See Sound therapy

**BioStim** FRINGE PHARMACOLOGY A non-FDA approved formulation made from an extract of bacteria, which is believed to stimulate the immune system, and help the body defend itself against bacterial, viral, and fungal infections; Biostim is believed by some to be useful in treating AIDS, cancer, bornchitis, and other conditions WARNING Patients with autoimmune-related diseases, eg multiple sclerosis or rheumatoid arthritis should not take Biostim; it should not be given to pregnant or lactating women, or to children. See Unproven methods for cancer management

**Bio-Strath Elixir** HERBAL MEDICINE A herbal formulation produced by F Pestalozzi in Switzerland, which was believed by some of the physicians who tested it, to have some efficacy in treating children with mental retardation and in post-operative recovery by increasing appetite, physical condition, and sense of well-being; Bio-Strath was never approved in Switzerland or in Britain, as its safety could not be proven, and ultimately research efforts were halted Note: Bio-Strath has been held as an example (by some providers of alternative health care) of the efficacy of the pharmaceutical industry's success in preventing natural therapies from reaching the masses, and governmental antagonism to clinical herbology

**biosynthesis** BODYWORK A system of 'spiritual' bodywork developed by David Boadella that combines features of bioenergetics and Reichian therapy; biosynthesis is based on the belief that there are 3 currents of energy flowing through the body, which emanate from the embryonal germ cell layers, the ectoderm, the mesoderm, and the endoderm; according to Boadella, stresses that may have begun in the uterus affect emotions in later life and interrupt the flow of energy; the intent of the system is to reintegrate the flow of energy, through breathing techniques, emotional centering, grounding the posture, and shaping ('facing') of experience through verbal communication and eye contact. See Bodywork

***Biota chinensis*** *Thuja orientalis*, see there

***Biota orientalis*** *Thuja orientalis*, see there

**biotin** CLINICAL NUTRITION Anti-egg white factor, factor H, factor S, factor W, skin factor, coenzyme R, vitamin H, W factor A D-isomer of the vitamin $B_2$ complex which is present in and required by most animals, as it participates in carboxylation; daily requirements are in the milligram

**biotin**

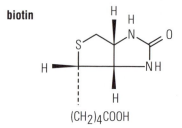

$(CH_2)_4COOH$

range; biotin deficiency is rare. See Biotin deficiency, Vitamins

**biotin deficiency** CLINICAL NUTRITION A condition characterized by anemia, dry skin, and hypercholesterolemia; biotin deficiency is rare, as it is formed by the intestinal flora, but may occur in those who consume raw egg whites, which are rich in avidin, an egg-white protein, which has a strong affinity for biotin. See Biotin

**BioToxic Reduction Program™** FRINGE MEDICINE A detoxification program developed by Zane Gard and Erma Brown, that is designed to reduce the body's internal load of toxic chemicals, heavy metals, drugs, and alcohol; the program requires a full medical work-up of supplementary vitamins, minerals, trace elements, amino acids, and oils, used in conjunction with daily exercise, followed by a sauna; it is claimed to be useful for pain, hearing and vision loss, and mood disorders (*Alternative Medicine, Future Med Pub, 1994*). See Chelation therapy, Detoxification therapy

**bird's nest** Queen Anne's lace, see there, *Daucus carota*

**bird pepper** Cayenne, see there, *Capsicum frutescens*

**BI-RG-587** AIDS PHARMACOPOEIA A dipyridodiazepinone that is a potent inhibitor of reverse transcriptase, and capable of in vitro inhibition of HIV-1 replication. See AIDS therapy It was hoped that BI-RG-587 might prove a useful adjunct to nucleoside analogs, eg zidovudine, ddC, ddI, or of use when HIV-1 became refractory to these agents (*Science 1990; 250:1411*)

**birth** see Natural childbirth, Primal (scream) therapy, Rebirthing

**birthroot** *Trillium erectum*, *T pendulum*, bethroot, Indian balm, stinking Benjamin, trillium, wake-robin HERBAL MEDICINE A perennial, the roots of which contain saponins, eg diosgenin, and volatile oils; it is antiseptic and astringent, and has been used for bites and dermal irritation, gastrointestinal complaints including hemorrhage and diarrhea, and to stop postpartum hemorrhage. See Herbal medicine

**bisabolol** HERBAL MEDICINE A volatile oil in German chamomile (*Matricaria chamomilla*) that is reported to be antimicrobial and accelerate wound healing. See Chamomile, Herbal medicine

**bistort** *Polygonum bistorta*, adderwort, patience dock, snakeroot, snakeweed HERBAL MEDICINE A perennial, the leaves and rhizomes of which contain oxalic acid, starch, tannins, and vitamin C; bistort is astringent, antiemetic, and antidiarrheal, and has been used for dysentery, menstrual bleeding, and oropharyngeal inflammation. See Herbal medicine

**bitter** ALTERNATIVE MEDICINE *noun* A preparation, usually of herbal origin, that is characterized by a bitter taste; the taste is alleged by some alternative health care practitioners to trigger a sensory nervous system, causing a cascade of responses including increasing the appetite, increasing the flow of gastric and bile juices, detoxifying the liver, and stimulating repair of the gastrointestinal tract. See Herbal medicine

**bitter almond** Apricot seed, see there, *Prunus armeniaca*

**bitter apple** *Colocynthis*, see there, *Citrullus colocynthis*

**bitter cucumber** *Colocynthis*, see there, *Citrullus colocynthis*

**bitter dock** *Rumex obtusifolius*, blunt-leaved dock, broad-leaved dock, common dock, red-veined dock, round-leaved dock HERBAL MEDICINE A perennial herb, the leaves of which have been used as a laxative, for skin blemishes, itching, and toothaches. See Herbal medicine

**bitter herb** European centaury, see there, *Centaurium umbellatum*

**bitter melon** ALTERNATIVE MEDICINE A plant from Asia administered as an extract in tea, capsules or in retention enemas; it is claimed to 'purify' the blood, prevent infections, and has been anecdotally reported to have antiretroviral activity (*Am Med News 21 Nov 1994 p13*); Cf AIDS fraud

**bitter root** Gentian, see there, *Gentiana lutea*

**black and blue foods** ALTERNATIVE NUTRITION A colloquial term for healthy foods that have a dark blue or black color, which is used outside of the context of color therapy; blue and black foods include black beans, blueberries, blue corn, fresh figs, and purple cabbage; see Diet; Cf Blue foods, Color therapy

**black box** HEALTH FRAUD A colloquial term for the Abrams generator, see there

**black cohosh** *Cimicifuga racemosa, Actaea racemosa*, black snakeroot, bugbane, rattle root, squawroot HERBAL MEDICINE A perennial herb, the roots and rhizomes of which contain triterpene glycosides (actein and cimigoside), cimicifugin, salycylates, isoferulic acid, tannins, and volatile oils; it is anti-inflammatory, antispasmodic, expectorant, sedative; it has been used internally for bleeding gums, cough, diarrhea, headaches, hypertension, menstrual disorders, neuralgia, postpartum cramping, and premenstrual syndrome, and topically for muscle spasms, neuralgia, rheumatic complaints, sciatica, and snakebites TOXICITY Black cohosh should not be used in pregnancy, as it may cause premature labor. See Botanical toxicity, Herbal medicine HOMEOPATHY See *Cimic*

**black dogwood** Alder buckthorn, see there, *Rhamnus frangula*

**black elder** Elderberry, see there, *Sambucus nigra*

**Black Forest mushroom** Maitake, see there, *Grifola frondosa*

**blackhaw** *Viburnum prunifolium*, American sloe, cramp bark, stagbush, sweet viburnum HERBAL MEDICINE A tall shrub (illustration, page 50), the root bark of which contains arbutin, resin, scopoletin, tannin, triterpenoid saponins, valeric acid, and viburnin; black haw has been used to treat menstrual cramps and postpartum pain, and is regarded by herbalists as a uterine tonic. See Herbal medicine

**black henbane** Henbane, see there, *Hyoscyamus niger*

**black medicine** Brown tonic FRINGE ONCOLOGY One of two cancer medicines promoted in the 1950s by Harvey Hoxsey, which consists of lactated pepsin and potassium iodide; the FDA evaluated the Hoxsey 'medicines', and concluded that they were ineffective. See Hoxsey treatment, Pink medicine, Unproven methods for cancer management

**blackhaw** *Viburnum prunifolium*

**black mustard** *Brassica nigra* HERBAL MEDICINE An annual herb, the seeds and leaves of which contain a glycoside–sinigrin, and an enzyme–myrosin, which on contact with water digests sinigrin, yielding allyl isothiocyanate (mustard oil); mustard oil is antibacterial and antifungal, but if applied topically in concentrated form, may cause vesicle formation*; mustard is antitussive, expectorant, and has been used as a circulatory tonic, and rheumatic complaints. See Herbal medicine; Cf White mustard

*Mustard oil forms the basis of one of the most devastating chemical weapons (dichlorodiethyl sulfide, or Yperite, in honor of the test site) ever deployed, mustard gas; it was first used at Ypres, Belgium during World War I, by the Germans and resulted in 15,000 casualties (*CL Taylor & LB Taylor, Chemical and Biological Warfare, Franklin Watts, New York 1992*)

**black pepper** *Piper nigrum, hu jiao* CHINESE MEDICINE A woody vine native to Asia, which is rich in piperine and piperidine; black pepper's dried unripe fruit is used in Chinese herbal medicine as a gastrointestinal tonic, and to treat constipation, food poisoning, obesity, sinusitis, and vomiting. See Chinese herbal medicine HERBAL MEDICINE In Western herbal medicine, black pepper is further believed to be a cardiostimulant, and enhance renal function. See Herbal medicine

**black poplar** Balm of Gilead, see there, *Populus* species

**black root** Culver's root, see there, *Veronicastrum virginicum*

**black Sampson** Echinacea, see there, *Echinacea angustifolia, E pallida, E pupura*

**black walnut** *Juglans nigra* HERBAL MEDICINE An eastern American tree, the bark of which contains iodine and tannins; it is analgesic, anthelmintic, antifungal, antiseptic, and laxative; it is used internally for constipation, oral ulcers, and intestinal parasites, and topically for acne, athlete's foot, eczema, fever blisters, jock itch, and psoriasis. See Herbal medicine

**blackwort** Comfrey, see there, *Symphytum officinale*

**bladder fucus** Bladderwrack, see there, *Fucus vesiculosus*

**bladder meridian** ACUPUNCTURE Leg greater yang meridian A meridian that begins at the nostrils, passes over the top of the head, down the side of the neck, body, and legs, and ends at the last joint of the great toe; stimulation of acupoints along the bladder meridian are used to treat conditions affecting the head and spine. See Acupuncture, The Twelve meridians

**bladder pod** Lobelia, see there, *Lobelia inflata*

**bladder training** A type of biofeedback therapy used for urinary incontinence, a condition that affects one-third of women older than age 60; bladder training is based on a combination of behavior modification, scheduling of voluntary micturition, and patient education that emphasizes neurological control of lower urinary tract function. See Biofeedback training, Behavioral modification

Bladder training decreases the episodes of incontinence by 57% and the volume loss by 54% in women with urinary incontinence who were urodynamically classified as having either urethral sphincteric incompetence or detrusor instability (*JAMA 1991; 265:609*)

**bladderwrack** *Fucus vesiculosus*, bladder fucus, kelp, kelpware, rockweed, seawrack HERBAL MEDICINE A seaweed with a long history of use as a medicinal plant; it contains iodine, mannitol, and mucilage; it has been used topically as an anti-inflammatory, and for rheumatic complaints, and internally for hypothyroidism, (given its high iodine content), radiation exposure, and heavy metal intoxication TOXICITY Kelp should not be used in patients receiving thyroid medication, with thyroid disease, or with hypertension. See Herbal medicine

**bland diet** CLINICAL NUTRITION A mechanically soft and nonirritating (as it has no spices or gastric irritants) diet that is commonly prescribed in inflammatory bowel disease and peptic ulcer disease, despite its uncertain efficacy. See Diet; Cf Spicy foods

**blastolysin** FRINGE ONCOLOGY A concentrate of fragmented cell walls from *Lactobacillus bulgaricus* that was reported to have an anticarcinogenic effect against leukemia, melanoma, sarcoma, and spontaneous tumors in experimental mice (*Moss, 1992*). See Unproven methods for cancer management

**blazing star** Fairywand, see there, *Chamaelirium luteum*

**bleeding heart** *Dicentra formosa* FRINGE MEDICINE-FLOWER ESSENCE THERAPY A floral essence that is believed to provide emotional freedom and facilitate unconditional love. See Flower essence therapy

**blessed thistle** *Cnicus benedictus, Cardius benedictus,* holy thistle, St Benedict's thistle, spotted thistle HERBAL MEDICINE An annual herb that contains alkaloids, cnicin, mucilage, and tannin; it has a long medicinal history, and was believed to be a cure-all; it is anti-inflammatory, diaphoretic, emetic, and hemostatic; it has been used as a cardiovascular and gastrointestinal tonic, to increase lactation, for arthritis, fever, headaches, and menstrual cramping, and applied topically for abscesses, itching, and wounds TOXICITY Blessed thistle is a potent emetic; it should not be used in pregnancy. See Herbal medicine

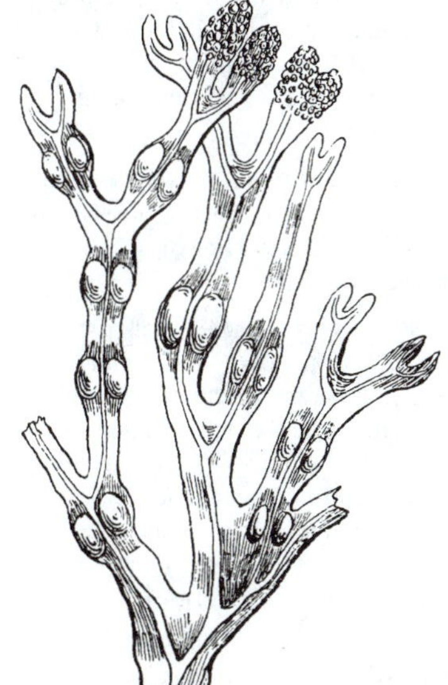

**bladderwrack** *Fucus vesiculosus*

***Bletilla hyacinthina*** *Bletilla striata*, see there

***Bletilla striata*** *Bai ji, Bletilla hyacinthina, lan hua* CHINESE MEDICINE A perennial orchid, the root/tuber of which is used in Chinese medicine as an anti-inflammatory, astringent, and hemolytic agent; it has been used topically for acne, burns, dermatitis, and eczema, and internally for tuberculosis, oral, gastrointestinal, and respiratory tract hemorrhage, and is believed to promote healing of traumatized tissues. See Chinese herbal medicine

**blessed thistle** *Cnicus benedictus*

**blister beetle** *Cantharis*, see there, *Cantharis vesicatoria, Lytta vesicatoria*

**blockade point** ALTERNATIVE PSYCHOLOGY Any form of impasse in a person's life that limits his (mental) growth potential and prevents him from achieving psychological health; blockade points can be external, eg constant bickering with a spouse, or being a victim of domestic violence, or internal, eg depression, extreme tension, and 'perpetual' unhappiness. See Humanistic psychology, Natural psychotherapy

**bloodroot** HERBAL MEDICINE 1. Erect cinquefoil, see there, *Potentilla erecta* 2. *Sanguinaria canadensis*, Indian paint, red puccoon, red root, tetterwort A perennial plant (see below), the roots and rhizomes of which contain alkaloids, including berberine, chloryethrine, copticine, proptopine, and sanguinarine; it is a strong expectorant and emetic, and was once used internally for asthma, bronchitis, cancers, colds, lung congestion, and sore throats TOXICITY It should not be used in pregnancy; it is listed by the FDA as 'unsafe'. See Berberine, Herbal medicine HOMEOPATHY see *Sanguinaria*

**bloodroot** *Sanguinaria canadensis*

**blood type → personality type** FRINGE MEDICINE A belief held in Japan, that a person's personality type is determined by his or her (ABO system) blood type

▶ **BLOOD/PERSONALITY TYPES**

- **A TYPE** Industrious, patient, punctual, and loyal
- **B TYPE** Creative and passionate individualists
- **O TYPE** Aggressive, athletic, eloquent, optimistic realists
- **AB TYPE** Rare and may have psychic abilities

**bloodwort** Yarrow, see there, *Achillea millefolium*

**blow ball** Dandelion, see there, *Taraxacum officinale*

**The Bloxham tapes** PARANORMAL PHENOMENA A series of audiocassettes recorded by a British hynotherapist, Arnell Bloxham from Jane Evans; while under hypnosis, she became a 12th century Jewess who was violently killed at a previously unknown crypt in a Catholic Church. See Past life/lives therapy; Cf Freudian psychoanalysis, Rebirthing therapy

**blue** FRINGE MEDICINE-COLOR THERAPY A color that is believed to be antibacterial, maintain the circulation in optimum condition, soothe, increase vitality, treat rheumatic complaints, and be of use in preventing cancer. See Blue foods, Blue metals & chemicals, Color breathing, Color therapy

**blue and black foods** Black and blue foods, see there

**bluebottle** European centaury, see there, *Centaurium umbellatum*

**blue cohosh** *Caulophyllum thalictroides*, blue ginseng, papoose root, squawroot, yellow ginseng HERBAL MEDICINE A perennial herb, the roots and rhizomes of which contain alkaloids, anangyrine, baptifoline, cystine, saponins, and resin; it was formerly used to ease labor and delivery, and for colic, and arthritis; it is now believed to be unsafe for pregnancy, and should not be used in those with cardiovascular disease or hypertension TOXICITY Blue cohosh seeds ('berries') are poisonous. See Herbal medicine

**blue eyes** FRINGE MEDICINE-IRIDOLOGY See Hydrogenic constitution, Iridology, Lymphatic constitution, Mesenchymal-pathological constitution, Neurogenic constitution

**blue flag** *Iris versicolor*, flag lily, liver lily, poison flag, water flag HERBAL MEDICINE A perennial herb, the dried rhizome of which contains alkaloids, salicylates, starch, and tannins; it is antiemetic and carminative, and has been used for eructation, headache, cramps, and rheumatic complaints, to increase the flow of bile, and is believed to remove toxins from the blood TOXICITY Fresh blue flag root is poisonous. See Herbal medicine

**blue foods** FRINGE MEDICINE–COLOR THERAPY Blue foods are believed to be soothing and include blueberries, plums, and grapes. See

Blue, Blue metals and chemicals, Color breathing, Color therapy; Cf Black and blue foods

**blue ginseng** Blue cohosh, see there, *Caulophyllum thalictroides*

**blue-green algae** Spirulina, see there

**blue gum** Eucalyptus, see there, *Eucalyptus globulus*

**blue metals & chemicals** FRINGE MEDICINE—COLOR THERAPY Blue metals and chemicals are believed to be mentally soothing and include copper, lead, oxygen, and tin. See Blue, Blue foods, Color breathing, Color therapy

**blue morning glory** *Pharbitis hederacea,* also known as black taurus, *chien niu, hei chou, Ipomoea hederacea, Pharbitis nil, qian niu* CHINESE MEDICINE A climbing vine, the seeds of which in traditional Chinese medicine are anti-inflammatory, cathartic, diuretic, and expectorant, it is used to treat constipation, edema, parasitosis, and shortness of breath. See Chinese herbal medicine

**Blue Mountain tea** Goldenrod, see there, *Solidago odora*

**blue flag** *Iris versicolor*

**blue pimpernel** Skullcap, see there, *Scutellaria lateriflora*

**blue sailors** Chicory, see there, *Chicorium intybus*

**blue skullcap** Skullcap, see there, *Scutellaria lateriflora*

**blue violet** Sweet violet, see there, *Viola odorata*

**bluet** European centaury, see there, *Centaurium umbellatum*

**blunt-leaved dock** Bitter dock, see there, *Rumex obtusifolius*

**BMI** Body mass index, see there

***bo dze ren*** *Thuja orientalis*, see there

***bo he*** Peppermint, see there, *Mentha piperita*

***bo zi ren*** *Thuja orientalis*, see there

**body armor** REICHIAN THERAPY A term coined by W Reich and used in bioenergetic and Reichian therapies in reference to a person's muscular and emotional blocks, which according to Reich, are caused by the repression of one's sexuality, and the cause of most disease; body armor is a constellation of postures and expressions that mold to a personality and protect it from the world; Reich divided body armor into 7 segments: eyes, mouth, neck, chest and arms, diaphragm, abdomen, and pelvis and legs; the Reichian therapist's role is to choose exercises that act on, and ultimately remove the body armor. See Orgone energy, Reich, Reichian therapy Cf Armoring

**body awareness therapy** Bodywork, see there

**body harmony** BODYWORK A permutation of bodywork that is believed to evoke natural healing energies, using the body's 'inner wisdom' to release the emotional component of past traumas. See Bodywork, Kinesics

**body integration** A process in which chronic holding patterns are released from a person's physical, mental, and emotional 'body'. See Ziaela/Dr Salomon

**body language** PSYCHOLOGY An informal, often culture-independent, form of communication in which emotions, feelings, motives, and thoughts are expressed by changes in facial expressions, gestures, posture, body positions, and other nonverbal signs (eg 'tight-lipped glare,' 'laid-back expression'). See Kinesics

**body manipulation** Bodywork, see there

**body mass index** A calculated value that correlates with body fat, which is used to define obesity; according to the World Health Organization, there is an increased risk of obesity-related conditions when the body mass index is greater than or equal to 25 (*Sci Am Aug 1996, p88*). See Fat balance

$$BMI = w/h^2$$

**w** is the weight in kilograms

**h** is the height in meters

**body-mind centering** FRINGE PSYCHOLOGY A type of meditation developed by Gay and Kathleen Hendricks, as a means of solving life problems by reconnecting one's 'inner self' with the 'outer self'. See Meditation

**body-mind link** Mind-body link technique ALTERNATIVE MEDICINE A general term for any form of alternative health care that views physical disease as a manifestation in part of a repressed psychoemotional substrate; methods used in linking the body to the mind include dialog, imagery and visualization, verbalization, or a formal format of specific routines; mind-body techniques include Alexander technique, autogenic feedback training, bioenergetics and body-oriented psychotherapy, biofeedback, Feldenkrais method, hypnosis, past life/lives therapy, rebirthing therapy, relaxation, shamanism, Tragerwork, and other techniques discussed elsewhere in this work

**body-oriented psychotherapy** A general term for any form of psychotherapy that views treatment of the mind and the body as an inseparable exercise. See Cf Biodynamic psychotherapy, Humanistic psychology

**body scan meditation** A type of meditation in which person focuses on breathing, starting from the toes, the individual focuses his attention of the body part being 'scanned,' while he visualizes the breath penetrating and relaxing the part of interest. See Meditation

**body therapy** FRINGE MEDICINE A general term for any '...*therapeutic or healing...system, modality, or session. Energy-based body therapies, such as acupuncture or reflexology, that emphasize free-flowing vital force...*' (*Gottschaulk Olsen, 1989*); or *chi*; these forms of body therapy apply pressure, but are not, in the true sense, massage therapies. See Bodywork, Energy medicine, Massage therapy, Mind/body medicine

**body type** FRINGE ENDOCRINOLOGY A hypothesis advanced in 1983 by an American physician, Elliot Abravanel, MD (*Body Type Diet & Nutrition Plan*, Bantam Books, 1983) that a person's body type is a function of the dominant endocrine organ, and that each type of person craves and overeats certain foods in an effort to stimulate that organ; according to this hypothesis, there are various forms of obesity and the role of the physician treating obesity is to determine the patient's body type and tailor a diet and exercise plan that addresses the person's body type. See Adrenal type, Gonadal type, Pituitary type, Thyroid type

**body weight fluctuation** Weight cycling, see there

**body wrap** FRINGE MEDICINE A technique that is believed by its promoters to enhance health and possibly induce weight loss; in a body wrap, the client is lathered with lotions containing vitamins and herbs and sheathed in plastic for an hour; once unwrapped, the client may be told she or he looks better and has lost mass or girth. See Contour cream NATUROPATHY Wet sheet pack A method for treating fever, and inducing relaxation, in which the body is swathed in sheets soaked with cold water, and the feet are kept warm with blankets or a foot bath. See Hydrotherapy, Naturopathy

**bodywork** Body manipulation ALTERNATIVE MEDICINE A generic term for the use of touch[1] to either improve bodily structure and function[2], or as a therapeutic modality, to reduce pain, and heal damaged musculoskeletal units (*Alternative Medicine, Future Med Pub, 1994*); central to all forms of bodywork is the belief that there are blocks in the flow of energy and fields that indirectly cause disease, and which, when unblocked, result in a return to the state of health. See Manipulation and restructuring technique, Structural integration; Cf Active muscle relaxation technique, Actualism bodywork, *Agni dhatu*, Alexander technique, Aston patterning, Awareness-oriented structural therapy, Bartenieff system, Behavioral kinesiology, Biodynamic massage, Biosynthesis, Body harmony, Body therapy, Bodywork for the Childbearing Year®, Bodywork plus, Core energetics, Deep tissue sculpting, Egoscue method,

Energy field work, Esalen massage, Feldenkreis method, Hellerwork®, Josephing, Ki-shiatsu® Oriental bodywork, Kripalu bodywork, Laban movement analysis, Life impressions bodywork, Massage parlor, Massage therapy, Manual organ stimulation therapy, Ortho-bionomy®, Postural integration, Rolfing®, Rosen method, Soma Neuomuscular Integration™, SomatoEmotional Release™, Strain-counterstrain therapy, Sotai, Swedish/Esalen massage, Thai massage, Therapeutic touch, Tibetan pulsing, Tragerwork; Transformational bodywork, Whole Person bodywork

[1]eg massage, deep tissue manipulation, movement awareness, energy balancing, exercise, and others [2]eg stimulate circulation and promote relaxation

**Bodywork for the Childbearing Year®** BODYWORK A proprietary permutation of bodywork developed in the 1980s in California, by K Jordan and C Osborne-Sheets; Bodywork for the Childbearing Year® incorporates massage and movement education as an emotional support for a woman during the entire year of her pregnancy, as well as labor, delivery, postpartum period, extending into the baby's first year of life, by helping the mother-child bonding process; the method increases body awareness and prepares the birthing muscle for the rigors of labor and delivery; it is believed to increase circulation, reduce swelling, prevent or alleviate varicose veins, reduce stress on muscles and ligaments and weight-bearing joints, reduce neck and back pain caused by poor posture, and imbalance caused by a shift in the center of gravity; trained therapists undergo a 32-hour intensive program, and ideally have had 500 or more hours of massage training before enrolling in the course. See Bodywork

**bodywork plus** ALTERNATIVE MEDICINE A general term for any system of bodywork that integrates other health-promoting modalities including energy balancing, imagery and visualization, shiatsu, Swedish massage, and others. See Bodywork

**bodywork tantra** ALTERNATIVE MEDICINE A meditation-based health philosophy developed by H Dill, that incorporates Zen shiatsu and chakra healing, and encompasses co-centering, tantsu, and watsu. See Co-centering, Tantsu, Watsu; Cf Meditation

**bogbean** *Menyanthes trifoliata*, buckbean, marsh trefoil, water shamrock, water trefoil HERBAL MEDICINE A perennial aquatic herb, which contains alkaloids, essential oil, flavonoids, glycosides, and saponin; it is a gastric tonic and mildly sedative and has been used for rheumatic complaints TOXICITY Large doses may cause vomiting and diarrhea. See Botanical toxicity, Herbal medicine

**bogbean** *Menyanthes trifoliata*

**bonding** NEONATOLOGY The emotional ties formed between the infant and mother or other caregiver that occur in the early postpartum period, which are regarded by some as analogous to imprinting in animals. See Companionship, Infant massage; Cf Anaclitic depression, Male bonding, Social isolation

**bone marrow *nei kung*** Iron shirt *chi kung* III ALTERNATIVE HEALING A health system that developed from Iron shirt *chi kung*, which is intended to increase internal strength

▶ **BONE MARROW *NEI KUNG* EXERCISES**
- 'Breathing' *chi* through fingertips and toes
- Contracting muscles to force *chi* into bones and marrow
- Hitting various parts of body with sticks (!)
- Massaging genitals to disseminate *chi* over body (!!)
- Attaching weights (4–5 kg) from genitals (!!!)

—Raso, 1994

see Iron shirt *chi kung*

**Bonefos®** A proprietary form of clodronate,

see there

**boneset** HERBAL MEDICINE 1. Comfrey, see there, *Symphytum officinal* 2. *Eupatorium perfoliatum*, agueweed, crosswort, feverwort, Indian sage, thoroughwort A perennial herb, which contains pyrrolizidine alkaloids, flavonoids (eg eupatorin, quercetin, rutin), terpenoids, volatile oil (tremerol), and resin; it is antipyretic and diaphoretic, and has been used for arthritis, colds, diarrhea, malaria, respiratory congestion, rheumatic complaints, snakebites, as a digestive tonic, and was regarded by some herbalists as a cure-all; boneset owes its name to its efficacy in treating breakbone fever TOXICITY Diarrhea, nausea, vomiting; fresh boneset contains a toxic chemical, tremerol, which causes vomiting, rapid breathing, and if in excess, coma and death; boneset is hepatotoxic due to pyrrolizidine alkaloids. See Herbal medicine

**boneset** *Eupatorium perfoliatum*

**bone-setter** A colloquial term for a person in Britain who practiced various forms of spinoskeletal manipulation until the mid-1800s; in 1853, the medical profession was consolidated into its current format, and physicians who referred patients to bone-setters for manipulation risked being erased from the Medical Register

**Bonnie Prudden myotherapy** A type of (contemporary) Western massage that is based on the application of manual pressure to sensitive or painful zones known as trigger points which result in muscle spasm; trigger points are believed to be caused by various types of trauma, including accidents, birth injury, childhood abuse, and sports injuries, and can be exacerbated by disease, substance abuse, and aging; Prudden's myotherapy was developed as a noninvasive alternative to injecting the trigger points with saline or procaine, a mainstream medical technique that has been used to control recalcitrant neuromuscular pain; Prudden divides the body into 5 zones with 17 distinct segments, which she believes can be manipulated to reduce trigger point pain; she believes that 5 to 7 seconds of deep pressure to the same zones being injected is as effective as the injections in interrupting the cycles of pain and muscle spasm. See Neuromuscular massage, Trigger points; Cf Trigger point injection therapy

**borage** *Borago officinalis*, bee bread, bugloss, burage, common bugloss, starflower FRINGE MEDICINE-FLOWER ESSENCE THERAPY A floral essence that is believed to provide buoyant courage and optimism. See Flower essence therapy HERBAL MEDICINE An annual herb that contains essential oils, mucilage, pyrrolizidine alkaloids, and tannins, which is antipyretic, a mucilage, and demulcent; it was once considered to be a cure-all, and administered as an infusion for urinary tract complaints, and dermatitis TOXICITY Borage may be harmful in large doses, given its known liver toxicity, and carcinogenic potential. See Botanical toxicity, Herbal medicine, Poisonous plants

***Borago officinalis*** Popularly known as borage, see there

**bore tree** Elderberry, see there, *Sambucus nigra*

**2-bornanone** Camphor, see there

**boron** ALTERNATIVE PHARMACOLOGY A trivalent nonmetallic element (atomic number 5; atomic weight 10.81) that is present in almonds, beans, honey, lentils, peas, peaches, pears, and raisins; although there is no known role for boron, and a deficiency state is not known to exist, boron is believed by some advocates of alternative therapies to be useful in pregnancy and menopause, as it may increase certain estrogens

***bo-shin*** CHINESE MEDICINE A traditional Chinese method of diagnosis, based on the analysis of the face; according to the Chinese construct, the auricula is a homunculus that can be exploited therapeutically in auriculotherapy. See Auriculotherapy, Homunculus

***Boswellia carterii*** Popularly known as mastic tree, see there

**botanical medicine** A general term that encompasses any plant-based therapeutic system, which may be formal, as in Chinese and Western herbal medicine, or informal, as in folk medicine, and ethnomedicine. See Herbal medicine, Pharmacognosy

**botanical toxicity** HERBAL MEDICINE A general term for any adverse effect caused by herbs or other plants; botanical toxicity has been documented in herbs with a narrow therapeutic range including aconite, *Aloe vera*, *Anemone pulsatilla*, *Arnica montana*, *Artemisia santonica*, belladonna, borage, broom, *Cactus grandiflorus*, chaparral, *Chenopodium anthelminticum*, *Cinchona ledgeriana,* coltsfoot, comfrey, ephedra, foxglove, henbane, juniper, licorice, lily-of-the-valley, *Lobelia inflata,* may-apple, pennyroyal, pokeweed, *Rauwolfia serpentina,* rue, sassafras, squill, white bryony, wormwood, yohimbe. See Poisonous plants; Cf Herbal medicine

**borage** *Borago officinalis*

**botanomedicine** Herbal medicine, see there

**bottlebrush** Horsetail, see there, *Equisetum arvense*

**bottled water** PUBLIC HEALTH A packaged potable water that has been processed, eg filtered or distilled, or obtained from a natural source, which is claimed* to be better than the drinking water from municipal sources. See Mineral water, Spring water, Water filters

*University of Delaware researchers found that 24 of 37 brands of bottled water violated one or more of 31 US drinking water standards (*M Castleman, 1996*)

**bouncing Bet** Soapwort, see there, *Saponaria officinalis*

**bourman's root** Culver's root, see there, *Veronicastrum virginicum*

**bourtree** Elderberry, see there, *Sambucus nigra*

**bowel toxemia** see Colon therapy

**bowman's root** Culver's root, see there, *Veronicastrum virginicum*

**boxberry** Wintergreen, see there, *Gaultheria pro-cumbens*

**boxwood** Dogwood, see there, *Cornus florida*

**6-Br-AA** FRINGE ONCOLOGY A form of ascorbic acid (vitamin C), which may have some efficacy in treating melanomas (*Moss, 1992*). See Unproven methods for cancer management

**Braidism** A permutation of hypnosis developed in the 1840s by a Scottish surgeon, James Braid. See Hypnosis

**brain waves** NEUROLOGY Oscillations per second that correspond to various types of cerebral activity, as measured on an electroencephalogram

▶ **BRAIN WAVES**

- **delta** < 3.5 Sleep
- **theta** 4–7 Dozing, deep meditation
- **alpha** 8–12 Relaxed wakefulness, meditation
- **beta** 13–22 Alert, focused on external events

**bran** CLINICAL NUTRITION A byproduct of milled wheat, that contains ± 20% indigestible cellulose, which serves as a bulk laxative; bran also contains water-soluble fiber with a high content of β-glycan*; bran has been recommended for cardiovascular disease, constipation, diarrhea, diverticular disease, hemorrhoids, and irritable bowel syndrome. See Dietary fiber; Cf Water-soluble fiber

*A substance which, by an unknown mechanism, reduces LDL-cholesterol by 5-15% (*JAMA 1991; 265:1833*); rice bran may be more effective in reducing cholesterol than oat bran as it may be defatted, which further reduces the cholesterol by 25%

***Brassica nigra*** Black mustard, see there

**BRAT(T) diet** Bananas, rice, apples, toast (and tea) CLINICAL NUTRITION A bland diet prescribed for viral gastroenteritis which, with water, replenishes liquids and electrolytes lost in pediatric diarrhea; other foods appropriate for diarrhea include boiled chicken, crackers, and potatoes. See Diet

Brat, *noun* A spoiled, tedious, ill-mannered child

**breast feeding** The provision of a neonate and infant with liquified lacteal products 'on tap'; lactation and breast feeding (≥ 6 months) before age 20 is associated with a relative risk of 0.54 (ie decreased risk) for the subsequent development of breast cancer in breast-fed mothers (*N Engl J Med 1994; 330:81OA*). See Breast milk, La Leche League, Natural family planning

**breast implant** An inert sac filled with silicone, (some breast implants are covered by polyurethane foam now), used to augment cosmetically the female contour; with time, the implants covered by polyurethane (composed of long chains of isocyanate monomers joined together in ester linkages), are hydrolyzed in vivo, yielding various breakdown products (eg toluene 2,4-diisocyanate, and toluene 2,6-diisocyanate diamines) from the polyurethane sponge covering the breast implants (BI)s, which were thought to have carcinogenic potential in humans (as these products are known to cause sarcomas in rats) the relationship of BIs with breast cancer is uncertain, and probably close to 'unity' (*N Engl J Med 1995; 332:1535OA*) STATISTICS 1-2 million US women had BIs since the early 1960s, when the silicone gel-filled elastomer envelope-type breast prosthesis was introduced, until the moratorium was placed in 1992 by the FDA on BIs, pending further evaluation of safety (*DA Kessler, N Engl J Med 1992; 326:1713OA*); implantation was performed for either cosmetic reasons (ie augmentation) or for post-mastectomy reconstruction; breast implants may be associated with an increased risk of connective-tissue and autoimmune phenomena, eg Hashi-moto's thyroiditis or primary biliary cirrhosis, sarcoidosis, or cancer (*N Engl J Med 1994; 330:1697OA*)

Asymptomatic rupture is estimated (by manufacturers) to occur in 0.2-1.1%; preliminary findings presented at the FDA's advisory panel (early 1992) suggested that 4-6% had ruptured; rupture may be detected by ultrasound mammography (*N Engl J Med 1993; 328:733c*), as well as by X-ray mammography Note: An expert panel from the Canadian Medical Association concluded that 'surgical removal of polyurethane-foam-covered breast implants solely for reasons of potential risk of cancer is not indicated' (*N Engl J Med 1992; 326:1649OA, 1695ED, 1696ED*)

**breast milk** Maternal milk NEONATOLOGY Human milk is similar to cow milk in the water content (88%, specific gravity, 1.030), fat content (3.5%), energy value (0.67 kcal/ml) and type of sugar (lactose); breast milk (BM) has less protein (1.0-1.5% versus 3.3% cow's milk, the latter due to a 6-fold increase in casein), more carbohydrate (6.5-7.0% versus 4.5%), less minerals and different vitamins (more vitamins C and D, less thiamin and riboflavin and equivalent amounts of vitamins A and B and niacin); breast milk is usually sterile, provides IgA and is more easily digestible, as reflected in rapid transit time; breast-fed infants have a better response to vaccines than formula-fed infants; breast milk also contains bradykinin, epidermal growth factor, gonadotropin-releasing hormone, insulin-like growth factor, melatonin, mammotropic growth factor, nerve growth factor, oxytocin. See Breast-feeding, La Leche league; Cf Certified milk, Humanized milk, Raw milk, White beverages

Note: It is considered unethical to feed children anything but human milk in Sweden, where there are banks of human milk for those who cannot breast-feed (*New York Times May 24, 1994; C1*)

**breast self-examination** The periodic palpation by a woman of her own breast, which is intended to detect new growths; although there is little evidence of the effectiveness of self-examination (*DeVita, et al, 1993*), it is the only means by which neoplasms can be detected between examinations by health care personnel; data suggest that it may result in an increased rate of detection of breast cancer, and possibly a decrease in mortality

**breathing** ALTERNATIVE MEDICINE Many forms of alternative health care and improvement emphasize proper breathing; the mechanical component of breathing is divided into chest breathing, which is under voluntary control, and the more rhythmic diaphragmatic breathing, which is primarily involuntary, and therefore more natural; the various breathing techniques focus on improving diaphragmatic breathing, which allows a fuller expansion of the lungs, and a decrease in carbon dioxide and lactic acid; improper breathing is believed by some alternative health care providers to have an adverse effect on the nervous system, resulting in anxiety, stress, insomnia, and exhaustion. See Breathing exercise, BRETH, Complete breath, Meditation; Cf Breath therapy

**breathing exercise** A generic term for any form of breath training, the most refined of which were developed in yoga; in breathing exercises, the individual switches from shallow and relatively rapid breaths to deeper slower breathing; breathing exercises are believed by their advocates to improve blood circulation, calm the nervous system, and draw in vital substances* that are not normally inhaled. See Meditation; Cf Breath therapy

*Of unspecified nature–Author's note

**breath therapy** ALTERNATIVE MEDICINE A technique in mind/body medicine for coping with stress, anxiety, and pain, which is based on the belief that fuller breathing supplies the body with more energy, which is used in healing; slow breathing evokes relaxation, which can be used in conjunction with other mind/body techniques, including meditation or imagery and visualization; forced breathing–known as evocative breath therapy–accompanied by music is used to elicit an emotional release that some believe enhances the immune system. See Autogenic training, Biofeedback, Biopsychosocial model, Flight-or-fight response, Hypnosis, Imagery (and visualization), Meditation, Mind/body medicine, Mindfulness, Progressive relaxation, Psychoneuroimmunology; Cf Breathing

**BRETH** Breath Releasing Energy for Transformation and Healing and/or happiness ALTERNATIVE MEDICINE A technique developed by an Australian, K Hope-Campbell, which is intended to release emotional and physical trauma and limiting thought patterns; the BRETH method involves 'conscious beathing' and 'high touch', which is directed by a 'sitter'. See 'High touch', 'Sitter'

**brewer's yeast** ALTERNATIVE PHARMACOLOGY Yeast that is produced *Saccharomyces cerevisiae* as a byproduct of brewing beer, which is regarded by some as being a healthy food product; it is rich in chromium, and has been shown to lower blood sugar in diabetes, reduce LDL cholesterol, and raises HDL cholesterol; it has been applied topically for athlete's foot, oily skin, and for flea control in domestic pets; see Healthy food

**bridewort** Meadowsweet, see there, *Filipendula ulmaria*

**bright light therapy** Light therapy, phototherapy The use of the visible range of the electromagnetic spectrum as a therapeutic modality; light acts via the hypothalamus and releases cascades of neurotransmitters and releasing factors after receiving neural impulses from the retina; it is the therapy of choice for seasonal affective disorder (SAD), and may be of use in bulimia, insomnia, lupus erythematosus, nonseasonal depression, prolonged menstrual cycles, and shift work-related drowsiness; modalities of LT include the use of full spectrum light (eg sunlight), bright light (10 000 lux*), UV light, colored light, hemoirradiation. See Heliotherapy, Seasonal affective disorder, Spring fever

*To place this in perspective, the average home is illuminated at 250 lux; noonday sun is 120 000 lux; there is no evidence in peer-reviewed journals to support the assertion that '*Malillumination contributes to ...tooth decay, depression, hostility, suppressed immune function, strokes, hair loss, skin damage ...and cancer.*' (*Alternative Medicine, Future Med, 1994*), or organic changes caused by AIDS, arthalgias, asthma, bulimia, dysmenorrhea, headaches, high cholesterol, infections, insomnia, or other conditions–Author's note

**brimstone** *Sulfur*, see there

**brinase** FRINGE ONCOLOGY An enzyme obtained from a mold (*Aspergillus oryzae*) that is reported to stimulate the immune system by increasing the T-cell counts in the elderly and those with cancer (*Br J Cancer 1975; 31:164*). See Enzyme therapy, Kelley methods, Metabolic typing, Unproven methods for cancer management

There is little recent data suggesting that enzyme therapy, as used by alternative health care providers, is beneficial in patients with malignancy–Author's note

**Brinton's root** Culver's root, see there, *Veronicastrum virginicum*

**bris** *pronounced* Briss The traditional religious rite (the Brith Milah) of circumcision as practiced by Jews; it is performed by the eighth day of life, not by a physician, but rather by a mohel (*pron* moil); see Circumcision

Note: The word bris (aka brith) translates from Hebrew as covenant (*L Rosten, The Joys of Yiddish, 1968*)

**Bristol diet therapy** ALTERNATIVE MEDICINE A diet devised by Dr Alex Forbes of the Bristol Cancer Self-help Centre; the Bristol diet's main staples are fresh vegetables, whole grains, yogurt, fresh juice, olive oil, and herbs and spices in lieu of salt and pepper; it also includes fish, free-range chicken, and organically grown meat; coupled with meditation and counseling, the Bristol diet is intended to improve the quality of life of patients with cancer. See Diet; Cf Unproven methods for cancer management

**broad-leaved dock** Bitter dock, see there, *Rumex obtusifolius*

**broad-leaved plantain** Plantain, see there, *Plantago major*

**bromelin** Bromelain, see there

**bromelain** Bromelin, plant protease concentrate A general term for any of a number of trypsin-like cysteine endopeptidase enzymes (thiol proteases) obtained from the 'fruit' and stem of the pineapple (*Ananas comosus*); bromelain is used as an anti-inflammatory agent, meat tenderizer, to lyse proteins, reduce edema and, in transfusion medicine, to increase agglutinability of red cells in the presence of an incomplete antibody. See Pineapple

**brominated vegetable oil** FOOD INDUSTRY A food additive used as an emulsifier in some foods, and as a clouding agent in some soft drinks, which is alleged to be extremely dangerous by alternative health care advocates TOXICITY Heart palpitations, head-aches, nausea, and nerve damage. See Nutrition therapy

**broom** *Sarothamnus scoparius, Cytisus scoparius*, broomtops, genista, Irish broom, Scotch broom HERBAL MEDICINE A branched shrub that contains alkaloids (eg genisteine, sarothamine, and sparteine), amino acids, tannin, and volatile oil; it is a cardiac depressant, diuretic, and laxative TOXICITY Broom causes vasoconstriction and should be avoided in pregnancy and hypertension; it is listed by the FDA as 'unsafe'. See Botanical toxicity, Herbal medicine

**broom grass** Belvedere cypress, see there, formally designated *Kochia scoparia*

**broomrape** *Cistanche salsa, rou cong rong, rou tsung rung* CHINESE MEDICINE An annual parasitic herb, the fleshy stem of which is emollient, laxative, and tonic; it is also used for constipation, impotence, and infertility; it is believed by some to be an aphrodisiac. See Chinese herbal medicine

**broomtops** Broom, see there, *Sarothamnus scoparius*

**brown eyes** FRINGE MEDICINE-IRIDOLOGY See Hematogenic constitution

**brown rice pillow** CHINESE MEDICINE An herbal pillow used in traditional Chinese medicine, that is recommended for young children; the aromatic rice is believed to promote sound sleep, normal brain development, and control hyperactivity; Chinese herbal medicine, Herbal pillow

**bruisewort** 1. *Bellis*, see there, *Bellis perennis* 2. Soapwort, see there, *Saponaria officinalis*

**brushing** MASSAGE A superficial massage technique, in which the skin surface is slowly, lightly, and rhythmically stroked, often as a 'finishing touch' after a full massage. See Massage therapy

**Milan Brych** An individual who was alleged to have falsified documents as to his medical qualifications, who practiced medicine in New Zealand during the 1970s, and claimed to have a secret cure to cancer*. See Unproven methods for cancer management

*For which he charged up to $9600 per injection for ingredients that cost $10; the National Medical Council of New Zealand concluded that Brych '*...had never qualified in medicine, and had never, in fact been to University.*' (*Mod Med Australia May, 1987, p51*); Brych's career in medicine spanned nearly 15 years; and after folding his tent in New Zealand, he reopened shop in Rarotonga in the Cook Islands, and subsequently in California, where he operated cancer treatment clinics; Milan Brych is believed to have belonged '*...to a long lineage of bogus cancer therapists...*'

***Bryonia*** *Bryonia alba*, common bryony, white bryony, wild hops HOMEOPATHY A remedy used primarily for acute conditions of slow onset; it has also been used internally for arthritis, breast-feeding-related mastitis, bursitis, colds with congestion, colic, cough, gastrointestinal complaints including constipation, gastritis, nausea, and vomiting, headache, inflammation of the serosa, influenza, low back pain, and rheumatic complaints. See Homeopathy

**bryostatin** ALTERNATIVE ONCOLOGY Any of a number of compounds known as lactones derived from coralline (sea mat, *Bugulia neritina*), a marine invertebrate; bryostatins stimulate the immune system, increasing T cell and interleukin-2 production, and inhibit growth of experimental leukemias and breast cancer (*Br J Cancer 1991; 64:671*). See Unproven methods for cancer management

**$B_T$ factor** Carnitine, see there

***bu gu jih*** *Psoralea corylifolia*, see there

***bu gu zhi*** *Psoralea corylifolia*, see there

***bu ji tien*** Morinda root, see there, *Morindae officinalis*

**bubble of light meditation** Bubble of light technique, see there

**bubble of light technique** Bubble of light meditation PARANORMAL PHENOMENA A method of 'magical healing' that is based on the belief that the unconscious mind has a 'magical place' where anything–including the healing of dread diseases, is possible. See Meditation

**buchu** *Agathosma* species HERBAL MEDICINE A South African shrub that is diuretic, which has been used for congestive heart failure, hypertension, bloating caused by premenstrual syndrome, and urogenital infections and kidney stones TOXICITY Buchu's diuresis causes a loss of potassium. See Botanical toxicity, Herbal medicine

**buckbean** Bogbean, see there, *Menyanthes trifoliata*

**buckeye** Horse chestnut, see there, *Aesculus hippocastanum*

**buckthorn** Alder buckthorn, see there, *Rhamnus frangula*

***budo*** Martial arts, see there

**buffalo herb** Alfalfa, see there, *Medicago sativa*

**buffer theory** CLINICAL NUTRITION A theory on food intake and weight autoregulation that holds that only changes in the original equilibrium or rapid fluctuations in the food intake or body weight are opposed; the metabolic set point is easily disturbed, with rapid weight loss when food is not available, or rapid gain when food is readily available. See Obesity; Cf Set point hypothesis, Settling point hypothesis

**bugbane** Black cohosh, see there, *Cimicifuga racemosa*

**bugloss** 1. Alkanet, *Anchusa officinalis* 2. Borage, see there, *Borago officinalis*

**building biology** A seemingly ad hoc term referring to the study of the effect that modern (high-rise) office buildings have on human behavior and disease. See Sick building syndrome

**bulk cathartic** Bulk-forming laxative, see there

**bulk-forming laxative** Bulk cathartic, bulk laxative Any of a number of laxatives (eg psyllium, calcium polycarbophil) that absorbs water and expands, resulting in an increase in stool volume, facilitating passage of stools, while increasing motility. See Laxative; Cf Stool softener, Stimulant laxative

In common parlance, the adjectival modifier, *–forming*, is usually eliminated; the term bulk laxative may be confusing to the non-cognoscenti–Author's note

**bulk laxative** Bulk-forming laxative, see there

**bull's-eye** Calendula, see there, *Calendula officinalis*

**bulrush** Cattail, see there, *Typha latifolia*

**bunny's ears** Mullein, see there, *Verbascum thapsus*

***Bupleurum chinense*** Hare's ear, see there, *Bupleurum falcatum*

***Bupleurum falcatum*** Popularly known as hare's ear, see there

***buqi*** *Qigong* therapy, see there

***buqi* therapy** *Qigong* therapy, see there

**bur** Burdock, see there, *Arctium lappa*

**burage** Borage, see there, *Borago officinalis*

**burdock** *Arctium lappa*, beggar's buttons, bur, clotbur, cockle buttons, cocklebur, *da li dze*, great burdock, great power seeds, lappa, *niu bang dze, niu bang zi,* thorny burr CHINESE MEDICINE A biennial herb rich in essential oils, arctiol, fukinone, volatile (acetic, butyric, isovaleric, and propionic) acids, inulin (up to 50% by weight), non-hydroxyl (lauric, myristic, palmitic, and stearic) acids, polyacetylenes, tannic acid, and taraxasterol; the seeds and roots are anti-inflammatory, antimicrobial, antipyretic, antitussive, diaphoretic, diuretic, expectorant, and laxative; burdock is used for abscesses, bronchitis, chickenpox, low back pain, pulmonary congestion, syphilis, and urethritis; the seeds are used to treat colds, measles, sore throat, and tonsillitis; the roots and leaves are used for rheumatic complaints and gout. See Chinese herbal medicine HERBAL MEDICINE Burdock is used by Western herbologists internally for bacterial and fungal infections, cystitis, fever, recuperation from strokes, renal disease, as a gastrointestinal tonic, to detoxify various organs, and topically for skin conditions including acne, bites, dandruff, eczema, and psoriasis, gout, and leprosy. See Herbal medicine TOXICITY Burdock should not be used in pregnancy, as it stimulates uterine contraction, or in young children. See Herbal medicine

**burdock** *Arctium lappa*

**burnout** SOCIAL MEDICINE A feeling of hopeless frustration often accompanied by depression, which is experienced by workers in certain fields; in the health care field, without an active, self-renewing support group, nurses, and social workers assigned to AIDS, cancer, and geriatrics patients–in which there is an endless parade of dementia, deterioration, and death, drift toward callousness and desire to change fields. See Burnout syndrome, Flight-or-fight response; Cf Adaptation response, Ala rm stage

**burnout syndrome** Compassion fatigue SOCIAL MEDICINE A form of chronic stress in which the subject gives of himself or herself 'until it hurts'; BS is described as a sensation of depletion without time for psychological 'replenishment'; these individuals (eg health care providers) suffer chronic fatigue, muscle tension, and engage in substance abuse, usually alcohol

**Laurence Burton** FRINGE ONCOLOGY The chief proponent of immunoaugmentive therapy, who has operated for-profit clinics providing this form of cancer management in various places, most recently, in the Caribbean. See Immunoaugmentive therapy, Unproven methods for cancer management

**Burton Treatment** Immuno-augmentive therapy, see there

**Stanislaw R Burzynski** See Antineoplaston

**bush tea** see Jamaican vomiting sickness

**bushmaster** *Lachesis muta*, see there

**butcher's broom** *Ruscus aculeatus* HERBAL MEDICINE A shrub native to the Mediterranean rim, the roots and rhizomes of which contain neuroscogenin and ruscogenin; it is astringent, diuretic, and laxative, and has been used internally or topically for hemorrhoids, rectal inflammation, and varicose veins. See Herbal medicine

**buttercup** *Ranunculus occidentalis* FRINGE MEDICINE-FLOWER ESSENCE THERAPY A floral essence that is said to provide radiant inner light. See Flower essence therapy

**butterfly weed** Pleurisy root, see there, *Aesclepias tuberosa*

**butylated hydroxyanisole** see BHA

**butylated hydroxytoluene** See BHT

**butyric acid** FRINGE ONCOLOGY A hydrocarbon present in cow's butter used as a flavoring agent, and thought to have anticarcinogenic activity, in particular the chemical derivative sodium butyrate (*Moss, 1992*). See Unproven methods for cancer management

**C.A.** Certified Acupunturist

**cabala** Cabbala, kabala, kabbala, kabbalah, kabbalism, Qabalah, Qabbalah PARANORMAL PHENOMENA A system of eclectic mysticism and healing based on ancient Jewish tradition, involving the study of angels ('angelology'), demonology, meditation, prayers, and ritual. See Shamanism; Cf Neo-Shamanism

**cabbage juice diet** ALTERNATIVE NUTRITION A diet that consists of only cabbage juice, and water, but no other solid foods; it is recommended for ulcers. See Fasting

**cabbala** Cabala, see there

***Cactus grandiflorus*** Night-blooming cactus HERBAL MEDICINE An herb that has been used as a cardiac stimulant; it should be used with caution, given its narrow therapeutic range TOXICITY Angina, heart spasms, headache, myocarditis, tachyarrhythmias; vertigo. See Botanical toxicity, Poisonous plants HOMEOPATHY A minor homeopathic remedy used for crushing anginal pain. See Homeopathy

**café coronary** Vallecular dysphagia Complete and abrupt upper airway obstruction by a bolus of food, often meat, resulting in occlusion of both the esophagus and larynx, so named as the sudden onset of symptoms simulates acute myocardial infarction; the victims are speechless, breathless and, without help (eg Heimlich maneuver), lifeless; cafe coronaries occur in the inebriated, bedentured, mentally retarded, demented, or gluttonous CLINICAL Violent coughing, cyanosis, collapse and death; Cf Steakhouse syndrome, Sushi syncope

Note: Although a café coronary was the alleged cause of death at age 33 of the famed siren of the 60s, (Mama) Cass Elliot, according to Dr K Simpson, forensic pathologist and G Thurston, Coroner of London, she in fact died of atherosclerotic heart disease

**cafeteria diet** Snack diet, 'trash' diet CLINICAL NUTRITION An experimental diet for studying obesity that allows rats free (cafeteria-style) access to cookies, candy, cake ('junk-food'); if the diet is begun before puberty, the animals remain lean despite excess intake; if the diet is begun as adults, they become obese, due to insufficient thermogenesis; the diet is a model for pure over-feeding type obesity, in which adipsin (a serine protease analog synthesized by adipocytes) levels are normal; genetically obese rats have low adipsin levels. See Diet, Fast food, Obesity

**caffeine** A methylxanthine that is the most widely used psychoactive substance in the world; it is present in coffee, tea, maté, soft drinks, cocoa, kola nuts, guarana products; low doses of caffeine (20 to 200 mg) produce positive subjective effects, feelings of well-being, alertness, energy; higher doses may have adverse effects, eg nervousness, anxiety (*JAMA 1994; 272:1043oc*). See Coffee

Note: Its use during pregnancy has not been linked to an increased risk of spontaneous abortion, intrauterine growth retardation, or microcephaly (*ibid, 1993; 269:593oc*)

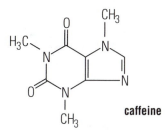

**caffeine**

**caffeine-dependence syndrome** SUBSTANCE ABUSE A clinical complex that can be defined by fulfilling 3 of 4 generic criteria for substance dependence from the Diagnosis and Statistical Manual of Mental Disorders, 4th edition (*DSM-IV*)

▶ **CAFFEINE DEPENDENCE SYNDROME, CRITERIA**

- **TOLERANCE** (Criterion 1, seen in 75% of cohort)
- **SYMPTOMS OF WITHDRAWAL** in absence of the use of caffeine (Criterion 2, seen in 94%)
- **PERSISTENT DESIRE** or unsuccessful attempt to reduce or control use of caffeine products (Criterion 4, seen in 81%)
- **CONTINUED USE DESPITE KNOWLEDGE** of a persistent or recurrent problem that is likely to have been caused or exacer-

bated by substance abuse (Criterion 7, seen in 94%) See Coffee, Tea; Cf Caffeine withdrawal syndrome Note: Certain DSM-IV substance dependence critera were excluded from the definition as they do not qualify as dependence per se; 16 of 99 subjects in one study (*JAMA 1994; 272:1043OC*), were caffeine dependent

**caffeine withdrawal syndrome** A complex of findings associated with the cessation of caffeine consumption of doses as low as 100 mg/day (equivalent to one cup of coffee/day); caffeine withdrawal syndrome is a defining criterion for the caffeine dependence syndrome, see there CLINICAL Head-ache, lethargy, muscle pain or stiffness, decreased performance, dysphoric mood changes including depression, occasionally nausea and vomiting (*N Engl J Med 1992; 327:1109OA, 1160ED*). See Caffeine, Caffeine-dependence syndrome, Coffee

**Calabar bean** *Physostigma venenosum* HERBAL MEDICINE A climbing vine native to Africa that contains physostimine, which causes death by inducing muscle contractions to the point of rigidity; the synthetic derivatives, including neostigmine are used in myasthenia gravis and in ophthalmology to prevent glaucoma. See Herbal medicine

**calamine lotion** A lotion containing zinc oxide (98% of volume) mixed with iron oxide, or zinc carbonate; it is mildly astringent and protective, and used for various skin conditions, including poison ivy and sunburn

**calamus** Sweet flag, see there, *Acorus calamus*

**calanolide A** A compound derived from a Malaysian tree (*Calophyllum lanigerum*), which was of transient interest as a therapy for AIDS, and reported to be active against AZT-resistant HIV-1 (*Sci Am 1993; 268/1:142*). See AIDS fraud

***Calc carb*** *Calcarea carbonica*, calcium carbonate HOMEOPATHY A homeopathic remedy formulated from the mother-of-pearl of oysters; it is used for allergies, arthritis, asthma, delayed bone and tooth development, candidiasis, chronic otitis media, conjunctivitis, constipation, eczema, slowly healing fractures, gastrointestinal complaints, right-sided headaches, insomnia, joint, bone, and low back pain, muscle cramps, teething and diarrhea in children, and menstrual dysfunction. See *Calc carb* type, Homeopathy

***Calc carb* type** HOMEOPATHY A constitutional type of person who is anxious, impressionable, obsessive, quiet, and sensitive; *Cal carb* types may be anxious, fatigued, sensitive to cold, and sweaty; they like sweet, starchy, or sour foods, cold drinks, eggs, and may have pica (a craving for nondigestible substances, eg chalk or dirt) WORSE Cold, humidity, premenstrual, spring, full moon FEARS Poverty, death, dread disease, darkness, enclosed spaces, rodents WEAKEST BODY REGIONS Bones and teeth, intestines, endocrine glands, skin, ears, nose, and throat. See *Calcarea carbonica*, Constitutional type, Homeopathy

***Calc phos*** *Calcarea phosphorica*, calcium phosphate *Calcarea carbonica*, calcium carbonate HOMEOPATHY A homeopathic remedy used for bone and teeth, including slowing healing fractures, and caries, growing pains in children, gastrointestinal complaints including indigestion and diarrhea, and swollen lymph nodes due to tonsillitis. See Homeopathy

**calcium** A bivalent metallic element (atomic number 20; atomic weight 40.08) which is the most abundant mineral in the body, and critical for bone and tooth formation; it is intimately linked to many metabolic processes including muscle contraction, neural transmission, coagulation, and inhibition of cell destruction; calcium levels in the blood are controlled by the counterbalancing actions of parathyroid hormone and calcitonin; it is present in dairy products, almonds, leafy vegetables, sardines, and salmon; proper absorption of calcium hinges on appropriate acidity of the stomach, presence of vitamin D, and a balance of other minerals, including phosphorus and mangesium. See Hypercalcemia, Hypocalcemia

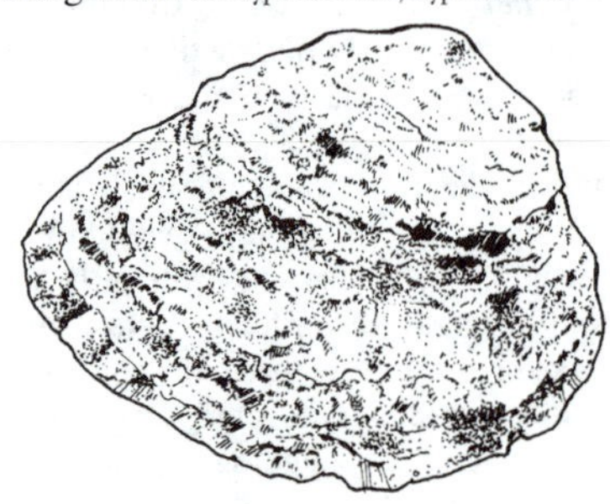

**oyster** *Ostrea* species

**calcium carbonate** HOMEOPATHY *Calc carb*, see there, *Calcarea carbonica*

**calcium deficiency** Hypocalcemia, see there

**calcium intoxication** Hypercalcemia, see there

**calcium phosphate** HOMEOPATHY *Calc phos*, see there, *Calcarea phosphorica*

**calendula** *Calendula officinalis*, bull's-eye, marigold, marybud, pot marigold HERBAL MEDICINE An annual that contains carotenoids, essential oils, flavonoids, mucilage, saponins, and sterols, which is antimicrobial and antiseptic; it is used topically for athlete's foot, bacterial and fungal infections, burns, chickenpox, diaper rash, impetigo, stings, and varicose veins, and internally for gallstones, gastritis, gastric ulcers, menstrual dysfunction and painful menses, and to promote the flow of bile; see Herbal medicine

**calendula** *Calendula officinalis*

***Calendula officinalis*** Calendula, see there,

**California poppy** *Eschscholzia californica* FRINGE MEDICINE-FLOWER ESSENCE THERAPY A floral essence that is believed to develop inner knowledge, spirituality, and love; see Flower essence therapy

**California wild rose** *Rosa californica* FRINGE MEDICINE-FLOWER ESSENCE THERAPY A floral essence that is believed to develop one's sense of serving others. See Flower essence therapy

**Calistoga** see Natural spring

**Callanetics®** A proprietary exercise program developed in the 1970s by Callan Pinckney, who was born with scoliosis and lordosis, and required leg braces as a child; the exercises consist of small delicate movements, activating the largest and deepest muscles of the body, and are believed to promote strength, endurance, and flexibility, improve balance, discipline, and speed, and decrease appetite; Cf Aerobic exercise

***Calluna vulgaris*** Popularly known as heather, see there

**Calming Essence™** Dr. Bach's Emergency Stress Formula, see there

**caloric restriction** The deliberate reduction in the intake of calories to levels that are up to 30% below a 'usual' diet; calorically restricted experimental animals live longer, remain healthier, and maintain better physiologic and behavioral functions than their well-fed counterparts; animals subjected to caloric restriction from birth are smaller, mature later, have lower blood levels of insulin and glucose, and have increased daytime activity; hypotheses to explain the anti-aging properties of caloric restriction include altered glucose utilization, decreased oxygen radical damage, decreased glycation of macromolecules, changes in patterns of gene expression, and levels of stress hormones (*Nature Medicine 1995; 1:414*). See Diet, Methuselah factor; Cf Protein restriction

**caltrop** *Tribulus terrestris*, see there

***Campanula grandiflora*** Balloon flower, see there, *Platycodon grandiflorum*

**camphor** 2-Bornanone PHARMACOLOGY Any of a family of bicyclic alcoholic or ketonic terpenes obtained from *Cinnamomum camphora* in the form of whitish crystals; camphor is used topically as an analgesic, antipruritic, rubifacient, as a counterirritant for inflamed joints, and as a mouthwash; internally it is carminative, decongestant, and expectorant TOXICITY Prolonged exposure to camphor's volatile oils are dangerous, and may be associated with nausea, vomiting, delirium, coma, and respiratory arrest

**camphor**

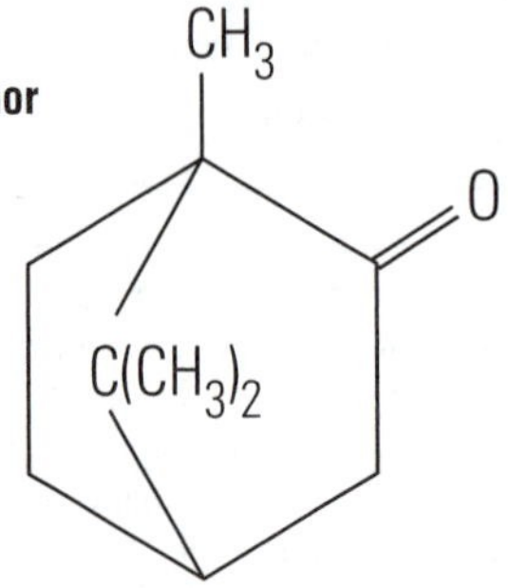

$CH_3$ $C(CH_3)_2$ O

**C.A.M.T.** Certified Acupressure Massage Therapist

**Canada root** Pleurisy root, see there, *Aesclepias tuberosa*

**CanCell** Entelev HEALTH FRAUD An unproven form of disease management consisting of 'plant-energized' water, which was promoted as a cure for AIDS, arthritis, cancer, diabetes, systemic lupus erythematosus, and other conditions; it was administered per cutaneously or per rectum, and determined by the FDA to be fraudulent (*Am Med News 21 Nov 1994 p13*). See AIDS fraud, Quackery, Unproven methods for cancer management

**cancer fallacy** FRINGE ONCOLOGY A general term for scientifically invalid reasoning about the nature of cancer, which may be used by purveyors of unproven cancer therapies to promote their products or services; Cf Cancer myth

The American Cancer Society listed these fallacies (table) in a professional publication (*CA 1986; 36:293-301*), and addressed each

▶ **CANCER FALLACIES**

- A person should be allowed to chose his/her own therapy, irrespective of proof of efficacy
- A person should be allowed to chose the therapy for his/her children, irrespective of proof of efficacy
- There is nothing to lose by trying an alternative therapy

**cancer myth** A general term for any of a number of popular beliefs about the nature of malignancy, that may contrast with available scientific evidence; there is a tendency on the part of purveyors of unproven methods of cancer management to play on these myths, and entice cancer victims to make health decisions that are not in their own interests. See Cancer fallacy, Unproven methods for cancer management

▶ **CANCER MYTHS**

- Cancer is a single disease
- Cancer spreads like wildfire
- Cancer's cause is unknown
- Cancer has no cure
- Cancer-free societies exist
- Cancer can be cured by diet
- There is a conspiracy (eg by physicians, pharmaceutical concerns) AGAINST curing cancer
- Cancer can be cured by a strong belief in the treatment
- Science is close-minded toward unorthodox therapies
- Alternative therapies offer a 'last chance' for patients

The American Cancer Society has addressed each in a professional education publication (*CA 1986; 36:293-301*)

**cancer phobia** An excessive fear of suffering the ravages of malignancy; this phobia commonly affects those who have directly cared for a loved one who suffered marked pain or disfigurement for a protracted period before death; cancer phobia is considered an indication for a simple mastectomy in patients with a diagnosis of carcinoma-in-situ, which may be treated more conservatively by close observation and periodic mammography and breast examination

**cancer-prone personality** ALTERNATIVE PSYCHOLOGY A personality profile that is believed to place a person at an increased risk for developing a cancer due to ill-defined internal conflicts; it is unclear whether such a personality actually exists, as evaluation of 'proneness' is based on subjective observation and personal data (*Prof Ed Pub, American Cancer Society*); nonetheless, Simonton and others have listed personality traits that they believe increase a person's susceptability to cancer

▶ **CANCER SUSCEPTIBILITY**

- Maternal domination
- Immatural sexual adjustment
- Inability to express emotions and hostility
- Inability to accept significant losses
- Pre-neoplastic feelings of despair, hopelessness, self-pity
- Poor self-image and interpersonal relationships
- Lack of closeness to parents

(*Watson, 1995*) Cf Psychoneuroimmunology, Psycho-oncology

**cancer screening** The testing of a large group of people for malignancies that are common to the group; screening tests must be inexpensive and, in order to detect all those who are abnormal for the analyte, highly sensi-

tive. See Cancer screening guideline, Cancer screening test

**cancer screening guideline** A general term for any guideline, often promulgated by an authoritative organization (eg, American Cancer Society), for early detection of a malignancy that is relatively common in a particular population, the diagnosis of which, in initial stages of development results in a complete cure or improved long-term survival. See Cancer screening, Cancer screening test; Cf Unproven methods for cancer management

▶ **CANCER SCREENING GUIDELINES**

- **BREAST CANCER** Self-breast examination on a monthly basis, a baseline mammogram at age 40 and mammography every 1-2 years thereafter, depending on risk factors
- **COLON CANCER** Recommendation by the National Cancer Institute, American Cancer Society, and American College of Physicians for colorectal carcinoma is annual fecal occult blood test after age 40 and flexible sigmoidoscopy every 3-5 years after age 50 (*N Engl J Med 1991; 325:37*)
- **PROSTATE CANCER** Annual digital rectal examination after age 40, and measurement of prostate-specific antigen in the serum
- **UTERINE CERVIX CANCER** Annual Pap smear and pelvic examination after initiation of sexual activity; after three normal years, the test may be reduced in frequency at the discretion of the patient's physician

**cancer screening test** Any measurable clinical or laboratory parameter that can be used to detect early malignancy; although these tests are relatively nonspecific, they are highly sensitive, and detect many individuals who are 'abnormal' for the parameter being measured; the most common cancer screening methods are those that detect occult blood in the stool, seen in colorectal cancer and mammography (to detect microcalcifications and geographic densities) for breast cancer. See Cancer screen, Cancer screening guideline

**cancer underground** A loosely cohesive network of providers and consumers of nonconventional cancer therapies, that have not been shown in formal clinical trials to have a positive impact on the tumor's outcome; the cancer underground's members share in common a disbelief in the efficacy of mainstream medical and surgical oncology, and an unwillingness to question the practices of providers of unproven cancer therapies. See Health freedom argument, Unproven methods for cancer management; Cf Health food movement

**candida syndrome** Candida hypersensitivity syndrome, see there

**candidiasis hypersensitivity syndrome** Candida syndrome, yeast syndrome A condition, the very existence of which is controversial, which is said to occur in women, due to an overgrowth of *Candida albicans* on mucosal surfaces, especially of the vagina and gastrointestinal tract ETIOLOGY Candidiasis hypersensitivity syndrome has been linked to various agents, ranging from overuse of broad-spectrum antibiotics to oral contraceptives, and pregnancy CLINICAL Chronic gastrointestinal complaints (eg bloating, heartburn, constipation, and diarrhea), anxiety, depression, loss of memory, poor concentration, fatigue, increased infections, irritability and mood swings, nasal congestion, weight gain DIAGNOSIS The diagnosis is made based on a questionnaire, rather than on blood or tissue studies TREATMENT Nystatin*. See Crook diet

*In a randomized study of oral and/or vaginal nystatin vs placebo, there was no difference in response (*N Engl J Med 1990; 323:1717*)

**candleberry** Bayberry, see there, *Myrica cerifera*

***cang zhu*** Thistle, see there, *Atractylodes chinensis*

***Cannabis sativa*** Marijuana, see there

***Canon of Medicine*** MEDICAL HISTORY—HERBAL MEDICINE A 131-work collection of medical thought based on the Greek writings of Aristotle; Dioscorides, Galen, Hippocrates, and others written by the Persian philosopher Avicenna (980-1037); although the *Canon* served as the standard medical text in Christian and Moslem universities, by the late 1400s it had been replaced by the works of the luminaries of the Renaissance, including Leonardo da Vinci in Italy, Paracelsus in Switzerland, and William Harvey in England. See Herbal medicine; Cf *Chakra Sambita*, *The Complete Herbal*, *De Materia Medica*, *Natural History*, *Nei Jing*, *Pen Ts'ao*, *Philosophy of Natural Therapeutics*, *Rigveda*,

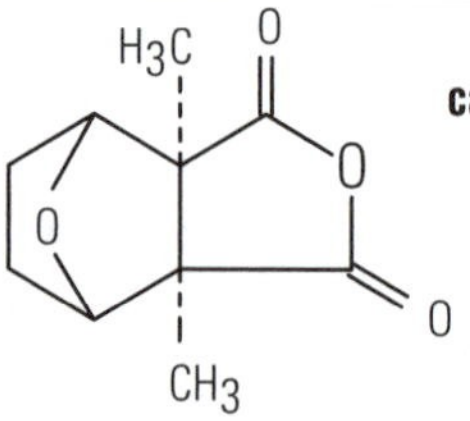

**cantharidin**

*Sushrita Samhita*, *Theatrum Botanicum*

**cantharidin** ALTERNATIVE ONCOLOGY The active component of Chinese fly and *Cantharis* (Spanish fly); it is highly irritating and causes vesicle formation; it has been used for warts, and other skin lesions (*Moss, 1992*). See *Cantharis*, Chinese fly

***Cantharis*** *Cantharis vesicatoria*, *Lytta vesicatoria*, blister beetle, Spanish fly HOMEOPATHY A homeopathic remedy used for acute cystitis, baldness, colic, acute tonsillitis, hypersexuality, and extreme emotional lability TOXICITY Applied in its pure form to mucocutaneous surfaces, *Cantharis* causes erythema, urticaria, and vesiculation; per os, it causes gastrointestinal irritation, nausea, vomiting, diarrhea, cramping, and collapse; as little as 60 mg of this highly nephrotoxic agent may be fatal; the active component is cantharidin, a rubifacient. See Homeopathy

**canthaxanthin** Carotaben plus, Food Orange 8, Roxaxanthin Red 10 A red-orange beta-carotene-like pigment that is produced naturally by some plants and marine animals; it is approved by the FDA as a dye for soups, fruit drinks, catsup, and other foods; canthaxanthin deposits in the skin, and results in a pink-orange hue; it has been illegally marketed as a tanning agent. See Artificial dye, Tanning FRINGE ONCOLOGY It stimulates the immune system and enhances the antioxidant activity of vitamin E; it is reported to decrease the development of spontaneous cancers in experimental animals TOXICITY Allergic reactions, hives, itching, hepatitis, and aplastic anemia, deposition in the macula (*Moss, 1992*). See Unproven methods for cancer management

**c'ao gio** Coining, see there

***Capsella bursa-pastoris*** Popularly known as shepherd's purse, see there

***Capsicum frutescens*** Popularly known as cayenne, see there

***Capsicum minimum*** Cayenne, see there, *Capsicum frutescens*

**capsule** *Jaio niang* CHINESE MEDICINE A gelatin capsule filled with finely ground powder, which allows the optimal delivery of pungent or bitter herbs. See Chinese herbal medicine, Powder–Chinese medicine

**caraway** *Carum carvi* HERBAL MEDICINE A biennial culinary herb that has fixed and volatile oils, proteins, and resin, which is antispasmodic and carminative, and has been used to treat indigestion. See Herbal medicine

**caraway** *Carum carvi*

***Carbo veg*** *Carbo vegitabilis*, charcoal HOMEOPATHY A remedy used for fatigue following an illness, shock, or surgery, as well as for suboptimal oxygenation; it has been used to treat asthma, bronchitis, gastrointestinal complaints including indigestion and bloating, morning headaches, varicose veins, and whooping cough. See Homeopathy

**carbohydrate drink** A type of sports drink that contains glucose polymers and is intended to replenish the reserves of energy during and after exercise (*New York Times 7 Dec 1994; C6*). See Sports drink

**cardamom** *Alpina oxyphylla*, *Amomum amarum*, *Elettaria cardamomum*, *yih jih ren*, *yih zhi ren* CHINESE MEDICINE A perennial herb, the seeds of which are astringent, carminative, and stimulatory; it is used for abdominal pains, impotence, premature ejaculation, spermatorrhea, urinary incontinence, and vomiting. See Chinese herbal medicine

**cardinal juices** The Four Humors, see there

**cardiovascular exercises** A general term for any form of vigorous aerobic exercise, which includes basketball, bicycling, cross-country skiing, dancing, hiking, jogging, race-walking, racquetball, running, skating, soccer, stair-climbing, and volleyball. See Aerobic exercise, Exercise, Vigorous exercise

**cardiovascular fitness** Fitness A benchmark of a subject's cardiovascular and respiratory 'reserve', which is assessed by exercise testing; improved cardiovascular fitness is associated with a decreased risk of acute myocardial infarction (*N Engl J Med 1994; 330:1550OA*). See Aerobic exercise, Exercise, MET, Vigorous exercise; Cf Anaerobic exercise

***Carduus benedictus*** Blessed thistle, see there, *Cnicus benedictus*

**CARET** Beta-Carotene and Retinol Efficacy Trial A large randomized, double-blind, placebo-controlled trial that examined the effect of dietary supplementation with beta carotene and retinol (vitamin A) on 18,314 smokers, former smokers, and asbestos workers. See Beta carotene

CARET was halted in 1996, as investigators found no benefit and, if anything, a slight increase in cardiovascular and/or pulmonary mortality and morbidity in those given the vitamin supplements; followup will continue for another 5 years (*N Engl J Med 1996; 334:1150OA*); Some members of the medical community believe that pure vitamins may lack factors that are present in whole fruits or vegetables; this may explain the discrepancy between the statistically significant decrease in the incidence of cancer in those consuming fruits and vegetables, which is not 'verified' by studies in which only the synthetic vitamins are administered–Author's note

***Carica papaya*** Papaya, see there

**caries** The destruction of tooth enamel and dentin, which is linked to infection by *Streptococcus mutans* and microaerophilic organisms that thrive when protected by a layer of hardened dental plaque; caries is most common in the young, who have refined carbohydrate-rich diets, especially when they 'snack' excessively (thereby increasing the oral pH); caries affects certain older patients, including those with diabetes, cancer, or immunodeficient states. See Fluoridation, Periodontal disease, Plaque; Cf Biological dentistry, Painless Parker

**carminative** Aromatic HERBAL MEDICINE An herb with a pleasant taste or odor, which is soothing to the gastrointestinal tract, and reduces bloating or flatulence; carminatives include angelica (*Angelica archangelica*), anise (*Pimpinella anisum*), balm (*Melissa officinalis*), cinnamon (*Cinnamomum zeylandicum*), cloves (*Eugenia carophyllus*), dill (*Anethum graveolens*), fennel (*Foeniculum dulce*), ginger (*Zingiber officinale*), and peppermint (*Mentha piperita*) (*R Trattler, 1985*). See Herbal medicine

**carnitine** $B_T$ factor, vitamin $B_T$ CLINICAL NUTRITION An amino acid that is involved in fat metabolism and synthesized in the body from lysine and methionine; carnitine is indicated for rare congenital metabolic defects, some endocrine diseases, and may be of use in treating heart disease. See Vitamins FRINGE NUTRITION Despite claims that carnitine enhances athletic performance, prevents heart disease, controls weight, and has antiaging properties, there is no evidence that carnitine deficiencies develop in normal individuals; moreover, the concentration of the over-the-counter carnitine supplements may be suboptimal. See Vitamins

**carnivora** FRINGE ONCOLOGY An extract of Venus flytrap (*Dionaea muscipula*) patented by a German physician, Helmut Keller, which he claims is effective against cancer; the active ingredient is said to be a substance known as plumbagin (*Moss, 1992*). See Unproven methods for cancer management

**carnivore** A meat-eater; Cf Omnivore, Vege-tarian

**carob** The sweet pulp of the Mediterranean evergreen leguminous tree, *Ceratonia siliquia*, which is a chocolate surrogate that is consumed by those who are allergic to chocolate, or adhere to the tenet that anything that is as good as chocolate must be evil; carob is high in palm kernel oil, ie, a 'tropical oil' and therefore atherogenic, and is high in sodium and thus linked to hypertension; Cf Chocolate, Cola tree

**Carolina jasmine** *Gelsemium*, see there, *Gelsemium sempervirens*, *G sempervitalis*

**Carolina jessamine** *Gelsemium*, see there, *Gelsemium sempervirens*, *G sempervitalis*

**Carolina yellow jasmine** *Gelsemium*, see there, *Gelsemium sempervirens*, *G sempervitalis*

**carotene** See Beta carotene

**carotenoid** CLINICAL NUTRITION Any of a family of nutrients that are precursors of vita-

min A and have antioxidant activity; although beta carotene[1] is the best known of the group, 600 carotenoids have been identified; 40 are common in fruits and vegetables[2]; high carotenoid[3] consumption is associated with a decreased incidence of bladder, colon, lung[4], and skin cancers and growth of cancer cells in general (*New York Times 21 Feb 1995; C1*). See Beta carotene, Vitamin A

[1]It had been long assumed that beta carotene was the major carotenoid responsible for the reduced incidence of strokes, cardiovascular disease, and cancers linked to increased consumption of vegetables [2]Tomato juice is highest in carotenoids, followed by kale, collard greens, spinach, sweet potato, chard, watermelon, carrots, and pumpkin [3]which include alpha-carotene, beta-carotene, beta cryptoxanthin, lutein, and lycopene [4]The cause-and-effect relationship is not clear; in a well-designed study from Finland, men who were heavy smokers and recieved beta carotene supplements had increases in both lung cancer (18% increase) and overall mortality (8% increase)

**carp gut** *Eclipta prostrata*, see there

**carpenter's square** Figwort, see there, *Scrophularia nodosa*

**carragheen** Irish moss, see there, *Chondrus crispus*

**carrier oil** Any oil used to dilute essential oils in producing cosmetics or for aromatherapy; carrier oils include those from almonds, apricot kernels, avocados, grapeseed, jojoba, soy beans, sunflowers, and wheat germ. See Aromatherapy

**carrot** ALTERNATIVE NUTRITION A vegetable (*Daucus carota*) that is rich in beta carotene which is widely regarded as a 'healthy food'; consumption of carrots reduces the risk of cancer, myocardial infarction and strokes, and macular degeneration of the retina. See Healthy foods

**carrot mono diet** ALTERNATIVE NUTRITION An alkaline diet in which the person ingests only carrots, carrot juice, and water, but no solid foods; it is recommended for colitis and gastric ulcers. See Fasting

**Cartilade** FRINGE ONCOLOGY A proprietary preparation of concentrated shark cartilage, which contains 740 mg of pure shark cartilage. See Shark cartilage

**cartilage-derived inhibitor** FRINGE ONCOLOGY An angiogenic macroprotein abundant in shark cartilage that is believed to be responsible for the absence of tumors in sharks (*Pelton, Overholser, 1994*); shark cartilage has not proven to be effective for treating cancer, and has been virtually abandoned by mainstream oncologists. See Shark cartilage, Unproven methods for cancer management

***Carum carvi*** Popularly known as caraway, see there

**cascara buckthorn** Cascara sagrada, see there, *Rhamnus purshiana*

**cascara sagrada** *Rhamnus purshiana*, cascara buckthorn, chittenbark, sacred bark HERBAL MEDICINE A deciduous tree, the bark of which contains anthraquinone glycosides; it has been, and continues to be, a widely used laxative; it is used by herbalists as a gastric tonic TOXICITY Cascara should not be used in pregnant women. See Herbal medicine

**caseweed** Shepherd's purse, see there, *Capsella bursa-pastoris*

**cassia** Cinnamon, see there, *Cinnamon cassia*

***Cassia tora*** Popularly known as sickle senna, see there

**castor bean** HERBAL MEDICINE The kernel of the seeds of *Ricinus communis*. See Castor oil

**castor bean** *Ricinus communis*

**castor oil** An oil that is cold-pressed from the kernels of the seeds of *Ricinus communis**, which contains glycerides of ricinoleic and isoricinoleic acids, eg dihydroxystearin, isoricinolein, palmitin, and triricinolein; it has been used externally as an emollient and internally as a laxative. See Castor bean

*The *R communis* seeds contain the highly toxic principles, ricin and ricinine

**cat's foot** Ground ivy, see there, *Glechoma hederacea*

**catalyst-altered water** FRINGE PHARMACOLOGY A concoction of water mixed with calcium chloride, castor oil, Epsom salt, and sodium metasilicate developed by John Willard, professor emeritus of the South Dakota School of Mines and Technology; it is claimed to be an effective cure for virtually any condition that affects humans, animals, or plants. See Unproven methods of cancer management; Cf CanCell

**category X drug** CLINICAL PHARMACOLOGY A therapeutic agent that has a confirmed teratogenic effect, which is contraindicated for use during pregnancy, eg vitamin A congeners used for severe recalcitrant acne, which cause a characteristic clinical complex in neonates. See Vitamin A embryopathy

**catmint** Catnip, see there, *Nepeta cataria*

**catnep** Catnip, see there, *Nepeta cataria*

**catnip** *Nepeta cataria*, catmint, catnep, cat's play HERBAL MEDICINE A perennial herb that contains volatile oils, including carvecrol, citronellol, geraniol, nepetallactones, nepetol, and thymol, and tannins; it is antidiarrheal, antipyretic, carminative, diaphoretic, sedative, stomachic, and tonic, and used as an enema for colicky infants; it has been used topically for cuts, and internally for colds, flu, viral infections in children, for 'nervous stomach', nervous headache, and menstrual cramps TOXICITY Catnip should not be used in pregnancy, or in young children. See Herbal medicine

**cat's play** Catnip, see there, *Nepeta cataria*

**cattail** *Typha latifolia*, bulrush, fragrant rush, *hsiang pu, pu huang, Typha orientalis* CHINESE MEDICINE A reed, the pollen of which is astringent, diuretic, fibrinolytic, hemostatic, and tonic for the cardiovascular system; it is used for dysmenorrhea, hepatitis, postpartum pain, posttraumatic hemorrhage, spermatorrhea. See Chinese herbal medicine

**catchweed** Cleavers, see there, *Galium aparine*

***Catha edulis*** Popularly known as khat, see there

***Catharanthus roseus*** Popularly known as Madagascar periwinkle, see there

**cathartic** HERBAL MEDICINE An herb that evokes intestinal evacuation; cathartics include black root (*Leptandra virginica*), butternut (*Juglans cinerea*), castor oil plant (*Ricinus communis*), jalapa (*Ipomoea jalapa*), mayapple (*Podophyllum peltatum*), mountain flax (*Linum catharticum*), rhubarb (*Rheum palmatum*), senna (*Cassia acutifolia*) (*Trattler, 1985*). See Herbal medicine

**catharsis** PSYCHIATRY Any of a number of psychoanalytical techniques in which the client is led to both recognize the underlying basis for his mental disease, and also release the associated suppressed emotions; the cathartic method is integral to primal therapy and Reichian therapy. See Primal therapy, Psychoanalysis, Reichian therapy

**cathode ray tube** see Video display unit

***Caulophyllum thalictroides*** Popularly known as blue cohosh, see there

**Edgar Cayce** 'The Sleeping Prophet' PARANORMAL PHENOMENA An insurance salesman (1877-1945) who rendered medical diagnoses while in a trance; his diagnostic accuracy was carefully documented and remains unexplained; in the 43 years that Cayce acted as

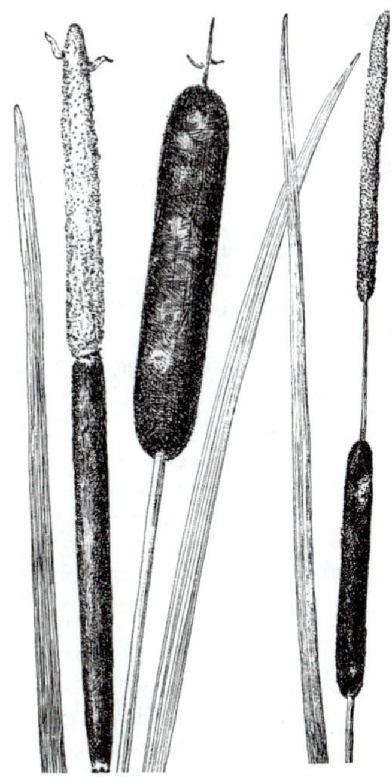

**cattail** *Typha latifolia*

a medical clairvoyant, he gave 30,000 diagnoses, which were recorded and form the basis for the Cayce therapies. See Cayce therapies, Cayce/Reilly massage; Cf Psychic surgery

**Cayce therapies** PARANORMAL PHENOMENA Any of the therapies recommended for the 30,000 diagnoses rendered by Edgar Cayce, a medical clairvoyant; the Cayce therapies included herbs, chemicals, oils, hydrotherapy, sweat baths, fume baths, colonics, hot and cold packs, electrotherapy, chiropractic, osteopathy, massage, exercise, nutrition and diet, and conventional medicine and surgery. See Edgar Cayce, Cayce/Reilly massage; Cf Psychic surgery

**Cayce/Reilly massage** PARANORMAL PHENOMENA Any of a number of massage techniques recommended by Edgar Cayce, and carried out by Dr. RJ Reilly (1895-1987); the techniques included deep massage, local massage, neuropathic massage, osteopathic massage, spinal massage, Swedish massage, and vibratory massage. See Edgar Cayce, Cayce therapies, Psychic diagnosis

**cayenne** *Capsicum frutescens*, *C minimum*, chillies, bird pepper HERBAL MEDICINE A shrub, the fruit of which has both culinary and medicinal use; it contains capsaicin, an alkaloid, carotenoids, flavonoids, pungent principles, vitamins A and C, and volatile oil; it is antibacterial, diaphoretic, hemostatic, stimulant, and used topically as a counterirritant for joint and muscle pain, neuralgias, low back pain, rheumatic pain, and sprains; internally, cayenne is a cardiotonic, and used for colds and respiratory complaints, indigestion, toothaches, hangovers, and fatigue, especially in the elderly TOXICITY In excess, cayenne may cause indigestion and vomiting. See Herbal medicine

Note: In a case-control study with 220 gastric cancers and 752 population-based controls, increased consumption of 'hot' (ie spicy) chili pepper was associated with ↑ risk of gastric cancer, with an odds-ratio of up to 17.1 in those with the highest consumption (*Am J Epidemiol 1994; 139:263*)

**C.C.H.** Certified Clinical Hypnotherapist

**CD4 immunoadhesin** A molecule formed by fusing CD4 (the receptor for HIV–human immunodeficiency virus) with an immunoglobulin that both binds HIV's gp120 and blocks HIV; this synthetic molecule was developed as a possible therapy for AIDS, as it mediates (antibody-dependent cell-mediated cytotoxicity) toward HIV-infected but not uninfected cells, and is easily transported across the primate placenta. See AIDS therapy

**CD4(178)-PE40** A recombinant protein consisting of the HIV envelope glycoprotein-binding region of CD4 linked to the translocation and ADP-ribosylation domains of *Pseudomonas aeruginosa* exotoxin A; this hybrid toxin ('magic bullet') selectively binds to and destroys HIV-1-infected human T cells, and was developed as a possible HIV-static agent. See AIDS therapy

**celandine** Greater celandine, see there, *Cheledonium majus*

**celery** A biennial plant (*Apium graveolens*) of the parsley family that is used as a folk therapy for hypertension, which has been

**celery** *Apium graveolens*

used to increase local circulation in bursitis and gout. See Herbal medicine

**cell salts** Schüssler's tissue salts, see there

**cell therapy** 1. Live cell therapy, see there 2. '*the injection of cellular material* from organs, fetuses, or embryos of animals to stimulate healing, counteract the effects of aging, and treat a variety of degenerative diseases such as arthritis, Parkinson's disease*, atherosclerosis, and cancer. ...methods include the use of live cells, freeze-dried cells...cells from specific organs, and whole embryo prepara-*

*tions.'* (*Alternative Medicine, Future Med Pub, 1994*). See Alternative medicine, Unproven methods for cancer management

Note: There is no data on the efficacy of cell therapy in peer-reviewed journals; it is not approved for use in the United States, but is regionally popular in other countries; *There is a vast difference between the therapeutic use of cells in a legitimate (ie 'mainstream') medical context and the pseudoscience that is intimately linked to 'cell therapy'; in conventional medical practice, the indications for such therapy are controlled by ethical 'standards of practice' if it is part of the accepted medical armamentarium (eg BM transplantation from a person with a defined HLA profile), or strictly delineated, if it is part of an experimental protocol (eg IL-2/LAK cells for adoptive immunotherapy or fetal mesenchymal cells for Parkinson's disease); the cells used in mainstream medicine are 'biologicals', the quality of which is regulated by the FDA; use of the term 'cell therapy' in mainstream and alternative medicine lends to confusion-Author's note

**Cellular Repatterning™** Neuro/Cellular Repatterning™, see there

**cellular memory** ALTERNATIVE MEDICINE A term referring to the Reichian conceptualization of disease being the result of negative emotions and fears that are maintained in the body at the deep muscular level; see Reich, Reichian therapy

**cellular therapy** ALTERNATIVE MEDICINE 1. Live cell therapy, see there 2. Cell therapy, see there

**cellular theta breath technique** ALTERNATIVE MEDICINE A form of self-healing, which is based on theta breathing, which is believed to provide 'transformation energy'

**'cellulite'** A term used by the lay public for cosmetically undesirable subcutaneous layer(s) of adipose tissue that cause(s) peau d'orange-like dimpling of the skin surface; cellulite is not an accepted medical term, either clinically or pathologically, as histologic examination reveals nothing more than 'garden variety' fat and adipocytes. See Obesity

***Centaurium erythraea*** European centaury, see there, *Centaurium umbellatum*

***Centaurium umbellatum*** Popularly known as European centaury, see there

**centaury** European centaury, see there, *Centaurium umbellatum*

**centaury gentian** European centaury, see there, *Centaurium umbellatum*

***Centella asiatica*** Gutu kola, see there, *Hydrocotyle asiatica*

**centering** A general term for any method that is used by people to calm themselves physically, mentally, or emotionally, usually in preparation for performing an activity requiring concentration, eg meditation, an examination, or competitive sporting event

**centesimal** HOMEOPATHY A dilution of 1:100, which is a factor used in potentization of homeopathic remedies; centesimals are expressed C—a 6C homeopathic remedy would have one active part in $10^{12}$ of diluent. See Avogadro's limit, Homeopathic remedy, Potentization; Cf Decimal

**central obesity** Abdominal obesity Obesity that is defined by increased waist-to-hip and waist-to-thigh ratios, waist circumference, and sagittal abdominal diameter, and an increased risk of cardiovascular disease (*JAMA 1996; 275:1160ED*). See Body mass index, Obesity

***Cephalis ipecacuanha*** Ipecac, see there

**cerebral allergy** Environmental disease, see there

**cerebral exhaustion** Neurasthenia, see there

**ceroid** A complex of alcohol-insoluble, oxidized polyunsaturated lipid pigment(s) resulting from the peroxidation of unsaturated lipids that are similar or identical to lipofuscin; ceroid accumulates in macrophages of the heart, liver, gastrointestinal tract, and brain in the elderly and is thus termed 'wear and tear' pigment; it has been inculpated in age-related organ dysfunction ('garbage can' hypothesis), hypovitaminosis E, cathartic colon, and hereditary conditions, eg Batten's disease, and sea-blue histiocytosis. See Garbage can hypothesis

**certified milk** ALTERNATIVE NUTRITION Raw (unpasteurized) milk that has been approved by a nongovernmental affiliate of the raw milk industry; certified milk has not been approved by a governmental body, or pasteurized (which would reduce the risk of infections to a minimum). See Milk, Raw milk; Cf Colostrum

**cervical segment** ALTERNATIVE PSYCHOLOGY One of the seven segments of the body according to Reich, which includes the neck, throat, and tongue; the cervical segment is believed to be linked to anxiety and depression, resulting in regional body armoring, which is believed to be resolved by tongue exercises and vigorous shouting. See Armoring, Body armor, Reich, Reichian therapy

**cesium** A rare alkali element (atomic number 55; atomic weight 132.91) FRINGE ONCOLOGY Cesium is said to have anticarcinogenic properties, and believed to protect against radiation toxicity by blocking sites on the red blood cells, thereby increasing the excretion and clearance of radioactive cesium TOXICITY Cesium chloride may cause diarrhea, nausea, and paresthesias (*Moss, 1992*). See High pH therapy, Unproven methods for cancer management

***Cetraria islandica*** Popularly known as Iceland moss, see there

**cevitamic acid** Vitamin C, see there

**CFS** Chronic fatigue syndrome, see there

**C.H.** 1. Certified Herbalist 2. Clinical Hypnotherapist

***cha*** Infusion–Chinese medicine, see there

***chai hu*** Hare's ear, see there, *Bupleurum falcatum*

***chakra*** AYURVEDIC MEDICINE Any of seven (or eight) centers present in the body, that are regarded as 'relay stations' for the flow of Life Forces, which create a luminous energy field known as an aura–a manifestation of the total body energy

▶ ***CHAKRAS***

- **ROOT (FIRST OR BASE) *chakra*** Governs the survival instinct, is located at the base of the spine, and associated with the color red
- **SEXUAL (SECOND OR SACRAL) *chakra*** Governs the sexual instinct and emotions, is located behind the navel, and is associated with the sex organs and spleen, and the color orange
- **SOLAR PLEXUS (THIRD) *CHAKRA*** Governs personal drives and sense of self worth, is located below the heart, and associated with the adrenal glands and the color yellow
- **HEART CENTER (FOURTH) *CHAKRA*** Governs love and harmony, is located in the heart, and associated with the circulation and the color green
- **THYMUS CENTER (EIGHTH) *CHAKRA*** The 'high heart,' governs generosity and compassion, and is associated with the thymus and the color tourquoise
- **THROAT CENTER (FIFTH) *CHAKRA*** Governs intelligence, creative expression, communication through sound, and truth, is located in the neck, and associated with the thyroid gland and the color blue
- **THIRD EYE (SIXTH) *CHAKRA*** Governs the mind, self, perceptions and intuition, is located deep in the brain behind the eyes, and associated with the pituitary gland and the color indigo (deep blue) or violet
- **CROWN (SEVENTH) *CHAKRA*** Governs the individual's relationship with the Force or Universal Self, is located at the top of the head, and associated with the pineal gland and the color purple or magenta

Illness is viewed as the result of blockage or restriction in the flow of the body's energy, which requires *chakra* balancing (*The New Age Catalog, Island Publishing Co, Dolphin, Doubleday, New York 1988*). See Ayurvedic medicine, Aura balancing, *Chakra* energy balancing, 'New Age'; Cf Aura

***chakra* balancing** *Chakra* healing, see there

***chakra* breathing** AYURVEDIC MEDICINE A form of self-healing, in which the flow of energy through the *chakras* (or energy centers) is brought into balance by proper breathing; *chakra* healing is believed to connect the body and soul. See Ayurvedic medicine, *Chakra*, Polarity therapy

***chakra* energy balancing** *Chakra* healing, see there

***chakra* energy massage** AYURVEDIC MEDICINE A permutation of foot reflexology which is intended to facilitate the flow of energy through the *Chakras*. See Ayurvedic medicine, *Chakra*, Polarity therapy

***chakra* healing** *Chakra* balancing, *chakra* energy balancing, *chakra* therapy, *chakra* work AYURVEDIC MEDICINE A form of hands-on polarity therapy (which is similar to aura balancing) that facilitates the even flow of energy through the nerve plexi or *chakras*, from the coccyx (first or root *chakra*) to the top of the head (seventh or crown *chakra*); a local block in the flow of the 'vital life energy' through the *chakras* is believed to cause specific diseases; eg a block in the throat *chakra* could result in metabolic defects related to thyroid dysfunction and defects in communication; methods used for *chakra* healing include color therapy, crystal/gem therapy, imagery and visualization, sound therapy, meditation, pressure point massage, and vibration therapy; *chakra* healing is believed to be useful in relieving anxiety, headaches, stress, and tension. See Ayurvedic medicine, *Chakra*, Polarity therapy

***chakra* inner tuning therapy** AYURVEDIC MEDICINE A permutation of *chakra* healing, which involves *chakra* 'alignment,' diet, dream interpretation, meditation and use of mantras, and yoga. See Ayurvedic medicine, *Chakra*

***chakra* therapy** *Chakra* healing, see there

***chakra* work** *Chakra* healing, see there

***Chakra Samhita*** HERBAL MEDICINE A comprehensive textbook of herbal medicines used in India, which includes 500 herbal remedies; see Herbal medicine; Cf *Canon of Medicine, The Complete Herbal, De Materia Medica, Natural History, Nei Jing, Pen Ts'ao, Philosophy of Natural Therapeutics, Rigveda, Sushrita Samhita, Theatrum Botanicum*

***Chamaelirium luteum*** Popularly known as fairywand, see there

**chamazulene** HERBAL MEDICINE One of the volatile oils in German chamomile (*Matricaria chamomilla*), which is reported to be analgesic, anti-inflammatory, antispasmodic, accelerate wound healing, and be of use in treating eczema. See Herbal medicine

***Chamomilla*** HOMEOPATHY A minor homeopathic remedy that has been used in chronic complainers who have a low threshold for pain; it has been used for teething in children, painful earaches, irritability, menstrual cramping and bleeding, tootheaches; see Chamomile, Homeopathy

**chamomile** *Matricaria chamomilla, M recutita* (German chamomile), *Anthemis nobilis* (Roman chamomile, babunah, romashka) AYURVEDIC MEDICINE Chamomile has been used for women's complaints, indigestion, and colicky children FRINGE MEDICINE-FLOWER ESSENCE THERAPY A floral essence believed to balance the emotions, calm the nerves, and brighten moods. See Flower essence therapy HERBAL MEDICINE An annual herb, the flowers of which contain choline, coumarins (eg umbelliferone), cyanogenic glycosides, flavonoids (eg rutin), salicylate derivatives, tannins, and volatile oils (eg bisabolol and chamazulene); chamomile is administered as a tea, an extract, tincture, or ointment; German chamomile tea is analgesic, anti-inflammatory, antimicrobial, antispasmodic, anxiolytic, carminative, expectorant, and sedative; it has been used to treat acne, anxiety, asthma, bacterial and fungal infections, colic in infants, diarrhea, flatulence, gout, headaches, indigestion, insomnia, irritable bowel, menstrual cramping, pruritus, rheumatic disease, and sciatica; in Russia, Roman chamomile is used for colds, gastric complaints, colitis, as a sedative, gargle, and topically for eczema and inflammation. See Bisabolol, Chamazulene, Herbal medicine HOMEOPATHY See *Chamomilla*

Note: Most herbalists use German chamomile and Roman chamomile interchangeably

***chan mi gong*** CHINESE MEDICINE A permutation of *qigong* meditation, which is based on Zen (*chan*) and Tantric (*mi*) Buddhism; see Zen Buddhism

**Chan Su** LoveStone A purported aphrodisiac prepared from toad venom, which contains cardioactive bufadienolides; those ingesting these substances are at increased risk of cardiovascular disease or death, as bufadienolides may cause a clinical picture reminiscent of digoxin toxicity

In the event of overdose, these patients appear to respond to digoxin Fab fragments (*JAMA 1996; 275:988*)

***chandrika*** Rauwolfia, see there, *Rauwolfia serpentina*

***ch'ang ch'uan*** *T'ai chi ch'uan*, see there

**channel** Channeler, see there

**channeler** Channeler, medium PARANORMAL PHENOMENA A person who serves as a conduit for channeled information from another

**chamomile** *Matricaria recutita*

plane of existence. See Channeling, Plane of existence

**channeling** Mediumship PARAPSYCHOLOGY The alleged communication with a dead person, either directly, or through a physically 'embodied' person (angel, deceased human, extraterrestrial being or another level of the same person's consciousness), from a source that is believed to exist on a level or dimension of reality other than the physical reality, as accepted or recognized by mainstream science; channeling has been anecdotally reported by 'entities' known as Lazaris (channeled via J Pursel), Ramtha (via JZ Knight), and Seth (via Jane Roberts) (*The New Age Catalog, Island Publishing Co, Dolphin, Doubleday, New York 1988*). See Channeling, George Chapman, Medium, Paranormal, Parapsychology, Plane of existence

**chaparral** *Larrea tridentata, Larrea divaricata, L mexicana,* and *Covillea tridentata,* creosote bush, greasewood, hediondilla ALTERNATIVE ONCOLOGY An evergreen shrub, the major component of chapparal is NDGA (nordihydroguaiaretic acid), which may be useful in treating certain gastrointestinal tumors, leukemia, and gliomas of the brain. See Nordihydroguaiaretic acid HERBAL MEDICINE Chaparal was once used by Native American herbalists as an antiarthritic and antitussive, for diarrhea and other gastrointestinal complaints, and topically for wounds. See Herbal medicine TOXICITY Chaparal may be associated with cramping, nausea, and vomiting. See Botanical toxicity

**George Chapman** PARANORMAL PHENOMENA A British fireman, who performs 'etheric surgery' on the eye through a spirit guide, Dr. Wm Lang, a well-known deceased ophthalmologic surgeon. See Psychic surgery

***Charak Samhita*** AYURVEDIC MEDICINE The sacred scripture of India written over 2000 years ago, which contains a comprehensive treatise that delineates the eight major branches of human health care and provided details on psychology, toxicology, rejuvenation, virilization, and others. See Herbal medicine; Cf *Canon of Medicine*, *The Complete Herbal*, *De Materia Medica*, *Natural History*, *Nei Jing*, *Pen Ts'ao*, *Philosophy of Natural Therapeutics, Rigveda, Sushrita Samhita, Theatrum Botanicum*

**charcoal** 1. Activated charcoal, see there 2. *Carbo veg*, see there, *Carbo vegitabilis*

**charismatic healing** PARANORMAL PHENOMENA A permutation of 'healing,' in which there is an attempt to restore Pentecostal elements (simplistically, 'fire and brimstone' preaching) to the process of Christian healing. See Christian healing, Psychic healing

**charlatan** Quack, see there

**charm** FOLK MEDICINE A talisman that is thought to ward off evil and promote health

**chaste tree** *Vitex agnus-castus* HERBAL MEDICINE A tree the berries of which contain phytoestrogens; the berries have been used in various forms for menstrual dysfunction, premenstrual syndrome, endometriosis, increased libido, acne in adolescence, and to promote lactation; it is believed by some to be an aphrodisiac. See Herbal medicine

**chat** Khat, see there, *Catha edulis*

**chaulamoogra** *Hydnocarpus wightiana* An oriental tree, the seeds of which contain chaulamoogric and hydrocarpic acids, which are antibacterial, and have been used against leprosy and sarcoidosis. See Chinese herbal medicine, Herbal medicine

***che chien dze*** Plantain, see there, *Plantago major*

***che qian zi*** Plantain, see there, *Plantago major*

**checkerberry** Wintergreen, see there, *Gaultheria procumbens*

**cheese disease** see Tyramine-induced hypertension

**cheirognomy** Hand analysis, see there

**chelation therapy** FRINGE MEDICINE A method for removing toxins and metabolic wastes from the bloodstream; chelation therapy consists of the administration of chelating agent, eg EDTA (ethylene diamine tetraacetic, edetic acid) usually intravenously, or penicillamine administered orally; some alternative health care practitioners believe that chelation therapy may be used to remove calcium from atherosclerotic plaques, and by extension is a viable alternative to bypass surgery and angioplasty; anecdotal reports suggest that chelation therapy may be useful in treating arthritis and connective tissue diseases, improving vision, hearing, sense of smell, and memory (*Alternative Medicine, Future Med Pub, 1994*); it is also believed by some practitioners of alternative health care to reverse the effects of degenerative diseases caused by poor circulation, cataracts, diabetes, emphysema, gallstones, hypertension, osteoporosis, Parkinson's disease, renal disease, and strokes SIDE EFFECTS Anorexia, headaches, bone marrow suppression, cardiac arrhythmias, hemolytic anemia, joint pain, muscle spasms, nausea and vomiting, osteoporosis, phlebitis, renal damage and failure, and death (*Butler, 1992*). See Oral chelation, Unproven methods for cancer management MAINSTREAM MEDICINE The only FDA-approved indication for EDTA chelation is for treating heavy metal (eg lead, mercury) poisoning; some practitioners of mainstream medicine believe that chelation therapy may also be effective in treating snake venom poisoning and digitalis intoxication

The American Heart Association, the American College of Physicians, and other professional organizations disapprove of alternative forms of chelation therapy; it is not approved by the FDA for conditions other than those listed above under mainstream medicine

***Cheledonium majus*** Popularly known as greater celandine, see there

**chelerythrine** PHARMACOGNOSY A chemical found in prickly ash (*Zanthoxylum americana*) that has been shown to have anticarcinogenic activity in animals (*Pelton, Overholser, 1994*). See Prickly ash, Folk cures for cancer

**chemical carcinogenesis** The induction of malignancy by a known or putative chemical carcinogen, which can be occupational (eg aromatic amines, arsenic, benzene, cadmium, chromium ores, soots, tars, vinyl chloride), environmental (eg aflatoxin, asbestos, tobacco), or iatrogenic (eg alkylating agents, anabolic steroids, phenacetin) PATHOGENESIS Initiation of the carcinogenic 'cascade' occurs when an electrophilically reactive chemical (initiator), or more often, one or more of its metabolites interacts with DNA, and repair of the damaged DNA is unsuccessful; this is followed by a sequence of events known as tumor promotion

**chemical colitis** Soap colitis An acute inflammatory reaction of the colonic mucosa that develops within hours after the administration of various types of 'cleansing' enemas; although classically associated with soapsuds, this form of acute colitis may also occur after rectal instillation of a wide range of 'insulting fluids' including herbal concoctions, hydrogen peroxide, and vinegar[1], as well as with potassium permanganate, sodium diatrizoate (Hypaque), glutaraldehyde, Fleet's Phospho-Soda enema[2] or other inappropriate fluids, which may have hypertonic, detergent, or directly toxic effects CLINICAL Chemical colitis may cause pain, cramping, anaphylaxis, serosanguinous diarrhea, hypovolemia, and acute hemoconcentration; if the mucosal damage is severe, bacteria may penetrate the mucosa, causing sepsis, hypokalemia, pseudomembrane formation, hemorrhagic necrosis, intestinal gangrene, and acute renal failure. See Colon therapy, Detoxification therapy, High colonic

[1]Agents preferred by alternative health practitioners [2]Primarily used in mainstream medications

**chemical pollutant** ENVIRONMENT A chemical substance that enters the environment through industry, agriculture, or other human activities, which poses an immediate or potential hazard to plant, animal, or human life; the major chemical pollutants are heavy metals (eg mercury and lead), aromatic hydrocarbons (eg benzene and other petrochemicals), organic solvents (eg toluene, and xylene), organohalides (eg polychlorinated biphenyls–PCBs and polybrominated biphenyls–PBBs), dioxins, and others (eg nitrogen dioxide and sulfur dioxides). See Air pollution, Environmental disease, Sick building syndrome

**chemoprevention** ALTERNATIVE NUTRITION The use of a drug, chemical, or other substance in the diet to prevent or decrease the incidence of a disease, usually understood to be cancer; agents with chemopreventive effects (supported by 'soft' epidemiologic data) are vitamins A, C, and E, bran and other dietary fibers, and cruciferous vegetables; see Antioxidant, Antioxidant therapy; Cf Unproven methods for cancer management

Statistical support for the efficacy of chemoprevention is weak; 'prophylactic' use of vitamin A or beta carotene has not been definitively shown to prevent breast, lung, or non-melanoma skin cancer; high doses of the vitamin A analog, isotretinoin, reportedly prevents second primary malignancies in the head and neck region

***chen hsiang*** Eagle wood, see there, *Aquilaria agallocha*

***chén pi*** Tangerine peel, see there, *Citrus reticu-*

*lata*

**chen xiang** Eagle wood, see there, *Aquilaria agallocha*

**Chen method** A form of personal physical training, which is believed by historians to be the precursor of t'ai chi ch'uan. See T'ai chi ch'uan

***Chenopodium scoparia*** Belvedere cypress, *Kochia scoparia*

**chest pack** NATUROPATHY An alternative therapy for various chest complaints, which consists of placing warm wet sheets or blankets over the patient's chest, and leaving them in place for 3 hours. See Hydrotherapy

**chewing gum diarrhea** A type of diarrhea caused by an excess of sugarless chewing gum, which contains hexitols, (eg sorbitol and mannitol); hexitols are major constituents of sugar-free dietary foods, are not metabolized by bacteria, remain in the intestinal lumen, and increase the intraluminal osmotic pressure, resulting in diarrhea

Note: The amount consumed may be large, eg 50-100 sticks of gum/day, which translates into 85-170 g sorbitol/day (*Am J Dig Dis 1978; 23:568*)

***chi*** *Ki, qi, pronounced* chee TRADITIONAL CHINESE MEDICINE The vital force that is believed to flow through the body, along routes known as meridians; illness is attributed to changes in the flow of *chi* which, according to the construct of Chinese medicine, can be treated by placing needles (acupunture) or pressure (acupressure) at specific points on the meridians (*Alternative Medicine, Future Med Pub, 1994*). See Acupressure, Acupuncture, Meridians, Vital force

***chi gong*** *Qigong*, see there

***chi gung*** *Qigong*, see there

***chi kung*** *Qigong*, see there

***chi kung* reaction** *Qigong* reaction

***chi nei tsang*** Healing light massage, internal organ *chi* massage, internal organ massage, organ *chi* transformation (massage), Taoist *chi nei tsang*, Taoist healing light technique CHINESE MEDICINE A traditional Taoist form of massage therapy, which is applied to the abdomen; *chi nei tsang* is used to stimulate and manipulate muscles and connective tissue, organs (stomach, intestine, liver, gallbladder, spleen, pancreas, uterus, kidneys, and lungs), and systems (lymphatic, circulatory, and nervous) located in the abdomen; internal organ massage is believed to release regional stress and tension, prevent stagnation of blood, improve the flow of energy into the abdominal region, allow detoxification, and enhance the immune system. See *Chi*

***chiang huo*** *Angelica pubescens*-purple, see there

***chiang mi*** Multiflowered rose, see there, *Rosa multiflora*

**chichism** Pellagra, see there

***Chicorum intybus*** Popularly known as chicory, see there

**chicken broth** Chicken soup, see there

**chicken head** Foxnut, see there, *Euryale ferox*

**chick and pellagra factor** Pantothenic acid, see there

**chicken soup** Chicken broth CHINESE MEDICINE Fresh chicken broth has been used in traditional Chinese medicine as a therapeutic tonic, and is recommended for children, the elderly, those with gastrointestinal complaints and those recuperating from chronic disease, pregnancy, and surgery. See Traditional Chinese medicine FOLK MEDICINE A fowl broth that has a long tradition as a home remedy for upper respiratory tract infections; it is reported to be a nasal decongestant, and inhibit growth of pneumococci in vitro (*JAMA 1994; 272:1104c*), and may stimulate immune responsiveness in white cells (*Castleman, 1996*); Cf 'Chicken soup'

Notes: In some regions, fish soup is regarded as the universal elixir

**'chicken soup'** A colloquial term for any drug, maneuver, or device that has virtually no recognized (or at most, minimal) efficacy, which may be used in absence of an effective therapy (*JAMA 1992; 268:1987MN&P*). See Band-Aid® therapy, 'Homeopathic', Placebo; Cf Chicken soup

**chickweed** *Stellaria media*, mouse-ear, satinflower, starweed, tongue grass, white bird's eye, winterweed HERBAL MEDICINE An annual herb, the aerial parts of which contain mucilage, saponins, and vitamin C; it has been used internally for bronchitis, pulmonary congestion, gastric ulcers, rheumatic complaints, and sore throat, and topically for abscesses, bites, cuts, dermatitis, eczema, and psoriasis. See Herbal medicine

**chicory** *Chicorium intybus*, blue sailors, coffeeweed, succory, wild succory HERBAL MEDICINE A perennial herb that contains fructose, inulin, lactucin, taraxasterol, pectin, resin, taraxasterol, and tannins; it is diuretic, laxative, and tonic, and has been used topically for skin inflammation, and internally for diabetes, gallstones, gout, hepatitis and other liver conditions, rheumatic complaints, splenomegaly, and caffeine-induced tachyarrhythmias TOXICITY Skin rash. See Herbal medicine

**chief of staff** Liver, see Twelve vital organs

***chien shih*** Foxnut, see there, *Euryale ferox*

***chien tsao*** Indian madder, see there, *Rubia cordifolia*

***chih chien*** *Gastrodia elata*, see there Placebo

**children massage** Massage for children A general term for the use of massage in children; mainstream medical indications for children massage include physical problems caused by birth defects, physical disabilities, trauma, and neuromuscular disease; advocates of alternative health care believe that massage is of use for children who suffer stress and tension related to emotional trauma. See Massage therapy; Cf Baby B.E.S.T., Bodywork for the Childbearing Year™

**chicory** *Chicorium intybus*

**chili pepper** Cayenne, see there, *Capsicum frutescens*

**chillies** Cayenne, see there, *Capsicum frutescens*

***chin dao*** *Justicia gendarussa*, see there

***China*** *China officinalis* HOMEOPATHY A homeopathic remedy derived from cinchona (Peruvian bark) that is used for exhaustion due to loss of body fluids and breastfeeding; it has been used for gastrointestinal complaints, explosive outbursts, gallbladder disease, headaches, restless insomnia, muscle fatigue and spasms, poor concentration, seizures, and vertigo. See Cinchona, Homeopathy

**China root** Tuckahoe, see there, *Porio cocos*

**Chinese angelica root** *Angelica sinensis*, see there

**Chinese asparagus** Shiny asparagus, see there, *Asparagus lucidus*

**Chinese balls** Chinese reflex balls, see there

**Chinese chive** Garlic, see there, *Allium sativum*

**Chinese clock** TRADITIONAL CHINESE MEDICINE A colloquial term for diurnal variations that are believed to occur in the flow of energy through the meridians; 'purist' practioners of the Oriental healing arts believe that acupressure and acupuncture should be performed at the times of the peaks and troughs of energy flow. See Acupuncture

**Chinese cornbind** *Polygonum multiflorum*, also known as *ho shou wu*, *jiao teng*, tangled vine CHINESE MEDICINE A perennial herb, the roots, stems, and leaves of which are used for anemia, canites, colitis, constipation, infertility, insomnia, malaria, nocturnal emission, postpartum pain, rheumatic complaints, skin infections, spermatorrhea, vaginal discharge, and vertigo; some data suggest that cornblind may be antibacterial. See Chinese herbal medicine

**Chinese date** Chinese jujube, see there, *Ziziphus vulgaris*

**Chinese dodder** Dodder, see there, *Cuscuta chinensis*

**Chinese ephedra** Ephedra, see there, *Ephedra sinica*

**Chinese fly** Mylabris ALTERNATIVE ONCOLOGY A Chinese 'herb,' that is the dried body of the Chinese blister beetle which, like Spanish fly, contains cantharidin, which is believed to have some therapeutic efficacy in liver cancer (*Moss, 1992*). See Cantharidin, *Cantharis*

**Chinese foxglove** *Rehmania glutinosa*, see there

**Chinese ginseng** Ginseng, see there, *Panax ginseng*

**Chinese goldthread** Coptis, see there, *Coptis sinensis*

**Chinese hand analysis** A type of medical palmistry, which is believed by its practitioners to inform about a person's health, sexuality, and other personal information. See Hand analysis

**Chinese health balls** Chinese reflex balls, see there

**Chinese herb** CHINESE MEDICINE Any of thousands of substances that is used in traditional Chinese medicine to treat illness; Chinese 'herbs' differ from Western herbs as they can be any natural material of plant, animal, or mineral origin; herbs are used to balance and harmonize the dynamic forces involved in disease, and are believed to have an intrinsic energy related to their concentration in the source material; Chinese herbs are administered as capsules, decoctions, extracts, herbal pillows, infusions, (teas), herbal liquors (medicine wines), ointments, pastes, pills, porridges, poultices, and steam decoctions, discussed elsewhere in this text. See Acupuncture, Chinese herbal medicine, Chinese medicine, Traditional Chinese medicine

**Chinese herbal formula** A general term for any of a number of preparations of Chinese 'herbs'; the average formula contains 6 to 15 substances; some (eg Composition A, Enhance) have been anecdotally reported to have antiretroviral activity (*Am Med News 21 Nov 1994 p13*); Cf AIDS fraud

**Chinese herbal medicine** A therapeutic system that classifies foods and herbs according to the four natures, the five flavors, the four directions, and the organs and meridians affected; the term Chinese herb encompasses any of nearly 6000 medicinal substances that have been used for 5000 years to treat various illness. See Chinese herb, Chinese medicine, the Five flavors, the Four directions, the Four natures, Organs and meridians affected, Traditional Chinese medicine, Yang, Yin

Note: Many of the basic formulas used in Chinese herbal medicine are from Chang Chung Chin's classics *Treatise on Febrile Diseases* and *Summaries of Household Remedies*, which have been used for over 2000 years; the more commonly used of these formulas are summarized in the appendix of Moshe Olshevsky's *The Manual of Natural Therapy* (*Facts on File, New York, 1989*)

**Chinese jujube** *Ziziphus vulgaris*, Chinese date, *da dzao, da zao, gan dzao*, sweet jujube CHINESE MEDICINE A perennial shrub, the fruits of which are used for coughs, fatigue, hypertension, insomnia, to increase internal secretions, treat malnutrition, retard aging, and as a tonic. See Chinese herbal medicine

**Chinese massage** *Amma, anma, pu tong an mo* A general term for any of a number of massage techniques used in traditional Chinese medicine, in which energy points (*tsubos*) are stimulated. See Massage therapy, Traditional Chinese medicine

**Chinese motherwort** *Leonurus heterophyllus*, benefit mother herb, *yi u cao* CHINESE MEDICINE A perennial shrub, the fruits of which are used for coughs, edema, fatigue, hypertension, infertility, insomnia, malnutrition, menstrual irregularies, postpartum pain, urinary delay, to increase internal secretions, retard aging, and as a tonic TOXICITY Chinese motherwort should not be used in pregnancy, as it may induce abortion. See Chinese herbal medicine

**Chinese peony** White peony, see there, *Paeonia albiflora*

**Chinese qigong** Qigong, see there internal qigong

**Chinese reflex balls** Chinese balls, Chinese health balls, health balls, *qigong* balls, reflex balls Two balls that are available in four different sizes, and manipulated for their health-enhancing effects; in addition to limbering the fingers and hands, they are believed—by stimulating the acupressure points on the hands—to enhance neural activity, improve memory and circulation, relax muscles and joints, tone internal organs, and balance the flow of *chi*; they are specifically intended to prevent arthritis and hypertension; the balls may be made of various materials, including brass, enamel, marble, or may be magnetized

**Chinese restaurant syndrome** An abrupt allergic reaction, the susceptibility to which is an autosomal recessive trait, caused by an increased sensitivity to monosodium glutamate (MSG, a seasoning used in Chinese restaurants, soy sauce, and other foods)

CLINICAL Severe headaches, numbness, palpitations, vertigo (especially with chronic MSG exposure), thirst, abdominal and chest pains, sweating, and flushing, which develop one-half hour after exposure, and last up to 12 hours. See MSG

**Chinese rhubarb** *Rheum officinale, R palmatum* A perennial plant, the roots and rhizome of which contain anthraquinone glycosides including sennosides A–F, free anthroquinones (eg emodin), and tannins CHINESE MEDICINE In traditional Chinese medicine, it is used for diarrhea in low concentrations and as a laxative at high concentrations; it is antipyretic, and a digestive tonic. See Chinese herbal medicine HERBAL MEDICINE Chinese rhubarb is used in Western herbal medicine in a fashion similar to that of traditional Chinese medicine. See Herbal medicine TOXICITY Chinese rhubarb should not be used in pregnancy, in those with arthritis, or renal or urinary tract disease

**Chinese wild raspberry** *Rubus coreanus, fu pen dze, fu pen zi, Rubus tokkura* CHINESE MEDICINE A perennial plant, the unripe fruit of which is astringent and tonic, and believed to be an aphrodisiac; it is used for male and female infertility, fatigue, sexual dysfunction, and urinary incontinence. See Chinese herbal medicine

**Chinese wolfberry** *Lycium chinense, L barbarum*, goat milk, *gao ji dze, gao di zi, yang ru* CHINESE MEDICINE A perennial shrub, the fruit of which is used for diabetes, fatigue, headache, impotence, low back pain, malnutrition, night blindness, nocturnal emision, poor vision, spermatorrhea, thirst, tinnitus, and tuberculosis. See Chinese herbal medicine

**Chinese yam** *Dioscorea opposita, shan yao* CHINESE MEDICINE A bean-like plant, the tuber of which is used for anorexia, bacterial infections, chronic fatigue, cough, diabetes, diarrhea, poor digestion, immune defects, nocturnal emissions, purulent discharges, spermatorrhea, urinary frequency, vaginal discharges, wheezing, and to stimulate internal secretions. See Chinese herbal medicine

**ching** Meridian, see there

**chirognomy** Hand analysis, see there

**chiropodist** Podiatrist, see there

**chiropody** Podiatry, see there

***chi* self-massage** *Tao* rejuvenation-*chi*, self-massage CHINESE MEDICINE A permutation of hand massage, which is believed to strengthen the organs and teeth. See Hand massage; Cf Massage therapy

**chiropractic** ALTERNATIVE MEDICINE A system of health care founded in 1895 by Daniel David Palmer (1845-1913), which is based on the belief that the nervous system is the most important determinant of a person's state of health; according to chiropractic theory, most diseases are the result of 'nerve interference,' caused by spinal subluxations, which respond to spinal manipulation

▶ **EFFECTS OF CHIROPRACTIC MANIPULATION**

- **MECHANICAL**–by improving the anatomical relationship between joints and muscles through manipulation
- **NEUROLOGICAL**–by changing the patterns of nerve signal by changing the patterns of nerve signaling and, by extension, physiological and mental functioning
- **EMOTIONAL**–through hands-on contact with a person who is playing an active role of healer

Abnormal nerve function may result in musculoskeletal derangements and aggravate pathological processes in other body regions or organ systems

▶ **PRINCIPLES OF CHIROPRACTIC**

- **VITALISM** The body has an intrinsic ability to heal itself; the chiropractor's role is to facilitate the body's ability to restore the vital or life force (termed innate intelligence) to its optimum level, and therefore be allowed to heal itself
- **HOLISM** All organs and systems function as one interconnected unit; anything that affects the nervous system has widespread effects elsewhere in the body
- **CORRECTION OF SUBLUXATION** Subluxation is defined as a malalignment of the vertebrae that causes pressure on the spinal cord, nerve roots, and nerves; chiropractics have labelled this subluxation-induced pressure on nerves 'nerve reflex' (which has a completely distinct definition for mainstream neurologists-Author's note)

See Chiropractic education, Chiropractic malpractice, Chiropractor, Medically-oriented chiropractic, Mixed chiropractic, Network chiropractic, Straight chiropractic, Subluxation-based chiropractic; Cf Massage therapy, Osteopathic medicine *RESOURCE: American Chiropractic Association, 1701 Clarendon Blvd, Arlington, VA 22209* ☎ *1.800.986.4636*

Mainstream medical practitioners are not, in general, opposed to patients seeking chiropractic manipulation when indicated, or under the Hippocratic principle of *primum non nocerum*; the difficulty lies when chiropractors claim to treat such diverse clinical conditions as bladder infections, anginal chest pain, sexual dysfunction, dysmenorrhea, disorders of speech, and mental disorders ranging from mild depression to schizophrenia, for which there is virtually no controlled data on efficacy; patient experience with chiropractic care has not been entirely favorable, and some consumers believe some practices are based in part on questionable ethical standards (*JAMA 1996; 275:1032BR*)

**chiropractic education** A four-year program of hands-on and classroom instruction, which is carried out at one of 16 schools of chiropractic; about one-half of the students have a bachelor of arts degree (four years of college or university) before entering chiropractic school; the curriculum consists of 4200 hours of course work, which is similar in some ways to the format of mainstream medical education, as the students are taught both basic and clinical sciences; course work includes anatomy, biochemistry, physiology, microbiology, pathology, laboratory medicine, physical examination of patients, dermatology, emergency medicine, ENT (otorhinolaryngology), geriatrics, obstetrics, gynecology, pediatrics, nutrition, physical therapy, orthopedics, psychology, radiology, spinal analysis, principles and practice of chiropractic, and adjustive technique; many practice 'straight' chiropractic, ie lumbar manipulation, which is widely believed (a belief shared by some mainstream physicians) to benefit patients with low back pain. See Chiropractic, Chiropractic education, Chiropractic malpractice, Chiropractor

**chiropractic malpractice** An event that occurs with uncertain frequency; it is believed by some that chiropractors may not always recognize serious problems requiring mainstream medical attention (*Peter J Modde: Chiropractic Malpractice. Columbia, MD, Hanlow Press, 1985*). See Chiropractic

**chiropractic therapy** Chiropractic treatment consists of adjustment and manipulation (*chiro–*, Greek, hand) of the vertebral column and extremities, which some chiropractors supplement with physical therapy, nutritional support, and radiography (for diagnostic purposes only); according to J Pammer, DC, president of the American Chiropractic Association, '*We categorize ourselves as mechanical engineers, while medical doctors are chemical engineers.*' (*personal communication to W Collinge, 1996*); conditions that may be regarded as the therapeutic domain of a chiropractor are arthritis, pain in the neck, shoulder, back, arms, and legs, pain described as 'pins and needles' and numbness, sports injuries, whiplash, migraine, sprains, strains, insomnia, nerve entrapment, muscle cramps, stiffness, occupational injuries, and degeneration of the lumbar disk (*Jacobs, 1996*); chiropractors may recommend that an individual return on a periodic basis for 'preventative maintenance'. See Chiropractic, Chiropractic education, Chiropractor

**chiropractor** A health care professional who is formally trained in chiropractic; chiropractors do not perform surgery or prescribe drugs; there are nearly 50,000 licensed chiropractors in the US. See Chiropractic, Chiropractic education, Chiropractic therapy

**chittenbark** Cascara sagrada, see there, *Rhamnus purshiana*

**chitterlings** 'Chitlins' NUTRITION An ethnic food popular especially among the blacks in the American south which, if improperly prepared, may result in bacterial infections by *Yersinia enterocolitica* O:3 (*N Engl J Med 1990; 322:984*)

Chitterlings consist of the seromuscular layer of the porcine large intestine, prepared by boiling several times in spices, and baking to a crisp consistency

***Chlorella pyrenoidosa*** ALTERNATIVE ONCOLOGY A one-celled alga that is reported to have anticarcinogenic activity in experimental animals, increasing the length of survival in breast cancer, leukemia, and Ehrlich ascites tumor; this activity is believed to be due to stimulation of the immune system (*Moss, 1992*). See Unproven methods for cancer management

**chloride** A compound containing chlorine with a valence of –1; chloride is a macromineral that interacts with sodium to maintain the fluid and electrolyte balance, which is critical for digestion of food; SOURCE table salt. See Chlorine

**chloride of potash** Kali muriaticum, see Schüssler's tissue salts

**chloride of soda** Natrum muriaticum, see Schüssler's tissue salts

**chlorination** PUBLIC HEALTH The addition of various chlorinated compounds to water as a disinfectant; although liquid chlorine ($Cl_2$) is the most commonly used disinfectant, given its ease of transportation, it is being replaced by sodium hypochlorite (NaOCl) solution, as $Cl_2$ is highly toxic; chlorination has been linked to an increased risk of bladder and colorectal cancer; ozonation had

been proposed as an alternative, but may be no less carcinogenic than chlorination (*Science 1995; 267:1771*); Cf Ozonation

**chlorine** A toxic gaseous element (atomic number 17, atomic weight 35.45), which is used as a bleaching agent; although clorine is critical for metabolism, it is present as chloride, which has a valence of –1. See Cloride

**Chorionic Gonadotropin Quantitative Test** Beard Anthrone Test, see there

**chlorophyll** FRINGE NUTRITION The green plant pigment pivotal in photosynthesis–the manufacture of carbohydrates from carbon dioxide and water; while chlorophyll resembles hemoglobin chemically, it has no role in human metabolism; there is no basis for using chlorophyll to treat allergies, anemia, arthritis, colitis, coughs, hypertension, infections, ulcers, and many other conditions, as has been recommended by some practitioners of alternative medicine

**chlorophyllin** ALTERNATIVE ONCOLOGY The sodium-copper salt of chlorophyll, which is reported to have antimutagenic activity by the Ames test and in experimental animals (*Moss, 1992*). See Ames test

**chocolate** A comestible prepared from ground and roasted beans of the cacao plant *Theobroma cacao*, native to South America; it is composed of cocoa butter, a substance high in stearic acid, which is converted in vivo to oleic acid, which may lower cholesterol levels; one-third of cocoa butter is palmitic acid which increases cholesterol; chocolate craving is thought to be more intense in women and may be associated with increased progesterone levels; theobromine may be the chemical in chocolate responsible for the intense cravings in those people who are facetiously known as 'chocoloholics'; Cf Carob

Note: Chocolate was the ceremonial brew of the Aztecs, Mayas, and Toltecs and returned with Columbus to the Royal Court of Spain, where it remained a state secret until it was stolen by the Italians in 1606; chocolate was first consumed in the solid form in 1847

**choke** Energy block, see there; see Reflexology

**chokecherry** Wild cherry, see there, *Prunus serotina*

**choline** Lipotropic factor, transmethylation factor A chemical present in most tissues, either free or combined with acetate (acetylcholine, critical for synaptic transmission), cytidine diphosphate, or lecithin (phosphatidylcholine); choline is considered to be one of the vitamin B complex FRINGE NUTRITION Choline has been recommended by some practitioners of alternative health care as therapy for body odor, convulsions, and tardive dyskinesia

***Chondrodendron tormentosum*** Periera

***Chondrus crispus*** Popularly known as Irish moss, see there

**Deepak Chopra** An Indian-born, US-based endocrinologist, who wrote *Perfect Health: The Complete Mind/Body Guide* (*New York, Crown Publishers, 1990*), *Ageless Body, Timeless Mind: The Quantum Alternative to Growing Old* (*1993*), and other books; Chopra has helped popularize alternative and ayurvedic health care. He was formerly medical director of the Maharishi Ayur-Ved Health Center in Massachusetts, and is now affiliated with SharpHealthCare in San Diego. See Weil

**Christian healing** PARANORMAL PHENOMENA The laying on of hands by a cleric, with the purpose of effecting a cure; mainstream medical thought has traditionally rejected the notion that organic disease can be substantially affected by spiritual intervention; '*...healing, like all treatment by suggestion, can be expected to be permanently effective only in cases of what are generally termd "functional" diseases. The alleged exceptions are so disputable that they cannot be taken into account.*' (*British Medical Association, in Inglis, West, 1983*). See Christian Science, Faith healing

**Christian Medical Research League** see Koch treatment

**Christian Science** A religious and healing doctrine established in 1879 by Mary Baker Eddy (1824-1910); Christian Science therapy for the sick consists of '*heartfelt, yet disciplined prayer*' by members of the Christian Science Church in lieu of drugs or measures used in mainstream medicine to alleviate pain; while anecdotal 'healing' testimonials available from the Christian Science Church imply that prayer therapy may be better than conventional medical therapy for the care of children, this has not been supported by some peer-reviewed reports (*JAMA 1989;*

*262:1657*); Christian Scientists do not smoke or drink

▶ **IMPACT OF CHRISTIAN SCIENCE ON MEDICINE**

- Christian Scientist parents may override the physician's medical judgment in the care of underage minor children, with potentially fatal consequences
- Christian Scientists may be difficult to treat (especially as unconscious victims of trauma), as they may refuse therapy (eg blood transfusion) deemed appropriate by conventional medical standards; if such therapy is administered, the medical team may be held liable for assault and battery
- Religious exemption statutes allow healers to perform their services ('healing') without liability and at standards of practice that are at variance for those expected of physicians
- Healing therapy can be billed to an insurance company, Medicare, or Medicaid (*JAMA 1990; 264:1379*)

**chromium** A metallic element (atomic number 24; atomic number 51.99), which is an essential mineral that potentiates the action of insulin and is present in trace amounts in various enzymes; chromium is present in various foods including brewers' yeast, whole grains, peanuts, wheat germ, and skim milk. See Chelation therapy, Chromium deficiency, Chromium intoxication

**chromium deficiency** A rare clinical condition characterized by weight loss, glucose intolerance, insulin resistance, decreased respiratory quotients, and peripheral neuropathy. See Chromium

**chromium intoxication** Poisoning caused by toxic levels of chromium, which may be from industrial exposure to chromium-laden fumes and dusts in electroplating, manufacture of steel, dyes, and chemicals, leather tanning, and photography CLINICAL Acute chromium poisoning causes allergic reactions, conjunctivitis, dermatitis, and edema; chronic exposure is associated with gastrointestinal symptoms, hepatitis, and an increased risk of lung cancer. See Chromium

**chromopathy** Color therapy, see there

**chromotherapy** Color therapy, see there

**chronic fatigue immune dysfunction syndrome** Chronic fatigue syndrome, see there

**chronic fatigue syndrome** A condition[1] first described in the mid-1980s in California, which often follows viral infections (eg herpes, hepatitis, cytomegalovirus–CMV), or may be induced by an unrecognized virus[2]; the polymerase chain reaction (PCR) reveals enteroviral RNA sequences in muscle, possibly also in the brain in 53% of CFS, in contrast to 15% of controls (*Br Med J 1991; 302:692*) TREATMENT None; the 'cures' reported are thought to be due to placebo response or spontaneous remission

[1]Synonyms include Akureyri disease, yuppie disease, chronic Epstein-Barr syndrome, postviral syndrome [2]Although CFS had been associated with EBV infection, more than half of those with the CFS improve without a change in EBV titers; chronic fatigue syndrome shares clinical features with epidemic neuromyasthenia, Iceland or Royal Free Hospital disease)

**chronic miasm** Miasm. see there

**chronic stress** A state of prolonged tension from internal or external stressors, which may cause various physical manifestions including asthma, back pain, cardiac arrhythmias, fatigue, headaches, hypertension, irritable bowel syndrome, and ulcers; chronic stress is believed to suppress the immune system. See Flight-or-fight response

**chronobiology** The formal study of circadian rhythms on an organism's activity; certain hormones have their peak secretions at specific times of the day, eg thyrotropin when falling asleep, growth hormone 1-2 hours after onset of sleep, ACTH and prolactin before waking (*Lab Med 1994; 25:372*). See Biorhythm, Chronotherapy, Circadian rhythm

**chronodesm** A time-specific range of an

**CHRONIC FATIGUE SYNDROME** (CDC case definition)

**MAJOR CRITERIA** (required)

1. Recent onset of debilitating or recurring fatigue of > 6 months duration and
2. Exclusion of clinically similar conditions

**MINOR CRITERIA** (eight of ten required)

1. Low-grade fever (< 38.6° C) or chills
2. Sore throat (or pharyngitis)
3. Painful anterior and/or posterior cervical and axillary lymphadenopathy
4. Unexplained muscular weakness
5. Myalgia
6. Generalized fatigue of > 24 hours for previously tolerated exercise
7. Severe generalized headache
8. Migratory arthralgia
9. Neuropsychological complaints, eg photophobia, irritability, inability to concentrate, depression
10. Sleep disturbance

acceptable hormone level that takes into account the difference in the levels of certain hormones at different times of the day (*Lab Med 1994; 25:372*). See Biorhythm, Chronotherapy, Circadian rhythm

**chronotherapy** ALTERNATIVE MEDICINE The process in which a person's daily activities are synchronized with a natural metabolic rhythm in a 24-hour cycle; chronotherapy entails the establishment of routines of exercise, eating, work or study, and rest or sleeping. See Bright light therapy, Chronobiology, Circadian rhythm, Seasonal affective disorder

**chrysanthemum** *Chrysanthemum moriflorum, C indicum, ju hua* CHINESE MEDICINE A perennial herb, the flowers of which are used topically for conjunctivitis, and blurred vision, and internally for inflammation, headaches, hearing loss, hypertension, ocular pain, paresthesias, poor vision linked to renal and hepatic dysfunction, vertigo, and as a blood tonic. See Chinese herbal medicine

**chrysanthemum and uncaria pillow** CHINESE MEDICINE An herbal pillow used in traditional Chinese medicine, which contains dried crysanthemum blossoms and *Uncaria rhynchophylla*; it is believed to control hypertension, hepatitis, blurred vision, and vertigo. See Chinese herbal medicine, Herbal pillow

***Chrysanthmum vulgare*** Tansy, see there, *Tanacetum vulgare*

***chua ka*** A self-administered technique of deep tissue massage rooted in an ancient Mongolian system of manipulation; *chua ka* is based on the belief that trauma and painful life experiences are stored in the body as muscle tension; *chua ka* divides the body into 27 regions or 'zones of karma', each of which is capable of storing a distinct form of psychological fear; as examples, the lower back stores the fear of losses, the scalp retains worries and preoccupations (*Kastner, Burroughs, 1993*); *chua ka* is a three-step technique in which the hands are applied to the muscles, followed by use of a flat massage tool known as a *ka* stick, and the application of long vertical strokes; the techniques are used to release tension, loosen the skin, connective tissue, and muscles; *chua ka* is believed by its advocates to release physical, emotional, and mental stress, reduce cellulite, increase vitality, awareness, and flexibility, and help in recuperation from injuries. See Massage therapy

***chuan hsiung*** *Ligusticum wallichii*, see there

***chuan jiao*** Szechuan pepper, see there, *Zanthoxylum piperitum*

***chuan xiong*** *Ligusticum wallichii*, see there

**church steeples** Agrimony, see there, *Agrimonia eupatoria*

***chyawanprash*** AYURVEDIC MEDICINE A 'metabolic' tonic that contains a veritable gallimaufry of herbs, which is used in ayurvedic medicine to promote health and prevent disease. See Ayurvedic medicine, *Pranayama*

**cicada** CHINESE MEDICINE *Crytotympana atrata* A winged insect which has long had currency as a Chinese 'herb'; it is used internally for swollen eyes with blurred vision, sore throat with hoarse voice, virus-related skin rashes, high fever in childhood infections accompanied by convulsions and delirium TOXICITY Cicada should not be used in pregnancy, as it may induce abortion. See Chinese herbal medicine

**ciguatera poisoning** CLINICAL NUTRITION The ciguatera, a coral reef fish, in its battle to remain a coral reef inhabitant, secretes ichthyosarcotoxin (ciguatoxin, a lipid-soluble, heat-stable substance isolated from bottom-dwelling fish in temperate and tropical zones), which is produced by the reef dinoflagellate, *Gambierdiscus toxicus*, and concentrated, unchanged up the food chain by herbivores and carnivores; ciguatera poisoning is the most common marine intoxication in the US; 400 species of fish are implicated, including barracuda, grouper, red snapper, amberjack, surgeonfish, sea bass and (unlike scombroid poisoning) may cause morbidity regardless of the form of preparation CLINICAL Onset 6 to 12 hours after ingestion with nausea, vomiting, cramping, diarrhea, paresthesias, reversal of temperature sense, arthralgias, myalgias, cranial nerve palsies, pruritus with alcohol ingestion, chills, hypotension, bradycardia, respiratory paralysis, or death, average duration of disease eight days. See Fish, Sushi; Cf Scombroid poisoning

***Cimicifuga dahurica*** *Cimicifuga foetida*, see there

***Cimicifuga foetida*** *C dahurica, sheng ma*, ascending

hemp, bugbane CHINESE MEDICINE A perennial herb, the roots of which are analgesic, anti-inflammatory, and diaphoretic; it is used for anal prolapse, bronchitis, canker sores, diarrhea, fever, headaches, pelvic organ prolapse (bladder, rectum, uterus), Raynaud's phenomenon, skin rashes, sore throat, spermatorrhea, and thyroid disease TOXICITY Skin rash. See Chinese herbal medicine; Cf *Cimic*, Black cohosh, Blue cohosh

***Cimic*** *Cimicifuga racemosa* HOMEOPATHY A homeopathic remedy used primarily for women, which acts on their reproductive organs; it is used to treat emotional lability, menstrual cramping, menopausal and pregnancy-related symptoms. See Black cohosh, Homeopathy

***Cimicifuga racemosa*** HERBAL MEDICINE Popularly known as black cohosh, see there HOMEOPATHY *Cimic*, see there

**cinchona** *Cinchona* species, *China* (homeopathy), *China officinalis*, bark, cinchona bark, Jesuits' bark, Peruvian bark, quina, quinaquina, quinine tree, quinquina HERBAL MEDICINE A tree native to South America that is the primary source of the alkaloids quinine, and quinidine, the first effective antimalarial agent; other alkaloids present in cinchona include cinchonidine and cinchonine TOXICITY Abdominal pain, deafness, delirium, headache, impaired vision, nausea, psychotic disorder, tinnitus, vomiting, and weakness. See Botanical toxicity, Herbal medicine HOMEOPATHY See *China*

**cinchona**

**cinchona bark** 1. *China*, see there 2. Cinchona, see there, *Cinchona* species

***Cinchona ledgeriana*** See Cinchona

***Cinchona pubescens*** See Cinchona

**cingulum sancti Johannis** Mugwort, see there, *Artemisia vulgaris*

**cinnamon** *Cinnamomum zeylanicum* HERBAL MEDICINE A tree native to the Indian subcontinent, the bark of which contains cinnamanic aldehyde, eugenol, and tannins; it is antibacterial, carminative, stimulates the appetite, and is used for gastrointestinal complaints. See Herbal medicine

***Cinnamon cassia*** Cassia, *mu gui, rou qui,* wood cinnamon CHINESE MEDICINE A tree native to southeast Asia, which has analgesic, astringent, diaphoretic, and sedative principles, including cinnamaldehyde; in Chinese herbal medicine, the bark and twigs are used for different indications; the bark is used for anorexia, abdominal pain, asthma, diarrhea, fatigue, impotence, infertility, loss of libido, and urinary frequency; the twigs are used for arthritis, colds, fibroids, low-grade fever, and painful menses; both may be used in Raynaud's phenomenon, to improve vision, and as a cardiovascular tonic TOXICITY Cinnamon should be used with caution in pregnancy, and in those with fever, inflammation, or active bleeding. See Chinese herbal medicine; Cf Cinnamon

**cinnamonwood** Sassafras, see there, *Sassafras albidum*

**cinquefoil** 1. Erect cinquefoil, see there, *Potentilla erecta* 2. *Potentilla reptans*, five fingers, five finger grass, five-leaf, sunkfield HERBAL MEDICINE A perennial herb; it is antidiarrheal, antipyretic, astringent, and tonic, and has been used to treat nasal and oral bleeding, sore throat, and toothaches. See Herbal medicine

**circadian pacemaker** A cluster of hypothalamic neurons, the activity of which fluctuates in ± 24 hour cycles, resides in the pineal gland,* weighs 100-180 mg, and derives embryologically from the ependyma at the roof of the 3rd ventricle; in rats, this 'biogenic oscillator' or internal clock resides in the ventral hypothalamus, in hamsters, in the suprachiasmatic nucleus; the circadian pacemaker influences the pineal gland, which produces melatonin at night

(*Lab Med 1994; 25:372*). See Bright light therapy, Chronotherapy, Circadian rhythm, Melatonin, Seasonal affective disorder, Zeitgeber

*An aggregate of parenchymal cells surrounded by a neuroglial network with direct retinal innervation (retinohypothalamic tract), which is thought to act by secreting melatonin

**circadian rhythm** The diurnal cadence which, in humans (without the cyclical cues provided by natural light), is 25.4 hours; 'photoperiodic' information from the eyes synchronizes the circadian pacemaker with the light-dark cycle; circadian rhythm affects drug metabolism[1], serum levels of various substances (in particular adrenocortical hormones) that are routinely measured to detect and monitor disease, physiologic activities, eg blood pressure, myocardial blood flow and oxygen demand (*JAMA 1991; 265:386*), psychosomatic disease and sleep cycles[2], cell division, hematopoiesis, and natural killer cell activity. See Biorhythm, Circadian pacemaker, Insomnia, Jet lag, Melatonin, Shift work

[1]eg antacids, halothane [2]Sleep patterns may become desynchronized by shiftwork, and may be reset or completely suppressed by a light stimulus at a critical time and strength (*Nature 1991; 350:59, 18*)

**circle walking** *Baguazhang*, see there

**circular breathing** Conscious-connected breathing, see there

**cinquefoil** *Potentilla reptans*

**circulation-sex meridian** Heart constrictor meridian, see there

**circumcision** Surgical removal of the foreskin, either by an obstetrician, or as a part of a religious rite (eg, a bris, performed by a rabbi in Judaism at birth and in Moslems in preadolescence); the American Academy of Pediatrics recommends circumcision as it decreases the incidence of balanitis, phimosis, colonization by *Escherichia coli* and other bacteria, and urinary tract infections, which are 10 to 20 times greater in uncircumcised boys; the lifetime risk for penile cancer in uncircumcised males is 600-fold greater than that of circumcised males; Cf Female circumcision

Note: The risk for cancer of the uterine cervix is closely linked to HPV infections (HPV-16 in 50% and HPV-18 in 10%) in uncircumcised males' partners; the incidence of STDs, eg genital herpes, syphilis, gonorrhea, chancroid, and HIV-1 is decreased in the circumspect and circumcised (*N Engl J Med 1990; 322:1308, 1312*)

**'circumcision', female** see Female circumcision

***Cirsium japonicum*** Popularly known as tiger thistle, see there

***cis* fatty acid** CLINICAL NUTRITION A natural fatty acid, in which the carbon moieties lie on the same side of the double bond; natural fats and oils contain only *cis* double bonds, eg oleic acid, a monounsaturated fatty acid with a *cis* configuration. See Fatty acid; Cf *Trans* fatty acid

***Cistanche salsa*** Broomrape, see there

***Citrullus colocynthis*** Known to homeopaths as *Colocynthis*, see there

**citrus fruit diet** See Grapefruit diet, Lemonade diet, Orange diet

**citrus oil** AROMATHERAPY An oil distilled or extracted from citrus fruits, eg lemon, lime, orange, and grapefruit, which is used in aromatherapy; citrus oil is believed to act on depression by creating a bright and uplifting environment. See Aromatherapy, Essential oil, Lemon balm, Limonene

**Citrus Red 2** A dye used to tint orange skins a bright orange color; it induces chromosomal damage, and is carcinogenic in animals when administered in extremely high doses; the impact that the low levels to which humans eating dyed oranges are exposed is uncertain, and probably minimal;* see Ames test, Artificial dye, FD&C Red No 3

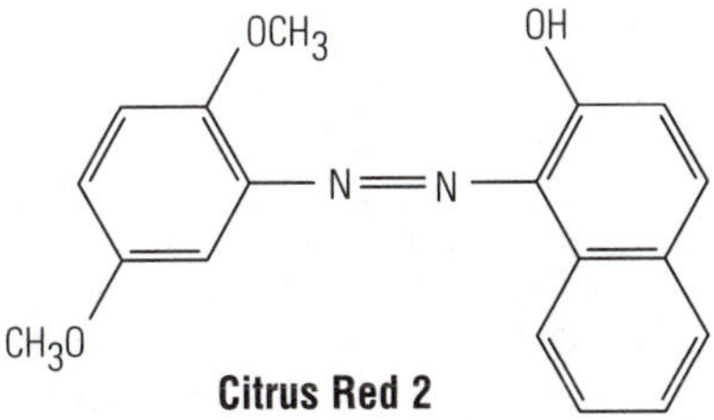

apy, Laying on of stones

**Citrus Red 2**

*Although alternative health care advocates and organic food aficionados may make statements to the contrary (*Alternative Medicine, Future Med Pub, 1994*)

***Citrus reticulata*** Popularly known as tangerine, see tangerine peel

**citrus shell** Trifoliate orange, see there, *Poncircus trifoliata*

***Citrus trifoliata*** Trifoliate orange, see there, *Poncircus trifoliata*

**clairvoyant diagnosis** Psychic diagnosis, see there

**clarified butter** Ghee, see there

**classical osteopathy** Pure osteopathy ALTERNATIVE MEDICINE A format of osteopathic medicine that resorts to prescription drugs and surgery only when absolutely necessary; classical osteopathy is in keeping with the original philosophy of osteopathy, as delineated by its founder, Andrew Taylor Still. See Osteopathy, Still

**clay therapy** Mud therapy, see there

**clear** PARANORMAL PHENOMENA A term used in Scientology® for an individual who has successfully erased the painful effects of traumatic memories (engrams). See Auditing, Scientology®

**clearing** FRINGE MEDICINE The removal from a therapeutic crystal or gemstone, of vibrations or 'imprints' from individuals who had previous contact with the crystal, before using it for crystal therapy; the concept of clearing is based on the belief that sounds, light, emotions, thoughts, and the physical environment can leave energy traces on therapeutic crystals; clearing is accomplished by soaking the stones in sea-salt water, passing them through a flame, smoke, or running water, or burying them in the ground for a period of time. See Crystal therapy, Laying on of stones

**cleavers** *Galium aparine*, bedstraw, catchweed, clivers, goosegrass, gripgrass, hedgeburs, sticky-willie HERBAL MEDICINE An annual herb that contains citric acid, coumarins, and tannins; it is diuretic and alterative, ie stimulates lymphatic circulation, and is used to treat kidney stones, arthritis, hypertension, skin conditions, eg eczema and psoriasis, and is believed to be of use in treating lymphomas. See Herbal medicine

**client-centered therapy** 1. A general term referring to any format of non-directive client counseling, first developed by Carl Rogers; see Humanistic psychology; Cf Confrontation therapy 2. Rogers' therapy, see there

**cliffhanger** An exercise performed in polarity therapy, that consists of slowly lowering the body from a standing position, while grasping a table from behind the back; the cliffhanger is intended to loosen the chest and shoulders, expand the lungs, stretch the vertebral cloumn, and release pelvic tension. See Polarity therapy

**clinical ecology** Environmental medicine, see there

**clinical ecologist** FRINGE MEDICINE A non-mainstream health care practitioner, who claims special expertise in diagnosing and treating 'environmental disease', a condition that is not believed to exist by many mainstream medical practitioners. See Environmental disease, Environmental medicine

**clinical remedy** AYURVEDIC MEDICINE An ayurvedic term for medication, strong herbs, and purification practices including purgation, medicated enemas, therapeutic vomiting, nasal medication, and therapeutic bloodletting

**clitoridectomy** HUMAN RIGHTS A type of female circumcision

▶ **CLITORIDECTOMY, TYPES OF**

- **TYPE I** Part or the entire female clitoris is removed, a procedure likened to penile amputation
- **TYPE II** Clitoridectomy and partial labia minora removal

The wound is closed with thread, grasses, or other suture materials, or with a poultice; clitoridectomy is deeply rooted in the culture of certain African countries, and symbolizes societal control over a woman's sex-

uality (*N Engl J Med 1994; 331:712SA*). See Female circumcision, Cf Infibulation

**clivers** Cleavers, see there, *Galium aparine*

**clodronate** A biphosphonate* that decreases cancer-induced hypercalcemia in patients with prostate cancer, multiple myeloma, and other malignancies by regulating osteoclastic activity (*Pelton, Overholser, 1994*)

*which is structurally similar to pyrophosphate; clodronate is produced by the Leiras Corporation of Finland under the trade name Bonefos; it is not available in the US

**clotbur** Burdock, see there, *Arctium lappa*

**clover broom** Wild indigo, see there, *Baptista tinctoria*

**clove cigarette** A cigarette made from a mixture of tobacco leaves, cloves, and spice prepared from the dried flowers of the tropical tree, *Eugenia aromatica*; clove cigarettes are produced in Indonesia, where they are the preferred smoking product, 30% to 40% of which is shredded clove buds, and the remainder, tobacco

Importation of clove cigarettes to the US peaked in the mid-1980s and is on the decline; eugenol is the main (85%) constituent of clove oil; while not carcinogenic or mutagenic in test animals, clove cigarettes cause respiratory depression, atelectasis, alveolar edema, bronchopneumonia, and may exacerbate asthma (*JAMA 1988; 260:3641*)

**clove tree** *Eugenia aromatica, Syzygium aromaticum* A tropical tree, the buds of which have a high concentration of essential oil containing eugenol and eugenyl acetate; it is analgesic, anti-emetic, antiseptic, and carminative, and has been used for abdominal bloating and athlete's foot HERBAL MEDICINE Cloves have been used for nausea and toothaches. See Herbal medicine CHINESE MEDICINE In Chinese medicine, cloves have been used for diarrhea and hernias. See Chinese herbal medicine; Cf Clove cigarette

**club moss** *Lycopodium*, see there, *Lycopodium clavatum*

**C.M.A.** Certified Movement Analyst

**C.M.T.** 1. Certified Massage Therapist 2. Certified Music Therapist

***Cnicus benedictus*** Popularly known as blessed thistle, see there

***Cnicus japonicus*** see Tiger thistle

***Cnicus spicatus*** see Tiger thistle

***Cnidium monnieri*** *Selenum monnieri, she chuang dze, she chuang zi* CHINESE MEDICINE An annual herb, the seeds of which contain essential oils, including borneol, camphene, pinene, and terpineol; it is antiseptic, astringent, and a stimulant; it is used topically for abscesses, eczema, itching and oozing skin lesions, ringworm, and scabies, as a douche for vaginal discharge and yeast infection, and internally for male impotence and female infertility. See Chinese herbal medicine

**coakum** Pokeweed, see there, *Phytolacca americana*

**cobalt** A metallic element (atomic number 27; atomic weight 58.93), which is critical to the formation of red cells, maintenance of neural tissue, and in certain metabolic reactions, and is the central ion in vitamin $B_{12}$; cobalt is present in dairy products, organ meats, shellfish, and sea vegetables

**coca shrub** *Erythroxylum coca* A South American shrub, the leaves of which contain cocaine; coca leaves continue to be used in the Andes for increasing concentration and reducing pain, fatigue, and hunger

**coca shrub** *Erythroxylum coca*

***Cochlearia armoracia*** Popularly known as horseradish, see there

**cockleburr** 1. Agrimony, see there, *Agrimonia eupatoria* 2. Burdock, see there, *Arctium lappa*

**cockle buttons** 1. Agrimony, see there, *Agrimonia eupatoria* 2. Burdock, see there, *Arctium lappa*

**co-carcinogenic K factor** FRINGE ONCOLOGY A substance which, according to Gaston

Naessens in Montreal, is secreted by cancer cells (which require and consume excessive amounts of nitrogen) and paralyzes the immune system; Naessens believes that intralymphatic administration of nitrogen-rich camphor provides the cancer cells with the required nitrogen, causing them to stop excreting co-carcinogenic K factor, resulting in an up-regulation of immune defenses. See 714X, Unproven methods for cancer management

**co-centering** ALTERNATIVE MEDICINE A component of bodywork tantra; co-centering refers to a system of 'pointwork', in which various points along acupuncture meridians or chakra channels are manipulated or stimulated. See Bodywork tantra

**co-counseling** Peer counseling PSYCHOLOGY A therapeutic philosophy that originated in the 1960s in Seattle; in a typical co-counseling session, each person has an allotted time to act as a counselee, while the peer counselor helps him recognize hidden or blocked emotions; once one person's allotted time ends, the roles are switched; co-counseling ideally occurs after one or more members in the counseling network have undergone a training (eg 40 hours) period; peer counseling can only work long-term, if the sessions are mutually beneficial; as co-counseling was popularized, breakaway groups added techniques of regression and guided fantasy, which provide a transpersonal element; despite these changes, the intent of co-counseling remains the same. See Encounter groups, Humanistic psychology

**cod-liver oil** CLINICAL NUTRITION An oil extracted from cod liver, that is rich in n-3 fatty acids, in particular eicosapentanoic acid (EPA); 10 grams of cod-liver oil contributes 1 gram of EPA to the diet. See Eicosapentanoic acid, Fish oil

***Codonopsis dangshen*** *Codonopsis pilosula*, see there

***Codonopsis pilosula*** *C dangshen*, bastard ginseng, *dang shen* CHINESE MEDICINE Any of a family of plants that resemble ginseng, which may be substituted for true ginseng; the root is used for anorexia, chronic cough, chronic fatigue, diabetes, diarrhea, dyspnea, edema, postsurgical and postpartum fatigue, hypertension, immune deficiency, indigestion, as a cardiotonic, for prolapsed rectum and uterus, and increased thirst. See Chinese herbal medicine; Cf Ginseng

**coenzyme R** Biotin, see there

**coenzyme Q10** Ubiquinone, CoQ10 A factor present in the mitochondria which extracts energy from foods; it has acquired a reputation among fringe nutritionists as being effective in detoxifying patients with an overdose of environmental pollutants; it is also claimed to be beneficial in treating hypertension, obesity, periodontal disease, preventing cancer, increasing longevity, and revitalizing the immune system; Cf Compound Q

***Coffea arabica*** 1. Coffee, see there 2. *Coffea*, see there

***Coffea cruda*** Coffee, see there, *Coffea arabica*

***Coffea*** HOMEOPATHY A minor homeopathic remedy produced from *Coffea arabica* which is used for mental hyperactivity resulting in insomnia and fatigue; it is used for pain, eg toothaches or childbirth. See Antidoting Caffeine, Coffee, Homeopathy

**coffee** *Coffea arabica* ALTERNATIVE MEDICINE A beverage prepared from dried ground beans of *Coffea arabica*; an African evergreen; the berries are rich in caffeine, which stimulates the nervous and cardiorespiratory systems; many practitioners of alternative medicine regard coffee in a negative light (with the exception of coffee enemas, which are part of the unusual Gerson therapy), as its effects are abrupt in onset– which is rarely seen in 'natural' therapies, is a psychoactive addictive agent, and has an 'antidoting' effect, and may cancel the effects of homeopathic remedies–patients being treated by a homeopath may be required to abstain from coffee. See Gerson therapy, Unproven methods for cancer management ALTERNATIVE NUTRITION On the positive side, coffee is a bronchodilator and decongestant, and therefore of use in asthma and congestion of common colds; it boosts stamina and performance in athletes, and may have analgesic effects. See Healthy foods HOMEOPATHY see *Coffea*

**coffee enema** ALTERNATIVE MEDICINE An enema that uses coffee to stimulate bile and hepatic glutathione-SH production, both of which are claimed to help detoxify the body in cancer patients; coffee enemas are a component of Gerson therapy, an unproven can-

cer therapy based on detoxification (*JAMA 1992; 268:3224sc*) TOXICITY Coffee leaches potassium and electrolytes from the body, and may cause fatal electrolyte imbalances (*JAMA 1980; 244:1608*); the large doses of caffeine contained in coffee enemas may result in anxiety, dehydration, and diarrhea. See Gerson therapy, Unproven methods for cancer management

**coffeeweed** Chicory, see there, *Chicorium intybus*

**cognitive therapy** PSYCHOLOGY A format of psychological therapy in which a person is taught to cope with internal conflicts—anxiety, stress, guilt, phobias, and emotional negativity by consciously changing the way in which he thinks. See Distorted thinking

**cohoba** A hallucinogen obtained from the bark of the *Anadenanthera* tree, *Acacia niopo*, *Piptadenia peregrina*, and other plants; cohoba

**coffee** *Coffea arabica*

is ingested in Central America as a snuff or as an enema

**coining** C'ao gio ETHNOMEDICINE The practice of rubbing the edge of a coin across warm, oiled skin as part of Southeast Asian (Vietnamese) folk therapy, for treating migraines, fever, and other conditions; skin subjected to 'coining' has darkened, linear, erythematous microecchymoses which, when seen in feverish children in the emergency room, may be confused with lesions associated with child abuse (*N Engl J Med 1995; 332:1552*). See Ethnomedicine

**coitus interruptus** A form of natural family planning in which an orgasm is achieved as an out-of-body experience. See Contraception, Natural family planning, Pearl index

**coix** *Coix chinensis*, popularly known as Job's tears, see there

***Coix chinenis*** Popularly known as Job's tears, see there

***Coix lacryma-jobi*** *Coix chinensis*, popularly known as Job's tears, see there

***Cola nitida*** Cola tree, see there

***Cola vera*** Cola tree, see there

**cola tree** *Cola nitida* HERBAL MEDICINE An evergreen shrub, the berries of which stimulate the cardiovascular and respiratory systems, and have been used for anorexia, asthma, diarrhea caused by 'nervous bowel,' fluid retention, headaches and migraines, hangovers, indigestion, and motion sickness TOXICITY Cola should not be used in those with anxiety, chronic hypertension, heart disease, high cholesterol, history of stroke, or in pregnancy. See Herbal medicine

**colchicum** Autumn crocus, see there, *Colchicum autumnale*

***Colchicum autumnale*** Autumn crocus, see there

**cold bath** NATUROPATHY A bath taken in ice-cold water, which is believed to act as a tonic; cold baths may be of use in treating asthma, fever, muscle soreness, low sperm count and decreased libido*. See Hydrotherapy; Cf Hot bath, Sauna

*Many believe that cold showers reduce the sexual drive, a belief that may not be correct (*Castleman, 1996*)

**cold compress** NATUROPATHY A cloth imbibed with ice-cold water that is apllied locally to relieve pain, stop bleeding, and reduce congestion and swelling caused by acute local trauma. See Hydrotherapy; Cf Hot compress

**cold mitten friction rub** NATUROPATHY A therapy that combines brisk massage with cool temperatures, using a cloth imbibed with ice-cold water; the rub is believed to increase circulation, strengthen the immune system, accelerate recuperation from respiratory tract infections, and be of use in treating chronic fatigue syndrome (*Gottlieb, 1995*). See Hydrotherapy

**cold pack** Full body wet sheet NATUROPATHY A therapy in which a patient is wrapped firmly in a sheet soaked in cold water, which may be beneficial for acute conditions, acting to eliminate various toxins. See Hydrotherapy

**cold remedy** POPULAR PHARMACOLOGY A general term for any product available without prescription (ie over-the-counter) that is intended to relieve one or more of the symptoms typical of the common cold; cold remedies include antihistamines and decongestants; they are not antimicrobial, do not enhance the immune system, and have no effect on the actual duration of the cold; they provide a modicum of relief by partially suppressing nasal congestion, runny nose, and cough

**cold sponge bath** NATUROPATHY An alternative to a cold bath, which minimizes the shock inherent in ice-cold water immersion, as only part of the body is subjected at one time to near-freezing temperatures. See Hydrotherapy; Cf Hot bath, Sauna

**cold therapy** Cryotherapy, ice therapy ALTERNATIVE MEDICINE A general term for the use of ice or cold compresses for therapeutic purposes; locally applied ice increases the circulation, and relieves pain, and is of use in acute trauma; practitioners of alternative therapies may advocate alternating ice and heat, as it is believed to 'flush' an area with fresh blood. See Cold compresses, Cold pack, Hydrotherapy

**Coley's toxin** IMMUNOLOGY A 'cocktail' of endogenous pyrogens from *Streptococcus pyogenes* and *Serratia marcesens*, which includes hemolytic streptococcal proteins, eg streptokinase and streptodornase, as well as endotoxin (lipopolysaccharide); the concoction was formulated in 1893 by a New York surgeon, William B Coley, who observed the cyclical regression of an inoperable head and neck cancer in a patient who had repeated attacks of eysipelas; during his life, Coley used the therapy on a wide range of inoperable tumors including cancer of the breast and ovaries, Hodgkin's disease, and melanoma, many of which resulted in regression and prolonged survival; recent studies indicate that Coley's toxin increases NK (natural killer) cell activity, production of interleukins and tumor necrosis factor TOXICITY fever, nausea, headache, back pain, and cold sores (*Moss, 1992*). See BCG, Heat therapy, Immune boosters, Unproven methods for cancer management

**colicroot** 1. Fairywand, see there, *Chamaelirium luteum* 2. *Aletris farinosa*, ague grass, ague root, aletris, aloeroot, crow corn, devil's-bit star grass HERBAL MEDICINE An annual herb that was used by Native Americans as an infusion for intestinal colic, dysentery, and dysmenorrhea, and topically as a poultice for back and breast pain. See Herbal medicine

**collateral** CHINESE MEDICINE An energy channel that is a subsidiary of a meridian, which contains acupressure points or acupoints. See Acupuncture, Meridian

**collective unconscious** A concept championed by Carl Gustav Jung, which he regarded as an inborn, symbol-rich psychological bedrock, common to humanity that differs slightly according to the culture; he postulated that the collective unconsciousness reflected a group mindset, which would allow telepathy. See Jungian psychoanalysis

**College of Electronic Medicine** See Oscilloscope, Radionics

***Collinsonia canadensis*** Popularly known as stoneroot, see there

**colloidal silver protein** ALTERNATIVE MEDICINE Any of a family of non-FDA-approved compounds that have been promoted as essential mineral supplements for adults, pregnant and lactating women, and children, and have been available in various forms (per os, injectable, vaginal douche); they are claimed to be antiviral (eg herpes, HIV), antifungal (eg *Candida*), antibacterial (eg tuberculosis), and antiparasitic (eg malaria), immunostimulatory, anti-inflammatory, and effective in treating diabetes, chronic fatigue syndrome, allergies, cancer, and more than 600 other conditions*; silver is NOT an essential mineral, and has no known physiologic role TOXICITY When consumed in excess, silver causes an irreversible condition, argyria, which is characterized by a slate-gray skin color, neurologic defects, diffuse deposition of silver in visceral organs, and renal damage; see Unproven

methods for cancer management

*There is no known therapeutic role of colloidal silver protein (*JAMA 1995; 275:1196c*)

**Colocynthis** *Citrullus colocynthis*, bitter apple, bitter cucumber HOMEOPATHY A remedy used for colic, neuralgia caused by suppressed emotions, gastric pain, headaches accompanied by nausea and vomiting, gout, rheumatic complaints, and vertigo. See Homeopathy

**colon cleansing** 1. Colonic therapy, see there 2. Colonic irrigation, see there

**colon hydrotherapy** 1. Colonic therapy, see there 2. Colonic irrigation, see there

**colon therapy** Colon cleansing, colon hydrotherapy, colonic, colonic irrigation, colonic lavage, colonic therapy, high colonic FRINGE MEDICINE A generic term for the use of various types of enema, which are believed to '...*balance body chemistry, eliminate wastes, and restore proper tissue and organ function.*' (*Alternative Medicine, Future Med Pub, 1994*); colon therapy is a controversial procedure in which a series of purging enemas is administered over a short period; a rubber tube is passed per rectum for a distance and warm fluids (often with herbs, coffee, or other substances) are pumped in and out with a gravity-dependent device, typically using 20 or more gallons; the technique may be practiced by chiropractors, 'colon therapists', 'nutrition therapists', naturopaths and 'homeopaths' with the purpose of 'detoxification'; it is believed to reduce the body's burden of impacted feces, microorganisms, and cellular debris, which cause the so-called 'bowel toxemia'; colon therapy is believed by its advocates to tone the intestinal muscles, decrease the transit time of intestinal toxins, and enhance the immune system, circulation, the eyes, muscles, joints, skin, gastrointestinal and genitourinary tracts; it is claimed to be effective for bloating, cardiovascular disease, constipation, depression, fatigue, gallbladder disease, halitosis, headaches, loss of memory, low back pain, nausea, obesity, parasites, psychosis, pulmonary congestion, sexual dysfunction, shock, sinusitis, skin disease, and other conditions; marketing literature from colon therapy clinics may claim that after treatment, the skin 'glows', the clients look younger, and lose significant weight with merely one treatment; colon therapy and detoxifying enemas are an integral component of 'metabolic therapy'; in contrast to enemas, which irrigate the sigmoid colon, colon therapy bathes the entire colon to the cecum, using 2-6 liters of herbs, wheatgrass, bentonite, clay, and oxygen in a filtered aqueous solution (oxygenated water) WARNING Colon therapy has been associated with a number of deaths due to amebiasis and other infections (*Butler, 1992*). See Coffee enema, Enema, Herbal enema, Unproven methods for cancer management; Cf Colonic irrigation

Note: In 1981, federal authorities traced 7 deaths and many cases of dysentery to a single machine that had been improperly cleaned (*Morbidity and Mortality Weekly Report 1981; 30:101*); in 1985, the California Department of Health's Infectious Disease Branch stated that neither physicians nor chiropractors should perform colonic irrigation (colon therapy)

**colonic lavage** 1. Colonic therapy, see there 2. Colonic irrigation, see there

**colonic therapy** Colonic therapy, see there

**colonic irrigation** ALTERNATIVE MEDICINE Colon therapy, see there SURGERY An intraoperative procedure for antegrade cleansing of the large intestine in an emergency colon resection, which can be used in elective left-sided colonic surgery in patients who are clinically stable, circumventing the need for a temporary colostomy; Cf Colon therapy

**color breathing** FRINGE MEDICINE A permutation of color therapy that involves imagery (visualization), meditation, and use of positive affirmations; according to the proponents of this form of pseudotherapy, the patient can balance his energy and relieve a condition by imagining that he is breathing one or more colors associated with healing a particular condition. See Affirmation, Color therapy

**color healing** Color therapy, see there

**color meditation** FRINGE MEDICINE A permutation of color therapy involving meditation on particular colors, which is believed to help a person balance energy and increase creativity. See Color therapy

**color projection** A permutation of color therapy in which light is passed through sheets or slabs of gelatin of various colors, onto the patient; according to the proponents of color projection, each color has a particular effect, eg red-filtered light increases hemoglobin, blue light reduces fevers, and so on. See Color therapy

**color therapy** Chromopathy, chromotherapy, color healing FRINGE MEDICINE A general term for any pseudotherapy in which a patient is exposed to various colors in the form of colored light, colored environment, colored clothing, or colored food, as a 'modality' for treating organic (ie not mental) disease. See Blue, Color breathing, Color meditation, Color projection, Green, Indigo, Orange, Purple, Red, Violet, Yellow ALTERNATIVE PSYCHOLOGY A general term for any form of sensory therapy in which a patient is exposed to various colors, either in the form of colors in the environment, in clothing, or colored lights; the efficacy of colored light therapy is uncertain, although some data suggest that the autonomic nervous system is aroused by the color red, and attenuated by blue; color therapy is integral to ayurvedic medicine, but is peripheral to mainstream psychiatric therapy. See Sensory therapy; Cf Color therapy, Music therapy

**colostrum** FRINGE MEDICINE The milk produced by mammals after giving birth which, given its high content of antibodies, is believed to serve as an immune system enhancer; bovine colostrum in the form of pills, powders, and ointments has been marketed as a treatment for arthritis, cancer, various infections, multiple sclerosis, and other conditions; see Breast milk, Certified milk, Raw milk

**coltsfoot** *Tussilago farfara*; ass's foot, cough wort, hall foot, horse hoof, *kuan dung hua*, son-before-the-father CHINESE MEDICINE A perennial herb that contains choline, inulin, saponins, and stearin; it is antitussive, expectorant, and anti-inflammatory, and is used for lung complaints, including smoker's cough, pulmonary infections and congestion. See Chinese herbal medicine HERBAL MEDICINE Coltsfoot has been used in Western herbal medicine internally for asthma, bronchitis, whooping cough, and emphysema by inhalation of smoking leaves; crushed leaves have been used topically for bites, burns, edema, ulcers, and other skin conditions TOXICITY Anorexia, diarrhea, jaundice, nausea, vomiting; coltsfoot should not be given to young children, nursing mothers, alcoholics, those with liver disease, or in pregnancy; it has carcinogenic potential. See Botanical toxicity, Poisonous plants

**combined tea** A general term for an infusion that is prepared from various herbs in specific proportions. See Herbal tea

**comfrey** *Symphytum officinale*, ass-ear, blackwort, bruisewort, healing herb, knitback, knitbone HERBAL MEDICINE A perennial herb, the leaves and roots of which contain allantoin, carotene, essential oil, glycosides, mucilage, resin, saponins, tannins, triterpenoids, vitamin $B_{12}$, and zinc; comfrey is a 'standard' medicinal herb, which promotes the growth of bone and connective tissue, and breaks down red blood cells (from whence its name, bruisewort); it is anti-inflammatory, and has been used internally for hemorrhage, to treat diarrhea, gastric ulcers, colitis, bronchitis, whooping cough, and other respiratory tract infections (see below toxicity); it is used topically for burns, bruises, sprains, boils, sore breasts, ulcers, gangrene, hemorrhoids, and varicose veins TOXICITY Liver tumors may develop in lab rats when exposed to high levels; it is a potential carcinogen; the American Herbs Products Association has recommended that comfrey be used only externally. See Botanical toxicity, Herbal medicine, Poisonous plants

***Commiphora molmol*** Popularly known as myrrh, see there

**coltsfoot** *Tussilago farfara*

**comfrey** *Symphytum officinale*

**The Committee for Freedom of Choice in Cancer Therapy, Inc** ALTERNATIVE MEDICINE An organization that was most active in the 1970s, which maintained an educational and advocacy group, and held seminars, symposia, conferences, and workshops, and distributed information on unproven methods for cancer management; past activities of the Committee included attempts to vindicate and legalize laetrile (aka 'vitamin B-17'), and decriminalize its use (*Fact Sheet, American Cancer Society, June 1978*). See Unproven methods for cancer management

**common alkanet** Alkanet, see there, *Anchusa officinalis*

**common barberry** Barberry, *Berberis vulgaris*

**common bryony** *Bryonia*, see there, *Bryonia alba*

**common bugloss** Borage, see there, *Borago officinalis*

**common chamomile** Roman chamomile, see there, *Anthemis nobilis*

**common chokecherry** Wild cherry, see there, *Prunus serotina*

**common dock** Bitter dock, see there, *Rumex obtusifolius*

**common elder** Elderberry, see there, *Sambucus nigra*

**common hops** Hops, see there, *Humulus lupulus*

**common horehound** Horehound, see there, *Marrubium vulgare*

**common marjoram** Marjoram, see there, *Origanum vulgare*

**common milkweed** Milkweed, see there, *Asclepia syriaca*

**common nettle** Stinging nettle, see there, *Urtica dioica*

**common oat** Oat, see there, *Avena sativa*

**common plantain** Plantain, see there, *Plantago major*

**common rue** Rue, see there, *Ruta graveolens*

**common sage** Sage, see there, *Salvia officinalis*

**common Saint John's wort** Saint John's wort, see there, *Hypericum perforatum*

**common silkweed** Milkweed, see there, *Asclepia syriaca*

**common thyme** Thyme, see there, *Thymus vulgaris*

**common willow** White willow, see there, *Salix alba*

**companionship** ALTERNATIVE PSYCHOLOGY A general term for an interactional relationship with one or more living beings; companions include spouses, lovers, children, parents, friends, pets, and others, who provide an individual with a sense of belonging and of being needed; companionship prevents social isolation, which is common in those with disabilities, in divorce, advanced age, mental disorders, and alcoholism, and is a risk factor for both suicide and deaths from all causes (*Castleman, 1996*). See Extended family, Marriage bonus, Most significant other, Pet therapy, Support group; Cf Social isolation

**compassion fatigue** Burnout syndrome, see there

**complementary cancer care** ALTERNATIVE ONCOLOGY A general term for any alteration in lifestyle or diet that is designed to

enhance—not replace—conventional (mainstream) cancer therapy; a widely used format of complementary cancer care is that of the Commonweal Cancer Help Program in Bolinas, California, which is based on a vegetarian diet, psychological support, moderate exercise, and personal growth through the arts (*Castleman, 1996*); Cf Unproven methods for cancer management

**complementary medicine** Alternative medicine, see there

**complementary physician** A physician who practices alternative medicine

**complementary therapy** Alternative therapy, see there

**complete breath** AYURVEDIC MEDICINE An exercise integral to yoga, which is intended to fully expand the lungs, allowing the alveolar capillaries to achieve the maximum exchange of carbon dioxide and oxygen; the complete breath consists of an abdominal breath, a diaphragmatic breath, and an upper breath, which are linked in a wavelike movement; the complete breath is believed to increase vitality, soothe nerves, and strengthen weak abdominal muscles. See Abdominal breath, Diaphragm breath, Upper breath, Yoga

***The Complete Herbal*** *The English Physician* MEDICAL HISTORY–HERBAL MEDICINE A classic treatise on herbal remedies published in the 1600s by Nicholas Culpepper, which described 369 English herbs. See Herbal medicine; Cf *Canon of Medicine*, *Charak Samhita*, *De Materia Medica*, *Natural History*, *Nei Jing*, *Pen Ts'ao*, *Rigveda*, *Sushrita Samhita*, *Theatrum Botanicum*

**Compostela** See Healing shrine

**compound Q** FRINGE PHARMACOLOGY A purified form of the plant protein tricosanthin, which is derived from Chinese cucumber root, and imported from China as an unproven therapy for AIDS; it has also had currency as an 'underground' agent for inducing second trimester abortions and treating choriocarcinoma. See AIDS fraud, Unproven methods for cancer management; Cf Coenzyme Q10

**concentration therapy** ALTERNATIVE PSYCHOLOGY A type of psychological therapy in which the client was encouraged to 'tune out' sensory distraction; concentration therapy gave rise to Gestalt therapy. See Gestalt therapy, Humanistic psychology

**concept-therapy adjusting technique** Zone testing, see there

**Concept Therapy® technique** ALTERNATIVE MEDICINE A permutation of chiropractic developed in 1931 by an American chiropractor, Thurman Fleet (1895-1983); it consists of a diagnostic component—zone therapy diagnosis or zone testing, and a therapeutic component—suggestive zone therapy, in which the patient is guided to 'think away' his disease through positive thoughts; Concept Therapy divides the body into six health zones, each of which may respond to chiropractic adjustments. See Chiropractic, Health zone

**concommitant symptom** HOMEOPATHY A general term for any symptom that accompanies the main symptom; as an example, if the main symptom is a migraine, accompanying nausea would be a concommitant symptom. See Homeopathic symptom, Homeopathy

**conditioning** ALTERNATIVE PSYCHOLOGY Behavioral intervention, see there

**condom** A diaphanous device[1] for preventing sexually-transmitted diseases[2]. See Contraception, Natural family planning, Pearl index

[1]The name condom was first used in English in 1705 by the Duke of Argyll; it is unclear whether a Dr Condom existed, nor, despite there being a ville de Condom in southern France, is there evidence linking the appliance with a French origin [2]In a longitudinal (20 months) study of couples in which one partner was HIV-positive, use of condoms prevented transmission to the other partner (episodes of intercourse ± 15,000, 124 couples); in 121 couples, condom use was sporadic, and HIV seroconversion occurred at a rate of 4.8/100 (*N Engl J Med 1994; 331:341*OA, *391*ED)

**conductant** CHINESE MEDICINE Any of a number of ingredients that are incorporated into a Chinese herbal formula that is intended to channel the effects of the medication to the *chi* (*qi*). See Chinese herbal medicine; Cf Correctant

**coneflower** Echinacea, see there, *Echinacea angustifolia*, *E pallida*, *E pupura*

**confrontation therapy** ALTERNATIVE PSYCHOLOGY A general term for any format of psychotherapy, first developed by Sandor Ferenczi, in which the client is confronted with the therapist's interpretation of what is occurring in the client's mind, which is often discordant with the client's view of the evolving events; Cf Client-centered therapy

**congestion** ALTERNATIVE MEDICINE A general term for any hypothetical blockage in the flow of vital energy or *qi* through the body; congestion is viewed by many of the practitioners of vibrational medicine as being the primary cause of internal disease. See Vibration medicine

***Conioselenium univittatum*** *Ligusticum wallichii*, see there

**conjugated linoleic acid** ALTERNATIVE ONCOLOGY A long-chain fatty acid that is a free radical scavenger, which is reported to prevent cancer formation in mice (*Moss, 1992*); Cf Gamma linoleic acid, Linoleic acid

**connective tissue massage** Bindegewebsmassage A form of massage that manipulates the connective tissues, eg fascia, ligaments, and tendons of the musculoskeletal system, with the aim of enhancing circulation, and by extension, healing, eg of sport injuries; the technique consists of dragging motions with hooked fingers, which are believed to stimulate the trigger zones that refer pain to other places in the body; see Massage therapy

**conscious breathing** Conscious-connected breathing, see there

**conscious-connected breathing** Circular breathing, conscious breathing, free breathing, vivation ALTERNATIVE PSYCHOLOGY A component of rebirthing therapy in which the client hyperventilates as a means of releasing tensions that are believed to have begun at birth; in the early forms of rebirthing, Leonard Orr (the developer of rebirthing therapy) had his clients submerge in water with nose clips in place, while breathing through a snorkel, a process he termed 'wet rebirthing'; he subsequently developed 'dry rebirthing' which appeared to have the same effect. See Humanistic psychology, Rebirthing therapy; Cf Primal scream therapy

**conscious manifestation** Manifesting, see there

**consormol** Comfrey, see there, *Symphytum officinale*

**constitution** FRINGE MEDICINE-IRIDOLOGY Iris constitution, see there HOMEOPATHY Constitutional type

**constitutional prescribing** HOMEOPATHY The selection of a homeopathic remedy based on a person's constitutional type, which is determined by a complete homeopathic evaluation. See Constitutional remedy, Constitutional type

**constitutional remedy** AYURVEDIC MEDICINE Any of a number of therapeutic maneuvers, including diet, mild herbs, mineral preparations, and lifestyle adjustments, which are intended to balance life forces, and return the body to its normal state of harmony HOMEOPATHY A therapeutic agent in the homeopathic formulary that is chosen based on a person's individual constitutional type, which takes into account the person's symptoms, personality, genetic, and familial characteristics; in some cases, acute and chronic homeopathic remedies may also be constitutional remedies. See Homeopathic remedy, Homeopathy, Proving, Remedy, Vital force

**constitutional type** HOMEOPATHY A person's inherited and acquired physical, mental, and emotional composition, personality, and temperament. See Constitutional prescribing, Constitutional remedy, Homeopathy

**consultation clause** MEDICAL HISTORY–ALTERNATIVE MEDICINE A ruling by the American Medical Association in the 1870s that any doctor who consulted a homeopath or other nonregular practitioner would lose his membership in the AMA, and in effect could not legally practice medicine; the consultation clause was eventually dropped, but not before discrediting homeopathic principles in the eyes of the public; Cf Chiropractic malpractice, *Wilks* v *AMA*

**contact healing** (the) Laying on of hands, see there

**contour cream** FRINGE MEDICINE Any of a number of lotions containing vitamins and herbs that are used in performing a body wrap; contour creams are claimed to help a person lose weight and increase a sense of well-being. See Body wrap

**contrast sitz bath** Alternating sitz bath, see there

**contraception** A general term for any form of family planning that does not rely on artificial agents (eg oral contraceptives, 'morning-after' pill, spermicidal foam, RU486) or devices (eg condoms, diaphragms, IUDs) to prevent conception; natural family planning hinges on the use of the rhythm (calendar) method, coitus interruptus, and prolonged breastfeeding as contraceptive maneuvers. See Breast feeding, Coitus interruptus, Contraception, Natural family planning, Pearl index, Rhythm method

**Contreras method** FRINGE ONCOLOGY A proprietary form of unproven cancer management based on the use of laetrile and administered in a private 'clinica' in Tijuana, Mexico; according to information from the American Cancer Society, Ernesto Contreras Rodriquez (born in 1915) also diagnosed cancer by the Beard Anthrone Test and the Hemacytology Index (*American Cancer Society, Unproven Methods of Cancer Management, 1971*); see Beard Anthrone Test, Hemacytology Index, Laetrile, Manner cocktail, Tijuana, Unproven methods for cancer management

**control measurement points** see Energy medicine

***Convalaria majalis*** Popularly known as lily-of-the-valley, see there

**conventional medicine** Mainstream medicine, see there

***Convolvulus sepium*** Popularly known as bindweed, see there

**cooking** CLINICAL NUTRITION The preparation of comestibles by heating, which is virtually required for meats prior to consumption; overcooking results in the production of carcinogenic polycyclic amines; undercooking carries the risk of parasitic (eg *Taenia solium*, *T saginatus*), or bacterial (eg *E coli* 0157:H7, *Salmonella* spp) infections (*Am Med News 20 May 1996, p16*)

**cooking utensil** ALTERNATIVE NUTRITION A tool used in the preparation of cooked comestibles; according to some interested in alternative health, aluminum and copper may leach from the cookware into the food, causing unknown and possibly detrimental effects; among those who adhere to a macrobiotic diet, preferred utensils for cooking include cast iron, stainless steel, and enamel pots, ceramic and tempered glass for baking, and wood or bamboo utensils for preparing the foods

**copper** A metallic element (atomic number 29; atomic weight 63.56) that is an essential trace mineral, which is linked to key metabolic reactions, including iron absorption and metabolism, and formation of red blood cells and nerves; it is present in mollusks, organ meats, nuts, legumes, and seeds HOMEOPATHY *Cuprum met*, see there, *Cupurm metallicum*

**copper bracelet** FRINGE MEDICINE A pure copper bracelet believed to be effective in ameliorating rheumatic symptoms. See Copper

**coptis** *Coptis sinensis, C teeta, C chinensis, C deltoidea*, Chinese goldthread, *huang lien*, mishmi bitter CHINESE MEDICINE A perennial herb, the root of which contains berberine; coptis is antimicrobial, antipyretic, and a general antidote, and is used for abscesses, alcohol and other intoxications, anginal pain, bloodshot eyes, diarrhea, halitosis, hematuria, high fever, gastritis, heatstroke, hepatitis, inflammatory bowel disease, jaundice, and intestinal parasitosis. See Chinese herbal medicine

***Coptis chinensis*** Popularly known as coptis, see there

***Coptis deltoidea*** Coptis, see there, *Coptis sinensis*

***Coptis sinensis*** Popularly known as coptis, see there

***Coptis teeta*** Coptis, see there, *Coptis sinensis*

***Cordalis ambigua*** *Yen hu suo* CHINESE MEDICINE A perennial herb, the root of which contains alkaloids including corybulbine, corycavadine, isocorybulbine, and others; *C ambigua* is analgesic, antispasmodic, cardiotonic, and sedative, and used for pain, menstrual disorders, and traumatic injuries. See Chinese herbal medicine

***Cordiceps sinensis*** Popularly known as winter worm-summer grass, see there

**core energetic therapy** Core energetics, see there

**core energetics** Core energetic therapy A type of bodywork developed in the late 1970s by JC Pierrakos, in which a person's 'energy field' (*chakra*) is balanced by an eclectic system; the system is based on Pierrakos' personal experience, Reichian therapy, and a series of lectures transmitted through his wife, Eva Pierrakos, by a spirit entity known as 'the Guide'. See Bodywork, *Chakra*

**core issue** A term coined by T Loowen for the visible effects of emotional, psychological, and physical trauma which, once identified, can be treated with LoowenWork™. See LoowenWork®

**coriander** *Coriandrum sativum* HERBAL MEDICINE An annual herb that contains volatile oils including corioandrol and pinene, which has been used as an appetite stimulant, carminative, and gastrointestinal tonic. See Herbal medicine

***Coriander sativum*** Coriander, see there

**coriander** *Coriandrum sativum*

**corkwood** *Duboisia myoporoides* HERBAL MEDICINE An Australian tree that is an important commercial source of scopolamine and atropine. See Herbal medicine

**cornflower** 1. European centaury, see there, *Centaurium umbellatum* 2. Cornflower, *Centaurea cyanus* HERBAL MEDICINE A flowering annual native to Europe and the Near East, which contains cyanine and phytosterols; it has been used for conjunctivitis and coughs. See Herbal medicine

***Cornus florida*** Popularly known as dogwood (tree), see there

***Cornus officinalis*** Popularly known as dogwood tree, see there

**corona discharge photography** Kirlian photography, see there

**correctant** CHINESE MEDICINE Any of a number of ingredients incorporated into a Chinese herbal formula that is intended to counter the side effects of one or more of the herbs used in the medicine. See Chinese herbal medicine; Cf Conductant

**corydalis** *Corydalis yanhusuo* CHINESE MEDICINE An herb, the root of which is used in Chinese medicine and regarded as a potent analgesic; it is used for abdominal, arthritic, chest, menstrual, and post-traumatic pain. See Chinese herbal medicine

**cosmic *chi kung*** Cosmic energy *chi kung*, see there

**cosmic energy *chi kung*** Cosmic healing *chi kung*, cosmic *chi kung* A permutation of *Qigong* therapy and self-healing that is believed to '...*cultivate, channel, and mix the cosmic force with the saliva to nourish chi.*' (*Raso, 1994*); the therapy is accomplished by using acupuncture points in the hand to activate the meridians in the body. See *Qigong* therapy

**cosmic healing *chi kung*** Cosmic energy *chi kung*, see there

**cosmic vibrational healing** PARANORMAL PHENOMENA A form of medical astrology

▶ **BELIEFS, COSMIC VIBRATIONAL HEALING**

- Humans absorb cosmic (celestial, stellar) energy
- Different stars have different effects
- The brighter the star, the greater its influence on a person
- Humans can attune themselves to a particular star by either meditation or through ingestion or application of 'starlight elixirs' (*Raso, 1994*)

See Medical astrology, 'Starlight elixir'

**cosmobiology** See Medicinal astrology

**costus** *Saussurea lappa, mu hsiang, mu xiang* CHINESE MEDICINE A perennial herb, the root of which contains an alkaloid (saussurine) and essential oils; costus is analgesic, antiseptic, antispasmodic, carminative, and is used for abdominal discomfort, angina pectoris, crushing chest pain, asthma, body odor, diarrhea, nausea, and is believed to calm the fetus during pregnancy. See Chinese herbal medicine

**costus root** Aucklandia. see there, *Aucklandia lappa*

**cottonweed** Milkweed, see there, *Asclepia syriaca*

**couch grass** *Agropyron repens*, dog grass, quack grass, quick grass, scutch, triticum, twitch grass, witch grass HERBAL MEDICINE A perennial grass, the rhizomes of which contain inositol, mannitol, mucilage, saponin, vitamins A and B, and volatile oil; it is antimicrobial, diuretic, and a liver tonic, and has been used to treat urinary tract disease, kidney stones, and prostatitis. See Herbal medicine

**Couéism** Autosuggestion therapy, see there

**cough wort** Coltsfoot, see there, *Tussilago farfara*

**counseling** PSYCHOLOGY A relationship in which a professional or trained individual attempts to help another understand and solve his difficulties in psychosocial adjustment; counselors may also advise, opine, and instruct, in order to direct another's judgement or conduct. See Psychotherapy; Cf Cocounseling

**counterirritant** A general term for any substance applied to the skin which, by acting as an irritant on a painful zone, serves to attenuate the sensation of pain; capsaicin, obtained from (hot) chili peppers is a well-known counterirritant. See Capsaicin

**countryman's treacle** Rue, see there, *Ruta graveolens*

***A Course in Miracles*** ALTERNATIVE PSYCHOLOGY A 3-volume, 1000-page self-study program by Marianne Williamson, which is regarded by some as a form of spiritual psychology

**cow clover** Red clover, see there, *Trifolium pratense*

**cowherd** *Saponaria vaccaria*, forbidden palace flower, *jin gung hua*, soapwort, *wang bu lio xing, wang bu liu hsing* CHINESE MEDICINE An annual herb, the seeds of which contain saponins; cowherd is analgesic, astringent, expectorant, laxative, stimulates secretion, and is used to treat abscesses, chronic cough, headaches, menstrual disorders, paresthesias, poor lactation in nursing mothers, and strokes. See Chinese herbal medicine

**cow manure factor** Vitamin $B_{12}$, see there

**cowslip** *Primula veris*, European cowslip, fairy cup, keyflower, key of heaven, paigle, palsywort HERBAL MEDICINE A perennial herb, the flowers and roots of which contain flavonoids, glycosides, and saponins; it is analgesic, antispasmodic, diuretic, expectorant, laxative, and sedative, and has been used internally to treat arthritis, headache, insomnia, measles, paralysis, repiratory tract infections, and restlessness, and topically for sunburns. See Herbal medicine

**cramp bark** 1. Black haw, see there, *Viburnum prunifolium* 2. *Viburnum opulus*, cranberry bush, cranberry tree, European cranberry bush, European Guelder rose, Guelder rose, highbush cranberry, pembina, pimbina, snowball tree, whitten tree HERBAL MEDICINE A deciduous shrub, the bark of which contains valeric acid, tannin, viburnin, bitter resin, and vitamin C; it is antispasmodic and used for pregnancy-related cramps, menstrual cramps, and other forms of colic TOXICITY Uncooked berries are poisonous and may cause severe gastrointestinal discomfort. See Botanical toxicity, Herbal medicine, Poisonous plants

**cramp bark** *Viburnum opulus*

**cranberry bush** Cramp bark, see there, *Viburnum opulus*

**cranberry juice** ALTERNATIVE NUTRITION The juice of the American cranberry (*Vaccinium macrocarpon*) that has a long folk tradition in treating urinary tract infections; it has been shown to inhibit the adherence of bacteria to the urothelial mucosa. See Healthy foods HERBAL

MEDICINE A juice pressed from cranberries which has long had currency as a folk remedy for urinary tract infections, an effect attributed to blocking of the attachment of bacterial pili to the urothelial mucosa, and to the presence of hippuric acid, which inhibits the growth of bacteria in urine. See Diuretic, Herbal medicine

**cranberry tree** Cramp bark, see there, *Viburnum opulus*

**crane style *chi gong*** Soaring crane *qigong*, see there

**cranesbill** *Geranium maculatum*

**cranesbill** *Geranium maculatum*, alumroot, dovefoot, old maid's nightcap, shameface, wild geranium HERBAL MEDICINE A perennial herb that is astringent and hemostatic, which has been used internally to treat diarrhea and menstrual bleeding, and topically to reduce swelling. See Herbal medicine

**cranial manipulation** 1. Cranial osteopathy, see there 2. CranioSacral Therapy®, see there 3. Sacro-occipital technique, see there

**cranial osteopathy** Cranial manipulation, cranial technique, cranial work, craniopathy, craniosacral balancing, craniosacral osteopathy OSTEOPATHY A form of alternative osteopathy developed by Dr William G Sutherland (1873-1954), who viewed life as pulsating contractions and expansions that he called the 'breath of life'; according to Sutherland, a healthy craniosacral system pulsates at a rate of 6 to 15 times/minute, which is achieved through therapy; in craniosacral therapy, bones of the skull and face are manipulated to facilitate the flow of the 'living forces', possibly by improving the flow of cerebrospinal fluid; the manipulation is believed to be effective for autism, cerebral palsy, dyslexia, ear infections, edema, epilepsy, headache, hypertension, hypotension, mood disorders, recurrent infections, spinal cord injury, stroke, temporomandibular joint syndrome, stress, tension, tinnitus, and other conditions; cranial osteopathy has three approaches, meningeal, reflex, and sutural–in which the sutures between the cranial bones are manipulated (*Alternative Medicine, Future Med Pub, 1994*). See Osteopathy; Cf CranioSacral Therapy®

**cranial technique** 1. Cranial osteopathy, see there 2. CranioSacral Therapy®, see there 3. Sacro-occipital technique, see there

**cranial work** 1. Cranial osteopathy, see there 2. CranioSacral Therapy®, see there 3. Sacro-occipital technique, see there

**craniopathy** 1. Cranial osteopathy, see there 2. CranioSacral Therapy®, see there 3. Sacro-occipital technique, see there

**craniosacral balancing** 1. Cranial osteopathy, see there 2. CranioSacral Therapy®, see there 3. Sacro-occipital technique, see there

**craniosacral osteopathy** 1. Cranial osteopathy, see there 2. CranioSacral Therapy®, see there 3. Sacro-occipital technique, see there

**craniosacral technique** 1. Cranial osteopathy, see there 2. CranioSacral Therapy®, see there 3. Sacro-occipital technique, see there

**CranioSacral Therapy®** ALTERNATIVE MEDICINE A proprietary form of therapeutic manipulation developed in the 1970s by Dr John E Upledger that is '...*soft tissue-oriented, fluid-oriented, membrane-oriented, and energy-oriented* ... (which is)...*more subtle than any other type of cranial work.*' (*J Upledger, personal communication to Collinge, 1996*); this method contrasts with bone-oriented cranial osteopathy, developed by Sutherland; according to Upledger, cerebrospinal fluid circulation in the craniosacral system can be sensed in a fashion similar to that of the peripheral pulse; CranioSacral Therapy™ consists of light touch over the various points of pulsation, which serves to reestablish a normal symmetrical pulse of the cerebrospinal fluid, and more efficient functioning of the nervous system; Upledger claims success in treating chronic pain, cerebral dysfunction, depression, dyslexia, learning disabilities, Ménière's disease, migraines, spasticity of cerebral palsy, strabismus, and other conditions. See Involuntary mechanism, Cf Cranial Osteopathy, Integrative massage, Massage, Reflexology, Zero balancing of Sacro-occipital technique *RESOURCE: Upledger Institute, 11211 Prosperity Farms Rd, Palm Beach Gardens, FL 33410-3487 ☎ 1.407.622.4334*

**'crash' diet** FRINGE NUTRITION A general term for a semi-starvation type of fad diet that has various formulations; in general, crash diets may be followed for a short time by a person wishing to rapidly lose weight; such radical approaches rarely result in the desired permanent loss of weight. See Diet

***Crataegus monogyna*** Popularly known as hawthorn, see there

***Crataegus oxyacantha*** Hawthorn, see there, *Crataegus monogyna*

**creationism** EVOLUTIONARY BIOLOGY A philosophy based on the Judeo-Christian concept that all forms of life, in particular human life, were created out of 'nothingness', ie de novo; creationism is the virtual opposite of Darwinism or evolution (as known to most scientists), in which all organisms are believed to have evolved from another; despite the lack of valid scientific evidence supporting its theories, creationist 'science' has accrued widespread sympathy in some states of the southeastern US. See Pseudocience, Gaia hypothesis

**creative arts therapy** HUMANISTIC PSYCHOLOGY A general term for nonverbal psychological therapies that are based on natural forms of an individual's expression in art, dance, drama, music, poetry, and other fine arts, as a vehicle for expressing a person's internal conflicts and emotional imbalances. See Art therapy, Dance therapy, Drama therapy, Music therapy, Poetry therapy

**creative imagery** Imagery (and visualization), see there

**creative visualization** Imagery (and visualization), see there

**creeping Charlie** Ground ivy, see there, *Glechoma hederacea*

**creeping lilyturf** *Liriope spicata, mai men dung* CHINESE MEDICINE A perennial herb, the root of which is anti-inflammatory, antitussive, cardiotonic, diuretic, and emollient; it is used for poor circulation, cough, diabetes mellitus, hypoglycemia, recuperation from labor, surgery, and disease, hemoptysis, and shortness of breath. See Chinese herbal medicine

**creosote bush** Chaparral, see there, *Larrea tridentata*, *Larrea tridentata*

**critical period** PARANORMAL PHENOMENA A point in a biological rhythm (biorhythm) that occurs when an individual crosses the middle of a cycle, either from a high to a low or a low to a high; during critical periods, the person is believed to be more accident- and illness-prone. See Biorhythm, Kosmos

**crocin** PHARMACOGNOSY A mixture of two flavonol glycosides (crocetin, a carotenoid-dicarboxylic acid and α-crocin, a di-gentiobiose ester of crocetin), which are abundant in the stigmas and styles of saffron (*Crocus sativus*) flowers, and have a prostaglandin-like structure; intramuscular injection of crocetin in rabbits increases oxygen diffusion in plasma, decreases serum cholesterol, and decreases incidence of atherosclerosis. See Saffron

***Crocus sativus*** Popularly known as saffron, see there

**Crook diet** ALTERNATIVE NUTRITION A diet developed by Dr Wm G Crook, which he believes to be of use in treating the so-called candidiasis hypersensitivity syndrome (yeast syndrome); eliminated from Crook's regimen are refined starches and sugars, foods made from yeasts including breads, pastries, alcohol, vinegar, soy sauce, buttermilk, sour cream or other food products produced by fermentation, coffee, tea, dairy products, dried fruits, vegetables, herbs, smoked fish and meats, fruits, mushrooms, or chocolate; he recommends that some foods be cleaned with dilute bleach; the Crook diet is high in fat and cholesterol. See Candidiasis hypersensitivity syndrome, Diet

**cross-fiber friction massage** Deep transverse friction massage A form of massage in which the therapist applies friction to the muscle perpendicularly to the length of the fibers, which is believed to mechanically reset the proprioceptors; cross-fiber massage is widely used

the collection from the Baroque. And the voices of North American writers and writers of color begin to be heard in the collection from the nineteenth century.

There is need to develop further these once-marginal strands in the representation of Western music history, and to draw in still others, perhaps in some future version of this series, and elsewhere—the musical cultures of Latin America for one example, whose absence is lamented by Murata, and the representation of the Middle Ages in their truly cosmopolitan aspect, for another.

This series of books remains at its core the conception and the work of Oliver Strunk. Its revision is the achievement of the editors of the individual volumes, most of whom have in turn benefited from the advice of numerous colleagues working in their fields of specialization. Participating in such a broadly collaborative venture has been a most gratifying experience, and an encouraging one in a time that is sometimes marked by a certain agonistic temper.

The initiative for this revision came in 1988 from Claire Brook, who was then music editor of W. W. Norton. I am indebted to her for granting me the privilege of organizing it and for our fruitful planning discussions at the outset. Her thoughts about the project are manifested in the outcome in too many ways to enumerate. Her successor Michael Ochs has been a dedicated and active editor, aiming always for the highest standards and expediting with expertise the complex tasks that such a project entails.

Leo Treitler
*Lake Hill, New York*



to have proceeded no further but to have left it off as shamefully as it was foolishly begun. But then being admonished by some of my friends that it were pity to lose the fruits of the employment of so many good hours, and how justly I should be condemned of ignorant presumption—in taking that in hand which I could not perform—if I did not go forward, I resolved to endure whatsoever pain, labor, loss of time and expense, and what not, rather than to leave that unbrought to an end in the which I was so far engulfed.[5]

OLIVER STRUNK
*The American Academy in Rome*

5. Thomas Morley, *A Plain and Easy Introduction to Practical Music,* ed. R. Alec Harman (New York: Norton, 1966), p. 5.

# FOREWORD TO THE REVISED EDITION

*Hiding in the peace of these deserts*
*with few but wise books bound together*
*I live in conversation with the departed,*
*and listen with my eyes to the dead.*
*—Francisco Gómez de Quevedo*
*(1580–1645)*

The inclusion here of portions of Oliver Strunk's foreword to the original edition of this classic work (to which he habitually referred ironically as his *opus unicum*) is already a kind of exception to his own stricture to collect in it only "historical documents as such, excluding the writing of present-day historians." For his foreword itself, together with the book whose purpose and principles it enunciates and the readings it introduces, comes down to us as a historical document with which this revision is in a conversation—one that ranges over many subjects, even the very nature of music history.

This principle of exclusion worked for Strunk because he stopped his gathering short of the twentieth century, which has been characterized—as Robert Morgan observes in his introduction to the twentieth-century readings in this series—by "a deep-seated self-consciousness about what music is, to whom it should be addressed, and its proper role within the contemporary world." It is hardly possible to segregate historian from historical actor in our century.

For the collection in each of the seven volumes in this series the conversation begins explicitly with an introductory essay by its editor and continues with the readings themselves. The essays provide occasions for the authors to describe the considerations that guide their choices and to reflect on the character of the age in each instance, on the regard in which that age has been held in music-historical tradition, on its place in the panorama of music history as we construct and continually reconstruct it, and on the significance of the readings themselves. These essays constitute in each case the only substantial explicit interventions by the editors. We have otherwise sought to follow Strunk's own essentially conservative guidelines for annotations.

The essays present new perspectives on music history that have much in common, whatever their differences, and they present new perspectives on the music that is associated with the readings. They have implications, therefore, for those concerned with the analysis and theory of music as well as for students of music history. It is recommended that even readers whose interest is focused on one particular age acquaint themselves with all of these essays.

The opportunity presented by this revision to enlarge the book has, of course, made it possible to extend the reach of its contents. Its broader scope reflects achievement since 1950 in research and publication. But it reflects, as well, shifts in the interests and attitudes that guide music scholarship, even changes in intellectual mood in general. That is most immediately evident in the revised taxonomy of musical periods manifest in the new titles for some of the volumes, and it becomes still more evident in the introductory essays. The collections for "Antiquity and the Middle Ages" have been separated and enlarged. What was "The Greek View of Music" has become *Greek Views of Music* (eight of them, writes Thomas J. Mathiesen), and "The Middle Ages" is now, as James McKinnon articulates it, *The Early Christian Period and the Latin Middle Ages.* There is no longer a collection for "The Classical Era" but one for *The Late Eighteenth Century,* and in place of the epithet "The Romantic Era" Ruth Solie has chosen *The Nineteenth Century.* The replacements in the latter two cases represent a questioning of the labels "Classic" and "Romantic," long familiar as tokens for the phases of an era of "common practice" that has been held to constitute the musical present. The historiographic issues that are entailed here are clarified in Solie's and Wye Jamison Allanbrook's introductory essays. And the habit of thought that is in question is, of course, directly challenged as well by the very addition of a collection of readings from the twentieth century, which makes its own claims to speak for the present. Only the labels "Renaissance" and "Baroque" have been retained as period



designations. But the former is represented by Gary Tomlinson as
fragmentation, for which "Renaissance" is retained only *faute de mieu*
to the latter, Margaret Murata places new emphasis on the indetermi
of its music.

These new vantage points honor—perhaps more sharply than he wo
expected—Strunk's own wish "to do justice to every age," to eschew th
ous unity" of a "particular point of view" and the representation of his
succession of uniform periods, allowing the music and music-directed
of *each* age to appear as an "independent phenomenon," as Allanbroo
have us regard the late eighteenth century.

The possibility of including a larger number of readings in this revisio
have been thought to hold out the promise of our achieving greater fa
with each age. But several of the editors have made clear—explicitly or
itly through their selections—that as we learn more about a culture i
"more, not less distant and estranged from ours," as Tomlinson writes
Renaissance. That is hardly surprising. If the appearance of familia
arisen out of a tendency to represent the past in our own image, we
hardly wonder that the past sounds foreign to us—at least initially—as w
it to speak to us more directly in its own voice.

But these words are written as though we would have a clear vision
image in the late twentieth century, something that hardly takes acco
the link, to which Tomlinson draws attention, between the decline
confidence about historical certainties and the loss of certainty abo
own identities. Standing neck-deep in the twentieth century, surround
uncountable numbers of voices all speaking at once, the editor of this
selection of source readings may, ironically, have the most difficult time
in arriving at a selection that will make a recognizable portrait of the a
Morgan confesses.

Confronted with a present and past more strange and uncertain than
we have been pleased to think, the editors have not been able to carry on
in the spirit of Strunk's assuredness about making accessible "those t
which [the student] must eventually read." Accordingly, this revision i
forward with no claim for the canonical status of its contents. That ai
necessarily yielded some ground to a wish to bring into the conversation
has heretofore been marginal or altogether silent in accounts of music his

The sceptical tract *Against the Professors* by Sextus Empiricus, among
readings from ancient Greece, is the first of numerous readings that run ag
a "mainstream," with the readings gathered under the heading "Music, M
Gnosis" in the Renaissance section being perhaps the most striking. The
sage from Hildegard's *Epistle* to the prelates of Mainz in the medieval col
tion is the first of many selections written by women. The readings grou
under the reading "European Awareness of Other Musical Worlds" in
Renaissance collection evince the earliest attention paid to that subject. A r
prominence is given to performance and to the reactions of listeners

# CONTENTS

# NOTES AND ABBREVIATIONS

Footnotes originating with the authors of the texts are marked [Au.], those with the translators [Tr.].

Omitted text is indicated by five spaced bullets (• • • • •); three spaced bullets (• • •) indicate a typographical break in the original.

# THE NINETEENTH CENTURY

in physical therapy, sports massage–where it is used on trigger points, to treat tendinitis—and as a means of preventing scar tissue formation; cross-fiber massage is believed to release knots (painful spasms). See Massage therapy, Proprioceptors

**cross-fiber frictioning** Cross-fiber friction massage, see there

**crosswort** Boneset, see there, *Eupatorium perfoliatum*

**crowberry** Bearberry, see there, *Arctostaphylos uva-ursi*

**crow corn** Colicroot, see there, *Aletris farinosa*

**crown *chakra*** AYURVEDIC MEDICINE The seventh *chakra*, that governs the individual's relationship with the cosmic force or universal self, which is located at the top of the head, and associated with the pineal gland and the color purple. See Ayurvedic medicine, *Chakra*

**cruciferous vegetable** CLINICAL NUTRITION Any of a family of indole-rich vegetables (eg broccoli, Brussels sprouts, cabbage, cauliflower and mustard), that have anti-tumor promoting activity in laboratory animals; colon cancer is associated with decreased consumption of cruciferous vegetables. See Indole; Cf Tumor promoter

**crude** HERBAL MEDICINE Pertaining or referring to an herb that is 'prepared' by drying, without any other form of manipulation or derivitization. See Herbal medicine

**crude calcium sulfide** *Hepar sulf*, see there, *Hepar sulfuris calcareum*

**cryonics** HEALTH FRAUD The placing of a dead person (fee $100,000 each) or his head and brain (fee $35,000 per head) in a frozen state; the cryonics industry 'sells' the hope that when medical science advances to the point of regenerating tissues and curing the disease that caused the person's death, the person will be brought back from a state of 'suspended animation' (the bodies being frozen are, in fact, legally dead) and continue with his life; brain tissue undergoes irreversible changes at death; there is no scientific data to support the claim that vitalization is possible. See Health fraud

**cryotherapy** ALTERNATIVE MEDICINE Cold therapy, see there

**crystal healing** Crystal therapy, see there

**crystal therapeutics** Crystal therapy, see there

**crystal therapy** Crystal healing, crystal therapeutics, crystal work, gem therapy FRINGE MEDICINE The use of certain types of crystals, in particular quartz, as a therapeutic vehicle; crystal therapy is based on the assertion that all life forms are immersed in an energy field which can be altered by crystals that emit negative ions; used in conjunction with meditation and breathing exercise, crystals are believed to help a person contact 'higher' powers; crystal therapy is believed by its proponents to be of use in treating various mental, physical, or emotional conditions; it has had a long tradition in ayurvedic medicine as a means of *chakra* balancing; it is an integral component of aura balancing, color therapy, and radiesthesia, and has been used as an adjunct to acupressure and self-healing; before a therapeutic gem can be used, it should be 'cleared' of vibrations or other imprints. See Clearing, Laying on of stones

**crystal work** Crystal therapy, see there

**CuDIPS** ALTERNATIVE ONCOLOGY A copper-based superoxide dismutase that inhibits the growth of experimental cancer cells in mice by penetrating the malignant cells and scavenging free radicals (*Moss, 1992*). See Unproven methods for cancer management

**cult** PSYCHIATRY 1. A religious, political, psychotherapeutic, or commercial organization or sect, often with bizarre or unorthodox practices, values, or beliefs that differ widely from mainstream or accepted thinking, which engenders conflict between the group and society, and uses unethical manipulative techniques of persuasion and control to advance the leader's goals (*JAMA 1994; 272:979BR*); cults are often led by a strong-willed person, while the members tend to be mentally pliable; cults may be linked to mass suicides and/or deaths[1] 2. A '...*system of treating disease based on some special or unscientific theory of disease causation*.'[2] (*Dorland's Medical Dictionary, 1994*); Cf Cancer underground, Health food movement

[1]Including the Jonestown mass suicide, in which the cult's 900 members died imbibing cyanide-laced Kool-Aid, the Branch Davidians in Waco, Texas, or the 39 members of the Heaven's Gate cult who committed mass suicide in late March, 1997, in California [2]This definition of the term cult is rarely used in the US

**cultural healing** Shamanism, see there

**culture-bound syndrome** Cultural psychosis ETHNIC PSYCHIATRY A generic term for any of a number of '...*recurrent, locality-specific patterns of aberrant behavior and troubling experience*...', many of which cannot be linked to a particular DSM-IV diagnostic entity; they '...*are generally limited to specific societies or culture areas and are localized, folk, diagnostic categories that frame coherent meanings for certain repetitive, patterned, and troubling sets of experiences and observations*...' (*Diagnosis and Statistical Manual-IV, 1994*); culture-bound syndromes are acting-out behaviors unique to certain, often primitive societies, which are commonly accompanied by a strong component of superstition; one classification divides these reactions into 'taxa' which may have some validity. See Qi-gong psychotic reaction

**Culver's physic** Culver's root, see there, *Veronicastrum virginicum*

**Culver's root** *Veronicastrum virginicum, Lepandra virginica, Verona virginicum*, black root, bourman's root, bowman's root, Brinton root, Culver's physic, physic root HERBAL MEDICINE A perennial herb, the root of which has leptandrin, resin, saponins, tannins, and volatile oil; it is laxative, and has been used for chronic indigestion and liver disorders. See Herbal medicine

**cumulative trauma disorder** Repetitive motion injury, see there

**cupping** CHINESE MEDICINE An ancient Chinese method that is similar to moxabustion, in which either a suction cup (or an 'ad hoc' suction cup, eg moxa, herbal concoctions, or alcohol-soaked cotton burned inside of a cup–which is then flipped over on the skin to create suction) is applied to flat surfaces of the skin, usually at acupuncture points, or on a meridian; the suction is applied for 5 to 10 minutes, and may be repeated elsewhere; anecdotal reports suggest that cupping may be useful for abscesses, arthritis, asthma, back pain, hypertension, increasing local circulation, decreasing muscle pain, pneumonia, and pleuritis; Cf Moxabustion MASSAGE THERAPY A technique in which the cupped hand is used to strike gentle blows on the skin surface, with the intent of increasing local circulation

***Cuprum met*** *Cuprum metallicum*, copper HOMEOPATHY A remedy that is used to treat cramps, fatigue, spasms, and neuralgic pain, as well as asthma and whooping cough. See Homeopathy

**Curaçao aloe** *Aloe vera*, see there

**curandero** ETHNOMEDICINE A native healer or shaman who uses herbal medicines in the primitive cultures of Central America. See Ethnomedicine, Shamanism

***Curculigo ensifolia*** *Hsien yu, hsien mao* CHINESE MEDICINE A biennial herb, the root of which is used for fatigue, impotence, urinary incontinence, paraesthesias, premature senility, and tinnitus; it is believed by some to be an aphrodisiac. See Chinese herbal medicine

**curcumin** A chemical extract from the food spice turmeric AIDS Curcumin was anecdotally reported to have antiretroviral activity, allegedly by inhibiting critical steps in viral replication (*Am Med News 21 Nov 1994 p13*); Cf AIDS fraud HERBAL MEDICINE Curcumin is anti-inflammatory, antioxidant, and inhibits tumor growth; it is used internally for gastric ulcers, cancer, and topically as an analgesic, and for ringworm (*Moss, 1992*). See Herbal medicine, Turmeric

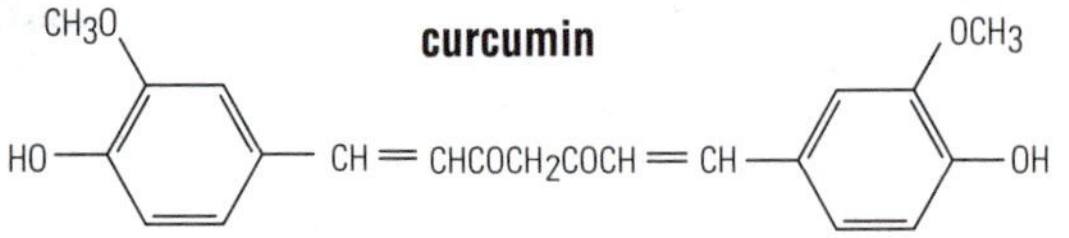

**curcumin**

$CH_3O$, HO — (ring) — $CH = CHCOCH_2COCH = CH$ — (ring) — $OCH_3$, OH

***Curcuma longa*** Turmeric, see there

**curse operation** PARANORMAL PHENOMENA A type of psychic surgery in which materialized objects are allegedly removed from the body. See Psychic surgery

**cuscuta** Dodder, see there, *Cuscuta chinensis*

***Cuscuta chinensis*** Popularly known as dodder, see there

***Cuscuta japonica*** Popularly known as dodder, see there

**cutaneo-organ reflex point** Reflex point, see Reflexology

**cuttlefish** *Sepia*, see there, *Sepia officinalis*

**cyanocobalamin** Vitamin $B_{12}$, see there

**cybernetics** The formal study of the functions

of human control and the mechanical and electronic devices designed to replace them

**cyberphysiology** FRINGE MEDICINE A general term for any technique (eg autogenic training, biofeedback training, imagery and visualization, meditation, use of placebos, self-hypnosis–all discussed elsewhere in this work) which is intended to enable the control of a physiologic process

**cyclamates** FOOD INDUSTRY A family (calcium cyclamate and its metabolites, cyclohexylamine, cyclamic acid, sodium cyclamate) of artificial sweeteners banned by the FDA in 1970, when they were linked to bladder cancer in rats given extremely high doses; subsequent studies have failed to reveal direct, intrinsic genotoxicity of cyclamate although, when added to saccharin (another artificial sweetener), there was an additive tumorigenic effect, causing a focal increase in tumors of the bladder epithelium. See Artificial sweeteners; Cf Sweet protein

**cymatic device** FRINGE MEDICINE An instrument used in energy medicine, in which a sound transducer replaces the electrodes of an electroacupuncture biofeedback device; it is used to generate harmonic signals that are believed to be specific for organs, tissues, and even molecules; health is said to be restored by matching the normal harmonic pattern of the ailing organ, tissues, or molecules (*Alternative Medicine, Future Med Pub, 1994*). See Energy medicine

**cymatic medicine** Cymatics, see there

**cymatic therapy** Cymatics, see there

**cymatics** Cymatic medicine, cymatic therapy FRINGE MEDICINE A form of 'vibrational bioenergetics' medicine developed by a British osteopath, PG Manners, which consists of the administration of high-frequency sound waves, either directly using various handheld applicators or other devices, or indirectly, by placing the patient in a bath with a device that causes 'whole body' vibration; cymatic therapy was believed by its earliest advocates to be effective in treating such diverse conditions as arthritis, gout, rheumatic diseases, sciatica, and slipped vertebral disk; more recently, cymatic therapy has been re-examined by mainstream medical practitioners, in particular orthopedic surgeons, and may accelerate the healing of bone fractures, relieve musculoskeletal tension, and have a positive impact on sports injuries. See Harmonic factor, Sound therapy, Toning

***Cynomorium coccineum*** Squaw root, *suo yang* CHINESE MEDICINE A biennial herb, the root of which is used for constipation, dry mouth, fatigue, impotence, leg weakness, paresthesias, premature ejaculation, and is believed by some to be an aphrodisiac. See Chinese herbal medicine

**cyperus** *Cyperus rotundus*, nutgrass rhizome CHINESE MEDICINE A marsh grass, the root of which is used in Chinese medicine for menstrual disorders and cramping, gastrointestinal complaints (eg bloating), and emotional lability (moodiness). See Chinese herbal medicine

***Cyperus rotundus*** Cyperus, see there

***Cypripedium calceolus*** Popularly known as lady's slipper, see there

***Cytisus scoparius*** Broom, see there, *Sarothamnus scoparius*

**cytotoxic testing** Leukocytotoxic testing FRINGE DIAGNOSTICS A test that was alleged to be useful in identifying food allergies, which consists of placing the patient's white cells on a glass slide coated with any of a number of food allergens; it was claimed that cytotoxic testing allowed laypersons to perform simple blood tests and diagnose food and chemical allergies that caused such diverse conditions as allergies, asthma, baldness, confusion, depression, fatigue, headaches, hormonal imbalances, obesity, ulcers, and many others; cytotoxic testing was determined to be of no diagnostic value by the FDA and banned from the marketplace in the late 1980s

**D need** Deficiency need, see Basic need

***da dzao*** Chinese jujube, see there, *Ziziphus vulgaris*

***da ji hua*** Tiger thistle, see there, *Cirsium japonicum*

***da li dze*** Popularly known as burdock, see there

***da suan*** Garlic, see there, *Allium sativum*

***da zao*** Chinese jujube, see there, *Ziziphus vulgaris*

**D.A.C.B.I.** Diplomate of the American Chiropractic Board of Internists

**D.A.C.B.N.** Diplomate of the American Chiropractic Board of Neurologists

**D.A.C.B.N.** Diplomate of the American Chiropractic Board of Nutrition

**D.A.C.B.O.** Diplomate of the American Chiropractic Board of Orthopedics

**D.A.C.B.R.** Diplomate of the American Chiropractic Board of Radiology

**daily value** CLINICAL NUTRITION A recommendation for the quantity (expressed in percentage) of a specific nutrient that an individual should consume per day in his or her diet; the food packaging labels that are affixed to foods in the US express the daily value in a percentage that corresponds to the total percentage of the daily requirements for a particular nutrient based on a hypothetical 2000-calorie diet; Cf Recommended daily allowance

**damiana** *Turnera diffusa* HERBAL MEDICINE An annual herb that contains cineole, thymol and other volatile oils, cymene, calamenene, a cyanogenic glycosideresin, and others; it is believed to be antimicrobial, laxative, may stimulate the production of sex hormones; it has been used for depression, lethargy, hormonal imbalances, and urogenital disorders; it is believed by some to be an aphrodisiac TOXICITY Headaches, and mild insomnia. See Herbal medicine

***dan gui*** *Angelica sinensis*, see there

**dance (movement) therapy** A therapeutic modality developed in the 1940s by Marian Chace, in which dance movements are used as surrogates of verbal communication; according to the construct of dance therapy, an individual learns to express his or her emotions through the vocabulary of dance, and ultimately to relieve inhibitions and tension; certain aspects of dance, eg synchrony and rhythm, are thought to promote healing; dance therapy may be effective in treating physical and learning disabilities, mental retardation, children with attention deficit-hyperactivity disorder, adolescents with anorexia or bulimia, and adults with problems in communication and in forming interpersonal relationships. See Art therapy, Alexander technique, Movement therapy, Music therapy, Play therapy, Recreational therapy

**dancing mushroom** Maitake, see there

**dandelion** A perennial herb that contains inulin, bitter principles, and sesquiterpenes; the roots are rich in vitamins A and C; Chinese and Western herbalists use two different species for different indications CHINESE HERBAL MEDICINE *Taraxacum mongolicum*, *huang hua di ding*, *pu gung ying* In Chinese herbal medicine, the entire plant has been used as an antidote, anti-inflammatory, to dissolve blood clots, reduce swelling, to promote internal secretions, and it may be antibacterial; dandelions have been used for breast disease and poor lactation, colitis, food poisoning, hepatitis and other liver diseases, gallstones, kidney stones, ocular pain and swelling, snakebites, tuberculosis, and urinary burning. See Chinese herbal medicine FRINGE MEDICINE-FLOWER ESSENCE THERAPY A floral essence believed to provide dynamic energy and promote inner peace. See Flower essence therapy HERBAL MEDICINE *Taraxacum officinale*, blow ball, fairy clock, lion's teeth, *Leontodon taraxacum*, pee in the bed, pissabed, priest's crown, tell-time In Western herbal medicine, dandelion root is used as a diuretic, laxative, tonic, and for poor digestion, gallbladder disease, hepatitis and other liver diseases, congestive heart failure, hypertension, menstrual pain, premenstrual syndrome, and arthritic pain. See Herbal medicine TOXICITY Contact dermatitis, mild diarrhea, heartburn, liver pain, flu-like symptoms; it should not be given to young children

***dang shen*** *Codonopsis pilosula*, see there

***dao-in*** *Do-in*, see there

**dandelion** *Taraxacum officinale*

**Daoist *chi kung*** Taoist *qigong*, see there

**DAS** Diallyl sulfide, see there

***Datura stramonium*** Popularly known as Jimsonweed, see there

***Daucus carota*** Popularly known as Queen Anne's lace, see there

**Dayan *Qigong*** Wild goose breathing exercises A series of 64 exercises based on a stylized interpretation of the movements of the wild goose; it is believed by its proponents to prolong life, and be useful for cardiac disease, chronic fatigue syndrome, gastrointestinal complaints, hepatitis, hypertension, hypotension, insomnia, low back pain, obesity, renal inflammation, rheumatoid arthritis, skin disease, and other conditions. See *Qigong*; Cf T'ai chi ch'uan

**dayflower** *Commelina communis* HERBAL MEDICINE A perennial herb that is native to Asia that is diuretic, which has been used for diarrhea, flu, urinary infections, and sore throats. See Herbal medicine

**Dzhuna Datavitashvili** A Russian former waitress, who in the 1970s achieved fame as a hand healer

**Davis, Adelle** FRINGE NUTRITION A deceased nutritionist, whose books continue to be widely read and sold, despite containing what are regarded as scientific fallacies; Davis believed in the ingestion of massive amounts of vitamins, and encouraged the consumption of high-protein, high-fat, and high-cholesterol foods; despite Davis' university education in nutrition and her advanced degree in biochemistry, her writing was rife with factual errors

▶ **DAVIS' ASSERTIONS**

- Eating too little fat causes obesity
- Americans eat too little protein
- 100,000 IU of vitamin A can be safely consumed for months
- Massive consumption of milk prevents cancer–she died of bone cancer
- Massive doses of vitamin E during pregnancy prevent miscarriage, mental retardation, and birth defects
- Calcium is a tranquilizer
- Magnesium can control epilepsy
- Inositol controls baldness
- All renal failure responds to potassium supplements
- All bruises are a sign of vitamin C deficiency
- PABA (para-amino benzoic acid) supplements can cure Rocky Mountain spotted fever and other rickettsial infections

(*Butler, 1992*)

**D.C.** Doctor of Chiropractic

**de la Warr box** FRINGE MEDICINE A washing machine-like radionics camera invented in the 1950s by a British civil engineer, George de la Warr, which he claimed could document biocurrents present in blood spotted on blotting paper; de la Warr also invented a 'colourscope', which emitted light of different wavelengths that was allegedly useful in treating various conditions; both instruments are regarded as having uncertain efficacy. See Radionics; Cf Abrams generator, Drown box, Emanometer

**De Materia Medica** HERBAL MEDICINE A 'classic' treatise on herbal remedies that was written by Dioscorides in the first century AD, which described more than 600 plants; *De Materia Medica* formed the basis for European herbal medicine, until the publication of *The Complete Herbal* by Culpepper; see Herbal medicine; Cf *Canon of Medicine, Charak Sambita, The Complete Herbal, Natural History, Nei Jing, Pen Ts'ao, Philosophy of Natural Therapeutics, Rigveda, Sushrita Sambita, Theatrum Botanicum*

**deadly nightshade** Belladonna, see there, *Atropa belladonna*

**deadmen's bells** Foxglove, see there, *Digitalis purpurea*

**(the) 'Dean of medical quacks'** Albert Abrams, MD, see there

**death layer** Implosive layer HUMANISTIC PSYCHOLOGY A term used in Gestalt therapy for a layer of the personality that corresponds to that of despair; individuals who function in the death layer are almost catatonic and unaware of their blocked emotions and contracted psychic energy

**decavitamin** CLINICAL NUTRITION A multivitamin preparation which contains vitamins A, $B_1$, $B_2$, $B_6$, $B_{12}$, C, D, E, folic acid, niacin (niacin amide), and calcium pantothenate. See Multivitamin

**decimal** HOMEOPATHY A dilution of 1:10, a factor used in potentization of homeopathic remedies; decimals are expressed X (or less commonly as D–a 6X homeopathic remedy would have one active part in $10^6$ of diluent. See Avogadro's limit, Homeopathic remedy, Potentization; Cf Centesimal

**decoction** HERBAL MEDICINE An herbal preparation, in which the substrate (eg cinnamon bark, ginger root, nuts, seeds, or coarse leaves) is hard or ligneous, making its extraction difficult; decoctions require grinding or pulverization and boiling to extract the volatile oil or substance of interest. See Herbal medicine; Cf Fluid extract, Infusion CHINESE MEDICINE *Tang* A preparation of traditional Chinese medicinal herbs in which the dried herbs are placed in water, boiled until the volume is markedly reduced, and the dregs strained off ADVANTAGE Virtually complete extraction of the herb's essence and medicinal potential and rapid absorption and onset of action DISADVANTAGE Labor-intensive. See Chinese herbal medicine, Steam decoction

**decosaenoic acid** One of the omega-3 (n-3) fatty acids found in fish, which has been shown to increase the high-density lipoprotein ('good') cholesterol in the blood. See Eicosapentanoic acid

**deep compression massage** ALTERNATIVE MEDICINE A type of massage, in which muscle bellies are pumped and squeezed in rapid succession; the muscle is thus treated as if it were the heart in open-heart massage; deep compression massage is believed to accelerate the healing of muscles that have an intrinsically low blood flow; Cf Deep compression massage, Deep tissue sculpting, Manual lymph drainage massage

**deep tissue friction massage** Cross-fiber transverse friction massage, see there

**deep tissue massage** ALTERNATIVE MEDICINE A type of massage, in which the fingers, thumbs, and elbows are used to release chronic muscle tension, using slow deep strokes and friction; the therapist may work perpendicularly to the length of the fibers of the superficial muscles, with the intent of massaging those that lie underneath–hence the name deep tissue massage; the therapy borrows from other forms of bodywork, including *Chua ka*, cross-fiber friction massage, deep tissue sculpting, Hellerwork®, Rolfing®, and others; it is believed to increase blood flow, and be of greatest use in 'problem' muscles for pain, rehabilitation, and arthritic complaints. See Massage therapy; Traditional European massage; Cf Cross-fiber friction massage, Deep compression massage, Manual lymph drainage massage, Neuromuscular massage, Sports massage, Swedish/Esalen massage

**deep tissue sculpting** Muscle sculpting ALTERNATIVE MEDICINE *'A type of bodywork (deep tissue massage) that is characterized by firm, constant compressions and strokes applied parallel to the muscle fibers.'* (*Kastner, Burroughs, 1993*); this sensitive penetrating form of therapeutic touch was developed in the 1970s by C Osborne-Sheets, who borrowed from Gestalt therapy, primal (re-education) therapy, *chua ka*, Swedish and Esalen massage, Rolfing®, and Tragerwork; the technique is performed by pressure or traction on a muscle, followed by releasing; the technique is used as an adjunct to psychotherapy, and is believed to be useful in relieving tension in muscles that are chronically tense due to injury, emotional trauma, or repetitive movements, as seen in athletes or in occupational medicine; it is also believed to be effective in treating poor posture, whiplash injuries, scoliosis, lordosis, and in rehabilitating shortened or tight muscles; the technique is taught to previously-trained massage therapists. See Bodywork, Massage therapy

**deer bamboo** *Polygonatum cirrhifolium*, see there

**deficiency need** Basic need, see there

**delayed sleep phase syndrome** Night-owl insomnia A sleep disorder characterized by the inability to fall asleep for several hours after going to bed; often related to abuse of alcohol or sleeping pills, the condition may respond to bright light therapy administered several hours before bedtime. See Bright light therapy, Seasonal affective disorder

**delta sleep** The deepest form of sleep, which is greatest in children and declines with age; it is thought that tissue repair and regeneration occur most efficiently during delta sleep. See Brain waves, Poor sleeping hygiene

**demulcent** HERBAL MEDICINE An herb that soothes, softens, and protects mucous membranes through a medical or mechanical effect; demulcents include chickweed (*Stellaria media*), coltsfoot (*Tussilago farfara*), comfrey (*Symphytum officinale*), Irish moss (*Chrondrus crispus*), marshmallow (*Althaea officinalis*), slippery elm (*Ulmus fulva*) (*Trattler, 1985*). See Herbal medicine

***Dendrobium nobile*** *Huang tsao, shih hu*, yellow grass CHINESE MEDICINE A perennial epiphyte, the root and stem of which are tonic, and stimulate peristalsis and secretion; it is used for adrenal insufficiency, dehydration, leg weakness, night sweats, and nervous exhaustion. See Chinese herbal medicine

**dental amalgam** ALTERNATIVE DENTISTRY A silver-copper-tin alloy with up to 50% mercury by weight, that has traditionally been used to fill carious teeth; although amalgams have been used in dental restoration since the early 1800s, it is unclear whether prolonged exposure to the relatively inert mercury in amalgam is entirely innocuous (*JAMA 1991; 265:2934/FDA*) and the wisdom of having a toxic heavy metal in the mouth has been questioned; the pulverization required to remove amalgam and substitute fillings with a non-toxic substance transiently increases serum levels of mercury; some data suggest that a single amalgam can release 3-17 μg of mercury/day; in some countries, eg Germany, Sweden, the use of dental amalgams has been either prohibited or severely restricted, with health insurers paying for the cost of replacement of the amalgams with less toxic alternatives, eg composite amalgams. See Alternative dentistry, Fluoridation, Mercury

Note: Some alternative health care providers believe that dental amalgams are responsible for chronic fatigue syndrome, chronic inflammation (eg rheumatoid arthritis, phlebitis, fibromyalgia), numbness, lowering of pain threshold, and immune defects (*Alternative Medicine, Future Med Pub, 1994*)

**depossession** Releasement PARANORMAL PHENOMENA A form of exorcism in which a practitioner of past-life/lives therapy rids the client of nonmaterial entities (ghosts, fairies, elves, and others). See Past-life/lives therapy

**deprenyl** Eldepryl ALTERNATIVE PHARMACOLOGY A prescription drug that is currently being used to treat Parkinson's disease, which has acquired currency among some practitioners of alternative medicine as an anti-aging substance; deprenyl acts on the substantia nigra (a region of the brain that is believed to age more rapidly than the rest of the brain) by blocking the degradation of dopaminergic neurotransmitters

**deprenyl**

$$C_6H_5CH_2CH(CH_3)N(CH_3)CH_2C\equiv CH$$

**deprivation dwarfism** Psychosocial dwarfism, see there

**Dermatron** FRINGE MEDICINE A device invented by a German physician, R Voll, which he believes is of use in monitoring energy disturbances in the body, and locate physical problems, including atherosclerosis, cardiac disease, hypoglycemia, multiple sclerosis, and others. See Electroacupuncture According to Voll; Cf Health fraud

**desensitization** ALLERGY MEDICINE A therapeutic modality that attempts to reduce IgE-mediated hypersensitivity to various substances, by administering ever-increasing amounts of an antigen (eg urushiol in poison ivy, sumac, and pollen), with the purpose of evoking the formation of blocking antibodies. See Elimination diet, Immune tolerance; Cf Bee venom therapy

**desirable weight** CLINICAL NUTRITION A general term for a person's optimal weight for a particular height. See Diet, Obesity

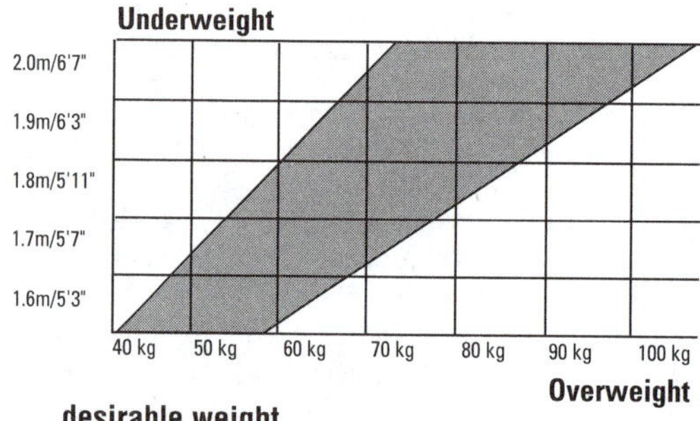


**desirable weight**

**deskercise** A colloquial term for exercises that can be performed while seated at the workplace, which are well-suited for those whose jobs require them to sit for prolonged periods of time, eg in front of a computer workstation; deskercises stretch and loosen the muscles of the upper body, including the back, neck, arms, fingers, and shoulders

**detoxication therapy** ALTERNATIVE MEDICINE A generic term for any maneuver that is intended to rid the body of a myriad of environmental toxins and pollutants (eg food preservatives and additives); detoxification* is a 'metabolic therapy' that includes such unproven maneuvers as enemas with coffee, soapsuds, herbs, and hydrogen peroxide, fasting, specific diets (eg water fasting, alkaline detoxification), colon therapy, vitamin C (ascorbic acid), chelation therapy (with wheat grass or EDTA), hyperthermia (heat stress detoxification), and others (*Alternative Medicine, Future Med Pub, 1994*). See Chelation therapy, Colon therapy INTERNAL MEDICINE A generic term for the removal of a toxic excess of any agent, including therapeutic agent, drug of abuse or toxic agent, eg pesticides, heavy metals, and venoms from the body, by induction of vomiting, administration of activated charcoal, hemodialysis, peritoneal dialysis or use of metabolic interference, eg treating methanol intoxication with ethanol overloading; the term often refers to medically supervised withdrawal from a substance of abuse and treatment of the symptoms of the withdrawal syndrome. See Activated charcoal

*There is little data in peer-reviewed literature to support claims that this form of detoxification therapy is useful for treating acne, arthritis, back pain, food and other allergies, headaches, hemorrhoids, insomnia, joint pain, moodiness, psoriasis, recurrent respiratory problems, sinus congestion, ulcers, and other conditions

**detoxosode** A term for homeovitics formulations (marketed by HoBoN in Naples, Florida), which are '...*vitalized substances that enhance detoxification by their transference of resonant energy to specific toxins in the living system, which is then eliminated.*' (*Raso, 1994*); detoxosodes may contain vitalized food additives, including dyes, mineral oil MSG (monosodium glutamate), sulfites, testosterone, and others. See Homeovitics

**devil's apple** 1. Jimsonweed, see there, *Datura stramonium* 2. Mayapple, see there, *Podophyllum peltatum*

**devil's bit** Fairywand, see there, *Chamaelirium luteum*

**devil's claw** *Harpagophytum procumbens* HERBAL MEDICINE A bitter African herb, the root of which contains harpagoside; it has been used topically for skin lesions, and internally for arthritis, diabetes, gallbladder disease, gastrointestinal complaints, and liver dysfunction. See Herbal medicine

**devil's eye** Henbane, see there, *Hyoscyamus niger*

**devil's plague** Queen Anne's lace, see there, *Daucus carota*

**devil's stone** *Argenticum nitricum*, see there

**dextran sulfate** AIDS FRAUD A high-molecular weight branched-chain polysaccharide polymer of D-glucose that is permeable to water and forms a viscid gelatinous material; it is synthesized commercially or naturally by glycosyl transferases on the surface of some bacteria; it was claimed to have anti-HIV activity;* see AIDS fraud, AIDS therapy

*Dextran sulfate was reported to inhibit HIV-1 and HIV-2 binding to CD4+ cells; therapeutic trials proved disappointing *(Science 1988; 240:646)*

**D.Ht.** Diplomate in Homeotherapeutics

**DHA** Decosahexaenoic acid, see there

**D.H.A.N.P.** Diplomate of the Homeopathic Academy of Naturopathic Physicians

***dhatus*** AYRUVEDIC MEDICINE An Indian term for body tissues; see Ayurvedic medicine

**DHEA** Dihydroepinandrosterone ALTERNATIVE PHARMACOLOGY A hormone that is believed by some to be an effective marker of a person's biological age; some data suggest that DHEA levels are inversely related to the risk for age-related conditions, including cardiovascular disease, diabetes mellitus, cancer, and degenerative diseases; it has been suggested *(Fox, 1996)* that DHEA may be administered to slow aging, increase longevity, and strengthen the immune system. See Unproven methods for cancer management

***di chien tsao*** Gutu kola, see there, *Hydrocotyle asiatica*

***di fu dze*** Belvedere cypress, see there, formally designated *Kochia scoparia*

***di fu zi*** Belvedere cypress, see there, formally designated *Kochia scoparia*

***di hsueh*** Indian madder, see there, *Rubia cordifolia*

***di qien cao*** Gutu kola, see there, *Hydrocotyle asiatica*

**diagnostic witness** FRINGE MEDICINE Witness, see there

**diallyl sulfide** ALTERNATIVE PHARMACOLOGY A substance present in garlic oil that is thought to neutralize various carcinogens and slow tumor growth. See Garlic

**Diamond approach (to inner realization)** Fit for Life program, see there

**Diamond method** See Fit for Life program

***dian xue an mo*** An aggressive form of Chinese *qigong* massage, which focuses on 'acupuncture cavities'. See Acupuncture, *Tui na*

**Dianetics®** A component of Scientology®, founded by L Ron Hubbard (1911-1986); Dianetics® redefines the manner in which the soul affects the body; it provides a means for handling life's energy, to enable a greater efficiency in a person's spiritual life, counseling a client to help him identify and rid himself of emotional and psychosomatic problems; its primary purpose its to erase traumatic memories (engrams) that the therapist ('auditor') may accomplish using an 'E-meter', which measures the galvanic skin response. See E-meter, Scientology®

**diaphoretic** HERBAL MEDICINE An herb that stimulates sweating (diaphoresis), which is often administered as an infusion; diaphoretics include boneset *(Eupato rium perfoliatum)*, catnip *(Nepeta cataria)*, chamomile *(Anthemis nobilis)*, ginger root *(Zingiber officinalis)*, peppermint *(Mentha piperita)*, pleurisy root *(Asclepias tuberosa)*, spearmint *(Mentha viridis)*, and yarrow *(Achillea millefolium)* *(Trattler, 1985)*. See Herbal medicine

**diaphragm breath** AYURVEDIC MEDICINE A type of breathing taught in yoga, in which the practitioner breathes through the nose, expanding only the diaphragm and rib cage; this is preceded by the abdominal breath, and followed by the upper breath, which are linked in a wavelike movement; the three comprise the so-called complete breath of yoga. See Complete breath, Yoga ; Cf Abdominal breath, Upper breath

**diaphragmatic segment** ALTERNATIVE PSYCHOLOGY One of the seven segments of the body according to Reich, which includes the diaphragm, duodenum, gallbladder, kidneys, liver, lower thoracic muscles, pancreas, solar plexus, and stomach, expresses fear and, according to Reich, results in diabetes, gastric ulcers, and liver disease. See Armoring, Body armor, Reich, Reichian therapy

**Diapulse™** ENERGY MEDICINE A therapeutic device that uses radio waves to produce short, intense electromagnetic pulses that penetrate to deep tissues; the heat generated by the pulses is said to improve blood flow, reduce pain, edema, inflammation, and promote healing *(Alternative Medicine, Future Med Pub, 1994)*. See Energy medicine

**diet** NUTRITION To eat and drink either sparingly or according to a prescribed regimen; diets are either for supplementation (ie weight gain) or restriction (ie weight loss); in restriction diets, the intent is to limit one or more dietary components, eg gluten or oxalate, or to globally decrease caloric intake; fat-rich diets are associated with an increased risk of cancers of the breast, colon, ovary, prostate, actinic keratosis, and some skin cancers (*N Engl J Med 1994; 330:1272oA*); the mechanism is unclear. See Affluent diet, Anti-cancer diet, Apple mono diet, Arthritis diet, Astronaut diet, Atkins diet, Balanced diet, Basic health diet, Beverly Hills diet, Bland diet, BRATT diet, Bristol diet, Cabbage juice diet, Cafeteria diet, Collagen diet, 'Crash' diet, Crook diet, Desensitization diet, Dong diet, Elemental diet, Elimination diet, Fad diet, Fasting, Feingold diet, Fit for Life Program, F-plan diet, Gerson therapy, Gluten-free diet, Gorging, Hay diet, Healthy diet, High-fat diet, Hippocrates diet, Hunter-gatherer diet, Juice therapy, *Kapha* diet, Lemonade diet, Life-extending diet, Life-extension formula, Lifestyle diet, Liquid diet, Liquid-protein diet, Low-fat diet, Low-protein diet, MacDougall diet, Macrobiotic diet, Magical diet, McDougall diet, Mediterranean diet, Moerman diet, Mono diet, Mucusless diet, Neo-Paleolithic diet, Nibbling diet, No-nightshade diet, Novelty diet, Numbers diet, nutritional therapy, On-off dieting, Onion mono diet, Orange mono diet, Ornish regimen, *Pitta* diet, Popcorn plus diet, Pritikin diet, Pyramid diet, Rainbow diet, Raw food diet, Rejuvenating diet, Restriction diet, Rice diet, Rotation diet, Scarsdale diet, Soft diet, Southampton diet, Standardized meal, Starvation diet, Step 1 diet, Stillman diet, Swank diet, Taoist five-element nutrition, TOPS, Total parenteral nutrition, *Vata* diet, Veganism, Vegeterianism, Very low calorie diet, Weight Watchers®, Western diet, Wheatgrass diet, Whole foods diet, yo-yo dieting, Zen macrobiotic diet, Zone-favorable diet

**diet pill** Any agent that either suppresses appetite or increases the basal metabolic rate, including amphetamines (available only by prescription) and over-the-counter dietary aids, including phenylpropanolamine, ephedrine, and caffeine, which in high doses, may cause marked agitation, hypertension, seizures, and, rarely, death due to cerebral hemorrhage. See Artificial sweeteners, Diet, Phenolpropanolamine, Starch blocker, Sugar blocker

**diet soda** A calorie-free carbonated beverage sweetened with saccharin or aspartame, which is widely believed to be useful in controlling weight; this belief may be unfounded as the soda is a substitute for water, rather than the high-calorie snacks that are in part responsible for obesity; sodas (diet and other) commonly contain caffeine and phosphoric acid, both of which increase the excretion of calcium, resulting in osteoporosis and caries. See Artificial sweeteners, Aspartame, Saccharin

**dietary fiber** Indigestible plant-derived residues that are composed predominantly of cellulose, hemicellulose, and cell wall polymers; cellulose is common to all plants, lignin is found in most, and pectin is present in fruits; dietary fiber (eg bran lignin, pectin), provides stool 'bulk', increasing the transit time for nutrients in (surgically) shortened gastrointestinal tracts, and decreasing the transit time in long or constipated gastrointestinal tracts; dietary fiber improves the plasma lipid ratios, resulting in a 10-17% decrease in cholesterol (including decreased LDL-cholesterol) as well as a decreased dietary intake of energy, fat, and cholesterol-rich foods; increased dietary intake of fiber is associated with decreased colon cancer and tumor regression in premalignant familial adenomatous polyposis and diverticulosis; low dietary fiber consumption is linked to colorectal cancer, diverticulitis, increased cholesterol, gallbladder disease, constipation, and appendicitis. See Bran, Oat bran, Pectin, Soluble fiber

**dietary guidelines** CARDIOLOGY A series of dietary recommendations (see table, facing page) from the Nutrition Committee of the American Heart Association, that promote cardiovascular health (*New York Times 25 April 1995, pC1*)

**diffusor** FRINGE MEDICINE-AROMATHERAPY Any device used to disperse volatile oils in a particular place, which may be effected by heat (candles or ceramic diffusors placed over a light bulb) or mechanical diffusors and dispersed by an electrical pump that mixes air and the oil. See Aromatherapy

**digestive aid** Any of a family of compounds, including proteins (eg, enzymes—bromelain, pancreatic lipase, papain), as well as betaine, lecithin, and ox bile, which are believed to be of use in helping digest foods. See Diet

***Digitalis*** *Digitalis purpurea*, foxglove HOMEOPATHY A minor homeopathic remedy used for heart failure, bradycardia, weakness, nausea evoked by food, and hepatitis. See Foxglove, Homeopathy

***Digitalis purpurea*** HERBAL MEDICINE Popularly known as foxglove, see there HOMEOPATHY See *Digitalis*

**dill** Anethum graveolens, dillseed, dillweed HER-BAL MEDICINE A culinary and medicinal plant, that has been used as an antimicrobial, appetite stimulant, carminative, and for colic. See Herbal medicine

**dillseed** Dill, see there, *Anethum graveolens*

**dillweed** Dill, see there, *Anethum graveolens*

**dimethylaminoethanol** DMAE ALTERNATIVE PHARMACOLOGY A substance that is believed by its users to prevent or slow mental deterioration and memory loss, increase energy, and stimulate the nervous system

***Dioscorea opposita*** Chinese yam, see there

**diosgenin** HERBAL MEDICINE A saponin that is closely related to human sex hormones, corticosteroids, vitamin D, and cardiac glycosides, which is present in bethroot (*Trillium erectum*). See Bethroot, Herbal medicine

**diphenylhydantoin** Phenytoin ALTERNATIVE PHARMACOLOGY A therapeutic drug used in mainstream medicine as an anticonvulsant; some physicians (*Fox, 1996*) believe phenytoin may be used to reverse age-associated mental impairment, and have recommended its use for certain 'off-label' uses including improvement of concentration by stabilizing electrical activity of neurons, and strengthening long-term memory. See Nervine

**DIETARY GUIDELINES**-AMERICAN HEART ASSOCIATION

1. Fat should be < 30% of total calories
2. Saturated fat should be < 10% of total calories
3. Polyunsaturated fat consumption should be < 300 mg/day
4. Carbohydrates (especially complex type) should constitute ½ of calories in diet
5. Protein constitutes the remainder, ie
   100% – (#1% + #4%)
6. Sodium should be < 3 g/day
7. Alcohol consumption should be ≤ 60 g (2 oz)/day[1]
8. Calories should be sufficient to maintain the body weight[2]
9. A wide variety of food should be consumed[3]

[1]This recommendation might be changed in the future-Author's note, see French paradox [2]see Caloric restriction [3]see Food pyramid

J Am Diet Assoc 1990; 90:223; Proc Nat Acad Sci 1989; 81:1290

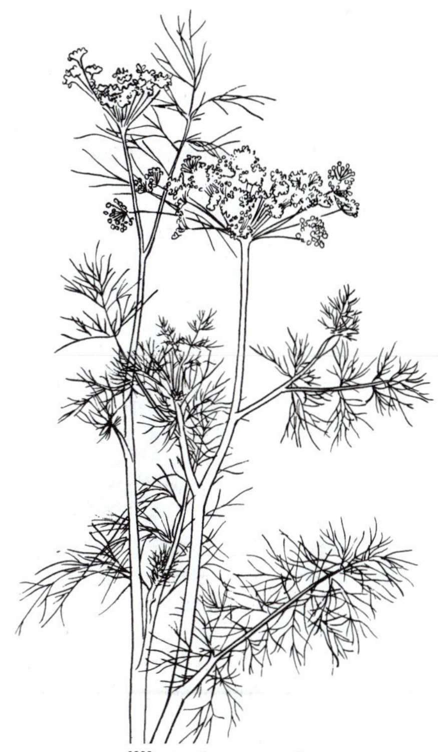

**dill** *Anethum graveolens*

**Dipl. Ac.** Diplomate in Acupuncture

***Dipsacus asper*** see Teasel

***Dipsacus japonicus*** see Teasel

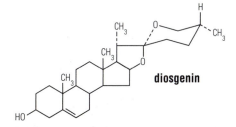

**diosgenin**

***Dipsacus sylvestris*** Popularly known as teasel, see there

**direct healing** Self-healing, see there

**directo** A repetitive, rhythmic thrust used in naprapathy, a system of soft tissue manipulation, which is designed to stretch painful and contracted soft tissues. See Naprapathy

**disease** ALTERNATIVE MEDICINE A state of

disharmonious vibration of the elements and forces affecting humans on one or more planes of existence (*Philosophy of Natural Therapeutics, H Lindlahr, Lindlahr Pub, Chicago, 1919*)

▶ **Disease–Alternative medicine construct**

- Accumulation of toxic material, eg through poor diet
- Incorrect or unbalanced diet
- Improper posture
- Destructive emotions
- The use of suppressive drugs and vaccines
- Use of alcohol, coffee, and tobacco
- Environmental hazards, eg air and water pollution
- Occupational hazards, eg dangerous chemicals, poor air quality, noise pollution, asbestos, and others
- Inherited factors and predispositions
- Infections, which are viewed in the naturopathic construct, as the result of disease (ie through weakening of the natural defenses and so on), and not a primary cause

See *Philosophy of Natural Therapeutics*; Cf Health

**distal point** ACUPUNCTURE A general term for any acupuncture point that is located at a distance from the diseased body region, often at the opposite end of the meridian linked to the affected organ

**distant biological detection** PARANORMAL PHENOMENA Telediagnosis, see there

**distance healing** 1. Prayer for the sick, see there 2. Absent healing, see there

**distant healing** 1. Prayer for the sick, see there 2. Absent healing, see there

**distillation** The process of vaporizing a liquid by heat, condensing it at a cooler temperature, and collecting the condensate; distillation serves to remove volatile impurities or undesired products or concentrate a volatile substance of interest. See Aromatherapy, Flower essence therapy

**distorted thinking** PSYCHOLOGY Any of a number of 'emotional traps' that prevent a person from dealing with negative emotions; David D Burns, MD (University of Pennsylvania) has listed elsewhere various forms of distorted thinking including all-or-nothing thinking, overgeneralization, mental filtering, and personalizing blame. See Cognitive therapy, Humanistic psychology

**diuretic** HERBAL MEDICINE An herb that stimulates urination, which includes bearberry (*Arctostaphylos uva-ursi*), burdock (*Arctium lappa*), couch grass (*Agropyrum repens*), hydrangea (*Hydrangea arborescens*), juniper (*Juniperus communis*), parsley (*Petroselinum sativum*), pellitory-of-the-wall (*Parietaria officinalis*), queen-of-the-meadow (*Eupatorium purpureum*), stone root (*Collinsonia canadensis*), wild carrot (*Daucus carota*), yarrow (*Achillea millefolium*) (*Trattler, 1985*). See Herbal medicine

**divine healing** Faith healing, see there

**divine herb** Ginseng, see there, *Panax ginseng*

**DLPA** D–, L– Phenylalanine, see there

**DMAE** Dimethylaminoethanol, see there

**DMSO** Dimethylsulfoxide A substance that occurs naturally in minute amounts in certain foods, which has been used for various purposes, both industrial and health-related; animal studies have shown it to have analgesic, anti-inflammatory, antimicrobial, vasodilatory, and other effects ALTERNATIVE MEDICINE Up to the 1960s, DMSO had been administered orally, topically, or parenterally by mainstream physicians for various conditions, including arthritis, bursitis, cancer, emphysema, mental illness, and pain; in the face of its association with lenticular degeneration, DMSO was removed from general use; some practitioners of alternative health care continue to recommend DMSO for these and other uses TOXICITY Topical DMSO is associated with burning, itching, and an unpleasant garlic-like odor MAINSTREAM MEDICINE DMSO is FDA-approved for treating interstitial cystitis, and may be of use in scleroderma, sprains, arthritis, cerebrovascular accidents, familial amyloidotic polyneuropathy, and acetaminophen hepatotoxicity; DMSO reduces the ice crystals formed in frozen section tissues from the operating suite, and may be an effective cryopreservative medium

**D.O.** Doctor of Osteopathy

**Dr Doom** MEDICAL HISTORY A colloquial term for Dr Benjamin Rush, see there

**Dr Elbows** A sobriquet for Dr Ida Rolf for her use of the elbows as a therapeutic tool. See Rolfing®

**doctor of osteopathy** D.O., see Osteopathy

**Dr (Edson de) Quiroz** see Psychic healing

**Dr Salomon** see Ziaela/Dr Salomon

**doctrine of contraries** MAINSTREAM MEDICINE A philosophical approach to treating illness, in which a symptom, eg fever, is treated by inducing its opposite, ie, cooling the body; this doctrine has been criticized by practitioners of alternative therapies as being overly simplistic

**doctrine of signatures** AROMATHERAPY A posit proposed by M Maury that the shape, appearance and scent of a particular flower provides information on its particular use. See Aromatherapy HISTORY–HERBAL MEDICINE A belief that was held in the prescientific era, that the shape and color of a particular plant provided information on its best use. See Herbal medicine

**dodder** *Cuscuta japonica, C chinensis*, Chinese dodder, cuscuta, jade woman, *tu seh dze, tu si zi, yeh hu sse, yu nu*, wild fox silk CHINESE MEDICINE A parasitic growth on plants, the seeds of which are tonic, nutritive, and general stimulants; dodder is used to strengthen the musculoskeletal system, retard aging, and improve vision, and has been used for impotence, premature ejaculation, urinary frequency and incontinence, diarrhea, low back pain, presenile dementia, prostate problems, threatened abortion, tinnitus, vertigo, and blurred vision. See Chinese herbal medicine HERBAL MEDICINE The European dodder, *Cuscuta epithymum* has been used by Western herbalists as a laxative, and to treat renal and hepatic disease. See Herbal medicine

**dog brier** Dog rose, see there, *Rosa canina*

**dog grass** Couch grass, see there, *Agropyron repens*

**dog rose** *Rosa canina*, dog brier, wild brier HERBAL MEDICINE A perennial shrub that contains niacin (nicotinamide), organic acids, pectin, tannin, and vitamins B, C, E, and K; it is astringent, diuretic, laxative, and tonic, and has been used to heal wounds; it is a rich source of vitamin C, commonly supplied as rose hips. See Herbal medicine, Rose hips

**dog tree** Dogwood, see there, *Cornus florida*

**dogwood (tree)** Dogwood, see there, *Cornus florida*

**dogwood** *Cornus florida*, boxwood, dog tree, flowering dogwood, Northamerican dogwood, Virginia dogwood HERBAL MEDICINE A tree (see illustration, 116) that was used by Native Americans as an antipyretic and laxative, and has been used by Western herbalists as an appetite stimulant, and to treat renal and hepatic disease. See Herbal medicine; Cf Dogwood tree

**dogwood** *Cornus florida*

**dogwood tree** *Cornus officinalis, rao dzao, shan ju yu, shan zhu yu* CHINESE MEDICINE A deciduous shrub native to eastern Asia, the fruit of which is astringent, diaphoretic, tonic, nutrient, hemostatic, and may also be antihypertensive and diuretic; it has been used

**dog rose** *Rosa canina*

for hypermenorrhea, impotence, night sweats, excessive sweating, low back pain, poor vision, urinary frequency and incontinence, and uterine prolapse. See Chinese herbal medicine; Cf Dogwood

**dogma** Any conviction or system held to encompass a truth

***do-in*** *Dao-in*, Taoist yoga A permutation of acupressure that evolved from a system (Tao-yin) of self massage developed by Chinese Taoist monks over 5000 years ago, in which the pressure is accompanied by stretching, proper breathing, and exercises. See Acupressure; Cf Shiatsu

**Edward Doiry, Sr** CLINICAL NUTRITION An American biochemist who identified vitamin K, for which he won the Nobel Prize in 1943. See Vitamin K

**dolomite** A general term for a specific form of calcium-magnesium carbonate that maybe used as a calcium supplement to ensure healthy bones, which is mined in the Dolomite mountains of Northern Italy (and elsewhere); some of the mineral deposits may be contaminated with heavy metals (lead, cadmium and others), for which there is a maximum ceiling of 5 ppm allowed by the FDA

Note: Dolomite has been claimed by some advocates of alternative health care to be the most natural (and therefore 'healthiest') calcium supplement available; ironically one of the most vocal of the advocates of dolomite's use, Adele Davis, died of a malignant bone tumor

**D.O.M.** Doctor of Oriental Medicine

**domestic kit** HOMEOPATHY A collection of homeopathic remedies selected by Dr Constantine Hering, a German emigrant and the Father of American homeopathy, which contained remedies identified by numbers (to help in home prescribing by laypersons) and accompanied by instructions for their use. See Hahnemann, Homeopathic remedy, Homeopathy

***dong chiung-xia cao*** Winter worm-summer grass, see there, *Cordiceps sinensis*

**Dong diet** CHINESE MEDICINE A diet developed in the 1930s by Dr C H Dong for treating arthritis and dermatitis that is based on traditional high-fiber, low-fat Chinese cuisine, which consists of fresh vegetables, rice, fish, and chicken. See Arthritis diet, Diet, No-nightshade diet

***dong quai*** *Angelica sinensis*, see there

**donkey's ear** Mullein, see there, *Verbascum thapsus*

**Kurt Donsbach** A self-proclaimed nutritionist, who has sold various vitamin and nutrition supplements of uncertain value, published various tracts on, and offered correspondance courses in, pseudonutrition; legal actions taken against him by state and federal authorities have been ineffective; he is currently the administrator of the Hospital Santa Monica in Baja, Mexico, which specializes in alternative therapies (*Butler, 1992*)

**dosed walking** Terrain therapy, see there

***dosha*** AYURVEDIC MEDICINE Any of three broad principles–*kapha* (earth and fire), *pitta* (fire and water), and *vata* (ether and air) which, according to the Ayurvedic construct, are the constituents that orchestrate a person's mental and physiologic functions, including metabolism and mind/body type; each person has some of all three *doshas*, and the individual's *dosha* doses constitute his or her *tridosha*, which has a unique pattern that is divided into 7 different patterns known as *prakriti*. See Ayurvedic medicine, *Kapha*; *Pitta*, *Prakriti*, *Prana*, *Vata*

**double-blinded study** A clinical trial in which both the patients and researchers are unaware of which arm (eg the gold standard therapy, the experimental, or placebo) of the study the patient has been placed in; Cf Anecdotal

A major criticism of alternative medicine by mainstream medical practitioners, is the inability of alternative practitioners to reproduce claimed therapeutic results with double-blinded studies, which are the standards by which mainstream therapies are tested, and approved by the FDA and other regulatory agencies–Author's note

**double-labeled water method** CLINICAL NUTRITION A technique used to measure a person's total energy expenditure, which is accurate to within ± 5%; the method is based on the calculation of $CO_2$ production from the differential disappearance rates of two stable radioisotopes ($^{16}O$ and $^{2}H$) from the body and may be used to determine whether diet resistant obesity is due to a discrepancy between the actual caloric intake and exercise, or due to an alteration in thermogenesis (N Engl J Med 1992; 327:1893 OA,1947ED). See Eye-mouth gap

**douche** HERBAL MEDICINE see Herbal douche

**doula** ALTERNATIVE OBSTETRICS According to the original Greek usage, a doula is an experienced woman who guides and assists a new mother in her infant care tasks; in a US study, the term doula was defined as a woman who provides emotional support to a primiparous woman during labor and delivery; the presence of a doula on the obstetric team is believed by some to decrease the need for a cesarean section, epidural anesthesia, use of oxytocin, and duration of labor (*JAMA 1991; 265:2197*). See Alternative birthing center, Alternative gynecology, Lamaze technique, Midwife, Natural childbirth

**dovefoot** Cranesbill, see there, *Geranium maculatum*

**Dover's Powder** QUACKERY A patent medicine that contained opium and ipecac that was sold in the late 1800s in the American frontier. See Frontier prescription, Patent medicine, Quackery

**dragon's mugwort** Tarragon, see there, *Artemisia dracunculus*

**drama therapy** ALTERNATIVE PSYCHOLOGY An eclectic approach to understanding and alleviating social and psychological conflicts using the vocabulary of theatre; the goal of drama therapy is to effect behavioral, emotional, and cognitive changes through active participation; it is believed to be effective for rehabilitating substance abusers, dysfunctional families, those with developmental disabilities, children, the elderly, prison inmates, AIDS patients, the homeless, and patients with mental disorders; methods used in drama therapy include role-playing, mime, puppetry, and mask work; Registered Drama Therapists have a master's degree, 500 hours of drama and theater experience, 300 hours of formal drama therapy training, and 1000 hours of internship; Cf Art therapy, Dance therapy, Music therapy, Psychodrama

**dread disease** Any of a number of diseases that have a significant impact on lifestyle (eg multiple sclerosis), longevity (eg AIDS, cancer), incur high costs (eg extensive burns, persistent vegetative state), and/or cause significant and permanent residual morbidity, ie loss of eyes or limbs

**dream-guessing ceremony** ETHNOMEDICINE A healing rite practiced by Iroquois medicine men who wear masks woven from cornhusks; among the Iroquois, dreams are believed to be the language of the spirit, and illness the result of a disconnection between the body and spirit. See Shamanism

**dream therapy** PSYCHIATRY A general term for the use of dreams as 'raw material' for analysis of a person's psyche; in Freudian and Jungian analysis, the dreams are interpreted from the therapist's vantage, in the format known as dream appreciation—described by M Ullman at Maimonides Medical Center in New York, the patient is guided to understand and appreciate his dreams and inner thoughts; see Psychoanalysis

**dreamtime** ETHNOMEDICINE A nonmaterial dimension which, in the construct of Australian aborigines, is believed to coexist with the material (physical) universe. See Shamanism

**dreamwork** Dreamworking PSYCHOLOGY The systematic inquiry into, or the use of, dreams for healing and self-actualization; the difference between dreamwork and dream therapy is subtle, but important to some, as the former adds a mystical component to the interpretive process; Cf Dream therapy

**dreamworking** Dreamwork, see there

**dress** *verb* To apply protective and/or absorptive materials to a wound

***Drosera*** *Drosera rotundifolia*, moorgrass, red rot, sundew, youthwort HOMEOPATHY A remedy used for severe coughs, growing pains and persecutory delusions. See Homeopathy

**Drown box** Drown stick pad HEALTH FRAUD A device invented by Ruth Drown, which she claimed measured biocurrents, by means of two rubber skeins, which she called a stick pad; Drown claimed that the box incorporated a therapeutic modality, but it was deemed fraudulent by the FDA; she died at age 72 of a stroke, while awaiting trial. See Radionics; Cf Abrams generator, de la Warr box, Emanometer

**Drown box** Drown stick pad, see there

**dry chamber** Isolation chamber, see there

**dry rebirthing** see Rebirthing therapy

**dry run surgery** ALTERNATIVE ANESTHSIOLOGY A simulated surgical operation that may include scrubbing the patient before the surgery, and providing the patient with the sights, sounds, and smells of a surgical operation; dry run surgery has been used to prepare the patient for use of hypnosis rather than general anesthesia; Cf Psychic surgery

***Dryopteris crassirhizoma*** see Fern-Chinese medicine

***du huo*** *Angelica pubescens*-yellow, see there

***du jong*** *Eucommia ulmoides*, see there

**dubious** Unproven, see there

**Duesberg, P** A respected molecular biologist from the University of California who has taken the unusual position that a cause-and-effect relation between AIDS and infection by human immunodeficiency virus (HIV) is unproven (*Nature 1991; 350:10c*)

**Duffy's Elixir** QUACKERY A bottled patent medicine that contained senna, a bulk laxative, which was sold in the late 1800s in the American frontier. See Frontier prescription, Patent medicine, Quackery

***Dulcamara*** *Solanum dulcamara*, woody nightshade HOMEOPATHY A minor homeopathic remedy used for those suffering from cold damp weather, or abrupt drops in temperature; it may be used to treat conjunctivitis, cough, cystitis, diarrhea, pruritus, and warts. See Homeopathy

***Dunaliela bardail*** ALTERNATIVE ONCOLOGY A beta-carotene-rich one-celled alga that inhibits the development of spontaneous breast cancer in mice and normalizes glucose and lactic acid; this activity is attributed to the beta-carotene's antioxidant activity, and normalization of the blood chemistries (*Moss, 1992*). See Unproven methods for cancer management

***dung chin*** Japanese wax privet, see there, *Ligustrum japonicum*

***dung chiung-hsia tsao*** Winter worm-summer grass, see there, *Cordiceps sinensis*

**DV** Daily value, see there

**dwale** Belladonna, see there, *Atropa belladonna*

**dwarf juniper** Juniper, see there, *Juniperus communis*

**dynamization** Potentization, see there

***dzang hung hua*** (Tibetan) saffron, see there, *Crocus sativus*

***dze hua di ding*** Wild Chinese violet, see there, *Viola yesoensis*

**E-meter** DIANETICS® A device that measures galvanic skin responses in a client being counseled for traumatic memories, known to Scientologists as 'engrams'. See Dianetics®, Engram, Scientology®

**eagle wood** *Aquilaria agallocha*, agila wood, aguru, aloes wood, *chen hsiang*, *chen xiang* CHINESE MEDICINE A deciduous tree, the resinous wood of which is a diuretic, stimulant, and tonic; it is used for angina and chest pain, fatigue, gastritis, hypertension, neurosis, paresthesias of the extremities, and mental stress. See Chinese herbal medicine

**ear acupuncture** Auricular acupuncture, see there

**earth smoke** Fumitory, see there, *Fumaria officinalis*

***eau d'arquebusade*** Musket-shot water, see there

**EAV** see Electroacupuncture according to Voll

**echinacea** *Echinacea angustifolia*, *Echinacea pallida*, *Echinacea pupurea*, black Sampson, coneflower, Missouri snakeroot, purple coneflower, rudbeckia FRINGE MEDICINE-FLOWER ESSENCE THERAPY A floral essence that is believed to provide a sense of self in the face of adversity. See Flower essence therapy HERBAL MEDICINE A perennial herb, the roots and rhizomes of which contain betain, essential oils including caryophylene and humulene, echinocoside (which has antibacterial activity), glycosides, inulin, isobutyl amides, resin, and sesquiterpene; it is antibacterial, antiviral, and diaphoretic, and has been used topically for eczema, herpes, insect and snake bites, itching, and wounds, and internally for gastrointestinal, respiratory, and urinary tract infections, infectious mononucleosis, septicemia, sore throat, toothaches, and to detoxify the blood. See Herbal medicine

**echinacea** *Echinacea angustifolia*

***Echinacea angustifolia*** Popularly known as echinacea, see there

***Echinacea pallida*** Echinacea, see there

***Echinacea purpurea*** Echinacea, see there

**eclectic** ALTERNATIVE MEDICINE *adjective* Pertaining or referring to a style of practice of a person trained in any of the forms of Oriental medicine, including auricular acupuncture, ethnic Chinese traditional medicine, five element acupuncture, medical acupuncture, and traditional Chinese medicine; Cf Traditional Chinese medicine

**Eclecticism** MEDICAL HISTORY-NATUROPATHY A health care movement founded by Dr Wooster Beach (1794-1868) that was rooted in Thomsonianism, a contemporary herb-based therapeutic system, but departed therefrom as the Beach et al were open to any therapy that made sense; legacies of the Eclectics include laboratory production of drugs and elimination of crude forms of drugs, and admission of women and minorities to their professional schools; Eclecticism disappeared by the mid-20th century, see Naturopathy; Cf Thomsonianism

**Eclipta prostrata** Carp gut, *han lien tsao, han lian cao*, ink vegetable, *li tsao, mo tsai* CHINESE MEDICINE An annual herb with black, nicotine-laden sap; it is astringent and hemostatic, and is used for internal hemorrhage including menorrhagia, epistaxis, and hematuria, as well as gray hair, loose teeth, loss of vision, and vertigo. See Chinese herbal medicine

**ecological disease** Environmental disease, see there

**Mary Baker Eddy** The founder (1821-1910) of Christian Science, see there

**edetic acid** Ethylene diamine tetraacetic acid, see Chelation therapy

**EDTA** Ethylenediaminetetraacetic acid, edetic acid A chelating agent that binds divalent, eg arsenic, calcium, lead and magnesium, and trivalent cations ALTERNATIVE MEDICINE see Chelation therapy CLINICAL TOXICOLOGY EDTA is used to treat lead and other heavy metal intoxication

**Harry Edwards** A British psychic healer (1893-1976), who believed himself to be a medium for healing, and claimed to have Joseph Lister and Louis Pasteur as his spirit guides

**effleurage** A 'soft tissue' form of massage therapy, which entails long slow, rhythmic, light and heavy pressure strokes from the fingertips, thumbs, knuckles, and palms; effleurage may be combined by some therapists with aromatherapy. See Massage therapy

**EGCG** Epigallocatechin gallate, see there

**'egg crate'** A foam mattress that has a chicken wire-like pattern of elevations and depressions, which has been likened to that of an egg carton; egg crates are most useful for patients with recalcitrant decubitus ulcers (bedsores)

**ego body technique** A form of dance therapy developed in the 1940s by an American dancer, Trudi Schoop, which has been used for patients with mental disorders including schizophrenia. See Dance therapy

**Egoscue method** BODYWORK A technique for treating muscle pain and for training athletes to achieve their peak performance that was developed in the 1970s by P Egoscue who, at the time, was recuperating from injuries sustained in Vietnam; the method places the responsibility of recuperation from pain and physical dysfunction on the individual; Egoscue believes that a main cause of disease is what he terms 'motion starvation,' ie the relative lack of movement by people in developed nations; 'low motion' conditions believed to be helped by the Egoscue method are carpal tunnel syndrome, low back pain, stiff neck, and general lack of energy. See Bodywork, Low-motion disease, Motion starvation

**eicosanoid** A 20-carbon cyclic fatty acid derived from arachidonic acid which is synthesized from membrane phospholipids; eicosanoids and other arachidonic acid metabolites, eg HETE, HPETE, leukotrienes, prostaglandins, and thromboxanes are site-specific, increase during shock and after injury, and have diverse functions, including bronchoconstriction, bronchodilation, vasodilation, and vasoconstriction. See Arachidonic acid, Bad eicosanoids, Good eicosanoids, Zone-favorable diet

**eicosapentaenoic acid** EPA One of the omega-3 (n-3) fatty acids found in fish that increases the high-density ('good') lipoprotein (HDL) cholesterol in the blood; EPA-rich fishes include mackerel, salmon, sardines, trout, and tuna. See Decosahexaenoic acid

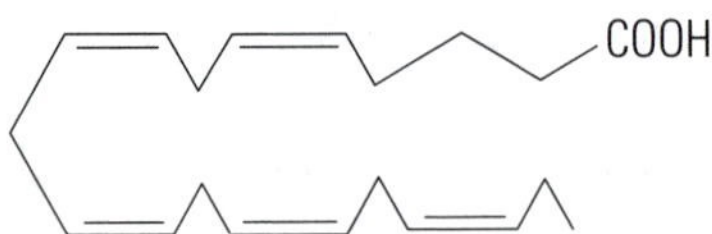


**eicosapentaenoic acid**

**The Eight Indicators** The Eight Principles CHINESE MEDICINE The 8 principles that influence the health care known as traditional Chinese medicine; the Eight Principles are in fact, 4 pairs of complementary opposites that describe the distinct qualities of the disharmony of the life force, *chi* (*qi*) in a person

▶ **THE EIGHT INDICATORS**

- **INTERIOR/EXTERIOR** Location of disharmony, either in the organs (interior) or in the skin or bones (exterior)
- **HOT/COLD** Qualities of the disease pattern–eg fever, chills, or the desire for a warm or cool environment
- **FULL/EMPTY** Whether the condition is acute or chronic, and whether the patient's responses are strong or weak

• **YIN/YANG** The most critical of the complementary opposites, discussed under yan and ying

See Acupuncture, Chinese herbs, Chinese medicine, Traditional Chinese medicine, Yang, Yin

**The Eight Principles** The Eight Indicators, see there

**eighteen *lohan* tiger/dragon *Qigong*** A health enhancing system based on a group of rarely performed *Qigong* exercises, which are believed to promote longevity and enhance the immune system. See *Qigong*

**Einsteinian medicine** Vibrational medicine, see there

**eldepryl** Deprenyl, see there

**elder** Elderberry, see there, *Sambucus nigra*

**elderberry** *Sambucus nigra*, black elder, bore tree, bourtree, common elder, elder, European elder, Mediterranean elderberry, pipe tree HERBAL MEDICINE A flowering shrub, the flowers and berries of which contain cyanogenic glycosides, essential fatty (linoleic, linolenic, and palmitic) acids, flavonoids, mucilage, pectins, resin, tannic acid, and vitamin C; it is antipyretic, diaphoretic, expectorant, laxative, and a mild stimulant, which has been used as an infusion for colds and respiratory tract infections, and topically for skin irritation and conjunctivitis. See Herbal medicine

**elderberry** *Sambucus nigra*

**elecampane** *Inula helenium*, gold coin flower, horse heal, *hsuan fu hua*, *Inula britannica*, *Inula chinensis*, *jin chien hua*, scabwort, *xuan fu hua*, yellow starwort, wild sunflower CHINESE MEDICINE A perennial herb that contains inulin (a starch), mucilage, pectin, resin, sterols, and volatile oil; in Chinese herbal medicine, the flower is used; it is analgesic, anthelmintic, antiemetic, antimicrobial, antitussive, carminative, diaphoretic, expectorant, laxative, and sedative; it is used to treat gastrointestinal complaints and fluid retention. See Chinese herbal medicine HERBAL MEDICINE In Western herbal medicine, the root and rhizome have been used for anemia, asthma, dysmenorrhea, and lung infections, including bronchitis and tuberculosis. See Herbal medicine

**elecampane** *Inula helenium*

**electric bath** HEALTH FRAUD A bath in which an individual is subjected to low currents of electricity, allegedly to increase the body's energy flow; popular at the turn of the 20th century, electric baths are widely regarded as useless*. See Galvanic Electric Belt, Quackery

*In 1989, Prime Minister Margaret Thatcher was reported to include electric baths in her health regimen (*Armstrong, 1991*)

**electric facelift** ALTERNATIVE MEDICINE The electrical stimulation of certain acupuncture points as a means of tightening the facial muscles. See Electrotherapy

**electric therapy** FRINGE ONCOLOGY A general term for the use of external electrical currents and induced electromagnetic fields to influence the course of a disease (*Moss, 1992*) The efficacy of this modality is uncertain–Author's note

**electrical acupuncture** Electro-acupuncture A permutation of acupuncture, in which low-voltage electric currents are passed through needles to stimulate the acupuncture points. See Acupuncture, Transcutaneous electrical nerve stimulation

It is uncertain whether this improves the efficacy of the usual (non-electric) format of acupuncture

**electrical muscle stimulator** Any device that stimulates muscle contraction by electrical impulses; these devices are used in (mainstream) physical therapy to reduce muscle spasms, prevent the development of blood clots after surgery or cerebrovascular accidents, and prevent disuse atrophy of muscle; electrical muscle stimulators (eg Relax-A-Cizor) have been promoted for body shaping, removing cellulite, and weight loss, indications that the FDA considers to be fraudulent (*Butler, 1992*) CONTRAINDICATIONS These devices may cause electric shock or burns, and should not be used in those with cardiac arrhythmias, pacemakers, cancer, seizures, or during pregnancy

**Electro-Acuscope™** FRINGE MEDICINE A computerized device that delivers weak (lower than that which causes muscle contraction) electric current to soft tissues, which is believed by its users to normalize acupressure points, and facilitate repair of traumatized tissues; anecdotal reports suggest that the Electro-Acuscope™ may be effective for arthritis, bruises, bursitis, carpal tunnel syndrome, chronic fatigue syndrome, herpes zoster, low back pain, migraines, muscle spasms, musculoskeletal pain, neuralgias, prolapsed vertebral disk, sports injuries, surgical wounds, TMJ syndrome, whiplash, and other conditions (*Alternative Medicine, Future Med Pub, 1994*). See Energy medicine

**electro-acupuncture** Electrical acupuncture, see there

**electro-acupuncture according to Voll** EAV FRINGE MEDICINE A system of pseudodiagnosis and pseudotherapy based on the 'Dermatron,' a type of galvanometer invented in the 1970s by a German physician, Reinhold Voll, which was believed to measure 'electromagnetic energy flow' along acupuncture channels, and provide information on organ functions (*Raso, 1994*); EAV practitioners claimed to treat 'imbalances' identified by such devices, either by electrically stimulating the acupuncture points and/or by adminstering homeopathic remedies; Cf Health fraud

**electroacupuncture biofeedback** ALTERNATIVE MEDICINE A technique that uses acupuncture meridians to screen for infections; an electrode is placed at the designated sites, a small electric current is applied, and the response is recorded; any deviation from a normal reading is said to indicate an infection or abnormality (*Alternative Medicine, Future Med Pub, 1994*). See Electrodiagnosis, Energy medicine

**electro-acuscope therapy** Acuscope therapy, see there

**electo-biomagnetics** 1. Magnet therapy, see there 2. Magnetic healing, see there

**electrocrystal therapy** FRINGE MEDICINE A pseudotherapeutic technique developed in the 1970s by Harry Oldfield, which he claims promotes health by 'energy restructuring,' a process that is said to rectify the imbalances in the flow of a person's vital energy; in electrocrystal therapy, crystals are sealed in a glass tube filled with a saline solution; the tubes are placed on the client's chakras and affected meridians, and an electric current is passed through the tubes, imparting healing vibrations; the technique is claimed to be of use in migraines, multiple sclerosis, and many other medical conditions (*Shealy, 1996*). See Kirlian photography, Polycontrast interface photography

**electrodermal skin response biofeedback** Galvanic skin response biofeedback, see there

**electrodermal screening** Electrodiagnosis, see there

**electrodiagnosis** Bioelectric testing, electrodermal screen ALTERNATIVE MEDICINE The use of an electric device to evaluate an internal organ, by measuring its 'electromagnetic energy balance'; as an example, the Accupath-100, a computerized galvanometer, is used to select and prepare homeopathic remedies and 'probe' the patient's acupuncture points on the hands; it is also used to interpret the values that appear on the computer's monitor; all electrodiagnostic devices are regarded by the FDA as ineffective

**electrography** Kirlian photography, see there

**electro-homeopathy** HOMEOPATHY A 'fringe' form of homeopathy, in which electrical devices are used in conjunction with homeopathic remedies; Cf Homeopathy

**electrogalvanism** ALTERNATIVE MEDICINE A term for the electricity generated by dental amalgams, where saliva acts as a conductant, and the dissimilar metals in the mouth form electric circuits to neutralize the ionic charge; electrogalvanism is allegedly responsible for the slow leaching of metals from amalgams, the most important of which is mercury; low-level mercury poisoning is believed by alternative health care providers to be responsible for lack of concentration and faulty memory, insomnia, mental disorders, tinnitus, vertigo, seizures, hearing loss, eye problems, and other conditions *(Alternative Medicine, Future Med Pub, 1994)*. See Biological dentistry; Dental amalgam

**electromagnetic field** PUBLIC HEALTH An invisible field of electromagnetic radiation on the spectrum of energetic particles that move as quanta (radiowaves, infrared, visible light, UV light, and gamma radiation); EMFs are generated by moving electric charges that propagate outward from any object carrying an electric current

▶ **ELECTROMAGNETIC FIELDS ARE DUE TO**

- **ELECTRIC FIELDS** that push or pull ions toward or away from the field; the electrical component of an EMF is blocked by most objects, from skin to concrete, and has a strength of 1 mV/m$^2$, which is similar to the strength of the cells' intrinsic electrical activity
- **MAGNETIC FIELDS** that act on moving particles, pushing them perpendicularly to their direction of motion, which passes through most matter without losing strength; the actual power generated by a magnetic field is a few milligauss (1% of the strength of the earth's magnetic field)

Tumor cells exposed in vitro to extremely low electromagnetic fields (ELF) of 60 Hz electromagnetic radiation from electrical distribution systems (powerlines, video display terminals, household appliances) have increased mitotic activity; some reports suggest that ELF radiation is linked to a ± 2-fold increase in leukemia, lymphomas, and intracranial malignancy, especially in children living near either 765 kV power lines or 15 kV distribution lines (*US Environmental Protection Agency, 1990, Science 1990; 249:1096, 250:23*), although ELF increases ornithine decarboxylase activity or cell membrane resistance with spontaneous lysis, a relationship of ELF with malignancy is uncertain

Note: With breast and other malignancies, the significance of EMF and ELF data that is not statistically significant is unclear; poor study design further hampers valid conclusions (*Science 1994; 264:1658n&c*)

**electromagnetic healing** A form of 'acupuncture without needles' that is believed by its proponents to involve 'tachyon energy'[1] or 'life energy,' which can be harnessed and used to create materials, eg mineral water, clothing, and jewelry that are said to be highly organized on the molecular level[2]

[1]A tachyon is a hypothetical physical particle that travels faster than the speed of light [2]These may be bought from Tachyon Energy Research, Beverly Hills, California

**electromyograph feedback** A type of biofeedback therapy in which the electrical activity of the muscles is monitored by the patient with an electromyograph; electromyograph feedback training is used to induce relaxation, treat anxiety, bruxism, phobias, neck and back pain, temporomandibular joint (TMJ) dysfunction, tension headaches, cerebral palsy, and to rehabilitate neuromuscular injuries. See Biofeedback device, Biofeedback training, Galvanic skin feedback

**electromedicine** FRINGE MEDICINE A general term for any form of energy medicine that uses electromagnetic fields, which is based on the belief that all living organisms are controlled by electrodynamic fields; Cf Radionics

**electronic medicine** see Oscilloscope, Radionics

**electrosleep** A system used to relax patients in some health spas of the former Soviet Union, which consists of connecting the client to a device that delivers low levels of electrical current to various parts of the body; it is believed by its users to remove stress and tension and induce deep and relaxing sleep

**electrotherapy** ALTERNATIVE MEDICINE A general term for any use of electric current as a therapy. See Electric bath, Electric facelift, Galvanism, Oscilloscope, Radionics, Transcutaneous electrical nerve stimulation

**elemental diet** CLINICAL NUTRITION A basic diet composed of oligopeptides and amino acids, disaccharides or partially hydrolyzed starch, and minimal fat; elemental diets provide proton (hydrogen ion) neutralization sufficient to maintain gastric pH above pH 3.5. See Diet

In patients with severe burns, only 3% of those receiving an elemental diet had major upper gastrointestinal hemorrhage compared to 30% of those fed with a regular diet; commercial elemental diets include Precision, Travasorb, and Vivonex (*Am J Surg 1980; 140:761*)

**elephant's gall** *Aloe vera*, see there

**elephantiasis asturiensis** Pellagra, see there

**elephantiasis italica** Pellagra, see there

***Elettaria cardamomum*** Cardamom, see there, *Alpina oxyphylla*

**eleuthero** Siberian ginseng, see there, *Eleutherococcus senticosus*

***Eleutherococcus gracilistylus*** *Wu jia pi* CHINESE MEDICINE A deciduous shrub, the epidermis of which is analgesic, cardiotonic, diuretic, and tonic to the musculoskeletal system; it is used to treat arthritis, cramps, impotence, low back pain, pruritus, and rheumatic complaints. See Chinese herbal medicine

***Eleutherococcus senticosus*** Popularly known as Siberian ginseng, see there

**elimination diet** A diet in which a food or small groups of foods are eliminated in turn, in order to detect the cause(s) of a food allergy or intolerance; commonly implicated causes of food allergies include milk, eggs, peanuts, and others; elimination diets are used in individuals, especially children with atopy, who are suspected of being allergic to certain foods, and to determine whether there is reduction of the symptoms attributed to allergy; these diets are time-consuming, onerous, and costly, and may not identify a specific dietary allergen; if the symptoms continue after a food has been eliminated, the symptoms are unlikely to be due to the eliminated food; elimination diets may also be used for gluten hypersensitivity. See Lactose intolerance; Cf Desensitization

**elixir** Panacea A general term for a therapy or agent that is said to be useful for treating any disease

Despite claims to the contrary advanced for various substances, including evening primrose oil, garlic, and others, no elixir is known to exist–Author's note

**ellagic acid** A phenol that is a potent antagonist of the mutagenicity induced by bay region diol oxides or aromatic hydrocarbons (eg the ultimate carcinogenic metabolite of benzo[*a*]pyrene); ellagic acid is present in cherries, strawberries, and grapes, and may explain in part the anticarcinogenic effects of a fruit-rich diet; although ellagic acid reduces mutagenicity, it appears to have a minimal chemopreventive effect (*Cancer Res 1990; 50:2068*)

**ellagic acid**

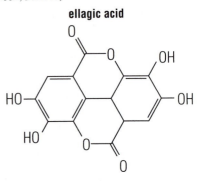

***Elsholtzia splendens*** *Hsiang rua, xiang ru* CHINESE MEDICINE A deciduous shrub that contains essential oils, including furane, ketones, pinene, and terpene; it is antiemetic, carminative, and diuretic, and is used for gastrointestinal complaints including nausea, vomiting, and bloating, as well as dry skin. See Chinese herbal medicine

**emanometer** UNPROVEN HEALTH CARE A device similar to the Abrams generator, that was invented by Dr WE Boyd, a British homeopath, which he believed could identify substances and chemicals at a distance. See Radionics; Cf Abrams generator, De la Warr box, Drown box

**EmBodyment** ALTERNATIVE MEDICINE A permutation of aura balacing and chakra healing that incorporates sacred touch–a type of craniosacral therapy, inner child therapy, and other techniques (*Raso, 1994*). See Inner child therapy

**emchi** Tibetan medicine, see there

**emergency stress formula** Dr Bach's Emergency Stress Formula, see there

**emergency stress relief formula** Dr Bach's Emergency Stress Formula, see there

**emetic** HERBAL MEDICINE An herb used to induce vomiting; emetics include ipecac (*Cephaelis ipecacuanha*), lobelia (*Lobelia inflata*), and mustard seed (*Brassica juncea*) (*Trattler, 1985*). See Herbal medicine

**emmenagogue** HERBAL MEDICINE An herb used to increase the menstrual flow; emmenagogues include black cohosh (*Cimicifuga racemosa*), blue cohosh (*Caulophyllum thalictroides*), life root (*Senecio aureus*), mugwort (*Artemisia vulgaris*), pennyroyal (*Hedeoma pulegioides*), pulsatilla (*Anemone pulsatilla*), southernwood (*Artemisia abrotanum*), squaw vine (*Mitchella repens*), and tansy (*Tanacetum vulgare*) (*Trattler, 1985*). See Herbal medicine

**emotivational therapy** see Imagineering

**empty calorie** CLINICAL NUTRITION A unit of carbohydrate-based energy derived from refined food products, which are high in sugars or salts, and essentially devoid of nutritive value, ie lacking protein, vitamins, dietary fiber, or essential fats; empty calories are typical of 'junk' or snack foods, and include potato chips (crisps), pastries, cakes, and soft drinks. See Cafeteria diet, Fast food, Junk food

**Empyrean® rebirthing** ALTERNATIVE MEDICINE A permutation of rebirthing therapy, which is based on the belief that the breath has intrinsic powers of healing, and the assumption that the rebirthing process increases this potential. See Rebirthing therapy

**emulsifier** FOOD INDUSTRY A substance added to foods which maintains the oils and fats mixed with a water base to give baked goods a light texture. See Food additives

**encounter group therapy** Sensitivity group therapy PSYCHOLOGY A therapeutic modality developed in the 1940s by an American psychologist, Carl Rogers; initially directed by a psychiatrist or psychotherapist, encounter groups have become therapeutic pow-wows in which similarly minded or afflicted individuals meet regularly to discuss mutual problems; with time, the group members become familiar enough with each other that honesty prevails, and the participants become each other's therapists. See Aversion therapy, Behavioral therapy, Flooding, Humanistic psychology, Image aversion therapy, Rogerian therapy, Systematic desensitization, Twelve-step program

**endogenous endocrinotherapy** ALTERNATIVE MEDICINE A general term for any therapy that is intended to rebalance the endocrine system without administering exogenous hormones; the goal of most alternative therapies is to reharmonize and rebalance life energy, and by extension heal disease, and thus can be regarded as forms of endogenous endocrine therapy. See Glandular

**endogenous pyrogen** Any of a number of compounds, usually cytokines, eg interleukin-6, interleukin-1$\alpha$, tumor necrosis factor-$\alpha$, interferon-gamma, and macrophage inflammatory protein-1, that induce a febrile reaction, typically in a background of an acute phase response (*Perspect Biol & Med 1993; 36:611*). See Coley's toxin, Immune booster

**endonasal acupuncture** Endonasal therapy A form of acupuncture in which acupoints inside of the nose are stimulated. See Acupuncture

**endonasal therapy** Endonasal acupuncture, see there

**endure winter** Japanese honeysuckle, see there, *Lonicera japonica*

**enema** see Barium enema, Colonic irrigation, Herbal enema

**energetic massage** Nonoriental massage, see there

**energy balance** ALTERNATIVE MEDICINE A general term for the 'harmony' in an individual's flow of life forces MAINSTREAM MEDICINE-PHYSIOLOGY A state in which the caloric intake equals the energy consumed, such that the body weight is stable. See Body mass index

**energy balancing** Energy balance technique ALTERNATIVE MEDICINE A general term for any form of alternative health care that actively seeks to restore the balance of 'life energy' by moving, unblocking, or balancing life forces over the physical, energetic, and spiritual body; these therapies include acupressure, acupuncture, Bach flower remedies, healing, homeopathy, polarity therapy, reiki, reflexology, and therapeutic touch, discussed elsewhere in this work. See Aura balancing, Vibrational medicine

**energy balance technique** Energy balancing, see there

**energy block** A putative reduction or impasse in the flow of life energy which, according to the practitioners of zone therapy and reflexology, can be resolved through massage and manipulation of the feet and other body regions

**energy channel** Energy zone REFLEXOLOGY Any of 10 distinct neural conduits believed by reflexologists to extend from the head to the feet; foot massage is believed by its advocates to increase the flow of healing energy through any or all of these channels. See Reflexology

**energy cyst** FRINGE MEDICINE A term coined by Drs JE Upledger and Z Kami, for a pocket of energy that represents a maladaptive response to physical forces that follow an injury; '...*if a person is harboring powerful negative feelings such as anger, resentment, fear, etc. at the time of the injury, the forces imposed on the body will be retained as energy cysts...the...Somato-Emotional Release® practitioner encourages the positive aspects of the mind-body and discourages the negative...helping to release the energy cysts from the body by facilitating the body's memory of the injury, thus ending suppression.*' (*Kastner, Burroughs, 1993*). See Bodywork, SomatoEmotional Release®; Cf Soma Neuromuscular Integration®

**energy diagnosis** Energy medicine, see there

**energy emission** see Aura therapy, Energy medicine

**'energy enhancer'** see Invalid claims of efficacy

**energy field work** A general term for any method used to analyze or balance the aura, with or without actually touching the client; these methods overlap with bodywork and may involve imagery and visualization, talking and verbal therapies. See Energy medicine

**energy medicine** Energy diagnosis, energy therapy FRINGE MEDICINE A generic term for a format of alternative medicine that uses '...*an energy field–electrical, magnetic, sonic, acoustic, microwave, infrared–to screen for, or treat health conditions by detecting imbalances in the body's energy fields and then correcting them.*' (*Alternative Medicine, Future Med Pub, 1994*); the patient is evaluated by 'electroacupuncture biofeedback,' in which a device measures electrical resistance at acupuncture points that correspond to specific organs and tissue, known as 'control measurement points'; therapy is effected by various devices including the cymatic device, Diapulse™, Electro-Acuscope™, Infratonic QCM, MORA, sound probe, TENS unit, and Teslar Watch; anecdotal reports suggest that energy medicine can detect aflavatoxin $B_1$ intoxication, chronic fatigue syndrome, failure to thrive, Hashimoto's disease, lung cancer, schistosomiasis, and other conditions; energy medicine has been used for allergies, angina pectoris, circulatory defects, dermatopathies, bacterial or viral infections, migraines, myopathies, myalgias, rheumatoid arthritis, sore throats, tendinitis, and other conditions. See Cymatic device, Diapulse™, Electroacupuncture according to Voll, Electro-Acuscope™, Infratonic QGM, Light Beam Generator, MORA, Sound probe, Teslar Watch, Transcutaneous Electrical Nerve Stimulator; Cf Electrogalvanism

**energy point** Tsubo, see there

**energy therapy** Energy medicine, see there

**energy zone** Energy channel, see there

**enfleurage** FRINGE MEDICINE–AROMATHERAPY A process by which oils are produced from flowers for use in aromatherapy; the flowers are pressed into pure vegetable fat or onto a filter; once dried, they are removed and other flowers put in their place until the fat or filter is saturated with the floral essence. See Aromatherapy, Essential oil, Flower essence therapy

**English chamomile** Roman chamomile, see there, *Anthemis nobilis*

**English hawthorn** Hawthorn, see there, *Crataegus monogyna*

***The English Physician*** *The Complete Herbal*, see there

**English valerian** Valerian, see there, *Valeriana officinalis*

**English violet** Sweet violet, see there, *Viola*

*odorata*

**engram** DIANETICS® A traumatic memory that prevents a person from achieving self-fulfillment; it is believed that engrams can be removed by a therapist ('auditor') using an 'E-meter,' which measures the galvanic skin response. See Dianetics®, Scientology®

**enneagram system** ALTERNATIVE PSYCHOLOGY A system of spiritual psychology of ancient Middle Eastern origin, which is based on the posit that there are 9 (ennea, Greek for 9) basic personality types (see table), which correspond to the roles people play in society; each type has a major fault or 'prime psychological addiction' (PPA); the goal of the system is to help each personality type 'neutralize' his prime 'psychological addictions,' and through self-knowledge, relate freely with himself, others, God, and the universe (*Raso, 1994*); despite the belief that the enneagram system has utility in interpreting personality types, one of the system's principal proponents, Dr Riso (*Enneagram Transformations: Releases and Affirmations for Healing Your Personality Type*, 1993), stated. '*If an interpretation or application of the enneagram does not clarify your own experience of people in the real world, it is not only relatively worthless, it is potentially dangerous.*' (*Raso, 1994*)

**enriching** FOOD INDUSTRY The addition of vitamins or minerals to a food, eg wheat, which may have been lost during processing. See White flour; Cf Whole grains

**ENNEAGRAM SYSTEM**

| PERSONALITY TYPE/SYNONYM | FEATURES | PPA | GOAL |
|---|---|---|---|
| Achiever/reformer | Rational, orderly self-righteous | Anger | Become a pathfinder |
| Helper | Generous, possessive, manipulative | Pride | Become a partner |
| Succeeder/motivator/status seeker | Ambitious, pragmatic, hostile | Deceit | Become a motivator |
| Individualist/artist | Sensitive, self-absorbed, intuitive | Envy | Become a builder |
| Observer/thinker | Analytical, original, provocative | Greed | Become an explorer |
| Guardian/loyalist | Responsible, engaging, defensive | Fear | Become a stabilizer |
| Dreamer/generalist | Manic and accomplished | Gluttony | Become an illuminator |
| Confronter/leader | Dominating, self-confident, combative | Lust for life and power | Become a philanthropist |
| Preservationist/peacemaker | Easygoing, receptive | Laziness | Become a universalist |

**Entelev** Cancell, see there

**enteroclysis** ALTERNATIVE MEDICINE Colon therapy, see there MAINSTREAM MEDICINE. Enteroclysis study, see there

**enteroclysis study** Enteroclysis MAINSTREAM MEDICINE. A double-contrast radiologic examination of the small intestine, in which the bowel loops are distended in succession as a means of detecting tumors, wall thickening, mucosal abnormalities, fistulas, bleeding sites; enteroclysis is more accurate and specific than the first-line screening procedure, the small bowel series, at a cost of slightly increased radiation exposure, and procedure time; in contrast to the small bowel series, enteroclysis is more sensitive in detecting bowel loop thickening (95% vs 61%) and tumors (90% vs 33%) (*MH Sleisenger, JS Fordtran, Eds, Gastrointestinal Disease, 5th ed, WB Saunders, Philadelphia, 1993*); Cf Colon therapy, Colonic irrigation

**entraining** A technique in which an individual is taught to focus on an extraneous factor (eg music) rather than on the normal focus of attention; entraining has been used to reduce the need for anesthetics in patients undergoing surgical procedures (*Insight; Dec 23, 1996, p41*), and has been shown to slow breathing and have a sedative effect

**entomophagy** ALTERNATIVE NUTRITION The dietary consumption of insects; outside of developed nations, insects and other arthropods are a major source of nutrition; they are rich in vitamins and lysine–an amino acid deficient in the diet of those subsisting on grains, and provide up to 60% of the dietary protein in rural Africa

Insect delicacies include chocolate cricket torte, honeypot ants, mealworm ganoush, roasted crickets, and wax worm fritters with plum sauce; cockroaches have not been popularized as menu items (*Sci Am 1992; 267/2:20*)

**environmental disease** FRINGE MEDICINE A hypothetical polysymptomatic condition[1] that is believed by 'clinical ecologists'[2] to be due to immune dysregulation induced by contaminants (eg allergens and chemicals including pesticides and petrochemicals) present in the air, water, food, soil; poor nutrition, infection, hereditary factors; and physical and psychological stress, resulting in various physical and mental disorders; the mainstream medical community[3] is largely skeptical of the existence of environmental disease, given the plethora of symptoms attributed to it, the lack of consistent laboratory abnormalities, and the use of unproven therapies to treat it; psychiatric disorders, eg depression, anxiety, and somatization are reported to be 2.5-fold greater in those with environmental disease (*JAMA 1990; 264:3166*), suggesting that the condition is not entirely organic in nature; clinical ecologists believe that the immune defects caused by environmental disease lead to mood and thought disorders, psychotic episodes, fatigue, vaguely defined gastrointestinal, respiratory, and urinary tract symptoms, rashes, arthritis-like symptoms, and cardiac arrhythmias DIAGNOSIS Environmental disease cannot be diagnosed by standard allergy tests or other standard examinations; clinical ecologists use a test of unproven validity known as neutralization DIFFERENTIAL DIAGNOSIS Allergies, early diabetes mellitus, chronic otitis media, infectious mononucleosis, nasal polyps, respiratory tract infections, sinusitis, thyroid disease, and other conditions may mimic environmental disease and, if misdiagnosed and treated incorrectly, delay more effective (mainstream) therapy TREATMENT Avoiding environmental pollutants, chemicals, and pesticides; consumption of organic foods; changing residence or place of employment; nutritional supplements; antifungal agents; hormones; gamma globulin; inhalation of pure oxygen; drinking urine. See Clinical ecologist, Environmental medicine (clinical ecology), Neutralization; Cf Candidiasis hypersensitivity syndrome

[1]Synonyms for environmental disease include cerebral allergy, ecological disease, environmental hypersensitivity, environmental hypersensitivity syndrome, environmental illness, environmental syndrome, hypersensitivity syndrome, immune dysregulation syndrome, total allergy syndrome, twentieth century disease, universal allergy, universal reactivity, universal reactor syndrome [2]a group of approximately 400 physicians in the English-speaking world have formed the American Academy of Environmental Medicine [3]The concepts and practices of environmental medicine (clinical ecology) have been evaluated by several professional bodies, including the American Academy of Allergy and Immunology; all have concluded that environmental disease has not been proven to exist and that environmental medicine (clinical ecology) is not a valid discipline

**environmental hypersensitivity** Environmental disease, see there

**environmental hypersensitivity syndrome** Environmental disease, see there

**environmental illness** Environmental disease, see there

**environmental medicine** Clinical ecology FRINGE MEDICINE A field that '...*explores the role of dietary and environmental allergens in health and illness...Virtually any chronic physical or mental illness may be improved by the care of a physician competent in this field.*' Environmental medicine is believed by its practitioners (clinical ecologists) to address allergies, cardiovascular (angina, arrhythmia, thrombophlebitis, vasculitis), pediatric (bedwetting, chronic otitis, learning disabilities), endocrine (autoimmune thyroiditis, hypoglycemia), ENT (allergies, sinus headaches, vertigo), gastrointestinal (bloating, constipation, gastritis, inflammatory bowel disease, irritable bowel syndrome), gynecologic (dyspareunia, premenstrual syndrome), skin (angioedema, eczema), neuromuscular (epilepsy, headaches, migraines, myalgias), psychiatric (anxiety, attention-deficit disorder, bipolar disorder, schizophrenia, sexual dysfunction), rheumatic (rheumatoid arthritis, systemic lupus erythematosus), and other conditions (*Alternative Medicine, Future Med Pub, 1994*); the intent of environmental medicine is to identify toxins in the environment through elimination diets, skin testing, provocation/neutralization testing, electroacupuncture, biofeedback, and radioallergosorbent testing, and to reduce patient exposure to noxious agents in the environment DIAGNOSIS Neutralization, a test of uncertain validity, consists of either subdermal injection or sublingual placement of the allegedly offending substance and evaluating the reactions; some clinical ecologists claim to identify offending substances using crystals, pendulums, galvanometers, and other devices. See Acid haze, Air pollution, Clinical ecologist, Environmental disease; Sick building syndrome

The concepts and practices of clinical ecology (environmental medicine) have been evaluated by several professional bodies, including the

American Academy of Allergy and Immunology; all have concluded that environmental disease has not been proven to exist and that clinical ecology (environmental medicine) is not a valid discipline; nonetheless, although there is little data to support the efficacy of EM in peer-reviewed journals, the concept that low levels of noxious components in the environment may cause disease has been attractive to some workers–Author's note

**environmental tobacco smoke** The smoke from burning tobacco products, to which a person is unintentionally exposed, in particular in public places* (ie restaurants, hospitals, government buildings, aircraft); environmental tobacco smoke is directly linked to acute exacerbations of asthma in children as measured by urinary cotinine levels (*N Engl J Med 1993; 328:1665oa*); the effects of second-hand smoke on the cardiovascular system are caused by carbon monoxide, nicotine, polycyclic aromatic compounds, and other, as yet not fully characterized or studied elements (*JAMA 1995; 273:1047*). See Passive smoking

*There has been a significant shift in the mentality in the US vis-`a-vis smoking; in 1986, several forward-thinking hospitals 'went smoke-free'; by 1990, few hospitals had not 'gone smoke-free'; the same shift has occurred in places of public access, such that aircraft, government buildings, restaurants are virtually all smoke-free—Author's note

**enzyme replacement therapy** A generic term for therapeutic administration of a congenitally defective or absent enzyme

▶ **ENZYMES CAN BE ADMINISTERED**

- **DIRECTLY**, by coupling the enzyme to a carrier molecule or by organ transplantation
- **INDIRECTLY**, by introducing the gene into the recipient

Cf Enzyme therapy

**enzyme therapy** ALTERNATIVE MEDICINE The administration of enzymes of plant or pancreatic origin '...*in complementary ways to improve digestion and absorption of essential nutrients*.' (*Alternative Medicine, Future Med Pub, 1994*); the enzymes are co-administered with food to predigest it and preserve internal enzymes '*for the important work of maintaining metabolic harmony*,' and may be effective in degrading circulating immune complexes as they pass through the kidneys; enzyme therapy is believed by its advocates to be effective in treating cancer, chronic degenerative diseases, pulmonary and periodontal infections, inflammation, multiple sclerosis, scarring, and other conditions; Cf Enzyme replacement therapy, Starch blockers CLINICAL MEDICINE A generic term for the supplementation of an enzyme present in adequate amounts under normal conditions with a related or identical enzyme to perform a specific task, eg rapid lysis of blood clots in an evolving myocardial infarction by tissue plasminogen activator, streptokinase, or urokinase

**eosinophilic-myalgia syndrome** An 'epidemic' intoxication that occurred in North America in the late 1980s, which was attributed to a chemically altered form of L-tryptophan* EPIDEMIOLOGY 1500 cases of EMS were described in 1990 in subjects who had ingested this particular form of L-trytophan CLINICAL Myalgia, myopathy, arthralgia, alopecia, angioedema, dermatoglyphism, morbilliform rash, sclerodermoid lesions, oral ulcers, restrictive lung disease, dyspnea, fever, lymphadenopathy, and edema of extremities LABORATORY Eosinophilia, increased creatinine kinase PATHOLOGY Sclerosing dermatopathy, arteriolitis; the responsible agent was an altered amino acid, DTAA (di-tryptophan aminal acetaldehyde), a contaminant introduced during tryptophan's manufacturing process (*Nature 1991;349:5n*), and EMS was linked to a new strain of *Bacillus amyloliquefaciens* used to produce high-dose tryptophan, while reducing the amount of powdered charcoal used in purification. See 'Peak E'; Cf Eosinophilic fasciitis

*This essential amino acid is ingested in adequate amounts in the diet, but is believed by some to be of use in treating insomnia, neurasthenia, premenstrual syndrome, and other conditions, and thus may be self-administered by 'health advocates'; tryptophan's subsequent metabolism to serotonin, gave rise to some claims that it could ameliorate obsessive-compulsive disorders and depression; high-dose L-tryptophan was recalled by the FDA in April 1990 (*JAMA 1992; 268:1828fda*)

**EPA** Eicosapentaenoic acid, see there

**ephedra** *Ephedra sinica*, Chinese ephedra, joint fir, *ma-huang* CHINESE & HERBAL MEDICINE A shrub, the stem of which contains ephedrine, which is a bronchodilator, diaphoretic, diuretic, and vasoconstrictor; it is used for asthma, bronchitis, fever, fluid retention, hypotension, paresthesias, to stimulate the central nervous system, and to suppress the appetite TOXICITY Ephedra should not be used in those with cardiac or thyroid disease, diabetes, glaucoma, hypertension, or in pregnancy; ephedra is an ingredient of some weight-loss aids, as it accelerates metabolism; it should only be used as such under (mainstream) medical supervision. See Botanical toxicity. Chinese herbal medicine, Herbal medicine, Poisonous plants

Note: *Ephedra vulgaris* has similar herbal properties

***Ephedra sinica*** Popularly known as ephedra, see there

***Ephedra vulgaris*** See Ephedra

**epigallocatechin gallate** A substance present in green and black tea that is an antioxidant ALTERNATIVE ONCOLOGY EGCG is reported to have a carcinoprotective effect against gastrointestinal and skin tumors in mice (*Moss, 1992*). See Black tea, Green tea, Unproven methods for cancer management ALTERNATIVE PHARMACOLOGY EGCG reduces blood pressure, and lowers the total and low-density lipoprotein-cholesterol, while raising the high-density lipoprotein cholesterol

***Epimedium macranthum*** Horny goat weed, see there, *Epimedium sagittatum*

***Epimedium sagittatum*** Popularly known as horny goat weed, see there

**Epsom salts** Magnesium sulfate heptahydrate ($MgSO_4$ $7H_20$) A bitter, water-soluble substance that occurs as white or colorless needle-shaped crystals; Epsom salts are used internally as purgatives and may be used as a mouthwash for treating toothaches

Epsom salts were first prepared from the mineral springs at Epsom, England (*The Columbia Encyclopedia, 5th ed, Columbia University Press, New York, 1993*)

**(hot) Epsom salt bath** NATUROPATHY A bath taken in hot water, into which 1-2 kg of Epsom salts are dissolved; it has been recommended (*Trattler, 1985*) that the water be as hot as can be reasonably borne by the patient, and ideally 20 minutes in duration; such baths are believed by their advocates to be both cleansing and antispasmodic. See Hydrotherapy

**Epsom salt rub** see Salt rub

**Equal™** Aspartame, see there

**equestrian therapy** PSYCHOLOGICAL THERAPY A general term for the mounting and riding of horses as a type of recreational therapy, which is believed to be of some use in those with mental or physical disabilites; Cf Hippotherapy; Cf Equestrian transformation expression

**equestrian transformation expression** Horseback to heaven PARANORMAL PHENOMENA A type of *chakra* healing which involves 'telepathic' horseback riding (*Raso, 1994*). See *Chakra* healing Cf Equestrian therapy, Hippotherapy

***Equestum arvense*** Popularly known as horsetail, see there

**Equipoise** HEALTH FRAUD A device invented at the turn of the 20th century by Heracles Sanche, the self-proclaimed 'Discoverer of the Laws of Spontaneous Cure of Disease'; according to Sanche, the device supplied the needed electrical force to the system, and optimized the absorption of oxygen from the lungs through heat; the device's opened metal cylinder proved to be empty (*Armstrong, 1991*). See Oxydonor, Quackery; Cf Equipoise

**equipoise** MEDICAL ETHICS A state of genuine uncertainty regarding the benefits or disadvantages of either therapeutic arm of a clinical trial; because an investigator may become biased as a clinical study progresses, given his perception of the benefits or adverse effects of one of the therapeutic regimens being evaluated, he may enroll fewer and fewer patients in the arm perceived to be less beneficial (due to ethical considerations), and may ultimately defeat the very purpose of the study for lack of patients in the control arm; a moral exit to this dilemma, known as 'clinical equipoise' is possible, as genuine uncertainty exists in the 'expert' medical community at large; the investigator may thus continue to enroll control patients 'blindly,' despite his bias (*N Engl J Med 1987; 317:141*); Cf Equipoise

***Er Mei Qigong*** An obscure form of *qigong* therapy developed by a Taoist priest, named after the Er Mei mountain. See *Qigong* therapy

**erect cinquefoil** *Potentilla erecta*, blood root, red root, tormentil, tormentilla; Cf Cinquefoil, *Potentilla reptans* HERBAL MEDICINE A perennial herb that contains catechols, tannins, resin, and tormentilline, a glycoside; it is antidiarrheal, antipyretic, astringent, and tonic, and has been used for sore throats, bleeding gums, hemorrhoids, open wounds, and in a weak topical solution, for conjunctivitis. See Herbal medicine

**ergogenic engineering** The implementation of refinements in physical and functional aspects of the workplace that improve efficiency and reduce work-related injuries. See Ergonomics, Social zone

**ergoloid mesylate** Hydergine ALTERNATIVE PHARMACOLOGY Any of a family of agents that are used in mainstream medicine to treat migraines; some physicians (*Fox, 1996*) believe the ergoloid mesylates may reverse age-associated mental impairment related to free radical damage, deposition of lipofuscin, and decreased flow of oxygen caused by vasospasm, and have recommended certain 'off-label' uses, eg, to improve memory, treat depression, decreased motor skills, and other forms of age-associated mental impairment

**ergonomic aid** see Invalid claims of efficacy

**ergonomic standards** OCCUPATIONAL MEDICINE A series of guidelines being developed (*NY Newsday 21 March 1995; A35*) by the OSHA,* intended to address activities in the workplace with a high risk for injury

▶ **HIGH-RISK WORKPLACE ACTIVITIES**

- **REPETITIVE MOTION** over prolonged periods of time of up to 4 hours
- Maintaining a **FIXED OR AWKWARD POSITION** for prolonged periods
- Use of **VIBRATING OR IMPACT TOOLS** for prolonged periods
- **LIFTING** heavy loads frequently during a shift

*Occupational Safety and Health Administration, a division of the US Department of Labor

**ergonomics** The formal study of the work environment, which evaluates, and if necessary, reconfigures a workplace by taking into account the anatomic, physiological, and psychological variables of those working in the environment. See Ergogenic engineering

**ergot** *Claviceps purpurea* HERBAL MEDICINE A fungus that infects rye, and is the primary source for ergonovine and ergotamine; its use in herbal medicine is confined to hemostasis and strengthening uterine contractions at the time of childbirth. See Herbal medicine

***Erica vulgaris*** Heather, see there, *Calluna vulgaris*

**Ericksonian hypnotherapy** A permutation of hypnotherapy developed by an American psychiatrist, Milton Erickson. See Hypnotherapy

***Eriocaulon sieboldianum*** *Gu jing tsao, gu jing cao* CHINESE MEDICINE An annual weed used as an herb, which is an analgesic, anti-inflammatory, and astringent; it is used to treat cataracts, glaucoma, headaches, sunstroke, and tonsillitis. See Chinese herbal medicine

**erythema endemicum** Pellagra, see there

***Erythraea centaurium*** European centaury, see there, *Centaurium umbellatum*

**erythrocyte maturation factor** Vitamin $B_{12}$, see there

**erythrosine** FD&C Red No. 3, see there

***Erythroxylum coca*** Coca shrub, see there

**Esalen Institute** An institute located in Big Sur, California, that was the spiritual home of the 1960s counter-culture, the Mecca of the 'human potential movement,' which combined a rest camp and 20th century religious retreat; it was the birthplace of the Gestalt movement, and Swedish/Esalen massage. See New Age

**Esalen massage** 1. Swedish/Esalen massage, see there 2. A form of bodywork developed in the 1960s at the Esalen Institute; while the movements of Esalen massage are virtually identical to those of Swedish massage,

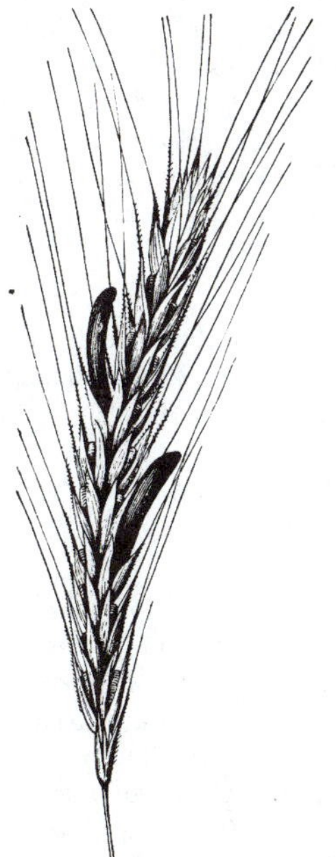

**ergot** *Claviceps purpurea*

they are not as vigorous; it is common practice to mix the 2 forms of massage, which is known as Swedish/Esalen massage, and thus Esalen massage is rarely practiced in its original form; Esalen massage therapists undergo a one-month training course. See Bodywork, Esalen Institute, Swedish/Esalen massage

**Esalen/Swedish massage** Swedish/Esalen massage, see there

**E.S.C.O.P.** European Scientific Cooperative for Phytotherapy

**esoteric healing** Ray methods of healing, see there

**essence of the body** Jing, see there

**essence therapy** Flower therapy, see there

**essential amino acids** A group of 8 amino acids (isoleucine, leucine, lysine, methionine, phenylalanine, threonine, tryptophan, and valine) that are essential for normal growth and development of humans; absence of an essential amino acid results in a negative nitrogen balance; in premature infants, histidine, arginine and cystine are also essential. See Amino acids

**essential dietary component** Essential nutrient CLINICAL NUTRITION A required dietary component, without which a deficiency state develops; essential dietary components include water (1-2 liters/day), calories (2000 to 2500 kcal/day), carbohydrates, fat, protein, vitamins, minerals and fiber. See Essential amino acids, Essential fatty acids, Fiber, Trace minerals, Vitamins

**essential fatty acids** Fatty acids that humans cannot synthesize, which contain double bonds more distal than the COOH end of the 9th carbon atom

▶ **ESSENTIAL FATTY ACIDS**
- Arachidonic acid
- Linoleic acid
- Linolenic acid

ALTERNATIVE NUTRITION It has been proposed by some practitioners of alternative health care that cystic fibrosis and attention deficit disorder in children may respond to an increased dietary intake of essential fatty acids See Arachidonic acid, Fatty acids, Linoleic acid, Linolenic acid

**essential nutrient** Essential dietary component, see there

**essential oil** Attar ALTERNATIVE MEDICINE An oil distilled or extracted from various plants, eg citrus fruits, eucalyptus, flowers, lavender, peppermint, rosemary, tea tree, and others, which is used in aromatherapy. See Aromatherapy, Citrus oil, Fixed oil, Floral oil, Flower essence therapy, Lavender oil, Peppermint oil, Rosemary oil, Tea tree oil; Cf Essential fats, Lorenzo's oil, Volatile oil

**Essiac** FRINGE ONCOLOGY An herbal cancer treatment formulated by a Canadian nurse, René Caisse (1888-1978), which consists of four principal herbs–burdock (*Arctium lappa*), Indian rhubarb (*Rheum palmatum*), sorrel (*Oxydendrum arboreum*), and slippery elm (*Ulmus fulva*), which is said to be useful for treating cancer; evidence of Essiac's efficacy is inconclusive (*Moss, 1992*). See Unproven methods for cancer management

**est** Est FRINGE PSYCHOLOGY A system of personal growth and behavior modification developed in the 1970s by Werner Hans Erhard (née Jack Paul Rosenberg) as a synthesis of other disciplines, including Esalen, Freud, Jung, mind control, mind dynamics, Scientology™, Silva mind control, transactional analysis, transcendental meditation, Zen Buddhism, and other philosophies; central to est (Erhard seminar training) is the concept of 'getting it,' in which participants are encouraged to treat life as a game, learn appropriate behavior, break agreements, tell lies, give space in relationships, and ultimately to take responsibility; '*Est is an individual experience rather than a belief...designed to give trainees a means to deal with the situations in their lives that are not working for them. They are taught the skills to work on a problem until they work out of it.*' (*Kastner, Burroughs, 1993*) . See Assertiveness training

Note: Est seminars are remarkable for their harshness—typically 250 people are crowded in a conference room complete with hard chairs for 15 hours, with no food and few opportunities to address bodily functions

**Colonel Oscar Estebany** A former Eastern European cavalry officer, who in the 1960s achieved fame as a hand healer. See Faith healing, Hand healing

**'etheric' body** see Anthroposophical medicine

**etheric surgery** PARANORMAL PHENOMENA A combination of aura balancing and psychic surgery that has been practiced by some American healers; in etheric surgery, the 'metaphysician' or practitioner performs all of the motions of the operation *above* the patient's body, ie in the 'ether'; it is claimed that etheric surgery has the same effect, despite the absence of physical contact between the psychic surgeon and the patient; some forms of etheric surgery are regarded as variants of absent healing or channeling. See Absent healing, Channeling, Psychic surgery; Cf Psychosurgery

**ethical diet** Religious diet, see there

**ethnic traditional Chinese medicine** CHINESE MEDICINE A term referring to a 'purist' form of Oriental medicine, which incorporates five element acupuncture, medical acupuncture, and traditional Chinese medicine

**ethnobotany** The field that studies the relationship between plants and a population, in particular the medicinal use of plants by an ethnic or aboriginal group; the ethnobotanical approach to drug discovery has been more efficient than random searches for plant-derived agents of therapeutic interest (*Sci Am 1994; 270/6:82*); ethnobotanical drugs include aspirin (*Filipendula ulmaria*), codeine (*Papaver somniferum*), ipecac (*Cephaelis ipecacuanha*), pilocarpine (*Pilocarpus jaborandi*), reserpine (*Rauwolfia serpentina*), theophylline (*Camelia sinensis*), and vinblastine (*Cantharanthus roseus*); Cf Herbal medicine, Pharmacognosy, Phytochemical

**ethnomedicine** Folk medicine Any of a number of traditional, often aboriginal, medical systems that use native plants and herbs, which may be administered by a medicine man, witch doctor, curandero or shaman; ethnomedical practitioners generally receive their education through a long apprenticeship and may administer the therapy in a ritual, and evoke the help of a deity; ethnic medical practice is waning in cultures changed by Western civilization. See Hot-cold syndrome, Shamanism; Cf Alternative medicine, Folk medicines

**ethylene diamine tetraacetic acid** see EDTA

**eucalyptus** *Eucalyptus globulus*, blue gum, fever tree, Tasmanian blue gum HERBAL MEDICINE An evergreen, the volatile oil of which contains eucalyptol, cineole, pinenes, and sesquiterpene alcohols; it is antiseptic and expectorant, and used internally as a steam inhalant for asthma and respiratory infections, and to soothe oral mucosae, and topically for dandruff, dry skin, arthritis and rheumatic complaints. See Eucalyptus oil, Herbal medicine

***Eucalyptus globulus*** Eucalyptus, see there

**eucalyptus oil** Steam-distilled oil from *Eucalyptus globulus*, which is expectorant and antiseptic; it is used as a steam inhalant for asthma and respiratory infections, and to soothe oral mucosae; an overdose of as little as 3.5 ml may be fatal TOXICITY Epigastric pain, nausea, vomiting, vertigo, ataxia, myasthenia, pallor, cyanosis, stridor, delirium, convulsions, stupor, transient coma, or death. See Eucalyptus

***Eucommia ulmoides*** *Du jung, mu mien*, wood cotton CHINESE MEDICINE An annual herb native to China, the bark of which is analgesic, antihypertensive, diuretic, and tonic; it is used for abdominal pain, chronic fatigue, poor circulation, headaches, hypertension, impotence, paresthesias, low back and leg pain, urinary frequency, vertigo, to calm the fetus in pregnancy, and threatened abortion. See Chinese herbal medicine

***Eugenia aromatica*** Popularly known as clove tree, see there

***Eupatorium perfoliatum*** Popularly known as boneset, see there

***Euphrasia*** *Euphrasia officinalis*, *E stricta*, eyebright HOMEOPATHY A remedy that has been used for eye complaints, particularly infections of the eye and surrounding tissues; it is also used for colds, hay fever, headaches, measles, menstrual dysfunction, and prostatitis. See Eyebright, Homeopathy

***Euphrasia officinalis*** Popularly known as eyebright, see there

***Euphrasia stricta*** HERBAL MEDICINE Eyebright, see there, *Euphrasia officinalis* HOMEOPATHY *Euphrasia*, see there

**eupsychology** Humanistic psychology, see there

**European barberry** Barberry, see there, *Berberis vulgaris*

**European centaury** *Centaurium umbellatum*, *Centau-*

*rium erythraea, Erythraea centaurium*, bitterherb, bluebottle, bluet, centaury, centaury gentian, cornflower HERBAL MEDICINE An annual or biennial that contains alkaloids, bitter principles, glycosides, and triterpenes; it is anthelmintic, anti-inflammatory, antipyretic, laxative, and a digestive tonic; it has been used for anemia, depression, gout, hypertension, kidney stones, and rheumatic complaints. See Herbal medicine

**European elder** Elderberry, see there, *Sambucus nigra*

**European cowslip** Cowslip, see there, *Primula vera*

**European cranberry bush** Cramp bark, see there, *Viburnum opulus*

**European daisy** *Bellis*, see there, *Bellis perennis*

**European Guelder rose** Cramp bark, see there, *Viburnum opulus*

**European mistletoe** see Iscador®

**European red raspberry** Raspberry, see there, *Rubus idaeus*

**European white birch** White birch, see there, *Betula alba*

**European willow** White willow, see there, *Salix alba*

***Euryale ferox*** Popularly known as foxnut, see there

**eutony (therapy)** Gerda Alexander method NATURAL PSYCHOTHERAPY A 'holistic' form of body-centered psychotherapy developed by Gerda Alexander, which resembles the Alexander technique, and is intended to re-establish muscle tone, by facilitating the flow of blocked energy through the collective unconscious of Jung; according to the eutony model, patients (pupils) are hypotonic, hypertonic, or eutonic. See Humanistic psychology; Cf Alexander technique

**evangelical healing** PARANORMAL PHENOMENA A boisterous form of faith healing, which in the US is practiced in person or over the airwaves by 'preachers' of various Christian denominations; evangelical healing combines 'fire-and-brimstone' preaching, often about the evils of Satan (who, some evangelists believe, may be the cause of all diseases) with speculative claims and promises of miracles

Note: Evangelical healing may be practiced by those with profit-oriented motives, and claims may be exaggerated (*Butler, 1992*)

**Herbert Evans** NUTRITION An American biochemist who identified vitamin E in 1922 at the University of California, Berkeley

**evening primrose** *Oenothera biennis, Oenothera lamarckiana*, evening star, king's cure-all, night willow herb, scabish, tree primrose HERBAL MEDICINE A biennial herb that contains essential fatty acids including gammalinoleic acid; it is not approved by the FDA TOXIC EFFECTS Headaches, nausea, seizures, skin rashes. See Evening primrose oil, Herbal medicine

**evening primrose** *Oenothera biennis*

**evening primose oil** HERBAL MEDICINE An extract of evening primrose that is rich in gamma-linoleic and gamma-linolenic acids; it is antihypertensive, anti-inflammatory, antispasmodic, antitussive, and thrombolytic; anecdotal reports suggest that evening primrose oil may be useful in treating alcoholism, post-binge-drinking depression, asthma, atopic dermatitis, attention-deficit disorder, breast engorgement, brittle hair, brittle nails, cardiovascular disease, dry eyes, eczema, migraines, multiple sclerosis, obesity, Parkinson's disease, premenstrual syndrome, rheumatoid arthritis, schizophrenia, and other conditions TOXICITY Headaches, nausea, rashes. See Evening primrose

**evening star** Evening primrose, see there, *Oenothera biennis*

**evening trumpet flower** *Gelsemium*, see there, *Gelsemium sempervirens*, *G sempervitalis*

**Evers' therapy** FRINGE ONCOLOGY An unproven method for cancer management developed by an American physician, H Ray Evers (who died in 1990), and administered at the International Medical Centers (IMC) in Juarez, Mexico, under the direction of Francisco R Soto, MD, and in El Paso, Texas; at the time of the initial evaluation at the IMC, patients undergo a complete workup, including physical examination, biochemical, bioelectrical, and blood (CBC) profiles, ultrasound, CT scans, and MRI; the therapy itself consists of diet, oxidative therapy (hyperbaric oxygen, ozone, and Koch vaccination), and antioxidant Eversol chelation therapy (*Alternative Medicine, Future Med Pub, 1994*). See Unproven methods for cancer management

**evocative breath therapy** MIND/BODY MEDICINE A permutation of breath therapy that is used in mind/body medicine for coping with stress, anxiety, and pain; evocative breath therapy accompanied by music is intended to elicit an emotional response, which some believe enhances the immune system. See Breath therapy; Cf Breathing

**evodia** *Evodia rutaecarpa* CHINESE MEDICINE A fragrant herb, the fruit of which is analgesic and a digestive tonic; it is used internally for abdominal pain, diarrhea, nausea, loss of taste, and topically for hypertension and indigestion. See Chinese herbal medicine

***Evodia rutaecarpa*** Evodia, see there

**exercise** The rhythmic contraction of muscles against a force; substantial literature supports the benefits of exercise in improving a sense of well-being, and promoting health BENEFITS Enhanced sexual pleasure, reduced risk of heart disease, stroke, osteoporosis, stress, anxiety; increased strength, flexibility, and stamina; improved reaction time, memory, moods, immune resistance, sleep, self-confidence, and control of arthritis and weight; exercise is divided into its effect on

▶ **MUSCLES**

- **ISOMETRIC** Exercise against an unmoving resistance; isometric exercises consists of muscle contraction with a minimum of other body movements; isometric exercises build muscle strength and include weight-lifting or squeezing a tennis ball
- **ISOTONIC** Also known as Dynamic exercise Isotonic exercise consists of continuous and sustained movement of the arms and legs; isotonic exercises are beneficial to the cardiorespiratory systems and include running and bicycling

▶ **WHOLE BODY**

- **LOW-IMPACT AEROBICS** Any type of aerobic exercise that promotes physical fitness, but does not stress musculoskeletal tissues and joints; low-impact aerobic exercises include walking, swimming, and bicycling
- **HIGH-IMPACT AEROBICS** Any type of aerobic exercise that promotes physical fitness, at the risk of stress to musculoskeletal tissues and joints; high-impact aerobic exercises include aerobic dancing, basketball, running, and volleyball

ALTERNATIVE MEDICINE Any of a number of regimens have been recommended to treat various conditions, including back and neck pain, balance the energy flow to the body, and to improve the harmony between the body and mind

Note: It is difficult to separate the benefits of exercise from the lifestyles of 'healthy' people, in that those who exercise regularly tend to have a more balanced diet and, if they abuse drugs and tobacco and drink alcohol at all, do so in extreme moderation

| **EXERCISE-KCAL CONSUMED/HOUR** | |
|---|---|
| Distance running (15 km/hour) | 1000 |
| Contact sports (wrestling, karate) | 900 |
| Bicycling (25 km/hour) | 800 |
| Swimming, freestyle | 800 |
| Basketball, volleyball | 700 |
| Jogging (9 km/hour) | 600 |
| Tennis | 500 |
| Coitus | 450 |
| Walking | 400 |

**exercise-associated amenorrhea** A finding in female long-distance runners; in prospective studies, although menstrual irregularities are present in the form of anovulatory cycles, irregular cycles and decreased endogenous production of progesterone with shortened luteal phases, true amenorrhea does not occur; the menstrual dysfunction may be accompanied by osteopenia, osteoporosis, and hypoestrogenic amenorrhea

**exercise-induced asthma** A condition* in which intense physical exertion results in acute airway narrowing in individuals with airway hyperreactivity PATHOGENESIS EIA is closely linked to thermal provocation that occurs when large volumes of cold air are 'conditioned' (heated and humidified), a scenario that is most common in winter; the limit of airflow is most intense with running, less so with jogging, and least with walking; the obstruction is greatest with cold dry air, and least with warm humid air CLINICAL Cough, wheezing, dyspnea, chest tightness, hyperinflation, airflow limitation, and hypoxia (*N Engl J Med 1994; 330:1329oa*)

*Although exercise-induced bronchospasm is the most correct term for this condition, exercise-induced asthma is firmly entrenched in the literature; other synonyms include exercise asthma, exercise-induced bronchial lability, and thermally induced asthma

**exercise/movement therapy** A general term for any of a number of health-enhancing systems of exercise and movement, which includes aikido, dance therapy, t'ai chi, and yoga, discussed elsewhere in this work. See Exercise

**exercise pyramid** A proposed schematic diagram that recommends the amount and types of exercise that should be performed for optimal health; at the bottom are non-structured physical activities, eg walking the dog and climbing stairs; higher on the pyramid are active recreational activities, eg basketball, swimming, tennis, and others; at the peak of the exercise pyramid is vigorous exercise, which is recommended at least 3 times/wk for at least 30 minutes each session (*N Y Times 29 March 1995, C1*). See Exercise, Vigorous exercise; Cf Food pyramid

**existential psychotherapy** Humanistic psychology, see there

**exorcism** PARANORMAL PHENOMENA A ritual that is intended to terminate the presence or trespassing of a non-material entity or spirit (or Satan) in a place (ie, a 'haunting') or a person (ie, a 'possession'); exorcisms are done by command or persuasion through rituals, special prayers, or symbolism in the Roman Catholic Church by a priest with authorization from the ordinary or other higher authority (*Inglis, West, 1983*)

**expectant faith** PARANORMAL PHENOMENA The hopeful confidence that a person has in a shamanic or faith healer, which is a function of the healer's reputation, the atmosphere created during the healing process, and the relevant healing paraphernalia. See Psychic healing

**exposure therapy** Systematic desensitization, see there

**extended family** SOCIAL MEDICINE A family unit that is related by blood or by marriage that extends over 3 or more generations, which may include 'collateral' relatives, spouses, and progeny; an extended family (EF) may also be defined as one composed of a core nuclear family unit of mother, father, children, and any other blood relative who lives either in the same household or closely proximal thereto, including in-laws, cousins, aunts, uncles, and grandparents; the EF provides an interactive system of moral, and often economic support; dissolution of the EF 'unit,' like the disintegration of the nuclear family, through the forces of divorces and economics, has been held responsible for decreased moral cohesion and an increase in some forms of mental illness in advanced societies. See Companionship, Pet therapy, Most significant other; Cf Nuclear family, Single-parent family, Social isolation

**extentional medicine** Alternative medicine, see there

**external *qi* healing** *Qigong* therapy, see there

**external *qigong* healing** *Qigong* therapy, see there

**extrasensory perception** Psi, psychism, sixth sense, voyand PARANORMAL PHENOMENA The alleged awareness of another person's thoughts, which is believed to be mediated by poorly-characterized 'factors.' See Psychic healing

**extrinsic factor** Vitamin $B_{12}$, see there

**eyebright** *Euphrasia officinalis, E stricta*, meadow eyebright, red eyebright HERBAL MEDICINE An annual that contains glycosides, saponins, tannins, and volatile oils; it is anti-inflammatory and astringent, and has a long tradition among herbalists as an eye tonic; it is administered as an infusion or applied topically for itchiness, and has been used for colds, hay fever, and sore throat. See Herbal medicine HOMEOPATHY see *Euphrasia*

**eye map** see Iridology

**eye-mouth gap** CLINICAL NUTRITION The discrepancy between a person's true and perceived caloric intake; a wide eye-mouth gap is typical of those with eating disorders and is not thought to represent conscious deception on the part of the individual; the 'gap' may result in the misdiagnosis of 'diet-resistant obesity,' a dilemma that can be resolved with the double-labeled water method, see there (*N Engl J Med 1992; 327:1947*)

**Eye-Robics®** ALTERNATIVE OPHTHALMOLOGY A proprietary permutation of Bates vision training developed in the 1970s by Dr JJ Taber; in addition to the Bates exercises, Eye-Robics® adds self growth techniques, addressing the emotional, mental, physical, and spiritual aspects of the whole person; Cf Bates vision training, Vision training

**eyeroot** Goldenseal, see there, *Hydrastis canadensis*

**eye training** Vision therapy, see there

**face massage** A self-performed technique that consists of stroking, pinching, rolling, squeezing, and otherwise stimulating the soft tissues and muscles of the face; face massage may be used to relieve tension and possibly control age-related phenomena including wrinkling. See Massage

**face modeling** A form of cosmetic massage promoted as an alternative to plastic surgery by the Arcadi Center in Amsterdam, Netherlands. See Massage

**face reading** FRINGE MEDICINE A pseudodiagnostic technique in which an individual's personality and emotional state are believed to be decipherable by evaluating facial features. See Metoposcopy, Physiognomy; Cf Phrenology

**facial rejuvenation** A type of head-centered reflexology, which is believed to increase the flow of energy to the shoulders, neck, and head, realign facial muscles, and promote inner harmony and healing. See Massage, Reflexology

**factor G** A general term for any factor that is necessary for the growth of an organism

**factor H** 1. Biotin, see there 2. Vitamin $B_{12}$ precursor or analogue

**factor R** Folic acid, see there

**factor S** 1. Biotin, see there 2. A general term for any factor believed to be increased in the brains of exhausted mammals

**factor U** Folic acid, see there

**factor W** Biotin, see there

**facilitated communication** ALTERNATIVE PSYCHOLOGY A form of behavioral therapy that may be successful in treating some cases of autism; in facilitated communication, a helper holds or braces the hands or arms of a person with autism, who uses one finger to type words on a keyboard, a task that initially is impossible in autistics; with time the facilitator reduces his control over the autistic person's movement, the expectation being that the individual will eventually initiate movement and activities spontaneously. See Humanistic psychology

Note: Many experts are unconvinced that facilitated communication is truly effective, and its reported success may be related to 'wishful thinking' (*New York Times 13 July 1993; C1*)

**factitious** *adjective* Pertaining or referring to consciously determined symptoms, driven by an unconscious, compelling need to assume a 'sick role,' usually in the absence of an external incentive (*Mayo Clin Proc 1996; 71:493oa*)

**factitious disorder** PSYCHIATRY Any of a number of self-produced lesions or biochemical changes seen in individuals with some mental disorders in order to gratify various self-motivated needs, including sympathy and narcotics; these conditions share the same raison d'etre, differing only in the site of injury and the agent used to produce the lesions. See Psychosomatic disorder

▶ **FACTITIOUS**

• **FACTITIOUS DERMATOPATHY** A skin condition produced by sharp objects, thermal, or chemical agents; the gross and histologic appearance reflects the damaging agent

• **FACTITIOUS DIARRHEA** The spurious increase in fecal volume, due to either excess use of laxatives, or dilution of the stool (*N Engl J Med 1994; 330:1418*OA); it is more common in women, and is related to excessive and inappropriate use of laxatives, and occurs in 1. Anorectics, who are often females, age 18 to 40 with an altered self image, for whom weight control is a central focus and laxatives an alternative to vomiting, and 2. Older perimenopausal females, who emphatically deny the abuse; here the motives for laxative abuse are complex and may be related to secondary gain of attention or may be a component of hysteria; side effects of prolonged laxative abuse include chronic diarrhea, colicky abdominal pain, nausea, vomiting, weight loss, weakness, hypokalemia, skin pigmentation, arthralgia, cyclic edema, nephrolithiasis (ammonium urates)

• **FACTITIOUS FEVER** A fever of unknown origin described in either young female health professionals that occurs after a legitimate disease, or in older neurotic women who are prone to self-mutilation

• **FACTITIOUS HYPOGLYCEMIA** Surreptitious ingestion of hypoglycemic agents, eg sulfonylureas or insulin; often by women ages 30-40, employed in the health professions who have highly variable levels of glucose

- **FACTITIOUS PURPURA** Devil's pinches Patchy self-inflicted lesions that may be produced by pinching flesh

**fad diet** Any of a number of weight-reduction diets that either eliminate one or more of the essential food groups, or recommend consumption of one type of food in excess at the expense of other foods; fad diets rarely follow sound nutritional principles for weight loss, which hinge on ingesting fewer calories and/or consuming more energy through exercise; fad diets are generally not endorsed by the medical profession. See Diet

**Fagan test of infant intelligence** PEDIATRIC NEUROLOGY A test designed to assess visual recognition memory, based on the time that an infant spends looking at a novel stimulus (*Pediatrics 1986; 78:1021*)

**fair lady** Belladonna, see there

**fairy clock** Dandelion, see there, *Taraxacum officinale*

**fairycup** Cowslip, see there, *Primula vera*

**fairy wand** *Chamaelirium luteum*, blazing star, colicroot, devil's bit, false unicorn root, helonias HERBAL MEDICINE A perennial herb, the rhizome and roots of which contain steroidal saponins; it is diuretic, and has been used by Native American and Western herbalists as a uterine tonic, for morning sickness, and to promote menstrual flow. See Herbal medicine

**faith factor** A term coined by H Benton, for a facet of deep spiritual conviction that may enable those who meditate to overcome insomnia, headaches, panic attacks, and enhance cancer therapies (*Bricklin, 1976*). See Meditation

**faith healing** Divine healing, spiritual healing PARANORMAL PHENOMENA An alternative form of health care, in which therapy consists of entrusting the healing process to a 'higher' (God in the Judeo-Christian construct) or other power(s) through prayer; in faith healing, active medical or surgical interventions are generally not administered, and if the patient deteriorates or dies, it may be viewed as the will of God. See Christian Science, Paranormal diagnosis, Paranormal therapy, Pentecostal healing; Cf Psychic healing, Psychic surgery

**falling-out** PSYCHIATRY A culture-bound episode described in the southern US, and regionally in the Caribbean, which is characterized by sudden and often unexpected collapse, which may be preceded by feelings of dizziness; it is thought to be a type of conversion reaction. See Culture-bound syndrome

**false jasmine** *Gelsemium*, see there, *Gelsemium sempervirens*, *G sempervitalis*

**false memory** PSYCHOLOGY A set of suggestions and cues that cause a person to believe an event occurred, which in fact did not; the mechanism by which this occurs is known as source amnesia (*New York Times 3 May, 1994; C1*)

**'false self'** ALTERNATIVE PSYCHOLOGY A term defined in the context of Swami Ajaya's inner self-healing process, as a false image that a person portrays to the world, which is a response to the constellation of 'raw deals' a person suffers in the course of life. See Inner self-healing process; Cf 'True self'

**false unicorn root** Fairywand, see there, *Chamaelirium luteum*

***fan hung hua*** (Tibetan) saffron, see there, *Crocus sativus*

***fang feng*** *Ledebouriella seseloides*, see there

***fang-hsiang*** *Angelica anomala*, see there

**fast food** CLINICAL NUTRITION Prepared food from a restaurant that specializes in providing a complete meal, often consisting of a permutation of hamburger or chicken, French fries, and a soft drink or milk shake, in a few minutes; a diet limited to fast foods is high in protein, fat, and calories, and low in vitamins, minerals, and fiber (*Consumer Reports 1988; 54:355*). See Cafeteria diet, Diet, Empty calories, 'Junk food,' Nibbling diet

Note: About 1/5 of the 250 million Americans consume at least one fast food meal daily

**fasting** ALTERNATIVE MEDICINE A generic term for a period of voluntary abstinence from foods and/or drinks; fasting is integral to many religions, as it is believed to purify the mind and spirit; fasting rests the gastrointestinal tract, and is believed to rid the body of toxins and undigested metabolites; it leads to a rapid loss of water, sodium, and potassium, resulting in postural hypotension; it decreases blood sugar resulting in depression, fatigue, decreased libido, and malaise, increased nitrogen in the circulation due to protein breakdown, and may result in premature childbirth (Yom Kippur effect); compete fasts (abstinence from all liquids and solids) should be limited to 24 hours or less, as they cause significant physiological stress; prolonged fasting causes anemia, decreased resistance to bacterial infections, osteoporosis, liver and kidney disease; according to advocates of alternative medicine, fasting may be advised in acute or chronic disease, during recuperation from disease, states of general weakness, and to 'clear the mind'; anecdotal reports suggest that fasting may be beneficial for allergies, arthritis, constipation, gastric ulcers, headaches, heart disease, hypertension, inflammation, mental disorders, rheumatoid arthritis, and other conditions CONTRAINDICATIONS Fasting is contraindicated in children, pregnancy, lactating women, and the elderly, and in those with asthma, cancer, diabetes, eating disorders, schizophrenia, tuberculosis, and ulcerative colitis. See Citrus juice fast, Diet, Fruit juice fast, Natural hygienist, Vegetable juice fast, Yom Kippur effect, Water fast

**fat** A general term for any of a class of neutral organic compounds formed by a molecule of glycerol linked to three fatty acids (a glycerol ester); fats are water-insoluble, ether soluble, solid at less than 20ºC, combustible, and energy-rich (9.3 kcal/g). See Fatty acids, Fish oil, Monounsaturated fatty acid, Olive oil, Polyunsatu-rated fatty acid, Saturated fatty acid, Tropical oil

**fat balance** A state of equilibrium in which the fatty acids in the circulation 'drive' a set level of fat oxidation; at the fat balance point, all consumed fat is metabolized, and weight is maintained at a status quo (*Sci Am Aug 1996, p88*). See Obesity

**fat burner** See Invalid claims of efficacy

**fat consumption** A general term for fats consumed in the diet, the amount and type of which correlate directly with the incidence of coronary artery disease

Note: Fats comprise 34% of the US diet (down from 42% in the mid-1960s); saturated fats comprise 12% (16% in mid-1960s); cholesterol levels average 205 mg/dL (213 mg/dL in 1978); reduction in dietary fats is credited with the 40% decrease in coronary artery disease-related mortality reported in the United States since 1968 (*New York Times 8 March 1994; C6*)

**fat distribution** The location of fat on the body; there are 2 patterns of body fat distribution, as measured by the ratio of the corporal diameter at the hips and waist, waist:hip ratio, normal: 0.7-0.8; these patterns differ significantly in co-morbidity

▶ **FAT DISTRIBUTION**

- **GYNECOID PATTERN** Female pattern–fat is deposited in the lower body (abdomen, buttocks, hips, thighs), by mesenchymal differentiation or hyperplasia
- **ANDROID PATTERN** Male pattern–fat is deposited in the upper body, especially around the abdomen; (gut fat) adipocytes are more sensitive to insulin and catecholamines; fat accumulates by hypertrophy, possibly a function of membrane receptor density; the android pattern has greater lipolytic and lipogenic potential, and thus has a greater risk for hypertension, cardiovascular disease, diabetes, and hyperinsulinemia

See Obesity; Cf Morbid obesity

**fat/fiber hypothesis** The posit that a diet with increased meat, fat, protein, and energy, and low in fiber is central to the pathogenesis of colorectal cancer (*JAMA 1992; 268:1573sc*). See Animal fat, Fiber

**fat fighter** see Invalid claims of efficacy

**fat metabolizer** see Invalid claims of efficacy

**'fat-mobilizing hormone'** A fanciful term for a non-existent 'factor,' the production of which was claimed to be induced by the Atkins' diet. See Atkins' diet, Diet, Cf Starch blocker

**fatigue syndrome** Chronic fatigue syndrome, see there

**fatty acid** A straight-chain monocarboxylic acid that can be either saturated (ie has no double bonds) or unsaturated, which is, in turn, either monounsaturated (having a single double bond), or polyunsaturated (having more than one double bond); the importance of saturation of the bonds in fatty acids is unclear, although saturated animal-derived and 'tropical' oils appear to increase the risk of atherosclerosis, while diets high in monounsaturated fats, in particular olive oil, decrease this risk. See Polyunsaturated fatty acid

Note: A table from the US Department of Agriculture is provided (facing page) to place these fats in context

**'fatty food attack'** A colloquial term for transient abdominal colic that occurs in response to ingesting fried or fat-laden foods, which is a common clinical sign of gallstones

**F.D.A.** Food and Drug Administration, see there

**FD&C Red No. 3** Erythrosine FOOD INDUSTRY A food dye that has been banned from cosmetics and most foods, as it causes thyroid tumors in rodents; it continues to be used in maraschino cherries, and in some pistachios. See Artificial dye, Food additives, Food dye

Note: In the US, approved colorants are designated by numbers under the Food, Drug, and Cosmetic Act, abbreviated as FD&C

**FD&C Yellow No. 5** Tartrazine A ubiquitous colorant used in foods and drugs that cross-reacts with aspirin, exacerbates asthma, and may cause life-threatening anaphylactic reactions, asthma, and urticaria. See Artificial dye, Food additives, Food dye

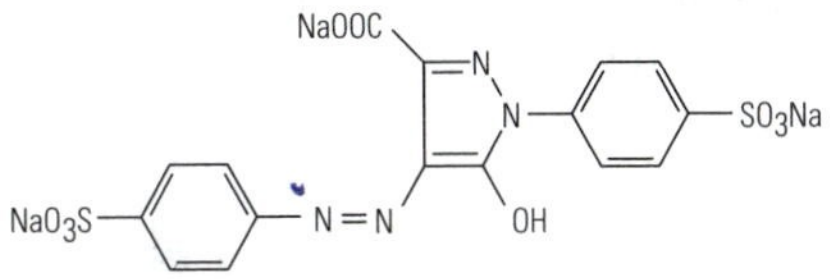

**FD&C Yellow No. 5**

**FD&C Yellow No. 6** Sunset Yellow FCF A food dye that has been used in candies and carbonated beverages, which in animals has been linked to adrenal and renal tumors, chromosomal damage, and in humans, to allergic reactions. See Artificial dye, Food additives, Food dye

**DIETARY FATS** (% SATURATION)

| | A | B | C |
|---|---|---|---|
| Safflower Oil | 9% | 13% | 72% |
| Sunflower Oil | 11% | 20% | 69% |
| Corn Oil | 13% | 25% | 62% |
| Olive Oil | 14% | 77% | 9% |
| Soybean Oil | 15% | 24% | 61% |
| Peanut Oil | 18% | 48% | 34% |
| Cottonseed Oil | 27% | 19% | 54% |
| Lard | 41% | 47% | 12% |
| Palm Oil | 51% | 39% | 10% |
| Beef Tallow | 52% | 44% | 4% |
| Butterfat | 66% | 30% | 4% |
| Palm-kernel Oil | 86% | 12% | 2% |
| Coconut Oil | 92% | 6% | 2% |

A % Saturated fatty acids

B % Monounsaturated fatty acids

C % Polyunsaturated fatty acids

**Feingold diet** An elimination diet developed in the 1970s by an American allergist, Benjamin Feingold MD, which was based on the belief that attention-deficit disorder (ADD) was influenced by diet; the Feingold diet eliminates artificial colors and flavors, and salicylate-like compounds; subsequently, white sugar was also viewed as a culprit and added to the list of items eliminated from the diet of children with ADD. See Diet, Sugar hypothesis

**Feldenkreis method** A technique of body and mind integration developed by a Russian-Israeli nuclear physicist, Moshe Feldenkreis, which is based on the posit that correction of poor habits of movement can improve one's self-image and health; the Feldenkreis method is carried out in 2 steps: in the first step, known as functional integration, the Feldenkreis practitioner uses touch to demonstrate techniques that will help the individual improve his breathing and body movements; in the second step, known as awareness through movement, the individual is taught to correct improper movements through 'floorwork'; anecdotal reports suggest that the Feldenkreis method is effective in treating the long-term effects of stress, accidents, back problems, and physical disabilities. See Structural integration; Cf Alexander technique, Aston patterning, Hellerwork®, Massage, Ortho-bionomy, Rolfing®, Rosen method, Tragerwork®
*Resource: Feldenkreis Guild, PO Box 489, Albany, OR 97321-0143* ☎ *1.800.775.2118*

**felon herb** Mugwort, see there, *Artemisia vulgaris*

**female circumcision** HUMAN RIGHTS The disfigurement and/or partial excision of the external female genitalia which is performed in many African countries and required for tribal identity; circumcision has deeply rooted cultural significance; male circumcision is a symbol of religious and ethnic identity, female circumcision is linked to women's sexuality and reproductive role in society, and is usually performed from age 4-10, but may be performed as early as infancy and as late as after the delivery of the first child; it is performed on 5-99% of women in 26 African countries, with ± 100 million women world-wide having undergone the procedure; female circumcision may be classified into two broad categories, clitoridectomies (type I and II procedures) and infundibulations (type III and IV procedures); the procedure is rarely if ever performed by trained physicians, but rather by village healers, shamans, or by local women 'specialized' in the procedure, who may use old razors or broken glass COMPLICATIONS-SHORT TERM Severe pain, hemorrhage, and potentially fatal shock; infection is very common and may be accompanied by abscesses, gangrene, septicemia, and tetanus COMPLICATIONS-LONG TERM Disfigurement in the form of dermoid cysts, stitch ('suture') neuromas, splitting of scars; if de-infibulation is not performed before childbirth, exit of the fetal head may be obstructed and the perineum torn; weak uterine contractions and delay in delivering the fetal head may result in fetal demise, vesicovaginal septal necrosis, fistula formation, and urinary incontinence TREATMENT De-infibulation, psychotherapy ETHICS Female circumcision is regarded in developed nations as genital mutilation and, when performed in the very young, a form of child abuse (*N Engl J Med 1994; 331:712*SA). See Clitoridectomy, Infibulation; Cf Circumcision

**female condom** Vaginal pouch An externally placed contraceptive device*, which consists of a 16.5 cm polyurethane sheath, held in place by two plastic rings, one at the cervix and the other outside the body (*New York Times 11 May 1993; C5*); the female condom offers some protection against both sexually-transmitted disease and pregnancy, with an annual pregnancy rate of 21-26% (vs ± 15% with a 'male' condom). See Contraception

*The first of which (Reality™) is marketed in the US by Wisconsin Pharmacal and in several European countries as Femidon™ (Chartrex Intl, Ltd, UK)

**female genital mutilation** see Female circumcision

***feng tsao*** *Gastrodia elata*, see there

**fennel** *Foeniculum vulgare, F dulce, F officinale, hui hsiang, hui xiang,* Muhammadan spice, sweet fennel, wild fennel A perennial herb that contains fixed oils (eg oleic, linoleic, and petroselenic acids), flavonoids, vitamins, and volatile oils (eg anethole, estragole, limonene, and pinene) CHINESE MEDICINE The seeds are antispasmodic, antitussive, diuretic, expectorant, and tonic, and used to treat colic, dyspepsia, hernias, nausea, and vomiting. See Chinese herbal medicine HERBAL MEDICINE In Western herbal medicine, fennel is regarded as a carminative; the seeds and roots are used internally for tired eyes, gastric discomfort, kidney stones, to increase breast milk, and stimulate the appetite; fennel is used topically for conjunctivitis, muscle pain, and rheumatic complaints; fennel's other uses are similar to those in Chinese herbal medicine TOXICITY Fennel should not be used in pregnancy, or in those with a history of liver disease, coagulopathy or estrogen-dependent breast tumors (ie those treated with tamoxifen), as fennel may contains phytoestrogens. See Herbal medicine

**fennel** *Foeniculum vulgare*

**fenugreek** *Trigonella foenum-graecum*, bird's foot, Greek hayseed, trigonella HERBAL MEDICINE An annual herb, the seeds of which contain alkaloids (eg choline and gentianine), flavonoids, minerals, mucilage, protein, steroidal saponins (eg diosgenin), and vitamins A, B, and C; fenugreek is used internally (herbal tea) for bronchitis, depression, diabetes, digestive complaints, hypercholesterolemia, hypertension, postmenopausal syndrome, rheumatic disease, sore throat, tuberculosis, and to increase lactation; it is used topically for cuts, gout, lymphadenitis, neuralgia, rashes, sciatica, skin infections, and wounds; it is believed by some to be an aphrodisiac TOXICTY Fenugreek should not be given to young children, or used in pregnancy as it stimulates uterine contraction. See Herbal medicine

**fermentation *Lactobacillus casei* factor** Folic acid, see there

**fern** CHINESE MEDICINE Any of a number of ferns (*Aspidium falcatum, Dryopteris crassirhizoma, Nephrodium filix, Onoclea orientalis, Woodwardia radicans*), the rhizomes of which are used in traditional Chinese medicine; all are referred to *guan jung* (*guan zhong*), and thus not differentiated by genus or species; ferns are anti-inflammatory, anthelmintic, and hemostatic, and are used to treat abscesses, menorrhagia, leukorrhea, intestinal parasites, and thyroiditis. See Chinese herbal medicine

**Ferreri technique** A permutation of applied kinesiology developed by a New York chiropractor, CA Ferreri

***Ferrum phos*** *Ferrum phosphoricum*, Iron phosphate HOMEOPATHY A remedy that has been used for infection and inflammation, anemia, colds, coughs with chest pain, diarrhea, earaches, fatigue, fever, menstrual disorders, nose bleeding, palpitations, rheumatic complaints, sore throat, vaginal discomfort, and vomiting. See Homeopathy

**feverfew** *Tanacetum parthenium, Chrysanthemum parthenium*, bachelor's button, featherfew, featherfoil, wild chamomile HERBAL MEDICINE A perennial herb that contains sesquiterpene lactones (eg parthenolide and santamarin), tannins, and volatile oil; it is anti-inflammatory and antipyretic; it may be effective for migraines due to its high parthenolide content, and has been used for asthma, colds, depression, diarrhea, gynecologic disorders, histrionic personality disorder, indigestion, insomnia, migraines, moodiness, nausea, and rheumatic complaints TOXICITY Oral ulcers; feverfew should not be used in pregnancy as it stimulates uterine contractions; it may interfere with coagulation. See Herbal medicine

**fever treegum** Eucalyptus, see there, *Eucalyptus globulus*

**feverwort** Boneset, see there, *Eupatorium perfoliatum*

**fiber** see Dietary fiber

***Ficaria major*** Figwort, see there, *Scrophularia nodosa*

**field balm** Ground ivy, see there, *Glechoma hederacea*

**field horsetail** Horsetail, see there, *Equisetum arvense*

**field mint** *Mentha haplocalyx, M arvensis* CHINESE MEDICINE A fragrant herb that is used internally for emotional lability, menstrual disorders, seizures in children, and virus-related skin rashes TOXICITY Field mint reduces the flow of milk and should not be used in those who are breastfeeding. See Chinese herbal medicine HERBAL MEDICINE Peppermint, see there, *Mentha piperita*

**fight-or-flight response** Flight-or-fight response, see there

**figwort** *Scrophularia nodosa*, carpenter's square, *ficaria major, l'herbe du siège*, rose noble, scrofula plant, square stalk, stinking Christopher, throatwort HERBAL MEDICINE A perennial shrub that contains flavonoids, resin, and saponins, which is used topically for hemorrhoids, ulcers, and wounds; it was formerly administered internally for tuberculosis and lymph node swelling TOXICITY Figwort should not be used internally, given its intense purgative, emetic, and cardioactive properties. See Herbal medicine

***Filipendula ulmaria*** Popularly known as meadowsweet, see there

**filler** CLINICAL NUTRITION Any of a number of agents that add bulk to the gastric content, and increase the sensation of fullness in dieters ingesting large quantities of food; fillers include various water-insoluble fibers, eg methylcellulose, or glucamannan, which is derived from the Japanese Konjac root; Cf Food additive

**finger walk** MASSAGE THERAPY Any of a number of methods in which the tips of the fingers adjacent to the fingernails are used to move slowly (walk) along a particular musculoskeletal group in reflexology. See Massage therapy, Reflexology

**fir balsam** Balsam fir, see there, *Abies balsamea*

**fir pine** Balsam fir, see there, *Abies balsamea*

**firewalking** PARANORMAL PHENOMENA The practice of walking barefoot across hot coals, often in the context of a religious or quasireligious ritual; firewalking ability may be ascribed to supernatural forces, deities, or a personal 'bioelectric field'; proponents believe firewalking is a vehicle for overcoming fears, doubts, inhibitions, and developing personal power; it is claimed that firewalking can cure addiction disorders, claustrophobia, depression, impotence, and obesity (*Raso, 1994*)

**fire yoga** Actualism, see there

**firming agent** FOOD INDUSTRY A substance added to canned fruits and vegetables as a means of maintaining their structural rigidity. See Food additive

**first-aid plant** *Aloe vera*, see there

**Fischer-Hoffman Process** Hoffman quadrinity process, see there

**fish** A high quality source of protein and essential oil, which is widely regarded as a healthy food

**HAZARDS OF FISH**[1] 1. Fish oil High levels of fish oil may cause nosebleeds due to impaired platelet function (*J Pediatr 1990; 116:139*) 2. Envenomation, see Ciguatera poisoning, Scombroid poisoning 3. Heavy metal poisoning, eg mercury, which concentrates up the food chain, especially in certain fish, eg tuna 4. Parasitosis, see Sushi

**BENEFITS OF FISH**[2] Fish is widely regarded as a 'healthy food'; the benefits of fish consumption are attributed to fish oil's omega-3 or n-3 fatty acids, including eicosapentanoic and docosahexanoic acids. See Fish oil, Healthy foods

[1]Damned if you do [2]Damned if you don't; those who consume greater than 35 grams of fish per day have one-third as much risk of nonsudden death from myocardial infarction as those who consume no fish (*N Engl J Med 1997; 336:1046*)

**fish oil** A product that is rich in n-3 (omega-3) fatty acids, including eicosapentanoic and docosahexanoic acids, which has a positive effect on the cardiovascular system[1,2], diabetes,[3] hypertension,[4] longevity,[5] and immunity[6]; fish oil's benefits may be a function of the length of the fatty acid acyl chain (C20 and C22) rather than to polyunsaturation; essential fatty acids are concentrated up the food chain from phytoplankton to fish to marine mammals; deep water trout has 3-fold more n-3 oil than other fish. See Essential fatty acid, Fish, Healthy foods

[1]ATHEROSCLEROSIS n-3 oil inhibits production of platelet-derived growth factor (PDGF) in endothelial cell cultures; PDGF causes smooth muscle proliferation, a factor in atherogenesis, possibly related to free radical production [2]CARDIOVASCULAR EFFECTS Myocardial infarction is 10-fold greater in Danes and Americans than Greenland Eskimos, despite similar levels of dietary fat; Danes consumed twice the saturated fat and more n-6 polyunsaturated fat than Eskimos, who consumed 5-10 g/d of long-chain n-3 polyunsaturated eicosapentanoic acid (C20:5n-3) and docosahexaenoic acid (C22:6n-3) [3]DIABETES MELLITUS n-3 lipids prevent the insulin resistance induced in rats by non-'aquatic' fat (n-6 fat derived from vegetables and meats rather than fish), replacement of 6% of the vegetable oil with n-3 fish oil circumvents the insulin resistance otherwise seen in the rats [4]HYPERTENSION Marine oils are high in n-3 polyunsaturated fatty acids (PFA); salad oils are high in n-6 fatty acids; vegetable PFAs are reported to decrease platelet aggregation, vaso-occlusive events and blood pressure, evoking low-level decrease in both diastolic and systolic pressures, and decrease thromboxane $A_2$ metabolites [5]LONGEVITY When n-3 fish oil replaces corn oil or lard in the laboratory rodent diet, they live longer, have decreased atherosclerosis, arterionephrosclerosis, and produce fewer autoantibodies [6]Fish oil enhances the immunosuppressive effects of cyclosporine in rats with heart transplants, and inhibits delayed hypersensitivity; addition of 6 g of dietary fish oil to cyclosporine therapy in renal transplant victims reduces the rejection episodes, but has no effect on survival (*N Engl J Med 1993; 329:769oa*); fish oil also results in decreased production of interleukin-1, interleukin-2, interleukin-6, tumor necrosis factor, and eicosanoids; cyclosporine-induced nephropathy is linked to increased production of thromboxane $A_2$, and leukotrienes $C_4$ and $D_4$; consumption of fish oil slows the progression of renal failure in IgA nephropathy (*N Engl J Med 1994; 331:1105oa*)

**Fit for Life Program** A lifestyle altering program developed in the 1980s by H and M Diamond that is based in part on specific rules for combining foods; in the program, proteins are not combined with starches, as it is believed that the body is not designed to digest more than one concentrated food at one time–any food that is not a fruit or vegetable is regarded as a concentrated food; according to the Diamonds, this diet consumes less energy and the body, having more energy available, automatically sheds excess weight. See Diet, Food combining, Natural Hygiene

**fitness** HEALTH see Cardiovascular finess

**fitness gadget** A generic term for any device that is intended to convert flab into firm muscle through exercise; fitness gadgets include rowing machines, treadmills, and proprietary devices, eg Dyna-bands, Nordic Track, Stairmaster, and Thigh Master

They are often purchased on impulse with the hope that one will obtain the advertised sleek physique (*N Y Times 29 March 1995, C1*)

**The Five Elements** AYURVEDIC MEDICINE

Earth, fire, water, air, and ether–the basic elements of nature in the ayurvedic construct of the universe; these elements are not distinct material entities, but rather manifestations of the Cosmic Conscious-ness; earth is manifest by ice, water's solid state, which with fire, melts to become, in turn, water and steam-the air principle, which disappears into the ether; in Avurveda, this fusing of matter and energy is intertwined with restoring and maintaining the harmony that corresponds to a state of health CHINESE MEDICINE Fire, earth, metal, water, and wood, the basic consitituents of nature according to the traditional Chinese construct; these elements are not static, but have dynamic qualities that undergo cyclical transformations, from one to another, such that wood creates fire, which creates earth, which creates metal, which creates water, which creates wood, and the cycle continues; health is achieved if the life energy flows in an uninterrupted manner. See Acupuncture; Five element acupuncture, Traditional Chinese medicine

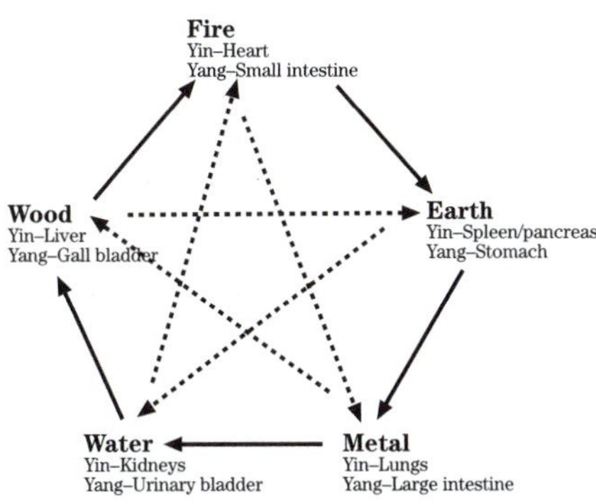


**Five elemental energies**

Their relationships in traditional Chinese medicine and corresponding 'yin' and 'yang' organs

**Five Element acupuncture** CHINESE MEDICINE The most established form of acupuncture, which is based on the five elements–fire, earth, metal, water, and wood, which undergo cyclical transformations, from one to another; health is achieved if the life energy flows in an uninterrupted manner; in acupuncture, the body is divided into five organ systems corresponding to these five elements: Wood corresponds to the liver and gallbladder, fire to the heart and small intestine, earth to the stomach and spleen, metal to the lungs and large intestine, water to the kidneys and bladder. See Acupuncture; Chinese herbal medicine, Chinese medicine, The Five Elements, Traditional Chinese medicine, Twelve Vital Organs

**five fingers** 1. American ginseng, see there, *Panax quinquefolius* 2. Cinquefoil, see there, *Potentilla reptans*

**five finger grass** Cinquefoil, see there, *Potentilla reptans*

**The Five Flavors** TRADITIONAL CHINESE MEDICINE The classification of foods and herbs in Chinese herbal medicine as sour, bitter, sweet, spicy, and salty, which relates to their physiological effect; each of the five flavors is further classified as being either yin or yang in nature. See Chinese herbal medicine, Yang, Yang foods, Yin, Yin foods

**five-flower formula** Dr Bach's Emergency Stress Formula, see there

**five food groups** NUTRITION An addition to the four food groups promulgated in 1956 by the US Department of Agriculture; the fifth group consists of fats, carbohydrate-rich foods (sweets), alcohol and other foods that do not fall into the Four Food Groups. See Balanced diet, Food groups, Food pyramid, Four food groups

**five-leaf** Cinquefoil, see there, *Potentilla reptans*

**50-minute hour** PSYCHIATRY A colloquial term for the time alloted by the therapist for a patient undergoing psychotherapy; the shortened time allows the therapist a 10-minute breather for taking notes, having coffee, and other activities

**fixed oil** HERBAL MEDICINE A general term for a type of essential oil produced by plants, which does not volatilize, ie is not aromatic. See Essential oil, Herbal medicine; Cf Volatile oil

**Jim Fixx** The author of *The Complete Book of Running*, a national bestseller; Fixx symbolized the fitness 'craze' and had converted himself from a 2-pack-a-day, 220-pound cigarette smoker into a long-distance runner; he died in 1984 at the age of 52 while on a 10-mile run. See Vigorous exercise

**flag lily** Blue flag, see there, *Iris versicolor*

**flagroot** Sweet flag, see there, *Acorus calamus*

**flag sign** CLINICAL NUTRITION The finding of sharply demarcated alternating bands of pigmented and depigmented hair, evidence of intermittent malnutrition, which occurs in kwashiorkor and marasmus type of malnutrition, or rarely, associated with chemotherapy, eg methotrexate (*Cancer 1983; 51:1356*)

**flannel leaf** Mullein, see there, *Verbascum thapsus*

**flavonoid** Bioflavonoid HERBAL MEDICINE Any of a family of yellow pigments that are chemically similar to tannins, and somewhat similar in use. See Herbal medicine, Tannins NUTRITION A family of biologically-active polyphenolic compounds found in fruits, in particular in the pulp thereof, vegetables, tea, and red wine, which are potent antioxidants and effective platelet inhibitors; flavonoids have been used for bruising, hay fever, and menorrhagia; a flavonoid-rich diet may protect against atherosclerosis and platelet-mediated thrombosis, due to flavonoids' platelet-inhibition (*JAMA 1995; 275:1197c*), and possibly also cancer

**flax** *Linum usitatissimum*, linseed, lint bell HERBAL MEDICINE An annual, the oil and seeds of which contain a cyanogenic glycoside, fixed oils (eg linoleic and linolenic acids), mucilage, and protein; it has been used internally as a laxative and antitussive and topically to treat burns. See Herbal medicine

**fleaseed** Psyllium, see there, *Plantago psyllium*

**fleawort** Psyllium, see there, *Plantago psyllium*

**flesh nut** Nutmeg, see there, *Myristica fragrans*

**fletcherize** *verb* To masticate food completely; the term was coined by Dr John Kellogg after Horace Fletcher (1849-1919), a wealthy healthy health advocate, who advised thorough chewing of solid foods and eating less than more

**Flexner report** A study of 155 medical schools in the US that was conducted by A Flexner in the early 1900s, and commissioned by the Carnegie Foundation; Flexner concluded that only Johns Hopkins Medical School provided an adequate medical education; the Report was instrumental in reforming American medical education; the report shifted the orientation of training physicians towards research and education, and led to the appointment of full-time faculty dedicated to the furtherance of medical science (*JAMA 1991; 265:1555, N Engl J Med 1993; 328:362br*)

**flight-or-fight response** Fight-or-flight response, general adaptation syndrome, stress response PHYSIOLOGY A constellation of physiologic responses to fear or perceived stress, which includes increased blood flow to muscle, increased blood pressure, heart rate, muscle tone, oxygen consumption, perspiration, and respiratory rate; Cf Relaxation response

**flint** *Silica*, see there

**'floater'** PARANORMAL PHENOMENA A colloquial term for a person who meditates for prolonged periods of time, floating in an isolation (samahdi) tank; floaters use the tank to alter their experiences by reducing external sensation to a minimum. See Flotation tank, Sensory deprivation

**flooding** Forced exposure PSYCHOLOGY A form of behavioral therapy for a specific phobia, in which the individual is 'intensely' exposed to the object (eg snakes, spiders) or situation that he normally tries to avoid; the hope is that by 'overloading' (ie flooding) the person's psyche with the dread event or object, his anxiety would be exhausted and learn to cope with what are, in essence, largely irrational fears. See Aversion therapy, Behavioral therapy, Encounter group therapy, Imaging aversion therapy, Systematic desensitization

**floorwork** see Feldenkreis method

**floral fragrance** *Angelica anomala*, see there

**floral oil** AROMATHERAPY An oil distilled or extracted from geranium, jasmine, roses, and other flowers that is used in aromatherapy; floral oils are believed by aromatherapists to relieve stress. See Aromatherapy, Essential oil, Volatile oil

**flossing** DENTAL HYGIENE The use of waxed or unwaxed synthetic thread to dislodge plaque, food, and microbes from the lateral borders of the teeth; regular flossing reduces halitosis and decreases the incidence of caries and periodontal disease. See

Alternative dentistry

**flotation tank** A type of isolation chamber in which a person floats in a tank filled with water maintained at body temperature, without tactile, auditory, or visual cues; such tanks have been used by those who wish to enhance the experience of meditation by eliminating sensory stimulation. See Isolation chamber, Sensory deprivation

**flotation therapy** ALTERNATIVE PSYCHOLOGY A therapeutic modality developed by an American physician, J Lilly, in which a person is placed in a warm tank filled with salt and mineral water, and isolated from sensory stimulation; by cutting off external stimulation and the sensations of sight, sound, smell, touch, and taste, the individual is believed to be free to examine his inner self or state of mind, and adjust his life circumstances to seek appropriate therapy; anecdotal reports suggest that floatation therapy may be effective in treating addiction disorders (alcohol, smoking), anxiety, insomnia, stress, and tension. See Floater, Isolation chamber, Sensory deprivation

**flower essence therapy** FRINGE MEDICINE 1. Aromatherapy 2. Bach flower remedy 3. A permutation and extension of the Bach flower remedies developed in the 1970s by R Katz, who added more than one hundred flower essences to Bach's original 38; therapeutic flower remedies are selected based on intuition and muscle testing. See Aromatherapy, Bach Flower remedy

**flower remedy** 1. Bach flower remedy, see there 2. Flower essence therapy, see there

**flowers of sulfur** *Sulfur*, see there

**flowering dogwood** Dogwood, see there, *Cornus florida*

**fluid extract** HERBAL MEDICINE A preparation that is the most concentrated form of an herb, and intended to preserve the herb's maximum efficacy; the simplest fluid preparation is a green extract, which is prepared from fresh leaves. See Green extract, Herbal medicine; Cf Fluid extract, Infusion

**fluidum** Animal magnetism, see Mesmerism

**fluoridation** The addition of small amounts of fluoride to drinking water to reduce the incidence of cavities FRINGE MEDICINE It is widely believed by some interested in alternative health that the addition of fluoride to the drinking water causes AIDS, Alzheimer's disease, birth defects, cancer, and a wide range of other conditions PUBLIC HEALTH Although most data suggest that fluoridation may decrease the incidence of caries, it is unclear whether fluoride actually has this effect; more than ½ of the US water supply has > 0.7 ppm of fluoride, a level that is considered adequate to reduce the incidence of caries (*JAMA 1991; 265:2934*). See Fluoride poisoning, Fluorosis

Soft data suggest that fluoride may be carcinogenic (*Science 1990; 247:276*)

**fluoride** A general term for a binary compound containing fluorinet. See Fluoridation, Fluoride poisoning, Fluorine, Fluorosis

**fluoride intoxication** Fluoride poisoning, see there

**fluoride of lime** Calcarea fluorica, see Schüssler's tissue salts

**fluoride poisoning** TOXICOLOGY An acute excess of fluoride may be fatal (either accidental or suicidal), given its affinity for calcium*; it is present in some rodenticides, insecticides, fertilizers, industrial chemicals, and anesthetics; it may cause acute intoxication by inhalation (causing coughing, choking, chills, and fever), ingestion (nausea, vomiting, salivation, paresthesias, diarrhea, and abdominal pain) or contact (hydrogen fluoride is similar to hydrogen chloride, and causes severe skin burns); acute intoxication may be due to an excess in the water supply (*N Engl J Med 1994; 330:950a*). See Fluorosis

*Acute fluoride poisoning caused the lowest serum calcium levels ever recorded, 0.85 mmol/L (US: 3.4 mg/dL) (*Pediatrics 1976; 58:90*)

**fluorine** A gaseous element (atomic number 9, atomic weight 18.99), which is used in health care for radiologic imaging and for dental amalgams. See Fluoridation, Fluoride, Fluoride poisoning, Fluorosis

**fluorosis** Chronic fluoride poisoning A chronic low-level intoxication that occurs where the drinking water's fluoride is > 2 ppm CLINICAL Weight loss, brittle bones, anemia, weakness, ill health, stiffness of joints, mottled enamel and chalky white discolored teeth that have a normal resistance to caries; fluorosis is common, given its availability in mouth rinses, toothpastes, and the injudicious use of fluoride treatments. See Fluoride, Fluoride poisoning, Fluorine

**flux root** Pleurisy root, see there, *Aesclepias tuberosa*

**FLV 23-A** AIDS FRAUD A drug derived from cyclohexane-based hexylene oxides that was claimed in clinical trials to assist in a patient's recovery from AIDS (*Nature 1990; 347:606n*); FLV 23-A was used to treat children infected with HIV-1 in Romania; the trials were halted when the manufacturer failed to provide data regarding the drug's chemical formula, mechanism of action, safety, and efficacy. See AIDS fraud, AIDS therapy

**foaming agent** FOOD INDUSTRY A substance added to liquid foods that puts bubbles on drinks, eg instant chocolate. See Food additives; Cf Anti-foaming agent

***Foeniculum dulce*** Fennel, see there, *Foeniculum vulgare*

***Foeniculum officinale*** Fennel, see there, *Foeniculum vulgare*

***Foeniculum vulgare*** Popularly known as fennel, see there

**folacin** Folic acid, see there

**folic acid** Factor R, factor U, folacin, *Lactobacillus bulgaris* factor, fermentation *Lactobacillus casei* factor, liver *Lactobacillus casei* factor, Norit eluate factor, pteroylmonoglutamic acid, *Streptococcus lactis* R factor, SLR factor, yeast *Lactobacillus casei* factor, vitamin $B_c$, vitamin $B_c$ conjugate, vitamin M A general term for pteroylglutamic acids and their related conjugates; this family of B vitamins are required for normal hematopoiesis (production of red blood cells), and is present in breakfast cereals, eggs, fish, leafy green vegetables, nuts, organ meats, and seeds; it is used to treat megaloblastic anemia and folate deficiency, prevent against cervical cancer, neural tube defects, may ward off coronary artery disease as it counteracts the effects of homocysteine, an amino acid that causes thrombotic vascular disease

**folk cure** Folk remedy, see there

**folk cures for cancer** FRINGE ONCOLOGY Any of a number of herbs and foods that are believed to have some effect in preventing or treating cancer; these include following list was compiled by Dr Jonathan Hartwell at the National Cancer Institute (*Bricklin, 1976*): Absinthe, arnica, atriplex, beets, black walnuts, borage, calendula, celery, chicory, chive, chufa, colocynth, crimson clover, crown vetch, cucumbers, cumin, flax, garlic, hot peppers, licorice, onions, peanuts, poke salad, safflower, salvia, stinging nettle, tamarind, tansy, tea, tomatoes; other herbs that are believed to have anticarcinogenic effects include chaparral, prickly ash, and stillingia. See Chemoprevention, Unproven methods for cancer management

**folk medicine** 1. A general term for any system of health care practiced among natives in a particular culture, which involves a belief in the effectiveness of the chosen treatment, eg plants, rituals, charms, and others. See Ethnomedicine; Cf Alternative medicine 2. Folk remedy, see there

**folk remedy** Folk cure, folk medicine ALTERNATIVE PHARMACOLOGY Any of a number of self-prescribed 'natural' drugs and products that are consumed in the US, and to a lesser degree in developed countries, most often by those with a categoric distrust of mainstream medicine; folk remedies may have significant co-morbidity (eg heavy metal poisoning–lead, mercury, arsenic, and cadmium) (*JAMA 1990; 264:2212c*). See Alternative medicine, Dolomite, Herbal medicine

**fomentation** Hot compress, see there

**food** See Chinese restaurant, Ciguatera poisoning, Diet, Dietary fiber, Fats, Fish, Food groups, Food pyramid, Four food groups, Scombroid poisoning, Spicy food, Succotash, Sushi

**food additive** FOOD INDUSTRY Any of a number of chemical and other products incorporated into processed foods including flavorings (eg monosodium glutamate, MSG), preservatives (eg BHA and BHT), dyes (eg nitrates and FD&C Yellow No. 5 or tartrazine), and other agents; these additives are used to alter the color, flavor, increase the nutritional value, and ease the processing, packaging and storage of foods; food additives may cause allergic reactions, and are believed by some to have a role in causing attention deficit disorder, cancer, migraines, and sinusitis. See Anti-foaming agents, Artificial dye, Artificial flavors, Emulsifier, Enrichment, Firming agent, Foaming agent, Food dye, Glazing agent,

Imitation ingredient, Leavening agent, Nutrient, Sequestrant, Thickener

**food allergy** A condition that is widely percieved to be a major health problem, the incidence of which (0.3-7.5%) has been obscured by controversial data and differing disease definitions; food-induced reactions of immediate-hypersensitivity type are well-recognized and include anaphylaxis, angioedema, and urticaria; food-induced reactions of delayed-hypersensitivity type or those mediated by antigen-antibody complex formation are rarely documented, and include a few specific reactions, eg gluten-sensitive enteropathy CLINICAL Edema and pruritus of oropharyngeal mucosa, followed by various responses in the gastrointestinal tract as the offending, and ultimately offensive, content traverses the system, including vomiting, colic, abdominal distension, flatulence, diarrhea, and less commonly, occult blood loss, malabsorption, protein-losing enteropathy, functional gastrointestinal obstruction, and eosinophilic gastroenteritis LABORATORY Elimination (challenge) diet, rotation diet, in vivo (intradermal, multitest, sublingual) testing, and in vitro (IgE, IgG, $IgG_4$, RAST, cytotoxic, histamine release) testing; Cf Food intolerance

**food color** Food dye, see there

**food colorant** Food dye, see there

**food coloring** Food dye, see there

**food combining** ALTERNATIVE NUTRITION A general term for any dietary practice that is based on the belief that a meal's healthfulness hinges on the compatibility of its components or on the sequence in which they are ingested (*Raso, 1994*)

**Food & Drug Administration** A federal agency of the US Department of Health and Human Services that is charged with ensuring that the American consumer is protected from injury, unsanitary food, and health fraud; the FDA was established in 1931 under the Department of Agriculture, in 1953 the FDA was transferred to the Federal Security Agency, and finally in 1979, to the Department of Health, Education, and Welfare; it enforces the Food, Drug, and Cosmetics Act (enacted in 1938, and amended several times since), the Fair Packaging and Labeling Act, the sections of the Public Health Service Act that relate to biological products, and the Radiation Control for Health and Safety Act; the FDA consists of centers for Biologicals Evaluation and Research, Drug Evaluation and Research, Food Safety, Radiological Health, and Toxico-logical Health (*The Columbia Encyclopedia, 5th ed, Columbia University Press, 1993*); the FDA's most visible roles in health care are in approving new drugs and medical devices, and in evaluating the efficacy of various therapies. See Kefauver-Harris Act

**food dye** Food color, food colorant, food coloring FOOD INDUSTRY Any of a number of natural (eg saffron) or synthetic (eg FD&C Yellow No. 5, also known as tartrazine) dyes added to foods to alter the color; food dyes may cause allergic reactions. See Artificial dye, FDA, FD&C Yellow No. 5, Food additive

**food group** NUTRITION A general term for any family of foods in the diet

▶ **FOOD GROUPS**

- **CARBOHYDRATES** Bread, cereal, rice, oats, pastas
- **CITRUS FRUITS** Grapefruits, lemons, melon, oranges, papaya, strawberries, tomatoes
- **DAIRY PRODUCTS** Cheese, milk, yoghurt
- **FATS** Butter, margarine, fish or vegetable oil, animal fat
- **GREEN/YELLOW VEGETABLES** Brussels sprouts, cabbage, carrots, celery, green beans, kale, spinach
- **HIGH PROTEIN FOODS** Eggs, fish, legumes, meat, nuts, poultry
- **OTHER FRUITS AND VEGETABLES** Apples, bananas, grapes, pineapples; beets, potatoes
- **YELLOW VEGETABLES** Carrots, corn, cauliflower

See Balanced diet, Essential dietary component, Food pyramid, Four food groups, Mineral, Vitamin

**food intolerance** FRINGE MEDICINE An adverse reaction to specific foods which, according to Dr Robert C Atkins, can be identified by applied kinesiology, cytotoxic testing, observing the patient after placing the food on the tongue, interpreting the elevations of blood sugar, and with electroacupuncture (*Butler, 1992*). See Atkins' diet MAINSTREAM MEDICINE Food sensitivity An adverse reaction to specific foods, which occurs in an estimated 10% of the population; food intolerances are often chronic and may cause severe illness; the term food intolerance has been mistakenly regarded as a synonym of food allergy; unlike food intolerances, food allergies are predictable, often severe, involve immunoglobulin E, and the release of histamine from the mast cells; Cf Food allergy

**food irradiation** PUBLIC HEALTH A generic term for the use of ionizing radiation (eg by $^{60}$Co, or $^{137}$Cs) to retard spoilage (1000 Gy prevents sprouting in potatoes, onions, and garlic), and destroys pathogens (> 1000 Gy kills bacteria in cereals, poultry, frog's legs, and other foods) in foods without causing deleterious organoleptic or nutritional changes; as the process induces only a minimal increases in temperature, the qualities typical of raw unprocessed food are preserved; a major criticism of irradiated foods is that the chemical compounds produced during irradiation may themselves be toxic; low level irradiation is designated radurization, so named as it has the same effect as pasteurization, ie improves shelf life and inactivates bacteria that cause food spoilage; higher dose irradiation of food intended to inactivate specific pathogens and parasites is termed radicidation; very high dose irradiation for producing commercial sterility is not commonly used, although it is approved and regarded in the same category as a food additive by the FDA, which requires that foods so preserved carry a radura label; although irradiation is considered safe, irrational fears and mass hysteria may prevent its broader use. See Radurization; Cf Food Preservatives, Organic food

**radura label**

**food preservative** Any of a group of chemical preservatives that the FDA regards as safe for human consumption; food preservatives include antioxidants (eg butylated hydroxyanisole–BHA and butylated hydroxytoluene–BHT), propylparaben, sodium nitrate, sodium nitrite, benzoic acid, and stannous chloride. See BHA, BHT, FDA, Food additive, Generally regarded as safe list

**food pyramid** NUTRITION A schematic guideline (see figure) promulgated by the US Department of Agriculture (USDA) for the proportions of food types that should be consumed daily basis in a healthy diet (*USDA, Human Nutrition Information Service, Home & Garden Bull, No 252, Aug 1992*); at the base of the pyramid are carbohydrates, followed by fruits and vegetables, dairy products,* fish, and meat; at the pyramid's peak are 'discouraged' foods, to be eaten sparingly, including fats, oils, and refined sugars; Cf Four food groups, Exercise pyramid, Five food groups, Mediterranean pyramid

*Dairy products include milk, yogurt, and cheese; proteins include meat, poultry, fish, eggs, dry beans, and nuts

**foot analysis** FRINGE MEDICINE A pseudodiagnostic technique developed in 1991 by A Grinberg in the Netherlands, in which the temperature, shape, and surface of the foot form the basis of the diagnosis; according to Grinberg, in-grown toenails indicate a susceptibility for headaches, calluses on the great toe indicate a defect in the cervical vertebrae, and so on (*Raso, 1994*). See Hand interpretation, Pseudodiagnosis

**foot bath** NATUROPATHY A bath taken in cold or warm water; given the importance of the feet in reflexology, immersion of the feet in extremes of temperature is thought by foot bath advocates to stimulate the entire body through nerve endings for various organs that are present in the feet; foot baths are said to reduce fever, lower blood pressure, treat headaches, improve the quality of sleep and renal function. See Hydrotherapy; Cf Cold bath, Hot bath, Sauna

**forbidden palace flower** Cowherd, see there

**forced exposure** Flooding, see there

**foreign saffron** Saffron, see there, *Crocus sativus*

***Forsythia suspensa*** Weeping golden bell, see there

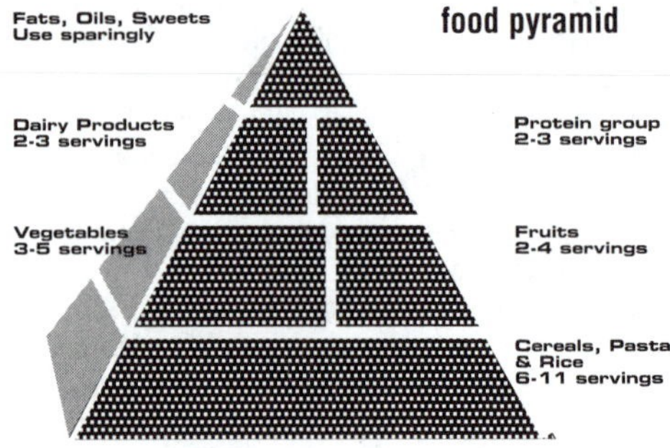


**food pyramid**

**fortified food** Any food, eg a cereal that has essential nutrients (eg iron and vitamins) added either in quantities that are greater than those present normally (supplementation), or which are not normally present in the fortified food ('fortification'). See Fortification; Cf Enriching, Refining

**fortified milk** PUBLIC HEALTH Processed and pasteurized milk with added vitamin D, usually 400 IU of vitamin $D_3$/quart (0.94 L). See Food additive; Cf Breast milk, Certified milk, Raw milk

Note: There is little consistency in the amount of vitamin D that is actually added; in the US and Canada, only 20% of milk purchased contains 80-120% of stated vitamin D; the remainder are either low (or even absent), increasing the risk of rickets, or too high (up to 3– to 9-fold greater than stated vitamin D content), increasing the risk of toxicity (*N Engl J Med 1993; 329:1507c*)

**The Four Directions** TRADITIONAL CHINESE MEDICINE The classification of foods and herbs in Chinese herbal medicine as sinking, rising, floating, or descending, which relates to how the substance reacts in the body; each of the four directions is further classified as having either yin (downward) or yang (upward) forces; light or yang herbs are used to treat superficial or acute conditions, eg colds, or inflammation; heavy or yin herbs are used to treat chronic conditions. See Chinese herbal medicine, Yang foods, Yin foods

**The Four Elements** MEDICAL HISTORY The four major forces—fire, water, earth, and air– in the universe, as understood at the time of Hippocrates. See (the) Four Humors

**four food groups** Basic four foods groups NUTRITION A series of nutritional guidelines published in 1956,* which divided foods into 4 groups (meat; milk/dairy; fruits and vegetables; cereals and grains); in a balanced diet, each food group would represent one-quarter of the foods consumed per day (*Science 1991; 252:917n*). See Food groups, Food pyramid, Balanced diet; Cf Five food groups

*By the US Department of Agriculture (USDA, and superseded in 1992, with the publication of the USDA's 'Food Pyramid')

**The Four Humors** Cardinal juices FRINGE MEDICINE The 4 major fluids in the body–yellow bile, phlegm, black bile, and blood, which the Greeks believed corresponded to the four elements—fire, water, earth, and air—in the universe; now largely of historic interest, the Four Humors or permutations thereof may be evoked or listed as part of a therapeutic philosophy or system that is usually not founded on accepted scientific principles; in general, such ad hoc classification systems are eschewed by alternative health care practitioners; (the) Four Humors

**The Four Natures** TRADITIONAL CHINESE MEDICINE The classification of foods and herbs in Chinese herbal medicine as cold, cool, warm, and hot, which relates to their ability to balance *chi*, the energy of life; each of the four natures is further classified as having either yin or yang forces; according to the Chinese construct a warm/hot or yang herb would be used to treat a cool/cold or yin disease; some of the herbs are nature-neutral and can be used to treat either yang or yin diseases. See Chinese herbal medicine, Yang food, Yin food

**foxberry** Bearberry, see there, *Arctostaphylos uva-ursi*

**foxglove** *Digitalis purpurea*, deadmen's bells, witch's bells HERBAL MEDICINE A biennial herb that contains the prototypic cardioactive glycoside, digitalis, as well as gitalin, gitonin, and gitoxin; it is no longer administered as an herb, given its cardiotoxicity TOXICITY Anorexia, drowsiness, impaired vision, nausea, and vomiting; when the intoxication is extreme, tachyarrhythmias, ventricular fib-

**foxglove** *Digitalis purpurea*

rillation, cardiovascular collapse, and possibly death. See Botanical toxicity, Herbal medicine HOMEOPATHY see *Digitalis*

**foxnut** *Euryale ferox*, chicken head, *chien shih, ji tou, qian shi* CHINESE MEDICINE An aquatic lily, the seeds and fruit of which are analgesic, astringent, nutrient, and tonic; it is used for premature aging, arthritis, impotence, leukorrhea, neuralgia, and nocturnal emissions. See Chinese herbal medicine

**F-plan Diet** CLINICAL NUTRITION A dietary regimen formulated by Audrey Eyton (*F-plan Diet, Crown Publishers, New York, 1983*) that is based on the consumption of low-fat, primarily vegetarian fare with high amounts (35 to 50 grams/day) of fiber, and reduction of calories to 1000 to 1500/day

**fragrant fruit** *Ligusticum wallichii*, see there

**Frankenfood** A highly colloquial generic term of uncertain utility for any food product produced by recombinant DNA technology, eg the genetically engineered tomato, see Flavr Savr (*Bio/Technology 1995; 13:540*)

Waggishly named in the tradition of Mary Shelley's hit, Frankenstein

**frankincense** *Boswellia thurifera* FRINGE MEDICINE-FLOWER ESSENCE THERAPY A flower essence that is believed to calm the nerves and enhance meditation. See Flower essence therapy

**Carlton Fredericks** A self-proclaimed nutritionist with a PhD in communications who has given nutritional and medical advice to millions through his books, lectures, and radio and television broadcasts (*Butler, 1992*)

**free-form amino acids** A general term for purified amino acids in powder, capsules, or pills that are used for a wide variety of therapeutic purposes. See Amino acid therapy, Essential amino acid

**Freeman surgery** see Psychosurgery

**free breathing** Conscious-connected breathing, see there

**free radical** PHYSIOLOGY Any of a family of highly reactive molecules containing an unpaired electron in the outer orbital, eg the excited variants of $O_2$; free radicals cause random damage to structural proteins, enzymes, macromolecules, and DNA, and play major roles in inflammation, hyperoxidation, post-ischemic tissue damage, infarction, and possibly also in carcinogenesis and tissue damage induced by organ transplantation; free radical production is increased by cigarette smoking, radiation, ultraviolet light, and chemical pollutants. See Antioxidants, Free radical scavenger, Free radical theory

**free radical inactivator** Free radical scavenger, see there

**free radical scavenger** Free radical inactivator Any compound that reacts with free radicals in a biological system, reduces free radical-induced damage, and protects against the indirect effects of free radicals produced by ionizing radiation and other sources; free radical scavengers include ceruloplasmin, cysteine, glutathione, superoxide dismutase,* transferrin, vitamins A, C, and E and D-penicillamine. See Antioxidant, Antioxidant therapy, Free radical, Free radical theory

*Superoxide dismutase is the major 'scavenger' enzyme, which catalyzes the reduction of reactive oxygen species to $O_2$ and $H_2O$; free radical production by endothelial cells during coronary artery ischemia, which is inculpated in myocytolysis may be reduced in experimental systems by pre-treatment with superoxide dismutase

**free radical theory** GERIATRICS A biological theory that posits that the changes seen in aging cells and organisms are due to an accumulation of molecules damaged by free radicals; the host cell's defenses against free radical damage include glutathione peroxidase, $\alpha$-tocopherol (vitamin E), and superoxide dismutase; intracellular superoxide levels are believed to correlate well with lifespan. See Antioxidants, Free radical, Free radical scavenger, Glutathione

**José de Freitas** see Psychic surgery

**French tarragon** Tarragon, see there, *Artemisia dracunculus*

**fresh cell method of cellular therapy** Live Cell Therapy, see there

**fresh cell therapy** Live cell therapy, see there

**fresh cell method of cellular therapy** Live cell therapy, see there

**Freudian analysis** PSYCHIATRY The prototypic form of psychoanalysis developed by Sigmund Freud (1856-1939), in which the patient and psychiatrist identify traumatic events and experiences that occurred in the person's childhood, which have been repressed in adult life; psychoanalysis differs from psychotherapy in that it is more formal, intense, and concerned with early sexuality and events of infancy, which may or may not be remembered as they actually occurred–as in the 'false memory' phenomenon; Cf Jungian analysis, Hypnotherapy, Psychotherapy

**friar's cap** Aconite, see there, *Aconitum napellus*

**friction** A 'soft tissue' massage technique, which entails the use of small circular pressure strokes from the fingertips, thumb pads, and palms, with the intent of freeing stiff joints, and enhancing the flow of blood to tendons and ligaments. See Massage therapy

**fringe** *adjective* Pertaining or referring to those health care methods and philosophies that lie between therapies that may represent viable alternatives to mainstream medical treatment (eg acupuncture, chiropractic, homeopathy, and others), and those that are purely speculative, questionable, or frankly unethical (eg laetrile, psychic surgery); Cf Alternative, Integrative, Mainstream

In the present work, the author uses the terms fringe medicine, fringe nutrition, fringe oncology, fringe pharmacology, and others to refer to this 'gray area' of alternative health

**fringe medicine** 1. Alternative medicine, see there 2. Quackery, see there 3. As used in this work Any health care doctrine that is not clearly fraudulent, but which is based on no recognized scientific principle, eg flower essence therapy and iridology

**fringe (medical) practitioner** 1. A generic term for any of a wide range of practitioners of alternative medicine, see there 2. Quack, see there 3. As used in this work, any health care worker who either believes in his 'medical' doctrine, or is not intentionally deceptive in his methods, but whose therapy is based on no recognized scientific principle

**fringe tree** *Chionanthus virginicus*, chionanthus, graybeard, old man's beard, poison ash, snowdrop tree, snowflower, white fringe HERBAL MEDICINE A deciduous tree or shrub, the bark of which contains a glycoside, phyllyrin and saponins; its bark is antipyretic, astringent, diuretic, laxative, and tonic; it has been used internally to stimulate the appetite, gastric secretions, and the flow of bile, and topically to treat wounds. See Herbal medicine

**frontier prescription** MEDICAL HISTORY-QUACKERY A colloquial term for the doses prescribed for medicines, in particular patent medicines, in the days of the 'wild West' (United States in the 19th century); medicines were to be swallowed, '*...one for a man, two for a horse*'. See Patent medicine

**fructose** ALTERNATIVE NUTRITION A molecule that is half sucrose (table sugar) and half glucose, which has been promoted as a sugar substitute ADVANTAGES It is 70% sweeter per calorie than other sugars and does not promote caries (tooth decay) DISADVANTAGES It is more expensive, loses sweetness with heating, and may increase serum lipids in some individuals. See Artificial sweeter

**fruit juice fast** ALTERNATIVE NUTRITION An 'elimination' fast in which the person ingests fruit (eg apple, grape, grapefruit, lemon, orange) juice and water, but no solid foods. See Fasting

**fruit and vegetable** PREVENTIVE MEDICINE A unit of food that has been widely regarded as healthy, given the content of potassium, antioxidants, carotenoids, ellagic acid, flavonoids, and other as-yet unidentified substances; an accumulating body of data suggests that F&Vs are indeed 'good for you'*. See Food pyramid

*In the population-based longitudinal Framingham study, there was a 22% decrease in incidence of strokes for every 3-servings/day increase in F&V intake (*JAMA 1995; 273:1113oa*)

**fruit vegetable** CLINICAL NUTRITION A type of vegetable that has a pulpy, seed-rich body which grows on a vine; fruit vegetables include eggplants, peppers, squashes, tomatoes, and zucchini which, while technically fruits, are used as vegetables; they are higher in calories than leafy vegetables, and are rich in vitamin C; Cf Leafy vegetable

**frutarian** Raw food eater A person who consumes only fruits, which some also define as including vegetables, nuts, and sprouted beans or grains; frutarians eschew the use of fats, oils, sugar, salt, and other flavorings

***fu ling*** Tuckahoe, see there, *Porio cocos*

***fu* organs** CHINESE MEDICINE Those organs (stomach, small intestine, large intestine, gallbladder, and urinary bladder) which, according to the construct of traditional Chinese medicine, are yang organs that transform food into energy and eliminate wastes; Cf *Zang* organs

***fu pen dze*** Chinese wild raspberry, see there, *Rubus coreanus*

***fu pen zi*** Chinese wild raspberry, see there, *Rubus coreanus*

***fu yao*** Herbal poultice, see there

***Fucus vesiculosus*** Popularly known as bladderwrack, see there

**full immersion bath** NATUROPATHY A bath in which the patient is completely 'dunked' in hot or cold water, which is believed to enhance the therapeutic effect achieved by a bath encompassing a smaller surface area. See Hydrotherapy

**fumitory** *Fumaria officinalis*, earth smoke, hedge fumitory, wax dolls HERBAL MEDICINE An annual herb that contains alkaloids, fumaric acid, mucilage, resin, and tannic acid; it is a mild laxative, diuretic, and stimulates the flow of bile, and has been used to treat skin conditions and liver complaints TOXICITY Large doses may cause stomach aches and diarrhea. See Herbal medicine

***Fumaria officinalis*** 1. Wild Chinese violet 2. Fumitory, see there

**functional integration** see Feldenkreis method

**fusion meditation** PARANORMAL PHENOMENA Any format of meditation that is believed to convert negative energy into 'quality energy' that can then fuse with negative energy; such meditation is based on the belief in chakras and an energy body (*Raso, 1994*). See Chakra balancing, Meditation

***fu-zhen*** CHINESE MEDICINE A class of Chinese herbs that has been used by practictioners of Chinese medicine to both prevent and to treat cancer; fu-zhen is believed to have a positive effect on the survival in stage II liver cancer (*Recent Can Res 1988; 108:327*). See Chinese herbal medicine, Chinese medicine, Folk cures for cancer, Traditional Chinese medicine

**gagroot** Lobelia, see there, *Lobelia inflata*

**Gaia hypothesis** ENVIRONMENT BACKGROUND According to Darwin, evolution of the species, ie life, is driven by a static, nonliving environment; Gaia[1] is the theoretical opposite, and assumes that living organisms control and modify the relative compositions of the sea, air, and environment, thus viewing all life (flora and fauna) on the planet as an interacting homeostatic macrocosm or 'organism' driving mutual coordinated evolution of the geophysical sphere and its living inhabitants; Gaia is viewed by its chief architect, J Lovelock, as not being endowed with the foresight to regulate the planet's temperature and composition, but rather to optimize it. [2]See Creationism

[1]Gaia, the Greek Goddess of the Earth, is an 'organism' from J Lovelock's book on a magical kingdom, Gaia, *A New Look at Life on Earth*, Oxford University Press, 1979 [2]Gaia-ists are often scientifically 'innocent,' while non-Gaia-ists are often mainstream biologists; '.... *We should be careful, however, not to pretend* (that) *Gaia is a testable hypothesis, much less a basis for managing the biosphere. The risk is this: a metaphor like Gaia, flexible enough to wrap around any data set, is also versatile enough to be invoked, ad hoc, to lend a spurious air of scientific legitimacy to almost any reckless conjecture.'* JW Kirchner, Caltech (*Nature 1990; 345:470c*)

***Galium aparine*** Popularly known as cleavers, see there

**gallbladder meridian** Leg lesser yang meridian ACUPUNCTURE A meridian that extends from the lateral foot to the lateral chest; stimulation of acupoints along the gallbladder meridian are used to treat conditions affecting the extremities and chest. See Acupuncture, Meridians, Twelve meridians

**Galvanic Electric Belt** HEALTH FRAUD A device marketed in the beginning of the 20th century, which was constructed of copper and zinc, separated by blotting paper, and worn discreetly under clothing; the belt delivered low-voltage electricity, which was believed to increase a person's energy level and to cure chronic nervous diseases. See Pulvermacher's Electric Belt, Quackery

**Galvanic skin response biofeedback** Electrodermal skin response biofeedback A type of biofeedback therapy in which subtle changes in the autonomic system are monitored by the patient with a device that measures the changes in skin conductivity, caused by a minimal sweating; galvanic skin response biofeedback is believed to be useful in treating asthma, desensitization of phobic disorders, psychotherapy, and stuttering. See Biofeedback device, Biofeedback training, Electromyograph feedback

**gamma-linolenic acid** A chemical form of linolenic acid, the richest source of which is evening primrose oil FRINGE ONCOLOGY GLA has been used as a cancer treatment for dogs (*Moss, 1992*); it is reported to repress the growth of experimental breast, lung, and prostate cancer cell lines, and neuroblastomas. See Unproven methods for cancer management FRINGE PHARMACOLOGY GLA has been used for diabetes, hypercholesterolemia, obesity, premenstrual syndrome, schizophrenia, and other conditions (*Moss, 1992*). See Evening primrose, Evening primrose oil

***gan cao*** Licorice, see there, *Glycyrrhiza glabra*

***gan di huang*** *Rehmannia glutinosa*, see there

***gan dzao*** Chinese jujube, see there, *Ziziphus vulgaris*

***gan jiang*** Ginger, see there, *Zingiber officinale*

***gan tsao*** Licorice, see there, *Glycyrrhiza glabra*

**ganja** See Marijuana

**ganoderma** Reishi, see there

***Ganoderma lucidum*** Popularly known as reishi, see there

***Gansheitstherapy*** Issels' whole body therapy, see there

***gao*** Paste–Chinese medicine, see there

**garden angelica** Angelica, see there, *Angelica archangelica*

**garden daisy** *Bellis*, see there, *Bellis perennis*

**garden heliotrope** Valerian, see there, *Valeriana officinalis*

**garden rue** Rue, see there, *Ruta graveolens*

**garden sage** Sage, see there, *Salvia officinalis*

**garden thyme** Thyme, see there, *Thymus vulgaris*

**gargle** A liquid preparation of herbs, hydrogen peroxide, or other substance that is used as an intraoral wash, eg for sore throat, which is not intended to be ingested

**garlic** *Allium sativum* A culinary and medicinal perennial plant that contains amino acids, volatile oils (eg allicin), and vitamins A, B, and C; garlic owes its aroma to the high content of selenium, which is eliminated through the lungs and skin as dimethyl selenide; it is used in herbal medicine as a rubefacient and antihelmintic, and regarded as 'healthy'

▶ **GARLIC**

- **INHIBITS TUMOR GROWTH** and activity of tumor promoters and has chemopreventive activity against methylcholanthrene-induced carcinogenesis
- **ENHANCES DEFENSES AGAINST SYSTEMIC TOXINS**, acting in antihepatotoxin, stabilizing liver microsomal membranes from lipid peroxidation and ameliorates cyclophosphamide toxicity in mice; it may reduce serum lead
- **IS ANTIMICROBIAL**, inhibits growth of *Entamoeba histolytica*, lipid synthesis by *Candida albicans* and attachment of *Candida* spp to buccal mucosa, possibly related to conversion of allicin to diallyldisulfide when exposed to air
- **INHIBITS PLATELET AGGREGATION & PLATELET RELEASE**
- **REDUCES CARDIOVASCULAR DISEASE**–allicin and ajoene decrease cholesterol

See Healthy foods; Cf Spicy foods CHINESE MEDICINE Chinese chive, *da suan* Garlic is used in traditional Chinese medicine as an antimicrobial and general tonic; it is used internally for colds, cough, diarrhea, gastrointestinal complaints, parasites, rheumatic disease, shellfish poisoning, tuberculosis, tumors, vaginitis, and to increase internal secretions; it is used topically for athlete's foot, fungal and parasitic infection. See Chinese herbal medicine HERBAL MEDICINE In Western herbal medicine, garlic is used internally for atherosclerosis, colds, coughs, flu, gastrointestinal complaints, hypercholesterolemia, hypertension, liver and gallbladder disease; garlic's topical uses are as with Chinese herbal medicine. See Herbal medicine

**gastric balloon** Garren's balloon A doughnut-shaped inflatable polyurethane cylinder designed to decrease the stomach volume, which may be used in morbid obesity to reduce hunger sensation; when in place for prolonged periods, the gastric balloon induces hyperplasia of the gastrin-producing cells or rarely, pressure ulcers. See Diet, Ileal bypass operation, Morbid obesity

***Gastrodia elata*** *Chih chien, feng tsao*, red arrow, *tien ma*, wind grass CHINESE MEDICINE A perennial alpine plant of the orchid family, the tubers of which are anticonvulsive, sedative, and nerve tonics; *G elata* is used for headaches, low back pain, neuralgia, seizures, stress, and vertigo. See Chinese herbal medicine

**René Maurice Gattefossé** A French chemist who published *Aromatherapie* in 1937 and, in effect, became the father of modern aromatherapy. See Aromatherapy

***Gaultheria procumbens*** Popularly known as wintergreen, see there

**Ge-132** An organically-bound form of germanium synthesized by Dr J Asai, which is said to be an effective therapy for cancer. See Germanium; it is reported to increase NK (natural killer) cell activity and interferon production (*Pelton, Overholser, 1994*). See Germanium, Unproven methods for cancer management

***geh gen*** Kutzu vine, see there, *Pueraria lobata*

***Gelidium cartilagineum*** Popularly known as agar, see there

***Gelsemium*** *Gelsemium sempervirens, G sempervitalis*, Carolina jasmine, Carolina jessamine, Carolina yellow jasmine, evening trumpet flower, false jasmine, jasmine, yellow jasmine, yellow jessamine HERBAL MEDICINE *Gelsimium* is a poisoning evergreen vine that is not used by herbologists HOMEOPATHY A remedy that has been used for the nervous system and mucosal membranes, and for anxiety, cardiac arrhythmias, earaches, fever-associated myalgias, flu, headaches that are worse with bright lights, insomnia, measles, menstrual dysfunction, phobias, shock, sore throat, and trembling. See Homeopathy

**gem therapy** 1. Crystal therapy, see there 2. A permutation of crystal therapy in which a person wears precious or semiprecious stones, which are believed to have specific healing properties, eg rubies for chills. See Crystal therapy

**general adaptation syndrome** Flight-or-fight response, see there

**generalist** A physician who sees the patient as a whole 'unit,' ie not as an 'organ system' (specialist); generalists include family practitioners, general internists, and general pediatricians. See Holistic approach

**generally regarded as safe list** PHARMACOLOGY An extensive list, compiled by the FDA, of compounds that are often used in foods, cosmetics, and drugs, which are widely regarded as having little or no adverse effects on humans; GRAS compounds are legally defined under the 1958 Amendment of the Federal Food, Drug and Cosmetics Act; GRAS compounds include food preservatives, coatings, and films that may be used on fruits and vegetables, special dietary and nutritive additives, anticaking agents, eg sodium ferrocyanide, flavoring agents, gum bases, and other multipurpose agents. See Food preservatives

**'genetic optimizer'** see Invalid claims of efficacy

**Genie** A girl who had been imprisoned by her parents from age 2 until age 13, when she was discovered by authorities in Southern California in 1970; her height was in the 10th percentile, she walked in a permanently stooped position, had little speech, and permanent calluses on the buttocks as she had been strapped to a potty seat for long periods; the case has raised various ethical and scientific issues, and she was seen in a light similar to that of the 'Wild Child' of France; she has remained in a foster home for adults (*N Engl J Med 1994; 331:1030 Genie, R Rymer, HarperCollins*). See Anaclytic depression, Psychosocial dwarfism, Social isolation, '*The Wild Child*'; Cf Companionship

**genista** Broom, see there, *Sarothamnus scoparius*

**genistine** ALTERNATIVE ONCOLOGY An isoflavone present in soy products that down-regulates some of the enzymes involved in the carcinogenesis cascade, and may block neoplastic angiogenesis (blood vessel formation induced by tumors). See Soy

**genogram** ALTERNATIVE PSYCHOLOGY A chart that displays in graphic form the complex psychological interactions that occur in a multigenerational family; genograms use some of the geneologic symbols used in creating pedigrees of patients with genetic diseases, and adds those that are germane to the cohort's psychology (see figure)

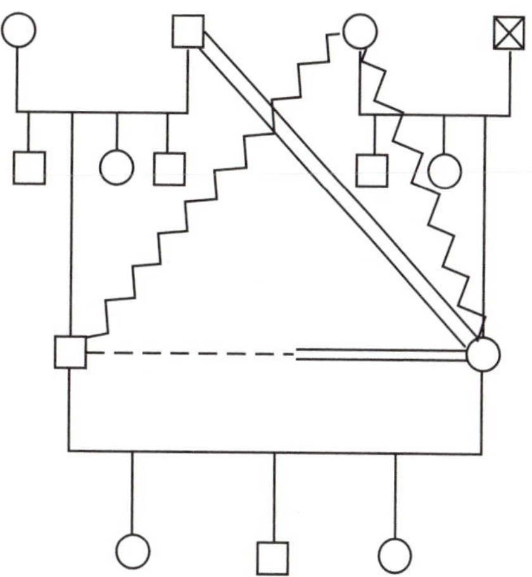


**genogram**

**gentian** *Gentiana lutea*, bitter root, gentian root, pale gentian, yellow gentian HERBAL MEDICINE A perennial herb (see figure, pg 158) that contains gentiopicrin, gentiamarin, gentisin, gentianose, triterpenes, volatile oil, and xanthones; gentian root is used in Western herbal medicine as a digestive tonic, to increase the appetite, peristalsis, and flow of bile; it is also used for arthritis, fatigue, and menstrual irregularity TOXICITY Large doses cause vomiting; it should not be used in those with hypertension, gastroenteritis, or in pregnancy. See Herbal medicine

**gentiana** *Gentiana scabra*, gentian root, *lung dan cao, lung dan tsao* A perennial herb that contains gentiopicrin, gentiamarin, gentisin, gen-

**gentian** *Gentiana lutea*

tianose, triterpenes, volatile oil, and xanthones CHINESE MEDICINE Gentiana root is used in Chinese medicine as an anti-inflammatory, and antipyretic, and is used to treat cholecystitis, diabetes, gallstones, hepatitis, ocular and rheumatic pain, pelvic inflammatory disease, seizures, sexually-transmitted diseases, and vaginal discharge TOXICITY Uncertain; it is not recommended in those with diarrhea. See Chinese herbal medicine

**gentian root** 1. Gentian, see there, *Gentiana lutea* 2. Gentiana, *Gentiana scabra*

***Gentiana lutea*** Popularly known as gentian, see there

***Gentiana scabra*** Popularly known as gentiana, see there

**gentle medicine** Alternative medicine, see there

**geranium** *Germanium maculatum* FRINGE MEDICINE-FLOWER ESSENCE THERAPY A floral essence believed to evoke relaxation. See Flower essence therapy. See Cranesbill

***Geranium maculatum*** Popularly known as cranesbill, see there

**geriatric massage** ALTERNATIVE MEDICINE A general term for any form of massage administered to an elderly person; older individuals may suffer long-term deleterious effects of poor nutrition, harsh climate, air and water pollution, accidents, intense physical activity, trauma, emotional and financial crises, which impact on the immune system; geriatric massage is intended to improve circulation, 'detoxify' cells and tissues, stimulate lymphatic drainage, soften indurated muscles, improve joint mobility, lower blood pressure, and increase energy; it may be of use in treating arthritis, hip and other joint problems, myofibrositis, neck and shoulder pain, poor circulation, and stiffening of the vertebral column. See Aging, Massage therapy; Cf Infant massage

**germ theory** The theory advanced by Louis Pasteur, and widely accepted in mainstream medicine that states, in brief, all infections are caused by microbes; the germ theory has been questioned by practitioners of alternative medicine, who may subscribe to the belief that infections only occur when the immune system is compromised

**German chamomile** *Matricaria chamomilla*, see Chamomile

**German rue** Rue, see there, *Ruta graveolens*

**German valerian** Valerian, see there, *Valeriana officinalis*

**germanium** FRINGE NUTRITION A metallic element used in 'high-tech' industries and believed in the 1920s to be an essential trace element; there is no known metabolic role for germanium in the body and in large quantities, it is toxic to the kidneys; germanium in tablets and other forms has been promoted as a therapy for AIDS, allergies, anemia, arthitis, cancer, chronic fatigue syndrome, diseases of the heart, liver, and nervous system, headaches, infections, sexual dysfunction, and other conditions; it is claimed to prevent birth defects and lower cholesterol levels. See Unproven methods for cancer management

**Gerovital** $GH_3$ ALTERNATIVE PHARMACOLOGY A formulation of procaine that was developed in Romania by Ana Aslan, which is administered by injection and has been used for rejuvenation, increasing longevity, enhancing the immune system, relieving depression, lowering blood pressure and levels of cortisone in the circulation, and treating arthritis (*Fox, 1996*); the agent is not officially available in the US

The US National Institute on Aging reviewed Aslan's data on Gerovital's effects; it was critical of her methods and concluded that the evidence for antiaging effects was unconvincing (*Butler, 1992*)

**Gerson dietary regimen** Gerson therapy, see there

**Gerson method** Gerson therapy, see there

**Gerson therapy** Gerson dietary regimen, Gerson method, Gerson treatment FRINGE ONCOLOGY An unproven method for managing cancer that was developed in the 1920s by Max Gerson, MD (1881-1959), which attempts to 'detoxify' the body with coffee enemas and 'sodium-poor, potassium-rich, poison-free' diets; in addition to cancer, Gerson therapies are believed to treat severe headaches and tuberculosis; Gerson's was the first of the so-called 'metabolic therapies,'[1] of which there are now 20; Gerson attributed the increased rate of cancer in the general population to the increased use of fertilizers in agriculture, which increases sodium and decreases potassium in fruits and vegetables; according to Gerson, food processing and cooking add more sodium, further altering the cells, causing a switch from oxidative to fermentative metabolism[2]; the Gerson regimen[3] is rigorous and includes enemas[4], medications[5], and various ancillary therapies[6], and because strict adherence to the Gerson method is regarded as critical to its success, it is very time-consuming[7] (*Fact Sheet from the American Cancer Society, Unproven Methods of Cancer Management*)

▶ **GERSON CLAIMS**

- **CLAIM 1** Anaerobic energy production causes cancer
- **CLAIM 2** Vital organs have been poisoned by toxic substances in processed foods and are detoxified by bile
- **CLAIM 3** Coffee enemas (see there) stimulate bile production
- **CLAIM 4** Cafestol and kahweol (compounds present in coffee enemas) enhance detoxification by stimulating liver enzymes
- **CLAIM 5** Enzymes from raw fruit, vegetables, and calves' liver restore normal function to poisoned organs
- **CLAIM 6** Once detoxified, the organs mount a tumoricidal allergic reaction

(*JAMA 1992 268:3224*) *Resource: Gerson Institute, PO Box 430, Bonita, CA 91908-0430* ☎ *1.619.472.7450*

[1]These methods claim to cure various diseases by 'detoxifying' the body, and 'boosting the immune system' [2]forbidden is the use of aluminum in cooking, salt, tobacco, alcohol [3]which includes once-hourly glasses of juices (orange juice, green leaf juice, carrot/apple juice, and pressed raw calf's liver-yum); forever forbidden foods include salt, oil, coffee, berries, nuts, drinking water, and any food that has been processed in any form (ie bottled, canned, refined, preserved, or frozen); temporarily forbidden fruits include dairy products, fish, and meat [4]with dilute coffee, castor oil, green leaves, and others [5]thyroid extracts, acidophilus pepsin, pancreatin, royal jelly, niacin, crude liver extracts [6]Laetrile–used for 'short-term relief from cancer-related pain,' 'polarizing treatments, Staphage lysate, and ozone enemas [7]according to one official of the Gerson Institute, 40-50 hours are spent of each week in order to purchase and process the foods properly

**Gerson treatment** Gerson therapy, see there

**Gestalt therapy** German, Configuration HUMANISTIC PSYCHOLOGY A type of psychotherapy developed by a German psychoanalyst, Fritz Perls, which focuses on the whole person, and thus is a 'holistic approach' to the psyche; Gestalt therapy takes into account the person's perceptions, and the effects of his environment and related stresses on his behavior; Gestalt therapists design 'experiments' in which the client play-acts and tries out new behaviors and responses to the experimental conditions, thereby increasing his self-awareness, and through it, self-liberation

▶ **SALIENT GESTALT INJUNCTIONS ARE**

- Live now
- Live here
- Stop imagining
- Stop unnecessary thinking
- Express rather than manipulate
- Give in to unpleasantness and pain-not just pleasure
- Accept no one else's image of yourself
- Take full responsibility for your actions
- Surrender to being as you are

(*C Naranjo, in Inglis, West, 1983*). See Est, Humanistic psychology, Psychotherapy

**GF-1** HERBAL MEDICINE A proprietary polysaccharide extracted from the fruiting bodies of the oriental mushroom, maitake (*Grifola frondosa*), which is reported to have antitumor activity against soft tissue tumors (sarcomas) and and cancers (*Moss, 1992*). See Chinese herbal medicine, Maitake, Unproven methods for cancer management

**GFL** HERBAL MEDICINE A lectin extracted from the fruiting bodies of the oriental mushroom, maitake (*Grifola frondosa*), which is reported to have antitumor activity (*Moss,*

*1992*). See Chinese herbal medicine, Maitake, Unproven methods for cancer management

**$GH_3$** Gerovital, see there

**ghee** Clarified butter AYURVEDIC MEDICINE The primary ingredient of many ayurvedic home remedies, which is prepared by boiling unsalted butter and discarding the strained cholesterol-rich curds

**Gill-over-the-ground** Ground ivy, see there, *Glechoma hederacea*

**GIM** Guided imagery and music, see there

**ginger** A deciduous plant rich in volatile oil with borneol, camphene, cineol, citral, gingerols, shogaols, zingerones, eg phenylalkylketones and phelandrene ALTERNATIVE NUTRITION Ginger has a long tradition as a 'healthy food,' and is used as a digestive aid, to prevent nausea due to motion sickness, morning sickness, or chemotherapy, for cardiovascular disease, as ginger reduces cholesterol, and may be useful in preventing cancer. See Healthy foods *Zingiber officinale, gan jiang* CHINESE MEDICINE Ginger is used in the Chinese kitchen, and in Chinese herbal medicine; the rhizomes are antiemetic, cardiotonic, carminative, rubifacient, and stimulate secretion; it is used topically for burns, and internally for abdominal pain, colds, hangovers, hypercholesterolemia, menstrual dysfunction, motion sickness, nausea, Raynaud's phenomenon, seafood intoxication, and vomiting. See Chinese herbal medicine HERBAL MEDICINE Ginger is used in Western herbal medicine for arthritic pain, colds, coughs, earache, gastrointestinal complaints, gout, headache, pancreatitis, hypertension, kidney conditions, menstrual cramping, motion sickness, sinusitis, and vertigo; some data suggest that ginger may be an antihypertensive and anticoagulant. See Herbal medicine

**gingko** *Gingko biloba* ALTERNATIVE PHARMACOLOGY A tree native to China, the leaves of which have terpenoid derivatives known as gingkolides A, B, and C, as well as bilobalide, and proanthocyanidins; as a group these compounds have anticoagulant activity, act as free radical scavengers, increase the peripheral blood flow, and are thought by some to slow age-associated memory impairment; the kernals are known in traditional Chinese medicine as *bai guo, Salisburia adiantifolia*, white nut, *ying hsing*, *ying xing*; the root is designated *bai guo gen* CHINESE MEDICINE Gingko roots and kernels (the latter are more potent) are anthelmintic, antitussive, astringent, cardiotonic, and sedative; gingko is used to treat alcoholic binges, asthma, bladder infections, cough, gonorrhea, and tuberculosis. See Chinese herbal medicine HERBAL MEDICINE Gingko is used to increase cerebral blood flow, prevent blood clots, and mood swings, and may be effective in Alzheimer's disease, asthma, decubital ulcers, diabetic vascular disease, phlebitis, Raynaud syndrome, tinnitus, and vertigo MAINSTREAM MEDICINE Mainstream pharmacologic research has shown gingkolides to be effective in treating cerebrovascular insufficiency, which causes lacunar defects of memory, migraines, strokes, and vertigo TOXICITY Gingko may cause hypersensitivity; it should not be used in pregnancy, or in those with coagulation defects

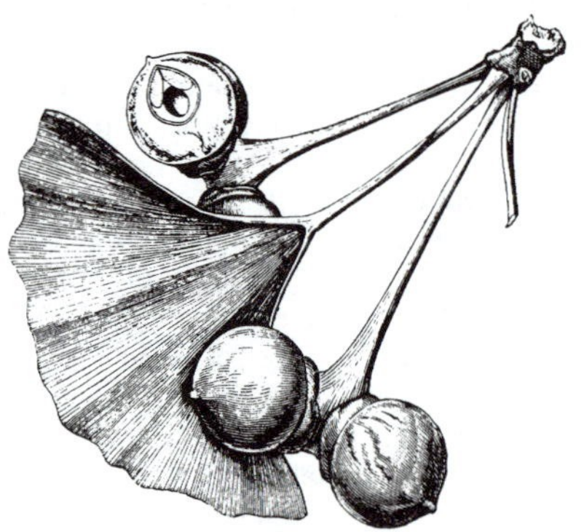

**gingko** *Gingko biloba*

**gingkolide B** ALTERNATIVE PHARMACOLOGY A chemical extracted from the ginkgo tree (*Gingko biloba*) that is of potential use in treating asthma and circulatory defects in the elderly. See Gingko

**gingkolides** ALTERNATIVE PHARMACOLOGY A large group of medicinal preparations from a tree in northern China, *Gingko biloba,* which are used by herbalists to treat cardiovascular and cerebrovascular disease, emotional lability, ocular defects, panic disorder, vertigo, other conditions. See Gingko, gingkolide B

**ginseng** 1. *Panax ginseng*; Asian ginseng, Chinese ginseng, divine herb, Japanese ginseng, Korean ginseng, Oriental ginseng, panax, *Panax schinseng*, *ren shen*, *shen tsao* CHINESE MEDICINE Any of 22 different deciduous plants, mostly of the Panax family, eg *Panax ginseng*, that are native to Southeast Asia; ginseng root contains panaxin, panax acid, panaquilen, panacen, sapogenin, and ginsenin; it is used in Chinese herbal medicine as a tonic and restorative, and believed to have immunologic, hormonal, and stress-reducing effects; it has been used for respiratory infections, gastrointestinal complaints including anorexia, bloating, depression, diarrhea, vomiting, fatigue, impotence, shock, shortness of breath, stress, and increased sweating PHYSIOLOGIC EFFECTS Increased testosterone, corticosteroids, gluconeogenesis, central nervous system activity, blood pressure, pulse, gastrointestinal motility, and hematopoiesis, and decreased cholesterol; evidence of ginseng's androgenic effect is anecdotal; it is widely consumed as an aphrodisiac TOXICITY Ginseng should not be used in those with asthma, arrhythmias, hypertension, or postmenopausal bleeding 2. American ginseng, see there, *Panax quinquefolius* 3. Siberian ginseng, see there, *Eleutherococcus senticosus* FRINGE ONCOLOGY Ginseng's purported efficacy in treating cancer is inconclusive (*Moss, 1992*), although it is thought to protect against cancer. See Unproven methods for cancer management

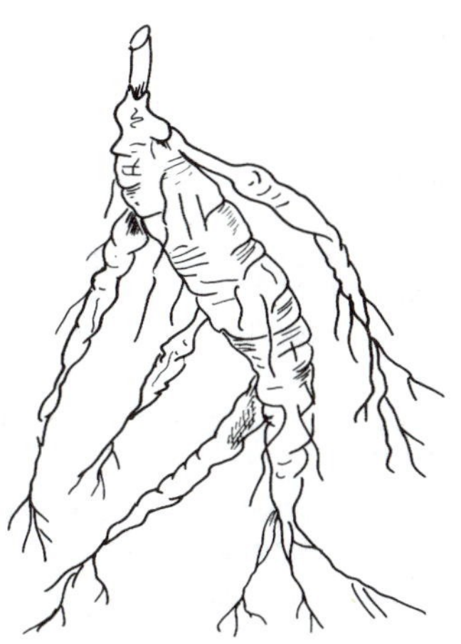

**ginseng** *Panax ginseng*

**ginseng abuse syndrome** A clinical complex caused by daily ingestion of 3 or more grams of ginseng CLINICAL Diarrhea, nervousness, insomnia, eruptive dermatosis, cognitive and motor hyperactivity. See Ginseng

**G-jo** Acupressure, see there

**GLA** Gamma-linolenic acid, see there

**glandular** Glandular extract, glandular remedy FRINGE PHARMACOLOGY A capsule, pill, or powder containing dried ground-up glandular (eg adrenal, ovarian, pancreatic, testicular, and other) and nonglandular (eg cerebral, hepatic, and renal) tissues of animal origin; glandulars are believed to enhance the function of the organ from which the extract was produced. See Endogenous endocrinotherapy

**glandular extract** Glandular, see there

**glandular remedy** Glandular, see there

**glazing agent** FOOD INDUSTRY A substance added to foods, in particular baked products, to make their surface shiny. See Food additive

***Glechoma hederacea*** Popularly known as ground ivy, see there

***Glonoin*** *Glonoinum*, glyceryl trinitrate, nitroglycerine HOMEOPATHY A minor homeopathic remedy that has been used for headaches, heatstroke, and circulatory lability. See Homeopathy

**glossy buckthorn** Alder buckthorn, see there, *Rhamnus frangula*

**glucan I** HERBAL MEDICINE A water-soluble polysaccharide obtained from the fruiting bodies of the edible Japanese mushroom, kikurage (*Auricularia auricula-judae*), which is reported to have antitumor activity against experimental tumors in mice (*Moss, 1992*). See Chinese herbal medicine

**glutathione** γ-Glutamyl-cysteinyl-glycine A ubiquitous antioxidant tripeptide involved in central nervous system metabolism, which serves as a coenzyme for some enzymes of oxidation-reduction systems, transmembrane amino acid transport, maintenance of RBC integrity, and prevention of $H_2O_2$ accumulation in red cells; glutathione is found in asparagus, avocado, broccoli, oranges, squash, strawberries, and watermelon. See Antioxidant, Antioxidant therapy, Free radical, Free radical scavenger, Free radical theory

**gluten** A wheat endosperm protein composed of gliadin and glutelin, which is inculpated in the pathogenesis of celiac disease, also known as gluten-sensitive enteropathy

**gluten-free diet** A diet that excludes all forms of gluten, including wheat, rye, oats, and barley, as well as beans, cabbage, cucumbers, dried peas, plums, prunes, and turnips; other foods that contain gluten include beer, instant coffee, malted milk, and Postum; grains allowed in a gluten-free diet include corn, rice, and gluten-free wheat, dairy products, seafoods, and poultry; the gluten-free diet is supplemented with vitamins, minerals, and digestive aids, including enzymes, eg bromelain, pancrelipase, and papain, as well as betaine, lecithin, and ox bile. See Celiac disease, Diet, Digestive aid, Gluten

**glyceryl trinitrate** *Glonoin*, see there, *Glonoinum*

**glycogen hypothesis** A theory that attempts to explain why some individuals never overeat; according to this hypothesis, glycogen stores affect the appetite in unknown ways; some individuals store very little glycogen, and when fat is available, burn it off immediately (*Sci Am Aug 1996, p88*). See Obesity; Cf Set point hypothesis; Settling point hypothesis

**glycogen loading** Carbohydrate loading, see there

**glycoside** HERBAL MEDICINE Any of a number of medicinally active compounds produced by plants, which include hydrocyanic (prussic) acid, which gives cough syrup its bitter almond flavor, digitoxin, a cardioactive agent, and salicin, which is the basis for salicylic acid. See Foxglove, Herbal medicine

***Glycyrrhiza glabra*** Popularly known as licorice, see there

**glycyrrhizin** A whitish crystalline extract from licorice (*Glycyrrhiza glabra*) roots, which is composed of calcium and potassium salts of glycyrrhizic acid; it is a demulcent, expectorant, and a flavoring agent for drugs, and claimed to have antibacterial and antiretroviral activity (*Am Med News 21 Nov 1994 p13*); Cf AIDS fraud

**glyoxylide** HEALTH FRAUD The active ingredient that was alleged to be present in the Koch treatments used for cancer victims; glyoxylide is believed by some to be distilled water. See Koch treatment, Unproven methods for cancer management

**gnidilatidin** PHARMACOGNOSY A chemical found in stillingia (*Stillingia sylvatica*) that has been shown to have anticarcinogenic activity in animals (*Pelton, Overholser, 1994*). See Folk cures for cancer, Stillingia

**'go' foods** NUTRITION A colloquial term for foods (eg fish, fruits, garlic, whole grains, and others) that can be eaten virtually ad lib in the diet. See Diet, nutritional Nutritional therapy; Cf 'No' foods

**'GO' FOODS--RECOMMENDED FOODS**

Cold pressed oils
Fish
Fresh fruits and vegetables and their juices
Honey
Onions and garlic
Nuts
Seeds
Whole grain breads and cereals
Yogurt, kefir, and other soured dairy products
Carroll, 1980

**goat milk** Chinese wolfberry, see there, *Lycium chinese*

**goatweed** Saint John's wort, see there, *Hypericum perforatum*

**gold** *Aurum metallicum*, see there

**gold coin flower** Elecampene, see there, *Inula helenium*

**gold no trade** *Gynura pinnatifida, see there*

**Golden Book Tea** *Jin gui shen qi* CHINESE MEDICINE An herbal tea thought to enhance the immune system, and possibly be an adjuvant in cancer therapy. See Chinese herbal medicine, Black tea, Green tea, Tea; Cf Unproven methods for cancer management

**golden bough** American mistletoe, see there, *Phoradendron flavescens*

**Golden Door** A luxury health spa in Escondido, California. See Health spa

**golden essence** *Polygonatum cirrhifolium*, see there

**goldenrod** FRINGE MEDICINE-FLOWER ESSENCE

**goldenrod** *Solidago odora*

THERAPY *Solidago californica* A floral essence that is believed to provide a sense of individuality. See Flower essence therapy HERBAL MEDICINE 1. *Solidago canadensis*, Aaron's rod, woundwort A flowering herb that contains essential oil, flavonoids, saponins, and tannins, which has been used to treat colds, kidney stones, and urinary tract infections; some herbalists believe it may also be used for arthritis, backache, diarrhea, and as an expectorant 2. *Solidago odora*, Blue Mountain tea, sweet goldenrod A perennial herb that is carminative, diaphoretic, diuretic and used by Native American medicine men to treat dropsy (presumably renal failure), and applied topically for bruises. See Herbal medicine

**goldenseal** *Hydrastis canadensis*, eyeroot, ground raspberry, Indian dye, Indian turmeric, orange root, yellow Indian paint, yellow puccoon, yellow root HERBAL MEDICINE A perennial herb that contains alkaloids (eg berberine and canadine), resin, and volatile oil, which was regarded by the Native American medicine men as an antimicrobial, antituberculotic, antiseptic, hemostatic, and hepatic; it has been used topically as an eyewash, for athlete's foot, contact dermatitis, eczema, ringworm, and other skin conditions, and internally for bleeding, cancer, colds, diarrhea, gallstones, gastritis, hepatitis, hypertension, irritable bowel syndrome, laryngitis, oral ulcers, sore throat, stomachache, morning sickness, postpartum hemorrhage, sore throat, yeast infections, gastrointestinal and vaginal inflammation TOXICITY It should not be used in pregnancy, as it may stimulate uterine contraction; it should not be used in those with diabetes, glaucoma, heart disease, hypertension, or history of stroke, as goldenseal stimulates the myocardium. See Herbal medicine

**golden yarrow** *Achillea filipendulina* FRINGE MEDICINE-FLOWER ESSENCE THERAPY A floral essence believed to aid in social interactions while maintaining a sense of self. See Flower essence therapy

**golf ball technique** MASSAGE THERAPY Any of a number of methods in which a golf ball is used to exert increased pressure on acupressure points in hand massage (*Gottlieb, 1995*). See Chinese reflex balls, Massage therapy, Reflexology; Cf Acuball technique

**gonadal type** FRINGE MEDICINE An endocrine profile based on a hypothesis advanced by E Abravanel, MD, that each person has a dominant endocrine organ, and that each type of person craves and overeats certain foods in an effort to stimulate that organ; all gonadal types are women and are believed to crave fats; gonadal type women gain weight in the 'cellulite'-prone regions (buttocks and upper legs); they are advised to consume more vegetables, leaner meats, and red clover tea. See Body type, Diet

**'good' cholesterol** A colloquial term for high-density lipoprotein-cholesterol. See HDL-cholesterol; Cf 'Bad' cholesterol

**good habit** Healthy habit CLINICAL MEDICINE A general term for any behavior that is considered to be beneficial to one's physical or mental health, which is often linked to a high level of discipline and self-control; good habits include regular exercise, consumption of alcohol only in moderation (if at all), consumption of a properly balanced diet, monogamy, and others; Cf Bad habit

**goosegrass** Cleavers, see there, *Galium aparine*

**gorge** *verb* To eat gluttonously. See Binging

**gossypol** An aromatic triterpene isolated from cotton (*Gossypium hirsutum*) seed oil ALTERNATIVE PHARMACOLOGY In low concentrations, gossypol inhibits cell proliferation, and was proposed as a possible cancer therapy; it has a narrow therapeutic range—at low doses it does not inhibit proliferation; at high doses, it is toxic (*Cancer Chemother Pharmacol 1985; 15:20*) ALTERNATIVE PHARMACOLOGY Gossypol is 90% effective in reducing sperm counts to the level of infertility, thus having potential as a male contraceptive DISADVANTAGE Nephrotoxicity, hypokalemia, one-fourth suffer irreversible sterility. See Contraception

**gotu kola** Gutu kola, see there, *Hydrocotyle asiatica*

***gou ji dze*** Chinese wolfberry, see there, *Lycium chinese*

***gou ji zi*** Chinese wolfberry, see there, *Lycium chinese*

**Graham, Sylvester** A Presbyterian minister and temperance advocate (1794–1851) turned public lecturer, who created the Graham cracker and, in the 1830s, founded the hygienic movement (Graham System), a spartan precursor of naturopathy. See Graham System, Graham cracker, Natural Hygiene, Naturopathy, Thomson

**Graham cracker** ALTERNATIVE NUTRITION A food product created in the 1860s by a Grahamite, James Jackson, that was intended to be a form of Graham's 'dyspepsia' bread, which could be packaged, stored indefinitely, and shipped, shaped in squares; the first successful Graham cracker was produced by National Biscuit Company (now Nabisco) in 1898 (*Armstrong, 1991*). See Battle Creek, Graham

Jackson failed, and ended with a fragmented product he called granula, the precursor to today's granola, which was to be consumed as a cold breakfast cereal; both were commercial failures

**Graham System** Hygienic movement MEDICAL HISTORY–ALTERNATIVE HEALTH A series of health reforms proposed by Sylvester Graham; an early advocate of abstinence from alcohol, he later extended his philosophy to all aspects of daily life; the system advocated regular exercise, fresh air, weekly bathing (at a time when once yearly bathing was a norm), control of sexual activity, and a drastic change in the diet; while the conventional wisdom of the early 1800s was that meats and wine led to good health and prevention of cholera, Graham advocated the substitution of meat with grains, fruits, and vegetables. See Graham, Natural Hygiene, Naturopathy, Thomsonianism

**Grahamite** MEDICAL HISTORY–ALTERNATIVE NUTRITION A follower of the Graham System, see there

**grains of paradise** *Amomum villosum*, *A xanthioides*, bastard cardamom, *sha ren* CHINESE MEDICINE An aromatic perennial, the seeds of which are analgesic, carminative, and sedative for the fetus; it is used for gastrointestinal complaints, eg abdominal pain, diarrhea, indigestion, nausea, vomiting, deep coughing, chest pain, morning sickness, urinary incontinence. See Carminative, Chinese herbal medicine

**grape diet** ALTERNATIVE MEDICINE A diet proposed in the 1920s by Johanna Brandt, which continues to be popular in some circles; the diet begins with grapes, followed by progressive introduction of other fruits, sour milk, raw vegetables, dried fruits, nuts, dairy products, honey, olive oil, and grapes galore; the hardened grape dieter is allowed one cooked meal daily without liquids or salad; grapes applied in various forms, to wit, gargles, douches, enemas, and poultices, are alleged to be useful in treating and preventing cancer. See Grape monodiet, Unproven forms of cancer management

**grape mono diet** ALTERNATIVE NUTRITION A diet in which the person ingests only grapes, grape juice, and water, but no solid foods; it is recommended for heart conditions. See Fasting, Grape diet

**grapefruit** ALTERNATIVE NUTRITION A citrus fruit that is widely believed to contain a special something that causes weight loss; there are no data to support its alleged increase in digestive efficiency, and other more interesting beliefs including enhancement of athletic performance, or reduction of fatigue or blood pressure. See Grapefruit mono diet

**grapefruit mono diet** ALTERNATIVE NUTRITION An acid diet in which a person ingests only grapefruits, grapefruit juice, and water, but no solid foods; it is recommended for colds, liver disease, and mucosal inflammation. See Fasting

Note: Grapefruit juice may cause marked hypotension in patients receiving nifedipine, a dihydropyridine calcium channel blocker (*Arch Fam Med 1996; 5:413*)

***Graphites*** HOMEOPATHY A homeopathic remedy formulated from graphite; it is used for skin disease in the form of eczema, psoriasis, keloids, nail defects, scars, hair loss, facial herpes, paresthesia, nosebleeds, and lymphadenitis. See Constitutional type, *Graphites* type, Homeopathy

***Graphites* type** HOMEOPATHY A constitutional type of person who is often heavy or overweight, moody, mentally and physically torpid, depressed, and pessimistic; *Graphites* types are prone to headaches and like sour foods WORSE Cold, humidity, morning, evening, sweet foods, seafood FEARS Insanity, death, thunderstorms WEAKEST BODY REGIONS Skin and nails, endocrine glands, mucosal membranes, left side of body. See Constitutional type, *Graphites*, Homeopathy

**graphochromotherapy** FRINGE MEDICINE A combination of color therapy and absent healing, in which a photograph of the patient *and* the ailing portion of his body is exposed to the appropriate colored filter, which is believed to be of therapeutic value. See Absent healing, Color therapy

**grapho-diagnosis** Medical graphology, see there

**graphotherapy** FRINGE MEDICINE A pseudodiagnostic technique that consists of the analysis of a person's handwriting as a basis for treating psychological problems (*Raso, 1994*). See Medical graphology; Cf Hand analysis

**GRAS** Generally regarded as safelist, see there

**grass** Marijuana, see there, *Cannabis sativa*

**greasewood** Chaparral, see there, *Larrea tridentata*

**great burdock** Burdock, see there, *Arctium lappa*

**great power seeds** Burdock, see there *Arctium lappa*

**great wild valerian** Valerian, see there, *Valeriana officinalis*

**greater celandine** *Cheledonium majus*, celandine, swallowwort, tetterwort HERBAL MEDICINE A perennial herb that is a potent skin irritant once used by herbalists of the Middle Ages for removing warts* TOXICITY Greater celandine is irritating to the skin and gastrointestinal tract and depresses the central nervous system, and should be administered with caution. See Doctrine of signatures, Herbal medicine

*It was further believed, in accordance with the so-called 'doctrine of signatures,' that its bright orange flowers signaled greater celandine's efficacy in treating jaundice

**Greco-Roman herbal medicine** HERBAL MEDICINE A system of classifying herbs based on the writings of Galen, in which herbs were classified according to four humors: Hot/moist–sanguine, cold/dry–melancholic, cold/moist–phlegmatic, and hot/dry–choleric. See Herbal medicine

**Greek cancer cure** FRINGE ONCOLOGY An unproven method for managing cancer, in which a blood test of an undisclosed type is used to diagnose, and determine the stage and progression of cancer; the chief proponent of the Greek cancer cure is Hariton Alivizatos*, who believes the test can determine a person's risk of cancer, and place that risk on a scale of 1 to 10; the treatment consists of injecting an unknown substance, possibly niacin, which is claimed to cure the cancer; according to the evidence available to the American Cancer Society, the Greek cancer cure has no known effect in treating malignancy (*Fact Sheet from the American Cancer Society's files on Unproven Methods of Cancer Management*). See Cancer myths, Unproven methods for cancer management

*Alizatos is a physician whose license to practice medicine had been twice suspended in Greece, and who has treated foreign tourists in various hotels in Athens

**green** FRINGE MEDICINE–COLOR THERAPY A mentally and physically soothing color that is regarded (in the context of color therapy) as the master healer; it is believed to disinfect and rebuild tissues, lower blood pressure, treat stress and fatigue, provide hope, and be of use in treating cancer. See Color breathing, Color therapy, Green foods, Green metals and chemicals

**green extract** HERBAL MEDICINE A simple fluid extract that is the most concentrated form of an herb; green extracts are prepared from fresh, juicy leaves that are pressed, and strained; one gram of green extract is equal to one gram of pure herb. See Fluid extract, Herbal medicine; Cf Fluid extract, Green mussel extract, Infusion

**green foods** FRINGE MEDICINE–COLOR THERAPY A general term for green colored foods, which are said to disinfect and rebuild tissues, and include green vegetables, peas, beans, kiwi fruit, and lentils. See Color breathing, Color therapy, Green, Green metals & chemicals

**green ginger** Wormwood, see there, *Artemisia absinthium*

**green metals & chemicals** FRINGE MEDICINE–COLOR THERAPY Green metals and chemicals are believed to disinfect and rebuild tissues, and include aluminum, carbon, barium, chlorine, chlorophyll, nickel, and sodium. See Green, Green foods, Color breathing, Color therapy

**green mussel extract** ALTERNATIVE RHEUMATOLOGY A substance obtained from green-lipped mussel in New Zealand, which is believed to relieve the arthritis-related inflammation; Cf Green extract

**green tea** A beverage prepared from the leaves of an eastern Asian evergreen shrub, *Camellia sinensis*, which is popular among Asians, and central to certain cultural rituals, eg the Japanese tea ceremony; green tea is believed to have a carcinoprotective effect greater than that of black tea (which is produced from green tea by a fermentation process). See Tea; Cf Caffeine, Coffee, Maté

Both have (–)-epigallocatechin gallate, an antioxidant responsible for the alleged protective effect (*Cancer Research 1 July 1994, in Science News 1994; 146:61*)

**greens** A general term for any 'green' vegetable, which includes leafy vegetables (eg cabbage, lettuce, spinach), fruit vegetables (eg green peppers), and others. See Leafy greens; Cf Fruit vegetable

**groats** Oat, see there, *Avena sativa*

**Grof breathwork** Holotropic Breathwork, see there

**gromwell** *Lithospermum officinale*, pearl paint, stoneseed HERBAL MEDICINE A perennial herb that was used by Native Americans as a diuretic and to treat kidney stones; clinical research has not confirmed gromwell's effectiveness as a diuretic. See Herbal medicine

**ground blood** Indian madder, see there, *Rubia cordifolia*

**ground coin grass** Gutu kola, see there, *Hydrocotyle asiatica*

**ground ivy** 1. Gutu kola, see there, *Hydrocotyle asiatica* 2. *Glechoma hederacea*, alehoof, cat's foot, creeping Charlie, field balm, Gill-over-the-ground, haymaids, hedgemaids HERBAL MEDICINE A low-lying perennial evergreen that contains vitamin C; it was used in colonial America for asthma, cough, fever, intestinal bloating, tuberculosis, ulcers, and other conditions; it is rarely used by modern herbalists. See Herbal medicine

**ground ivy** *Glechoma hederacea*

**ground juniper** Juniper, see there, *Juniperus communis*

**ground raspberry** Goldenseal, see there, *Hydrastis canadensis*

**grounding** BIOENERGETICS The degree of awareness of a person's physical experience, sexuality, and pleasure orientation, as reflects his realities; achieving a grounded state is a goal of bioenergetics and body-oriented psychotherapies, as a 'grounded' person is better able to handle emotional crises, painful memories, and psychological exploration. See Armoring, Bioenergetics, Reichian therapy

**growth need** Self-actualization need, see there

**GSR-2** A proprietary biofeedback device based on the Galvanic skin response, which is produced by Thought Technology, Inc. See Biofeedback training

***gu jing cao*** *Eriocaulon sieboldianum*, see there

***gu jing tsao*** *Eriocaulon sieboldianum*, see there

**guaiac** Lignum vitae, see there, *Guaiacum officinale*

**guaiacum** Lignum vitae, see there, *Guaiacum officinale*

***Guaiacum officinale*** Lignum vitae, see there

***guan jung*** see Fern

***guan zhong*** see Fern

**Guelder rose** Cramp bark, see there, *Viburnum opulus*

**guided imagery** Imagery (and visualization), see there

**guided imagery and music** ALTERNATIVE PSYCHOTHERAPY A stress management technique developed in the early 1980s by an American psychologist, Helen Bonny, at the Maryland Psychiatric Research Center in Baltimore; in GIM, the patient listens to music in a relaxed state, allowing deep emotions and images to rise to the conscious mind. See Affirmation, Imagery and visualization, Music therapy, Sensory therapy

**gum** *Acacia senegal* HERBAL MEDICINE A tree from Africa that produces a resinous sap that has been used for treating sore throat, coughs and diarrhea. See Herbal medicine

**gutu kola** *Hydrocotyle asiatica*, *Centella asiatica*, *di chien tsao*, *di qien cao*, gotu kola, ground copin grass, ground ivy, Indian pennywort, *man tien hsing*, pennywort, sky full of stars A low-lying plant, the leaves and stalk of which contain asiaticosides, triterpene acid, glycoside, tannin, and volatile oil AYURVEDIC MEDICINE Gutu kola is used in India for gastrointestinal complaints, psoriasis, leprosy, tuberculosis, and sexually transmitted disease CHINESE MEDICINE Gutu kola is believed to promote longevity, and was reported to be responsible for Lee Ching-yuen—a Chinese herbalist's—256 year lifespan; in Chinese medicine, it is antipyretic, diuretic, and tonic for the immune and nervous systems; it is used for convulsions, hair loss, recuperation from trauma, premature aging, memory loss, learning impairment, mental disorders, sexually-transmitted disease, and seizures. See Chinese herbal medicine HERBAL MEDICINE In Western herbal medicine, gutu kola is used internally for edema and poor circulation of the legs, and topically for burns, cuts, eczema, and psoriasis TOXICITY Gutu kola is poisonous; its use is restricted, as large doses may cause vertigo and coma; it should not be used in pregnancy, when breast-feeding, or in young children. See Herbal medicine

***Gynura pinnatifida*** Gold no trade, *jin bu huan*, mountain varnish, *san chi*, *shan chi* CHINESE MEDICINE A perennial herb, the root of which is highly regarded in traditional Chinese medicine for hemostasis and rapid healing of wounds; it is anti-inflammatory, astringent, and hemostatic, and used for internal and external hemorrhage, epistaxis, bleeding ulcers, hepatitis, liver and intestinal cancer, and bloodshot eyes. See Chinese herbal medicine

**gypsum pillow** CHINESE MEDICINE A type of pillow used in traditional Chinese medicine which contains crushed mineral gypsum, which is believed to have antipyretic and anti-inflammatory properties. See Chinese herbal medicine, Herbal pillow

**H factor** Harmonic factor, see there

**Samuel Christian Friedrich Hahnemann** A German physician (1755-1843) who founded homeopathy, and whose *Organon der rationellen Heilkunde* (*Principles of Rational Medicine*) delineated its key principles

▶ **HOMEOPATHIC PRINCIPLES**

- **LIKE CURES LIKE** (Law of similars)
- **LAW OF INFINITESIMALS**—the more diluted the remedy, the greater its action
- **DISEASE IS SPECIFIC** for an individual

See Constitutional remedy, Homeopathy, Kent, Law of the infinitesimal dose, Law of similars

**hair analysis** The use of scalp hair as an analytical specimen FRINGE MEDICINE Hair analysis is believed by some providers of alternative health care to be of use in evaluating a person's health and nutritional status, by allegedly measuring proteins and vitamins; given the variability of interlaboratory and intralaboratory results (*JAMA 1985; 254:1041*), hair analysis for this purpose is unscientific, costly, possibly illegal, and is believed by many mainstream medical practitioners to be fraudulent '...*hair analysis has appealed to pseudonutritionists, who perform the test without taking into account its limitations* (extrapolating) *results far beyond what has been scientifically demonstrated* (*NW Tietz, Textbook of Clinical Chemistry, WB Saunders, Philadelphia, 1986*) DRUG TESTING The use of samples of hair to detect chronic drug abuse* METHODS Radioimmunoassay, enzyme immunoassay, gas chromatography-mass spectroscopy DRUGS DETECTED Amphetamines, cocaine, heroin LEVELS OF DETECTION 10 pg/mg in 10 ng of hair CONFOUNDING FACTORS Variations in drug levels occur in different races (Asians absorb most, whites less), hair color (light hair is preferred for analysis) and environmental contamination (eg passive absorption of cocaine, which may occur in children of drug-abusing parents) (*CAP Today June 1995, p14*) TOXICOLOGY The most well-studied and reliable use of hair analysis is for detecting chronic heavy metal (eg arsenic, lead, and mercury) poisoning

*The use of hair as a source for drug testing has certain advantges, as it is non-intrusive, clean and difficult to cheat on, providing a long-term 'record' of drug ingestion

**hakim** A practitioner of herbal medicine in arabic and ayurvedic medicine

**hakomi** Hakomi body-oriented psychotherapy, see there

**hakomi body-centered psychotherapy** Hakomi body-oriented psychotherapy, see there

**hakomi body-oriented psychotherapy** Hakomi, hakomi method, hakomi therapy, hakomi body-centered psychotherapy ALTERNATIVE MEDICINE A Reichian-based therapeutic system* that combines Eastern philosophies (Buddhism, Taoism, meditation, mindfulness, and nonviolence) with Western body-oriented psychotherapy, bioenergetics, Feldenkreis method, Gestalt therapy, neurolinguistic programming, structural bodywork and others; hakomi therapists attempt to return the client to unpleasant childhood memories, examine the experience, and find strategies for new attitudes and behavior (*Gottschalk Olsen, 1989*); Cf Reichian therapy

*The word Hakomi is a Hopi word meaning where do you stand in relation to these many realms, which translates as '*Who are you?*' (*Kastner, Burroughs, 1993*)

**Hakomi bodywork** A therapeutic modality that incorporates hands-on work in the form of massage, structural work, movement and body awareness; Hakomi bodywork and Hakomi psychotherapy are used simultaneously, and thus their separation is somewhat arbitrary. See Hakomi body-oriented psychotherapy

**hakomi method** Hakomi body-oriented psychotherapy, see there

**hakomi therapy** Hakomi body-oriented psychotherapy, see there

**halfway house** A semi-sheltered environment for individuals who are in rehabilitation for mental illness or addiction disorders, including drug and alcohol abuse, who do not require in-patient hospitalization; halfway houses are often staffed by their own 'graduates' or by professionals who provide guidance and if necessary, treatment. See Co-counseling; Cf Homelessness, Shelter

**hallfoot** Colt's foot, see there, *Tussilago farfara*

**halo effect** The beneficial effect of a physician or other health care provider on a patient during a medical encounter, regardless of the therapy or procedure provided. See Hawthorne effect, Placebo effect, Placebo response, White coat hypertension

Note: A halo is a shimmering ring of light floating above the heads of angels of Judeo-Christian dogma, endowed with mystical healing powers, as in the 'healing hands' of the physician

***Hamamelis*** *Hamamelis virginiana*, witch hazel HOMEOPATHY A remedy that has been used for poor venous circulation and varicose veins, as well as bloodshot eyes, depression, irritability, headaches, hemorrhoids, and menstrual disorders. See Homeopathy, Witch hazel

***Hamamelis virginiana*** HERBAL MEDICINE Popularly known as witch hazel, see there HOMEOPATHY *Hamamelis*, see there

**hamma** ALTERNATIVE MEDICINE A traditional Japanese form of massage used to treat muscle complaints. See Massage

***han lian cao*** *Eclipta prostrata*, see there

***han lien tsao*** *Eclipta prostrata*, see there

**hand healing** Palm healing PARANORMAL PHENOMENA A technique in which a 'healer's' hands are passed over the body of a sick person, with or without physical contact; hand healing predates the wonder drug era; it is believed by some to be effective in treating pain and rheumatic complaints, effects that are difficult to verify

**hand interpretation** Palmistry The interpretation of various aspects of the hands as a means of determining specific characteristics of an individual, which has three distinct formats

▶ **HAND INTERPRETATION**

• **CHIROGNOMY** Cheirognomy The study of the shape, flexibility, color, texture, and the manner in which its owner uses it, which is believed by some to indicate various organ defects

• **CHIROMANCY** Palmistry The mystical interpretation of the lines of the hand, which is shunned by mainstream medical thought, see figure

• **DERMATOGLYPHICS** The study of skin patterns, which were studied by Sir Francis Galton (1822-1910), whose pioneering work on fingerprints resulted in their classification into 3 patterns, loops, arches, and whorls

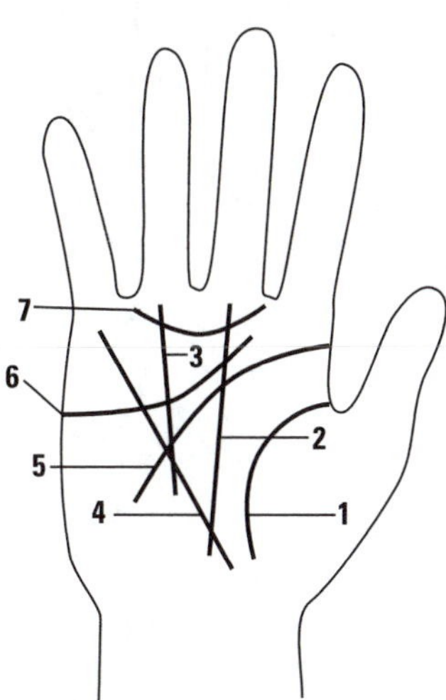


**hand interpretation** Chiromancy, palmistry

1. Line of life Reveals vitality; breaks indicate illness or major changes
2. Line of fate Reveals things may come to bear on the person
3. Line of the sun Reveals artistic inclinations
4. Line of health Not always present; if present may indicate health problems
5. Line of head Reveals intelligence
6. Line of heart Reveals emotional and sexual life
7. Girdle of Venus Reveals restlessness, volatile personality

**hand massage** A form of reflexology in which parts of the hands (see figure, pg. 170) are rubbed with the fingers, knuckles, and blunt or sharp objects, with the intent of stimulating nerve endings for various organs that are believed to be present in the hands—as they are believed to be present in the feet; Cf Reflexology

**HANES** Health And Nutrition Examination survey A series of dietary surveys first carried out in 1971 by the NIH (US); HANES I determined that Americans consumed suboptimal levels of iron, calcium, and vitamins A and C; HANES III is in progress and under the auspices of the National Center for Health Statistics and will determine the weights of Americans

**Hanna somatic education** Somatic education, somatics A method developed in 1973 by Dr T

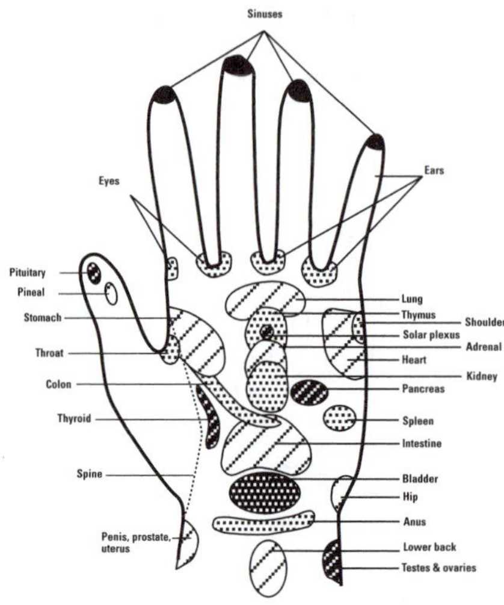


**hand massage chart**
Redrawn from Carroll, 1980

Hanna, which is based on the belief that muscles that are chronically contracted due to stress and trauma eventually reach a point where they can no longer remember how to relax; Hanna calls this phenomenon sensory-motor amnesia; the intent of somatic education is to input new sensory information that will allow the person's muscles to relearn how to relax. See Sensory-motor amnesia

**'happy foods'** ALTERNATIVE NUTRITION A term coined by Stuart Berger, the creator of the *Southampton Diet*, for those foods that he believed produced positive neurotransmitters in the brain; in his first diet book (*The Southampton Diet, 1981*), Berger regarded whole grains, dairy products, eggs, fish, leafy greens, fruits, and poultry as happy foods, which could be eaten ad lib* . See Diet, Southampton diet; Cf 'Sad foods'

*In his subsequent book (*Dr Berger's Immune Power Diet, New American Library, 1985*), these same foods were regarded among what he then termed the sinister seven foods, which could cause immune damage

***hara*** ORIENTAL MEDICINE The region of the solar plexus or abdomen, which as viewed in the context of oriental medicine, is said to be the spiritual center of the soul and the body's life processes; various types of pressure may be exerted on the abdomen in shiatsu to stimulate the flow of energy through the hara. See Acupressure, Ohashiatsu®, Shiatsu

***hara* center** ALTERNATIVE PSYCHIATRY One of four 'ontological being centers' defined in the construct of organismic psychotherapy, a permutation of Reichian therapy; the *hara* center is located in the abdomen and allows self-love and self-acceptance. See Ontological being center, Organismic psychotherapy

**hardback** Stoneroot, see there, *Collinsonia canadensis*

**hard water** Water that has a high content of calcium and magnesium salts (eg carbonates and sulfates), which may interfere with certain tests in the laboratory. See Mineral water, Spring water; Cf Soft water

**hardening** CLINICAL NUTRITION Hydrogenation of the unsaturated fatty acids in triglycerides into saturated fatty acids. See Browning reaction, Tropical oils

**hardening of the arteries** Atherosclerosis

**hare's ear** *Bupleurum falcatum*, *B chinense*, *chai*, thorowax root CHINESE MEDICINE A perennial herb, the root of which is analgesic, antipyretic, and an immune stimulant; it is used for amenorrhea, bloating, cancer, chest pain, cirrhosis, irritability, low-grade fever, malaria, menstrual dysfunction (eg cramping, premenstrual syndrome), nausea, rectal and uterine prolapse, and vertigo TOXICITY Nausea, vomiting. See Chinese herbal medicine

**harmonic factor** H factor ALTERNATIVE MEDICINE A substance believed by practitioners of sound therapy to be produced by cells subjected to sound at various wavelengths; the harmonic factor has not been characterized chemically, or identified by any standard method. See Sound therapy

**harmonics** SOUND THERAPY A system of chanting developed and practiced by Tibetan monks, which is thought to be therapeutic; it is believed that certain sounds correspond to certain energy centers. See Cymatics, Toning

**Harner method** PARANORMAL PHENOMENA A format of neo-shamanic psychology in which clients are induced into a shamanic state of altered consciousness through audiotapes of ritual drumming; the client relates his journey into the spirit realm, while being coached by the therapist or counselor; the session is taped for subsequent analysis. See Holotropic Breathwork®, Neo-shamanism; Cf Shamanism

**Harvest Moon phenomenon** A decrease in mortality in a person or population that occurs before a symbolically meaningful event or occasion

Note: Epidemiologists usually examine the impact of external factors in establishing cause-and-effect relations to disease; cultural factors are rarely examined and usually viewed as having a negative impact on disease; one study (*JAMA 1990; 263:1947*) revealed a positive impact of culturally significant events on mortality to 2 populations, older Chinese women (event: Harvest Moon festival) and older Jewish men (event: Passover); each group proved itself capable of staving off death, especially of cardiovascular disease and cancer; mortality decreased 35% before the event and increased 34.6% thereafter; the phenomenon also increases before the birthdays of men who perceive themselves as failures, and decreases in women who anticipate getting more attention from friends and family at the time of their birthday

**hashish** Marijuana, see there, *Cannabis sativa*

***hatha* yoga** An 'integrative' form of yoga that seeks the pathway to a higher power by integrating the self (*ha*—sun and *tha*—moon) through relaxation, postures, *pranayama*, purification practices (*kriyas*), and promoting harmony of the body and mind; *hatha* yoga is a 'gentle' yoga, and is the form best known to Westerners. See Yoga

**Gayelord Hauser** A German-American (1895-1972), née Helmut Eygene Bengamin Gellert Hauser, who became the health 'guru' to the Hollywood stars; he advocated a primarily vegetarian diet, but adopted some unconventional methods, eg abundant use of laxatives (*Armstrong, 1991*)

**Hawaiian healing** Kahuna healing, see there

**Hawaiian temple bodywork** *Lomi ha'a mauli ola* A permutation of lomilomi massage, that combines bodywork, music, the hula dance, and breathing exercise. See Lomilomi massage, Shamanism

**haw** Hawthorn, see there, *Crataegus monogyna*

**hawthorn** *Crataegus monogyna*, *Crataegus oxyacantha*, English hawthorn, haw, mayblossom, maybush, whitethorn HERBAL MEDICINE A general term for any of a number of deciduous trees or shrubs; hawthorne contains flavonoid glycosides, saponins, tannins, and trimethylamine, which is best known for its cardiovascular activity; the active principles in hawthorn cause vasodilation, bradycardia, and normalize blood pressure, in both hypotension and hypertension; hawthorn has been used for angina pectoris, spasms of peripheral arteries (eg Raynaud's phenomenon), tachyarrhythmias, insomnia, nervousness, and sore throat; the berries are used in Chinese herbal medicine as a digestive tonic TOXICITY Hawthorn may cause hypotension; it should not be self-prescribed as a cardiotonic; it should not be used in young children, pregnancy, or when breast-feeding. See Herbal medicine

**Hawthorne effect** ALTERNATIVE PSYCHOLOGY A beneficial effect that health care providers have on the workers in virtually any environment when an interest is shown in the workers' well-being; the studies were conducted in the 1930s at Western Electric's Hawthorne plant and evaluated the effects of improving the social environment and laborer-management relations in the workplace. See Halo effect, Placebo effect, Placebo response

Note: This phenomenon differs from both 1. The 'Halo' effect, in which the contact with health care personnel is personal and occurs in a legitimate medical context and 2. The placebo effect, in which the subject may believe a therapeutic effect is present, where none exists, ie *cogito ergo sum*; Cf 'Nocebo'

**Hay diet** ALTERNATIVE NUTRITION A diet described by an American, William Howard Hay, in which major food groups are eaten in separate sessions; as an example, carbohydrates are not eaten within four hours of ingesting proteins and acidic fruits; Hay divided carbohydrates two groups: 1. Grains (eg breads, flour, rice), some dried fruit (eg bananas, figs, dates, raisins), and vegetables (potatoes and Jerualem artichokes) and 2. Acidic fruits (eg fresh and dried apples, apricots, pears, prunes), which according to Hay, should not be eaten with the other carbohydrates; proteins (eg meat, fish, poultry, and yogurt) may be eaten with the acidic fruits; Hay's 'neutral' food groups include dairy products, cooking oils, vegetables (except for above), which can be eaten any time; refined and processed foods are forbidden; alcoholic beverages are allowed, but differ according to whether one is ingesting a 'carbohydrate' or a protein meal; anecdotal reports suggest that the diet may be effective in promoting health and a sense of well-being, and for treating arthritis, constipation, diabetes, heart disease, hypertension, indigestion, obesity, and ulcers. See Diet

**haymaids** Ground ivy, see there, *Glechoma hed-*

*eracea*

**hazel eyes** FRINGE MEDICINE-IRIDOLOGY See Biliary constitution

**HDL-cholesterol** Good cholesterol Cholesterol that is bound to high-density lipoprotein; an increased HDL-C: total cholesterol and increased HDL-C ratios are associated with increased longevity and decreased morbidity and mortality from coronary artery disease. See HDL/LDL ratio; Cf LDL-cholesterol

**HDL/LDL ratio** The ratio of cholesterol carried by high-density lipoprotein to that carried by low-density lipoprotein, which allows a risk stratification for atherosclerosis-related cardiac disease; the HDL/LDL ratio is decreased by increased consumption of saturated fatty acids (eg from meat) in the diet. See HDL cholesterol, LDL-cholesterol

**head-reading** Phrenology, see there

**Head's zones** Pressure points, see there

**heal-all** *Prunella vulgaris*, all-heal, prunella, self-heal HERBAL MEDICINE A perennial of the mint family that contains alkaloids, bitter principles, and volatile oils; it is astringent, and may be used as a throat gargle; it is rarely used by herbalists, given its uncertain efficacy. See Herbal medicine

**heal-all** *Prunella vulgaris*

**healer** One who heals FRINGE MEDICINE A person (eg a faith healer) who alleges to manipulate a person's internal forces to effect therapy. See Psychic healer ETHNOMEDICINE A healer (curandero) is one who uses various plants, concoctions (potingues), rites and rituals to treat various diseases or to rid the sufferer of various culture-bound syndromes. See Culture-bound syndrome, Curandero MAINSTREAM MEDICINE Physician

**healing crisis** HOMEOPATHY A transient exacerbation of symptoms of a particular condition being treating by homeopathy; such crises indicate that the remedy chosen was appropriate for the patient. See Homeopathy, Law of cures, Remedy

**healing food** Healthy food, see there

**healing hands kung fu** Healing light kung fu, see there

**healing herb** Comfrey, see there, *Symphytum officinale*

**healing humor** Laughter therapy, see there

**healing imagery** Imagery and visualization, see there

**healing light kung fu** Healing hands kung fu A form of kung fu in which the exercises are believed to process the 'Cosmic Force' and nourish the *chi*. See *Chi*

**healing light massage** *Chi nei tsang*, see there

**healing love** Healing love meditation, seminal and ovarian kung fu ENERGY MEDICINE A method of sexual intercourse that is believed to convert sexual energy into a self-healing force; for men, it entails intercourse without ejaculation, which is termed 'power draw'. See Energy medicine, Vital force

**healing shrine** PARANORMAL PHENOMENA A place that has been deemed to be sacred by the clerics of an organized religious body, who believe it to be vested with healing attributes; the most well-known healing shrine in the Catholic Church is that of Lourdes, southern France; others include the Basilica of Our Lady of Guadelupe in Mexico, and Compostela in Spain. See Lourdes, Miracle, Saint Bernadette

**healing *tao* system** Healing *tao* warm current meditation, International healing *tao* system A 'subtle energy system' developed in the 1980s by a Thai-American, M Chia, which is a synthesis of bone marrow *nei kung*, *chi nei tsang*, *chi* self-massage, fusion meditation, healing light kung fu, healing love, inner smile, iron shirt *chi kung*, microcosmic orbit meditation, the 6 healing sounds, t'ai chi ch'uan, and Taoist five element nutrition; the system's goal is to help its practitioner transcend physical boundaries by developing the spirit and soul (*Raso, 1994*)

**healing *tao* warm current meditation** Healing *tao* system, see there

**healing touch** Therapeutic touch, see there

**healing visualization** ALTERNATIVE MEDICINE A permutation of imagery (and visualization) central to Simonton's method for cancer therapy, which is based on the belief that psychological forces are a factor in the pathogenesis of cancer; in healing visualization, the patient places himself in a state of mental tranquility and visualizes his conventional therapy attacking the cancer cells; this is followed by imagining the immune system ridding the body of the remaining malignant cells DOSE 15 minutes, three times daily; Simonton recommends the method only in conjunction with conventional anticancer therapy in a highly motivated patient trained in visualization; anecdotal reports suggest that healing visualization may also be effective in treating asthma, heart conditions, pain, phobias, stress, tension, and other conditions. See Imagery and visualization, Simonton method, Unproven methods for cancer management

**health** ALTERNATIVE MEDICINE The '...*normal and harmonious vibration of the elements and forces composing the human entity on the physical, mental, and moral (emotional) planes of being, in conformity with the constructive principle (great law of life) in nature*.' (*Philosophy of Natural Therapeutics, H Lindlahr, Lindlahr Pub, Chicago, 1919*). See *Philosophy of Natural Therapeutics*; Cf Disease MAINSTREAM MEDICINE A condition defined by the World Health Organization as '...*a state of complete physical, mental, and social well-being and not merely the absence of disease or infirmity*.'

**health advocacy** Health promotion, see there

**health balls** Chinese reflex balls, see there

**health food** A non-medical term defined by the lay public as a food that has little or no preservatives, has not undergone major processing, enrichment, or refinement and, usually, is grown without pesticides; health foods are believed by some alternative health advocates to possess the mystical ability to prevent disease (eg atherosclerosis, aging phenomena, rheumatic disease, cancer) or treat dread diseases (eg AIDS, cancer, and others). See Food preservatives, 'Go' food, Healthy food, Organic food; Cf Diet, Junk food, 'No' food

**health food movement** Natural food movement A loosely cohesive network of producers and consumers of 'health foods,' which are almost invariably grown organically; members of the movement share a distrust of varying intensity for mainstream medical practices, industry, and society in general; Cf Cancer underground

**health fraud** A general term used for those practices in which health services are promised and/or paid for, but not provided at an appropriate standard of professionalism or skill

▶ **HEALTH FRAUD, TYPES**

- **FINANCIAL FINAGLING** in any form committed against third-party payer of health care; 43% of health fraud is in the form of services not rendered, 33% for fraudulent diagnoses
- **DECEIT FOR PROFIT**, including false representation of efficacy and concealment of adverse effects of medications or 'natural curatives'

See AIDS fraud, Health freedom argument, Pseudovitamins, Quackery, Unproven methods for cancer management

**health freedom argument** UNPROVEN MEDICINE A defense that has been periodically used in public debate, in attempts to legalize[1] various forms of alternative health care, for which there is evidence that the therapy is ineffective, and may have considerable adverse effects[2]; the argument hinges on an individual's freedom to choose his therapy regardless of its potential harm. See Cancer underground, Unproven methods for cancer management

[1]And/or legitimize [2]eg Laetrile

**health hydro** Health spa, see there

**health-promoting food** Healthy food, see there

**health promotion** Any activity that seeks to improve a person's or population's health by providing information about, and increasing awareness of, 'at risk' behaviors associated with various diseases, with the intent of reducing those behaviors; in the US, health promotion has been successful in reducing cardiovascular and tobacco-related disease; health-promoting behaviors include smoking cessation, avoidance of substances of abuse, use of safety belts in cars, moderate or nonconsumption of alcohol, reduced consumption of saturated fats, and engaging in daily exercise (*N Engl J Med 1996; 334:996d*)

**health spa** Water cure establishment ALTERNATIVE MEDICINE A general term for a facility in which a person resides for a period of days to weeks, where various therapeutic or health-promoting modalities may be administered; some spas are located near a natural spring—in which the waters are alleged to have some health benefit—hence the phrase 'taking the waters'; some natural springs have increased concentrations of zinc, chloride, and others—the actual benefit of bathing in such waters is uncertain; other spas are located in regions where the air or climate (eg mountains, desert) are believed to be beneficial; common to most spas is the availability of massage therapy, dietary regimens or forced fasting, and exercise programs. See Hydrotherapy

**Health Watch** A British watchdog organization (formerly known as the quackbusters) dedicated to evaluating the methods of alternative medicine. See Health fraud, Quack, Quack buster, Quackery

**health zone** CHIROPRACTIC Any of six divisions of the body: circulatory, digestive, eliminative, glandular, muscular, and nervous, based on a form of chiropractic known as Concept Therapy; according to the Concept Therapy construct, each of these six zones has a corresponding reflex point located in the occipital region of the head, and four corresponding vertebrae; in zone therapy, the chiropractor analyzes the head to identify the most sensitive point in the occipital zone, then adjusts the corresponding four vertebrae; successful adjustment is indicated by decreased tenderness in the occipital zone. See Chiropractic, Concept Therapy, Zone testing

**health zone analysis** Zone testing, see there

**healthy diet** CLINICAL NUTRITION A general term for any diet based on sound nutritional principles; the healthy diet philosophy is often coupled with the (largely unsubstantiated) belief that organic and/or unprocessed foods (ie those produced without pesticides, and chemical preservatives) are superior to adulterated foods

▶ **HEALTHY DIETS, FEATURES OF**

- High consumption of fruits and vegetables
- Low consumption of red meat and fatty foods
- Raw foods and whole grains are preferred to processed or refined foods
- Protein is derived primarily from fish, dairy products, nuts
- Consumption of salt, pepper, sugar, coffee and other caffeinated beverages, and often alcohol, is discouraged

See Coffee, Diet, Health food, Healthy food

**healthy food** Healing food, Health-promoting food ALTERNATIVE NUTRITION A general term for any of a number of foods that are widely believed to be 'good for you,' which include foods high in fiber, natural vitamins, fructose, and other (at present) unidentified 'factors'; among other effects, healthy foods are believed to lower cholesterol and risk of cardiovascular disease including strokes, help control glucose, halt the progression of osteoporosis, reduce infections, and risk of cancer; healing foods include apples, beans, carrots, coffee, cranberry juice, fish, garlic, ginger, nuts, oats, olive oil, soy foods, tea, and yogurt, which are discussed elsewhere in this work. See Fiber, Fruit and vegetables; Cf Health food, Junk food, Unhealthy foods

Note: While the terms healthy food and health food may refer to the same comestibles, the latter term has a mystical overtone as health foods are believed by alternative health care advocates to prevent or cure diseases

**healthy habit** Good habit, see there

**heart center *chakra*** AYURVEDIC MEDICINE The fourth *chakra*, which governs love; it is located in the heart, and associated with the circulation and the color green. See Ayurvedic medicine, *Chakra*

**heart meridian** Arm lesser yin meridian ACUPUNCTURE A meridian that begins at the armpit, extends down the arm, and ends at the little finger; stimulation of acupoints along the heart meridian are used to treat conditions affecting the heart and nervous system. See Acupuncture, (the) Twelve meridians

**heat stress detoxification** Hyperthermia, Induced hyperthermia ALTERNATIVE MEDICINE The application of external heat to a person whose fever responsiveness is viewed as being inadequate; external temperature can be increased by saunas, steam baths, local hot compresses, and friction, and is claimed to be useful either alone or as an adjunctive therapy in bladder and lung infections, AIDS, cancer, and viral infections; 'high-tech' hyperthermia (eg diathermy, extracorporal heating, infrared, ultrasound) is being examined for possible health benefits; there is little peer-reviewed data to support induced hyperthermia as an effective therapeutic modality. See Alternative medicine, Unproven methods for cancer management

Note: Although the term hyperthermia is more popular among alternative health care practitioners than heat stress detoxification, hyperthermia is widely used in mainstream medicine and thus lends to considerable 'cross-cultural' confusion

**heat therapy** Hyperthermia FRINGE ONCOLOGY A general term for the deliberate induction of hyperthermia (from 40° to 43° C, or 104° to 109° F),* through the application of external sources of heat, including microwave heaters; heat therapy stimulates the immune system and enhances the activity of macrophages; in cancer hyperthermia increases the therapeutic reponse rate by 25 to 35%, and may be used in combination with chemotherapy, radiotherapy, and biological response modifiers including tumor necrosis factor and interferon-gamma (*Moss, 1992*)

*Higher temperatures have been recommended by some workers in this field–Author's note

**heath** Heather, see there, *Calluna vulgaris*

**heather** *Calluna vulgaris*, *Erica vulgaris*, heath, ling, Scotch heather HERBAL MEDICINE An evergreen shrub that contains arbutin, carotene, citric and fumaric acids, flavonoids, tannins, and volatile oils; it is antitussive, mildly sedative, a urinary tract antiseptic, and has been used to treat rheumatic complaints and gout. See Herbal medicine

**hedge bindweed** Bindweed, see there, *Convolvulus sepium*

**hedgeburs** Cleavers, see there, *Galium aparine*

**hedge fumitory** Fumitory, see there, *Fumaria officinalis*

**hedgemaids** Ground ivy, see there, *Glechoma hederacea*

**hediondilla** Chaparral, see there, *Larrea tridentata*

**Hegsted's score** A formula for determining a diet's relative lipid composition, where a high value indicates increased saturated fatty acids and cholesterol and low polyunsaturated fatty acids (*N Engl J Med 1985; 312:811*)

**Heidelberg test** NATUROPATHY An unconventional test that may be used to measure acidity of the stomach, which is alleged to indicate adequacy of digestion. See Naturopathy

**heliotherapy** Sunshine treatment, sunbathing A form of light therapy in which an individual is exposed to direct sunlight for varying periods. See Bright light therapy

**Hellerwork®** ALTERNATIVE MEDICINE A form of bodywork developed in the late 1970s by an American aerospace engineer, Joseph Heller; like Rolfing® (Heller was a Rolfer before he became a Heller), Hellerwork® is based on the belief that certain diseases are caused by musculoskeletal malignment; Hellerwork® seeks to realign the physical balance and integrate the mind and body

▶ **HELLERWORK® COMPONENTS**

- **BODYWORK**–manipulation to release tension
- **DIALOGUE**–with the patient about the effects of strong emotions and rigid thought on an individual's physical and mental state, and
- **MOVEMENT EDUCATION**–the client is counseled to increase his awareness of his body and release tensions, and poor ('health-threatening') posture, specifically by realigning the natural balance of the fascia in relationship to the muscles, tendons, and bone

Integral to Hellerwork® is movement reeducation in the form of exercises that teach stress-free methods of performing everyday movements, including standing up, sitting down, and bending over. See Bodywork, Structural integration; Cf Alexander technique, Aston patterning, Feldenkreis method, Massage, Ortho-bionomy, Rolfing®, Rosen method, Tragerwork®

**hellstone** *Argenticum nitricum*, see there

**helmet flower** Skullcap, see there, *Scutellaria lateriflora*

**helonius** Fairywand, see there, *Chamaelirium luteum*

**hemacytology index** UNPROVEN MEDICINE A test that measures unspecified alterations of blood cells; the hematology index was championed by Dr Ernesto Contreras, who believed it to be highly accurate in both diagnosing cancer and monitoring its progress (*American Cancer Society, Files on 'Unproven Methods of Cancer Management,' 1971*).

See Beard Anthrone test, Contreras method(s), Laetrile, Kelley index of malignancy, Unproven methods for cancer management

**hematogenic constitution** FRINGE MEDICINE-IRIDOLOGY A brown iris which, according to the construct of iridology, belongs to a person who is prone to anemia, cardiovascular disease, hepatitis, hepatobiliary disease, pancreatic insufficiency, malabsorption, and diabetes mellitus. See Iridology, Iris constitution

**hematogenic oxidation therapy** FRINGE ONCOLOGY A component of Issels' whole body therapy, an unproven method for cancer management, in which the patient's blood is removed, bubble oxygenated, irradiated with ultraviolet light, left to settle, then returned to the patient. See Issels' whole body therapy, Unproven methods for cancer management

**Hemi-Sync™** An audiocassette system that is claimed by its developer (*Monroe Institute, Faber VA*) to be useful for addiction disorders, eating disorders, hypertension, metabolic disease, pain, recuperation from surgery, strokes and other conditions, and for increasing strength (*Raso, 1994*)

**hemlock** Any of a family of poisonous herbs of the carrot family; in particular, *Conium maculatum*, but also *Tsuga* species, which contains the alkaloid conine TOXICITY Conine produces central nervous system hyperactivity, followed by medullary depression and respiratory failure TREATMENT Activated charcoal

Note: Socrates died from hemlock in 399 BC when he was tried and convicted for corrupting Athen's youth, two of whom, Alcibiades and Critias, betrayed Athens

**hemp** Marijuana, see there, *Cannabis sativa*

**hemlock** *Tsuga heterophylla*

**henbane** *Hyoscyamus niger*, black henbane, devil's eye, hog bean, Jupiter's bean, poison tobacco, stinking nightshade HERBAL MEDICINE An herb that is the primary source of atropine, hyoscyamine, and scopolamine; henbane was formerly used by herbalists; it is regarded as unsafe by the FDA TOXICITY Blurred vision, convulsions, delirium stupor, vertigo, and in high amounts, death. See Botanical toxicity, Herbal medicine, Poisonous plants

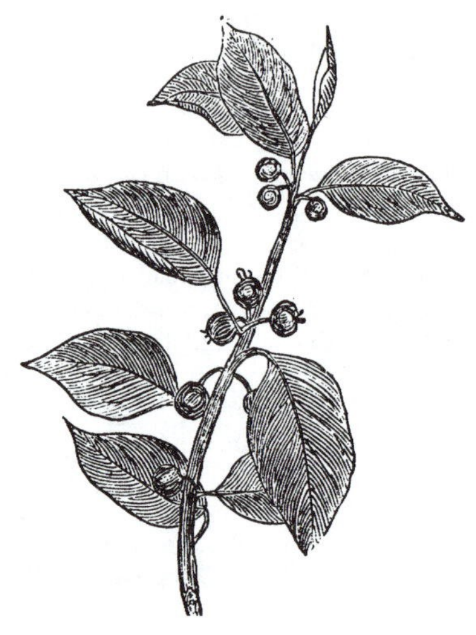

**henbane** *Hyoscyamus niger*

**HEPA filter** High-efficiency particulate air filter An air filter that markedly reduces dust, pollen and other particles in the air; HEPA filters are believed to relieve the symptoms of asthma in 10 to 30 minutes. See Air pollution

***Hepar sulf*** *Hepar sulfuris calcareum*, crude calcium sulfide HOMEOPATHY A remedy that has been used for acute suppurative infections of the head and neck, associated with the common cold; it is also used for asthma, constipation, croup, emphysema, genital herpes, joint pain, and paroxysmal coughing. See Homeopathy

**hepatic** ALTERNATIVE MEDICINE *noun* A medicinal preparation, usually of herbal origin that is used to 'tone' and strengthen the liver, increase the flow of bile, and detoxify the liver MAINSTREAM MEDICINE *adjective* Pertaining or referring to the liver

**herb** ALTERNATIVE PHARMACOLOGY A general term for a plant or part thereof that is used to produce a medicine, which may include roots, bark, stems, leaves, flowers, fruit, and seeds; according to the WHO, three-fourths of plant-derived pharmaceuticals are used in the same fashion as when they were first identified by native herbalists (*Alternative Medicine, Future Med Pub, 1994*). See Alternative medicine, Herbal medicine, Pharmacognosy

**herb of the cross** Vervain, see there, *Vebena officinalis*

**herb of grace** Rue, see there, *Ruta graveolens*

**herbal** *adjective* Pertaining or referring to an herb *noun* A book or treatise on herbs. See *Canon of Medicine*, *Charak Samhita*, *The Complete Herbal*, *De Materia Medica*, Herbal medicine, *Natural History*, *Nei Jing*, *Pen Ts'ao*, *Philosophy of Natural Therapeutics*, *Rigveda*, *Sushrita Samhita*, *Theatrum Botanicum*

**herbal douche** HERBAL MEDICINE The application of a decoction or infusion of herbs, apple cider vinegar, or yogurt directly to the vaginal mucosa. See Herbal medicine, Hydrotherapy

**herbal enema** HERBAL MEDICINE A format for delivering herbs directly to the large intestinal mucosa, using either a decoction or infusion. See Herbal medicine, Hydrotherapy

**herbal liquor** Medicine wine, *yao jiao* CHINESE MEDICINE A general term for a therapeutic preparation, in which chopped herbs are placed in alcohol, eg brandy, rum, vodka, and allowed to steep for three months to a year; the process allows virtually complete extraction of an herb's energies and essences, and forms the basis of many of the tonics used in Chinese medicine. See Chinese herbal medicine, Powder-Chinese medicine

**herbal medicine** Botanical medicine, botanomedicine, herbalism, phytomedicine, phytotherapy, vegotherapy As usually defined in alternative medicine, herbal medicine refers to the use of substances extracted from flowers, fruits, roots, seeds, and stems, either alone or as an adjunct to other forms of alternative health care or physical manipulation, eg massages; 'subspecialties' of herbal medicine include aromatherapy, ayurvedic herbal medicine, Bach flower remedies, and Chinese herbal medicine, which are discussed elsewhere in this work; anecdotal reports suggest that herbal medicine may be effective in treating abcesses, acidity, acne, addiction disorders, adenoids, agoraphobia, alcoholism, allergies, anemia, anxiety, arthritis, asthma, atherosclerosis, athletes' foot, bedwetting, bites and stings, bladder problems, blisters, bone fractures, bronchitis, bruxism, bruises, bunions, burns, bursitis, candidiasis, celiac disease, chickenpox, chronic fatigue syndrome, circulatory defects, claustrophobia, the common cold, coughs, cramps, dandruff, depression, earache, eczema, emphysema, eyestrain, fatigue, fever, flatulence, fluid retention, food poisoning, frozen shoulder, gallstones, gastrointestinal complaints (eg anal changes, gastritis, nausea, vomiting, indigestion, diarrhea, and irritable bowel syndrome), gout, halitosis, hangover, hay fever, headaches, heat rash, heartburn, hemorrhoids, hiccups, hives, hypertension, hypotension, incontinence, infertility, insomnia, jaundice, jet lag, laryngitis, low back pain, measles, menopausal disorders, menstrual dysfunction, migraines, mineral deficiencies, mood swings, morning sickness, mumps, neurologic complaints, obesity, painful conditions (eg neuralgia), panic attacks, parasites, periodontal disease, phobias, post-partum depression, premenstrual syndrome, prolapsed vertebral disks, prostate disease, psoriasis, renal disease, rheumatic disease, sciatica, sexual dysfunction, shortness of breath, sinusitis, sleep disorders, sports injuries, stasis (decubitus) ulcers, stress, tension, thyroid disease, tics, tinnitus, vaginitis, vertigo, warts, wheezing, whooping cough, and other conditions

▶ **CLASSIC HERBAL TEXTS**

- *Canon of Medicine*
- *Charak Samhita*
- *The Complete Herbal*
- *De Materia Medica*
- *Natural History*
- *Nei Jing*
- *Pen Ts'ao*
- *Philosophy of Natural Therapeutics*
- *Rigveda*
- *Sushrita Samhita*
- *Theatrum Botanicum*

The above are described in the text *Resource: American Herbalist Guild, PO Box 1683, Soquel CA, 95073 ☎ 1.408.464.2441*

See Alterative, Alternative medicine, Analgesic, Anthelmintic, Antibiotic, Antiseptic, Antispasmodic, Astringent, Botanical toxicity, Carminative, Cathertic, Decoction, Demulcent, Diaphoretic, Diuretic, Douche, Emetic, Emmenagogue, Enema, Ethnomedicine, Fluid extract, Green extract, Hepatic, Infusion, Laxative, Naturopathy, Nervine, Ointment, Poultice, Stomachic, Suppository, Syrup, Tincture

Note: The term herbal medicine may also loosely refer to alternative medicine, ethnomedicine, naturopathy, some unproven forms of herb-based therapies, and unproven methods for cancer management, as well as the use of herbs as therapeutic agents

**herbal pillow** CHINESE MEDICINE A drug delivery device used primarily in traditional Chinese medicine, in which a concoction of dried herbs is stuffed inside of a small pillow; heat from the head and neck is believed to volatilize therapeutic essences and release them to a person while sleeping; popular herbal pillows in the Chinese herbal formulary include those made from brown rice, crysanthemum and uncaria, gypsum, *Ligusticum wallichii* and *Angelica anomala*, and tea, described elsewhere in this work. See Chinese herbal medicine, Hops pillow

**herbal porridge** *Yao jou* CHINESE MEDICINE A general term for a therapeutic combination of herbs mixed with foods, usually grains, eg brown rice, barley, and millet, and ingested with meals. See Chinese herbal medicine

**herbal sleeping aid** HERBAL MEDICINE A general term for any herb that is believed to promote sleep at bedtime; such herbs include balm, catnip, hops, passionflower (due to meltol and ethyl-maltol), skullcap, and valerian. See Herbal medicine

**herbal tea** *Cha* HERBAL MEDICINE An infusion made from various plants, which may be beneficial for or ameliorate various conditions; some plants are toxic and tonic, and may affect the cardiovascular, gastrointestinal, and central nervous systems. See Herbal medicine

▶ **HERBAL TEAS WITH TOXIC EFFECTS**

- **CHAMOMILE** *Matricaria chamomilla* Anaphylactic shock, contact dermatitis
- **COMFREY** *Symphytum officinale* Veno-occlusive disease, hepatic failure, possibly a hepatic carcinogen
- **FOXGLOVE** *Digitalis purpurea* Malignant arrhythmias, cardiac arrest
- **JIMSONWEED** *Datura stramonium* Atropinic and hallucinogenic effects, central nervous system intoxication, ataxia, blurred vision
- **MAYAPPLE** *Podophyllum peltatum* Scopolaminic and anticholinergic effects
- **MATÉ** *Ilex paraguariensis* Veno-occlusive disease, possibly hepatic failure
- **POKEWEED** *Phytolacca americana* High saponin content causes gastroenteritis, bloody diarrhea, respiratory depression, mitogenic effects
- **SASSAFRAS** *Sassafras albidum* Hepatic carcinogen
- **SNAKEROOT** *Polygonum bistorta* Reserpinic, central nervous system intoxication (*Arch Environ Health 1987; 42:133*)

See Botanical toxicity, Infusion, Poisonous plants, Unproven methods for cancer management.

**herbalism** Herbal medicine, see there

**herbalist** An individual who administers or prescribes herbal medicines

***l'herbe du siege*** Figwort, see there, *Scrophularia nodosa*

**herbe royale** Basil, see there, *Ocimum basilicum*

**Constantine Hering** An American student of Samuel Hahnemann, the founder of homeopathy, who returned to the US; he has been called the father of American homeopathy, and is best known for his Law of Cures. See Hahnemann, Homeopathy, Kent, Law of Cures

**Hering's Law of Cures** see Law of cures

**heroic surgery** SURGICAL ONCOLOGY An aggressive surgical operation, eg radical mastectomy for malignancy, in which wide resection margins are obtained, as the tumor has spread beyond a resectable size; heroic surgery may be performed in order to alleviate pain or improve the quality of life of those who are terminally ill; Cf Heroic therapy

**heroic therapy** MEDICAL HISTORY The use of draconian measures (eg blood-letting and preparations of mercury) to save a person's life in absence of valid studies justifying their use; heroic therapies are believed to have hastened the death of George Washington and countless others in the 18th century (*Armstrong, 1991*) MAINSTREAM MEDICINE Aggressive treatment of a dread disease that is regarded by the patient's caregivers as incurable with standard therapies at usual and prudent doses of potentially toxic drugs; Cf Heroic surgery

Note: In the latter context, the use of intense (heroic) therapy is justified by peer-reviewed data, which may reveal a minimal increase in survival in those with a dread disease, often at the price of a poor quality of life

**heterocyclic amine** Any of a family of potentially carcinogenic compounds present in grilled meat, which include PhIP and AαC, compounds that volatilize and may represent a risk factor for malignancy in 'short-order' cooks (*Science News 1994; 146:103*). See Animal fat

**hexuronic acid** Vitamin C, see there

**HGP-30** An experimental AIDS vaccine based on a synthetic HIV core protein, p17; HGP-30 has been added to the growing list of failed AIDS vaccines. See AIDS fraud, AIDS therapy

**H.H.D.** Doctor of Holistic Health

**H.H.P.** Holistic Health Practitioner

**hibiscus** *Hibiscus sabdariffa,* Jamaica sorrel, roselle HERBAL MEDICINE A tropical flower that contains ascorbic, citric, and glycolic acids, which is diuretic and laxative; it is used internally for constipation, nausea, and bladder infections, and topically for sunburns. See Herbal medicine

**hierotherapy** Prayer therapy. See Christian Science

**highbush cranberry** Cramp bark, see there, *Viburnum opulus*

**high colonic** ALTERNATIVE MEDICINE Colon therapy, see there SEXOLOGY High colonics (enemas) have had some currency as a vehicle for erotic transport in the context of homosexual practices

**high-density, high-glycemic carbohydrates** CLINICAL NUTRITION A general term that encompasses breads, grains, pasta, rice, and other starches

**high density lipoprotein cholesterol** see HDL-cholesterol

**high-fat diet** A diet rich in fats, usually understood to be saturated (animal or tropical oils) fats; adverse health effects of a high-fat diet include arthritis, cancer, cardiovascular disease, diabetes mellitus, hypertension, obesity, and stroke. See Fat, Fatty acids, Saturated fat acis; Cf Low-fat diet

**high-impact aerobics** Any type of aerobic exercise that promotes physical fitness, at the risk of stress to musculoskeletal tissues and joints; high-impact aerobic exercises include aerobic dancing, basketball, jogging, and running. See Aerobic exercise, Exercise, High-impact exercise; Cf Low-impact aerobics

**high-impact sport** SPORTS MEDICINE A generic term for any physical activity or sport in which there is intense and/or frequent wear and trauma of weight-bearing joints, in particular the foot, knee, and hip; high-impact sports include baseball, basketball, football, handball, hockey, karate, racquetball, running, soccer, and waterskiing; participation in high-impact sports is discouraged after hip and knee arthroplasty (*Mayo Clin Proc 1995; 70:342oa*); Cf Low-impact sport, Moderate impact sport, No-impact sport

**high pH therapy** A hypothetical therapy for cancer based on epidemiologic data that suggest that regions with high amounts of alkali metals in the soil have a low incidence of cancer; it has been postulated that alkali metals, eg cesium and rubidium, might be beneficial in treating cancer; the clinical efficacy of high alkali therapy is uncertain (*Moss, 1992*). See Cesium, Unproven methods for cancer management

**'high touch'** ALTERNATIVE MEDICINE A component of the BRETH technique, in which a 'sitter' touches the client through 'soul-to-soul' contact, creating a 'sacred space' for 'deep inner journeys' (*Raso, 1994*). See BRETH technique, 'Sitter'

**high velocity-low amplitude technique** Articulatory technique, see there

**highway hypnosis** PSYCHOLOGY A light hypnotic state induced by the monotony of driving a motor vehicle, usually on straight roads that are uninterrupted by crossings, municipalities, and other visually distracting factors; highway hypnosis most commonly occurs in a background of fatigue. See Hypnosis, Poor sleeping hygiene

**hipberry** Rose hip, see there

**Hippocrates diet** Living foods diet ALTERNATIVE NUTRITION A diet formulated by an American, A Wigmore, which consists of uncooked 'living foods,' including fruits and vegetables and their juices, sprouts, nuts and seeds, fermented foods, eg miso and sauerkraut, and raw honey. See Hippocrates health program

**Hippocrates health program** A health enhancing system developed by an American, A Wigmore, which consists of a vegetarian diet, food combining, enemas, deep breathing, brushing the skin, and various exercises; the program is believed to integrate the body, mind, and spirit to achieve optimal health (*Raso, 1994*). See Diet, Food combining, Hippocrates diet

**hippotherapy** ALTERNATIVE MEDICINE The use

of a specially trained horse as a therapeutic 'vehicle,' for improving a person's balance; as the horse sways and rocks, the mounted patient's pelvic muscles are required to compensate; hippotherapy has been used in Europe, and is believed to be useful in patients with cerebral palsy and multiple sclerosis; Cf Equestrian therapy, Equestrian transformation expression

**HIV conspiracy** A broad deception allegedly being committed by mainstream retrovirology researchers, the majority of whom subscribe to the belief that AIDS is intimately linked to infection by HIV; according to one politician, the US '*Federal AIDS effort–based on the conclusioin that HIV causes AIDS–will be seen as the greatest scandal in American history...*' (*Science 1995; 268:191*). See AIDS fraud, Peter Duesberg

**HIV wasting syndrome** AIDS A clinical complex linked to HIV infection, and characterized by a marked decrease in weight[1] associated with chronic renal insufficiency, and caused by poor nutrition and anorexia, endocrine dysfunction, and catabolic stresses, eg infection (*N Engl J Med 1992; 327:329rv*), uremia, and dialysis; the wasting syndrome is mediated by tumor necrosis factor (as well as by interleukin-1 and interferons), which decreases lipoprotein lipase, fatty acid synthesis, and increases lipolysis in fat cells TREATMENT Recombinant human growth hormone[2]. See AIDS therapy

[1]In absence of disease, starvation results in death at 66% of ideal body weight; in AIDS, cell mass at death is 54% [2]Which increases lean body mass by ± 3 kg and increases the capacity for physical work (*Bio/Technology 1995; 13:206*)

***ho shou wu*** Chinese cornbind, see there, *Polygonum multiflorum*

**hoarhound** Horehound, see there, *Marrubium vulgare*

***hochu-ekki-to*** JAPANESE HERBAL MEDICINE An herbal formulation that is reported to increase the production of tumor necrosis factor and stabilize cell membranes, and may be of use as an adjuvant in treating cancer in patients who require chemotherapy and/or radiotherapy (*Moss, 1992*). See Unproven methods for cancer management

**Hoffman quadrinity process** Fischer-Hoffman Process, quadrinity process ALTERNATIVE PSYCHOLOGY A program developed from the 1960s to the 1980s by R Hoffman, in which a person undergoes a 7-day 'retreat'; the intent of the process is to help a person recognize negative behaviors, moods, and attitudes, which Hoffman termed 'negative love,' and implement positive personality changes; the quadrinity process is believed to help individuals become more loving, accepting, and forgiving of family, friends, and others. See Negative love syndrome

**hog apple** Mayapple, see there, *Podophyllum peltatum*

**hog bean** Henbane, see there, *Hyoscyamus niger*

**hogberry** Bearberry, see there, *Arctostaphylos uva-ursi*

**hog cranberry** Bearberry, see there, *Arctostaphylos uva-ursi*

**holding** ALTERNATIVE MEDICINE An ad hoc term used in the Rosen method of massage therapy that refers to muscular tension, which is believed to be caused by repressed emotions. See Holding, Massage therapy, Rosen method

**holistic approach** ALTERNATIVE MEDICINE A term used by alternative health care providers for a philosophical approach to health care, in which the entire patient is evaluated and treated; mainstream medicine has been criticized by alternative health care providers for patients only by organ systems. See Alternative medicine, Holistic medicine

**holistic dentistry** Alternative dentistry, see there

**holistic health** A health attitude in which an individual's physical and mental state and life experiences form the basis for his state of health. See Alternative medicine, Holistic medicine, Wellness

**holistic medicine** The term 'holistic medicine' is generally regarded as synonymous with alternative medicine, and in this work will be discussed as such. See Alternative medicine

The purist (*Gottschalk-Olsen, 1989*) would note that the adjective *holistic* refers to a philosophical approach to health care in which all aspects of a patient's physical and mental condition are evaluated, which may or may not occur with a practitioner of alternative medicine

**holistic nursing** Alternative nursing A format of nursing care that integrates the patient's body, mind, and spirit, through therapeutic touch, bodywork, reflexology, and other maneuvers. See Alternative medicine

**holistic obstetrics** Alternative gynecology,

see there

**holistic palpate energy therapy** A permutation of aura balancing. See Aura balancing, Chakra healing

**holistic Reiki** A synthesis of Reiki and *chakra* healing, developed M and B Abraham. See *Chakra* healing, Reiki

**holonomic breathwork** Holotropic Breathwork, see there

**holonomic therapy** Holotropic Breathwork, see there

**holotropic breath therapy** Holotropic Breathwork, see there

**holotropic breathing** Holotropic Breathwork, see there

**Holotropic Breathwork®** Groff breathwork, holonomic breathwork, holonomic therapy, holotropic breath therapy, holotropic breathing ALTERNATIVE MEDICINE A technique developed in 1976 by a Czech-American psychiatrist, Dr Stanislav Grof, as a means '...*of self-exploration based on ancient spiritual practices and modern conscious research*...(combining) ...*breathing, evocative music, and a specific form of bodywork*.' (*Kastner, Burroughs, 1993*); Holotropic Breathwork is presented in workshops by Grof-certified 'facilitators,' many of whom themselves are mental health care professionals; in the sessions, participants lie flat in a dimly-lit room, and learn breathing techniques while listening to the pounding of African drums; incorporated into the process are focused bodywork and mandala drawing; the participants are encourage to access various 'levels' of experience: sensory, biographical, prenatal, transpersonal, and 'buried' memories; certified Breathwork® facilitators undergo a 500-hour training program. See Harner method, Neo-shamanism

**Holtism** PEDIATRICS-HISTORY A 'hands-off' approach to child-rearing espoused by LE Holt, MD, professor of pediatrics at Columbia University; his book, *The Care and Feeding of Children* published in 1895, influenced turn-of-the-century child-rearing, as he recommended that children not be molly-coddled or held, and be allowed to cry and suffer pain; Holtism became intimately linked to marasmus, a condition then associated with wasting and death by age two; frequent physical contact with a care giver is now believed to be as necessary to an infant's survival as food; Cf Mothering

**holy thistle** Blessed thistle, see there, *Cnicus benedictus*

**homeoacupuncture** A non-traditional form of homeopathy, in which homeopathic remedies are injected into acupoints. See Homeopathy

**homeopath** HOMEOPATHY A practitioner of homeopathy; as of the early 1990s, there were an estimated 3000 practicing homeopaths in the US. See Homeopathy

**homeopathic** ALTERNATIVE MEDICINE *adjective* Pertaining or referring to homeopathy MAINSTREAM MEDICINE Because homeopathy is based on the counterintuitive posit that smaller concentrations of a particular remedy have greater therapeutic effects (law of the infinitesimal dose), 'homeopathic' has also been used by mainstream physicians to refer to a dose or therapeutic level of a particular substance that is too low to be clinically effective

**homeopathic first aid kit** HOMEOPATHY A collection of homeopathic remedies in the form of tablets, ointments, and tinctures, that are used by laypersons to treat common complaints including diarrhea, itching, motion sickness, nausea and vomiting, rashes, stagefright, and others. See Homeopathy

**homeopathic medicine** 1. Homeopathic remedy, see there 2. Homeopathy, see there

**homeopathic remedy** Homeopathic drug, homeopathic medicine A general term for any of the nearly 2000 preparations of medicines used in homeopathy

▶ **SOURCES, HOMEOPATHIC REMEDIES**

- **MINERALS**, eg *Cuprum metallicum* (copper), *aurum* (gold), *mercurium* (mercury), or mineral salts, eg *Kali carbonicum* (potassium carbonate), *Natrum sulfuricum* (sodium sulfate)
- **PLANTS**, eg *Belladonna* (deadly nightshade), *Pulsatilla* (wind flower), *Rhus toxicodendron* (poison ivy); plants are the primary source of homeopathic remedies
- **ANIMALS**, eg *Lac canensis* (canine breast milk), *Lachesis* (bushmaster snake venom), and *Tarantula* (the spider)

PREPARATION The raw material is extracted, then reduced in concentration by a process known as potentization, placed in a lactose base, and compressed in a small pill; homeopathic remedies are of three broad types–acute, chronic, and constitutional, which are usually administered sublingually; the concentrations are designated as X for a homeopathic remedy that is diluted one part in 10—commonly used concentrations are 6X (one part in $10^6$), 30X (one part in $10^{30}$), and 200X (one part in $10^{200}$); in Europe, homeopathic remedies may be diluted one part in 100 and designated C, the letter D may be used for concentrations of one part in 10; the remedies are dispensed, in order of decreasing size, as tablets, pillules, granules, and powder. See Antidote, Constitutional remedy, Homeopathy, Isopathy, Law of cures, Law of infinitesimal dose, Law of similars, Modality, Potentization, Proving; Cf Naturopathy

**homeopathic symptom** The manifestation of a condition; the homeopathic approach to evaluating symptoms differs from that of mainstream medicine; in general, four chracteristics are considered

▶ **HOMEOPATHIC SYMPTOMS, CHARACTERISTICS**

- **SENSATION**, eg pain, which is described as burning, throbbing, tearing and so on
- **LOCATION,** eg headache, the exact location is described, as is the region to which it extends
- **MODALITY**, eg factors that alleviate or aggrevate a main symptom, which is an expression of the uniqueness of the individual; a chest pain that is worsened by *cold air* or *in the morning* are two examples of modalities
- **COMCOMITANT SYMPTOM** Any symptom that accompanies the main symptom; as an example, if the main symptom is menstrual pain, a craving for certain foods would be a concomitant symptom

Evaluation of all above noted components are required to create a symptom picture. See Homeopathy

**homeopathy** Homeopathic medicine, homeotherapeutics A system of health care, formulated by a German physician, Samuel CF Hahnemann

## HOMEOPATHIC REMEDIES

| LATIN NAME | COMMON NAME |
|---|---|
| *Aconitum napellus* | Aconite |
| *Allium cepa* | Onion |
| *Antimonium crudum* | Antimony |
| *Apis melliflora* | Crushed honeybee |
| *Arnica* | Mountain daisy |
| *Arsenicum album* | Arsenic |
| *Aurum iod* | Gold iodide |
| *Aurum metallicum* | Gold |
| *Baryta carbonica* | Barium carbonate |
| *Belladonna* | Deadly nightshade |
| *Bellis perennis* | Daisy |
| *Berberis* | Bayberry |
| *Borax* | Borax |
| *Bryonia alba* | Wild hops |
| *Cactus grandiflora* | Night-blooming cactus |
| *Calcarea carbonica* | Calcium carbonate |
| *Calc fluor* | Calcium fluoride |
| *Calendula* | Marigold |
| *Cantharis* | Spanish fly |
| *Caulophyllum* | Blue cohosh |
| *Chamomilla* | Chamomile |
| *China officinalis* | Cinchona |
| *Cimifuga* | Black snakeroot |
| *Coffea cruda* | Coffee |
| *Colocynthis* | Bitter cucumber |
| *Cuprum metallicum* | Copper |
| *Dulcamara* | Woody nightshade |
| *Euphrasia* | Eyebright |
| *Ferrum phos* | Iron phosphate |
| *Gelsimium* | Yellow jasmine |
| *Hepar sulph* | Calcium sulfide |
| *Iodum* | Iodine |
| *Ipecacuanha* | Ipecac |
| *Kali bichromicum* | Potassium dichromate |
| *Kali sulphuricum* | Potassium sulfate |
| *Lachesis* | Bushmaster snake venom |
| *Ledum pallustre* | Marsh tea |
| *Lillium tigrum* | Tiger lily |
| *Magnesia phosphorica* | Magnesium phosphate |
| *Mercurius* | Mercury |
| *Natrum muriaticum* | Table salt |
| *Natrum carbonicum* | Sodium carbonate |
| *Nux vomica* | Poison nut |
| *Oscillococcinum* | Duck liver and heart |
| *Pulsatilla* | Windflower |
| *Rhus toxicodendron* | Poison ivy |
| *Ruta graveolens* | Rue |
| *Sarsaparilla* | Wild licorice |
| *Sepia* | Cuttlefish |
| *Sulphur* | Sulfur |
| *Urtica urens* | Stinging nettle |
| *Zincum met* | Zinc |

(1755-1843) that was heretical at the time for its opposition to the medical therapy of the day, which consisted of blood-letting, emetics, and cathartics; homeopathy is based on the principle of *'similia similibus curantur'* (like cures like), ie a disease caused by a substance, eg arsenic, could be cured by that same substance in highly diluted doses; homeopathy was popular in the US until the early 20th century, after which it was actively suppressed by mainstream medical practitioners; homeopathy continued to be popular in Europe, Brazil, Argentina, and in India, and has recently resurged in popularity in the US

▶ **HOMEOPATHY, FORMS OF**

- **CLASSICAL HOMEOPATHY** This form is closest to Hahnemann's original precepts, as it seeks to identify and use constitutional remedies; these remedies are selected based on an in-depth interview, which provides information on current symptoms, as well as psychological, emotional, physical, and familial background
- **COMBINATION HOMEOPATHY** Formula homeopathy The use of a 'shotgun' approach, in which 2 to 8 homeopathic remedies known to be effective against a particular condition (eg arthritic pain, dry cough, earache, tension headache, and others) are mixed together, with the hope that one will have an effect on the symptoms affecting the patient
- **FORMULA HOMEOPATHY** See Combination homeopathy
- **NONCLASSICAL HOMEOPATHY** A format of homeopathy that is somewhat similar in philosophy to mainstream medicine, in that the remedy is chosen based on the nature of the condition, and whether it is acute or chronic, rather than on the individual's constitution
- **SINGLE-REMEDY HOMEOPATHY** A permutation of classical homeopathy, in which only acute conditions are treated, and then with single agents, a format that is well-suited for self-treatment by a knowledgeable amateur

A metanalysis of 107 controlled trials of homeopathy (from 1966 to 1990) revealed widespread benefits in treating allergies, chronic problems, mild deficiency states, mental disorders, hay fever, pain, rheumatologic disease, cardiovascular disease, upper respiratory tract and other infections, recuperation from surgery, and other conditions (*Brit Med J 1991; 302:316*); anecdotal reports suggest that homeopathy may also be effective in treating such diverse conditions as acidity, acne, addiction disorders, adenoids, agoraphobia, anemia, anxiety, arthritis, asthma, atherosclerosis, athletes' foot, baldness, bedwetting, bereavement, bipolar (manic-depressive) disorder, bites and stings, bladder problems, blisters, bone fractures, bronchitis, bruxism, bruises, burns, bursitis, candidiasis, chickenpox, chronic fatigue syndrome, claustrophobia, colds, constipation, conjunctivitis, cough, cramps, depression, earache, eczema, eyestrain, fainting, fatigue, fever, flatulence, fluid retention, food poisoning, frozen shoulder, gallstones, gastrointestinal problems including constipation, diarrhea, gastritis, nausea, vomiting, indigestion, and irritable bowel syndrome, gout, halitosis, headaches, heat rash, heartburn, hemorrhoids, hives, hyperactivity, hypertension, infertility, insomnia, jaundice, laryngitis, measles, menopausal disorders, menstrual defects, migraines, mood swings, mumps, neurologic complaints, obesity, panic attacks, phobias, post-partum depression, premenstrual syndrome, prostate disease, slipped or prolapsed vertebral disks, psoriasis, renal disease, sciatica, sexual problems, shock, shortness of breath, sinusitis, sleep disorders, sports injuries, stasis (decubitus) ulcers, stress, tension, thyroid disease, tics, tinnitus, travel sickness, urinary incontinence, vaginitis, vertigo, viral infections, wheezing, whooping cough *Resource: National Center for Homeopathy, 801 N Fairfax St, Suite 306, Alexandria, VA 22314 ☎ 1.703.548.7792*

See Alternative medicine, Antidote, Homeopath, Homeopathic remedy, Homeopathic symptom, Isopathy, Law of cures, Law of the infinitesimal dose, Law of similars, Modality, Potentization, Proving; Cf Naturopathy

**'homeopathy of bodywork'** Ortho-Bionomy, see there

**homeotherapeutics** Homeopathy, see there

**homeovitics** A form of homeopathy based on principles that differ from mainstream homeopathy; there are 22 different homeovitics formulations sold by HoBoN in Naples, Florida; the selection of these remedies can, according to HoBoN's literature, can be determined by applied kinesiology and electrodiagnosis (*Raso, 1994*). See Detoxosode, Homeopathy

**homuncular acupuncture** A general term for any form of acupuncture in which a region or set of acupoints is believed to represent a miniature version (homunculus) of the entire person; according to this theory, stimulation of the homuncular acupoints would be as effective as treating the traditional acupoints; an example of this format is auricular acupuncture

**honey** A sweet golden-brown sticky fluid produced by honeybees from the nectar of flowers and stored in hives for food; honey has long been advocated as a healthy food that is superior to sugar, as it contains small amounts of vitamins and minerals. See Healthy food, Mad honey, Royal jelly; Cf Artificial sweeteners

**honeybee** *Apis mellifera*, see there

**honey grass** Licorice, see there, *Glycyrrhiza glabra*

**honeysuckle** *Lonicera japonica* CHINESE MEDICINE An ornamental plant, the flowers of which have been used for abcesses, bacterial infections, colds, conjunctivitis, inflammation, and urinary burning; some data suggest that honeysuckle may be antibacterial, and lower cholesterol. See Chinese herbal medicine

**honeywort** *Angelica sinensis*, see there

**honorable minister of the central clearing department** Gallbladder, see Twelve vital organs

**hoodwort** Skullcap, see there, *Scutellaria lateriflora*

**hook-up** A term used by Tragerwork® workers that refers to the linking of the mind and body; hook-up allows a person to perform work in a relaxed and meditative state and transmit a sense of freedom and playfulness. See Tragerwork

**hops** *Humulus lupulus*, common hops HERBAL MEDICINE A perennial vine that contains amino acids, flavonoids, glycosides (astralagin, quercitrin, rutin), and various other compounds including citral, geraniol, humulone, linionine, lupulin, lupulone, serolidol, and bitter resin; hops are known for their use in producing beer; hops are anti-bacterial (due to humulone and lupulone), mildly sedative, and have been used for anxiety, headaches, insomnia, neuralgias, to relax smooth muscle and, in combination with other herbs, for irritable bowel syndrome TOXICITY Given its soporific effect, hops should not be used by those who drive or operate heavy machinery; hops should not be used in pregnancy or women with estrogen-dependent breast cancer (ie those who respond to tamoxifen), as hops contain phytoestrogens; hops may cause contact dermatitis, constipation, diarrhea, and heartburn. See Herbal medicine, Hops pillow, Lupulin

**hops pillow** HERBAL MEDICINE A pillow filled with hops (*Humulus lupulus*), which is believed by its users to induce sleep, an effect attributed to the valeronic acid and active principles in the volatile oil. See Herbal medicine, Herbal pillow, Hops

**(the) Horder report** UNPROVEN HEALTH CARE An investigation headed by Lord Thomas Horder that examined the efficacy of the emanometer, a radionics device invented by Dr WE Boyd, a British homeopath, which he believed could identify substances and chemicals at a distance. See Emanometer, Radionics; Cf Abrams box, De la Warr box, Drown box

The investigation concluded that the device was ineffective (*Inglis, West, 1983*)

**horehound** *Marrubium vulgare*, common horehound, hoarhound, marrubium, marvel, white horehound HERBAL MEDICINE A perennial herb (figure, facing page) that contains marrubin, diterpene alcohols, resin, saponins, sesquiterpenes, tannins, and volatile oils; it is diaphoretic, expectorant, laxative, mildly sedative, and vasodilatory, and has been used as an appetite stimulant, a liver tonic, and for cardiac arrhythmias. See Herbal medicine

**horny goat weed** *Epimedium sagittatum*, also known as *Aceranthus sagittatum*, *E macranthum*, *hsien ling pi*, immortal spirit gall, *yin yang huo* CHINESE MEDICINE A perennial herb, the leaf of which is tonic, regarded as an aphrodisiac, and used for impotence, infertility, paresthesias, low back pain, and rheumatic complaints. See Chinese herbal medicine

**horseback to heaven** Equestrian transformational expression, see there

**horse balm** Stoneroot, see there, *Collinsonia canadensis*

**horse chestnut** *Aesculus hippocastanum*, buckeye HERBAL MEDICINE A deciduous tree, the bark or fruit of which contains coumarins, flavonoids, saponins, and tannins; it is believed to be anti-inflammatory, and is administered as an extract or decoction for arthritis, hemorrhoids, varicose veins, and to stimulate the circulation; it may be used topically for muscle pain and cramps TOXICITY The nuts are poisonous, and may be fatal in children. See Herbal medicine

**horsefly weed** Wild indigo, see there, *Baptista tinctoria*

**horse heal** Elecampane, see there, *Inula helenium*

**horse hoof** Coltsfoot, see there, *Tussilago farfara*

**horseradish** *Cochlearia armoracia*, *Armoracia rusticana* HERBAL MEDICINE A perennial culinary vegetable that contains asparagin, resin, sinigrin (which converts to mustard oil), and vitamin C; horseradish is antimicrobial, antiseptic, diaphoretic, diuretic, and a cardiovascular and gastrointestinal tonic; it is used internally and externally to treat respiratory and urinary tract infections, rheumatic diseases and gout, neuralgias, neck pain, stiffness; the leaves have been used by herbalists for food poisoning TOXICITY Excess use on the skin causes blistering; horseradish may depress thyroid activity. See Herbal medicine

**horse savin** Juniper, see there, *Juniperus communis*

**horsetail** *Equisetum arvense*, bottlebrush, field horsetail, mare's tail, pewterwort, scouring rush, shave grass HERBAL MEDICINE A branching shoot that contains alkaloids, flavonoids, minerals, saponins, silica, and tannins; it is antimicrobial, astringent, diuretic, and hemostatic, and has been used topically to treat cuts and internally to treat anemia, atherosclerosis, bedwetting, brittle nails and hair, fatigue, fractures, gastric ulcers, kidney stones, prostatitis, respiratory infections including tuberculosis, urinary tract infections, rheumatic complaints, and other conditions. See Herbal medicine

**horehound** *Marrubium vulgare*

**horse chestnut** *Aesculus hippocastanum*

**horse thistle** Tiger thistle, see there, *Cirsium japonicum*

**horseweed** Stoneroot, see there, *Collinsonia canadensis*

**Hoshino exercises** ALTERNATIVE MEDICINE A series of four exercises (shoulder exercise, knee exercise, chest exercise, and twisting) used in Hoshino therapy; they are intended to maintain optimal biochemical function and prevent the recurrence of musculoskeletal disease. See Hoshino therapy

**Hoshino therapy** ALTERNATIVE MEDICINE A permutation of acupressure developed in the 1950s by Professor T Hoshino that uses 250 pressure points located directly over the muscles, tendons, and ligaments, to evaluate biomechanical function and identify local musculoskeletal defects; Hoshino therapy has been used to treat bursitis, fatigue, headache, low back pain, muscle pain, nausea, numbness, sciatica, slipped (vertebral) disk, tendinitis, and vertigo; it is complemented by Hoshino exercises; training consists of 400 hours of instruction, which is offered to health care professionals. See Acupuncture, Hoshino exercises

**hot bath** NATUROPATHY A bath taken in very hot water, which is believed to be useful for arthritis, eczema, hemorrhoids, insomnia, muscle soreness, premenstrual syndrome and has been used to stimulate menstruation WARNING Hot tub use in early pregnancy has been associated with a 2-fold increase in neural tube defects; use of hot baths is linked to decreased sperm counts; prolonged periods of time in excessively hot water may result in fatigue, mental lethargy, and poor circulation. See Hydrotherapy; Sitz bath; Cf Cold bath

**hot-cold disease system** A therapeutic system rooted in classical Greco-Roman and Persian-Arabic medicine that arrived with 'los Conquistadores' and merged with local Mayan medicine; the system is practiced in its waning years by 'curanderos' in Central America; illnesses are viewed as either 'hot' and treated with their opposite, ie 'cold' remedies, eg limes, cauliflower, and roses, or 'cold,' treated with 'hot remedies,' eg rue (*Ruta graveolens*), garlic, and crude brown sugar (*Soc Sci Med 1985; 21:807*)

**hot compress** Fomentation NATUROPATHY A locally applied cloth imbibed with hot water, which is analgesic, antispasmodic, sedative, and vasodilatory. See Hydrotherapy; Cf Cold compress

**hot tub rash** Whirlpool dermatitis PUBLIC HEALTH A dermatopathy caused by *Pseudomonas aeruginosa*, a normal skin inhabitant; when immersed for a prolonged period in hot water, as typically occurs in hot tub parties, *P aeruginosa* reproduces rapidly and causes an itchy rash most prominent on the body regions covered by a bathing suit

**Hoxsey medicine** FRINGE ONCOLOGY Either of 2 preparations (popularly known as the 'pink medicine' and the 'black medicine' or brown tonic), which were formulated by Harvey Hoxsey, and promoted in the 1950s as cancer therapies; the FDA's investigation on the efficacy of the Hoxsey 'drugs' concluded that they were ineffective. See Alternative medicine, Black medicine, Hoxsey tonic, Hoxsey treatment, Pink medicine, Unproven methods for cancer management

**Hoxsey tonic** FRINGE ONCOLOGY A mixture of herbs and potassium iodide used by Mildren Nelson at the Bio-Medical Center (Hoxsey Clinic) in Tijuana, Mexico, which is said to be effective against cancer; the tonic contains barberry (*Berberis vulgaris*) bark, buckthorn (*Rhamnus purshiana*), burdock root (*Arctium lappa*), cascara amarga (*Picramnia antidesma*), chaparral (*Larrea tridentata*), licorice root (*Glycyrrhiza glabra*), potassium iodide, prickly ash (*Zanthoxylum americana*), red clover (*Trifolium pratense*), and stillingia (*Stillingia sylvatica*); evidence of the efficacy of the Hoxsey tonic in treating cancer is inconclusive (*Pelton, Overholser, 1994*). See Hoxsey medicine, Hoxsey treatment, Unproven methods for cancer management; Cf Essiac

**Hoxsey treatment** FRINGE ONCOLOGY An unproven cancer therapy consisting of a 'brown tonic' containing potassium iodide, licorice, and herbs (barberry root, buckthorn bark, burdock root, cascara amarga, pokeweed, prickley ash bark, red clover, and stillingia root); the brown tonic is administered for internal malignancies; another group of Hoxsey tonics are topically applied escharotic formulations used for skin cancer; Hoxsey treatment also requires a 'positive attitude' and a special elimination diet (no sugar, salt, or alcohol); Hoxsey tonics are banned by the FDA, but may be available at some alternative health centers in Tijuana, Mexico. See Unproven methods for cancer management; Cf Alternative medicine

**hsi hsin** *Asarum sieboldi*, see there

**hsiang dan** *Aloe vera*, see there

**hsiang guo** *Ligusticum wallichii*, see there

**hsiang pu** Cattail, see there, *Typha latifolia*

**hsiang ru** *Elsholtzia splendens*, see there

**hsien ling pi** Horny goat weed, see there, *Epimedium sagittatum*

**hsien mao** *Curculigo ensifolia*, see there

**hsien yu** *Curculigo ensifolia*, see there

**hsu duan** Teasel, see there, *Dipsacus sylvestris*

**hsuan fu hua** Elecampene, see there, *Inula helenium*

**hsueh** ACUPUNCTURE A term that translates from Chinese as cave or hollow and corresponds to an acupressure point. See Acupoint

***hu bo*** *Pinites succinifer*, see there

***hu buo*** *Pinites succinifer*, see there

***hu jiao*** Black pepper, see there, formally designated *Piper nigrum*

***hua wang*** Tree peony, see there, *Paeonia moutan*

***huang chi*** Astragalus, see there, *Astragalus membranaceous*, *Astragalus boantchy*

***huang hua di ding*** Dandelion, see there, *Taraxacum officinale*

***huang jing*** *Polygonatum cirrhifolium*, see there

***huang lien*** Coptis, see there, *Coptis sinensis*

***huang qi*** Astragalus, see there, *Astragalus membranaceous*, *Astragalus boantchy*

***huang tsao*** *Dendrobium nobile*

***hui hsiang*** Fennel, see there, *Foeniculum vulgare*

***hui xiang*** Fennel, see there, *Foeniculum vulgare*

**human adjuvant disease** A human correlate to adjuvant disease of animals, which was first described in the mid-1960s in Japanese women who had undergone injections of silicone, paraffin, and other unknown materials into their breasts; up to one-half of women with silicone breasts implants have circulating anti-collagen antibodies; this condition is thought to be an uncommon complication of the systemic leakage of silicone and is characterized by rheumatoid arthritis, systemic sclerosis, malignant hypertension, and other manifestations of chronic connective tissue disease (*N Engl J Med 1994; 331:1231c*). See Breast implants

**human energetic assessment and restorative technique** A healing method developed by GM DeLalio and based on the belief that the brain produces healing energy that travels along etheric pathways; this energy can be interrupted by adverse lifestyles and negative thoughts, diagnosed by scanning the human electromagnetic field, and restored by re-establishing the etheric pathways

**humanistic psychology** Eupsychology, existential analysis ALTERNATIVE PSYCHOLOGY A philosophy of psychotherapy based on a belief in a person's intrinsic potential for personal growth and development; central to humanistic psychology is the posit that a person is subject to multiple negative genetic, familial, environmental, and social factors, which can be altered by attaining a positive attitude; humanistic psychology eschews the 'medical sickness' model and embraces one of personal mental growth and emancipation; humanistic psychotherapies differ from both Freudian psychoanalysis and behaviorism (championed by BF Skinner); the more common forms are listed in the accompanying table. See Natural psychotherapy

See Behavioral intervention, Co-counseling, Encounter groups, Freudian analysis, Gestalt therapy, Metamorphic technique, Primal therapy, Psychodrama, Psychotherapy, Reichian therapy (bioenergetics), Rebirthing, Reflective communication, Rogerian therapy, Transactional analysis; Cf Behavioral intervention, Psychoanalysis

**'humanized' milk** NEONATOLOGY A modified formulation of cow milk, the fat ratio of which (40% casein, 60% whey) closely mimics human milk; humanized milk is indicated for infants weighing less than 2000 grams. See Breast milk; Cf White beverages

**humor** A fluid or gel-like substance. See The Four Humors

**HUMANISTIC PSYCHOTHERAPIES**

| | |
|---|---|
| Client-oriented | Jungian/mythopoetic |
| Constructivist | Narrative |
| Ericksonian | Primal integration |
| Ethno-cultural | Psychodrama |
| Existential | Reichian/bioenergetics |
| Experiential/Focusing | Rogerian therapy |
| Expressive arts | Self-in-relation |
| Family process | Self psychology |
| Feminist | Transactional analysis |
| Gestalt | Transpersonal |

J Jacobs, 1996

**humoral doctrine** MEDICAL HISTORY The medical philosophy of the ancient Greeks in which the state of health and disease was determined by the four body 'humors' (blood, yellow and black bile, and phlegm), and their relationship with the four humors (air, fire, earth, and water). See The Four Humors

***Humulus lupulus*** Popularly known as hops, see there

**huna** 1. The native philosphy of the Hawaiian islands, which is based on healing and a belief in extrasensory perception 2. Kahuna healing, see there

**hundred ounces of gold** Tree peony, see there, *Paeonia moutan*

***hung geh*** Indian madder, see there, *Rubia cordifolia*

**hunter-gatherer** ANTHROPOLOGY A step in the societal evolution of man that preceded the farmer; the few remaining hunter-gatherer societies, eg the !Kung San of Botswana have been closely examined by anthropologists, and are thought to approximate features of Stone Age foragers (*JAMA 1993; 269:1477mn&p*). See Hunter-gatherer diet

**hunter-gatherer diet** MEDICAL HISTORY–CLINICAL NUTRITION A diet rich in animal protein, fruits, and plants, and virtually devoid of grains and dairy products, which is the presumed fare of primitive man; consumption of grains and use of dairy products translate as the ability to cultivate and harvest plants and domesticate milk-producing animals, both of which represent later development of early man; some alternative health care providers believe that the allergies commonly seen in modern man may be due to changes in the human diet. See Diet, Neo-paleolithic diet, Zone-favorable diet

**hydrastine** HERBAL MEDICINE A major alkaloid present in the rhizomes and roots of goldenseal (*Hydrastis canadensis*), which is reported to be antihypertensive, antimicrobial, and sedative. See Goldenseal, Herbal medicine

***Hydrastis canadensis*** Popularly known as goldenseal, see there

**hydrazine sulfate** ALTERNATIVE ONCOLOGY A chemical that has been shown be beneficial in tumor-related cachexia, improve survival, eg in non-small cell carcinoma of the lungs (*J Clin Oncol 1984; 2:857; 1990; 8:9*), and shrink breast, colorectal, lung, ovarian, prostatic, and thyroid cancers, Hodgkin's disease, lymphoma, and melanoma (*Pelton, Overholser, 1994*); hydrazine sulfate is reported to reduce cancer-related weight loss and cachexia, slow tumor growth, and increase appetite and survival (*Moss, 1992*) TOXICITY Drowsiness, euphoria, itching, nausea, vertigo, and paresthesia, which respond to vitamin $B_6$ supplements. See Unproven methods for cancer management, Warburg effect

**hydro** see Health spa, Hydrotherapy

***Hydrocotyle asiatica*** Popularly known as gutu kola, see there

**hydrochromotherapy** FRINGE MEDICINE A form of color therapy, in which a patient drinks spring water that has been 'charged' with filters of various colors. See Color therapy

**hydrogen peroxide enteritis** An inflammatory response of the intestinal mucosa to varying concentrations of hydrogen peroxide ($H_20_2$), which causes mucosal damage and contact injury ETIOLOGY $H_2O_2$ enemas are used for various clinical indications, eg removal of inspissated meconium, demonstration of rectovaginal fistulae, and treatment of constipation and fecal impaction; $H_2O_2$ has been used by radiologists to help eliminate gas from the intestine during diagnostic procedures PROGNOSIS Ranges from reversible and self-limited to toxic fulminant ulcerating (not ulcerative) colitis associated with perforation and death (*Gastrointest Endosc 1989; 35:428*). See Colon therapy, Enteroclysis, Hydrogen peroxide therapy

**hydrogen peroxide therapy** Hyperoxygenation therapy ALTERNATIVE MEDICINE A form of 'oxidative' therapy in which hydrogen peroxide ($H_2O_2$) is administered parenterally, or more commonly locally, per rectum to induce oxidative inactivation of various organisms or toxins in the body through free radical production, and stimulation of NK (natural killer) cell activity; hydrogen peroxide therapy is believed to be of use in treating AIDS, arthritis, cancer, candidiasis, chronic fatigue syndrome, depression, emphysema, fractures, headaches, multiple sclerosis, systemic lupus erythematosus, varicose veins, and other conditions (*Alternative Medicine, Future Medicine Pub, 1994*); hydrogen peroxide therapy was claimed to have antiviral (anti-HIV), antimicrobial, and antitumoral activity, claims determined by the FDA to be fraudulent (*Am Med News 21 Nov 1994 p13*). See AIDS fraud, Alternative medicine, Oxygen therapy, Ozone therapy, Unproven methods for cancer management

**hydrogenic constitution** FRINGE MEDICINE-IRIDOLOGY A type of lymphatic constitution (blue eyes) of the iris which, according to the construct of iridology, belongs to a person with many features of a person with lymphatic constitution; those with hydrogenic constitutions are believed to have more chronic disease and lower resistance to infections; the hydrogenic 'types' are believed to be susceptible to rheumatic disease, bacterial infections, and fluid and toxin retention by the kidneys. See Iridology, Iris constitution

**hydropathy** Hydrotherapy, see there

**hydrosol** FRINGE MEDICINE-AROMATHERAPY The water from a distillation of a plant which contains water-soluble components and minimal amounts of essential oils. See Aromatherapy

**hydrotherapy** Hydropathy, water cure ALTERNATIVE MEDICINE A therapeutic modality, dating to ancient China, Greece, and Rome, that consists of the use of steam, hot or cold water, or ice, to maintain and/or restore health by immersion in baths, saunas, or other forms of hydration, either externally in the form of baths or compresses, or internally, eg colonic irrigation or enemas; hydrotherapy is loosely based on the physiological responses to cold (vasoconstriction, pallor, gooseflesh, shivering, increased pulse, shallow and rapid respiration, and cooling of skin) and to heat (vasodilation, redness, slowed, followed by quickened pulse, sweating, nervous excitation, and increased muscle irritability), and the subsequent responses to each; anecdotal reports suggest that hydrotherapy may be beneficial for patients with acne, adenoids, AIDS, anemia, anorexia, anxiety, arthritis, asthma, bedwetting, bladder problems, bronchitis, bruises, bunions, burns, bursitis, cancer, chickenpox, chronic fatigue syndrome, circulatory defects, claustrophobia, colds, conjunctivitis, cramps, croup, cystitis, depression, fever, fissures, fluid retention, gallstones, gastrointestinal tract problems (eg anal changes, gastritis, nausea, vomiting, indigestion, constipation, diarrhea, and irritable bowl syndrome), gout, headaches, heat rash, hemorrhoids, hypertension, infertility, insomnia, jaundice, jet lag, laryngitis, low back pain, measles, menopause, menstrual disorders, migraines, painful conditions including neuralgia, mood swings, muscle weakness, neurological complaints, obesity, panic attacks, parasites, periodontal disease, phobias, post-partum depression, premenstral syndrome, prostate disease, rheumatic disease, sexually-transmitted disease, slipped or prolapsed vertebral disks, psoriasis, renal disease, sciatica, sinusitis, sleep disorders, sports injuries, stasis (decubitus) ulcers, stress, tension, urinary incontinence, vertigo, wheezing, whooping cough, and other conditions (*Alternative Medicine, Future Medicine, 1994*). See Alternating sitz bath, Body wrap, Cold bath, Cold compress, Cold mitten friction rub, Cold pack, Cold sponge bath, Epsom salt bath, Full-immersion bath, Hot bath, Hot compress, Hot pack, Hot tub rash, Jacuzzi, Local bath, Mud bath, Natural spring, Russian bath, Salt rub, Sauna, Sitz bath, Spring water, Steam inhalation therapy, Sweat lodge, Tepid bath, Turkish bath *Resource: National College of Naturopathic Medicine, 11231 SE Market St, Portland OR 97216 ☎ 1.503.255.4860*

**Hygienic movement** see Graham system

***Hyoscyamus niger*** Popularly known as henbane, see there

**hyperbaric oxygen** The intermittent administration of oxygen in a chamber maintained at greater than sea-level atmospheric pressures (3 atmospheres), which increases oxygen dissolved in the blood from 1.5g/dl to 6.0 g/dl and oxygen tension in tissues to nearly 400 mm Hg; this surfeit of oxygen has various beneficial biochemical, cellular, and physiologic effects ALTERNATIVE MEDICINE Hyperbaric oxygen has been administered by some alternative health care providers as an 'oxidative' therapy, which is believed to reverse aging and canites, and be useful for treating AIDS, alcohol and drug addiction, multiple sclerosis, strokes and vascular problems, and other conditions (*Alternative Medicine, Future Medicine Pub, 1994*). See Oxygen therapy INTERNAL MEDICINE Hyperbaric oxygen is used in decompression sickness,* arterial gas embolism, smoke inhalation, cyanide intoxication, acute carbon monoxide poisoning, extreme blood loss anemia, traumatic ischemia, as seen in compartment syndrome(s) and crush injury, to enhance healing of recalcitrant or necrotic wounds, as an adjunct therapy for clostridial myonecrosis (which is associated with acute tissue hypoxia), compromised skin grafts and flaps, chronic osteomyelitis, and in preventing osteoradionecrosis (*N Engl J Med 1996; 334:1642*) COMPLICATIONS

Barotrauma (air embolism, pneumothorax, tympanic membrane damage), oxygen toxicity of central nervous system, lungs, and eyes, fire or explosion (due to oxygen), and claustrophobia

*Which is due to inert gas (nitrogen) bubbles in blood vessels and tissues, and air embolism

**hypercalemia** Calcium intoxication A condition that may be caused by an increase in parathyroid hormone due to parathyroid tumors or hyperactivity, excess ingestion of milk and/or vitamin D, increased bone turnover or aluminum intoxication CLINICAL Anorexia, arrythmias, constipation, depression, EKG abnormalities (shortened QT interval), nausea and vomiting, renal tubular defects, increased urination, and calcification of tissues; if severe (serum levels above 3.7 to 4.5 mmol/L or 15 to 18 mg/dL), coma and cardiac arrest occur. See Calcium; Cf Hypocalcemia

**hyperforat** ALTERNATIVE PHARMACOLOGY A proprietary agent derived from hypericin, an extract of St John's wort (*Hypericum perforatum*) that may be an effective virucidal agent against HIV, herpesvirus, and influenza virus. See Hypericin, St John's wort

**hypericin** A polyhydroxypolycyclic hydrocarbon extract from the St John's wort (*Hypericum* spp), which causes photosensitization in grazing animals, and has been anecdotally reported to prevent retroviral infection (*Am Med News 21 Nov 1994 p13*). See Hyperforat, St John's wort ; Cf AIDS fraud

***Hypericum*** *Hypericum perforatum*, St John's wort HOMEOPATHY A remedy that is used for neuralgias, or injuries that affect a nerve-rich body region, eg the fingers or lips; it is used for asthma, bites, stings, back pain, crush injuries, puncture and surgical wounds, and toothaches. See Homeopathy, St John's wort

***Hypericum perforatum*** HERBAL MEDICINE Popularly known as St John's wort, see there HOMEOPATHY *Hypericum*, see there

**hypermagnesemia** Magnesium intoxication An uncommon condition associated with end-stage renal failure, or which may be caused by excess ingestion of magnesium compounds, eg antacids, or may be deliberately induced in patients with eclampsia CLINICAL Excess magnesium reduces neuromuscular transmission and depresses the central nervous system; the symptoms correspond to the serum levels of magnesium; nausea occurs between 2 and 2.5 mmol/L (4 to 5 mEq/L); this is followed by sedation, decreased tendon reflexes and muscle weakness; at 2.5 and 5 mmol/L (5 to 10 mEq/L), hypotension, bradycardia, and systemic vasodilatation appear; areflexia, coma, and respiratory paralysis appear above these levels. See Magnesium

**hyperoxygenation therapy** Hydrogen peroxide therapy, see there

**hyperthermia** ALTERNATIVE MEDICINE 1. Heat stress detoxification, see there 2. Heat therapy, see there

**hypervitaminosis** A general term for any clinical condition attributed to the ingestion of vitamins in extreme excess of physiologic or pharmacologic levels. See Vitamins

**hypnosis** ALTERNATIVE PSYCHOLOGY The induction of a trance state in an individual, which is defined by the presence of trance phenomena in the form of objective physical changes (see trance state), subjective perceptual changes, and a cooperative interaction with the hypnotist; hypnosis has theoretical currency in behavior modification and biofeedback, in which a person learns to focus his attention on thoughts or images that are unrelated to a particular stimulus, eg cancer-related pain; hypnosis has some support in mainstream psychiatry and anesthesiology; the major effect of hypnosis is relaxation, and possibly control of habits; hypnosis is claimed to be useful in speech therapy, smoking cessation, ameliorating panic disorders and in low back pain. See Imaginative involvement; Cf Hypnotherapy–note, Mesmerism

Note: Hypnotizability appears to hinge on the degree to which a person can engage in fantasy, and be distracted; 20% of individuals are easily hypnotized, 20% are virtually 'hypnosis-proof'; children are less confined by reality-based thinking, and thus more easily hypnotized

**hypnotherapy** ALTERNATIVE MEDICINE A form of health care in which a trance-like state is induced in an individual, allowing a therapist to contact the unconscious mind, and (in theory) effect changes in the mental status and behavior; for some, hypnotherapy evokes atavistic regression–a return to a state in which instinct is allowed a freer reign than is the norm in the current consciousness-oriented society

▶ **HYPNOTHERAPY FORMATS**

- **SUGGESTIVE** Once in a trance, the hypnotist suggests that the patient's symptoms will disappear
- **UNCOVERING** The intent is de-repress memories, and help the client to re-experience childhood and adolescence

Hypnotherapy has been used as an adjunct for controlling acute and chronic pain (and may be used in place of anesthetics); it is useful in addiction (alcohol, tobacco, and abuse substance) disorders; anecdotal reports suggest that it may be effective in treating allergies, amnesia, anorexia, anxiety, arthritis, bedwetting, bulimia, chronic fatigue syndrome, claustrophobia, depression, dermatopathies, fear, flatulence, forgetfulness, gastrointestinal tract problems including colitis and irritable bowl syndrome, gout, hypertension, hyperventilation, insomnia, jet lag, low back pain, menstrual defects, migraines, pain and neuralgias, mood swings, panic attacks, phobias, post-partum pain, premenstrual syndrome, psychosomatic disease, sciatica, sexual dysfunction, sleep disorders, sports injuries, stress, stuttering, tension, tics, and warts; Cf Hypnosis, Hypnotic ageregression, Mesmerism *Resource: American Board of Hypnotherapy, 16842 von Karman Ave, Suite 475, Irvine CA 92714-4950 ☎ 714.251.4632*

Note: While the terms hypnosis and hypnotherapy are essentially synonymous, the author believes that it is appropriate to separate them, given the potential for confusion; thus hypnosis would be a regarded as a tool of possible use in the 'mainstream' medical fields of psychiatry and psychology, while hypnotherapy might be viewed by some as a treatment modality a sui generis, in the context of alternative medicine

**hypnotic age regression** ALTERNATIVE PSYCHOLOGY A technique used in primal scream therapy, in which a therapist attempts to return a client to the trauma of birth through the use of hypnosis. See Primal scream therapy; Cf Rebirthing therapy

**hypocalcemia** Calcium deficiency A condition characterized by decreased calcium (serum concentrations below 2.1 mmol/L or 8.5 mg/dL), which may be due to decreased ingestion or malabsorption of calcium, magnesium, or vitamin D, absent or ineffective parathyroid hormone, acute renal failure, cancer, or vitamin D-resistant rickets CLINICAL Neurological and neuromuscular symptoms in the form of irritability, depression, and psychosis, muscle spasms, laryngeal spasms, convulsions, cardiac arrhythmias, intestinal cramping, and chronic malabsorption. See Calcium; Cf Hypercalcemia

**hypoglycemia** FRINGE MEDICINE A 'fad' condition, which is believed by some promoters of fringe health care products to affect 10 to 25% of the US population and be responsible for chronic fatigue, criminal behavior, depression, drug addiction, mental disorders including schizophrenia, sexual impotence, and a wide range of other conditions

Note: Hypoglycemia is in fact rare, and should be diagnosed only the context of a legitimate endocrine disorder by a mainstream physician

**hypoglycin** A toxic amino acid derived from the unripe ackee fruit that evokes hypoglycemia, and inhibits the catabolism of branched-chain amino acids and the other symptoms of Jamaican vomiting sickness, see there

**hypomagnesemia** Magnesium deficiency A condition defined as a serum magnesium ≤ 1.5 mg/dL, which is manifest by muscular hyperirritability ETIOLOGY Alcohol abuse, burns, dehydration, diabetic ketoacidosis, diarrhea, hypercalcemia, hyperaldosteronism, hypokalemia, hypoparathyroidism, post-bowel resection, malabsorption, malnutrition, pancreatitis, renal insufficiency, therapy with amphotericin B, calcium gluconate, diuretics, insulin, and neomycin CLINICAL Cramping, increased tendon reflexes, tremors. See Magnesium

Hypomagnesemia present in the first 24 hours after admission to a health care facility is associated with decreased survival (9.3 vs 17.9 days) in acutely ill patients, independently of the APACHE II scores (*Crit Care Med 1993; 21:203*)

**hyssop** *Hyssopus officinalis* HERBAL MEDICINE A perennial herb that contains flavonoids, hyssopin (a glycoside), insolic acid, resin, tannins, and volatile oils (including camphene, pinenes, terpinene, and others); it was first used by Hippocrates and Galen, internally for upper respiratory tract infections, coughs, and sore throat (which continues to be its primary use), as well as anxiety, hysteria, and petit mal seizures; it is used topically for cuts and bruises, and rheumatic pain TOXICITY Hyssop should not be used in pregnancy as it stimulates uterine contraction–it was formerly used as an abortifacient. See Botanical toxicity, Herbal medicine, Poisonous plants

**I.B.M.** Ideal body mass. See Body mass index

**ice therapy** Cold therapy, see there

**Iceland lichen** Iceland moss, see there, *Cetraria islandica*

**Iceland moss** *Cetraria islandica*, Iceland lichen HERBAL MEDICINE A lichen that contains fumaric acids, iodine, and mucilage, which is antimicrobial and expectorant; it has been used for respiratory tract infections including tuberculosis, and as a bitter to stimulate and soothe the gastrointestinal tract. See Herbal medicine

**Iceland moss** *Cetraria islandica*

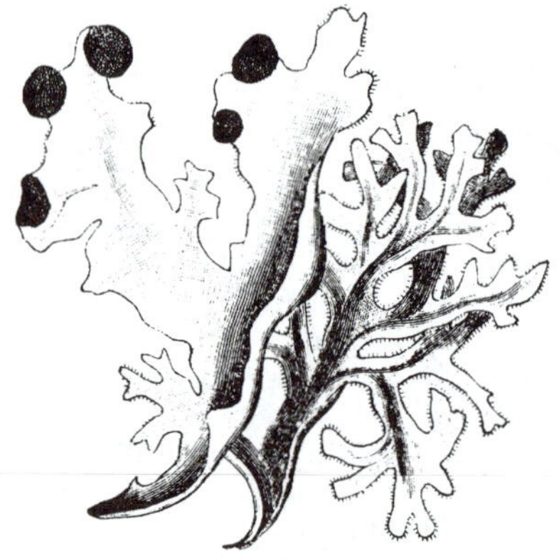

**idea therapy** see Imagineering

**identity process** ALTERNATIVE PSYCHOLOGY A process that allows a person to use his '*...limitations as a doorway to an inner core not reached by other neurolinguistic programming processes...a symptom becomes a gateway to pervasive changes that go beyond the ...symptom itself.*' (*Raso, 1994*). See Neurolinguistic programming

***Ignatia*** *Ignatia amara, Strychnos ignatii* HOMEOPATHY A homeopathic remedy prepared from the St Ignatius bean; it is used to treat extreme emotional tension not accompanied by the normal reactions of bereavement, depression, rage, and shock; it may also be used for anxiety, coughs, hemorrhoids, hysteria, insomnia, irritable bowel syndrome, mood swings, tension headaches, sore throat, and fever. See *Ignatia*, Homeopathy

***Ignatia* type** HOMEOPATHY The *Ignatia* constitutional type of person often suppresses moods; he is sensitive to pain, claustrophobic, dislikes crowds, is prone to headaches and tics, and likes sour foods, dairy products, and breads WORSE Cold, emotional stress, touching, tobacco FEARS Loss of self-control, emotional pain, and crowds WEAKEST BODY REGION Nervous system. See Constitutional type, *Ignatia*, Homeopathy

***Ilex paraguariensis*** Maté, see there

**image aversion therapy** PSYCHOLOGY A permutation of aversion therapy in which the individual attempting to modify a particular behavior, imagines something bizarre, or at least unsettling, associated with carrying out the undesired behavior, eg eating an excessive meal in front of a starving individual from a developing nation. See Aversion therapy, Behavioral therapy, Encounter group therapy, Flooding, Systematic desensitization

**imagery (and visualization)** Creative imagery, creative visualization, guided imagery, healing visualization, imaging therapy, mental imagery, visualization therapy ALTERNATIVE MEDICINE A form of health care in which the power of the mind is used '*...to evoke a positive physical response...reduce stress, slow heart rate, stimulate the immune system, and reduce pain.*' (*Alternative Medicine, Future Med Pub, 1994*); imagery consists of the creation of positive thoughts and images and communicating them with the body as a means of healing a diseased organ or tissue; it is believed to act on the newly conceptualized psychoneuroimmune system, by placing 'mind over matter'; anecdotal reports suggest that imaging may be effective for allergies, anesthesia, cancer, chronic pain, control of habits, dysmenorrhea, headaches, hypertension, enhancing the immune system, performance anxiety (stage fright), premenstrual syndrome, stress-related gastrointestinal symptoms, recuperation from surgery, and urinary incontinence. See Anodyne imagery, Simonton method

**imagineering** FRINGE PSYCHOLOGY A synthesis of creative visualization and self-healing methods developed by S King, who believes that prevention and healing of disease hinges on instinct, and that disease is induced by a conflict of ideas

▶ **IMAGINEERING TECHNIQUES**

- **EMOTIVATIONAL THERAPY** Self-administered therapeutic touch or other technique
- **IDEA THERAPY** Repetition of affirmations, eg I am immune to AIDS
- **VERBAL THERAPY** Repetition of words or sounds, regardless of whether they have meaning
- **VISUAL THERAPY** Visualization of eight colors, which have been linked to psychological conditions (*Raso, 1994*)

**Imaginetics, Inc** FRINGE MEDICINE A company in Bayside, New York, that sells magnetic products, eg cushions, insoles, masks, pendants, and others; these products are claimed to precisely regulate the activities of every cell; what Imaginetics terms 'North pole energy' is claimed to have anti-inflammatory effects, and 'South pole energy,' to relieve muscle tension and endocrine hypofunction. See Magnet therapy, Magnetic healing

**imaging therapy** Imagery (and visualization), see there

**imitation ingredient** FOOD INDUSTRY A substance added to foods that replaces the natural ones, as means of reducing the calories, cholesterol or cost. See Food additives

**immortal spirit gall** Horny goat weed, see there, *Epimedium sagittatum*

**immune booster** A general term for any substance, eg BCG, Coley's toxin, levamisole, muramyl dipeptide, tuftsin, ubenimex (Bestatin®), and zinc, that nonspecifically stimulate the immune system; immune boosters activate macrophages, increase T-cell proliferation. and increase interleukin production and secretion. See BCG, Coley's toxin, ubenimex (Bestatin®)

**immune quotient quiz** FRINGE MEDICINE A multiple-choice test devised by Stuart Berger, MD, that is believed to determine how much, if any, nutritional supplements are required in the diet, which may be up to 150 times the recommended daily allowance

**immuno-augmentive therapy** Burton treatment FRINGE ONCOLOGY An unproven method for cancer management developed in the 1980s by an American biochemist, L Burton, which is based on the assertion that the immune system is enhanced by four substances present in tissue: 'blocking' and 'deblocking proteins,' tumor antibody and 'complement' (which differs from complement as understood by immunologists); the therapy consists of parenteral administration of tumor cell lysates and serum from cancer patients and normal subjects; analysis of some of the sera used revealed contamination with various organisms (*Science 1988; 241:1285; JAMA 1988; 260:3435*); there is no scientific evidence of efficacy nor safety of immunoaugmentive therapy. See Unproven methods for cancer management

Immuno-augmentive therapy is expensive ($50,000) and has been administered in clinics in the Bahamas, Mexico and Germany (*Science 1990; 249:1369*)

**immunotherapy** Hypo-sensitization therapy ALLERGY MEDICINE A therapy in which an allergen, eg hymenopteran (bee, wasp) venom, is administered in increasing doses to individuals with potentially fatal hypersensitivity to the allergen; immunotherapy elicits production of blocking IgG antibodies, interferes with antigen-Fab (a portion of an Ig molecule) binding, prevents fixation of IgE (which causes anaphylaxis), down-regulates T-cell responses, inhibits inflammatory responses to allergens, and attenuates anaphylactic reactions; immuno-therapy in patients with seasonal ragweed-exacerbated asthma and allergic rhinitis evokes objective improvement of symptoms that are not sustained with time (*N Eng J Med 1996; 334:501oa*) ONCOLOGY A therapy that nonspecifically stimulates the immune system to destroy malignant cells; anecdotal success has been reported with BCG immuno-therapy* (which may be effective in treating melanomas, acute myelogenous leukemia, and solid tumors), Coley's toxin and heat-killed, formalin-treated *Corynebacterium parvum*, an immunopotentiator and immunomodulator in animals that evokes reticuloendothelial hyperplasia, stimulation of macrophages and B cells and which may enhance T-cell function by increasing its blastogenic response to T-cell mitogens. See BCG, Coley's toxin, Immune booster; Cf Immunoaugmentive therapy

*BCG is instilled in the bladder to control early transitional cell cancer

**implantation trauma** HUMANISTIC THERAPY The physical trauma that is allegedly experienced by the fertilized ovum, as it 'struggles' to implant itself in the endometrium; RD Laing believes that this trauma may translate into subconscious 'festering' that manifests itself later in life (*Inglis, West, 1983*). See Primal (scream) therapy

**implosive layer** Death layer, see there

**I.M.T.A.** International Movement Therapy Association, see there

**Indian apple** Mayapple, see there, *Podophyllum peltatum*

**Indian balm** Birthroot, see there, *Trillium erectum*

**Indian bread** Tuckahoe, see there, *Porio cocos*

**Indian cress** Nasturtium, see there, *Tropaeolum majus*

**Indian dye** Goldenseal, see there, *Hydrastis canadensis*

**Indian elm** Slippery elm, see there, *Ulmus rubra*

**Indian madder** *Rubia cordifolia*, *chien tsao*, *di hsueh*, ground blood, *hung geh*, Mandjuchaka, *qian cao*, red vine CHINESE MEDICINE A perennial plant that is hemostatic, purifies the blood, and increases cardiovascular tone; it is used for amenorrhea, postpartum uterine bleeding, internal hemorrhage, hepatitis, hepatic toxicity, kidney stones, and cancer. See Chinese herbal medicine

**Indian paint** Blood root, see there, *Sanginaria canadensis*

**Indian paintbrush** *Castilleja miniata* FRINGE MEDICINE-FLOWER ESSENCE THERAPY A floral essence that is said to provide energetic creativity. See Flower essence therapy

**Indian pennywort** Gutu kola, see there, *Hydrocotyle asiatica*

**Indian plume** Bergamot, see there, *Monarda didyma*

**Indian sage** Boneset, see there, *Eupatorium perfoliatum*

**Indian snakeroot** Rauwolfia, see there, *Rauwolfia serpentina*

**Indian tobacco** Lobelia, see there, *Lobelia inflata*

**Indian turmeric** Goldenseal, see there, *Hydrastis canadensis*

**indican test** FRINGE DIAGNOSTICS A nonconventional test that may be used by naturopaths; indican in the urine is believed to indicate the degree of intestinal putrefaction. See Naturopathy

**indicator muscle** ALTERNATIVE MEDICINE A muscle which, according to R Utt, developer of Applied Physiology, is in perfect balance or homeostasis, and neither over- nor understressed. See Applied Physiology

**indigo** FRINGE MEDICINE–COLOR THERAPY The color indigo is believed to purify the blood and strengthen the immune system. SeeColor breathing, Color therapy, Indigo metals and chemicals

**indigo broom** Wild indigo, see there, *Baptista tinctoria*

**indigo metals & chemicals** FRINGE MEDICINE-COLOR THERAPY Indigo metals and chemicals are believed to purify the blood and strengthen the immune system, and include bismuth, potassium and strontium. See Color breathing, Color therapy, Indigo

**individualization** PSYCHIATRY A term coined by Carl Jung for a point in an individual's personal development, in which a partner (eg lover, wife) is no longer viewed as a 'complementary opposite' of himself, but rather as an individual sensient being (*Watson, 1995*). See Animus, Jungian psychoanalysis

**indole** 2,3-Benzopyrrole ALTERNATIVE PHARMACOLOGY A heterocyclic compound that is the

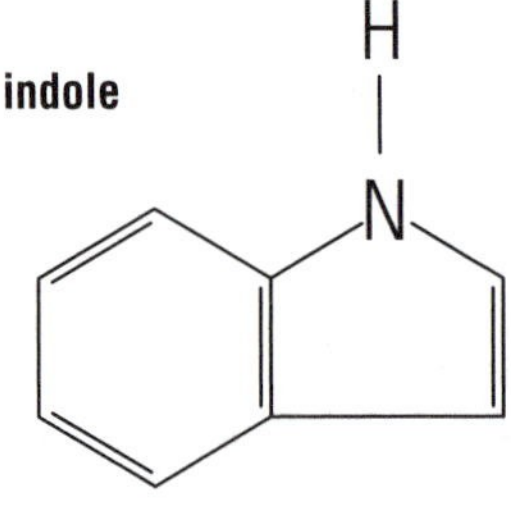

parent molecule for serotonin, tryptophan, and other alkaloids; indoles are present in broccoli, Brussels sprouts, cabbage and other cruciferous vegetables and may have anticarcinogenic activity. See Cruciferous vegetable

**induced hyperthermia** ALTERNATIVE MEDICINE Heat stress detoxification, see there

**inductive healing** Jin shin jyutsu, see there

**infant massage** ALTERNATIVE PEDIATRICS A general term for stroking of an infant, a physical interaction between parent or caregiver that fosters bonding; human touch is thought to be as important as essential nutrients for the growth and development of infants; premature infants who have been massaged for 15-minute periods, 3 times per day, have a significantly higher weight gain than control infants; stroking is believed to strengthen and regulate gastrointestinal and cardiorespiratory activity, relieve stress, tone muscles, and relax the infant. See Bodywork for the Childbearing Year®, Bonding, Massage therapy; Cf Anaclytic depression, Geriatric massage, Holtism

**Infratonic QCM** FRINGE MEDICINE A device that emits low-frequency (8 to 14 Hz) or infratonic sound waves; infratonic therapy was developed in the 1980s by a Chinese engineer, LY Fang, based on his observation that *qigong* masters emit high levels of infratonic waves, known as secondary sound, from their hands; according to Fang, everyone emits secondary sound, but that produced by *qigong* masters is 100 to 1000-fold more than normal individuals; Fang's device is believed to be effective for improving blood circulation, depression, migraines, and muscle relaxation; it is sold in the US as a massage device (*Alternative Medicine, Future Med Pub, 1994*). See Energy medicine

**infusion** HERBAL MEDICINE An herbal preparation in which a ground herb or plant component (eg bark, root, nuts, or seeds) is boiled in water to obtain an extract of interest, eg chamomile, peppermint, and rosehips. See Herbal medicine; Cf Decoction, Fluid extract CHINESE MEDICINE *Cha* A general term for a therapeutic tea made from ground herbs, which is boiled, steeped, and ingested. See Chinese herbal medicine, Powder-Chinese medicine

Note: Here the terms herbal tea and infusion are interchangeable

**Ingham Reflex Method of Compression Massage** Ingham method, see there

**Ingham method** Ingham Reflex Method of Compression Massage, Ingham technique A massage therapy developed in the 1930s by an American physical therapist, Eunice Ingram, which is a permutation of reflexology. See Reflexology

**Ingham technique** Ingham method, see there

**inhalation** see Steam inhalation therapy

**ink vegetable** *Eclipta prostrata*, see there

**innate** Innate intelligence CHIROPRACTIC '*The focus of the divine mind expressed through the mortal, challenging the latter to recognize its essence as divine.*' (*DD Palmer's son, as told to M Bach and quoted in Raso, 1994*); innate is, in the chiropractic construct, a form of personal energy based in the nervous system, and equated to the spirit or vital force. See Vital force

**innate intelligence** 1. CHIROPRACTIC Innate, see there 2. See Bio energetic synchronization technique

**inner bonding** A permutation of 'inner child therapy' developed by an American psychologist, Margaret Paul, as a means of becoming 'spiritually connected' (*Raso, 1994*). See Inner child therapy; Cf Bonding, Male bonding

**inner child therapy** Inner child work ALTERNATIVE PSYCHOLOGY A type of psychotherapy developed in the 1990s by an American theologian, John Bradshaw, which is based on the belief that individuals from dysfunctional families suffered 'spiritual wounds' during their formative years, caused by an awareness that they were not loved; Bradshaw's therapy consists of having the client relive early development, and have conversations with his 'inner infant' by writing letters to it, ideally with the non-dominant hand, which is believed to enhance the experience; at the end of the successful therapy, the inner child has evolved into a 'wonder child' who has a sense of a higher purpose

**inner child work** Inner child therapy, see there

**inner infant** see Inner child therapy

**'inner self'** True self, see there

**inner self-healing process** ALTERNATIVE PSYCHOLOGY A system of psychotherapy developed by an American psychologist, Swami Ajaya that is based on the belief in a 'true self' and a 'false self'; the self-healing process is believed to reconcile the disparity between the two through psychotherapy, attunement, and meditation

**inner shouting** HUMANISTIC PSYCHOLOGY A process used in 'natural' psychotherapy, in which a person spontaneously screams or shouts to himself (without actual verbalization), ideally accompanied by relaxation; inner shouting is believed to help a person work through his inner conflicts, in lieu of actually shouting at someone. See Humanistic psychology, 'Natural' psychotherapy

**inner smile** FRINGE MEDICINE A method of relaxation in which the individual projects positive feelings toward his internal organs, glands, and other tissues, as a means of increasing the flow of *chi*. See *Chi*

**innovative medicine** Alternative medicine, see there

**inosine** An intermediate in purine metabolism that enhances various immune functions in vivo and in vitro, which blunts the toxic effects of methotrexate. See Inosine prabonex

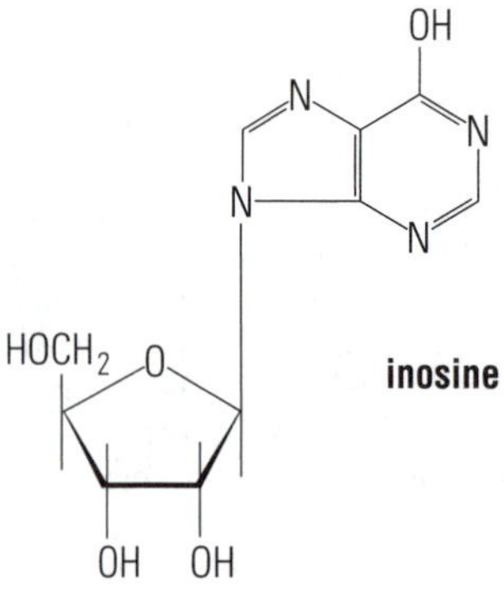

**inosine**

**inosine prabonex** Isoprinosin® AIDS A complex inosine-based salt that enhances various immune functions in vivo and in vitro, possibly by increasing interleukin-1 and/or interleukin-2 production, resulting in T-cell proliferation and increased natural killer cell activity; it has been used for other viral infections including flu, hepatitis, herpes simplex, and HPV; inosine is present in meat, meat extracts, and sugar beets. See AIDS therapy

In a trial of HIV-positive subjects, less than 0.5% of those treated with inosine prabonex developed AIDS versus 4% in the placebo group(*N Engl J Med 1990; 322:1757, 322:1807ed*)

**Inosiplex®** see Isoprinosine®

**Institute of Psychostructural Balancing** International Professional School of Bodywork

**Integral yoga** A form of yoga developed by guru Sri Ghose Aurobindo that synthesizes traditional forms (*bhakti* yoga, *hatha* yoga, *jnana* yoga, *karma* yoga, *raja* yoga and others) of yoga, but eliminates the excesses of some forms of yoga, in which the students may pursue physical feats at the expense of spiritual enlightenment. See Yoga

**integrative acupressure** A permutation of acupressure that emphasizes a technique known as acupuncture lymphatic release (*Raso, 1994*)

**integrative bodywork** Integrative massage, see there

**integrative massage** ALTERNATIVE MEDICINE A general term for the use of both mainstream and alternative massage therapies (bodywork and mind/body medicine) to treat musculoskeletal disease. See CranioSacral Therapy®, Reflexology, Zero balancing; Cf Energetic massage, Massage, Oriental massage, Physical therapy, Structural integration, Swedish massage, (contemporary) Western massage

**integrative medicine** The 'new medicine' Integrative medicine is a term used by Andrew Weil for the incorporation of alternative therapies into mainstream medical practice; the integrative philosophy accepts that mainstream medicine has succeeded in treating certain diseases, in particular acute conditions, eg bacterial infections and trauma, but has failed in chronic conditions, eg immune-mediated and rheumatic diseases; an acceptance that mainstream medicine has failed in the latter areas would open its practitioners to the possibilites of using different tools, including more aggressive preventive measures, and the vast array of possible alternative therapies including ayurvedic medicine, Chinese medicine, chiropractic, herbal medicine, homeopathy, naturopathy, and other systems. See Alternative medicine, Integrative technique; Cf Mainstream medicine OSTEOPATHY The incorporation of alternative therapies in patient managment; incorporated methods include ayurvedic medicine, bodywork, Chinese medicine, homeopathy, mind/body medicine, and naturopathy. See Osteopathy

**integrative technique** ALTERNATIVE MEDICINE A general term for any form of alternative health care that uses techiques affecting the mind, body mechanics, and flow of life energy; integrative techniques include ayurvedic medicine, bioenergetics and body-centered psychotherapy, Feldenkrais method, Hellerwork®, iridology, certain martial arts (eg aikido), neuromuscular motivation, Rosen method, Tragerwork®, yoga, and others, discussed elsewhere in this work. See Integrative medicine

**integrative therapy** ALTERNATIVE PSYCHOTHERAPY A type of psychotherapy that combines psychosynthesis and Jungian psychoanalysis. See Jungian psychoanalysis, Psychosynthesis

**interactive guided imagery** ALTERNATIVE PSYCHOTHERAPY A form of psychotherapy that combines psychosynthesis and Jungian psychoanalysis, as a means of diagnosing and monitoring disease. See Imagery and visualization

**internal organ *chi* massage** *Chi nei tsang*, see there

**internal *qigong*** *Qigong*, see there

**International Association of Cancer Victors and Friends, Inc** ALTERNATIVE MEDICINE A nonprofit organization with 5000 members and 13 active chapters, founded in 1963 by a woman who had been treated for breast cancer with amygdalin (Laetrile)*; the IACVF's purpose is to inform the general public about specific humane and effective cancer therapies that could be considered as therapeutic options for those seeking alternatives to mainstream oncology (*Fact Sheet, Sept 1988–from the American Cancer Society's files on Unproven Methods of Cancer Management*). See Unproven methods of cancer management

*Who later (1969) died of metastatic cancer

**International healing *tao* system** Healing *tao* system, see there

**International Movement Therapy Association** A credentialing body that certifies movement therapists trained in the Alexander technique, Feldenkreis method, or movement therapy

**International Primal Association** see Primal scream therapy

***Inula britannica*** Elecampene, see there, *Inula helenium*

***Inula chinensis*** Elecampene, see there, *Inula helenium*

***Inula helenium*** Popularly known as elecampene, see there

**invalid claims of efficacy** FRINGE MEDICINE A general term for an erroneous and/or misleading assertion used to market over-the-counter products intended to improve health or enhance mental or physical performance; invalid claims of efficacy made for amino acid and mineral supplements and multivitamins include such phrases as 'anabolic enhancer,' 'energy enhancer,' 'ergonomic aid,' 'fat burner,' 'fat fighter,' 'fat metabolizer,' 'performance booster,' 'strength booster,' 'strength enhancer,' and others. See Unproven methods for cancer management

**involuntary mechanism** OSTEOPATHY A general term for slight rhythmic contractions and expansions identified on the skin surface of the head and neck that are believed to correspond to the flow of cerebrospinal fluid; the symmetry and quality of the involuntary mechanism is evaluated by practitioners of cranial osteopathy, and may provide useful information on the health of the tissues of the head and neck. See CranioSacral Therapy®; Cf Cranial osteopathy

**iodine** 1. A nonmetallic element (atomic number 53; atomic weight 126.90) which is critical for certain metabolic processes and central to thyroid metabolism; it is present in iodized salt, dairy products, and seafood 2. *Iodum*, see there

***Iodum*** Iodine HOMEOPATHY A remedy that has been used for those with thyroid dysfunction, nonfocused hyperactivity, and forgetfulness; it is also used to treat cardiovascular disease, coughs, and laryngitis. See Homeopathy

**ion generator** A device that generates negative ions; in the 1950s these devices were claimed to cure cancer, heart disease, and other conditions, claims that the FDA deemed fraudulent; in the 1970s, ion generators resurfaced with claims that they increase energy levels and a sense of well-being. See Air ionization therapy

**ionization therapy** Air ionization therapy, see there

**ipecac** *Cephalis ipecacuanha* HERBAL MEDICINE An amazonian shrub that contains an alkaloid (emetine) and cephaeline; it is anthelmintic, emetic, and expectorant, and used for coughs, dysentery, and gastrointestinal parasites. See Herbal medicine HOMEOPATHY A homeopathic remedy that is used for asthma, mucocutaneous bleeding, colic, diarrhea, nausea, cold or hot sweats, flu, menstrual cramping, and paroxysmal coughing. See Homeopathy

**ipecacuanha** Ipecac, see there

**ipes** Pau d'arco, see there, *Tebebuia impetiginosa*

**IQ quiz** Immune quotient quiz, see there

**iridiagnosis** Iridology, see there

**irido-diagnosis** Iridology, see there

**iridology** Iridiagnosis, irido-diagnosis, iris copy, iris diagnosis, iris interpretation FRINGE MEDICINE A system of alternative diagnosis, which is based on the belief that each body region and/or organ is represented by one of six corresponding regions on the iris; iridologists claim to be able to diagnose imbalances in the body by studying the shape, color(s), and qualities of the iris; interpretation of the changes seen differs according to the iridologist–while all agree that color changes are significant, for some, whitish discoloration is believed to indicate overstimulation, while for others, these same spots indicate an accumulation of toxins, eg uric acid or cholesterol; all agree that clarity of the iris indicates healthiness; once identified, the defects can (in theory) be treated, using vitamins, herbs, minerals, and other substances; anecdotal reports suggest that various diseases can be identified by changes in the iris including anemia, cardiac conditions, trauma, hepatic, adrenal, and renal stress; according to Bernard Jensen, the iris can be divided into 6 zones or rings; the innermost corresponds to the stomach; the second to the small and large intestine, the third to the circulation of blood and lymph; the fourth to the organs and endocrine system; the fifth to the musculoskeletal system; the sixth (outermost zone) to the skin and organs of elimination. See Alternative medicine, Iris constitution; Cf Rayid model *Resource: National Iridology Research Association, PO Box 33637, Seattle WA 98133* ☎ *1.206.363.5980*

Note: Formal studies by the American Medical Association and the American Optometric Association have shown iridology to be ineffective as a diagnostic tool (*Gottschalk Olsen, 1989*); in a well-controlled study of diagnostic accuracy of iridology, three iridologists examined photographs (without knowing the diagnosis) from the irises of 24 patients with severe and 24 with moderate renal disease, as well as 95 individuals with no known disease; the iridologists were unable to diagnose the presence or absence of renal disease with any accuracy—most of those in the general population who have moderate to severe kidney disease could be told they have normal kidneys (*JAMA 1979; 242:1385*)

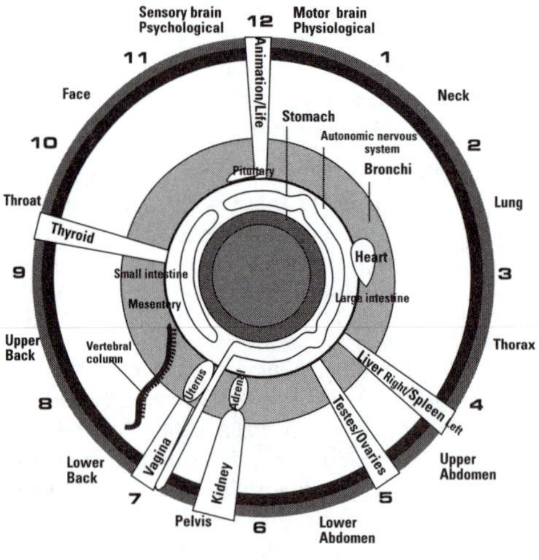

**left iris** Relationship with organs
modified from Inglis, West, 1983

**irimi-nage** Bamboo swaying in the wind MARTIAL ARTS A movement of aikido that is typical of the harmonious balance integral to the philosophy of this Japanese martial art; in irimi-nage, the defender connects with the attacker's forward thrust, absorbs its energy, and fluidly continues with the flow of the blow, bringing the attacker off balance, while adding his force to the defensive action. See Aikido, Martial arts

**iris** *Iris douglasiana* FRINGE MEDICINE-FLOWER ESSENCE THERAPY A floral essence believed to provide artisitic vision radiance, and perspective. See Flower essence therapy

**iris constitution** FRINGE MEDICINE-IRIDOLOGY Any of a number of types into which patients consulting an iridologist are divided; the principal constitutions (colors) of the iris are lymphatic constitution (blue-gray eyes, subdivided into neurogenic, hydrogenic, and mesenchymal-pathological constitutions), hematogenic constitution (brown eyes), and biliary or mixed constitution (hazel eyes). See Biliary constitution, Hematogenic constitution, Hydrogenic constitution, Iridology, Lymphatic constitution, Mesenchymal-pathological constitution, Neurogenic constitution

**iris copy** Iridology, see there

**iris diagnosis** Iridology, see there

**iris interpretation** Iridology, see there

***Iris pseudoacorus*** Popularly known as yellow flag, see there

***Iris versicolor*** Popularly known as blue flag, see there

**Irish broom** Broom, see there, *Sarothamnus scoparius*

**Irish moss** *Chondrus crispus*, carragheen HERBAL MEDICINE A marine lichen, the dried fronds of which contain carrgheenans, which are polysaccharide complexes; it is demulcent, and emollient, and has been used to soothe coughs and gastric ulcers. See Herbal medicine

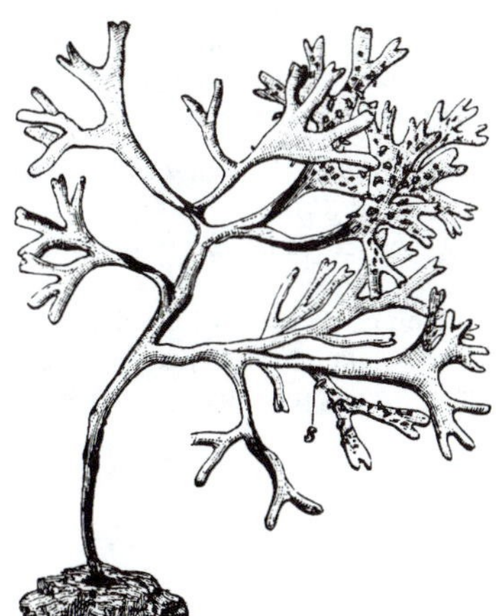

**Irish moss** *Chondrus crispus*

**iron phosphate** *Ferrum phos*, see there, *Ferrum phosphoricum*

**iron shirt *chi kung*** A system of breathing techniques, exercises, and positions, that are believed to allow its practitioner to absorb and discharge energy through the tendons, and resist disease. See Bone marrow *nei kung*, Healing *tao* system

**iron shirt *chi kung* III** Bone marrow *nei kung*, see there III

**irregular medicine** Alternative medicine, see there

**Iscador®** ALTERNATIVE PHARMACOLOGY A proprietary (*Weleda AG, Switzerland, Germany*) preparation of European mistletoe (*Viscum album*) that stimulates the immune system by increasing NK (natural killer) cell activity and antibody-dependent cell cytotoxicity; it is said to be directly toxic to foreign cells, damaged 'self' cells, and malignant cells; it is thought to be useful for cancers of the breast, cervix, colon, lungs, ovaries, and stomach, and has been used for proliferative breast disease (mastopathy), gastric ulcers, intestinal polyps, papillomatosis of the bladder, senile keratosis, and ulcerative colitis (*Pelton, Overholser, 1994*). See Unproven methods for cancer management

Iscador is prepared by grinding in water, fermenting with *Lactobacillus plantarum*, then filtering; it is administered to cancer patients by injection near the site of the tumor

**isoflavone** ALTERNATIVE PHARMACOLOGY Any of a number of hormone-like substances found in peanuts, beans, and lentils, which are thought to have anticarcinogenic properties. See Unproven methods for cancer management

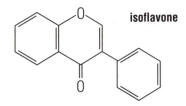

**isoflavone**

**isolation chamber** Samahdi tank A tank in which a person relaxes on a bed with a mattress that conforms to one's body; the chamber is lightproof, and soundproof; isolation chambers can be tolerated for longer (24 to 28 hours) periods of time, while floatation tanks are believed to be better for relaxation. See Flotation tank, Sensory deprivation

**isolation tank** A type of isolation chamber in which a person is placed and deprived of all sensory input; isolation tanks are divided into flotation (wet) tanks and isolation (dry) chambers or Samahdi tanks; some have used these tanks for meditation, as they believe sensory deprivation enhances their meditation experience. See Flotation tank, Isolation chamber, Sensory deprivation

**isometric exercise** An exercise against an unmoving resistance, which consists of muscle contraction with a minimum of other body movement; isometric exercises build muscle strength and include weight-lifting or squeezing a tennis ball. See Exercise; Cf Isotonic exercise

**isopathy** A format of homeopathy in which the remedy is chosen based on identifying the offending substance thought to cause the symptoms in a patient; isopathy is thought to be effective in only about $^1/_3$ of cases, as the remedy ignores a person's individual constitution. See Homeopathy

**Isoprinosine®** ALTERNATIVE PHARMACOLOGY A combination agent that may slow replication of various viruses, including HIV, herpes, poliovirus, and common cold viruses; isoprinosine has been reported to delay the onset of AIDS in HIV-infected individuals (*Fox, 1996*); it is reported to activate NK (natural killer) cell activity and interferon production, and stimulate the production of T and B lymphocytes, and to be of use in treating viral infections in patients with leukemia, Hodgkin's disease, and gastrointestinal cancer (*Pelton, Overholser, 1994*). See AIDS therapy, Unproven methods for cancer management

It is marketed in other countries under the names Methisoprinol and Inosiplex

**isotonic drink** A generic term for a type of sports drink, which is used to simply replace fluid and electrolytes lost during lengthy exercise (*New York Times 7 Dec 1994; C6*). See Sports drink

**isotonic exercise** Dynamic exercise An exercise that consists of continuous and sustained movement of the arms and legs; isotonic exercises are beneficial to the cardiorespiratory system, and include running and bicycling. See Exercise; Cf Isometric exercise

**Issels' whole body therapy** *Ganzheitstherapie*, whole body therapy FRINGE ONCOLOGY An unproven method for cancer management developed by a German physician, Joseph Issels, which is based on the belief that cancer has a systemic etiology and local manifestations in the form of a neoplasm; he attributed cancer to adverse changes in metabolism and natural resistance due to 'causal factors,' including genetic defects, microbes, dental amalgams, infections, abnormal intestinal flora, poor diet, neural interference, chemical toxins, and radiation; Issel's therapy most unique feature is the so-called hematogenic oxidation therapy, in which the patient's blood is removed, oxygenated, irradiated with ultraviolet light, then returned to the patient; Issels' therapy also incorporates dietary (consumption of organic foods) and behavioral (cessation of smoking and consumption of tea, coffee, and alcohol) alterations, and informal psychotherapy to rid the patient of 'toxic emotions' such as stress and anger. See Hematogenic oxidation therapy, Unproven methods for cancer management

**Iyengar-style yoga** A 20th century form of 'high-impact' yoga developed by BSK Iyengar, which adapts *hatha* yoga, incorporating *pranayama*-breathing exercises, and the brisk performance of certain *asanas*, eg the Sun salutation into quasi-aerobic exercises, known as jumping. See *Pranayama*, Yoga

**jaborandi tree** *Pilocarpus jaborandi* HERBAL MEDICINE A shrub-like tree that contains pilocarpine and volatile oils; it is diaphoretic, diuretic, and expectorant, and has been used to treat bladder infections and rheumatic pain; pilocarpine is a standard glaucoma drug. See Herbal medicine

**Jacob's staff** Mullein, see there, *Verbascum thapsus*

**jacuzzi** NATUROPATHY A permutation of the whirlpool, in which the water is moved by powerful jets over the body, which is believed to promote relaxation, and be useful in treating arthritic complaints, musculoskeletal injuries, and sports injuries. See Hydrotherapy; Cf Whirlpool

**jade woman** Dodder, see there, *Cuscuta chinensis, Cuscuta japonica*

**Jamaica quassia** *Picrasma excelsa* HERBAL MEDICINE A tree that contains a bitter resin rich in quasin, a natural insecticide, laxative, and a stimulant of appetite and secretion of bile and gastric juices. See Herbal medicine

**Jamaican sorrel** Hibiscus, see there, *Hibiscus sabdariffa*

**Jamaican vomiting sickness** An intoxication by 'bush tea' made from unripe fruit of the Jamaican ackee tree (*Blighia sapida*), caused by hypoglycin, a propionic acid derivative that inhibits isovaleryl CoA dehydrogenase, provoking violent vomiting, prostration, drowsiness, convulsions and hypoglycemia as low as 0.56 mmol/L (US: 10 mg/dl) MORTALITY High, often within 24 hours of ingestion

The condition is caused by the metabolites of hypoglycin A, an amino acid converted to coenzyme A thioesters and carnitine derivatives, which sequester intracellular carnitine and inhibit fatty acid oxidation, causing accumulation of isovaleric acid with continued fatty acid esterification, resulting in fine-droplet fatty liver (*N Engl J Med 1976; 295:461*)

**James Fever Powder** MEDICAL HISTORY-QUACKERY A bottled patent medicine containing antimony that was sold in the late 1800s in the American frontier. See Frontier prescription, Patent medicine, Quackery

**Jamestown weed** Jimsonweed, see there, *Datura stramonium*

**Japanese acupuncture** ALTERNATIVE MEDICINE A permutation of acupuncture which at one time differed from Chinese acupuncture, as thinner (less traumatic) needles were used; thinner needles have become standard, and the differences between the forms are minimal. See Acupressure, Acupuncture, Chinese medicine

**Japanese catnip** *Schizonepeta tenuifolia*, also known as *jing jie*, *Nepeta japonica, Nepeta tenuifolia* CHINESE MEDICINE A perennial plant, the stem, leaves, and flowers of which are analgesic, antipyretic, hemostatic, and diaphoretic; it is used for abscesses, fevers, headache, menstrual dysfunction, postpartum hemorrhage, and recuperation from strokes. See Chinese herbal medicine

**Japanese ginseng** Ginseng, see there, *Panax ginseng*

**Japanese honeysuckle** *Lonicera japonica*, endure winter, *jin yin hua*, *ren dung*, woodbine CHINESE MEDICINE A shrub, the stems, leaves, and flowers of which are anti-inflammatory, antipyretic, diuretic, and believed to purify the blood; it is used for abscesses, allergies, hemorrhoids, obesity, infection, internal hemorrhage, and sore throat. See Chinese herbal medicine

**Japanese medicine** ALTERNATIVE MEDICINE A therapeutic system that is rooted in ancient Chinese tradition, and altered to fit the Japanese philosophy; Japanese medicine includes shiatsu, herbal medicine-commonly known as kanpo, spa baths, folk remedies, and spiritual healing using prayer and talismans. See Kanpo

**Japanese prickly ash** Szechuan pepper, see there, *Zanthoxylum piperitum*

**Japanese wax privet** *Ligustrum japonicum, L*

*lucidum, dung chin, la shu, nu jen dze, nu jen zi*, wax tree, wintergreen CHINESE MEDICINE An evergreen, the berries of which are diuretic, stimulate the immune system, and antitumoral; it is used for anorexia, fatigue, and immune deficiencies. See Chinese herbal medicine

**jasmine** *Gelsemium*, see there, *Gelsemium sempervirens*, *Gelsemium sempervitalis*

**Jason Winters Products cancer tea** An herbal tea marketed by Tri-Sun International (Fargo, North Dakota), that contains chaparral, red clover, and herbaline, which is said to be effective in preventing and curing cancer (*Butler, 1992*). See Chaparal, Red clover, Unproven methods for cancer management

**jaundice berry** Barberry, see there, *Berberis vulgaris*

**Jazzercise®** ALTERNATIVE HEALTH A proprietary form of aerobic exercise developed in the 1970s by J Sheppard Missett; each session consists of a warmup, followed by aerobics, muscle toning, and cool-down and flexibility segments. See Aerobic exercise

**jeevani** Indian ginseng ETHNOBOTANY An active ingredient of *Trichopus zeylnicus*, a plant known to the Kani tribe (in the southern state of Kerala in India) as an instant source of energy; it is believed by some workers to be superior to ginseng as it does not have steroidal activity (*Nature 1996; 381:182n*)

**Jen Chung** VG26, see there

***jen tan*** Sandlewood, see there, *Santalaum album*

**Jerusalem cowslip** Lungwort, see there, *Pulmonaria officinalis*

**Jerusalem sage** Lungwort, see there, *Pulmonaria officinalis*

**Jesuits' bark** 1. *China*, see there 2. Cinchona, see there, *Cinchona* species

**jewelweed** *Impatiens capensis* HERBAL MEDICINE An annual, the crushed leaves and stem juice of which is used topically for bites, eczema, and poison ivy. See Herbal medicine

***jhana yoga*** The intellectual form of yoga that seeks the pathway to *prajna* (transcendental wisdom) through meditation and thought. See Yoga

***ji ke*** Trifoliate orange, see there, *Poncircus trifoliata*

***ji li dze*** *Tribulus terrestris*, see there

***ji li zi*** *Tribulus terrestris*, see there

***ji tou*** Foxnut, see there, *Euryale ferox*

***jiao niang*** Capsule–Chinese medicine, see there

***jiao teng*** Chinese cornbind, see there, *Polygonum multiflorum*

***jie geng*** Balloon flower, see there, *Platycodon grandiflorum*

***jie gu*** Teasel, see there, *Dipsacus sylvestris*

***jih mu*** *Anemarrhena asphodeloides*, see there

***jih shih*** Trifoliate orange, see there, *Poncircus trifoliata*

**Jimsonweed** *Datura stramonium*, apple-of-Peru, devil's apple, Jamestown weed, mad apple, stinkweed, thornapple HERBAL MEDICINE A malodorous annual herb (see illustration, page 204) that contains tropane alkaloids including atropine, hyoscamine, hyoscine; it was used to reduce bronchospasms during asthmatic attacks and for Parkinson's disease, and used topically for rheumatic pain and sciatica TOXICITY Confusion, double vision, hallucinations, tachyarrhythmias, and thirst; it is classified by the FDA as poisonous; it is contraindicated in pregnancy, in those taking antidepressants, or with prostatic disease or tachycardia. See Herbal medicine

***jin bu huan*** *Gynura pinnatifida, see there*

**jewelweed** *Impatiens capensis*

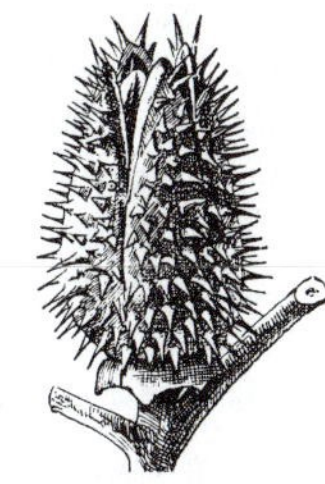

**Jimsonweed**
*Datura stramonium*

**jin chien hua** Elecampene, see there, *Inula helenium*

**jin gui shen qi** Golden Book Tea, see there

**Jin Shin Acutouch®** BODYWORK A proprietary form of therapeutic touch developed in the 1970s by an American asthmatic, B Clark, which is intended to stimulate the flow of vital energy through the body; the technique combines elements of breath therapy, *gigong*, kung fu, meditation, and Taoist yoga, with nutritional support using vitamins and herbs to form a complete health system, reflecting the translation of Jin Shin Acutouch–compassionate spirit penetration through touch; in this system, 26 pressure points (energy centers or keys of the body) are recognized, based on Clark's observation of the places people touch when they are in pain; Cf Jin Shin Do® Bodymind Acupressure™

**jin shin do** 1. Aupressure massage, see there 2. Jin Shin Do® Bodymind Acupressure™, see there

**Jin Shin Do® Bodymind Acupressure™** BODYWORK A proprietary form of Oriental massage that was developed by an American psychotherapist, IM Teeguarden, which applies deep and prolonged acupressure, to release 'armoring'–muscular tension of emotional origin; Jin Shin Do® incorporates acupuncture, Jungian therapy, Reichian theory, shiatsu, and Taoist breathing; the technique promotes relaxation, increased awareness, and inner peace, and is said to be effective for allergies, attention-deficit disorder, bedwetting, eyestrain, fatigue, coughs, headaches, insomnia, low back pain, lung congestion, mood disorders (eg anger, anxiety, depression, guilt), nosebleeds, tension, and other conditions. See Acupressure, Reichian therapy, Shiatsu, Taoist breathing; Cf Jin Shin Acupressure, Jin Shin Jyutsu, Reflexology

**jin shin jitsu** Jin Shin Jyutsu, see there

**jin shin jyutsu** Inductive healing, jin shin jitsu BODYWORK A Japanese form of acupressure that uses gentle touching and cradling of the body rather than massage; the practitioner identifies zones of compromised flow of energy *chi* (life force) by pulse diagnosis, and then attempts to harmonize the body, mind, and spirit, simultaneously touching a combination of 2 of 26 'safety energy locks' located along the body's energy pathways, and redirect the patient's intrinsic life forces to unblock the flow of energy. See Acupressure, Bodywork, Oriental massage, Shiatsu; Cf Jin Shin Do™ Bodymind Acupressure®, Reflexology

**jin yin hua** Japanese honeysuckle, see there *Lonicera japonica*

**jing** Kidney essence, essence of the body ALTERNATIVE MEDICINE A life force of the body said to be seated in the kidney. See Chinese herbal medicine, Chinese medicine, Traditional Chinese medicine; Cf *Hara*

**jing jie** Japanese catnip, see there, *Schizonepeta tenuifolia*, see there

***jnana* yoga** *Nana* yoga The intellectual form of yoga that seeks the pathway to *prajna* (transcendental wisdom) through meditation and thought, and understanding of the laws of the universe. See Yoga

**Job's tears** Coix, *Coix chinensis*, *C lacryma-jobi*, *yi yi ren* CHINESE MEDICINE A grass, the seeds of which are anti-inflammatory, antipyretic, decongestant, diuretic, and nutrient; it is used for arthritis, diarrhea, eczema, epistaxis, gastric ulcer, hernias, gastrointestinal and lung abscesses, plantar warts, rheumatic complaints, and urinary retention, see Chinese herbal medicine

**joint fir** Ephedra, see there, *Ephedra sinica*

**joint mobilization** OSTEOPATHY An osteopathic technique in which the joints are passively moved through their entire range of motion, with the intent of expanding the range of motion and eliminating restrictions. See Osteopathy

**Josephing** BODYWORK A manipulative technique developed in 1982 by Spencer Burke, based on a series of dreams that he had of a Native American tribal Chief Joseph (*Raso, 1994*). See Bodywork

**Joshua tree** *Yucca brevifolia* HERBAL MEDICINE An evergreen from the southwestern US that contains steroidal saponins and phytoestrogens, which may be of use in treating menstrual disorders. See Herbal medicine

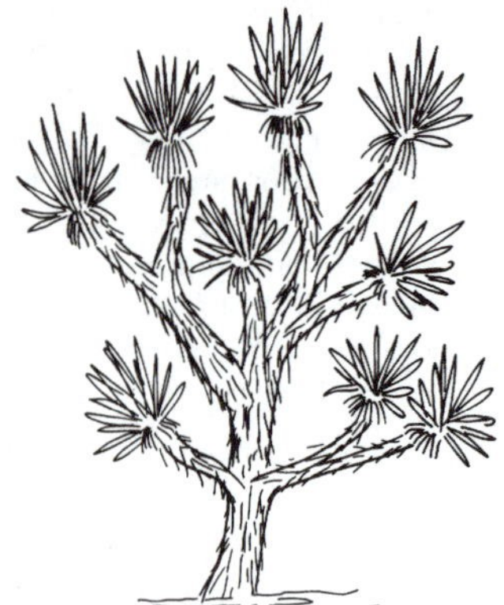

**Joshua tree** *Yucca brevifolia*

***ju hua*** Crysanthemum, see there, *Chrysanthemum moriflorum*

***jue ming dze*** Popularly known as sickle senna, see there, *Cassia tora*

***jue ming zi*** Sickle senna, see there, *Cassia tora*

**juice therapy** ALTERNATIVE NUTRITION The ingestion of fresh raw fruit and vegetable juices to 'replenish' the body and provide nutritional support; juice therapy is believed by its advocates to have anticarcinogenic and detoxifying effects, and is believed to be an effective adjunctive therapy for AIDS, allergies, cancer, rheumatic diseases, and other conditions. See Apple juice therapy, Carrot juice, Fruit juice therapy, Mono therapy, Vegetable juice therapy

Note: Fruits and vegetables are prepared for juicing by scrubbing, peeling–especially if they have been coated by wax or mineral oil, removal of seeds and pits, removal of stems and greens–especially of carrots and rhubarb, which contain toxins; imported fruits are, in general ill-advised as pesticides are more liberally used outside of the US; certain fruits, eg bananas and vegetables, eg avocados have low content of water, and virtually defy juicing; for maximum benefits, the juice should be consumed at the time of juicing, as the nutritional value decreases due to the presence of enzymes and other components

**Jungian psychoanalysis** PSYCHIATRY A form of psychoanalysis developed by Carl Gustav Jung (1875-1961), who trained with Freud, but subsequently formed his own school of psychoanalysis; in contrast to Freud, for whom a person's past–in particular those of psychosexual development, serves as the substrate for all future events, Jung viewed the mind as a result of past experiences and future expectations; Jungian psychoanalysis guides the patient to merge his or her personal unconscious mind with that of the 'collective unconscious'; psychoanalysis differs from psychotherapy in that it is more formal, intense, and concerned with early sexuality and events of infancy, which may or may not be remembered as they actually occurred–as in the 'false memory' phenomenon. See False memory; Cf Freudian analysis, Hypnosis, Psychotherapy

**juniper** *Juniperus communis*, dwarf juniper, ground juniper, hackmatack, horse savin HERBAL MEDICINE An evergreen shrub, the berries of which contain flavonoids, gallotannin, vitamin C, and volatile oils including camphene, juni-perin, limonene, myrcene, pinene, sabinene, terpinene, and thujone; juniper is antiseptic, antitussive, carminative, diuretic and an expectorant, and has been used internally for digestive complaints, hypertension, menstrual irregularities, neuralgia, premenstrual syndrome, sciatica, urinary tract infections; it is used topically for rheumatic complaints and gout TOXICITY Juniper should not be used internally in pregnancy as it stimulates uterine contraction, nor in those with renal disease. See Botanical toxicity, Herbal medicine

**juniper** *Juniperus communis*

***Juniperus communis*** Popularly known as juniper, see there

**junk food** A popular term for any food that is low in essential nutrients and high in carbohydrates; junk foods may be highly salted (eg potato chips/crisps, pretzels), high in refined carbohydrates (empty calories, eg candy, soft drinks) and high in saturated fats and cholesterol (eg cake and chocolates). See Cafeteria diet, 'Fast' food

**Jupiter's bean** Henbane, see there, *Hyoscyamus niger*

***Justicia gendarussa*** *Chin dao* CHINESE MEDICINE An annual plant, the root of which is anti-inflammatory, antipyretic, antirheumatic, diuretic, and sedative, and used for alcohol abuse, diarrhea, fever, jaundice, and rheum-atic complaints. See Chinese herbal medicine

***juzen-taiho-to*** JAPANESE HERBAL MEDICINE An herbal formulation containing angelica, astragalus, cinnamon, foxglove, ginseng, licorice, nettle, and peony, which has been used for patients with anemia and fatigue; it is reported to increase NK (natural killer) cell activity, production of tumor necrosis factor, and stabilize cell membranes, and may be of use as an adjuvant in treating cancer in patients who require chemotherapy and/or radiotherapy (*Moss, 1992*). See Unproven methods for cancer management

***ka*** A flat, handheld and self-deployed device used in *chua ka*, a Mongolian form of massage. See *Chua ka*, Massage

**kabala** Cabala, see there

**kabbalah** Cabala, see there

**kabbalism** Cabala, see there

***kahuna*** PARANORMAL PHENOMENA A priest and medicine man (or woman) of the Hawaiian Islands, who uses tropical plants for shamanic medical rituals that predate recorded history; the kahuna is believed to be capable of foretelling the future, reviving the dead, and controlling a person's *mana*. See Lomilomi massage, *Mana*

***Kali bich*** *Kali bichromicum*, potassium dichromate, potassium bichromate HOMEOPATHY A remedy used for diseases of the head and neck, gastrointestinal, and genital tract mucosa, and for acute bronchitis, arthritis, colds, croup, indigestion, migraines, nausea, nasal congestion and sinusitis, and vomiting. See Homeopathy

***Kali phos*** *Kali phosphoricum*, potassium phosphate, phosphate of potash HOMEOPATHY A remedy used for mental and physical exhaustion due to stress, tension, overwork, nervous breakdowns and fatigue. See Homeopathy

**kalium** Potassium, see there

**kampo** Kanpo, see there

**kanpo** 1. Japanese medicine, see there 2. Japanese herbal medicine The system of herbal medicine practiced by herbologists in Japan

***kapha*** Moon force AYURVEDIC MEDICINE The *dosha* that represents the earth and water forces according to the ayurvedic construct of the universe; *kapha* is the densest of the elements, and is related to organic tissues, fluids, and other substances; *kapha* forces heal, impart physical strength, and resiliency; *kapha* energy flows at its peak in the winter and early spring. See Ayurvedic medicine, *Dosha*; Cf *Pitta*, *Prakriti*, *Prana*, *Vata*

***kapha* diet** AYURVEDIC MEDICINE A diet that is believed to be optimal for a person with a '*kapha*' *dosha*, which consists of a low-calorie diet of pungent, bitter, and astringent foods; fats should be avoided. See *Dosha*, *Kapha*; Cf *Pitta* diet, *Vata* diet

***kapha* personality** AYURVEDIC MEDICINE A personality profile with a '*kapha*' *dosha*; *kapha* individuals tend to be 'solid,' methodical, and may be sensuous, physically stronger, more softly spoken, wiser, more stable, and calmer than other *dosha* types; they often have sluggish metabolism, and tend to be middle managers; *kapha* energy flows at its peak in the winter and early spring, the times when the *kapha* personality is most susceptible to allergies, bronchitis, headaches, lung disease, sinusitis, and tonsilitis. See *Kapha*; Cf *Pitta* personality, *Vata* personality

Note: *Pitta* persons are 'low-key' and calm, and thus similar to the type 'B' personality of Western medicine

**karaya tree** *Sterculia urens* HERBAL MEDICINE A tree of subtropical India that produces a polysaccharide-rich sap known as mucara, kadaya, sterculi or karaya gum, which is used as a bulk laxative, and in dentistry, as an adhesive. See Herbal medicine

***karma*** A concept central to Hinduism that states that a person's condition in this life is the result of physical and mental actions that occurred in past incarnations, and actions in the present life will influence one's destiny in future incarnations. See Yoga

***karma yoga*** The service form of yoga that seeks to serve others as a pathway to a higher power. See Yoga

**Kasper Hauser syndrome** Psychosocial dwarfism, see there

**kat** Khat, see there, *Catha edulis*

***kathakali* massage** AYUVEDIC MEDICINE A

type of massage used in ayurvedic medicine, in which the various body parts are stretched to allow greater access to points that are being massaged. See Massage therapy

**kava** *Piper methysticum*, kava kava A broad-leafed shrub native to Oceania, which contains alkaloids, lactones, kawain, methysticin, mucilage, starch, and yangonin ETHNIC MEDICINE Kava plays a central role in the tribal life of Oceania, and is ground and fermented to produce an hallucinogenic narcotic; it is used to celebrate birth and marriage, to mourn death, to placate the gods, cure illness, and remove curses HERBAL MEDICINE It is antiseptic and diuretic; kava is used by by Western herbalists is to treat prostatitis, urinary tract infections, rheumatic complaints, gout, anxiety, depression, insomnia, and muscle spasms TOXICITY Chronic use of kava is associated with dermal, hepatic, ocular, and spinal cord damage. See Herbal medicine

**kedlock** White mustard, see there, *Sinapsis alba*

**Keeley cure** MEDICAL HISTORY A treatment for alcoholism and other addictions that was promulgated in the late 19th century by an American physician, Leslie E Keeley (1834-1900); Keeley's remedies were packaged in triangular bottles, contained trace amounts of gold, and marketed as therapies for 'drunkenness,' 'opium habit,' and 'neurasthenia'. See Patent medicine

**Kefauver-Harris Bill** An amendment to the 1938 Food, Drug, and Cosmetic Act, passed in 1962 which required, in addition to being proven to be safe, a pharmaceutical must be proven effective (*Mayo Clin Proc 1984; 59:707*). See Food and Drug Administration

***keis-bukuryo-gan*** JAPANESE HERBAL MEDICINE An herbal formulation that has been used to treat benign prostatic conditions, including prostatitis (*Moss, 1992*)

**Kelley's cancer theory** A hypothesis on cancer causes proposed by an American dentist

▶ **CAUSES OF CANCER, ACCORDING TO KELLEY**

- **PANCREATIC INSUFFICIENCY** The pancreas does not produce enough, or the right type of enzymes
- **MINERAL IMBALANCES**
- **INADEQUATE DIGESTION OF PROTEINS**
- **CANCER CELLS PROTECT THEMSELVES** by producing electromagetic forces that weaken the host's immune response

See Kelley's Index of malignancy, Kelley's nutritional-metabolic therapy, Unproven methods for cancer management

**Kelley index of malignancy** FRINGE ONCOLOGY A questionnaire developed in the late 1960s by William Kelly, who believed that cancer resulted from a deficiency of pancreatic enzyme; the questionnaire was believed to localize and determine the growth rate of tumors, which were then treated with laetrile. See Kelley's cancer theory, Kelley's nutritional-metabolic therapy, Laetrile, Metabolic therapy, Tijuana, Unproven methods of cancer managment

**Kelley's nutritional-metabolic therapy** FRINGE ONCOLOGY Any of a number of regimens based on Kelley's cancer theory; in addition to a specific diet, the patients are to consume supplements of pancreatic enzymes, raw beef concentrates, vitamins and minerals, and are treated with coffee enemas. See Gerson therapy, Kelley's cancer theory, Kelley's index of malignancy, Unproven methods for cancer management

**kelp** 1. Bladderwrack, see there, *Fucus vesiculosus* 2. Kelp, *Laminaria digitata*, tangleweed 3. Kelp, *Laminaria saccharina*, seawrack

**kelpware** Bladderwrack, see there, *Fucus vesiculosus*

**Kempner rice diet** Rice diet, see there

**Kemron** A low-dose formulation of interferon-α that was reported by some workers in Kenya as a cure or potential cure for AIDS, a claim that has not been substantiated. See AIDS fraud

**James Tyler Kent** HOMEOPATHY An American homeopath (1849-1916) who introduced the concept of constitutional types. See Constitutional remedy, Constitutional type, Hahnemann, Homeopathy

**keyflower** Cowslip, see there, *Primula vera*

**key of heaven** Cowslip, see there, *Primula vera*

**key of the body** ALTERNATIVE HEALTH CARE A colloquial term for any of the 26 pressure points (energy centers) identified by B Clark, the developer of Jin Shin Acutouch®, see there

**khat** *Catha edulis*, chat, kat, qat HERBAL MEDICINE A shrub, the leaves of which have a high content of D-norpseudoephedrine, a central nervous system stimulant; consumed as a leaf (in a similar fashion to that of coca), khat increases alertness, relieves hunger and fatigue, and produces mild euphoria. See Herbal medicine

**khella** *Ammi visnagi* HERBAL MEDICINE An Arabian shrub, the leaves of which have a high content of khellin, which is diuretic, broncho- and vasodilatory, it was once used for angina pectoris, asthma, and kidney stones but, given its toxicity, is rarely used by Western herbologists TOXICITY Nausea and vomiting. See Botanical toxicity, Herbal medicine

***ki*** see *Chi*

***ki* breathing** A health-enhancing system that combines *tanden* breathing, massage, and *ki-ren* exercises. See *Tanden* breathing

***Kiai!*** MARTIAL ARTS A shout used in aikido and other Japanese martial arts that expresses the energy accumulated during a period of meditative build-up. See Aikido, Martial arts, T'ai chi ch'uan

**kidney essence** Jing, see there

**kidney meridian** see Twelve meridians

**Kilner screen** PARANORMAL PHENOMENA A device invented by Dr WJ Kilner (1847-1920) of St Thomas Hospital in London which consists of two plates of glass, separated by $\frac{1}{8}$ inch, and filled with a dye (eg carmine or coal-tar dye) in alcohol; an individual stands adjacent to the screen and (in theory) his aura can be analyzed. See Aura analysis, Kirlian photography Raso reference

**kinesiology** ALTERNATIVE MEDICINE see Applied Kinesiology

**king's bodyguard** Pericardium, see (the) Twelve vital organs

**king's cure-all** Evening primrose, see there, *Oenothera biennis*

**king of flowers** Tree peony, see there, *Paeonia moutan*

**king of the vital organs** Heart, see The Twelve vital organs

**kinnikinnick** Bearberry, see there, *Arctostaphylos uva-ursi*

**Kirlian diagnosis** PARANORMAL PHENOMENA A method of pseudodiagnosis based on Kirlian photography, see there

**Kirlian photography** Corona discharge photography, electrography PARANORMAL PHENOMENA A technique developed in the 1970s by Semyon Kirlian, an electrician from Kuban (the former Soviet Union), in which a high-voltage, high-frequency electric field interacts with the material being photographed and is delivered to an aluminum plate overlaid with photographic film; the resulting image is that of wispy radiations emanating from the skin surface, which is claimed to correspond to the aura of living beings; the intensity of the image is alleged to be decreased in sick patients, and increased by 'energy-enhancing' maneuvers, eg acupuncture, homeopathy, nutritional supplements, transcendental meditation and yoga; the Kirlian effects are a function of the degree of pressure on the imaging plate, the moisture of the part being imaged, the type of photographic paper, the length of development time, and length of exposure; Kirlian photography enthusiasts believe it can be used to diagnose cancer, confusion, depression, nutritional deficiencies, mental disorders, drug addiction, and other conditions; despite these assertions, '*No use of Kirlian photography in diagnosing, treating, or preventing disease of any type is legitimate.*' (*Butler, 1992*)

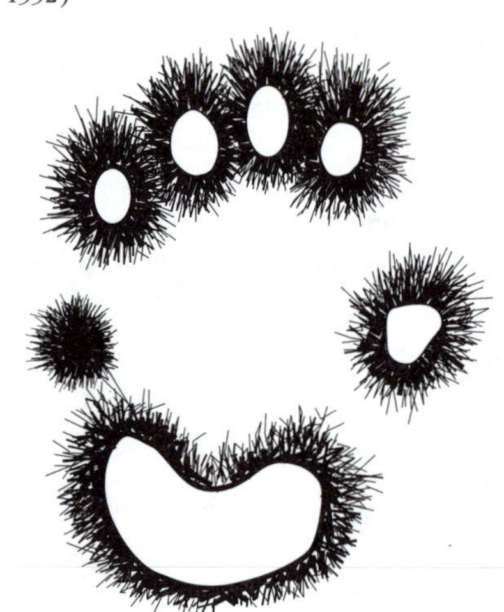

**Kirlian photography** (schematic of hand)

**Kirlian technique** Kirlian diagnosis, see there

**Ki-shiatsu®/Asian bodywork (therapy)** Shiatsu oriental bodywork A proprietary healing system based on various manual methods and breathing techniques; the intent of Ki-shiatsu® is to balance and nurture the whole person, and is believed to release mental and physical tension, improve the circulation, vitality, relieve pain, and tone the immune and digestive systems (*Raso, 1994*). See Bodywork

**klamath weed** Saint John's wort, see there, *Hypericum perforatum*

**Kneipp cure** Kneipp therapy, see there

**Kneipp therapy** Kneipp cure, kneipping, *Kneipptherapie* NATUROPATHY A health care system developed in the 19th century by Father Sebastian Kneipp (1821-1897), that was based on hydrotherapy (eg morning dew walks or walking on freshly fallen snow), followed by a brisk dry massage to increase circulation; in addition to hydrotherapy, Kneipp recommended light and fresh-air therapies and herbal teas; Kneipp therapy eventually gave rise to what is now known as naturopathy. See Hydrotherapy, Naturopathy

**kneipping** Kneipp therapy, see there

***Kneipptherapie*** Kneipp therapy, see there

**knitback** Comfrey, see there, *Symphytum officinale*

**knitbone** Comfrey, see there, *Symphytum officinale*

**knobroot** Stoneroot, see there, *Collinsonia canadensis*

**knotroot** Stoneroot, see there, *Collinsonia canadensis*

***koan*** PARANORMAL PHENOMENA An unanswerable question, eg '*what is the sound of one hand clapping?*,' which is regarded as a key to freeing oneself from the confines of conventional logic, which can be pondered during meditation

**Koch treatment** HEALTH FRAUD A cancer cure promoted in the 1940s by Dr William Koch of Detroit, and administered to cancer victims through an organization known as the Christian Medical Research League, which continued to operate after his retirement to South America; the Koch therapy hinged on administration of glyoxylide, an allegedly curative substance diluted to parts per trillion in distilled water; workers who have examined glyoxylide, identified only distilled water. See Quackery, Unproven methods for cancer management

***Kochia scoparia*** Belvedere cypress, see there

**kofutu system** FRINGE MEDICINE A system of spiritual healing and personal development, which incorporates absent healing, aura balancing, and therapeutic touch, as a means of enhancing a person's creativity and balancing *karma*. See Absent healing, Aura balancing, *Karma*, Therapeutic touch

**kola** Cola, see there

**konzo** A distinct upper motor neuron spastic paraparesis described in Africa due to cyanide poisoning, which is related to consumption of carbohydrate-rich cassava; in droughts, cassava produces more cyanogenic glycosides and, due to the food shortage, causes the food manufacturers to take short-cuts in the steps designed to remove the cyanide. See Cyanide

**Korean ginseng** Ginseng, see there, *Panax ginseng*

**kosher** ETHNIC NUTRITION *adjective* Pertaining or referring to foods that are prepared according to Jewish dietary law (*Lev 11 and Deut 14*); kosher meat is the flesh of animals that both chew the cud and have cloven hoofs (cows and sheep); the animals must be killed with a single skilled stroke; unless the meat is broiled, it must be salted and soaked to remove all traces of blood; kosher fishes are those with scales and fins; simulataneous preparation or consumption of dairy products and meats is tref, ie is not kosher (*The Columbia Encyclopedia, 5th ed, Columbia University Press, New York, 1993*); to be designated as kosher, the foods must be approved by a rabbi; Cf Pareve

Note: The adjective kosher entered mainstream English in the mid-1920s, as a synonym for correct, genuine, or legitimate

***kosht*** AYRUVEDIC MEDICINE The usual location of a life force, according to the ayurvedic construct of the body. See Ayurvedic medicine

**kosmos** PARANORMAL PHENOMENA A calculator-like device used to determine a person's biorhythm, which is based on the physical, emotional, and spritual aspects of an individual's personality; the kosmos is used to signal critical time periods in the individual's life, in which a person is at greatest risk of suffering accidents or illness. See Biorhythm, Critical period

**Krebiozen** FRINGE ONCOLOGY A substance promoted in the late 1940s as an effective therapy for cancer which, in samples obtained by the NCI and the FDA, consisted of creatine monohydrate in mineral oil; Krebiozen was particularly controversial as it was sponsored by Andrew C Ivy, MD, PhD, professor emeritus of the University of Illinois. See Quackery, Unproven methods for cancer management

Of the 4307 Krebiozen-treated cases investigated by the FDA, less than one-half of the medical records were complete enough to allow evaluation; only 3 of these 1526 cases had what would be considered to be objective responses, and the 3 cases may have represented spontaneous regression of cancer; the health care professionals of the Krebiozen Research Foundation were indicted on 49 counts of fraud and conspiracy, but were acquitted

**krestin** PSK® HERBAL MEDICINE A substance extracted from a mushroom, *Coriolus versicolor,* that stimulates the immune system, by enhancing cytotoxic (killer) T-cell activity; it has been used in Japan as an adjuvant to conventional therapy for gastrointestinal cancer and leukemia, and is reported to improve survival; it is not approved for sale in the US (*Moss, 1992*). See Unproven methods for cancer management

***kripalu* bodywork** A bodywork based in *kripalu yoga*, a variant of *hatha yoga*, a meditation-oriented yoga

***kriya yoga*** A form of yoga founded by Paramahansa Yogananda, which requires purification practices (*kriyas*). See Yoga

***kuan dung hua*** Coltsfoot, see there, *Tussilago farfara*

**Kulkarni naturopathy** AYURVEDIC MEDICINE A system of naturopathy developed in the 1930s by an Indian, VM Kulkarni, which incorporated a diet of 'natural' food, fasting, hypnotism, massage, magnetic healing, heliotherapy, *pranayama*, and yogic postures (*Raso, 1994*). See Naturopathy, *Pranayama*

***kum nye* relaxation** A T'ai chi ch'uan-like healing system developed in Tibet, that consists of breathing exercises, slow movements, and self-massage, which is believed to free constrictions in the natural flow of energy, and allow a person's natural healing energy to be tapped

***kundalini yoga*** A form of yoga that seeks the pathway to a higher power by activating *kundalini*, the primal force of nature, which resides like a coiled snake at the spine through contemplation and/or *tantra*, a sexual means of evoking *kundalini;* activation of *kundalini* may result in enlightenment, insanity, malignancy, weakness or death. See Ayurvedic medicine, Yoga

**Michio Kushi** A Boston-based, Japanese-American (1926–) who formulated the macrobiotic diet in response to the nutritionally deficiencies of the Zen macrobiotic diet of George Ohsawa. See Macrobiotics, Ohsawa, Zen macrobiotic diet

**kutzu vine** *Pueraria lobata*, *Pachyrhizus thunbergianus*, *geh gen* CHINESE MEDICINE A ligneous vine, the root of which is antipyretic, diuretic, and a nerve tonic; it is used to treat alcohol and other intoxications, convulsions, diarrhea, fever, headache, neck pain, and skin conditions. See Chinese herbal medicine

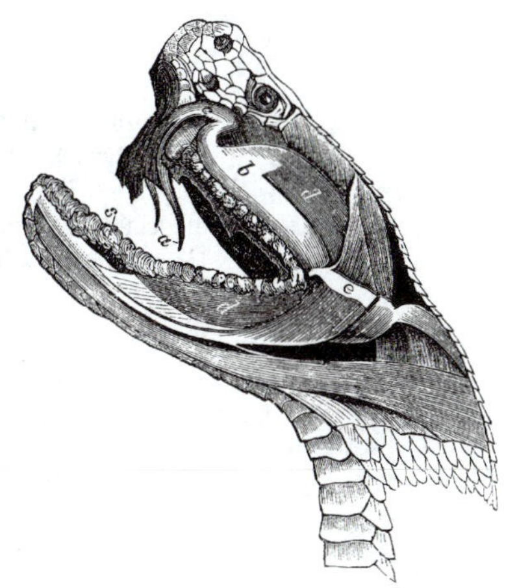

***Lachesis*** *Lachesis muta*

**Labanalysis** Laban movement analysis, see there

**L.Ac.** Licensed Acupuncturist

**La Leche League** An organization founded in 1956 by mothers who wished to breast-feed their infants; information is available on request from the International La Leche League. See Breast-feeding, Breast milk, White beverage *Resource La Leche League International; 9616 Minneapolis Avenue; Franklin Park IL 60131 ☎ 708.455.7730*

***la shu*** Japanese wax privet, see there, *Ligustrum japonicum*

**Laban movement analysis** Labanalysis A type of movement analysis developed in 1930s by an Austro-Hungarian dancer, Rudolph Laban for describing and interpreting the elements that comprise a particular movement; acording to Laban, there are 3 primary elements in a moving body: The body itself, the space surrounding it, and the intention of the movement; Laban analysis is of use to those who perform bodywork and movement therapy; Laban-Certified Therapists undergo 500 hours of instruction and evaluation. See Bodywork, Dance therapy

***Lachesis*** *Lachesis muta, Trigonocephalus lachesis*, bushmaster, surukuku HOMEOPATHY A remedy formulated from bushmaster snake venom; it is used to treat cardiac problems including tachycardia, arrhythmias, and angina, as well as choking coughs, croup, fever, hemorrhoids, hot flashes, throbbing headaches, indigestion, insomnia, nosebleeds, premenstrual syndrome, petit mal seizures, sciatica, varicose veins, and weeping wounds. See *Lachesis* type, Homeopathy

***Lachesis* type** HOMEOPATHY The *Lachesis* constitutional type individuals are egocentric, jealous, contradictory, sporadically creative, and 'hyper'; they like seafood, sour foods, starchy foods, and alcohol WORSE Heat or direct sun, tight clothing, menopause FEARS Water, poisoning, suffocation, death WEAKEST BODY REGIONS Nervous system, circulation, female organs, left side of body. See Constitutional type, *Lachesis*, Homeopathy

***Lactobacillus acidophilus*** A bacterium present in yogurt, and in the colon of infants; it is believed by some health care workers that the consumption of *Lactobacillus acidophilus* and *L bulgaricus* are of therapeutic value as they prevent the overgrowth of opportunistic and/or potentially pathogenic bacteria and fungi; lyophilized concentrates of *Lactobacillus* species are available commercially, and have been used to treat canker sores, colitis, diarrhea, halitosis, oral thrush and other and yeast infections. See Yogurt

***Lactobacillus bulgaris* factor** Folic acid, see there

**lacto-vegetarian** A vegetarian who consumes the same food groups as vegans (vegetables, fruits, grains, beans, and nuts), and in addition consumes dairy products, but no eggs. See Vegetarian, Vegetarianism

**lacto-ovo-vegetarian** Pythagorean A vegetarian who consumes the same food groups as vegans (vegetables, fruits, grains, beans, and nuts) and, in addition, consumes dairy products, *and* eggs. See Vegetarian, Vegetarianism

**lactose** Milk sugar A reducing disaccharide hydrolyzed by β-galactosidase into D-galactose and D-glucose; it is synthesized by mammalian mammaries, and causes intolerance to milk products that occurs in some adults. See Lactose intolerance, Lactose tolerance test; Cf Lactulose

**lactose intolerance** The inability to digest lactose, which is most often due to the inability to produce lactase, and occurs with aging; lactose intolerance is more common in African Americans and Asians CLINICAL Abdominal bloating, cramping, and diarrhea MANAGEMENT All dairy products should be eliminated from the diet unless pretreated with lactase; cultured milk products, eg yogurt and buttermilk may be well tolerated. See Lactose, Lactose tolerance test

**lactose tolerance test** A clinical test for lactase deficiency, in which 100 g of lactose, is administered orally, and serum glucose is monitored as in the glucose tolerance test; lactose intolerance is presumed to exist if the glucose levels rise less than 20 mg/dL; extreme lactase deficiency is evident by osmotic diarrhea. See Lactose, Lactose intolerance. Cf Glucose tolerance test

***Lactuca virosa*** Popularly known as wild lettuce, see there

**lactulose** A synthetic disaccharide used to treat hepatic encephalo-pathy, which is administered by mouth, acting as a laxative; lactulose reduces intraluminal $NH_3$ which, via the extracellular fluid, reduces $NH_3$ in the blood; Cf Lactose

**ladder-to-heaven** Lily-of-the-valley, see there, *Convallaria majalis*

**lady's foxglove** Mullein, see there, *Verbascum thapsus*

**lady's mantle** *Alchemilla vulgaris*, bear's foot, leontopodium, lion's foot, nine hooks, stellaria HERBAL MEDICINE A perennial herb that contains tannins, which is astringent and hemostatic; it has been used internally for diarrhea and heavy menses, and topically for cuts and wounds. See Herbal medicine

**lady's slipper** *Cypripedium calceolus*, American valerian, moccasin flower, nerve root, whippoorwill's shoe, yellow Indian's shoe, yellow lady's slipper HERBAL MEDICINE A perennial herb that contains glycosides, resins, tannins, and volatile oil, which is antispasmodic and sedative; it has been used for anxiety, insomnia, menstrual and muscle cramps, nervous tension, neuralgias, and seizures TOXICITY Contact dermatitis, giddiness, hallucinations, and headaches. See Herbal medicine

**lady's washbowl** Soapwort, see there, *Saponaria officinalis*

**ladle medicine** White peony, see there, *Paeonia albiflora*

**laetrile** Amygdalin, vitamin $B_{17}$ FRINGE ONCOLOGY A preparation from bitter almonds, apricot or peach pits that is high in cyanide, which has been claimed to be effective in treating cancer; a clinical study involving 178 cancer patients at the Mayo Clinic and 3 major cancer centers found that no one was cured, stabilized or relieved of cancer-related symptoms. See Manner cocktail, Tijuana, Unproven methods of cancer management

The use of laetrile arises from a modernization of the 'Trophoblastic theory of cancer' espoused by the Scottish zoologist and embryologist, James Beard (1857-1924); laetrile has no proven effect in cancer treatment, and is alleged to have been associated with a number of cancer-related deaths Note: The agent was named by its discover, ET Krebs, as it is levo-rotatory (left-handed) and amygdalin is chemically a mande-

**laetrile**

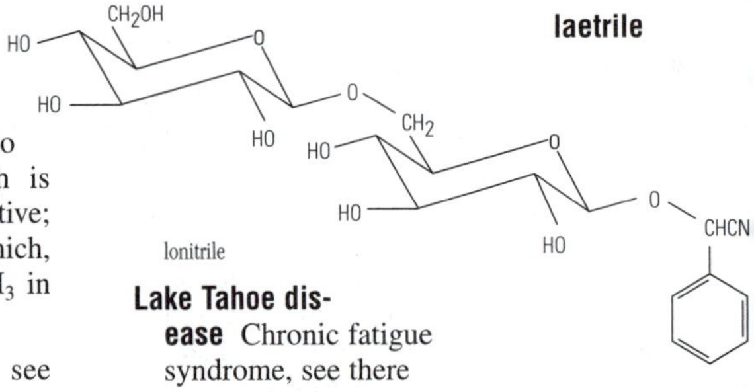

CH2OH HO O HO O CH2 HO HO O HO O CHCN HO

lonitrile

**Lake Tahoe disease** Chronic fatigue syndrome, see there

***lama yoga*** A form of yoga that is believed to promote health by means of union with a higher power. See Yoga

**Lamaze technique** ALTERNATIVE OBSTETRICS A program of instruction which orients first-time and, less commonly, 'experienced' mothers towards an uncomplicated vaginal delivery, with participation of the father or 'significant other'; the technique teaches the mother how to breathe and relax during parturition, which reduces the anxiety associated with childbirth, and often the amount of anesthesia required to deliver a baby. See Alternative gynecology, Doula, Midwife, Natural childbirth

***lan hua*** *Bletilla striata*, see there

**Lane system** Lane system of multilayer bioenergy analysis and nutrition FRINGE MEDICINE A permutation of applied kinesiology developed by an American massage therapist, based on an eclectic system that includes advanced dowsing, aura and *chi* balancing, and vitamin and mineral supplements; according to the Lane construct, there are more than 100 bioenergy energy layers of the human body, which can be subjected to three-dimensional *chi* analysis. See Applied kinesiology

**lapacho** Pau d'arco, see there *Tebebuia impetiginosa*

***Lapacho colorado*** Pau d'arco, see there

***Lapacho morado*** Pau d'arco, see there

**lapachol** Lapachone ALTERNATIVE ONCOLOGY A quinone from the Brazilian tree, pau d'arco (*Tebebuia impetiginosa*), which may be effective against leukemia and other cancers. See Pau d'arco, Unproven methods for cancer management

**lapachone** Lapachol, see there

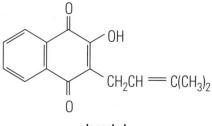

O
OH
$CH_2CH = C(CH_3)_2$
O

**lapachol**

**lappa** Burdock, see there, *Arctium lappa*

**larch moss** Usnea, see there, *Usnea* species

**large intestine meridian** Arm sunlight yang meridian ACUPUNCTURE A meridian that begins at the tip of the index finger, extends up the arm, neck and face, ending at the corner of the mouth or eye; stimulation of acupoints along the large intestine meridian are used to treat conditions affecting the head and neck, ears and oral cavity. See Acupuncture, Traditional Chinese medicine, Twelve meridians

**latherwort** Soapwort, see there, *Saponaria officinalis*

**laughter therapy** Healing humor NATURAL PSYCHOTHERAPY The use of humor to cope with major life traumas of stress, personal loss, and disappointment PHYSIOLOGY Laughter evokes endorphin release, decreases blood pressure, increases oxygenation of blood, and immunoglobulin A production

Note: Recognizing the health benefits to patients with dread diseases, some hospitals have begun social service programs that bring humor to the wards, in the form of clowns or carts with comedy videotapes (*Castleman, 1996*)

***Lavandula angustifolia*** Popularly known as lavender, see there

***Lavandula officinalis*** Popularly known as lavender, see there

**lavender** *Lavandula officinalis, L angustifolia* HERBAL MEDICINE A perennial herb that contains coumarins (eg coumarin and umbelliferone), flavonoids, tannins, triterpenoids, and volatile oils; lavender is believed to be antibacterial, carminative and sedative, and has been used topically as a mouthwash and for burns, eczema, fungal infections, and open wounds; lavender is used internally for colds, coughs, depression, flatulence, gastrointestinal discomfort, headaches, insomnia, nausea, nervous tension, neuralgias, and rheumatic pain. See Herbal medicine, Lavender oil

**lavender** *Lavandula angustifolia*

**lavender oil** AROMATHERAPY An oil distilled or extracted from lavender that contains borneole, camphor, cineole, limonene, pinene, terpinenol, and others; lavender oil is applied topically for cuts, bruises, and insect bites, or used in aromatherapy, by adding it to a bath to relieve stress TOXICITY Lavender oil should not be used internally. See Aromatherapy, Essential oil FRINGE MEDICINE-FLOWER ESSENCE THERAPY A floral essence believed to cause relaxation. See Flower essence therapy. See Lavender

**law of cures** HOMEOPATHY A guiding principle of homeopathy, delineated by Constantine Hering, which states, the '*...cure proceeds from above downward, from within outward, from the most important organs to the least important organs, and in the reverse order of appearance of symptoms*.' (*Gottschalk Olsen, 1989*); as an example, the primary symptom may shift from a stomach ache to a skin rash, which indicates the evolution towards a cure; often in the course of a homeopathic treatment, the patient may suffer a 'healing crisis'. See Healing crisis, Homeopathy, Potentization, Remedy

**law of inifitesimal dose** Law of infinitesimals, law of minimum dose, law of potentization HOMEOPATHY A guiding principle of homeopathy that the lower the concentration of a homeopathic remedy, the more potent is its action; the law is regarded as the essence of homeopathy, as the goal is to cure a disease without exacerbating the symptoms. See Homeopathy, Potentization, Remedy

**law of infinitesimals** Law of infinitesimal dose, see there

**law of minimum dose** Law of infinitesimal dose, see there

**law of potentization** Law of infinitesimal dose, see there

**law of similars** *Similia similibus curantur*, like cures like HOMEOPATHY A guiding principle of homeopathy, that any substance that causes a morbid process will, when diluted–a process known as potentization, serve to treat that same condition. See Homeopathic remedy, Homeopathy, Law of infinitesimal dose, Potentization

**laxative** Purgative HERBAL MEDICINE An herb used to purge the bowels; laxatives include cascara (*Cascara sagrada*), castor oil plant (*Ricinus communis*), flax seed (*Linum usitatissimum*), licorice root (*Glycyrrhiza glabra*), olive oil (*Olea europaea*), psyllium (*Plantago psyllium*), rhubarb (*Rheum pal-matum*), and senna (*Cassia acutifolia*) (*Trattler, 1985*). See Bulk-forming laxative, Herbal medicine, Stimulant laxative, Stool softener

***Laya yoga*** A form of yoga that entails activation of *kundalini*, balancing of *chakras*, and purification practices (*kriyas*). See Yoga

**the laying on of hands** Contact healing PARANORMAL PHENOMENA A type of psychic therapy sanctioned by many religions, in which a cleric, acting as a divine intermediary, touches a member of the 'flock' in order to pass on divine healing powers. See Faith healing, Prayer for the sick, Therapuetic touch; Cf Absent healing

**the laying on of stones** FRINGE MEDICINE An ancient form of crystal therapy, in which practitioners place certain crystals and gemstones on various parts of the body of someone who is sick, with the intent of balancing their energy flow. See Crystal therapy

**Lazarus complex** Near-death experience, see there

**LDL-cholesterol** Bad cholesterol Cholesterol that is transported in the body by low-density lipoprotein which, when elevated, is a major risk factor for atherosclerosis. See HDL/LDL ratio; Cf HDL-cholesterol

**leafy green** Leafy vegetable, see there

**leafy green vegetable** Leafy vegetable, see there

**leafy vegetable** Leafy green, leafy green vegetable CLINICAL NUTRITION A type of vegetable that may grow in tight or loose heads, or as individual leafs on a stem, or atop root vegetables (eg turnips or beets); leafy vegetables include cabbage, collards, cabbage, kale, radicchio, spinach, and watercress; leafy vegetables are low in calories, and rich in carotenoids, vitamin C, fiber, folic acid, and water, and supply varying amounts of iron and calcium; Cf Fruit vegetable

***Learea tridentata*** Popularly known as chaparral, see there

**leavening agent** FOOD INDUSTRY A substance in yeast and baking powder that causes baked products to rise. See Food additive

**lecithin** Phosphatidylcholine ALTERNATIVE NUTRITION A phospholipid extracted from soybeans, which is believed to 1. Improve memory—based on lecithin's choline, which is incorporated into acetylcholine, a neurotransmitter, and 2. Improve the lipid profile, by increasing HDL ('good') cholesterol and decreasing LDL ('bad') cholesterol

Despite the lack of evidence either confirming or refuting lecithin's efficacy for the above indications, lecithin is widely sold in health food emporia, either as a powder or liquid concentrate

***Ledebouriella seseloides*** *Siler divaricatum, fang feng* CHINESE MEDICINE A perennial plant, the root of which is analgesic, antipyretic, antitussive, and expectorant; it is used for headaches, pain, and poor vision. See Chinese herbal medicine

***Ledum*** *Ledum palustre*, marsh tea, wild rosemary HOMEOPATHY A homeopathic first-aid remedy used for acute trauma in the form of animal and insect bites, stings, bruises, contusions, and eye injuries; *Ledum* is also used for rheumatic and gouty pain. See Homeopathy

**leg absolute yin meridian** Liver meridian, see there

**leg greater yang meridian** Bladder meridian, see there

**leg greater yin meridian** Spleen meridian, see there

**leg lesser yang meridian** Gallbladder meridian, see there

**leg lesser yin meridian** Kidney meridian, see there

**leg sunlight yang meridian** Stomach meridian, see there

**legume** CLINICAL NUTRITION Any of a number of edible seeds enclosed in pods, which includes soy beans, lima beans, peas, lentils, and others; legumes are a rich source of proteins, complex carbohydrates, dietary fiber, B vitamins, and minerals (calcium, iron, magnesium, potassium, and zinc). See Beans, Diet

**leiki** Reiki, see there

**LELFD** HERBAL MEDICINE A proprietary polysaccharide extracted from the cultured broth of the oriental mushroom, maitake (*Grifola frondosa*), which is reported to have antitumor activity against soft tissue tumors (sarcomas) and and cancers (*Moss, 1992*). See Chinese herbal medicine, Maitake

**lemon** *Citrus limon* CLINICAL NUTRITION A vitamin C-rich citrus fruit HERBAL MEDICINE A citrus fruit, the leaves of which are thought to be mildly sedative and antibacterial. See Herbal medicine, Lemon oil; Cf Lemon balm

**lemon balm** *Melissa officinalis*, balm, bee balm, melissa, sweet balm FRINGE MEDICINE-FLOWER ESSENCE THERAPY A floral essence believed to be antidepressive, and brighten moods. See Flower essence therapy HERBAL MEDICINE 1. A perennial herb, the oil of which contains citral, citronellal, eugenol acetate, flavonoids, geraniol, polyphenols, tannin, and triterpenoids; lemon balm is antihistaminic, antipyretic, antispasmodic, antiviral, carminative, sedative, and tonic; it has been used to treat allergies, colds, depression, eczema, flu, headaches, insomnia, menstrual disorders, vomiting. See Herbal medicine 2. An extract of lemon (*Citrus limon*) that has been used topically to treat herpes simplex-induced cold sores

**lemon cleansing** Lemonade diet, see there

**lemon cocktail** NATUROPATHY A mixture of fresh lemon juice, warm water and cayenne pepper, which is alleged to loosen mucus, stimulate upper respiratory mucosa, and stimulate the circulation in patients with upper respiratory tract infections. See Naturopathy

**lemon juice diet** Lemonade diet, see there

**lemon juice fast** Lemonade diet, see there

**lemonade diet** Lemon cleansing, lemon juice diet, lemon juice fast, master cleanser (diet) FRINGE NUTRITION An 'elimination' fast in which the person ingests only lemon juice, sweeteners, cayenne pepper, and water, but no solid foods for periods of 10 days or more; the diet is believed by some to be of use in treating asthma, atherosclerosis, flu, gastric ulcers, skin conditions, and many other acute and chronic conditions (*Raso, 1994*). See Fasting

**lemongrass** *Cymbopogon palustre* HERBAL MEDICINE A tropical plant that contains myrcene, which is analgesic; lemongrass is used internally for diarrhea, fever, flu, headache, stomachache, and other types of pain; it is used topically for acne, athlete's foot, and circulatory defects. See Herbal medicine

**lentinan** An immune enhancing extract from the oriental mushroom, shiitake (*Lentinan edodes*) AIDS Lentinan was believed to have anti-HIV activity. See AIDS fraud; Cf AIDS therapy

ALTERNATIVE ONCOLOGY Lentinan is reported to have antitumor activity against breast and stomach cancer*. See Chinese herbal medicine, Shiitake; Unproven methods for cancer management

*It is approved in Japan for treating stomach cancer (*Moss, 1992*)

**leontopodium** Lady's mantle, see there, *Alchemilla vulgaris*

***Leontodon taraxacum*** Dandelion, see there, *Taraxacum officinale*

***Leonurus cardiaca*** Popularly known as motherwort, see there

***Leonurus sibericus*** Siberian motherwort, *yi mu tsao, yi mu cao* CHINESE MEDICINE An annual plant, the seeds of which are diuretic, hemostatic, and cardiotonic, and used to treat menstrual disorders, postpartum bleeding, female infertility, and breast swelling. See Chinese herbal medicine

**leopard's bane** Arnica, see there, *Arnica montana*

***Lepandra virginica*** Culver's root, see there, *Veronicastrum virginicum*

**LePore technique** A permutation of applied kinesiology developed by Donald LePore (*Raso, 1994*). See Applied kinesiology

**LeShan therapy** An approach to increasing survival in patients with malignancy based on the research of Lawrence LeShan, PhD, a pioneer in the psychotherapeutic treatment of cancer; according to LeShan, the greatest survival in cancer patients is seen in those who function at all levels of human existence–the physical, the psychological, and the spiritual (*Lerner, 1994*). See Unproven methods for cancer management

**leukocytotoxic testing** Cytotoxic testing, see there

**levamisole** Tetramisole ALTERNATIVE ONCOLOGY An agent that was introduced as a broad-spectrum anthelmintic, which stimulates the immune system by enhancing hypersensitivity reactions; it has been used in combination with the chemotherapeutic agent, 5-FU (fluorouracil), to increase survival in advanced colorectal and other cancers (*Moss, 1992*). See Unproven methods for cancer management

***Levisticum officinale*** Popularly known as lovage, see there

***li tsao*** *Eclipta prostrata*, see there

***lian qiao*** Weeping golden bell, see there, *Forsythia suspensa*

**'liberal' chiropractic** Mixed chiropractic, see there

**Lic.Ac.** Licensed Acupuncturist

**Licensed Massage Therapist** Bodywork trainer A person with 500 hours of education in massage techniques, certified by the National Certification Board for Therapeutic Massage and Bodywork. See Massage therapy

**licorice** A preparation from the root of the perennial European legume, *Glycyrrhiza glabra*, which contains asparagine, betaine, chalcones, choline, coumarins, flavonoids, glycyrrhizin, gums, isoflavonoids, saponins, and sugars; licorice has a particularly high content of glycyrrhizic acid (glucuronic acid + glycyrrhetinic acid) which is structurally similar to corticosteroids, explaining its anti-inflammatory, antipyretic, and antirheumatic effects; it is also antitussive, demulcent, expectorant, laxative, sedative, and reduces blood sugar and cholesterol CHINESE MEDICINE Licorice, *gan cao, gan tsao*, honey grass, *mi tsao*, sweetwood Licorice is one of the major herbs used in traditional Chinese medicine; the species used include *G glabra*, *G echinata*, and *G uralensis*; it is used topically for abscesses and wounds, and internally for abdominal pain and spasms, alcohol and other intoxications, asthma, cholecystitis, cirrhosis, colds, coughing and wheezing, constipation, diabetes, fever, gastritis, gastric ulcers, heartburn, hepatitis, respiratory congestion, and sore throat. See Chinese herbal medicine HERBAL MEDICINE In Western herbal medicine, the species used is *G glabra*; licorice is used topically for eczema, herpes, and skin infections, and internally for arthritis, colic, constipation, cough, gastric ulcers, and hepatitis, as well as the other indications for licorice as used in Chinese herbal medicine TOXICITY Excess licorice consumption causes a syndrome of mineralocorticoid excess,* with sodium and water retention, hypertension hypokalemia and myopathy with myoglobulinuria; it should not be used in those with glaucoma, hypertension, renal disease, or in pregnancy. See Botanical toxicity, Herbal medicine

*Acting not by molecular mimicry, as had been previously postulated, but rather by suppressing both 11 β-hydroxysteroid dehydrogenase and

the renin-angiotensin-aldosterone axis (*N Engl J Med 1991; 325:1223*)

***lien chiao*** Weeping golden bell, see there, *Forsythia suspensa*

***lien dze*** Lotus, see there, *Nelumbium nucifera*

***lien zi*** Lotus, see there, *Nelumbium nucifera*

**life energy analysis** Behavioral kinesiology, see there

**life energy technique** Behavioral kinesiology, see there

**life extension** A general term for any maneuver intended to increase longevity and vitality; life-extending activities include an appropriate diet, smoking cessation, drinking alcohol only in moderation, exercise, and general reduction in stress; some life-extending modalities, eg Gerovital and Live Cell Therapy, are of uncertain efficacy, and not available in the US. See Diet, Gerovital, Life-extending diet, Live Cell therapy, Melatonin

**life-extending diet** Anti-aging diet NUTRITION A general term for any dietary maneuvers that are believed to slow the aging process; central to a life-extending diet is caloric restriction–up to 40% less than is currently considered normal, while maintaining adequate levels of essential macronutrients–ie protein, fats, and carbohydrates, and micronutrients–ie minerals and vitamins; such low-calorie diets reduce blood pressure, glucose and insulin resistance, cholesterol, and triglycerides. See Diet, Melatonin, Zone-favorable diet; Cf Life-extension formula

**life-extension formula** FRINGE NUTRITION An antioxidant supplementation formula recommended by D Pearson and S Shaw, which includes vitamins A, C, and E, and most of the B vitamins, in daily doses up to 600 times the recommended daily allowance, as well as certain amino acids including arginine, cysteine, ornithine, and tryptophan, and sometimes phenylalanine and tyrosine, which are also recommended in doses far in excess of that required to treat any form of nutritional deficiency; Cf Life-extending diet

**life force** AYURVEDIC MEDICINE *Prana*, see there CHINESE MEDICINE *Chi*, see there CHIROPRACTIC Vitalism, see there ENTERTAINMENT INDUSTRY The Force HOMEOPATHY Vital force RUSSIAN PSYCHICS Bioplasmic energy

**life force balancing** FRINGE MEDICINE A 'healing science' developed by Barbara West that combines the laying on of hands, psychological 'adjustments,' and psychic healing, which is believed to result in intercellular regeneration (*Raso, 1994*)

**life impressions bodywork** FRINGE MEDICINE A 'healing science' developed by Ravi Dosnée Donald Van Howten, which borrows from ayurvedic medicine, craniosacral therapy, fluid balancing, hakomi psychotherapy, and soft tissue restructuring; according to Howten, humans are spirits embodied in physical form, and the body has an 'historic imprint' of experiences stored in the tissue, which can be 'updated' by releasing bound beliefs and energy (*Raso, 1994*)

**Life Science** Natural Hygiene, see there

**lifestyle** PUBLIC HEALTH The constellation of habitual activities that are unique to an individual, and lend consistency to his activities, behavior, manners of coping, motivation, and thought processes, and which define the way in which he lives; lifestyle activities include diet, level of physical activity, substance abuse, and social and personal interactions

Note: It is increasingly recognized that alteration of lifestyle activities has a significant impact on the risk of suffering from a wide range of diseases including cardiovascular disease, malignancy, and hypertension (*JAMA 1994; 272:842nib*)

**lifestyle diet** NUTRITION A generic term for a dietary regimen that reflects personal preferences, rather than well-founded scientific principle, including various vegetarian diets and diets claimed to treat cancer, enhance virility, or others (*N Engl J Med 1993; 328:282ed*). See Fast food, Junk food, Natural food, Nibbling diet, Snacking

**Light Beam Generator™** FRINGE MEDICINE A device that emits photons of light as a means of restoring cells to their normal energy state; the Generator is believed to penetrate deep tissues, and heal internal organs; its efficacy is attributed to stimulation of the lymphatic system and the opening of sealed and calcified blood vessels; the Light Beam Generator™ is used in conjunction with a dietary regimen for allergies, arthritis, bruises, bursitis, edema, premenstrual syndrome, sore throat, tendonitis, drainage of varicose veins and elimination of toxins, treatment of sports injuries; the Light Beam Generator may be used in conjunction with the Sound Probe™ (*Alternative Medicine, Future Med Pub, 1994*). See Energy medicine, Sound Probe™

**light therapy** The use of certain segments (in particular, the visible range) of the electromagnetic spectrum for therapy; light therapy is thought to act via the hypothalamus, which releases neurotransmitters and releasing factors, after receiving impulses from retina; light therapies include full spectrum light (eg sunlight), bright light (2 to 10,000 lux), ultraviolet light, colored light, hemoirradiation FRINGE MEDICINE There is little data to support claims that light therapy is effective in treating AIDS, arthalgias, asthma, bulimia, cancer, dysmenorrhea, headaches, high cholesterol, infections, insomnia, or other conditions. See Alternative medicine; Cf Light work MAINSTREAM MEDICINE Light therapy is thought to be effective in treating seasonal affective disorder (SAD), and shiftwork-related sleep disorders. See Bright light therapy 2. Bright light therapy, see there 3. Heliotherapy, see there

**light work** ALTERNATIVE MEDICINE Actualism, see there PARANORMAL PHENOMENA A permutation of aura balancing that involves use of spiritual guides. See Alternative medicine; Cf Bright light therapy, Light therapy

***Ligisticum levisticum*** Lovage, see there, *Levisticum officinale*

**lignan** ALTERNATIVE PHARMACOLOGY Any of a number of substances found in flaxseed oil that are thought to have anticarcinogenic properties

**lignum vitae** *Guaiacum officinale*, tree of life, guaiac HERBAL MEDICINE A Caribbean tree rich in saponins, resin, guaiaretic and guaiacolic acids; it is anti-inflammatory, laxative, and stimulatory, and has been used to treat arthritis and gout; its products have been commercialized in mainstream medicine in the guaiac test for occult bleeding of the large intestine, which is often a sign of colorectal cancer. See Herbal medicine

***Ligusticum* and *Angelica* pillow** CHINESE MEDICINE A type of herbal pillow used in traditional Chinese medicine, that contains *Ligusticum wallichii* and *Angelica anomala*; the pillow is recommended as an analgesic for severe headaches, postnasal drip, and watery eyes, and is believed to enhance cardiovascular circulation. See Chinese herbal medicine, Herbal pillow

***Ligusticum wallaichii*** *Chuan hsiung, chuan xiong, Conioselinium univittatum*, fragrant fruit, *hsiang guo* CHINESE MEDICINE An annual herb, the root of which is analgesic, sedative, tonic, and cardiotonic; it is used to treat anemia, blood toxicity, hypertension, menstrual disorders, and postpartum pain. See Chinese herbal medicine

***Ligustrum japonicum*** Popularly known as Japanese wax privet, see there

***Ligustrum lucidum*** Japanese wax privet, see there, *Ligustrum japonicum*

***Lilium*** *Lilium tigrinum*, tiger lily HOMEOPATHY A minor homeopathic remedy used for female reproductive disorders, as well as for anginal pain. See Homeopathy

***Lilium humboldtii*** FRINGE MEDICINE-FLOWER ESSENCE THERAPY Tiger lily, see there, *Lilium tigrinum* HOMEOPATHY *Lilium*, see there

**lily convalle** Lily-of-the-valley, see there, *Convallaria majalis*

**lily-of-the-valley** *Convallaria majalis*, ladder-to-heaven, lily convalle, May lily, Our Lady's tears HERBAL MEDICINE A perennial herb (see illustration, page 220) that contains aspargine, cardioactive glycosides (eg convalloside, and gluconvalloside), flavonoids, and saponins; like foxglove, lily-of-the-valley was formerly used as a cardiotonic, as well as diuretic and vasodilatory TOXICITY Arrhythmias, confusion, hypertension, and possibly death due to circulatory collapse; it is listed as poisonous by the FDA. See Botanical toxicity, Herbal medicine, Poisonous plants

**limonene** Cajeputene, cinene ONCOLOGY A monoterpene (see figure, right) which is a component of essential oils in plants, and found in the oil of citrus fruits, which is thought to have anticarcinogenic properties; it is currently in clinical trials as a therapy for advanced cancer (*JAMA 1996; 275:1349oa*). See Monoterpene; Cf Unproven methods for cancer management

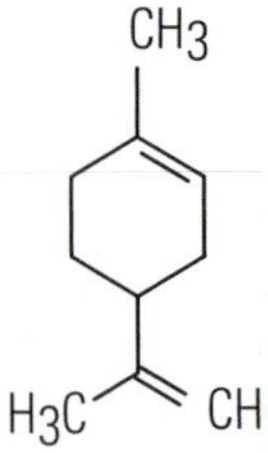

$CH_3$ $H_3C$ $CH_2$

**Lincoln therapy** see Staphage lysate

**lily-of-the-valley** *Convallaria majalis*

**ling** Heather, see there, *Calluna vulgaris*

***ling zhi*** Reishi, see there, *Ganoderma lucidum*

**liniment** HERBAL MEDICINE A vehicle for delivering herbal medicine, in which an extract of the herb is infused in an oil, alcohol or other volatile base, often heated and applied topically. See Herbal medicine

**linoleic acid** An essential 18-carbon fatty acid with 2 unsaturated bonds, derived from plant oils. See Essential fatty acids

**linolenic acid** An essential 18-carbon fatty acid with 3 unsaturated bonds, derived from either plants (α-linolenic acid) or animals (γ-linolenic acid). See Essential fatty acids

**linseed** Flax, see there, *Linum usitatissimum*

**linseed oil** Flaxseed oil FRINGE ONCOLOGY A vegetable oil obtained from flax or linseed (*Linum usitatissimum*) that is rich in essential fatty acids (arachidonic acid, linoleic acid, and linolenic acid), which has been used in ayurvedic medicine as a stool and skin softener, and for enemas; it is said to prevent the development of cancers, in particular of the small intestine (*Moss, 1992*). See Flax, Unproven methods for cancer management

**lint bells** Flax, see there, *Linum usitatissimum*

***Linum usitatissimum*** Popularly known as flax, see there

**lion's ear** Motherwort, see there, *Leonurus cardiaca*

**lion's foot** Lady's mantle, see there, *Alchemilla vulgaris*

**lions's teeth** Dandelion, see there, *Taraxacum officinale*

**lion's tail** Motherwort, see there, *Leonurus cardiaca*

**lion's tart** Motherwort, see there, *Leonurus cardiaca*

**lion's tooth** Dandelion, see there, *Taraxacum officinale*

**lipid therapy** Revici therapy, see there

**lipochrome** A general term for any natural, fat-soluble pigment including lipofuscin, carotenes, and lycopenes

**lipotropic factor** Choline, see there

**liquid diet** CLINICAL NUTRITION A very low-calorie diet that fulfills the daily fluid requirements and places little functional demand on the gastrointestinal tract; liquid diets have little fiber and do not provide adequate protein or calories (circa 1000 kcal/day). See Bland diet, Diet; Cf Liquid-protein diet

**liquid-protein diet** FRINGE NUTRITION A very low-calorie weight-reduction diet that provided 800 calories, and protein in the form of hydrolyzed collagen; the quality of protein in collagen is so poor that it is immediately converted to glucose, resulting in a negative nitrogen balance; liquid-protein diets have been linked to sudden cardiac death, and have been abandoned by mainstream medical practitioners. See Diet, Starvation diet; Cf Liquid diet

***Liriope spicata*** Popularly known as creeping lilyturf, see there

**lithium** A rare alkali element (atomic number 3; atomic weight 6.94) FRINGE ONCOLOGY Lithium is believed by Hans Nieper, MD, a German physician, to have anticarcinogenic properties; data supporting this hypothesis is weak (*Moss, 1992*). See High pH therapy, Unproven methods for cancer management

***Lithospermum officinale*** Popularly known as gromwell, see there

***liu wei di huang*** Six Flavor Tea, see there

**live food** ALTERNATIVE MEDICINE A term coined by Dr Virginia Wuerthe-Caspe Livingston, for any fresh fruit or vegetable that has retained its natural enzymes, which is a component of the Livingston therapy; the term live food is also used in the context of polarity therapy. See Liver flush, Livingston treatment, Polarity therapy *Progenitor cryptocides*, Unproven method for cancer management

**live cell analysis** FRINGE MEDICINE A pseudo-diagnostic technique in which a drop of blood is evaluated by darkfield microscopy; the red and white blood cells stand out against a dark background which, when shown to an unsophisticated individual, is an impressive 'finding' that can be used to convince a patient that he is suffering from virtually any condition that the 'practitioner' wishes to 'treat'. See Health fraud, Quackery

**live cell therapy** Cell therapy, cellular therapy, fresh cell therapy, fresh cell method of cellular therapy ALTERNATIVE MEDICINE A technique developed in the 1930s by a Swiss surgeon and endocrinologist, Paul Niehans, that consists of the implantation of healthy cells, in particular from the fetus of various animals, into humans with the intent of stimulating the immune system, extending life, and general revitalization; live cell therapy is claimed to increase libido, skin health, treat arthritis, improve children with Down's syndrome, and to repair cell damage TOXICITY Fatigue, fever, injection site pain, arthritis, and severe allergic reactions. See Gerovital, Life-extending diet, Life extension

Note: Live cell therapy has been used on such notables as Conrad Adenauer, Charlie Chaplin, Charles De Gaulle, Dwight Eisenhower, Bob Hope, and Elizabeth Taylor

**live yeast-cell derivative** Preparation H An extract of live yeast that has been used to treat hemorrhoids

**liver filtrate factor** Pantothenic acid, see there

**liver flush** A concoction of lemon juice, olive oil, garlic, and ginger root, consumed in conjunction with live foods, eg fruits and vegetables; the liver flush is used in polarity therapy as part of a two-week cleansing program intended to eliminate bodily toxins. See Polarity therapy

**liver *Lactobacillus casei* factor** Folic acid, see there

**liver lily** Blue flag, see there, *Iris versicolor*

**liver meridian** Leg absolute yin meridian ACUPUNCTURE A meridian that runs from the inside of the foot at the great toe, and extends to the anterior chest; stimulation of acupoints along the liver meridian are used to treat conditions affecting the hepatobiliary, reproductive and urinary systems. See Acupuncture, Twelve meridians

**living foods lifestyle diet** Hippocrates diet, see there

**Livingston therapy** Livingston treatment, Livingston-Wheeler therapy FRINGE ONCOLOGY An unproven method for cancer management (*CA 1990; 40:252*) developed in 1971 by an American physician, Dr Virginia Wuerthe-Caspe Livingston, which is based on the belief that cancer is caused by a microbe she called *Progenitor cryptocides*, that develops in a background of a compromised immune system, and facilitated by the consumption of non-living foods, which lack critical enzymes, and poultry which she believed to be contaminated by *P cryptocides*; central to Livingston therapy is the production of 'vaccines' against *P cryptocides*, using blood and urine from each patient; the full therapy consists of a diet of raw vegetables, and fresh fruits, vitamin and mineral supplements, and a plant hormone abscisic acid; some states require that the vaccine be generic and not produced from an individual's body fluids–presumably for safety reasons. See Live foods, *Progenitor cryptocides*, Unproven method of cancer management

**Livingston treatment** Livingston therapy, see there

**Livingston vaccine** Livingston therapy, see there

**Livingston-Wheeler therapy** Livingston therapy, see there

**LLD factor** Vitamin $B_{12}$, see there

**L.M.T. Licensed Massage Therapist**

**lobelia** *Lobelia inflata*, asthma weed, bladderpod, gagroot, Indian tobacco, pukeweed, vomitroot, wild tobacco HERBAL MEDICINE An annual or biennial that contains alkaloids (isolobinine, lobelanidine, lobeline, lobinaline), chelidonic acid, fats, and resin; it is emetic and expectorant, and was formerly used to treat asthma, respiratory complaints (asthma, bronchitis, pneumonia, and smoking-related morbidity), and for tobacco withdrawal syndrome (due to the content of lobeline); it is used topically for bites, poison ivy, and fungal infections TOXICITY Nausea, vomiting, coma, and possibly death by paralysis; the FDA has declared it poisonous. See Botanical toxicity, Herbal medicine, Poisonous plants

**lobelia** *Lobelia inflata*

**lobeline** The active component in *Lobelia inflata*, which usually evokes emesis (vomiting), which, when absorbed in excess, may have toxic effects. See Lobelia

**local bath** NATUROPATHY A method in which a part of the body, eg an extremity or part thereof, is immersed in hot water, cold water, or alternating between hot and cold water; one recommended regimen is the use of 3 minutes of hot water followed by 1 minute of cold water, repeated 3 times (*Trattler, 1985*). See Hydrotherapy

**logos center** ALTERNATIVE PSYCHIATRY One of four 'ontological being centers' defined in the construct of organismic psychotherapy, a permutation of Reichian therapy; the logos center is located in the upper back and facilitates understanding. See Ontological being centers, Organismic psychotherapy

**Lombardy erysipelas** Pellagra, see there

***Lomi ha'a mauli ola*** Hawaiian temple bodywork, see there

**lomilomi massage** An ancient Hawaiian energy-based massage technique used by the kahunas (the Hawaiian native healers), in which deep muscles are rigorously manipulated to interrupt muscle spasms, coupled with cross-fiber friction and strokes directed away from the heart; a specially carved stick may be used for massaging deeper tissues; lomilomi massage is believed to be useful for chronic stress and tension, musculoskeletal disease, and for increasing local blood and lymphatic circulation. See Massage therapy

Note: Lomilomi has increased in popularity through the efforts of Aunty Margaret Machado, who teaches the method at her school in Hawaii

**longevity vine** Shiny asparagus, see there, *Asparagus lucidus*

***Lonicera japonica*** Popularly known as Japanese honeysuckle, see there

**Loo Point** FRINGE ACUPUNCTURE A new acupuncture point discovered by Cyrus Loo, MD, located near the ankle; he believes that needling the Loo Point can cure a wide range of conditions, including hepatitis, herpes, macular degeneration of the retina, pain, psoriasis and other skin conditions, as well as cancer; his claimed 95% success rate in treating such patients has not been subjected to peer review

**loosening the prenatal pattern** See Polarity therapy

**LooyenWork®** A proprietary '...*synthesis of painless deep tissue body therapy, movement re-education, and environmental evaluation.*' (*M Kastner, H Burroughs, Alternative Healing, Halcyon Publishing, La Mesa, California, 1993*), developed in 1973 by a Dutch-Australian therapist, T Loowen, based in California; LoowenWork® borrows from Aston patterning, Feldenkreis method, Postural Integration, Rolfing®, and other techniques; central to LoowenWork® is the identification of the 'core issue,' a constellation of traumatic experiences unique to the individual; the patient and practitioner form a partnership for healing, but given the individual nature of each person's problems, there is no standard LoowenWork® treatment; the therapy consists of deep penetrating massages that release connnective tissue adhesions, lengthen contracted muscles, and separate tendons; LoowenWork™ certification requires 500 hours of training. See Bodywork, Core issue, Massage therapy

**Lorenzo's oil** A concoction of oleic and erucic acids alleged to be useful in treating adrenoleukodystrophy or adrenomyeloneuropathy SIDE EFFECTS Thrombocytopenia, neutropenia, and lymphocytopenia with immunosuppression and recurrent infections (*N Engl J Med 1993; 329:745c, 1994; 330o:577*). See Alternative medicine

Note: The popular term for this mixture of fatty acids originates from a popular movie, *Lorenzo's Oil*. The film left the impression with many laypersons that the oil was therapeutically useful.

**loss of boundaries** Meditation sickness, see there

**lotus** *Nelumbium nucifera, lien dze, lien zi* CHINESE MEDICINE A perennial aquatic herb, which is highly regarded in traditional Chinese medicine as it is a symbol of purity and spirituality; lotus seeds are hemostatic, nutritive, tonic to the nerves, and regarded as an aphrodisiac; lotus seeds are used to treat diarrhea, fatigue, heart failure, insomnia, menstrual disorders, pancreatitis, sexual dysfunction, and sexually-transmitted disease. See Chinese herbal medicine

**Louisiana hot sauce** A condiment of various formulas (horseradish, lemon, tabasco, ketchup, etc) that has been shown to inhibit the in vivo growth of *Vibrio vulnificus* and other vibrio that often contaminate raw shellfish, eg oysters

Note: The component responsible for the protective effect has not been identified (*New York Times 19 Oct 1993; C3*)

**Lourdes** PARANORMAL PHENOMENA A healing shrine located in southern France, where in 1858, Bernadette Soubirous, received 18 visions of the Virgin Mary at Massabielle Rock; the healing powers of the hidden spring at Lourdes became widely known; Lourdes became, and has remained, the Catholic Church's major healing shrine; approximately 100 medically confirmed miracles have occurred at Lourdes. See Healing shrine, Miracle, Saint Bernadette

**lovage** *Levisticum officinale, Ligisticum levisticum*, love parsley, sea parsley, smallage HERBAL MEDICINE A perennial herb that contains coumarins (eg bergapten, coumarin, umbelliferone), isovaleric acid, and volatile oils (eg phthalides, pinene, terpinene, terpineol), and resin; it is carminative, diaphoretic, and sedative; it has been used as a digestive tonic and to relieve menstrual cramping. See Herbal medicine

**love-lies-bleeding** *Amaranthus caudatus* FRINGE MEDICINE-FLOWER ESSENCE THERAPY A floral essence that is believed to help a person transcend personal pain and suffering, and empathize with others. See Flower essence therapy

**love parsley** Lovage, see there, *Levisticum officinale*

**LoveStone** Chan su, see there

**low-fat diet** A diet low in fats, particularly saturated fats; low-fat diet foods include fruits, vegetables, beans, pastas, grains, breads, nuts, chicken and turkey (white meat is lower in fat), seafood (cod, flounder, lobster, scallops, and shrimp are low in fat), and minimal red meat, except for venison; low-fat diets have a positive effect on arthritis, cancer, cardiovascular disease, diabetes, hypertension, obesity, and strokes. See Diet, Low-fat snack; Cf Animal fat, High-fat diet

**low-fat snack food** A noshable comestible low in fats, particularly saturated fats, which is regarded as providing a viable alternative to 'junk food' type snacks, which are high in salt, sugar, and/or fats; low-fat snacks include fruits, salads, vegetables, air-popped popcorn, and packaged products labeled as 'fat-free,' 'nonfat,' and 'low-fat'. See Low-fat diet

**low-impact aerobics** Any type of aerobic exercise that promotes physical fitness, but does not stress musculoskeletal tissues and joints; low-impact aerobic exercises include walking, swimming, and bicycling. See Exercise, Low-impact sport; Cf High-impact aerobics

**low-impact sport** SPORTS MEDICINE A generic term for any physical activity or sport in which there is minimal wear and trauma to weight-bearing joints, in particular of the foot, knee, and hip; LISs include bicycling, bowling golfing, sailing, swimming, scuba diving; participation is LISs is encouraged in those who wish to engage in physical activities after hip and knee arthroplasty (*Mayo Clin Proc 1995; 70:342*); Cf High-impact sport, Moderate impact sport, No-impact sport

**low motion disease** A general term for any condition associated with a sedentary lifestyle and inadequate physical activity and exercise, including arthritis, osteoporosis, and general weakness. See Egoscue method, Motion starvation

**low-protein diet** CLINICAL NUTRITION A diet that provides less than 1.5 g/kg/day of protein during growth periods, or less in adults; adults with renal failure should receive no less than 0.6 g/kg/day of protein, to avoid a negative nitrogen balance; low-protein diets are indicated for patients with renal failure, as reduction of protein reduces anorexia, nausea, vomiting, and if begun early, may slow the progression of the disease. See Diet

**low-quality protein** CLINICAL NUTRITION A protein, usually of plant origin that lacks one or more essential amino acid, eg corn,* which is low in lysine, or beans,* which are low in tryptophan; the poor quality of protein is a major impediment to progress in developing nations. See Liquid diet; Cf Succotash

*Succotash, a gruel containing corn and lima beans solves this protein quality dilemma; low quality protein in the form of the 'liquid diet' had transient currency in the US 'weight loss industry' and resulted in a number of deaths prior to its abandonment

**lower burner** see Triple burner

***lu hui*** *Aloe vera*, see there

**lucern** Alfalfa, see there, *Medicago sativa*

**lunar caustic** *Argenticum nitricum*, see there

***lung dan cao*** Gentiana, see there, *Gentiana scabra* (other species may be used)

***lung dan tsao*** Gentiana, see there, *Gentiana scabra* (other species may be used)

**lung meridian** Arm greater yin meridian ACUPUNCTURE A meridian that begins at the second rib, extends to the shoulder and passes back down the arm, ending at the tip of the thumb; stimulation of acupoints along the lung meridian are used to treat pulmonary and related conditions. See Acupuncture, Twelve meridians

**lungwort** *Pulmonaria officinalis*; beggar's basket, Jerusalem cowslip, Jerusalem sage, maple lungwort HERBAL MEDICINE A flowering plant that contains allantoin, mineral salts, mucilage, saponin, silica, and tannin; it is astringent and expectorant, and has been used to treat lung disease, hemorrhoids, and wounds. See Herbal medicine

**lupulin** HERBAL MEDICINE A term for the two major components of hops: bitter resin (which contains humulone, lupulone, and valeronic acid) and volatile oils (which contains beta-caryophyllene, farnescene, humulene, and myrcene). See Herbal medicine, Hops

**lutein** CLINICAL NUTRITION A carotenoid abundant in broccoli, greens (collard, turnip), spinach, and linked to a decreased risk of lung cancer (*New York Times 21 Feb 1995; C1*). See Carotenoid. Lycopene

***Lycium chinense*** Chinese wolfberry, see there

**lycopene** CLINICAL NUTRITION A carotenoid abundant in tomatoes, as well as watermelon, pink grapefruit, and red peppers, which is a potent antioxidant; lycopene consumption is linked to a decreased risk of pancreatic, prostate, bladder, colon, and cervical cancers and cancer cell growth in vitro; some data suggest that lycopene may be the most cardioprotective of the carotenoids (*New York Times 21 Feb 1995; C1*) see Carotenoid

$CH_3$ $CH_3$ $CH_3$ $CH_3$ $H_3C$ $CH_3$ $CH_3$ $CH_3$ $CH_3$ $CH_3$

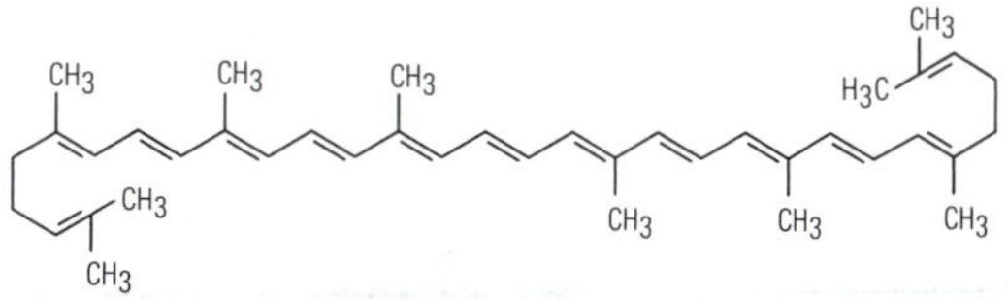

**lycopene**

***Lycopodium*** *Lycopodium clavatum*, club moss, running pine, staghorn moss, wolfsclaw HOMEOPATHY A homeopathic remedy formulated from *L clavatum* that is used for gastrointestinal complaints including bloating, constipation, nausea, and vomiting, as well as arthritic pain, back pain, bedwetting, chronic fatigue syndrome, colds, cystitis, flu-related fatigue, hair loss, hemorrhoids, kidney stones, nasal congestion, nervous headaches, prostatitis, psoriasis, and increased libido with decreased performance. See *Lycopodium* type, Homeopathy

***Lycopodium* type** HOMEOPATHY The *Lycopodium* constitutional type individuals are apprehensive, have a low self-esteem, and may be sexually-promiscuous; they prefer hot foods and drinks, vegetables, pastries, and shellfish WORSE Tight clothing, fasting, early morning, early evening FEARS Failure, death, darkness WEAKEST BODY REGION Digestive and urogenital tracts, brain, lungs, skin, and right side of body. See Constitutional type, *Lycopodium*, Homeopathy

***Lycosa tarantula*** *Tarantula*, see there

**lymphatic constitution** FRINGE MEDICINE-IRIDOLOGY A blue iris which, according to the construct of iridology, belongs to a person who produces excess lymph, and who is prone to lymphadenitis, allergies, lung and skin disease, and vaginal discharge. See Iridology, Iris constitution

**lymphatic drain** Organ drain, see there

**lymphatic drainage** ALTERNATIVE MEDICINE Manual lymphatic drainage, see there CONVENTIONAL MEDICINE A general term referring to the passive drainage of lymph to the nearest unobstructed lymphatic vessels

**lymphatic pump** Thoracic pump, rib raising OSTEOPATHY An osteopathic technique in which the rib cage and thoracic spine are manipulated with the intent of improving the lymphatic circulation of the chest; in this technique, the osteopath pushes upward on the anterior chest wall, or pulls the posterior chest wall in an anterosuperior direction. See Manual lymphatic drainage massage, Massage therapy, Osteopathy

**LZ-8** HERBAL MEDICINE A water-soluble immunomodulatory protein extracted from the oriental mushroom, reishi (*Ganoderma lucidum*), which is reported to have antitumor activity (*Moss, 1992*). See Chinese herbal medicine, Reishi, Unproven methods for cancer management

**M4** Amrit Nectar™, see Maharishi Amrit Kalash™

**M5** Ambrosia™, see Maharishi Amrit Kalash™

***ma huang*** Ephedra, see there, *Ephedra sinica*

[a]***ma ji*** Tiger thistle, see there, *Cirsium japonicum*

**MacDougall diet** ALTERNATIVE NUTRITION A diet, formulated by Roger McDougall, a victim of multiple sclerosis, which he credited with freeing him of symptoms; the diet is devoid of gluten (no wheat, oats, barley and rye), fatty meats (eg bacon, pork, water fowl), alcohol, and soft drinks; refined sugars and saturated fats (butter, cream, rich cheeses) are reduced to a minimum; the diet is supplemented with large doses of vitamins B, C, and E, lecithin, calcium, and magnesium (*Bricklin, 1976, 1983*). See Diet, Ornish regimen, Pritikin diet; Cf McDougall diet

**Bernarr Macfadden** King of Fitness ALTERNATIVE HEALTH A flamboyant American (1890-1944, née Bernard Adolphus McFadden), who founded the physical culture movement and became a cult figure, whose name was synonymous with health; Macfadden built his body with weights and his fortune by publishing his health-promoting theories (*Armstrong, 1991*). See Physical culture

**macrobiotic diet** see Macrobiotics

**macrobiotic shiatsu™** ALTERNATIVE MEDICINE A preventive holistic health care system developed by S Yamamoto (who also developed Barefoot Shiatsu™) as a means of 'balancing' the individual through health-promoting lifestyle changes; the system stresses proper (ie macrobiotic) diet, abundant exercise, especially out-of-doors regardless of the season, proper breathing, and a regulated sex life; in addition to shiatsu, Macrobiotic Shiatsu™ therapists may use moxabustion, tapping, and cupping to treat health problems; certified Macrobiotic Shiatsu™ therapists undergo 350 hours of training. See Cupping, Moxabustion, Shiatsu

**macrobiotics** ALTERNATIVE MEDICINE A dietary and lifestyle philosophy taught by George Ohsawa (1893-1966) and Michio Kushi, and popularized in the 1960s in the US, which is based on an idiosyncratic version of the ancient concept of the yin and yang forces in the universe; the macrobiotics construct assigns a unique 'male' (yang) or 'female' (yin) quality to various foods; Kushi described 13 types of diagnosis: astrological, aura and vibrational, behavioral, conscious and thought, environmental (by analyzing external forces, eg temperature and occupational factors, which may cause disease), meridian, parental and ancestral, pressure point, psychological, pulse, spiritual, visual, and vocal. See Kushi; Cf Zen macrobiotic diet

**macrobiotic diet** ALTERNATIVE NUTRITION A diet consisting of whole grains (eg barley, millet, oats, rice, and wheat, comprising 50% of the dietary intake), vegetables (freshly picked and in season, 20 to 30% of intake), soups (eg vegetables, seaweed, grains, 5-10% of intake), oils, juices, nuts, seeds (eg sunflower), herbs, pulses (beans, lentils, peas, and seaweed, 5-10% of intake) and enough animal foods (eg 'white meat' fish, 5-15% of intake) to prevent malnutrition; foods avoided in the macrobiotics diet are animal fats, canned and frozen foods, coffee, dairy products, eggs, meats, nightshade vegetables (eggplant, peppers, potatoes, and tomatoes), poultry, refined sugars, semi-tropical and tropical fruits, and tea. See Kushi, Macrobiotic Shiatsu™, Raw food diet, Zen macrobiotic diet Cf Unproven methods for cancer management

Note: Macrobiotics proponents may believe that conventional (non-macrobiotic) diets carry an increased risk of cancer, and may believe that any diet that can prevent cancer is also appropriate in its treatment; Kushi himself recognizes that the diet must be used in conjunction with mainstream cancer therapies; macrobiotics received considerable adverse publicity in the 1960s and 1970s when some of its advocates consumed brown rice, to the virtual exclusion of other foods, and suffered malnutrition or death

**macronutrient** CLINICAL NUTRITION A general

term for an essential dietary component—protein, fats, and carbohydrates, which is consumed in large amounts. See Diet; Cf Micronutrient, Non-nutritive dietary component

**mad apple** Jimsonweed, see there, *Datura stramonium*

**mad dog skullcap** Skullcap, see there, *Scutellaria lateriflora*

**mad dogweed** Skullcap, see there, *Scutellaria lateriflora*

**mad honey** Nectar derived from the pollens of certain plants, including rhododendron, western azalea, California rosebay, mountain laurel, and sheep laurel, which contain toxic diterpenes (grayanotoxins); 'mad honey' consumption may evoke severe anginal pain CLINICAL Vertigo, weakness, diaphoresis, nausea, vomiting, profound hypotension, bradyarrhythmia, heart block, and convulsions; all victims recover within 24 hours (*JAMA 1988; 259:1943c*); Cf Bee pollen, Honey, Royal jelly

**madweed** Skullcap, see there, *Scutellaria lateriflora*

**Madagascar periwinkle** *Catharanthus roseus*, *Vinca rosea* HERBAL MEDICINE A subtropical plant that contains two anticancer alkaloids, vinblastine and vincristine; it has been used as an herb to treat stings and bleeding, and as a gargle for sore throat and respiratory complaints. See Herbal medicine

**Madagascar periwinkle** *Catharanthus roseus*

**madderwort** Wormwood, see there, *Artemisia absinthium*

**magic pill syndrome** A colloquial term for any positive response, in particular to placebos containing inert substances, eg lactose. See Placebo

**magical diet** FRINGE NUTRITION A scientifically naive system of classifying foods devised by a writer, Scott Cunningham, which attributes magical energies to various foods, which can provide a vehicle for improving and enhancing one's life *(Raso, 1994)*. See Diet, Magical herbalism

**magical herbalism** FRINGE MEDICINE A system of herbal medicine created by a writer, Scott Cunningham, who defined herbs as magical, and infused with Earth's energy; Cunningham accepts absent healing, amulet healing, and autosuggestion, as valid means for effecting a cure *(Raso, 1994)*; he believes that 'banishing rituals,' eg wart removals, should be performed during a waning moon. See Herbal medicine, Magical diet

**magnesium** An alkaline earth element (atomic number 12; atomic weight 24.3) which is an essential mineral required for bone and tooth formation, nerve conduction, and muscle contraction; it is required by many enzymes involved in carbohydrate, protein, and nucleic acid metabolism; magnesium is present in almonds, apples, dairy products, corn, figs, fresh leafy greens, legumes, nuts, seafood, seeds, soybeans, wheat germ, and whole grains; magnesium may be useful in anxiety, asthma, cardiovascular disease (it is thought to prevent blood clots, raise HDL-cholesterol, lower total and LDL-cholesterol, decrease arrhythmias and blood pressure), depression, fatigue, hyperactivity, and migraines. See Hypermagnesemia, Hypomagnesemia, Minerals; Cf Manganese

**magnetic pass** FRINGE MEDICINE A component of Mesmer's 'occult' hypnosis, in which a person's trance is allegedly deepened by passing the hypnotist's hands in front of the patient's eyes. See Hypnosis, Hypnotherapy, Mesmerism, Silva mind control; Cf Autosuggestion therapy, Mantra, Meditation, Yoga

**magnet therapy** Biomagnetic therapy, biomagnetics, biomagnetism, electro-biomagnetics, magnetic healing, magnetic energy therapy, magnetic therapy, magnetotherapy FRINGE MEDICINE A general term for the therapeutic use of special magnets or magnetic fields, which has had a long tradition with many cultures including the Arabs, Chinese, Egyptians, Greeks, Hebrews, Romans, and subcontinental Indians; therapeutic magnetism is said to stimulate the body's intrinsic healing capacities and has been used for acute (eg fractures and musculoskeletal trauma) and chronic conditions including Alzheimer's disease, cancer, diabetes mellitus, diverticulitis, gastric ulcers, glaucoma, headaches, hypertension, hypotension, menstrual dysfunction, schizophrenia, sinusitis, tension, osteoarthritis, diabetic ulcers, and other conditions; the State of California has banned licensed health practitioners from using magnets as therapeutic tools (*Kastner, Burroughs, 1993*); Cf Magnetic healing

**magnetic energy therapy** 1. Magnet therapy, see there 2. Magnetic healing, see there

**magnetic healing** 1. Magnet therapy, see there 2. A general term for any method that is believed to transfer vital and/or healing energy from a 'healer' to a patient, which is believed to occur in absence of a need for physical contact; Cf Magnet healing 3. Mesmerism, see there

**magnetic microcapsule** Microcapsule EXPERIMENTAL ONCOLOGY A vehicle for delivering chemotherapy, in which a toxic drug (eg mitomycin C) is 'wrapped' in a zinc ferrite shell; the microcapsules are guided to the site of their desired action using an external or intraluminal magnet (*Moss, 1992*); Cf Pulsing magnetic field

**magnetic therapy** 1. Magnet therapy, see there 2. Magnetic healing, see there

**magnetizer** FRINGE MEDICINE A practitioner of animal magnetism. See Magnetic pass

**magnetotherapy** 1. Magnet therapy, see there 2. Magnetic healing, see there

**magnolia** *Magnolia liliflora, M denudata* CHINESE MEDICINE An herb, the buds of which are used for nasal congestion and sinusitis. See Chinese herbal medicine

**Maharishi Amrit Kalash™** Amrit FRINGE MEDICINE An herbal formulation containing Amrit nectar or M4 (composed of herbs, fruit, ghee, and sugar) and Ambrosia or M5 (herbal tablets), which is marketed by Maharashi Ayur-Ved™ Products Intl, Inc, as an antioxidant

**Maharishi Ayur-Ved™** FRINGE MEDICINE A proprietary system that incorporates transcendental meditation into the practice of ayurvedic medicine; Maharashi Ayur-Ved™ is very similar to traditional ayurvedic medicine, in Maharashi Ayur-Ved™, treatment requires analysis of a person's behavior, consciousness, environment, and physiology; it uses herbs, diet, massage and hatha yoga to promote healing; Maharashi Ayur-Ved™ is believed to be effective for anxiety, arthritis, emotional lability, gastrointestinal complaints, headaches, hypertension, insomnia, obesity, and other conditions, as well as for rejuvenation and increasing longevity; Maharashi Ayur-Ved™ training programs are available at the Maharishi International University in Fairfield, Iowa; Cf Ayurvedic medicine

**Maharishi effect** PARANORMAL PHENOMENA The alleged ability of group meditation to alter crime, acts of war, and natural and man-made disasters occurring at a distance (*Butler, 1992*)

**Maharishi Mahesh Yogi** Mahout The founder of the International Meditation Society, an organization that is intimately involved in teaching and promoting transcendental meditation as a means of self-enlightenment; Maharishi Mahesh Yogi's path to enlightenment began in the 1940s under Jagadguru Bhagwan Shankaracharya (Guru Dev), a major religious leader at the time in India, and continued for 13 years. See Maharishi Ayur-Ved™, Transcendental meditation; Cf Ayurvedic medicine The mystic Maharishi Mahesh Yogi is viewed by some as representative of the turbulent 1960s, in which the Beatles, 'hippies', and assorted truth-seekers sought to understand their inner selves through a spiritual guide or guru

**mahikari** PARANORMAL PHENOMENA A spiritual movement and healing method founded in 1959 by a Japanese businessman, Kotama Okada; mahikari (divine light) is similar to the radiance technique, and ascribes to the belief that most mental and physical illness is caused by spirits that were wronged by a person's ancestors; mahikari practitioners wear a divine talisman that is believed to allow them to both produce and focus light energy through the palms of the hand, in absence of physical contact

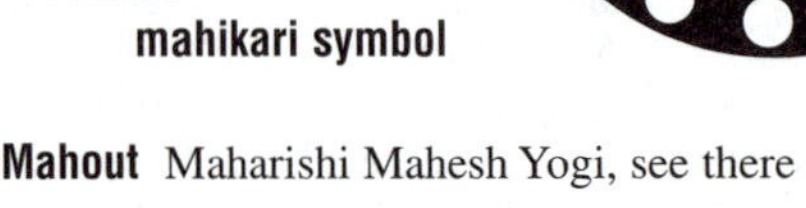

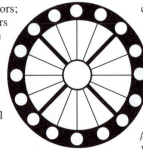

**mahikari symbol**

**Mahout** Maharishi Mahesh Yogi, see there

**maidism** Pellagra, see there

**Maillard reaction** NUTRITION A non-enzymatic heat-activated chemical reaction between sugars (especially ribose) and amino acids, that occurs in foods as they form glycosylamines and Amadori compounds; the Maillard reaction is responsible for 'browning' of baked or cooked foods, eg bread crusts and barbecued steak, which are mutagenic by the Ames assay; it is possible that the age-related changes in collagen are partially mediated through the Maillard reaction; it has been suggested a similar, if not identical, reaction is involved in certain neurodegenerative diseases, eg Alzheimer's, Creutzfeldt-Jakob, and Parkinson's diseases (*Nature Medicine 1995; 1:189*). See Browning reaction; Cf Rancidity

**mainstream medicine** Allopathic medicine, allopathy, conventional medicine, modern medicine, orthodox medicine, traditional medicine, Western medicine CLINICAL MEDICINE A general term for the approach to health care most commonly practiced in developed nations, which is based on scientific data for the validity of the diagnosis and the efficacy of its treatment; mainstream medicine assumes that all physiologic and pathological phenomena can be explained in concrete terms; the scientific tools used in mainstream medicine include use of nonhuman model systems, blinded studies, and statistical analysis, which seek to verify the reproducibility of therapeutic results; Cf Alternative medicine

**maitake** Dancing mushroom HERBAL MEDICINE A rare mushroom (*Grifola frondoa*) that decreases blood pressure and enhances the immune system, by increasing NK (natural killer) cell activity, increasing release of interleukin-1, and stimulating cytotoxic T cells; it appears to have a wide range of effects on cancer including the inhibition of growth of experimental tumors in mice (*Moss, 1992*). SeeGF-1, Lentinan, PSK, Unproven methods for cancer management

**MAK-4** AYURVEDIC MEDICINE A proprietary (Maharishi Amrit Kalash) *chyanwanprash* (metabolic tonic) that contains aloewood, butterfly pea, cardamom, catkins, cinnamon, cyperus, ghee, honey, Indian gallnut, Indian gooseberry, licorice, nutgrass, pennywort, raw sugar, shoeflower, turmeric, and white sandlewood; MAK-4 is thought to be a potent antioxidant, and inhibit the formation of neoplasms. See Ayurvedic medicine, *Pranayama*, Unproven methods for cancer management

**MAK-5** AYURVEDIC MEDICINE A proprietary (Maharishi Amrit Kalash) *chyanwanprash* (metabolic tonic), which contains black musale, butterfly pea, elephant creeper, *Gymnema aurentiacum*, *Sphaerantus indicus*, *Vanda spatulatum*; MAK-5 is regarded as an antioxidant that inhibits tumor formation. See Ayurvedic medicine, *Pranayama*, Unproven methods for cancer management

**making faces** see Unmasking

**makko-ho** A Japanese system of stretching based on traditional Chinese medicine, which is believed to strengthen internal organs

**mal de la rossa** Pellagra, see there

**mal rosso** Pellagra, see there

***mala*** AYURVEDIC MEDICINE Any of the waste products—sweat, urine, and feces, which may be studied as part of an ayurvedic diagnostic workup. See Ayurvedic medicine, *Pranayama*

**male bonding** PSYCHOLOGY The formation of a close relationship between men, which is usually nonsexual in nature; Cf Bonding

**male obesity** Upper body obesity, see there

**malnutrition** A general term for any number of nutritional defects including decreased proteins, minerals, vitamins, or calories

▶ **MALNUTRITION, CAUSES OF**

- **EXOGENOUS DEFECTS** Poverty, alcohol, mental disorders (eg severe depression), infection (eg tuberculosis), malignancy, or may be iatrogenic and occur in a hospital environment, when a patient is receiving all nutrients IV

- **ENDOGENOUS DEFECTS** Metabolic defects (congenital or acquired), malabsorption

LABORATORY Decreased folic acid, iron, magnesium, protein, vitamin $B_{12}$. See Kwashiorkor, Marasmus

***man tien hsing*** Gutu kola, see there, *Hydrocotyle asiatica*

***mana*** Biomagentism PARANORMAL PHENOMENA A term for the paraphysical force that is believed by inhabitants of Oceania and the Hawaiian Islands to exist in the universe; tribal witch doctors are chosen based on their ability to tap into *mana* from heaven, which they may demonstrate, by either exhibiting psychokinetic skill-levitating objects, or making them appear or disappear, or by displaying a second sight or clairvoyance that tells them when and where game animals are plentiful, or how to treat a person's illness. See Psychic healing

***manang*** PARANORMAL PHENOMENA A native healer or shaman in the aboriginal cultures of Borneo. See Healer, Shamanism

**Mandarin orange peel** Tangerine peel, see there, *Citrus reticulata*

**mandela** PARANORMAL PHENOMENA A symbolic design that is usually created from dyed sand, but also from painted wood which symbolizes the wisdom from a deity, and helps a person in the Buddhist construct tap into the healing powers of the mind through meditation. See Sand painting

**Mandjuchaka** Indian madder, see there, *Rubia cordifolia*

**mandrake** HERBAL MEDICINE 1. Mayapple, see there, *Podophyllum peltatum* 2. Mandrake, *Mandragora officinale* A Mediterranean perennial of the nightshade family, which contains alkaloids including hyoscyamine, mandragorin, and podophyllin; it was formerly used as an anesthetic and sedative. See Herbal medicine

**manganese** An essential trace metal (atomic number 25; atomic weight 54.9) required by certain enzymes, eg arginase and cholinesterase, which is ingested in the diet with coffee, tea, egg yolks, whole grains, leafy greens, nuts, and seeds. See Minerals; Cf Magnesium

**manifestation** Manifesting, see there

**manifesting** Manifestation, conscious manifestation Any of a number of wish-fulfillment techniques which involve visualization and positive thinking. See Affirmation, Imagery and visualization

**manipulation and restructuring technique** BODYWORK A general term for any alternative healing art intended to correct structural or positional problems, or disorders of balance, by intervening in the relationship between body parts; these methods focus on muscles and joints, and on the alignment of bones and include the Alexander technique, Bonnie Prudden myotherapy, chiropractic, neuromuscular massage, osteopathy, Rolfing®, and others discussed elsewhere in this work

**Manner cocktail** FRINGE ONCOLOGY A 'cocktail' (containing Laetrile, dimethylsulfoxide–DMSO, vitamins A and C) formulated by Harold W Manner, and administered daily as unproven method for cancer management. See Contreras method, DMSO, Laetrile, Tijuana, Unproven methods for cancer management

**Matthew Mannings** PARANORMAL PHENOMENA A British psychic hand healer, who believed himself capable of treating allergies, arthritis, back pain, cancer, multiple sclerosis,

**mandrake** *Mandragora officinale*

and other conditions; '...*Manning represents what can be regarded as the modern school of healing. He lays particular emphasis on the need for patients to explore self-help.*' (*Inglis, West, 1983*). See Hand healing, Psychic healing; Cf Cayce

**mantra** PARANORMAL PHENOMENA A word or phrase used in yoga, meditation, and in autosuggestive therapy, which is intended to maintain the mind in a state of spontaneous immobilization; in yoga, the droning *ommmm* might be used; in autosuggestive therapy, Coué used the phrase '*every day, in every way, I am getting better and better*'; other devices that may be used in meditation to help focus the mind are objects (eg a candle flame), or sensations (eg slow breathing). See Autosuggestion therapy, Meditation, Yoga

***mantra* yoga** *Nada* yoga A sensual form of yoga that seeks the pathway to a higher power through mind control and by focusing on vibrations and radiations, using sounds (bells, drums and music), which are believed to affect the endocrine system. See Toning, Yoga

**manual lymphatic drainage** Lymphatic drainage, manual lymphatic drainage massage ALTERNATIVE MEDICINE A type of (contemporary Western) massage developed in France in the 1930s by a Danish physical therapist, Dr E Vodder; manual lymphatic drainage consists of various manipulations intended to stimulate the lymphatic drainage of various organs and tissues and eliminate bacteria, toxins, viruses, wastes, and excess water, and address blocks in lymphatic circulation, which may cause congestion and peripheral edema; four basic techniques are used, including stationary circles, pumping, rotation, and scooping, followed by stroking the tissues toward the sites of normal lymphatic drainage; manual lymphatic drainage has been used for various conditions, including acne, arthritis, burns, edema, inflammation, and sinusitis. See Massage; Traditional European massage; Cf Ayurvedic massage, Deep tissue massage, Neuromuscular massage, Swedish/Esalen massage, Sports massage; Cf Lymphatic drainage

**manual organ stimulation technique** BODYWORK A type of bodywork developed by an American chiropractor, George DeLalio, which is based on the belief that energy imbalances in a particular organ can be detected through reflex points in the skin; according to MOST (manual organ stimulation technique) proponents, the afflicted organs can be reharmonized through manipulation. See Bodywork

**manzanita** *Arctostaphylos viscida* FRINGE MEDICINE-FLOWER ESSENCE THERAPY A floral essence that is believed to help integrate the spiritual self with the physical world. See Flower essence therapy

**MAP-30** FRINGE PHARMACOLOGY A protein derived from bitter melon, an Asian plant, which is administered as an extract in tea, capsules, or in retention enemas; MAP-30 has been claimed to 'purify' blood, prevent infections, and has been anecdotally reported to have antiretroviral activity (*Am Med News 21 Nov 1994 p13*); Cf AIDS fraud, Unproven methods for cancer management

**maple lungwort** Lungwort, see there, *Pulmonaria officinalis*

**marbling** FOOD INDUSTRY Increased intramuscular fat in carcass meat from cattle, which increases the tenderness of beef ('select' beef has 4% fat; 'choice' beef has 5% fat)

Note: Ultrasonography may eventually replace the 'eyeball' technique traditionally used by meat inspectors for evaluating fat content (*Science News 1994; 145:7*)

**mare's tail** Horsetail, see there, *Equisetum arvense*

**margarine disease** A condition of historic interest that was characterized by erythema multiforme-like lesions linked to the use of an emulsifier in oleomargarine, which was described in Germany and the Netherlands

**Marian thistle** Milk thistle, see there, *Silybum marianum*

**MariEL** A healing system developed by Reiki master, Ethel Lombardi, that is believed to be faster and more powerful than standard Reiki; the method is believed to provide a transformation healing energy that acts on the cellular level and helps a person discover and release emotional and physical traumas. See Reiki

**marigold** 1. Calendula, see there, *Calendula officinalis* 2. Marigold, *Tagetes patula* HERBAL MEDICINE A bushy annual native to Central America that is rich in esters, phenols and volatile oils, which is analgesic, antiseptic and a stimulant. See Herbal medicine

**marigold** Marigold, *Tagetes patula*

**marijuana** *Cannabis sativa*, bhang, ganja, grass, hashish, hemp, Mary Jane, pot, reefer, weed HERBAL MEDICINE Marijuana has a long history of use as an herb, is listed in ancient pharmacopeias of China, and has been used for pain, insomnia, and various nervous complaints; it has been subjected to more recent scrutiny by the mainstream medical community as a therapy for appetite stimulation, asthma, glaucoma, seizures, and for nausea from chemotherapy (*JAMA 1997; 277:867*). See Herbal medicine, THC

**marijuana** *Cannabis sativa*

**mariposa lily** *Calochortus leichtlinii* FRINGE MEDICINE-FLOWER ESSENCE THERAPY A floral essence that is said to omote maternal consciousness and mother-child bonding, and heal the inner child. See Flower essence therapy, Inner child therapy

**marjoram** *Origanum marjorana*, common marjoram, wild marjoram HERBAL MEDICINE A perennial herb that is carminative, and possibly diuretic. See Herbal medicine

***marma*** AYURVEDIC MEDICINE Any of 107 pressure (energy) points stimulated in *abhyanga* (ayurvedic massage); *marmas* are analogous to those used in acupressure and acupunture. See *Abhyanga*, Ayurvedic medicine, *Rasayana* Cf *Charak Samhita, Sushrita Samhita*

***marma* therapy** Ayurvedic massage, see there

**marriage bonus** PSYCHOLOGY A colloquial term for the health and longevity benefits that are linked to being married; the 'bonus' is attributed to better diet, fewer bad habits, lower risk-taking, improved medical care, and companionship in married individuals (*Castleman, 1996*). See Companionship, Extended family, Most significant other, Nuclear family; Cf Social isolation

**marrubium** Horehound, see there, *Marrubium vulgare*

***Marrubium vulgare*** Popularly known as horehound, see there

**Maruyama vaccine** ALTERNATIVE ONCOLOGY An immune stimulant derived from the supernatant from a culture of tuberculosis (Aoyama B strain of *Mycobacterium tuberculosis*), which is administered as one of two different vaccines, Z-100 and the concentrated form SSM; it has believed to ameliorate the adverse effects of radiotherapy in cancer patients *(Moss, 1992)*. See Unproven methods for cancer management

Note: An estimated 50,000 Japanese receive the vaccine each year, although it is not approved by the Japanese Ministry of Health

**marybud** Calendula, see there, *Calendula officinalis*

**marsh tea** HOMEOPATHY *Ledum*, see there, *Ledum palustre*

**marsh trefoil** Bogbean, see there, *Menyanthes trifoliata*

**marsh mallow** *Althea officinalis*, althea, mortification root, sweetweed HERBAL MEDICINE A perennial herb that contains asparagin, mucilage, and tannins, which is a mild diuretic and expectorant; it is used internally for inflammation and upper gastrointestinal ulcers, and to soothe the respiratory and urinary tracts, eg for urinary tract infections and kidney stones; it is used topically for abscesses, burns, cuts, ulcers, varicose veins, and for intraoral infections and inflammation. See Herbal medicine

**martial arts** *Budo* Any of a number of physical and mental disciplines based on self-defense, that are intended to achieve self-awareness and expression in movement; many of the oriental martial arts evolved from ritual dances, or from exercises intended to relieve tension caused by hours of meditation; martial arts have been divided into an 'outer family' of arts (*wai chia*), and an 'inner family' of arts (*nei chai*); the outer family is rooted in Buddhism from outside of China, stresses muscle strength, conditioning, and endurance, and includes judo, karate, and kung fu; the inner family of martial arts is rooted in Taoist traditions from China, stresses economy of strength and enhancement of vital energy, and includes t'ai chi ch'uan, *hsing i ch'uan*–a series of rising and falling movements, and *pa kua chang*–a series of spiraling exercises; it is believed that training in the martial arts curbs violence and increases a person's control over his mind and body; the health benefits of martial arts training include improved balance, coordination, and stamina; it is believed to improve circulation and strengthen the intestines, alleviate rheumatic complaints, and enhance neuromuscular function; the best known martial arts include aikido, *arnis* (from the Philippines), *chi kung* (*qi gong*), copeira (from Brazil), jujitsu, judo, karate, kendo, kung fu, tae kwan do, t'ai chi ch'uan. See Aikido, Chi kung (qi gong), T'ai chi ch'uan

**marvel** Horehound, see there, *Marrubium vulgare*

**Mary Jane** Marijuana, see there, *Cannabis sativa*

**massage** Massage therapy, see there

**massage parlor** A colloquial term for an establishment that provides manipulation and massage services, often by 'sex workers,' who may also provide sexual services; the term is unfortunate, as it detracts from legitimate massage therapy; Cf Massage therapy

**massage therapy** *Anmo, nuad bo-rarn, toogi-toogi* ALTERNATIVE MEDICINE A general term for any of a number of techniques in which the body surface and musculoskeletal system are stroked, kneaded, pounded, and yanked; massage has a time-honored history in medicine that stretches back to ancient Greece; Hippocrates was an early advocate of massages, and recommended them on a daily basis to ease pain and prevent stiffness; massages are intended to relax the body (and mind), mobilize stiff joints, improve the flow of blood and lymph, reduce muscular tension and chronic pain, reduce swelling and inflammation, and reduce tension and stress; massages are believed to integrate the mind and body, improve skin tone, increase the flow of energy through the nervous system and wastes through the gastrointestinal tract, and enhance all the body systems

▶ **GENERAL MASSAGE TECHNIQUES**

- **BRUSHING** A superficial technique in which the skin surface is slowly, lightly, and rhythmically stroked, often as a 'finishing touch' after a full massage
- **CONNECTIVE TISSUE TECHNIQUE** Massage that specifically manipulates the connective tissues, eg fascia, ligaments, and tendons of the musculoskeletal system, with the aim of enhancing circulation, and by extension, healing, eg of sport injuries
- **CUPPING** A technique in which the cupped hands are gently clapped on the skin surface with the intent of increasing local blood circulation
- **EFFLEURAGE** A 'soft tissue' technique, which entails long slow, rhythmic, light and heavy pressure strokes from the fingertips, thumbs, knuckles, and palms, which may be combined with aromatherapy
- **FRICTION** A 'soft tissue' technique, which entails the use of small circular pressure strokes from the fingertips, thumb pads, and palms, with the aim of freeing stiff joints, and enhancing the circulation in tendons and ligaments
- **NEUROMUSCULAR TECHNIQUE** A technique in which pressure is applied to neural reflex and trigger points in a fashion analogous to that of shiatsu and acupressure, with the aim of enhancing neuromuscular interaction
- **PERCUSSION** Tapotement A 'soft tissue' technique, which entails painless chopping and drumming motions delivered by the sides of the hands to 'fleshy' regions, eg the back, buttocks, and thighs
- **PÉTRISSAGE** A 'soft tissue' technique, in which fascicles of muscles are kneaded, lifted, grasped, squeezed, rolled, and released, with the intent of stimulating locoregional circulation, and relaxing contracted muscles
- **STRETCHING** The pulling of body region or extremity away from its most anatomically neutral position, which may be active (with) or passive (without) the active assistance from the patient
- **TAPOTEMENT** Percussion, see above
- **TWISTING** A technique in which the skin and soft tissues are wrung between the hands in opposite directions, which

serves to stimulate the nerves and promote vasodilation

- **VIBRATION** A 'soft tissue' technique, which entails delivery of vibrating movement, often using an electrical device

There are more than 80 individual styles of massage therapy

▶ **MASSAGE THERAPY, TYPES OF**

- **TRADITIONAL EUROPEAN MASSAGE**
- **CONTEMPORARY WESTERN MASSAGE**
- **STRUCTURAL (FUNCTIONAL/MOVEMENT) INTEGRATION**
- **ORIENTAL METHODS**
- **ENERGETIC METHODS**
- **OTHERS**

Anecdotal reports suggest that massage therapy may be useful for anxiety, arthritis, asthma, bereavement, bruxism, carpal tunnel syndrome, chronic fatigue syndrome, circulatory defects, common cold, cramps, depression, fatigue, fibrositis, fluid retention, foot problems, frozen shoulder, gallstones, gastrointestinal complaints including indigestion, gout, headaches, hyperactivity, insomnia, jet lag, laryngitis, low back pain, measles, menopausal disorders, migraines, pain, neuralgia, mood swings, muscle weakness, neck pain, neurological complaints, palpitations, panic attacks, post-partum depression, pregnancy, premenstrual syndrome, rheumatic disease, schizophrenia, sciatica, shock, sinusitis, sleep disorders, sports injuries–eg tennis elbow, sprains, strains, stress, tension, and other conditions CONTRAINDICATIONS Patients with certain conditions should be evaluated in a formal (mainstream) medical setting before undergoing massage therapy; these conditions include aneurysms, arthritis, bone disease, nonhealing bone fractures, cancer, diabetes mellitus, frostbite, hypertension, muscle disease, musculoskeletal trauma, osteoporosis or brittle bones, pregnancy, renal disease, skin disease, thrombosis, torn ligaments, and varicose veins. See Amma, Applied kinesiology, Applied Physiology, Benjamin system of massage therapy, Bodywork, Children massage, *Chua ka*, Connective tissue massage, Cross-fiber transverse friction massage, Deep compression massage, Deep tissue massage, *Dian xue an mo*, Energetic massage, Esalen massage, Geriatric massage, Hamma, Hand massage, Hellerwork, Infant massage, Ingham method, *Kathakali* massage, *Licensed Massage therapist,* Lomilomi massage, manual lymphatic drainage massage, Naprapathy, Neuromuscular massage, Organ drain, Oriental massage, Parasympathetic massage, Pfrimmer technique, Physical therapy, Proprioceptor neuromuscular facilitation stretching, Rehabilitation massage, Rolfing®, Russian massage, Shiatsu, Sports massage, Structural integration, Subtle touch massage, Swedish massage, Swedish/Esalen massage, Thai massage, Therapeutic touch, Traditional European massage, (contemporary) Western massage; Cf Acupressure, Massage parlor, Reflexology *RESOURCE: American Massage Therapy Association, 820 Davis St, Suite 100, Evanston IL 60201-4444 ☎ 1.708.864.0123*

Note: There is little data in peer-reviewed literature to verify the claims of therapeutic efficacy; massages are invigorating, despite absence of scientific basis for this reaction

**master cleanser** Lemonade diet, see there

**mastic tree** *Boswellia carterii*, *B glabra*, *B thurifera*, kunduru, olibanum, *ru hsiang*, *ru xiang* CHINESE MEDICINE A deciduous tree, the resinous wood of which is analgesic, astringent, stimulates muscle growth, and enhances circulation; it is used to treat abdominal and chest pain, abscesses, menstrual disorders, seizures, and sexual dysfunction. See Chinese herbal medicine

**maté** *Ilex paraguariensis* An evergreen shrub native to South America, that is rich in caffeine, neochlorogenic and chlorogenic acids, and theobromine catechols; maté is a stimulant and tonic, and the leaves are used to make a very hot tea that is habitually ingested in southeastern South America. See Herbal medicine; Cf Coffee, Tea

Note: High volume drinkers are 2.2-fold more likely to have esophagitis, and have a relative risk of 1.47 for esophageal cancer; ingestion of more than 2.5 liters/day is reported to be associated with a relative risk of 12.2 for esophageal cancer (*Cancer Res 1990; 50:426*)

**materia medica** HOMEOPATHY A reference encyclopedia that lists the effects of homeopathic remedies. See Homeopathic symptoms; Cf Repertory

**maternal milk** Breast milk, see there

**matrix point** A type of trigger point that is a primary site of local pain, or referred pain located at a distance, eg in the shoulders or neck muscles, from the primary site of the pain, eg the head. See Bonnie Prudden myotherapy, Trigger point; Cf Satellite point

**maturation factor** Vitamin $B_{12}$, see there

**MaxEPA®** CLINICAL NUTRITION A proprietary fish oil product that is high in omega-3 (n-3) fatty acids which, in experimental animals, is associated with a reduced incidence of transplantable breast tumors. See Eicosapentanoic acid, Fish oil, N-3 fatty acid, Unproven methods for cancer management

**mayapple** *Podophyllum peltatum*, American mandrake, devil's apple, hog apple, Indian apple, mandrake, umbrella plant, wild lemon HERBAL MEDICINE A perennial herb that was once used as an anthelmintic, emetic, purgative, and liver tonic; its marked purgative activity virtually precludes its therapeutic use; a semisynthetic derivative, etoposide, is used to treat certain cancers TOXICITY Dermatitis, diarrhea, nausea, vomiting, severe gastroenteritis, and possibly death; mayapple is regarded by the FDA as 'unsafe'. See Botanical toxicity, Herbal medicine, Poisonous plants

**mayapple** *Podophyllum peltatum*

**May blossom** Hawthorn, see there, *Crataegus monogyna*

**May bush** Hawthorn, see there, *Crataegus monogyna*

**May lily** Lily-of-the-valley, see there, *Convallaria majalis*

**maypop** Passionflower, see there, *Passiflora incarnata*

**mayidism** Pellagra, see there

**Elmer V McCollum** CLINICAL NUTRITION An American biochemist who identified the first vitamin, vitamin A in 1913 at the University of Wisconsin; he identified vitamin D in 1922 at Johns Hopkins University

**McCollough effect** A phenomenon observed by individuals who have worked for a prolonged period with a computer monitor that displays green lettering on a darkened background, who find that white paper acquires a pink hue; the effect is caused by adaption of cortical neurons to specific combinations of color and form; it may last for several weeks and is of no clinical significance. See Video display unit

**McDougall diet** CLINICAL NUTRITION A vegan (strictly vegetarian) diet formulated by Dr John A McDougall, MD, that is low in fats, sugars, and salt, high in fiber and complex carbohydrates, and has virtually no cholesterol; the McDougall diet is based on whole grains, whole grain flours, pasta, legumes, squash, root vegetables, and is supplemented with fresh fruits and vegetables (*Kastner, Burroughs, 1993*). See Diet, Ornish regimen, Pritikin diet; Cf MacDougall diet

**McHerb** HERBAL MEDICINE A colloquial term for a medicinal herb available in capsule form, a convenient vehicle that is widely preferred by American consumers of alternative therapies. See Herbal medicine

The term derives from McDonald's, an American fast food restaurant that has been linked to the concept of instant gratification which for some, is typical of Americans

**Aimee Semple McPherson** PARANORMAL PHENOMENA An American faith healer (1890-1944) who founded the Angelus Temple, an evangelist organization dedicated to preaching the gospel and performing medical miracles (*Armstrong, 1991*). See Faith healing

**meadow anemone** *Pulsatilla*, see there, *Anemone pratensis*

**meadow clover** Red clover, see there, *Trifolium pratense*

**meadow eyebright** Eyebright, see there, *Euphrasia officinali*

**meadow saffron** Autumn crocus, see there, *Colchicum autumnale*

**meadow sage** Sage, see there, *Salvia officinalis*

**meadowsweet** *Filipendula ulmaria*, *Spiraea ulmaria*, bridewort, queen-of-the-meadow HERBAL MEDICINE A perennial herb that contains flavonoids, salicylates (eg gaultherine and salicin), tannin, vitamin C, and volatile oil; it is anti-inflammatory, antiseptic, and diuretic, and has been used for diarrhea, fever, and rheumatic pain. See Herbal medicine

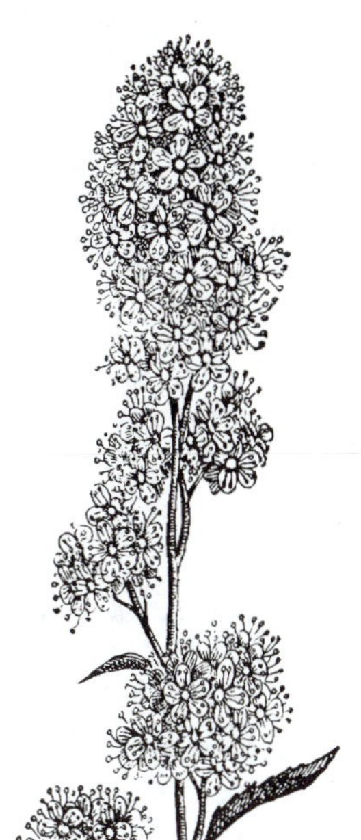

**meadowsweet** *Filipendula ulmaria*

**mealberry** Bearberry, see there, *Arctostaphylos uva-ursi*

**mechanotherapy** A nonspecific term for any method, eg massage, bodywork, or device, used to mechanically stimulate a part, usually on the outside of the human chassis. See Bodywork, Massage therapy

**media malpractice** The misuse of the press or other forms of mass media to slander a person or group, provide an unbalanced viewpoint, or otherwise misinform the public; media malpractice can encompass talk shows that promote quack theories and pseudoscientific doctrines, or publishers that promote books that are popular (ie lucrative), but based on no known scientific principles

***Medicago sativa*** Popularly known as alfalfa, see there

**medical astrology** Astral healing, astrologic medicine, astrological healing, astromedicine PARANORMAL PHENOMENA A system based on the pseudoscientific concept of cosmobiology, which holds that specific mental and physical conditions are in part due to the positions of celestial bodies; medical astrology assumes that a person's personality is 'assigned' at the time of birth–based on the position of the planets, and that the 12 signs of the zodiac rule different parts of the anatomy–males (illustration below) and females (illustration on facing page) differ somewhat in these influences; according to the medical astrology construct, certain positions of celestial bodies in relationship with each other are capable of triggering disease in a susceptible host. See Astrology, Radiesthesia

Medical astrology is peripheral to all forms of health care; its validity is, at best, uncertain, as reflected by the following '*In one study, approximately 150 people who responded to an advertisement from 'Astral Electronics' were given a free 'ultra-personal horoscope' interpretation. More than 90% were happy with the interpretation and said they recognized themselves. The horosocpe was that of mass murderer Dr Marcel Petiot.*' (*Butler, 1992*)

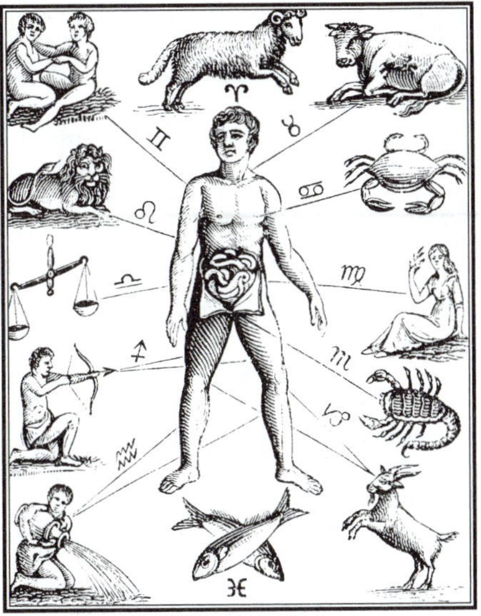

**medical dowsing** Radiesthesia, see there

**medical graphology** Grapho-diagnostics FRINGE MEDICINE A pseudodiagnostic method in which a person's handwriting forms the basis for diagnosing physical and mental disease

**medical massage** Rehabilitation massage, see there

**medical orgonomy** Orgone therapy, see there

**medical palmistry** FRINGE MEDICINE 'The application of palmistry–an offshoot of fortunetelling–to pseudodiagnosis.' (*Raso, 1994*);

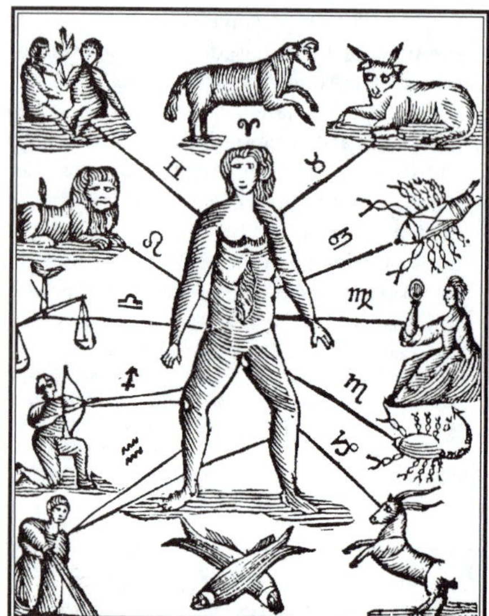

medical palmistry is based on chirognomy–the interpretation of the shape, size, and texture of the various parts of the hands and skin surface, and on chiromancy–the interpretation of lines and other markings on the hands; medical palmistry is believed by its proponents to be useful for evaluating specific organs. See Hand interpretation

**medical *qigong*** *Qigong* therapy, see there

**medical radiesthesia** Radiesthesia, see there

**medical tattooing** ANTHROPOLOGY A practice among some primitive cultures that is regarded as a precursor of acupuncture

Note: The oldest known medical tattooing was on the Ice Man, a 5000-year-old man found mummified in the Tyrolean Alps (*Science 1995; 268:33*)

**medically-oriented chiropractic** CHIROPRACTIC A chiropractic philosophy that diverges from the principles delineated by DD Palmer, the founder of chiropractic; medical orientation refers to the adoption of a mainstream (allopathic) medical perspective for understanding disease, a broadening of the chiropractors' 'scope of practice,' and subspecialization in areas that are not the usual domain of alternative forms of health care, eg obstetrics and surgery. See Chiropractic; Cf Chiropractic malpractice, Mixed chiropractic, Straight chiropractic, Subluxation-based chiropractic

Note: 20% of chiropractics are subluxation-based practitioners

**medicinal charcoal** Activated charcoal, see there

**medicinal dew** Steam decoction, see there

**medicine bundle** ETHNOMEDICINE A collection of objects (eg animal skins, powders, stones, and others) that may be carried by Native Americans; these objects are believed to be the physical homes of the spirits (which may correspond to animals, humans, rocks, trees, and the elements including the wind, sun, and others), upon which a person calls when he is sick. See Rattle, Sand painting, Shamanism, Sweat lodge, Vision quest

**medicine show** QUACKERY An itinerant spectacle that was most commonly used in the American West from the late 1800s until the early 1900s as a vehicle to huckster various patent medicines; traveling medicine shows borrowed elements and performers from circuses, vaudeville, Wild West extravaganzas, and theater troupes who provided the supporting cast to a pitch 'doctor' selling the medicines. (*Armstrong, 1991*) See Frontier prescription, Patent medicine, Pitch doctor Quackery

**medicine wine** Herbal liquor, see there

**Medipatch™ system** FRINGE MEDICINE A proprietary healthcare system that is loosely based on homeopathy; the kits are claimed to treat migraines, carpal tunnel syndrome, and other conditions, and protect a person from low-level electromagentic field radiation; the kits have homeopathic tablets to be taken sublingually, a bracelet with homeopathic remedies, and a digitally-encoded magnetic strip, the latter two of which, when worn on the wrist or ankle, are believed to interface with the 12 acupuncture pulse points, strengthen a person's electromagentic filed, and enhance the production of *chakra* energy. See Electromagnetic field; Cf Homeopathy

**meditation** ALTERNATIVE MEDICINE A general term for a technique in which a person empties his mind of extraneous thought, with the intent of elevating the mind to a different level, and transcend (hence the term transcendental meditation) mundane concerns; physiologic effects of meditation include decreased heart and breathing rates, blood pressure, and activity of the cerebral cortex

▶ **BASIC FORMATS FOR MEDITATION**

- **BODY CONTROL**–through hatha yoga, as a means of uniting the body and mind
- **MIND CONTROL**–through contemplation and visualization, or use of a symbol, object, or mantra to increase one's concentration
- **'LETTING GO' OF THE BODY** Deliberate relaxation of muscles, and regions under voluntary control
- **'LETTING GO' OF THE MIND** Emptying the mind of thoughts to allow others to enter

Anecdotal reports suggest that meditation may be effective for anxiety, asthma, bronchitis, cancer, cardiovascular disease, chest pain, circulatory defects, depression, fear, hypertension, infertility, insomnia, menopausal disorders, muscle tension, pain management, panic attacks, phobias, psoriasis, shock, sleep disorders, stress, tension, wheezing, and other conditions; other benefits attributed to meditation include increased job satisfaction, creativity, and speed in performing tasks, improved academic performance, attention span, and interpersonal relationships SIDE EFFECTS Excess meditation can result in meditation sickness or increased mental plasticity and susceptibility to manipulation by a cult. See Auto-suggestion therapy, Body scan meditation, Bubble of light technique, Mantra, Meditation sickness, Yoga *RESOURCE: Insight Meditation Society, 1230 Pleasant St, Barre MA 01005 ☎ 1.5078.355.4378*

**meditation in motion** See T'ai chi ch'uan

**meditation sickness** A 'toxic' side effect of prolonged meditation which, because it induces profound relaxation, makes a person more aware of painful emotions and memories; such individuals are said to have lost their boundaries and become, in effect, 'bundles of "raw" nerves;' some believe that long-term meditation causes a plethora of mental residua, including anxiety, confusion, hallucinations, headaches, memory loss, paranoia, and others. See Meditation, TM-EX

**Mediterranean diet** A loosely defined diet that differs according to the country, and includes an increased consumption of olive oil, complex carbohydrates, vegetables, and decreased consumption of red meat (*N Engl J Med 1992; 327:52c*). See Diet, Mediterranean diet pyramid; Cf Affluent diet

**Mediterranean diet pyramid** A schematic representation of recommendations* on the amounts of specific food groups that should be consumed daily; in contrast to the US Department of Agriculture's food pyramid, which lumps all high protein foods (meat, poultry, fish, and beans) in one category, the Mediterranean pyramid recommends increased fish and olive oil and decreased red meat consumption, passes beans into the nuts & legumes group, and categorizes wine as optional (*N Y Times 29 March 1995, C1*). See Diet; Cf Exercise pyramid, Food pyramid

*By The WHO, Harvard School of Public Health, and Oldways Preservation and Exchange Trust

**Mediterranean elderberry** Elderberry, see there, *Sambucus nigra*

**medium** Channeler, see there

**mediumship** Channeling, see there

**megavitamin therapy** The administration of excess or 'hyper-doses' of water-soluble vitamins, either physician-guided, usually to treat diseases of the nervous system, or self-prescribed by health-food advocates; water-soluble vitamins include niacin (nicotinic acid) and niacinamide (nicotinamide), $B_6$ (pyridoxine, pyridoxal, pyridoxamine) and vitamin C

▶ **MEGAVITAMINS, ADVERSE EFFECTS**

- **THIAMIN** Central nervous system hyperresponsiveness (convulsions), Parkinson's disease (thiamin antagonizes L-dopa), sensory neuropathy (destruction of dorsal axon roots)
- **NIACIN & NIACINAMIDE** Exacerbation of asthma (histamine release), cardiac disease (arrhythmias), gastrointestinal symptoms, eg nausea, vomiting, diarrhea, anorexia, diabetes mellitus (hyperglycemia), gout (increased uric acid), liver disease (enzyme leakage, hepatocellular injury, portal fibrosis or massive necrosis, cholestatic jaundice), peptic ulcer disease (histamine release and increased acidity), skin disease
- **VITAMIN $B_6$** Paresthesia, headaches, asthenia, irritability
- **VITAMIN C** Increased iron absorption, possibly iron overload, evoking diarrhea, renal calculus formation and possibly inhibiting the bacteriolytic activity of neutrophils, G6PD deficiency (increased red cell lysis), megaloblastic anemia (decreased vitamin $B_{12}$ absorption), nephrolithiasis (oxaluria) (*Diagn Clin Testing 1990; 28:27*)

Some alternative health advocates believe that megavitamin therapy is effective for acne, addiction disorders (eg alcoholism, smoking), chronic fatigue syndrome, depression, neurological disease, panic attacks, premenstrual syndrome, schizophrenia, viral infections, and other conditions. See Decavitamin, Orthomol-ecular medicine,

Vitamin(s)

**melanocyte-inhibiting substance** Melatonin, see there

**melatonin** Melanocyte-inhibiting factor A hormone formed by methylation and acetylation of serotonin,[1] which is produced in a diurnal cycle by the pineal gland,[2] in response to light[3] PHYSIOLOGY Melatonin secretion is intimately linked to the light-dark cycle, peaks ± midnight, and is highest in winter; melatonin secretion decreases with age,[4] it may be markedly increased in patients with hypothalamic or hypogonadotropic hypogonadism, or delayed puberty, and may be decreased in precocious puberty (*N Engl J Med 1992; 327:1356oa*); it helps sleep, stimulates the immune system, may reverse aging phenomena, and be of use in treating depression ALTERNATIVE MEDICINE Melato-nin has acquired currency in the alternative health care community as a self-administered tonic; some believe melatonin can be used to slow the aging clock, extend a person's lifespan, invigorate one's sex life, slow the growth of cancer cells, treat insomnia, prevent heart disease, and revive the immune system (*W Pierpaoli, et al, The Melatonin Miracle, Simon & Schuster, 1995*) ADVERSE EFFECTS Melatonin should not be used in those with leukemia, Hodgkin's disease, or multiple myeloma; it should not be used in pregnancy. See Circadian rhythm, Seasonal affective disorder

[1]L-tryptophan → 5-hydroxytryptophan → serotonin → N-acetyl-serotonin-melatonin)[2]A tissue that is similar to the 'third eye' or photosensory organ of lower vertebrates [3]Its binding sites are concentrated in the suprachiasmatic nucleus of the hypothalamus (directly connected to the eyes and possibly also to the biological clock [4]measuring 1080 pmol/L (250 pg/ml) age 1-3, 520 pmol/L (120 pg/ml) age 8-15, 86 pmol/L (20 pg/ml) age 50-70; daytime levels in all ages is 17-43 pmol/L (4-10 pg/ml) (*N Engl J Med 1992; 327:1378ED*), melatonin profoundly influences the reproductive system in seasonally breeding animals

**melissa** Lemon balm, see there, *Melissa officinalis*

***Melissa officinalis*** Popularly known as lemon balm, see there

**mend bones** Teasel, see there, *Dipsacus sylvestris*

**menstrual extraction** FRINGE OBSTETRICS A type of abortion that consists of the suction extraction of an early (up to 8 weeks of gestation) conceptus, often performed by lay persons EQUIPMENT A sterile syringe, a rubber stopper, a one-way valve, plastic tubing, and jars; there are pros and cons to this unconventional, do-it-yourself procedure; while somewhat similar to an abortion performed by a physician, the procedure is not without danger and women so treated may not seek timely medical intervention when needed; as the data are anecdotal, claims for menstrual extraction's success may be bloated, and the real or potential complications (uterine perforation, ectopic pregnancy, gram-negative sepsis and continued pregnancy) minimized by its advocates. See Alternative gynecology

**mental filtering** PSYCHOLOGY The selective evaluation of a complex situation with both positive and negative elements; positive mental filtering occurs when a person ignores or downplays negative aspects of a situation or criticism; it is typical of manic reaction and indicates a loss of reality sense; negative mental filtering prevents a person from coping with internal conflicts and emotions. See Cognitive therapy, Distorted thinking

**mental gymnastics** Mentastics, see there

**mental imagery** Imagery (and visualization), see there

**mental imaging** see Visualization therapy

**Mentastics** Trager Mentastics, see there

***Mentha piperita*** Popularly known as peppermint, see there

**menthol** PHARMACOGNOSY An aromatic oil first obtained from peppermint (*Mentha piperita*), now primarily produced synthetically; it is used topically for arthritic pain, hemorrhoids, itching, and sore muscles; it is added to cough medicines and throat lozenges TOXICITY Pure menthol oil is toxic–as little as 5.0 mL may be fatal. See Botanical toxicity, Herbal medicine, Poisonous plants; Cf Peppermint, Wintergreen

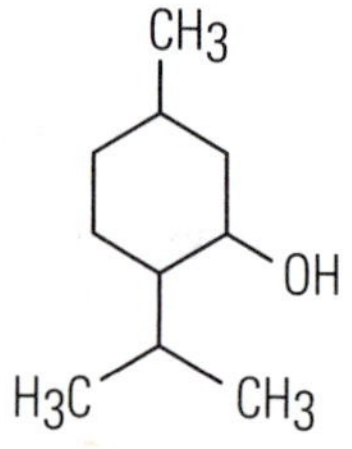

$CH_3$ / OH / $H_3C$ / $CH_3$

**menthol**

***Menyanthes trifoliata*** Popularly known as bogbean, see there

**meridian** CHINESE MEDICINE Any of 12 channels that are believed to extend over the length of the body (see figure, next page),

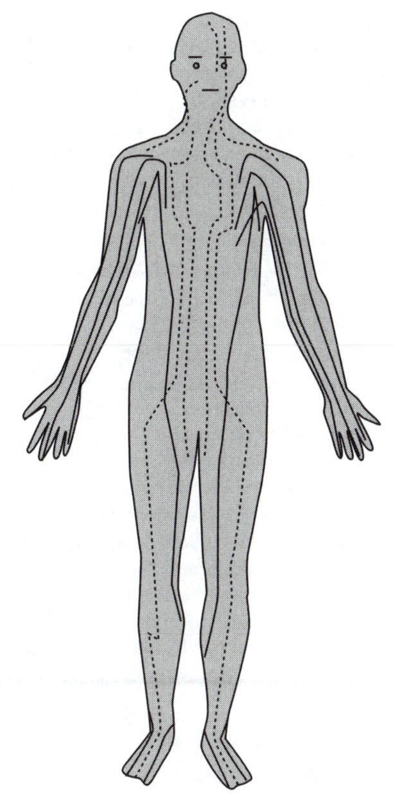

**meridians–general locations**

and believed to carry *chi* (vital energy) through the body; the meridian concept is central to acupuncture and other forms of oriental medicine; mainstream (Western) medicine has been frustrated by its inability to verify the presence of meridians; data from R Melzack et al (*Inglis, West, 1983*) suggest that the 'trigger points' (which, when stimulated, ameliorate pain elsewhere in the body) identified by neurologists may be identical to acupuncture points. See Acupuncture, *Chi*, the Twelve meridians Cf Acupressure, Shiatsu

***Mercurius solubilis*** Mercury HOMEOPATHY A homeopathic remedy formulated from cinnabar, the major mercury ore; *Merc sol* is used for abscesses, burning discharges, chickenpox, conjunctivitis, cough, cystitis, painful diarrhea, fevers with chills and sweating, flu, gingivitis, halitosis, severe headaches, itching, oral thrush, periodontal disease, rheumatic complaints, runny nose, burning sore throat, and toothaches. See *Merc sol* type, Homeopathy

***Merc sol* type** HOMEOPATHY A constitutional type of person who is anxious, restless, shy, and has a low self-esteem; when sick, *Merc sol* types may become mentally torpid; *Merc sol* types prefer cold drinks, bread, and lemons WORSE Night, sweating, temperature changes FEARS Dread disease, insanity WEAKEST BODY REGIONS Gastrointestinal and respiratory tracts, mucosal membranes, liver, oral cavity, bones and joints, and skin. See Constitutional type, *Mercurius solubilis*, Homeopathy

***Mercurius vivus*** *Mercurius solubilis*, see there

**mercury** Hydrargyrum, quicksilver A liquid metallic element (atomic number 80; atomic weight 200.59) often obtained from cinnabar, the major mercury ore; mercury is used in medicine for pressure devices, eg manometers, as topical antiseptics, in diuretics, dental amalgams, and historically in calomel ALTERNATIVE DENTISTRY see Dental amalgam HOMEOPATHY *Merc sol*, see there, *Mercurius solubilis* TOXICOLOGY Mercury is a highly toxic heavy metal absorbed through the skin and lungs; exposure to inorganic mercury is associated with nausea, diarrhea, and renal toxicity; organic mercury causes mental changes that have been misinterpreted as mental disorders, as occurred in the 19th century with the so-called 'mad hatter' disease

**mesenchymal-pathological constitution** FRINGE MEDICINE-IRIDOLOGY A blue iris which, according to the construct of iridology, belongs to a person who is prone to cardiovascular disease, hernias, hemorrhoids, spinal weakness, and other connective tissue diseases. See Iridology, Iris constitution

**Franz Anton Mesmer** MEDICAL HISTORY-UNPROVEN METHODS An Austrian physician (1734-1815) who lived in France and developed the pseudoscientific doctrine of animal magnetism, a form of hypnosis that was discredited by the medical practitioners of the time. See Hypnosis, Magnetic pass, Mesmerism

**mesmerism** Animal magnetism UNPROVEN METHODS IN MEDICINE A method of hypnosis developed in the early 1800s by Mesmer, which he claimed put patients in a trance-like state deep enough to allow major surgery to be performed without pain, or awareness of the operation; mesmerism fell into disrepute, as it was associated with the occult and other non-scientific components. See Hypnosis, Mesmer; Cf Autosuggestion therapy, Mantra, Meditation, Yoga

**MET** Met, metabolic equivalent, metabolic equivalents of oxygen consumption PHYSIOLOGY A metabolic unit used to quantify the intensity of physical activity, which is defined as the ratio of the metabolic rate during exercise to the metabolic rate at rest; one MET corresponds to an energy expenditure of approximately 1 kcal/kg of body weight/hour, or an oxygen uptake of 3.5 ml of $O_2$ consumption/kg/hour (*N Engl J Med 1994; 330:1550*) the MET unit is of use when planning the rehabilitation of patients who have had a myocardial infarction; Sleeping (1.0 MET), desk work (1.5-2.5), coitus (2.0-5.0), walking 3 mph (3.0), medium housework (3.0-5.0), bicycling (3.5-15.0), shoveling snow (4.0-7.0), jogging 6 mph (10.0). See Exercise

► **METABOLIC EQUIVALENTS (MET)**

**1.** Sleeping, reclining, 'couch potatoing'

**2.** Sitting, eg desk work, highway driving

**3.** Very light exertion, eg office work, city driving

**4.** Light exertion with normal breathing, eg slow walking, mopping, golfing with a cart

**5.** Moderate exertion with deep breathing, eg normal walking, golfing on foot, calisthenics, raking leaves, downhill skiing, hunting, fishing, slow dancing, interior painting

**6.** Vigorous exertion with panting; overheating, eg slow jogging, speed-walking, tennis, swimming, cross-country skiing, fast biking, shoveling snow, heavy restaurant work, laying bricks, heavy gardening, heavy household repairs

**7.** Heavy exertion with gasping and sweating, eg fast jogging, running, continuous racquetball, touch football, moving heavy rocks, mixing cement, using a jackhammer, shoveling deep or heavy snow, hanging drywall

**8.** Peak or extreme exertion, eg fast running, jogging uphill, aggressive sports with no rest, extreme work, pushing or pulling with one's entire strength

From N Engl J Med 1993; 329:1677

**metabolic equivalents of oxygen consumption** MET, see there

**'metabolic' therapy** FRINGE ONCOLOGY An unconventional form of cancer management that originated with Dr Max Gerson in the 1920s, which consists of bowel enemas to rid the body of unspecified toxins accumulated by an 'unhealthy' lifestyle, unnatural foods, preservatives, pesticides, and industrial pollution), as well as dietary modifications, often supplemented with vitamins or minerals; metabolic therapies include Gerson therapy, Kelley therapy, and the Manner cocktail. See Colon therapy, Gerson therapy, Kelley therapy, Manner cocktail, Tijuana, Unproven methods for cancer management

**metabolic typing** FRINGE MEDICINE A method proposed by Nicolas J Gonzales, MD, for classifying humans into one of three genetically distinct groups

► **GONZALEZ'S METABOLIC TYPES**

- **SYMPATHETIC DOMINANT** Individuals with an efficient sympathetic nervous system
- **PARASYMPATHETIC DOMINANT** Individuals with an efficient parasympathetic nervous system
- **BALANCED TYPE** Individuals whose sympathetic and parasympathetic nervous systems are in complete balance

According to Gonzalez, sympathetic dominant types should eat a primarily (80%) vegetarian diet, while the parasympathetic dominants should consume primarily fatty meats, and dairy products (50% of total) in their diet *(Moss, 1992)*. See Parasympathetic dominant, Sympathetic dominant

**metabolic unit** MET, see there

**metamorphic technique** Metamorphosis, prenatal therapy ALTERNATIVE MEDICINE A technique developed in the 1960s by a British naturopath, Robert St John, as an extension of reflexology; the method is based on the belief that a person's physical and psychological profiles develop in utero, ie before birth; treatment hinges on massage of specific parts of the foot, hand, head, and ear, with the intent of loosening prenatal patterns; the specific goal of the technique is to meliorate the effects of prenatal imprints or fears, which are believed to cause behaviors and emotional stresses resulting in poor health; metamorphic therapists view themselves as catalysts that connect a patient with his own intrinsic healing ability—which has been termed 'innate intelligence,' freeing the 'life forces' from genetic and karmic influences; the technique is believed to be beneficial for chronic conditions including physical or mental disabilities, eg Down's syndrome and autism. See Humanistic psychology

**metamorphosis** Metamorphosis, see there

**metaneed** Self-actualization need, see there

**metaphor** SOCIOLOGY '...*a high-level similarity between different things or different processes. It can reflect a deep structural resonance or merely a superficial resemblance. Most of our most basic cultural assumptions rest on the foundations of a metaphor. Metaphors are incisive and misleading, valuable and dangerous.*' (*Nature 1994; 369:287br*)

**metaphysical healing** Prayer for the sick, see there

**Methuselah factor** A colloquial term for any of a number of contributors to longevity; those with the Methuselah syndrome more often have consumed a moderate or light diet with little meat, worked out-of-doors, had a good night's sleep, rose early, were female, and usually married (*D Georgakas, The Methuselah Factors, Simon & Schuster, New York, 1980*). See Life-extending diet; Cf Life-extension formula

The name derives from the biblical 969-year-old Methuselah, who was the longest-living of a line of long-lived antediluvian Hebrews

**methylcobalamin** Vitamin $B_{12}$, see there

**methylene blue** ALTERNATIVE ONCOLOGY A synthetic bacteriostatic dye that inhibits the growth of several experimental cells lines, which has been proposed as a therapy for certain cancers; used in combination with phototherapy, it may be useful for superficial bladder cancer (*J Urol 1990; 144:164*). See Unproven methods for cancer management

**metoposcopy** FRINGE MEDICINE A pseudodiagnostic technique in which an individual's personality and emotional state are believed to be decipherable by evaluating the lines on his or her forehead. See Face reading, Phrenology, Physiognomy

**M.H.** Master Herbalist

***mi tsao*** Licorice, see there, *Glycyrrhiza glabra*

**miasm** Chronic miasm HOMEOPATHY A term coined by Samuel Hahnemann for any of three 'hereditary' conditions that are resistant to homeopathic treatment

▶ **MIASMS**

- **PSORIC** Refers to scabies-like skin eruptions
- **SYCOTIC** Refers to gonorrhea-like manifestations
- **SYPHILITIC** Refers to syphilis-like manifestations

Not all homeopaths accept the miasmatic theory. See Hahnemann, Homeopathy; Cf Psora

**microcapsule** Magnetic microcapsule, see there

**microcosmic orbit meditation** PARANORMAL PHENOMENA A technique that forms the basis for the healing *tao* system, which is believed to reduce stress, connect its advocates with terrestrial and ethereal forces, enhance *chi* and circulate *chi* through the primary acupuncture meridians. See *Chi*, Healing *tao* system

**micronutrient** CLINICAL NUTRITION Any of the necessary minor components of a well-balanced diet, including vitamins and minerals, which are ingested in relatively large amounts, thus known as macrominerals, or in minimal amounts, known as trace minerals. See Diet; Cf Macronutrient, Minerals, Non-nutritive dietary component, Vitamins

**microwave** A 1-100 gigaHerz ($10^9$) wave on the electromagnetic spectrum with a wavelength of 1-1000 mm; exposure to minimal amounts of microwaves is common with the advent of domestic microwave ovens; leakage of infrared waves ranges from 1 milliWatt/cm$^2$ at the time of sale of a microwave oven to 5 mW/cm$^2$, measured at a distance of 2 inches; older pacemakers tended to misfire when the wearer was exposed to early consumer microwave ovens, which were also linked to an increase in cataracts HAZARDS Mechanical-eggs and popcorn are particularly hazardous, as they can explode, causing a transient loss of visual acuity (*N Engl J Med 1991; 325:1749c*)

Note: There is little substantive data to suggest that microwave exposure is associated with increased morbidity

**mid-arm muscle area** A derived value for estimating lean body mass as a function of skeletal muscle; ≥ 30% below a standardized value (52 to 55 for males; 31 to 35 for females) from the Health and Nutritional Examination Surveys (HANES) data indicates a depletion of lean body mass, ie malnutrition; Cf Triceps skin fold

**middle burner** see Triple burner

**middle pillar meditation** Middle pillar technique PARANORMAL PHENOMENA A system of mental healing developed in 1907 by a British chiropractor, Francis Regardie, that synthesizes rhythmic breathing, mantra mummering, and prayer; central to the technique is the visualization of 5 balls of light, corresponding to the 5 specific chakras which the practitioner imagines emit a single beam of light, known as the middle pillar (*Raso, 1994*). See Meditation

**middle pillar technique** Middle pillar meditation, see there

**midwife** OBSTETRICS A formally trained person, often an advanced practice registered nurse, who assists in childbirth; midwifery is undergoing a renaissance, as it provides obstetric services for lower-income women, and is a delivery option chosen by some upper-income women who desire a greater involvement in childbirth. See Alternative birthing center, Alternative gynecology, Doula, Natural childbirth; Cf Lamaze technique

Note: There is an accelerating trend in litigation-oriented societies for obstetricians and gynecologists to shift their practice away from obstetrics, given the high cost (up to $150 000/year) of obstetric malpractice insurance and, regionally (eg inner cities, economically-depressed rural regions), increased numbers of financially disadvantaged women, which has made obstetrics a 'loss leader' service

**Milan Brych** see Brych affair

**milfoil** Yarrow, see there, *Achillea millefolium*

**millefoil** Yarrow, see there, *Achillea millefolium*

**milk** See Breast milk, Humanized milk, Unpasteurized milk

**milk intolerance** Lactose intolerance, see there

**milk-rejection sign** An anecdotal clinical observation that breast-fed infants will not take milk from a breast affected by carcinoma (*Cancer 1966; 19:1185*); infants also tend to suck less when the mother has ingested alcohol before breast feeding (*N Engl J Med 1991; 325:981*), which is attributed to objective changes in the quality of the milk. See Breast milk, La Leche league

**milk ring test** A simple test for the surveillance of dairy herds for brucellosis. See Certified milk, Raw milk; Cf Breast milk

In the milk ring test, a stained suspension of *Brucella abortus* organisms is added to small sample of pooled fresh milk or cream from 25 cows or less; if agglutinins against *B abortus* are present in the milk, the organisms will clump together, adhere to the fat globules in the milk and rise to the top of the test tube, resulting in a stained ring on the top of the milk

**milk stool** PEDIATRICS The viscid dark green neonatal feces, ie meconium, which gives rise to yellow-green and more liquid stools that later develop into the firm caramel-to-milk chocolate-colored stool of milk-fed infant. See Breast milk

Note: The stool of human milk-fed infants is looser and less malodorous than those fed ruminant (eg bovine, caprine) milk

**milk sugar** Lactose, see there

**milk thistle** *Silybum marianum*, Marian thistle HERBAL MEDICINE An annual or biennial herb thought to be effective for cirrhosis, gallbladder inflammation (cholecystitis), and hepatitis, possibly related to its high content of the flavonoid derivative, silymarin; it has also been used as an appetite stimulant, a digestive tonic, for mushroom poisoning and, topically, for psoriasis TOXICITY Milk thistle should not be used in those with liver disease. See Herbal medicine

**milk thistle** *Silybum marianum*

**milk-vetch root** Astragalus, see there, *Astragalus membranaceous*

**milkweed** Pleurisy root, see there, *Aesclepias tuberosa*

**milkweed** *Asclepia syriaca*, common milkweed, common silkweed, cottonweed, silky swallowtail, Virginia silk, wild cotton HERBAL MEDICINE A perennial herb with a milky white sap, which was used topically by Native Americans for skin complaints including fungal infections, poison ivy, and warts; it was once used internally for gastrointestinal and respiratory conditions; the roots are poisonous. See Herbal medicine

**mind** Psyche PSYCHOLOGY The consciousness

**milkweed** *Asclepia syriaca*

that originates in the brain, and is evident in emotion, imagination, memory, perception, throught, and volition

**mind-body link** Body-mind link, see there

**mind/body medicine** 1. Alternative medicine, see there 2. Behavioral medicine ALTERNATIVE MEDICINE An evolving field of health care based on the belief that a complex interplay of external and internal factors influence the mind, and therefore a person's response and recuperation from disease; these interactions are genetic, environmental, psychological, and socioeconomic; integral to mind/body medicine is the belief that stress–which evokes a flight-or-fight response will, if repeated over time, weaken the immune system, resistance to disease, and healing capacity; to counteract the stress response, mind/body medicine seeks to develop in an individual, the capacity to reduce these adverse effects, teaching relaxation responses to reduce blood pressure, heart rate, muscle tone, oxygen consumption, perspiration, and respiratory rate; the individual copes with stressants based on his personality type (types A, B, or C) or by changing lifestyle; methods for reducing stress include autogenic training, biofeedback training, breath therapy, hypnosis, meditation, mindfulness, progressive relaxation, and visualization therapy or mental imagery–all discussed elsewhere in this work; data suggest that mind/body medicine may be effective in treating or ameliorating certain symptoms of AIDS, arthritis, common cold, diabetes, headaches, and infertility. See Behavioral medicine, Biopsychosocial model, Body-mind technique, Evocative breath therapy, Flight-or-fight response, Movement and exercise technique, Psychoneuroimmunology

For some, the terms behavioral medicine and mind/body medince are synonymous; because the term behavioral medicine appears to be more acceptable, and possibly embraced by more mainstream medical practitioners, while the term mind/body medicine may be more accepted to advocates of alternative health care they are, in this work, listed as separate entries–Author's note

**mindfulness** PARANORMAL PHENOMENA A zen-like approach to meditation, in which the individual focuses completely on the activity or event occurring at that moment; mindfulness contrasts with traditional meditation, in which the intent is to free the mind of all thought. See Autogenic training, Biofeedback training, Biopsychosocial model, Breath therapy, Flight-or-fight response, Hypnosis, Imagery and visualization, Meditation, Mind/body medicine, Progressive relaxation, Psychoneuroimmunology, Zen therapy

**mind mirror** FRINGE BIOFEEDBACK A rudimentary electroencephalograph connected to the scalp of a person to record the electrical activity of both hemispheres, or to the scalp of two people to compare their responses to various forms of external stimulation; the claimed efficacy of the mind mirror for either diagnostic or therapeutic purposes is uncertain; Cf Biofeedback training

**minerals, dietary** Those metallic elements that are required for optimal functioning of the body (see table, pages 245-246) dietary requirements for minerals range from molar to trace amounts/day; some, eg nickel, tin, and vanadium, may be required by some plants or animals, but are not known to have a role in human nutrition

▶ **DIETARY MINERALS**

- **MAJOR MINERALS, BONE** Calcium, phosphate, magnesium
- **MAJOR MINERALS, ELECTROLYTES** Sodium, potassium, chloride
- **MINOR MINERALS, FOUND IN METALLOPROTEINS** Iron, copper, manganese, iodine, cobalt, molybdenum, selenium, chromium, fluoride and zinc
- **TRACE MINERALS** Nickel, silicon, vanadium and tin

**mineral oil** A mixture of liquid petroleum-derived hydrocarbons (specific gravity, 0.818-

0.96); mineral oil was formerly used with impunity as a vehicle for drugs applied to the nasal mucosa and internally as a laxative; when applied too liberally, mineral oil may evoke exogenous lipid pneumonia; although mineral oil may be used as a laxa-

| MINERALS | RDA†/DV‡ | FOOD SOURCES | BENEFIT |
|---|---|---|---|
| Calcium | 0.8 g/1.0g | Almonds, broccoli, dairy products, dairy products, fish, fortified orange juice, turnip greens | Bone and teeth growth and maintenance, neuromuscular function, blood clotting |
| Chloride | 750 mcg/none | Salt, salty foods | Electrolyte and fluid balance |
| Chromium | 50-200 mcg/none | Black pepper, broccoli, brewers' yeast, brown sugar, dairy products, grape juice, molasses, whole grains | Carbohydrate metabolism |
| Copper | 1.5-3.0 mg/2.0 mg | Cherries, cocoa, eggs, fish, gelatin, mushrooms, legumes, shellfish, whole grain cereals | Blood cells and connective tissue |
| Fluoride | 1.5-4.0 mg/none | Fish, fluoridated water, tea | Strengthens tooth enamel |
| Iodine | 150 mcg/150 mcg | Iodized salt, milk, shellfish, spinach | Maintains thyroid metabolism |
| Iron | 10 mg/20 mg | Asparagus, clams, meats, poultry, prunes, pumpkin seeds, raisins, soybeans, spinach | Oxygen transportation in red blood cells, maintains metabolism |
| Magnesium | 350 mg/400 mg | Bananas, broccoli, dairy products molasses, nuts, pumpkin seeds, seafood, spinach, wheat germ | Neuromuscular function, strong bones |
| Manganese | 2-5 mg/none | Dairy products, dried fruits, leafy green vegetables, legumes, nuts, tea, whole grain cereals | Carbohydrate and fat metabolism, bone and connective tissue metabolism |
| Molybdenum | 75-250 mcg/none | Breads, cereals, dairy products, legumes, meats, whole grain cereals | Nitrogen metabolism |
| Phosphorus | 0.8 g/1.0 g | Cereals, dairy products, eggs fish, meats, poultry | Energy metabolism, co-acts with calcium to maintain bones |
| Potassium | 2000 mg/3500 mg | Avocados, bananas, cantaloupe, dairy products, dried fruits, mushrooms, tomatoes | Maintains pH in blood, co-acts with sodium to maintain fluid balance |
| Selenium | 70 mcg/none | Brazil nuts, dairy products, fish, meats, mushrooms, shellfish, whole grain cereals | Co-acts with vitamin E as antioxidant |

| | | | |
|---|---|---|---|
| Sodium | 500 mg/2400 mg | Salt, salty foods, soy sauce | Nervous system function, co-acts with chloride to maintain fluid balance |
| Zinc | 15 mg/15 mg | Dairy products, fish, lean beef, legumes, lima beans, nuts, oysters, poultry, wheat germ | Wound healing, sperm production, many enzyme reactions |

†Recommended daily allowance ‡Daily value *International Units

tive without major adverse effect; excess use of mineral oil as a laxative may cause anorexia, malabsorption of fat-soluble vitamins, and absorption of the oil itself

**mineral supplement** ALTERNATIVE NUTRITION A general term for any mineral ingested with the intent of increasing the body's load of the mineral; in developed countries, most mineral deficiencies are rare in those with a balanced diet, although iron deficiency may occur in menstruating women, and in those with bleeding caused by colon cancer or gastric ulcers; self 'prescribed' mineral supplements are potentially dangerous; iron can be absorbed in excess when ingested with vitamin C, and may cause constipation, and the growth of certain tumors; excess calcium causes kidney stones, excess magnesium causes diarrhea, excess zinc causes bone marrow suppression, anemia, and may increase cholesterol; Cf Minerals–dietary

**mineral water** A general term for water that contains dissolved mineral salts, elements, or gases, which is obtained from natural sources (spring water) or prepared from municipal or other sources; mineral water is believed to be of therapeutic use; from the 1870s until the enactment of the Pure Food and Drug Act in 1906, fantastic claims for health benefits were commonly made regarding the ability of mineral waters to cure anemia, asthma, bronchitis, constipation, diabetes, dyspepsia, eczema, gout, hemorrhoids, hysteria, liver disease, 'nervous prostration,' pain of all types, paralysis, psoriasis, urinary tract infections, and a host of other conditions; in 1918, the American Medical Association published a pamphlet panning the properties of mineral water as a therapeutic modality (*Armstrong, 1991*). See Natural spring, Spring water

**minimum dose** See Law of the infinitesimal dose

**minister of dikes and dredges** Triple burner, see there, The Twelve vital organs

**minister of the granary** Spleen and pancreas, see The Twelve vital organs

**minister of the mill and the sea of nourishment** Stomach, see The Twelve vital organs

**minister of power** Kidney, see The Twelve vital organs

**minister of reception** Small intestine, see The Twelve vital organs

**minister of the reservoir** Bladder, see The Twelve vital organs

**minister of transportation** Large intestine, see The Twelve vital organs

**mint** See Peppermint, Spearmint

**miracle in the mouth** Psychic dentistry, see there

**miraculous cure** PARANORMAL PHENOMENA A return to health that is regarded as a religious miracle; defining a cure as miraculous is based on guidelines, first promulgated in the 18th century by Pope Benedict XIV, that have become more rigorous in recent years; use of the adjective *miraculous* in connection with cures is restricted to a disease that is extremely serious; the cure is not regarded as one of spontaneous recovery; the recovery must be abrupt (ie shortly after visiting a healing shrine); no relapse of symptoms have occurred; the cure passes the muster of medicos examining the supposed cure. See Healing shrine, Lourdes

Less than one case every two years passes this stringent litmus test for a miraculous cure

**mirroring** see Psychodrama

**mishmi bitter** Coptis, see there, *Coptis sinensis*

**Missouri snakeroot** Echinacea, see there, *Echinacea angustifolia, E pallida, E pupura*

**mistletoe** HERBAL MEDICINE 1. American mistletoe, see there, *Phoradendron flavescens* 2. European mistletoe, *Viscum album* A parasitic evergreen plant that has been used for hypertension and cancer TOXICITY Mistletoe is poisonous; the FDA lists it as 'unsafe' and does not approve its use. See Herbal medicine, Iscador, Unproven methods for cancer management

**Mithridates antidote** THERAPEUTIC HISTORY An antipoisoning concoction (theriac) formulated by Mithridates VI, king of Pontus. See Mithradatism, Theriac

Mithridates' stormy lifestyle and penchant for expediting the permanent departure of friends and family, made him understandably concerned that he would be poisoned; he consumed ever-increasing doses of his antidote, which consisted of various poisonous ingredients, including the blood from ducks that had been raised on poisonous plants; he had himself killed by a bodyguard

**mithridatism** FRINGE TOXICOLOGY Tolerance developed against a toxin, which is induced by gradually incrementing the toxin, a technique likened to tolerization therapy used in allergy medicine. See Mithradates, Theriac

It is named after Mithridates VI (131-63 BC), the king of ancient Pontus; Grigori Rasputin (1872-1916), the 'mad monk' was thought to have ingested increasing amounts of strychnine for this purpose

**'mixed' chiropractic** Liberal chiropractic CHIROPRACTIC A method of chiropractic which diverges from the fundamental principles delineated by DD Palmer, the founder of chiropractic; mixed chiropractic represents an individual style of practice, and incorporates a wide range of modalities, which may include a gamut of alternative therapies, eg ayurvedic medicine, Chinese medicine, diet and nutritional supplementation, homeopathy, massages, mind/body medicine, naturopathy, and other methods of healing; approximately 85% of chiropractics are 'mixed' practitioners. See Chiropractic; Cf Medically-oriented chiropractic, Straight chiropractic

**mixed constitution** Biliary constitution, see there

**MK-639** AIDS An HIV-1 protease inhibitor that has therapeutic potential for HIV infection. See AIDS therapy

When first administered, MK-639 results in a rapid and precipitous (up to 1000-fold) drop in HIV replication and a transient recuperation in the CD4 cell counts, but eventually is bested by the emergence of MK-639-resistant HIV-1 variants (*Nature 1995; 374:569, 493, Bio/Technology 1995; 13:206*)

***mo tsai*** *Eclipta prostrata*, see there

**mobility testing** Motion palpation OSTEOPATHY A technique used in classic osteopathy, in which the examiner evaluates each spinal segment for proper mobility in all planes of motion, and in relationship to the above and below vertebrae. See Classic osteopathy, Osteopathy

**moccasin flower** Lady's slipper, see there, *Cypripedium calceolus*

**modality** HOMEOPATHY A general term for any factor that alleviates or aggravates a main symptom, which is an expression of the uniqueness of the individual; a chest pain that is worsened by heat, by sitting, or at night are three examples of modalities. See Homeopathy

**moderate-impact sport** SPORTS MEDICINE A generic term for any physical activity or sport in which there is relatively intense wear and trauma of weight-bearing joints, in particular of the foot, knee, and hip; moderate-impact sports include aerobics, backpacking, ballet, cross-country skiing, downhill (alpine) skiing, ice-skating, softball, speedwalking, tennis, and volleyball; these sports are allowed after hip and knee arthroplasty if the participant uses viscoelastic shoe inserts and sport- and joint-specific therapy (*Mayo Clin Proc 1995; 70:342*); Cf High-impact sport, Low-impact sport, No-impact sport

**modern medicine** Mainstream medicine, see there

***mo-ehr*** HERBAL MEDICINE A black tree fungus reported to protect against coronary artery disease and cancer *(Moss, 1992)*. See Unproven methods for cancer management

**Moerman's anticancer diet** Pigeon diet FRINGE NUTRITION A dietary regimen formulated by a Dutch physican, Cornelis Moerman, based on the belief that poor eating habits interrupt the body's immune defense and allow cancer to develop, and is fashioned after the eating habits of pigeons, which rarely get cancer; the Moerman diet consists of fresh fruits and vegetables (ideally, organically grown) and their juices, whole grain cereals and breads, buttermilk, natural seasonings, small amounts of diary products, and eggs, which is supplemented with multi-vitamins, iron, iodine, and sulfur. See Diet, Unproven methods for cancer management

**molybdenum** CLINICAL NUTRITION An essential trace element (atomic number 42, atomic weight 95.94) which is required for the function of certain enzymes, eg xanthine oxidase; it is present in legumes, liver, and whole grains FRINGE ONCOLOGY Molybdenum is a free radical scavenger, and is believed by some to have anticarcinogenic properties *(Moss, 1992)*; cereals, dark green vegetables, legumes, meats. See High pH therapy, Unproven methods for cancer management

***Monarda didyma*** Popularly known as bergamot, see there

**monellin** A sweet protein produced by the African fruit, serendipidy, *Dioscoreophyllum cumminsii,* which, like thaumatin, has a high affinity for sweet taste receptors, eliciting a sensation of sweetness that is $10^5$ times greater than D-glucose on a molar basis (*Bio/Technology 1992; 10:561*). See Sweet protein, Thaumatin; Cf Artificial sweetener

*This 94-residue heterodimeric carbohydrate-free protein has a 44-residue A chain and a 50-residue B chain linked by weak noncovalent bonds

**monkshood** Aconite, see there, *Aconitum napellus*

**(juice or) mono diet** ALTERNATIVE NUTRITION An 'elimination' diet in which the person ingests only one fruit (eg apple or grape) or vegetable (carrot or onion), its juice, and water, but no solid foods. See Fasting

**monoclonal antibody** Any of a family of antibodies created in the laboratory, which are generated when B lymphocytes–which form antibodies after being stimulated by antigens-are fused with myeloma cells-which are malignant cells that provide immortality; monoclonal antibodies have been viewed as a possible therapy for cancer, as they directly inhibit the growth of certain tumors, can be chemically bound to toxins that are lethal to malignant cells, stimulate the complement system (a nonspecific arm of the immune system), which may destroy malignant cells, can be used to purge the bone marrow of malignant cells, and form the basis for cancer vaccines ALTERNATIVE ONCOLOGY A number of alternative health care providers include the use of monoclonal antibodies in their therapeutic regimens, see below note *(Moss, 1992)*. See Unproven methods for cancer management

Monoclonal antibodies have thus far been largely disappointing to mainstream efforts to treat cancer–Author's note

**monosodium glutamate** see MSG

**monoterpene** ALTERNATIVE PHARMACOLOGY Any of a number of antioxidants found in various fruits and vegetables that have anticarcinogenic properties EXPERIMENTAL BIOLOGY Any of a number of substances (eg limonene, perillyl alcohol) that are major components of essential oils present in various plants; limonene and perillyl alcohol are currently in clinical trials as possible cancer therapies (*JAMA 1996; 275:1349oa*). See Unproven methods for cancer management

Monoterpenes induce the expression of phase I and II hepatic detoxification enzymes, selectively inhibit protein isoprenylation (which targets proteins to membrane), and induce expression of the mannose G-phosphate/IGF-II receptor and TGF-β; monoterpenes have antitumor properties, acting by an unknown mechanism, which may be related to the above indicated enzyme activities

**monounsaturated fat** A saturated fatty acid (ie an alkyl chain fatty acid with one ethylenic (double) bond between the carbons in the fatty acid chain. See Fatty acid, Saturated fatty acid; Cf Polyunsaturated fatty acid, Unsaturated fatty acid

**montebank** Quack, see there

**moon force** *Kapha*, see there

**moorgrass** *Drosera*, see there, *Drosera rotundifolia*

**moose elm** Slippery elm, see there, *Ulmus rubra*

**MORA** FRINGE MEDICINE A device created by F Morrel, MD, a colleage of Reinhold Voll, which is believed to receive electromagnetic waves directly from a person's body, manipulate the aberrant waveforms, normalize them by increasing or decreasing their amplitude, and then return the 'treated' normal waves to the individual, thereby effecting a cure; the MORA is said to be effective for headaches, skin diseases, muscle pain, circulatory defects; it may be used for color therapy, and in combination with homeopathic remedies (*Alternative Medicine, Future Med Pub, 1994*). See Energy medicine

**moral treatment** MEDICAL HISTORY An early therapeutic philosophy for mental disorders, based on Wm Tuke's retreat model; moral treatment consisted of removing the afflicted from their homes and placing them in a surrogate 'family' of 250 members or less, often under the guidance of a physician (*JAMA 1995; 273:923ed*)

**morbid obesity** Superobesity CLINICAL NUTRITION A condition defined as 45 kilograms over the ideal body weight, 2 times greater than the ideal or standard weight or, for children, a triceps skin fold greater than the 95th percentile of all children (*Am J Dis Child 1987; 141:535*) PHYSIOPATHOLOGY Superobese subjects react to the 'stress' of weight loss by increasing lipoprotein lipase, which in the capillaries of adipose tissue, hydrolyzes triglycerides from circulating lipoproteins into free fatty acids, that are taken up by adipocytes, increase lipid storage, and make weight loss difficult; surgical therapy is rarely successful and some previously used surgical procedures (jejunocolostomy, jejunoileostomy) have been abandoned; despite significant weight loss following jejuno-ileal bypass, the procedure is complicated by steatorrhea, hepatic failure, cirrhosis, oxalate deposition, bile stone formation, electrolyte imbalance (decreased calcium, magnesium, and potassium), hypovitaminosis, psychological problems, polyarthropathy, hair loss, pancreatitis, colonic pseudo-obstruction, intussusception, pneumatosis cystoides intestinalis, and blind loop syndrome). See Gastric balloon, Obesity, Pickwick syndrome

**morinda root** *Morindae officinalis, Polygala reina, ba ji tien* CHINESE MEDICINE An evergreen shrub, the root of which is astringent, tonic to the nervous and musculoskeletal systems, and believed to be an aphrodisiac; it is used for low back and abdominal pain, lack of volition, and sexual dysfunction. See Chinese herbal medicine

***Morindae officinalis*** Popularly known as morinda root, see there

**morning dew walk** NATUROPATHY A barefooted saunter on wet morning grass, which is recommended as a year-round activity, and believed by its advocates '*channel the body's vital energies toward health*.' (*Trattler, 1985*). See Hydrotherapy

**Morter B.E.S.T.** Bio Energetic Synchronization Technique, see there

**Morter HeathSystem** A health care system developed in 1980 by an American chiropractor, MT Morter, which includes bio energetic synchronization technique–BEST, Baby BEST, a videocassette stress-management program, and nutritional supplements, which are intended to restore the body to its natural alkaline state (*Raso, 1994*). See Baby BEST, Bio energetic synchronization technique

**mortification root** Popularly known as marshmallow, see there, *Althea officinalis*

**MOST** Manual organ stimulation technique, see there

**most significant other** SOCIAL MEDICINE The person in a patient's universe, upon whom the patient most heavily depends for moral and physical support, during periods of crisis and stress; MSOs include parents, spouses, children, lovers, siblings, or friends; the help of a patient's MSO may be enlisted by the medical team in patients with terminal disease. See Bonding, Companionship, Extended family, Marriage bonus, Mothering; Cf Anaclytic depression, Holtism, Nuclear family, Social isolation

Notes: In the working parlance, 'most' is being slowly deleted, such that 'significant other' is the term likely to prevail by the end of the 20th century; for some, most significant others can also include pets

**mother's heart** Shepherd's purse, see there, *Capsella bursa-pastoris*

**mother tincture** HOMEOPATHY A concentrate of a raw materials used in homeopathy which is prepared by placing it in alcohol and distilled water for one month, followed by pressing and filtering. See Homeopathy, Potentiza-tion, Succussing

**mothering** ALTERNATIVE PEDIATRICS A general term for the constellation of physical interactions, eg holding, cuddling, rocking, and others, that a caregiver has with an infant; mothering has been shown to be as critical to an infant's survival as physical nourishment. See Bonding; Cf Anaclytic depression; Holtism, Social isolation

**motherwort** *Leonurus cardiaca*, lion's ear, lion's tail, lion's tart, throw wort HERBAL MEDICINE A perennial herb, that contains alkaloids (eg leonurinine and stachydrine), bitter glycosides (eg leonurine and leonuridin), tannins, vitamin A, and volatile oil; it is a sedative, spasmolytic, and antihypertensive, and classically used to regulate menses; it has also been used for tachyarrhythmias, to prolong life, for rabies TOXICITY It should not be used in pregnancy, as it may cause uterine contractions; it should be avoided in those cutaneous allergies. See Herbal medicine

**motherwort** *Leonurus cardiaca*

**motion palpation** Mobility testing–Osteopathy, see there

**motion starvation** ALTERNATIVE MEDICINE A term coined by P Egoscue for the relative lack of physical activity, which he believes to be a main cause of illness in advanced nations; 'low motion' illnesses include carpal tunnel syndrome, low back pain, stiff neck, and general fatigue. See Egoscue method

**mountain aspen** White poplar, see there, *Populus tremuloides*

**mountain celery** *Angelica sinensis*, see there

**mountain cranberry** Bearberry, see there, *Arctostaphylos uva-ursi*

**mountain daisy** Arnica, see there, *Arnica montana*

**mountain essence** Thistle, see there, *Atractylodes chinensis*

**mountain ginger** *Polygonatum cirrhifolium*, see there

**mountain jujube** Wild Chinese jujube, see there, *Ziziphus jujuba*

**mountain savory** Winter savory, see there, *Satureia montana*

**mountain tea** Wintergreen, see there, *Gaultheria procumbens*

**mountain tobacco** Arnica, see there, *Arnica montana*

**mountain varnish** *Gynura pinnatifida*, see there

**mouse-ear** Chickweed, see there, *Stellaria media*

**movement analysis and performance** A component of movement therapy, which consists of the assessment of the 'quality' of a movement as it relates to a particular task; the intent is to optimize the movement's ease and efficiency within a defined space. See Laban analysis, Movement therapy

**movement and exercise technique** ALTERNATIVE MEDICINE A general term for any method of health maintenance that attempts to optimize the flow of energy through the body by means of exercise, movement, and stretching; these may be accompanied by breathing exercises and meditation; movement and exercise techniques include aikido and other martial arts, aerobics, dance therapy, Rolfing®, Rosen method, T'ai chi ch'uan, Tragerwork, yoga, and others, discussed elsewhere in this work. See Bodywork, Mind/body medicine

**movement observation techniques** See Laban analysis

**movement analysis and performance** A component of movement therapy, which consists of the assessment of the 'quality' of a movement as it relates to a particular task; the intent is to optimize the movement's ease and efficiency within a defined space. See Laban analysis, Movement therapy

**movement therapy** A process in which a person learns to re-educate his body's movement, and improve on patterns of movement that cause stress-related emotional conditions

▶ **TECHNIQUES OF MOVEMENT THERAPY**

• **PHYSIOLOGICAL REPATTERNING** The appraisal of cognitive-motor functional defects related to poor usage of the musculoskeletal system; the therapist addresses the perceptual, neurological, and musculoskeletal defects by studying the relationship of the biomechanical structures with the environment and the environmental tasks, and employs the appropriate corrective measures

- **Movement analysis and performance** The assessment of the 'quality' of a movement as it relates to a particular task; the intent is to optimize the movement's ease and efficiency within a defined space
- **Psychological and emotional expression** The observation of an individual's nonverbal interactions with himself and others
- **Health maintenance and improvement** The use of primarily noncardiovascular exercises to reduce stress, and enhance the immune system, and the patient's overall health and quality of life

Registered movement therapists undergo 700 hours of training, instruction, and postgraduate experience. See Laban analysis

**moxa** Mugwort, see there, *Artemisia vulgaris*

**moxabustion** Moxibustion TRADITIONAL CHINESE MEDICINE A variation of acupuncture that uses heat, in which mugwort (*Artemisia vulgaris*) is rolled into a pea-sized cone, placed point up, and burned almost to the skin; the smoldering cone is extinguished after a few seconds, and the warmth passes into the acupuncture needle. See Acupuncture, Alternative medicine, Mugwort

**moxibustion** 1. Moxabustion, see there 2. The application of heat to an acupuncture point, either by moxabustion, or by use of an electrical source of heat

**MRT** Metabolic response testing, see there

**MSG** Monosodium glutamate FOOD INDUSTRY A flavor-enhancing amino acid used in processed, packaged, and fast foods which is an excitatory neurotransmitter and neurotoxin; often added to Chinese food; other sources with up to 40% MSG include autolyzed yeast, calcium caseinate, sodium caseinate, hydrolyzed and texturized proteins (*Vitality June 1993*) TOXICITY Headaches, heart palpitations, skin flushing, tightness of the chest. See Chinese restaurant syndrome

Note: MSG may cause convulsions when injected into the peritoneal cavity of experimental animals, stimulating neurons until they die, an effect that has been implicated in brain damage in strokes, hypoglycemia, trauma, seizures, Huntington's disease, Parkinson's disease, Alzheimer's diseases, and Guam-type amyotrophic lateral sclerosis; domoic acid, a potent glutamate analogue, may cause toxic envenomation in mussel eaters, in some resulting in an Alzheimer-like disease

**M.T.** Massage Therapist

**MTH-68** FRINGE ONCOLOGY A vaccine formulated by LK Csatary of Fort Lauderdale, which is based on the belief that certain viruses can be used to interfere with the growth and proliferation of cancers; this interference is viewed as being similar to the manner in which one virus interferes with the growth of another when both are present either in vitro (in experimental cell lines) or in vivo (in experimental animals or humans); Csatary believes that many cancers are induced by viruses or of viral origin. See Unproven methods for cancer management

The anticarcinogenic effects of the MTH-68 vaccine have been interesting, but inconclusive *(Moss, 1992)*, and like other similar vaccines, is not part of the current therapeutic armamentarium against cancer–Author's note

***mu dan pi*** Tree peony, see there, *Paeonia moutan*

***mu gui*** Cinnamon, see there, *Cinnamon cassia*

***mu hsiang*** Costus, see there

***mu mien*** *Eucommia ulmoides*, see there

***mu* point** ACUPUNCTURE An alarm point located on the front of the body. See Alarm point

***mu tong*** *Akebia quinata*, see there

***mu tung*** *Akebia quinata*, see there

***mu xiang*** Costus, see there

**mucusless diet (healing system)** CLINICAL NUTRITION A dietary regimen developed in the early 20th century by a German artist, Professor Arnold Ehret, which consisted of fresh fruits and fasting

**mud therapy** Clay therapy NATUROPATHY The therapeutic use of certain earths which are believed to contain trace elements missing from the modern diet; some advocates believe that the mud may also have beneficial radioactive properties that cure both internal and external conditions; mud therapy is removed from the mainstream practitioners of alternative medicine, given the absence of viable data, but continues to be popular in various forms for cosmetic purposes, as when used for nightly 'facials'. See Hydrotherapy

**mugwort** *Artemisia vulgaris, A argyi, cingulum sancti Johannis*, felon herb, moxa, St John's herb, St John's plant ACUPUNCTURE See Moxabustion HERBAL MEDICINE A perennial shrub that contains absinthin, flavonoids, tannin, and volatile oil, which is used for menstrual dysfunction and cramping, threatened abortion, and as a natural insect repellant TOXICITY Mugwort should not be used in pregnancy. See Herbal medicine

**Muhammadan spice** *Foeniculum vulgare*, fennel, see there

**mullein** *Verbascum thapsus*, Aaron's rod, bunny's ears, donkey's ears, flannel leaf, Jacob's staff, lady's foxglove HERBAL MEDICINE A biennial herb that contains flavonoids, glycosides (eg aucubin), mucilage, saponins, and volatile oil, which is anti-inflammatory, diuretic, expectorant, and sedative; it is used to treat respiratory conditions, including asthma, bronchitis, colds, and whooping cough, insomnia, urinary tract infections, and rheumatic pain; it has been used topically for skin inflammation and infections, hemorrhoids, and earaches TOXICITY Mullein should not be used in those with cancer, as it has cancer-promoting activity; it should not be used in pregnancy or while nursing; the seeds are toxic. See Herbal medicine

**mullein** *Verbascum thapsus*

**multidimensional entity** PARANORMAL PHENOMENA A person who presents himself as one who is both in this 'plane of existance' and has incorporated into his body a spirit or entity from another plane of existence. See Body integration, Plane of existence, Spirit, Ziaela/Dr Salomon

**multiflowered rose** *Rosa multiflora, bao chiang wei, chiang mi, Rosa indica*, wall rose CHINESE MEDICINE A rose bush, the root of which is an astringent, carminative, and emmenagogic; it is used for dysmenorrhea, nocturnal emission, urinary frequency, and uterine prolapse. See Chinese herbal medicine

**multivitamin** An over-the-counter and often self-prescribed combination supplement containing lipid-soluble vitamins (vitamin A, vitamin D, vitamin E, and vitamin K) and water-soluble vitamins (thiamin–vitamin $B_1$, riboflacin–vitamin $B_2$, vitamin $B_6$, vitamin $B_{12}$, vitamin C), folic acid, niacin, pantothenic acid, and biotin; these dietary 'supplements' may also contain minerals, including calcium, phosphorus, iron, iodine, magnesium, manganese, copper, and zinc. See Decavitamin, Neural tube defects; Cf Megavitamin therapy

The use of periconceptual multivitamins is reported to decrease the incidence of neural tube defects (*N Engl J Med 1992; 327:1832*), an effect that may be due to folic acid (*ibid, 327:1875*); multivitamins may also decrease the risk of anencephaly and spina bifida

**mumbo-jumbo** Quackery, see there

**muroctasin** ALTERNATIVE ONCOLOGY A non-specific immune stimulant derived from muramyl dipeptide, which is obtained from gram-positive bacterial cell walls; muroctasin stimulates macrophages which release interleukin-1, which in turn increases production of colony-stimulating factors; muroctasin also evokes an increased production of neutrophils; it is used in Japan for chemotherapy-induced leukopenia (*Moss, 1992*). See Unproven methods for cancer management

**muscle energy manipulation** OSTEOPATHY Any of a number of osteopathic techniques in which the patient actively moves against resistance to a muscle group held in position by the physician; the intent of muscle energy manipulation is to expand the muscle's range of motion and correct muscle dysfunction, which may be related to trauma or injury; '*the counterforce applied by the practitioner varies in intensity depending on whether* (the resistance) *is isometric (practitioner equally resisting the patient's force), isotonic (patient overcomes the practitioner's resistance), or isolytic (practitioner overcomes patient's force).*' (*Collinge, 1996*). See Osteopathy

**muscle response testing** FRINGE CHIROPRACTIC A permutation of applied kinesiology developed by chiropractor Mark Grinims and acupuncturist Walter Fischman; they believe that the technique can be used to detect allergies, nutritional deficiencies, and diagnose virtually any disease in adults, children, and animals, circumventing the need to test blood, urine, or other body fluids. See Applied kinesiology, Chiropractic

**muscle sculpting** Deep tissue sculpting, see there

**music** The art of making sounds that are beautiful, pleasing, and/or interesting, founded on the principles of melody, harmony, rhythm, tempo, and timbre NEUROLOGY Music instruction in preschoolers may strengthen cross-communication among brain regions involved in complex mathematics, navigation, sculpting, and others, and increased spatial intelligence (*Science News 1994; 146:143*) NEUROPHYSIOLOGY The complexity of the production of music and its role in mental development, emotion, language, and intelligence is poorly understood (*NY Times 16 May 1995, C1*) SURGERY Early data suggest that the addition of performance-shaping factors,* eg surgeon-selected music, is associated with decreased cardiovascular (autonomic) reactivity and improved performance* of stressful nonsurgical laboratory tasks, eg serial number subtraction. See Music therapy

*The data may be confounded by the participant's personal bias toward or against the use of performance-shaping factors, the potential negative effect such factors might have on other participants in the surgical team, different levels of experience by the surgeons being studied, bodily position, duration of the test, and so on; investigator-selected (Pachebel's Canon in D) music is less effective than surgeon-selected music, which is more effective than no music (*JAMA 1994; 272:882OA, 1995; 273:1090C*)

**music healing** Music therapy, see there

**music therapy** Music-facilitated psychoeducational strategy PSYCHOLOGY The use of music as an interventional modality; music therapy is of use in children and adults with learning disabilities or with mental and/or emotional disorders; it is used for those with anxiety, depression, distress, low self-esteem, and moodiness; the use of music therapy in older adults is reported to be a cost-effective strategy for treating depression in housebound persons (*J Gerontol 1994; 49:265*), and may have a secondary effect of 'jogging' one's memories, through the use of music known to have been played during certain time periods of a person's life, eg 'Big Band' music for the elderly; music therapy is associated with decreased heart rate and blood pressure, less anxiety, improved sleep hygiene, less need for analgesics (in cancer and childbirth and during surgery), and more positive emotional state; it may have a positive impact on mental, physical, and work performance, insomnia, heart attacks and strokes, migraines; anecdotal reports suggest that it may be effective in improving Alzheimer's disease, autism, behavior, breathing, communication, emotional lability, mental illness and retardation, nervous conditions, orthopedic and other physical limitations, schizophrenia, sensory impairment, speech defects, stress, and tension. See Guided Imagery and Music, New Age music, Noxious music, Sedative music, Sensory therapy, Stimulative music; Cf Art therapy, Color therapy, Dance therapy, Play therapy, Recreational therapy *RESOURCE: American Association of Music Therapy, PO Box 80012, Valley Forge PA 19484 ☎ 1.610.265.4006*

**musket-shot water** *Eau d'arquebusade* HERBAL MEDICINE A preparation of agrimony leaves and seeds, used since the Middle Ages as an herbal cure for wounds. See Agrimony, Herbal medicine

**mustard** 1. Black mustard, see there, *Brassica nigra* 2. White mustard, see there, *Sinapsis alba*

**myofascial release therapy** A technique used primarily in osteopathy to reactivate previously restricted musculoskeletal groups; it is believed that chronic tension and trauma cause the fascia, which envelop muscle, to become stuck and fixed in a particular position, known as a myofascial restriction; manipulation of the myofascial group results in a 'release', which dissolves the restriction back into the '...*wholeness of the body*.' (*Y Erskine, in Collinge, 1996*). See Osteopathy

**myotherapy** Neuromuscular massage, see there

***Myrica cerifera*** Popularly known as bayberry, see there

***Myristica fragrans*** Nutmeg, see there

***Myristica moschata*** Nutmeg, see there, *Myristica fragrans*

**myristicin** An aromatic ether extracted from nutmeg, carrots, and parsley, which has narcotic properties; excess consumption of nutmeg, based on the belief that nutmeg is an abortifacient, results in delirium and disorientation. See Nutmeg

***Myroxylon balsamum*** Popularly known as balsam of Peru, see there

**myrrh** *Commiphora molmol* HERBAL MEDICINE A flowering plant, which contains volatile oils (eg cinamaldehyde, cuminaldehyde, eugenol, heerabolene, limonene, pinene, and others), resin, and gum; it is antifungal, antiseptic, astringent, cardiotonic, and expectorant, and has been used as a mouthwash for sore throats and laryngitis; topically for athlete's foot and wounds, and as a mosquito repellent; myrrh has been used internally for asthma, colds, coughs, chest congestion, and sinusitis; some data suggest that myrrh may lower cholesterol and prevent blood clot formation TOXICITY Myrrh should not be used in pregnancy or in those with renal failure. See Herbal medicine

**myrtle root** Sweet flag, see there, *Acorus calamus*

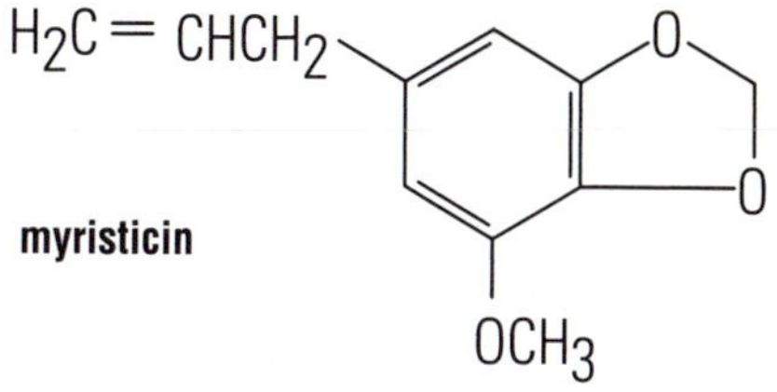

$H_2C=CHCH_2$ O O $OCH_3$

**myristicin**

**N-acetylcysteine** A precursor (via cysteine) of glutathione, the principal antioxidant that mops up free radical-induced oxidative damage; N-acetylcysteine deficiency has been linked to the pathogenesis of AIDS; in one proposed sequence, tumor necrosis factor, produced in the early inflammatory response to HIV, enters T cells, generates free radicals, depletes intracellular stores of glutathione, and ultimately causes T cells to self-destruct; this scenario may explain the death of T cells that are not infected with HIV; NAC is in therapeutic trials (*New York Times May 3, 1994; C3*). See AIDS therapy

**n-3 (polyunsaturated) fatty acids** Omega-3 fatty acids A family of long-chain polyunsaturated fatty acids, primarily eicosapentaenoic (C20:5) and docosahexanenoic acid (C22:6)[1]; increased dietary n-3 fatty acids are cardioprotective and have a positive impact on inflammatory conditions, interfering with the production of mediators of inflammation, including leukotrienes, platelet-activating factor, interleukin-1, and tumor necrosis factor; increased consumption of dietary n-3FAs and/or fish[2] is reported to benefit patients with chronic inflammatory conditions, including rheumatoid arthritis, ulcerative colitis, and chronic obstructive pulmonary disease (*N Engl J Med 1994; 331:228*); following ingestion, n-3FAs are rapidly incorporated into phospholipids of plasma and blood vessels; n-3FAs decrease plasma levels of VLDL-cholesterol, decrease platelet aggregation, cause vasodilation (*N Engl J Med 1995; 332:977*), and protect against coronary artery disease (*Arch Pathol Lab Med 1993; 117:102*) and atherosclerosis[3] See Fish; Cf Olive oil, Tropical oil

[1]Which have a double bond between carbons 3 and 4 [2]Fish oils are predominantly n-3 (omega-3) [3]They have also been reported to decrease plasma LDL, increase HDL, decrease prostaglandin production and synthesis of leukotrienes and possibly also IL-1

***nada* yoga** *Mantra yoga*, see there

**Naessens** See 714-X

**naked ladies** Autumn crocus, see there, *Colchicum autumnale*

***nan dzao*** Southern jujube, see Chinese jujube

***nan jiao*** Szechuan pepper, see there, *Zanthoxylum piperitum*

***nana* yoga** *Jnana yoga*, see there

**naprapathy** A system for gentle manipulation of soft tissues—muscles, tendons, and ligaments—that was developed in 1907 by a chiropractor, O Smith, which is intended to release tension and restore the normal flow of energy through the body; naprapathy is based on the belief that normal physiologic activities, eg circulation and flow of neural information, can be compromised by connective tissue that has become contracted and rigid through improper posture, poor nutrition, trauma, and mental and emotional conflicts; the naprapathic practitioner explores soft tissues for 'knots' and painful areas, which are kneaded, stretched, and pounded upon (the thrusts being known as 'directos') until the tension in the contracted tissue is released, the compromised nerve(s) reactivated, and the circulation restored to a state of normalcy. See Directo, Massage therapy; Cf Nutripathy

**N.A.S.H.** North American Society of Homeopaths

**nasturtium** 1. *Tropaeolum majus*, Indian cress HERBAL MEDICINE A flowering plant that contains glucotrapeoline, which hydrolyzes to form sulfur-based antibiotics; it is antimicrobial, hematopoietic, and purgative, and has been used for respiratory and urinary tract infections. See Herbal medicine 2. Watercress, see there, *Nasturtium officinale*

***Nasturtium officinale*** Popularly known as watercress, see there

***nasya*** AYURVEDIC MEDICINE The intranasal administration of herbs in ayurvedic medicine to eliminate *ama* (physiologic impurities). See Ayurvedic medicine, *Panchakarma*, *Prana*

**National Cancer Institute** An institute which, like the others in the National Institutes of Health, is under the US Public Health Service; the NCI has a focused interest on cancer research, conducts its own research, and guides the peer-review process for the funding of (mainstream) experimental protocols for treating malignancy. See Cancer screening; Cf International Association of Cancer Victors and Friends, Inc, National Health Federation, Office of Alternative Medicine; Unproven methods for cancer management

**National Commission for Certification of Acupuncturists** ALTERNATIVE MEDICINE An organization chartered in 1984, which promotes national (US) standards for safety and competence in the practice of acupuncture; the NCCA conducts a two-part (written and practical) examination that certifies acupuncturists, who are designated as Diplomates in Acupuncture or Dipl. Ac. (NCCA). See Acupuncture, Chinese medicine, Traditional Chinese medicine

**National Council Against Health Fraud** An anti-quackery group (*NCAHF Box 1276, Loma Linda, CA 82354*) founded in 1977 that has 2500 members and chapters in 17 states

▶ **NCAHF purposes**

- **CONDUCT STUDIES** and investigations on the claims made for health care products and services
- **EDUCATE** the public, professionals, legislators, business people, organizations, and agencies about untruths and deceptions
- **PROVIDE A COMMUNICATION CENTER** for individuals and organizations concerned about health misinformation, fraud, and quackery
- **SUPPORT SOUND CONSUMER HEALTH LAWS** and oppose legislation which undermines consumer rights, and
- **ENCOURAGE LEGAL ACTIONS AGAINST LAW VIOLATORS**

See Health fraud, Quackery

**National Health Federation** FRINGE MEDICINE An organization based in Washington DC, that exerts political pressure to secure 'health freedom' and 'freedom of medical choice' on behalf of alternative medicine practitioners, their families, and 'health food' consumers; the organization has neither medical nor scientific affiliations, and subscribes to the belief that organized medicine, the pharmaceutical industry, and other 'special interest' groups have controlled legislation that does not serve the interests of the American public in terms of health care (*Encyclopedia of Associations, 1990*); the Federation was founded in 1955* by FJ Hart, and claims 20,000 members in 74 chapters (*Committee on Questionable Methods of Cancer Management, American Cancer Society-March 7, 1990*). See Alternative medicine; Cf National Council Against Health Care Fraud, Quackery, Unproven methods for cancer management

*Shortly after his company, the Electronic Medical Foundation, was forced by the FDA to cease distribution of 'radionics' devices including the 'depolaray' machine and 'oscilloclast'

***Natrum muriaticum*** Sodium chloride, table salt HOMEOPATHY A remedy formulated from rock salt; it is used to treat anxiety and depression—especially if caused by the suppression of emotions, anal fissures, anemia, back pain, bereavement-related depression, cold sores, constipation, eczema, genital herpes, gingivitis, halitosis, hay fever, indigestion, menstrual dysfunction, migraines with fortification phenomena, runny nose, urinary hesitation, and watery discharge. See *Natrum mur* type, Homeopathy

***Natrum mur* type** HOMEOPATHY The *Natrum mur* constitutional type of person is serious, conscientious, moody, impatient with others, and mentally rigid WORSE Cold, damp, hot sun, overexertion, before midnight FEARS Failure, emotional pain, loss of self-control, lateness, crowds WEAKEST BODY REGION Gastrointestinal tract, blood, muscle, skin, mind. See Constitutional type, *Natrum muriaticum*, Homeopathy

**natural antibody** Normal antibody An antibody present in the circulation, without there being previous exposure to the antigen

**natural carcinogen** A substance normally present in foods, which is carcinogenic when tested by mutagenic assays in rodents or bacteria, eg Ames' test; it is unclear whether the 14 ppm of 5-8-methoxypsoralen present in parsley and parsnips, which is carcinogenic to rodents, or the 50-200 ppm of caffeic acid, present in apples, carrots, cherries, and others, actually have a carcinogenic potential in humans.* See Ames' test, Toxicity testing

*Or as Ames et al have implied (*Proc Natl Acad Sci, USA 1990; 87:7777*), there is a threshold at which critical mutation occurs (*Science 1990; 250:743*)

**natural childbirth** ALTERNATIVE OBSTETRICS A

vaginal delivery in which the mother is more actively involved in the parturitional mechanics than in the 'unnatural' birth; the 'natural' mother is awake during delivery, often without general anesthesia, has actively 'trained' in the birthing process, and is 'attended' by the father (or 'significant' other) at the time of delivery. See Alternative gynecology, Bonding, Breast milk, Doula, Lamaze method, Naturopathic obstetrics

**natural family planning** A general term for any form of family planning that does not rely on artificial agents (eg oral contraceptives, the 'morning-after' pill, spermicidal foam, and RU486) or devices (eg condoms, diaphragms, and IUDs) to prevent conception; natural family planning hinges on the use of the rhythm (calendar) method, coitus interruptus, and prolonged breastfeeding as contraceptive maneuvers. See Breast feeding, Coitus interruptus, Contraception, Pearl index, Rhythm method

**natural food movement** Health food movement, see there

**natural healing** Alternative healing A general term for any of a number of healing techniques that may be rooted in supernaturalistic methods; natural healing methods include absent healing, acupuncture, acupressure, aikido, Alexander technique, applied kinesiology, ayurvedic medicine, bioenergetics, Cayce therapies, charismatic healing, cranial osteopathy, Dianetics®, exorcism, hydrotherapy, iridology, Jin Shin Acutouch, jin shin jyutsu, Jin Shin Do®Bodymind Acupressure™, Jungian psychology, laying on of hands, lomilomi massage, macrobiotics, medical astrology, nature cure, naturopathy, neo-Shamanism, orgonomy, past life/lives therapy, polarity therapy, primal therapy, psychic healing, radiesthesia, radionics, rebirthing therapy, reflexology, reiki, Rolfing®, shamanism, t'ai chi ch'uan, therapeutic touch, Touch for health, transcendental meditation, yoga, and vibrational medicine, all discussed elsewhere in this work

***Natural History*** HERBAL MEDICINE A 37-book collection on plants written by Pliny (the Elder) of the Greek empire, which served as a source of information for herbalists until the 17th century; books 20 through 27 address plant pharmacology. See Herbal medicine; Cf *Canon of Medicine, Charak Samhita, The Complete Herbal, De Materia Medica, Nei Jing, Pen Ts'ao, Philosophy of Natural Therapeutics, Rigveda, Sushrita Samhita, Theatrum Botanicum*

**Natural Hygiene** A health system (formerly Life Science), formally formulated in 1982 by Dr HE Stevenson, in which the individual is taught to live in harmony with nature by consuming a properly balanced natural diet, fasting when sick, and maintaining a healthy lifestyle. See Fit for Life Program; Cf Graham system, Macfadden, Thomsonianism

**natural hygienist** A disciple of the Natural Hygiene philosophy. See Fasting, Natural Hygiene

**natural medicine** 1. Naturopathy, see there 2. A general term for any form of health care (eg diet, exercise, herbs, hydrotherapy) that depends on the body's natural healing powers

**natural psychotherapy** ALTERNATIVE PSYCHIATRY A general term for any format of client-oriented psychotherapy that accepts the person with his flaws and foibles, and nurtures him in order to maximize his emotional and spiritual potential; natural psychotherapy attempts to teach the client to relax and give of himself, identify his goals in life, and achieve a sense of vitality; skills required of the natural psychotherapist include effective listening and reflective communication. See Blockade point, Humanistic psychology, Reflective communication

**natural spring** HYDROTHERAPY Any of a number of natural sources of water, around which the occasional entrepreneur may erect a health spa or retreat that touts the water's efficacy in treating various evil humors; Hot Springs, Arkansas and Calistoga, California are two of the more famous American hot springs, where the health seeker may go to get soaked. See Health spa, Hydrotherapy, Mineral water, Spring water

**natural therapeutics** Naturopathy, see there

**naturalism** A guiding principle of the physical universe and understanding thereof, that holds that all that exists and all phenomena can be explained without recourse to supernatural concepts; Cf Supernaturalism

**natural care** Nature cure, see there

**nature cure** Natural care A general term for any

of a number of methods of self-healing, which are based on fasting, rest, and often hydrotherapy. See Fasting, Hydrotherapy

**naturology** Naturopathy, see there

**naturopathic education** There are 3 colleges that conduct 4-year programs in naturopathy, which are accredited by the Naturopathic Medical Council of North America: the Bastyr University of Natural Health Sciences, Seattle WA, the National College of Naturopathic Medicine, Portland OR, and the Canadian College of Naturopathic Medicine, Toronto; the entrance requirements are believed by some to be as stringent as those required for students of mainstream medicine. See Naturopathy

**naturopathic medicine** Naturopathy, see there

**naturopathic obstetrics** ALTERNATIVE OBSTETRICS A 'cross-platform' speciality that emphasizes 'natural' prenatal care, 'natural' childbirth, non-use of anesthesia, noninvasive interventions in the birthing process, and postnatal care in the form of massage and herbal infusions for the mother and infant. See Alternative gynecology, Bonding, Breast milk, Doula, Lamaze method, Natural childbirth

**naturopathic therapy** Naturopathy, see there

**naturopathy** Natural medicine, natural therapeutics, naturopathic medicine, naturology ALTERNATIVE MEDICINE An approach to healing that espouses the philosophy that disease is caused by a violation of the laws of nature, and uses the forces of nature as therapeutic modalities; naturopathy was founded in the US in 1902 by a German, Benedict Lust

▶ **LUST'S HEALTH PHILOSOPHY**

- **ELIMINATE BAD HABITS**, eg alcohol consumption, coffee, drugs, erratic hours, gluttony, meat, sexual or social excess
- **ACQUIRE GOOD HABITS**, eg proper breathing, exercise, posture, mental state
- **CHANGE HEALTH PHILOSOPHY**, eg proper foods, periodic fasting, use of chiropractors, enemas, osteopaths, and other alternative practitioners

Naturopaths believe that disease is caused by the body's attempt to purify itself, and treatment requires that the body's vital force be enhanced by ridding the body of toxins

▶ **NATUROPATHY'S SIX PRINCIPLES**

- **FIRST, DO NO HARM**–*primum non nocere*
- **PREVENT RATHER THAN CURE**
- **NATURE HAS INNATE HEALING POWERS**–*vis medicatrix naturae*
- **HOLISTIC APPROACH**–the 'whole person' is treated
- **TREAT CAUSE OF DISEASE**, not symptoms–*tolle causum*
- **TEACH**–*docere*, and patient learns prevention

Naturopathy encompasses a gamut of alternative therapies, and is not bound by any particular orthodoxy; modalities used in naturopathic medicine include 'natural food' diets, vitamins, herbs, teas, tissue mineral salts, live cell therapies, manipulation, massage, use of natural forces (ie earth, wind fire, light, heat, cold, air)—known to some as physiotherapy, exercise, acupressure, acupuncture, auricular acupuncture, autogenic training, biofeedback training, Chinese herbal medicine, chiropractic, herbal remedies, homeopathy, hydrotherapy, *jin shin do*, Jungian psychotherapy, massage therapy, minor surgery, moxibustion and cupping, ortho-bionomy, osteopathy, reflexology, *tui na*, and other natural modalities; some naturopaths may believe that the treatment of virtually all diseases is within their scope of practice, since their role is to free the body of toxic encumberments (eg conventional drugs, food preservatives, pesticides), and allow it to heal itself; anecdotal reports suggest that naturopathy may be effective in treating abcesses, acidity, acne, addiction disorders (eg alcoholism, smoking), adenoids, anemia, angina pectoris, anorexia, anxiety, arthritis, asthma, atherosclerosis, bites and stings, blisters, bronchitis, bruises, bunions, burns, bursitis, candidiasis, cataracts, chickenpox, chronic fatigue syndrome, circulatory defects, the common cold, conjunctivitis, corns, cough, cramps, cystitis, dandruff, depression, eczema, emphysema, eyestrain, fainting, fatigue, fever, fissures, flatulence, flu, fluid retention, food poisoning, frozen shoulder, gallstones, gastrointestinal problems (eg anal changes, gastritis, nausea, vomiting, indigestion, constipation, diarrhea, and irritable bowel syndrome), gout, halitosis, hangover, hay fever, headaches, hemorrhoids, herpes (genital and oral), hives, hypertension, hypoglycemia, hypotension, hypothermia, infertility, insomnia, itching, laryngitis, low back pain, measles, menopausal disorders, menstrual defects, migraines, mineral deficiencies, mood swings, morning sickness, mumps, muscle weakness, neuralgias, neurologic complaints, obesity, osteoporosis, panic attacks, parasites, periodontal disease, phobias, post-partum depression, premenstrual syndrome, prostate disease, rheumatic disease, psychosomatic disease, sciatica, seizures, sexual problems, shortness of breath, sinusitis, sleep disorders, sports injuries, stasis (decubitus) and gastric ulcers, stress, tension, tics, tinnitus, urinary incontinence, varicose veins, vertigo, warts, wheezing, whooping cough, and other conditions. See Chiropractic, Herbal medicine, Homeopathy RESOURCE: *American Association of Naturopathic Physicians, 2355 Eastlake Ave E, Suite 322, Seattle WA 98102 ☎ 1.206.323.7610*

**N.C.C.A.** National Commission for Certification of Acupuncturists, see there

**N.D.** Doctor of Naturopathy, Naturopathic Physician

**NDE** Near-death experience, see there

**NDGA** Nordihydro-guaiaretic acid, see there

**near and far focusing** Accommodation ALTERNATIVE OPHTHALMOLOGY One of the exercises used in the Bates method of vision training, which consists of changing the point of focus from near to far distances 10 to 20 times. See Bates vision training

**near-death experience** Lazarus complex PARANORMAL PHENOMENA A phenomenon of unclear nature that may occur in patients who have been clinically dead and then resuscitated; the patients report a continuity of subjective experience and may recall visitors and other hospital events despite virtually complete suppression of cortical activity; near-death experiences are considered curiosities with no explanation in the context of an acceptable biomedical paradigm The trivial synonym, Lazarus complex, refers to the biblical Lazarus, who was raised from the dead by Jesus of Nazareth

**need** see Basic need, Self-actualization need

**needle treatment** Acupuncture, see there

**negative emotion** A general term for any of a number of adverse emotions, including anger, envy, cynicism, and others

**negative love syndrome** ALTERNATIVE PSYCHOLOGY A 'condition' which, according to R Hoffman, developer of the Hoffman quadrinity process, is a constellaton of negative attitudes, behaviors, emotions, and moods, that is the key to all neuroses, which consists of negativity, low self-esteem, and an inability to love. See Hoffman quadrinity process

***Nei Jing*** The Yellow Emperor's Classic of Internal Medicine MEDICAL HISTORY-ALTERNATIVE MEDICINE A textbook of internal medicine compiled by 7 medical scholars in the Han dynasty (± 2000 years ago) that contained the medical thought and philosphy known at the time; *Nei Jing* forms the basis for Chinese medicine as it is currently practiced. See Chinese medicine, Herbal medicine, Traditional Chinese medicine; Cf *Canon of Medicine, Charak Samhita, The Complete Herbal, De Materia Medica, Natural History, Pen Ts'ao, Philosophy of Natural Therapeutics, Rigveda, Sushrita Samhita, Theatrum Botanicum*

***Nelumbium nucifera*** Popularly known as lotus, see there

**neo-Paleolithic diet** CLINICAL NUTRITION A diet similar to that consumed in the Paleolithic period (100,000 years ago), which is believed by some to be an optimal diet for humans; the diet consists of fruits and fiber-rich vegetables as sources of carbohydrates, provides a 2-5-fold greater amount of micronutrients (ie minerals and vitamins) than is currently consumed in the US–based on recommended daily allowances promulgated by the FDA; the diet also has a low protein-to-carbohydrate ratio, given the relative lack of protein-rich foods in the environment; a modern variant of the neo-Paleolithic diet is the Zone-favorable diet. See Diet, Zone-favorable diet

**neo-shamanism** New Age shamanism PARANORMAL PHENOMENA A general term for a modern Western interpretation of the spiritual and medical tradition of shamanism, which draws on the use of rituals and 'tribal' psychology for therapy; in addition to the shamanic state of altered consciousness through rituals and psychotherapy, neo-shamanism uses such tools as flotation tanks, strobe lights, active-alert hypnosis, and other devices intended to alter a person's reality sense. See Harner method, Holotropic breathwork; Cf Shamanism

***Nepeta cataria*** Popularly known as catnip, see there

***Nepeta japonica*** Japanese catnip, *Schizonepeta*

*tenuifolia*, see there

***Nepeta tenuifolia*** Japanese catnip, see there, *Schizonepeta tenuifolia*, see there

***Nephrodium filix*** see Fern-Chinese medicine

**neroli** *Citrus aurantium* FRINGE MEDICINE-FLOWER ESSENCE THERAPY A floral essence from the bitter or sour orange tree believed to calm the nerves, relieve anxiety, and induce sleep. See Flower essence therapy

**nerve interference** CHIROPRACTIC A general term for an interruption in the flow of neural impulses, which is believed to be the primary process that causes disease in patients needing chiropractic care. See Chiropractic, Rule of the nerve

**nerve root** Lady's slipper, see there, *Cypripedium calceolus*

**nervine** HERBAL MEDICINE *noun* A medicinal preparation, usually of herbal origin, that is believed to act on the nervous system, reduce anxiety and tension (nervine relaxant), stimulate neural function (nervine stimulant), or strengthen and restore the entire nervous system (nervine tonic)

▶ **NERVINES**

- **Nervine relaxants** include betony (*Betonica officinalis*), catnip (*Nepeta cataria*), hops (*Humulus lupulus*), lady's slipper (*Cypripedium pubescens*), mistletoe (*Viscum album*), passion flower (*Passiflora incarnata*), skullcap (*Scutellaria lateriflora*), valerian (*Valeriana officinalis*)
- **Nervine stimulants** include cayenne (*Capsicum fruticens*), ginger (*Zingiber officinale*), horseradish (*Cochlearia armoracia*), poplar (*Populus tremuloides*), prickly ash (*Xanthoxylum americanum*), snake root (*Aristolochia reticulata*), and wintergreen (*Gaultheria procumbens*)
- **Nervine tonics** include Belvedere cypress (*Kochia scoparia*), black pepper (*Piper nigrum*), broomrape (*Cistanche salsa*), Chinese jujube (*Ziziphus vulgaris*), dodder (*Cuscuta japonica*), dogwood (*Cornus officinalis*), fennel (*Foeniculum vulgare*), garlic (*Allium sativum*), ginseng (*Panax ginseng*)

(*Trattler, 1985*). See Bitter, Herbal medicine

**nervous exhaustion** Neurasthenia, see there

**nervous prostration** Neurasthenia, see there

***netra vyaayamam*** AYURVEDIC MEDICINE A system of yoga-based eye exercises (horizontal, perpendicular, circular movements) and manipulations (warming the eyes with the palms of the hands) that are used for stress management. See Yoga; Cf Bates vision training

**nettle** Stinging nettle, see there, Urtica dioica

**network chiropractic** CHIROPRACTIC A permutation of chiropractic developed in 1979 by D Epstein, DC, based on traditional chiropractic adjustments; network chiropractic uses a unified sequence of 12 techniques, which consist of gentle touching and tapping to release tension in the brain and spinal cord, to return a patient to his state of harmony, vitality, and health; Epstein reports that some patients respond to the release reaction with laughter, screams, or assume strange postures; if the network method does not have the desired effect, the practitioner will then 'reflect' into standard chiropractic techniques. See Chiropractic

**neural organization technique** NOT A permutation of cranial osteopathy developed by an American chiropractor, Carl Ferreri; the treatment consists of applying vise-like pressure to the roof of the mouth and eye sockets, which is believed to remove static from the nervous system

Note: In 1988 the Del Norte, California, schools sponsored a NOT treatment program for children with cerebral palsy, Down's syndrome, dyslexia, learning disabilities, seizure disorders, and other conditions; the residua from NOT included seizures, violent behavior, and loss of self-motivation and drive (*Butler, 1992*)

**neurasthenia** American nervousness, americanitis, cerebral exhaustion, nervous exhaustion, nervous prostration, neurasthenia americana MEDICAL HISTORY-ALTERNATIVE HEALTH A condition described in the late 1800s as being uniquely American, that was believed to most commonly affect physicians, lawyers, and inventors, who performed cerebral work; the symptoms included a loss of interest in mental labor and heart disturbances; neurasthenia was viewed as a reflection of the natural superiority of the American culture and a product of the progess and refinement of modern civilization; treatments included cold water cures, diets, exercise, arsenic and many others; the modern translation of neurasthenia is 'stress' (*Armstrong, 1991*)

**neurasthenia americana** Neurasthenia, see there

**neurocalometer** A device invented in 1924 by BJ Palmer, son of DD Palmer, that was claimed to be able to locate sublocations (*Armstrong, 1991*). See Chiropractic, BJ Palmer

**Neuro/Cellular Repatterning®** Cellular Repatterning® '...*a process that integrates spiritual psychology with body/mind therapy to release negative cellular memory*...(it)...*works on the physical, mental, emotional, spiritual, and etheric levels to* ...*release emotional and physical dysfunctions*.' (*Kastner, Burroughs, 1993*); Neuro/Cellular Patterning® was developed in the late 1970s by a psychologist, AH Martin, and uses love and forgiveness as its therapeutic tools; Neuro/Cellular Patterning practitioners view their role as that of teaching a person to love himself and others, and to improve self-esteem; biofeedback devices may be used in unusual ways, eg as a means of validating responses from the subconscious mind, and for identifying blocked traumatic events

**Neuro-Emotional Technique** A therapy developed in the late 1980s by an American chiropractor, Scott Walker, which is a synthesis of acupuncture (meridian therapy), kinesiology (muscle testing), chiropractic activator technique, nutritional support, and homeopathy; the technique is based on Walker's belief that many physical conditions, eg myofascial tension, pain, TMJ syndrome, and others, are due to the long-term effects of negative emotions (*Visions Maga-zine, Jan 1996*). See Negative emotion

**neurogenic constitution** FRINGE MEDICINE-IRIDOLOGY A blue iris which, according to the construct of iridology, belongs to a person who is prone to colds, inflammation, tuberculosis, pericarditis, peritonitis, and rheumatic complaints. See Iridology, Iris constitution

**neurolinguistic programming** Neurolinguistics ALTERNATIVE PSYCHOLOGY A behavior modification technique developed in 1975 by Richard Bandler and John Grinder, that is based on a reciprocal relationship said to exist between a person's behavior and the external manifestations of his personality, including vocal tone, posture, eye movements, and physiology

**neurolinguistics** Neurolinguistic programming, see there

**neuromuscular massage** Trigger point massage, myotherapy ALTERNATIVE MEDICINE A type of deep massage, in which the fingers are used to knead individual muscles, increase blood flow and, according to its advocates, release 'trigger points'*; neuromuscular massage is applied to the neural reflex and trigger points in a fashion analogous to that of shiatsu and acupressure, to enhance neuromuscular interaction; the technique is believed to be useful in controlling pain and reducing neuromuscular spasms. See Bonnie Pruden myotherapy, Massage therapy; Traditional European massage, Trigger point; Cf Deep tissue massage, Swedish/Esalen massage, Manual lymph drainage, Shiatsu

*Here, trigger point refers to a circumscribed 'knot' of tense muscle which, when stimulated, triggers a pain response elsewhere in the body; this contrasts with the term trigger point or trigger zone, as used by neurologists, which refers to a region on mucocutaneous surfaces which, when stimulated, evokes intense ('lightning') locoregional pain, as occurs in trigeminal neuralgia, glossopharyngeal neuralgia, tic doloreaux, and myofascial pain syndrome

**neuro-muscular motivation** ALTERNATIVE MEDICINE An integrative method of health care created by J Lowe, who divided body therapies into a continuum of relaxation, stimulation, and manipulation, in which the client sets the pace at which he or she undergoes health improvement and achieves his or her maximum potential for health. See Integrative technique

**neuromuscular reeducation** REHABILITATION MEDICINE The use of any manipulation-based therapeutic modality, eg use of biofeedback training, that is intended to help a patient recuperate functional activity, after trauma or a cerebrovascular accident. See Biofeedback training

**neuromuscular therapy–St John's method** St John's neuromuscular therapy, see there

**neuropeptide Y inhibitor** NUTRITION Any of a number of agents that act in the central nervous system to decrease neuropeptide Y, an appetite stimulant that increases carbohydrate absorption and decreases its metabolism. See Obesity

Note: Early trials are in progress with various neuropeptide Y inhibitors (*Sci Am Aug 1996, p88*)

**neutral bath** Tepid bath, see there

**neutralization (test)** Provocation (test) FRINGE MEDICINE A test of uncertain validity used by clinical ecologists (practitioners of environmental medicine) to identify various conditions, in particular, environmental disease; the test consists of either subdermal injection or sublingual placement of the allegedly offending substances (eg formaldehye, toluene) and evaluating reactions thereto; the substances are then 'neutralized' with lower doses of the same substances; some clinical ecologists diagnose illness and identify noxious substances by crystals, pendulums, galvanometers, and other devices of uncertain diagnostic efficacy. See Clinical ecologist, Environmental disease, Environmental medicine

**New Age** '*...a metaphor for the expression of a transformative, creative spirit...for being in the world in a manner that opens us to the presence of God...in the midst of our ordinariness; New Age ...calls us to live in a delicate balance between transformation and routine, between metamorphosis and maturation, between the birth of what could be and the care of what is, between empowerment and surrender.*' (*The New Age Catalogue, Island Pub Co, Dolphin, Doubleday, New York, 1988*)

A vast array of philosophies, activities, belief systems, and concepts have either aligned themselves or been identified with the New Age movement, including astral projection, channeling, graphology, global concerns, medical astrology, mysticism, near-death experiences, New Age music, transformational travel, visionary art, and others

**New Age music** MUSIC THERAPY A style of music first written in the 1970s by S Halpern, that is designed to relax the listener, and realign the mind, body, and spirit; unique to New Age music is the deliberate absence of specific harmonies, melodies, or rhythms–this lack of thematic distraction is believed to enhance meditation and yoga, and facilitate massage, movement therapy, and other alternative health care practices. See Music therapy

**New Age shamanism** Neo-Shamanism, see there

**New Age shiatsu** A type of shiatsu developed by Reuho Yamada. See Shiatsu

**the 'new medicine'** Integrative medicine, see there

**niacin** Nicotinic acid, vitamin $B_3$ A water-soluble 'B complex' vitamin that is integrated in the coenzyme nicotinamide adenine dinucleotide (NAD), one of the $H^+$ acceptors for dehydrogenases; niacin is formed in the body from tryptophan, and is present in high-protein foods (eg fish, poultry, meats, liver, yeast, enriched bread and cereals); niacin prevents heart attacks by lowering the total and LDL cholesterol, and is used for alcoholism and migraines, and believed by some alternative health advocates to be useful for anxiety, arthritis, autism, depression, diabetes, hypoglycemia, and schizophrenia TOXICITY Skin flushing, arrhythmias, defects in glucose and urea metabolism, diarrhea, nausea, gastric bleeding, headaches, itching, hepatic toxicity, psychotic reactions. See Vitamins

**niacin**

N

COOH

**niacin deficiency** Pellagra, see there

**niacinamidosis** Pellagra, see there

**nibbling diet** NUTRITION The consumption of food 'á petit pas,' between the 'normal' three meal-a-day regimen followed by most individuals, and either binging (gorging) or snacking diets. See Binge, Junk food

In one study, a nibbling diet reduced the total cholesterol, LDL-cholesterol, and apo-B by 8.5%, 13.5%, and 15.1% respectively; during the nibbling diet, mean serum insulin, urinary C-peptide, and 24-hour excretion of cortisol decreased by 28%, 20%, and 17% respectively (*N Engl J Med 1989; 321:929*); the terms snacking and nibbling may be used interchangeably; American colloquial usage might define snacking as the 'off-hour' (ie, off mealtime) consumption of food, usually of junk ('snack') foods; in contrast, nibbling is a similarly staccato, but temporally periprandial, consumption, often of healthy foods

**NICE** ALTERNATIVE PSYCHOLOGY A colloquial acronym for a technique used to reduce the stress of new situations, which can be viewed as being new, interesting, and challenging experiences, rather than with FUD (fear, uncertainty, and doubt)

**nickel** A metallic element (atomic number 28; atomic weight 58.69) that has been linked to deficiency states in some plants and animals; in some biological systems, nickel protects against heat-induced ribosomal damage; its role in humans is uncertain; in large amounts, it is toxic. See Nickel toxicity, Trace element; Cf Trace mineral

**nickel toxicity** A condition caused by nickel excess, which may be due to nickel-based jewelry, resulting in contact dermatitis, or occupational, resulting in liver necrosis and pulmonary congestion; long-term nickel exposure increases the risk for nasopharygeal and lung cancer. See Minerals, Nickel

**nicotinic acid** Niacin, see there

**nicotinic acid deficiency** Pellagra, see there

**night-blooming cactus** *Cactus grandiflora*, see there

**night-owl insomnia** Delayed sleep phase syndrome, see there

**nightshade vegetable** ALTERNATIVE NUTRI-

TION Any vegetable of the nightshade family (*Solanaceae*) which includes eggplant, peppers[1], white potatoes, tomatoes, and others[2] which, according to the macrobiotic construct of nutrition, are foods to be avoided. See Macrobiotics, No-nightshade diet

[1]Bell peppers, chili peppers, jalapeño, and others [2]Tobacco belongs to this family, but is not comestible

**night willow herb** Evening primrose, see there, *Oenothera biennis*

**nimodipine** AIDS An L-type calcium channel antagonist that preferentially binds to the channels when the cells are depolarized, maintaining them in an opened state, theoretically preventing the accumulation of glutamate, which has been pathogenically linked to AIDS dementia complex (*N Engl J Med 1995; 332:934*). See AIDS therapy

**nine hooks** Lady's mantle, see there, *Alchemilla vulgaris*

***niou hsi*** *Achyranthes bidentata*, see there

**nitidine** PHARMACOGNOSY A chemical found in prickly ash (*Zanthoxylum americana*) that has been shown to have anticarcinogenic activity in animals (*Pelton, Overholser, 1994*). See Prickly ash, Folk cures for cancer

**nitrates** BIOCHEMISTRY A family of chemically stable forms of inorganic nitrogen; nitrates are formed as part of the natural breakdown of organic matter, and are ingested in vegetables and absorbed from the gastrointestinal tract; an estimated 25% of absorbed nitrates are released into the saliva; 20% of the nitrates in the saliva are converted into nitrites; nitrates are manufactured for use as fertilizers and explosives, and tend to accumulate in the environment, as the uptake of nitrates by plants is relatively slow; Cf Nitrites, Nitrogen, Nitrosamines

**nitrites** FOOD INDUSTRY A family of chemically stable forms of inorganic nitrogen that are not present in significant amounts in the environment; nitrites in the blood originate from bacterial conversion of nitrates present in vegetables, and from nitrites ingested as preservatives; nitrites are regarded as potentially hazardous, given their conversion to carcinogenic nitrosamines; nitrites (eg sodium nitrite) are manufactured primarily as preservatives for fish and meats (hot dogs, bacon, corned beef, ham, liverwurst, salami); nitrites have been associated with allergic reactions and formation of methemoglobin. See Sodium nitrite; Cf Nitrates, Nitrogen, Nitrosamines

**nitrogen** A gaseous element (atomic number 7; atomic weight 14.01) present in biological systems as the molecular form, $N_2$, or bound to other elements including oxygen, as in nitric oxide (NO), a neurotransmitter; nitrogen is critical to all biological systems, and is present in proteins and DNA, without which life cannot occur. See Nitrates, Nitrites

**nitrogen balance** CLINICAL NUTRITION A crude indicator of the adequacy of nutrition is the protein lost (in the urine) in a 24-hour period, which is calculated by urinary excretion of nitrogen products produced by the urea cycle; usually 0.5 g/kg of dietary protein is adequate to maintain an adequate nitrogen balance; in a negative nitrogen balance, loss exceeds intake, as occurs in aging, burns, and protein-losing enteropathy Note: In the induction phase of chemotherapy, a 'physiologic' negative balance occurs due to massive lysis of malignant cells; a positive balance is typical of growth periods, ie in the young, in pregnancy and in convalescence from burns

**nitroglycerin** HOMEOPATHY *Glonoin*, see there, *Glonoinum*

**nitrosamines** CLINICAL TOXICOLOGY A class of complex organic nitrogen molecules, formed in the stomach by a reaction between nitrites and the amine groups of certain proteins, or ingested preformed in beer and certain drugs, or absorbed from cigarette smoke (the nitrosamine levels in smokers is up to 8-fold that of nonsmokers); the reaction between of nitrites and amines can be inhibited with antioxidants including vitamins C and E, and other antioxidants; nitrosamines are carcinogenic, and are implicated in cancers of the stomach, esophagus, nasopharynx, and urinary bladder; Cf Nitrates, Nitrites, Nitrogen, Sodium nitrate

***niu bang dze*** Popularly known as burdock, see there, *Arctium lappa*

***niu bang zi*** Popularly known as burdock, see there, *Arctium lappa*

***niu hsi*** *Achyranthes bidentata*, see there

**NLP** Neuro linguistic programming, see there

**N.M.D.** Naturopathic Medical Doctor

**'no' foods** HEALTH A colloquial term for those

foods and substances (eg alcohol, junk foods, refined sugars, tobacco, and others) that should be severely curtailed or deleted from the diet. See Nutritional therapy; Cf 'Go' foods

**'NO' FOODS--FOODS & CONSUMPTIONS TO AVOID**

Alcohol (allowed in moderation)
Artificial sweeteners
Bleached flours
Cakes, pastries, pies
Candy, ice cream, chocolate
Carbonated soft drinks
Coffee and other caffeinated beverages
Drugs of abuse
'Fast' foods, eg pizza, hamburgers, hot dogs
'Junk' foods, eg pretzels, potato chips
Refined sugar
Salt
Tobacco

D Carroll,1980

**no-impact sport** SPORTS MEDICINE A generic term for any physical activity or sport in which there is virtually no wear or trauma to weight-bearing joints; NISs include bicycling, sailing, scuba diving, and swimming (laps); NISs are encouraged after hip and knee arthroplasty for those who wish to participate in physical activities (*Mayo Clin Proc 1995; 70:342*); Cf High-impact sport, Low-impact sport, Moderate-impact sport

**The Noble Experiment** MEDICAL HISTORY-SUBSTANCE ABUSE A term attributed to Herbert Hoover that referred to Prohibition, the period between 1918 and 1933, during which the sale of alcohol was banned in the United States

**'nocebo'** A negative placebo effect that may occur when patients in a clinical trial of a drug therapy recognize (or think they recognize) that they are getting a placebo (ie not receiving therapy), and fare worse due to the effect of negative suggestibility (*Lancet 1991; 338:899*); Cf Placebo

**noise** A term defined in electronics as the random variation in signals of the electromagnetic spectrum that carries no useful information from the source; OSHA requires that anyone with occupational exposure to greater than 89 decibels should wear ear protection. See Cymatics, Music therapy, Sound therapy

**noise pollution** PUBLIC HEALTH The unexpected or undesired contamination of the spectrum of electromagnetic waves audible to the human ear; loud noises destroy the ciliary hair in the inner ear, which does not regenerate. See Cymatics, Sound therapy, Toning

Common sounds in decibels: 60 normal conversation, 70 restaurant, 80 vacuum cleaner, 90 motorcycle, 100 jackhammer, 100-130 rock concert, 140 gunshot

**nomenclature** ALTERNATIVE MEDICINE The names used in alternative health care often overlap with those of mainstream medicine as well as other fields and may cause confusion to the practitioners of both types of medicine, as well as to patients

▶ **ALTERNATIVE MEDICAL TERMINOLOGY–SOURCES OF CONFUSION**

- **DIFFERENT USES FOR SAME TERM** As an example, colonic irrigation is used by mainstream practitioners for the flushing of the large intestine in preparation for emergency surgery, and used by alternative practitioners as a synonym for colon therapy, the practice of performing multiple enemas to flush out putative toxins; the same problem occurs when herbologists use the same names for medicinal plants as used by horticulturists, which may or may not refer to the same plants; an example of such confusion is the use of geranium by both for the ornamental use of the plant and its medicinal use
- **DIFFERENT TERMS FOR THE SAME ENTITY** As an example, homeopaths use a Latinized term, *Natrum muriaticum*, for table salt (sodium chloride); similarly, some herbs are known by the trivial name, eg rue and blood root, while the homeopathic remedies based on these same plants take the Latin name, *Ruta* and *Sanguinaria*, respectively

To resolve these dilemmas, and aid the reader, in this work, the author uses extensive cross-referencing

**no-nightshade diet** ALTERNATIVE NUTRITION A diet developed by a professor of horticulture, N Childers, that is devoid of nightshade family vegetables–eggplant, peppers, potatoes, and tomatoes—which he believes can cause and/or exacerbate arthritis and rheumatic complaints. See Arthritis diet, Diet, Dong diet, Nightshade vegetable

**non-epileptic seizure** Psychogenic seizure, see there

**non-nutritive dietary component** CLINICAL NUTRITION Any critical component of a well-balanced diet that has an 'ancillary' function; non-nutritive components include water, fiber (soluble and insoluble), and a host of molecules present in plant and animal foods with as-yet unknown functions; Cf Micronutrients, Non-nutritive dietary component

**non-operative cranioplasty** Head shaping, see there

**nonoriental massage** Energetic massage ALTERNATIVE MEDICINE A general term for any form of massage therapy (polarity therapy, reiki, therapeutic touch) intended to balance the flow of energy; nonoriental massages are based on principles other than that of harmonizing *chi*–which is the principle underlying oriental massage therapy. See Polarity therapy, Reiki, Therapeutic touch; Cf Massage therapy, Oriental massage, Structural integration, Traditional European massage, (contemporary) Western massage

**nonresting energy expenditure** PHYSIOLOGY A metabolic value that corresponds to the energy cost of physical activity, which represents approximately 30% of the total energy expenditure, see there (*N Engl J Med 1995; 332:621*). See MET, Total energy expenditure

**nonscientific** Unproven, see there

**non-traditional cancer therapy** Unproven method for cancer management, see there

**non-traditional medicine** Alternative medicine, see there

**nordihydroguaiaretic acid** A relatively nontoxic quinone obtained from the oily resin of the evergreen shrub, chaparral, or creosote bush (*Larrea divaricata*, *Covillea tridentata*) ALTERNATIVE PHARMACOLOGY NDGA appears to have a broad spectrum of anticancer properties; its efficacy is attributed to NDGA's antioxidant activity, its virtually complete inhibition of anaerobic glycolysis, and inhibition of DNA synthesis; NDGA may be useful in treating choriocarcinoma, gastrointestinal tumors, gliomas of the brain, leukemia, lymphoma, and melanoma (*Moss, 1992*). See Chaparral, Unproven methods for cancer management

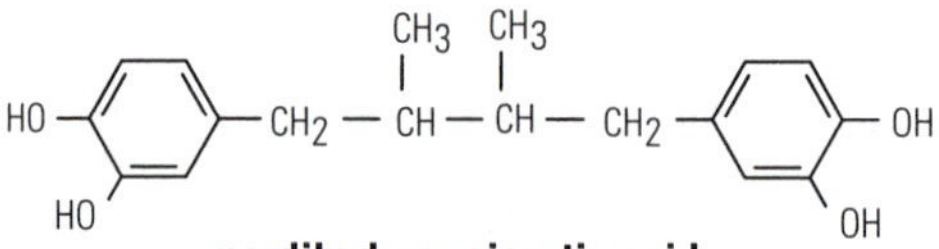

**nordihydroguaiaretic acid**

**Norit eluate factor** Folic acid, see there

**'North Pole energy'** see Imaginetics

**Northern jujube** See Chinese jujube

**Northern prickly ash** *Zanthoxylum americanum*, angelica tree, prickly ash, suterberry, toothache tree HERBAL MEDICINE A deciduous shrub that contains alkaloids, coumarins, resins, tannins, and volatile oil; prickly ash bark and berries have a long tradition among herbalists–they are regarded as carminative, diuretic, and vasodilatory, and have been used for toothaches, rheumatic pain, and may protect against cancer. See Herbal medicine

**nosebleed** Yarrow, see there, *Achillea millefolium*

**NOT** Neural organization technique, see there

**not proven** Unproven, see there

**notoginseng** *Panax notoginseng*, pseudoginseng CHINESE MEDICINE An herb, the root of which is analgesic and hemostatic; it is used internally for bleeding from the nose, upper respiratory tract, in the urine, and in stool; it is used topically for contusions, swelling, injuries, gunshot wounds, and other external trauma, and has been used in sports medicine to increase stamina; some data suggest that notoginseng may lower cholesterol, blood pressure, decrease anginal pain, and possibly be of use in acute exacerbations of inflammatory bowel disease TOXICITY It should not be used in pregnancy. See Chinese herbal medicine; Cf Ginseng

**nouthetic counseling** Biblical counseling, see there

**novelty diet** see Diet, Fad diet

**noxious music** A general term for strident music that is capable of inducing seizures or other adverse responses. See Noise, Noise pollution; Cf Music therapy, Sedative music, Stimulative music

**N.P.L.EX.** Naturopathic Physician Licensing Examination

***nu jen dze*** Japanese wax privet, see there, *Ligustrum japonicum*

***nu jen zi*** Japanese wax privet, see there, *Ligustrum japonicum*

***nuad bo-rarn*** Massage, see there

**nuclear family** SOCIAL MEDICINE The core family unit, which classically consists of heterosexually-oriented male and female partners and their direct (usually unmarried) genetic progeny; disintegration of this unit and its central role in society is held responsible for losses in mental equilibrium (*Science News 1994; 146:106*); Cf Companionship, Extended family, Marriage bonus, Most significant other, Social isolation

**Numbers diet™** FRINGE NUTRITION A weight-loss diet developed in 1990 by Jean Simpson based on numerology, in which a important numbers in a person's life are believed to have an effect on a person's weight. See Atkins' diet, Diet, Numerology

**numerology** PARANORMAL PHENOMENA The study of the mystical significance of numbers and the influence they are alleged to have on human behavior, health, and other activities

**nuts** ALTERNATIVE NUTRITION Dry fruits with an edible kernel enclosed in a leathery or woody shell, eg peanuts, almonds, and walnuts, which are a vegetarian food staple; in the past, conventional wisdom held that the high fat content of nuts made them a suboptimal source of protein, and thus had been restricted in those on low-fat diets; nuts are now widely regarded as 'healthy foods'; they are high in omega-3 fatty acids and unsaturated (good) fats; increased consumption of nuts is associated with decreased cholesterol, decreased myocardial infarction, and decreased osteoporosis. See Healthy foods

**nutgrass** Cyperus, see there, *Cyperus rotundus*

**nutmeg** *Myristica fragrans*, flesh nut, *Myristica moschata*, *rou dou kou*, *rou guo* HERBAL MEDICINE A tropical tree, the seeds of which are astringent, carminative, and sedative in small doses and stimulating in large doses, possibly related to the high content of myristicin; nutmeg has been used for abdominal pain and discomfort, anorexia, diarrhea, flatulence, insomnia, malabsorption, pancreatitis, sexual dysfunction, and urinary incontinence; in some cultures, it is regarded as an aphrodisiac TOXICITY Consumed in large amounts, the myristin in nutmeg may cause delirium and disorientation; it should not be used in pregnancy. See Herbal medicine, Myristicin

**Nutrasweet™** Aspartame, see there

**nutrient** FOOD INDUSTRY A substance added to foods that increases their vitamin, mineral, and protein content. See Food additives

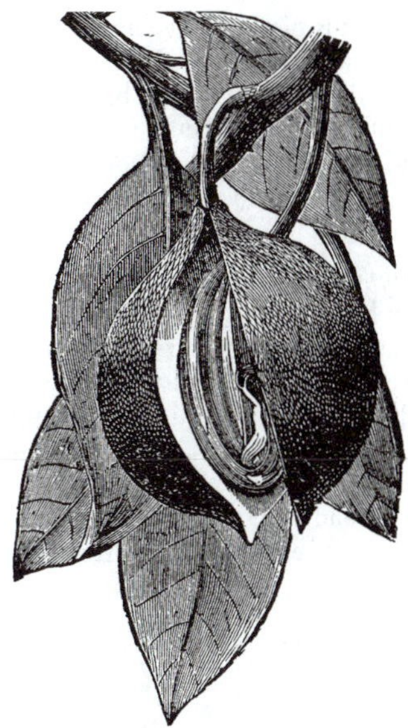

**nutmeg** *Myristica fragrans*

**nutripathy** FRINGE MEDICINE A system of pseudodiagnosis and pseudotherapy developed in the 1970s by a nontraditional Christian minister, Gary Martin; nutripathy combines "spiritual" analysis of saliva and urine, food combining lifestyle alterations, and dietary supplements. See Food combining; Cf Naprapathy

**Nutritional Herbology** FRINGE MEDICINE A proprietary system of herbal medicine developed in 1987 by a US-based 'nutritional chemist,' Mark Pedersen, who divides herbs into 5 groups based on their active components: aromatic (volatile oils), astringent (tannins), bitter (alkaloids, phenols, and saponins), mucilaginous (polysaccharides), and nutritive; in the construct of nutritional herbology, diseases are divided into those of excess or paucity, which can be treated by any of 80 combinations of herbs; Cf Herbal medicine

**nutritional therapy** CLINICAL NUTRITION A general term for the use of foods to cleanse the body and to promote health ('go' foods); nutritional therapy addresses 3 broad categories of disease—allergies, toxic overload, and nutritional deficiency—and is an adjunct to naturopathy, homeopathy, and other forms of alternative health care; nutritionists who adhere to the alternative 'philosophy' of diet generally believe there are certain foods and dietary 'exposures' that should be minimized if not eliminated in their entirety ('no' foods). See Diet, Go foods, No foods

**Nux vomica** *Strychnos nux vomica*, poison nut, Quaker buttons HOMEOPATHY A homeopathic remedy formulated from the strychnine tree native to western Asia and Australia; it is used for colds, coughs, gastrointestinal complaints including colic, cystitis, diarrhea, and indigestion, hangovers, headache with vertigo, hemorrhoids, hypersensitivity, irritability, laryngitis, menstrual cramping and dysfunction, morning sickness, nasal congestion, sinusitis, urinary frequency, and vomiting. See *Nux vomica* type, Homeopathy

**Nux vomica type** HOMEOPATHY The *Nux vomica* constitutional type of person is aggressive, ambitious, hyperactive, irritable; these types may have a strong sex drive and tend to abuse alcohol or drugs; they like rich fatty foods, meat, alcohol, coffee, and spicy foods WORSE Cold, dryness, noise, mental stress, eating, spicy foods, before dawn FEARS Failure, death, crowds WEAKEST BODY REGIONS Gastrointestinal tract, liver, lungs, nerves. See Constitutional type, *Nux vomica*, Homeopathy

**oat** *Avena sativa*, common oat, groats ALTERNATIVE NUTRITION Oats are regarded by some as a 'healthy food'; they are rich in a type of soluble fiber, beta-glucans, and reduce serum cholesterol by up to 10%. See Healing foods HERBAL MEDICINE An annual grass that contains alkaloids (avenine and trigonelline) fats, minerals (calcium copper, iron, magnesium, and zinc), saponins, a sterol flavonoid, and vitamin B; they are used as a nerve tonic, for depression and insomnia. See Herbal medicine, Healthy food

**oat bran** NUTRITION A convenient source of soluble fiber from oats (*Avena sativa*), which reduces serum cholesterol levels by replacing dietary fats (*N Engl J Med 1990; 322:147*). See Bran, Diet, Dietary fiber

Bran derived from oats was believed by some workers to be superior to bran from other grains, a posit that is not supported by current data

**obesity** A state of excess body fat, which for some is a premorbid addiction disorder, defined as 10% to 20% above an individual's standard weight; the ideal body weight is 21 kg/m$^2$ EPIDEMIOLOGY 33% of US adults are obese and weigh an average excess of 25.5 kg/m$^2$; 59% of Americans are overweight according to a 1995 report by the Institute of Medicine, there has been a 54% increase in obesity and a 98% increase in superobesity in children 6-9 years of age); an obese child is often an obese adult and the patterns may be established as early as 3 months of age and due to decreased energy expenditure in infants of obese mothers; Diet-resistant obesity is characterized by an inability to lose weight despite decreased caloric intake and increased exercise; a certain percentage of diet-resistant obesity is related to underreporting of actual caloric consumption and/or overreporting of physical activity, rather than due to low energy expenditure, which is known as the 'eye-mouth' gap ETIOLOGY Endocrine-hypothyroidism, Cushing syndrome, hypogonadism (Fröhlich syndrome), polycystic ovaries, pseudohypo-parathyroidism PATHOGENESIS Increased lipid deposit in fat cells, decreased mobilization of lipids from adipocytes, and decreased lipid utilization

▶ **OBESITY, CLASSIFICATIONS OF**

**ANATOMIC**

- **ANDROID OBESITY** Central obesity, 'beer-gut' obesity This form is more common in males, more central or truncal in distribution and places the subject at increased risk for diabetes mellitus
- **GYNECOID OBESITY** This form is more common in women, the fat is distributed in the lower abdomen and legs and is less commonly associated with atherosclerosis

**PRIMARY OR SECONDARY**

- **PRIMARY** Primary obesity is a component of Allström, Blount, Cohen, Carpenter, Laurence-Moon-Biedl, Prader-Willi, and other eponymic syndromes
- **SECONDARY** Secondary or acquired obesity comprises the bulk of obesity

**AGE OF ONSET**

eg juvenile, mature, in pregnancy or other

**TYPE OF TISSUE CHANGE,**

eg hyperplastic or hyperplastic-hypertrophic

Obesity mimics the laboratory findings of non-insulin-dependent diabetes mellitus, which include insulin resistance, increased glucose, cholesterol and triglycerides, decreased HDL-cholesterol and norepinephrine and depression of the sympathetic and parasympathetic nervous systems CONDITIONS LINKED TO OBESITY Cardiovascular disease, thromboembolism, cholecystitis, cholelithiasis, abnormal gastrointestinal transit, poor wound healing, atelectasis, hepatic steatosis and fibrosis TREATMENT Diet, exercise, behavior modification; Cf Diet, Gastric balloon, Morbid obesity, Superobesity

**'obe-tension'** A colloquial term for the relatively common clinical association of obesity with hypertension; Cf Diabesity

**object reading** Psychometry FRINGE MEDICINE A pseudodiagnostic technique described in the early 20th century by Dr JR Buchanan, which is based on the alleged ability to obtain information about people, places, and events, by merely touching an object owned by the person

***Ocimum basilicum*** Popularly known as basil, see there

**octasanol** SPORTS MEDICINE A solid alcohol that is the principal active ingredient of wheat germ and some vegetable waxes; it was transiently popular with some atheletes as it was believed to improve stamina, strength, and reaction time (*JC DeLee, D Drez, Jr, Eds, Orthopedic Sports Medicine WB Saunders, Philadelphia, 1994*). See Wheat germ

***Oenothera biennis*** Popularly known as evening primrose, see there

***Oenothera lamarckiana*** Evening primrose, see there, *Oenothera biennis*

**Office of Alternative Medicine** A section of the US National Institutes of Health established by the US Congress, the purpose of which is to investigate the claims of efficacy for various forms of alternative therapy, and their possible health benefits; the OAM's first director resigned

▶ **OAM, PILOT PROJECTS**

- **CHINESE MEDICINE** Acupuncture for unipolar depression, acupuncture for attention deficit-hyperactivity disorder, *chi kung* (*qi gong*) and reflex sympathetic dystrophy, *tai chi ch'uan* and balance disorders
- **AYURVEDIC MEDICINE** Health promotion, heroin addiction, obsessive disorder, Parkinson's disease
- **NATUROPATHIC MEDICINE** Antioxidant vitamins and cancer, macrobiotic diet and cancer
- **MIND/BODY MEDICINE** Biofeedback in diabetics, guided imagery for asthma, hypnosis for accelerated fracture healing
- **OTHERS** Homeopathy, massage therapy for HIV, music therapy for psychosocial adjustment after brain injury, prayer intervention for substance abuse (*Am Med News 17 October 1994 p13*). See Alternative medicine

Note: Criticism has been leveled that the very existence of such an agency has the potential for legitimizing virtually any form of unproven therapy that claims to be 'alternative' (*Sci Am 1993; 269/3:39*)

**Ohashiatsu®** ALTERNATIVE MEDICINE A proprietary health system developed by a Japanese-American, Wataru Ohashi, which combines shiatsu, exercise, and meditation into a form of 'touch communication' (*Raso, 1994*); the system is believed to integrate and rejuvenate the client's mind, body, and spirit, and increase awareness of his *hara*, the solar plexus, which is thought to be the spiritual center of the soul

**Ohsawa, George** A Japanese-American (1893-1966) who formulated the Zen macrobiotic diet, and Macrobiotics–a cult-like movement and lifestyle that was popular in the US during the 1960s. See Kushi, Macrobiotics, Simon, Zen macrobiotic diet

**oils** ALTERNATIVE MEDICINE See Aromatherapy, Bach's flower remedies NUTRITION The relative health benefits of the different types of dietary fats are not clear, as definitive studies have not been performed, although it is known that the more saturated (ie the greater the number of double bonds in the carbon chain) the fatty acid, the greater is the risk for atherosclerosis. See Fatty acids, Fish, Olive oil, Tropical oils; Cf Mineral oil

**ointment** *Yio* CHINESE MEDICINE A general term for any of a number of therapeutic balms that are applied topically for various complaints; an ointment consists of a finely ground herbal powder in any of a number of oil bases, including almond oil, beeswax, lanolin, lard, petroleum jelly, and sesame oil. See Chinese herbal medicine, Powder-Chinese medicine, Tiger Balm HERBAL MEDICINE A mixture of herbs heated in cocoa butter, lanolin, oils, or hardeners, eg beeswax, and applied externally, eg for bites, burns, cuts, and hemorrhoids. See Herbal medicine

**oki-do** Japanese, way of the great spirit An eclectic lifestyle philosophy that incorporates herbal medicine, purification through diet, meditation, Taoism, traditional oriental medicine, yoga, and Zen Buddhism

**old maid's nightcap** Cranesbill, see there, *Geranium maculatum*

**old maid's pink** Soapwort, see there, *Saponaria officinalis*

**old man** Rosemary, see there, *Rosmarinus officinalis*

**old man's beard** Usnea, see there

**oleoresin** HERBAL MEDICINE An oily resin from the male fern (*Aspidium oleoresin*) which has been used as a vermifuge

**Olestra®** Sucrose polyester NUTRITION A proprietary FDA-approved (1996) synthetic (no-calorie) fat used in savory snack foods, eg tortilla chips, potato chips, and crackers; Olestra has an appearance, taste, and texture virtually identical to fat, but unlike most dietary fats (which are composed of 3 fatty acids linked to a glycerol), it is composed of 6-8 fatty acids linked to glucose and is too large for digestion by the body's enzymes; Olestra may reduce passive overconsumption, as it flows undigested through the GI tract (*Sci Am Aug 1996, p88*). See Obesity

Note: Concern has been expressed that the product's safety was addressed in only one study performed by Proctor & Gamble, Olestra's developer, which involved 194 adults for 56 days, although in its status as a food additive (rather than a therapeutic agent), no more stringent testing for product safety is required (*N Engl J Med 1996; 334:984ED*)

**olive oil** CLINICAL NUTRITION A vegetable oil obtained from the ripe fruit of *Olea europaea*, which is used in foods, and as a demulcent, and laxative; it is widely regarded as a healthy food that reduces the risk of cardiovascular disease (heart attacks, hypertension, and strokes), by reducing cholesterol. See Healthy foods; Cf Fish oil, Tropical oils

Olive oil contains the highest (77%) level of monounsaturated fatty acids of all cooking oils; in one study of polyunsaturated fat-supplemented diets, $HDL_2$-cholesterol increased by 50%, $HDL_3$-cholesterol decreased by 7%, resulting in a 23.5% total increase in HDL-cholesterol); apolipoprotein-B is increased by 5.4% over those consuming monounsaturated fats, data that contradicts some reports that olive oil is optimal for lowering cholesterol; nonetheless, the high olive oil consumption and low incidence of cardiovascular disease in Italians suggests a cause-and-effect relation between the two

**O.M.D.** Doctor of Oriental Medicine

**OMEGA** A permutation of reiki, in which a healer is believed to be capable of transferring healing energy without physical contact with the healee. See Laying on of hands, Reiki, Therapeutic touch

**omega-3 fatty acids** n-3 fatty acids, see there

**omnivore** A meat-eater; Cf Carnivore

**O.M.T.** Osteopathic manipulative technique, Osteopathy

**Onconase®** P30 Protein EXPERIMENTAL ONCOLOGY An enzyme-like protein that is structurally similar to ribonuclease, which is derived from the embryos of the North American frog, *Rana pipiens*; it appears to be effective in treating experimental cancers in mice, but in larger animals is associated with cumulative central nervous system toxicity and muscle degeneration; in FDA Phase I trials it is associated with anorexia, flushing, and vertigo *(Moss, 1992)*. See Unproven methods for cancer management

**onion** *Allium cepa*, common onion HERBAL MEDICINE A perennial herb that contains volatile oils, and vitamins B and C, which has a long tradition among herbalists; it is antidiabetic, antihypertensive, and antiseptic; onions inhibit platelet aggregation by blocking the synthesis of thromboxane, reducing glucose in diabetes, and may contain a natural enzyme inhibitor that blocks the growth of cancer cells; raw slices may be applied topically for insect bites or as a poultice for bruises or sprains; onions appear to reduce cholesterol and lipids. See Herbal medicine

**onion** *Allium cepa*

**onion mono diet** FRINGE NUTRITION A diet in which the person ingests only onions, onion juice, and water, but no solid foods; it is recommended for lung complaints and inflammation of the mucosal surfaces of the head and neck. See Fasting

***Onoclea orientalis*** see Fern-Chinese medicine

**on-off dieting** CLINICAL NUTRITION A form of dieting in which a person undergoes a draconian diet, loses the desired weight, then regains it, resulting in the yo-yo syndrome PHYSIOLOGY As caloric intake decreases, the basal metabolic rate decreases to a minimum (known as the starvation response) to conserve energy; when the calories become available at the end of the diet, the weight is rapidly regained. See Binge, Diet, Yo-yo dieting

**ontological being center** PARANORMAL PHENOMENA Any of four arbitrarily defined anatomic regions of the 'embodied soul' which, according to the construct of organismic psychotherapy, are believed to mediate specific interactions with the external environment. See Organismic psychotherapy

**operant conditioning** see Biofeedback training

**ophresiology** Aromatherapy, see there

**opium poppy** *Papaver somniferum* HERBAL MEDICINE An annual, the unripe seeds of which contain alkaloids, including morphine, codeine, and papaverine; the poppy has been used for than 5000 years in cultural rituals for inducing euphoria, and reducing anxiety, and inhibitions; the alkaloids are analgesic, antispasmodic, and antitussive, and have been used for pain, colic, and asthmatic attacks; ripe poppy seeds have virtually no alkaloids, and are used as condiments TOXICITY Opium can cause fatal respiratory paralysis. See Herbal medicine

**opium poppy** *Papaver somniferum*

**OPT** Organic process therapy, see there

**oral chelation therapy** FRINGE MEDICINE The use of any agent or combination of agents, including enzymes, minerals, vitamins, and other compounds, which are claimed to bind to and remove 'dangerous' minerals or other substances from the circulation; these products may contain potentially toxic amounts of vitamins, eg vitamin A; they are not approved by the FDA; Cf Colon therapy

**orange** FRINGE MEDICINE–COLOR THERAPY A color that combines the healing power of red and yellow light; it is believed to stimulate the thyroid gland, lungs, and circulation, integrate mental and physical energy, and promote a sense of well-being; orange color therapy is claimed to be useful for gout, rheumatism, and tumors. See Color breathing, Color therapy, Orange foods, Orange metals & chemicals

**orange foods** FRINGE MEDICINE–COLOR THERAPY Orange foods are believed to release energy to the body and promote a sense of well-being, and include oranges, cantaloupe, and mangoes. See Color breathing, Color therapy, Orange, Orange metals and chemicals

**orange metals & chemicals** FRINGE MEDICINE–COLOR THERAPY Orange metals and chemicals are believed to release energy to the body and promote a sense of well-being, and include aluminum, antimony, rubidium. See Color breathing, Color therapy, Orange, Orange foods

**orange mono diet** ALTERNATIVE NUTRITION An alkaline diet consisting of oranges, orange juice, and water, but no solid foods; it is recommended for lung and mucosal disease, but should be used with caution, as oranges may irritate the liver. See Fasting

**orange root** Goldenseal, see there, *Hydrastis canadensis*

**orange swallow-wort** Pleurisy root, see there, *Aesclepias tuberosa*

**organ *chi* transformation (massage)** *Chi nei tsang*, see there

**organ drain** Lymphatic drain MASSAGE THERAPY A type of massage in which internal organs (eg kidneys, liver, and intestines) are kneaded and squeezed, with the intent of stimulating their drainage, allowing the entry of fresh blood. See Manual lymphoatic drainage massage, Massage therapy

**organ-based specialty** MAINSTREAM MEDICINE A generic term for any specialty (or subspecialty) of medicine or surgery that is focused on the diagnosis and treatment of diseases of a particular organ or organ system, eg neurology, neuropathology, neuroradiology, neurosurgery, and others

**organic** *adjective* ALTERNATIVE NUTRITION Pertaining or referring to foods that are grown without pesticides or artificial growth enhancers, which are processed and preserved without chemicals CLINICAL MEDICINE Pertaining or referring to a disease process that can be objectively evaluated, as it is organ-based, in contrast to mental disorders, which are not organic

**organic food** Organically-grown food A broadly-defined category of comestibles, which in the purest form, are grown without use of chemical fertilizers or pesticides, and sold to the consumer without addition of preservatives and synthetic food additives; it is widely believed by advocates of alternative health care that organically grown foods are safer, more nutritious, and taste better;* organic products may be certified by voluntary organizations or governmental bodies; organic foods may be labeled as 'Farm-Verified organics,' and 'California Certified Organic Farmers'. See Health food, Health food movement; Cf Enriched food, Food additives, Fortified food, 'Health food', Preservatives, Refining

*Heuristic logic to the contrary, there are no compelling data that demonstrate clear superiority of organic over nonorganic foods

**organic process therapy** ALTERNATIVE PSYCHIATRY A format of psychotherapy believed to help a person return to his 'organic self,' by rediscovering his body, emotions, mind, and spirit; according to this construct, a person's physical and mental problems can be traced to infancy, birth, and to previous lives. See Past life/lives therapy, Rebirthing therapy

**organicism** See Alternative medicine

**organismic psychotherapy** ALTERNATIVE PSYCHIATRY A permutation of Reichian therapy developed in the 1960s by Malcolm Brown, who divided the body into four 'ontological being centers' that interact with the external environment

▶ **ONTOLOGICAL BEING CENTERS**

- **AGAPE-EROS CENTER** Chest; mediates open interactions with others
- ***HARA* CENTER** Abdomen; allows self-love and self-acceptance
- **LOGOS CENTER** Upper back; facilitates understanding
- **PHALLIC-SPIRITUAL-WARRIOR CENTER** Lower back and extremities; mediates perseverance

See Reichian therapy

**organ meat** CLINICAL NUTRITION Any of a number of edible parts from slaughtered animals, which consist of, or form part of an internal organ, eg brain, heart, kidney, liver, and lungs; more commonly eaten muscle-based meats are known in the food industry as carcass meats

***Organon of Medicine*** HOMEOPATHY The first book on homeopathy, written by Samuel Hahnemann (1755-1843), the founder of homeopathy. See Hahnemann, Homeopathy, Materia medica, Repertory

**organotherapy** MEDICAL HISTORY The ingestion of any of a cornucopia of human and nonhuman tissues to cure diseases or improve performance, eg the heart for courage, brain to treat idiocy, and other body parts and fluids, including bile, blood, bone, feces, feathers, and placenta, each intended to address various evil humors. See Endogenous endocrinotherapy, Glandular

*Organotherapy with testicular tissues was reported by CE Brown-Séquard, which was a founding event of modern endocrinology (*Sci Am 1995; 272/2:77*), who in 1889 at the age of 72 reported that he had reversed his own aging by using liquid extracts from the testicles of dogs and guinea pigs; modern workers believe the positive effects reported by BS were placebo in nature; however, his principle of hormonal replacement therapy is correct

**organotellurium** Tellurium that is combined with organic molecules, some of which (eg AS-101) are thought to have anticarcinogenic properties (*Moss, 1992*). See Unproven methods for cancer management

**organs & meridians affected** CHINESE HERBAL MEDICINE A classification of Chinese herbal medicine that takes into account the effect that specific foods and herbs have on the 12 organs and the 12 meridians. See Chinese herbal medicine, Twelve Meridians, Twelve Vital Organs

**Orgone Accumulator** FRINGE MEDICINE A device invented by Wilhelm Reich, which was alleged to recharge a person's orgone–the energy associated with for the energy associated with sexual orgasm; Reich was imprisoned for selling the device, which was widely believed to be inefficacious, and died in prison in 1957. See Health fraud, Orgone energy, Orgone therapy, Reich, Reichian therapy

**orgone energy** FRINGE MEDICINE A term coined by Wilhelm Reich, an Austrian psychiatrist, for the energy associated with sexual orgasm; Reich believed that the inability to achieve a satisfactory orgasm caused many physical conditions, based on the assumption that the body needs the convulsions and transient (complete) loss of control inherent in an orgasm; without this release of sexual energy, various mental disorders (in particular 'neurosis') eventually develop; as a person matures, he develops an 'armor'–a constellation of postures and expressions to fit his personality and protect it from the world. See Body armor, Orgone Accumulator, Orgone therapy, Reichian therapy; Cf Bioenergetics

**orgone therapy** Medical orgonomy, orgonomic medicine FRINGE MEDICINE A general term for the use of a device (eg Orgone Accumulator) believed to emit orgone energy, which charges and fills the cosmos. See Orgone Accumulator, Orgone energy, Reichian therapy

**orgonomic medicine** Orgone therapy, see there

**orgonomy** FRINGE MEDICINE A science that is claimed to incorporate new approaches to child-rearing, medicine, and psychiatry, which may be accomplished by an Orgone Accumulator. See Orgone Accumulator, Orgone energy, Orgone therapy, Reichian therapy

**Orgotein®** ALTERNATIVE ONCOLOGY A timed release superoxide dismutase believed to have some efficacy in treating cancer and arthritis; it is not approved for sale in the US (*Moss, 1992*). See Unproven methods for cancer management

**Oriental ginseng** Ginseng, see there, *Panax ginseng*

**oriental massage** ALTERNATIVE MEDICINE A general term for massage intended to balance and harmonize the flow of *chi* (the life force) through the energy pathways (meridians); the various forms of oriental massage stimulate the same points stimulated in acupuncture (see cross-references). See Acupressure, Jin Shin Jyutsu, Jin Shin Do®, Bodymind Acupressure™, Reflexology; Cf Energetic (nonoriental) massage, Massage therapy, Structural integration, Traditional European massage, Western massage

***Origanum vulgare*** Popularly known as marjoram, see there

**Orionic healing system** FRINGE MEDICINE A philosophy developed by a rebirther and hypnotherapist, Janna Zarchin, which is believed to release emotional traumas and negative thought patterns through the use of time and space, and mediated by a god or goddess as a healer. See Rebirthing therapy; Cf Past life/lives therapy

**orlistat** Xenical® An agent approved by the FDA in 1997 as a therapy for obesity, Orlistat interferes with pancreatic lipase, and allows up to one-third of ingested fat to pass undigested through the body (*Sci Am Aug 1996, p88*). See Obesity

**Ornish regimen** CLINICAL NUTRITION A health enhancing program developed by Dean Ornish, MD, which is designed to reduce the risk of cardiovascular disease

▶ **ORNISH REGIMEN**

- **DIET** Low-fat, vegetarian diet of beans, bean curd, grains, fruits, vegetables
- **STRESS MANAGEMENT** Daily meditation and yoga
- **EXERCISE** 30 minutes/day
- **RESTRICTED** Alcohol, fat-free yogurt
- **ABSTINENCE** Meat, poultry, fish, egg yolks, caffeine, dairy products, and tobacco; no fat or oil added to foods

RESULT Weight loss; 40% decrease in total cholesterol, 60% decrease in LDL-cholesterol. See Diet, 'Health food', Organic food

**Orobronze** see Tanning pill

**Orphan Drug Act** A US federal law (*Public Law 97-414*) designed to provide tax incentives, developmental grants, and a 7-year marketing monopoly for drugs for orphan diseases

Note: Some 'orphan drugs' have been very successful (PEG-ADA, for severe combined immunodeficiency, Enzon Corp; erythropoietin, for anemia in chronic dialysis, Amgen Corp; human growth hormone, Genentech), allowing significant revenues

**Ortho-Bionomy®** 'Homeopathy of bodywork' A method of structural integration that was developed in the 1970s by a British osteopath and bodyworker, AL Pauls; the goal of Ortho-Bionomy® is to restore structural alignment and balance through gentle movement and postural adjustment, with the intent of releasing tension and holding patterns; the patient is encouraged to adopt postures that are comfortable, rather than idealized postures; Ortho-Bionomy® replaces long-term patterns of misuse with new patterns of balance and self-awareness; the technique is believed to be effective for arthritis, stress, muscle pain, occupational disorders including repetitive motion injury, rheumatic complaints, and sports injuries. See Structural integration; Cf Alexander technique, Aston patterning, Feldenkreis method, Hellerwork®, Massage, Repetitive motion injury, Rolfing®, Rosen method, Tragerwork®

**orthodox medicine** Mainstream medicine, see there

**orthomolecular medicine** A term coined by Linus Pauling, for the administration of the exact amount of a substance (eg a vitamin or mineral) needed to maintain health; this contrasts with the megavitamin therapy, in which excess vitamins are administered without attempting to determine the necessary quantity of each vitamin; proponents of orthomolecular medicine advocate its use for aging, AIDS, alcoholism, allergies, arthritis, depression, hyperactivity, hypoglycemia, learning disabilities, substance abuse, and other conditions. See Orthomolecular psychiatry, Vitamin(s); Cf Megavitamin therapy

**orthomolecular psychiatry** A term coined by Linus Pauling, for the administration of the exact amount of a substance (eg a vitamin or mineral) for normal mental health, which Pauling attributed to biochemical imbalances. See Orthomolecular medicine, Vitamin(s); Cf Megavitamin therapy

**orthoptics** Vision therapy, see there; Cf Orthotics

**orthotics** Arch supports, inner soles, inserts PODIATRY A device that is placed on the insole of shoes to either make them more comfortable and provide added support, or to modify a person's balance in the shoe; Cf Orthoptics, see Vision therapy

**γ-oryzanol** SPORTS MEDICINE A rice-derived product that was transiently popular among some atheletes as it was believed to stimulate growth hormone release, and act as an anti-oxidant (*JC DeLee, D Drez, Jr, Eds, Orthopedic Sports Medicine WB Saunders, Philadelphia, 1994*)

**oscilloclast** FRINGE MEDICINE A device alleged to be useful in the diagnosis and treatment of cancer, based on scientifically uncertain proposals by Dr Albert Abrams of San Francisco, who died in the 1920s; the device allegedly operated on the hypothesis that since electrons are the basic biological unit, disease in general, and cancer in particular, represented a disequilibrium in electronic harmony; the oscilloclast consisted of a box in which slots were cut in the side, with the top bedecked in lights, dials, and knobs; mainstream health care professionals submitted blood samples blotted on paper to Abrams' College of Electronic Medicine, which were analyzed by the device; the FDA found that the oscilloclast could not distinguish between colored water, and the blood of a human, living or dead. See Abrams, Radionics therapy, Unproven methods for cancer management

**osteopath** A physician trained in osteopathic medicine; the differences between doctors of medicine (MDs) and doctors of osteopathy (DOs) have been largely erased; the chief distinction between osteopaths and mainstream physicians is that osteopaths rely more on 'manipulation' of various body parts; otherwise, DOs prescribe drugs and may train in the same teaching hospitals as MDs; there is a greater tendency for osteopaths to provide primary care as general practitioners of medicine, obstetricians, and pediatricians; 5% (39,000) of physicians in the US are DOs, they treat 10% of the US population; 70% are in private practice (*Am Med News 12 October 1992 p32*); there were 15 schools of osteopathy in the US with 6632 students enrolled in 1986

**osteopathic lesion** ALTERNATIVE MEDICINE A term coined by Andrew Taylor Still, the founder of osteopathy, which refers to a musculoskeletal defect that responds to 'classic' osteopathic manipulation. See Osteopathy

**osteopathic manipulation** Osteopathic manipulative technique, ten-finger osteopathy OSTEOPATHY A general term for 'classic' osteopathic manipulation in which the ten fingers are used, operating on the principle of a lever, ie pressure on one part connected through a joint is intended to overcome the resistance from the opposite part. See Osteopathy

**osteopathic manipulative technique** Osteopathic manipulation, see there

**osteopathy** ALTERNATIVE MEDICINE A school of medicine practiced predominantly in the US, that is based on Dr Andrew Taylor Still's theory of healing, first delineated in 1874; osteopathic theory holds that a body in a state of wellness is correctly adjusted, and that disease represents a loss of coherency of structure and/or function, and the inability to mount a normal defense against infection, malignancy, inflammation, toxins, and other inciting agents

▶ **OSTEOPATHY, KEY PRINCIPLES**

- **HOLISM** The body is an integrated unit or balanced musculoskeletal system which holds the key to optimal physiologic function
- **STRUCTURE AND FUNCTION ARE INTERRELATED** Any alteration in the body's structure leads to defects in function
- **HOMEOSTASIS** The body has intrinsic mechanisms to heal itself; osteopathic manipulation, exercise, and medication are intended to enhance the body's intrinsic healing ability; chronic conditions are believed to occur when the healing capacity is compromised

Rational osteopathic therapy is based on the above three tenets; other osteopathic principles include

- **PREVENTION** Central to the school of osteopathy is the teaching of lifestyle alteration, in particular through diet and exercise
- **RULE OF THE ARTERY** All illness responds to improved blood circulation, which provides essential nutrients and releases toxins
- **SOMATIC DYSFUNCTION** A premorbid state in which tissues are functioning in a suboptimal state, but structural defects are not yet present

See Articulatory techniques, Cranial manipulation, CranioSacral Therapy™, Integrative medicine, Joint mobilization, Lymphatic pump, Muscle energy manipulation, Myofascial release, Positioning techniques, Rule of the artery, Somatic dysfunction, Strain-Counterstrain Therapy™, Visceral manipulation; Cf Chiropractic, Naturopathy *RESOURCE: American Osteopathic Association, 142 E Ontario St, Chicago IL 60611 ☎ 1.312.280.5800*

**osteopuncture** A technique for pain relief, developed by an American neurologist, RM Lawrence, in which needles are inserted into the periosteum in one of 120 areas, where the bone is relatively accessible to the skin surface; once the needle is inserted, it may be stimulated with low-voltage electricity for up to one-half hour; osteopuncture stimulates the bone in regions that are adjacent to sites of pain; this differs from acupuncture, as the acupoints along meridians often correspond to body regions and organs located at a distance from the site of the needle's insertion; osteopuncture is believed to be of use in treating arthritic pain, back and neck pain, osteoarthritis, phantom limb pain, and rheumatoid arthritis; Cf Acupuncture

**Oswego tea** Bergamot, see there, *Monarda didyma*

**Our Lady of Guadelupe** See Healing shrine

**Our Lady's tears** Lily-of-the-valley, see there, *Convallaria majalis*

**overseas mail-order drug** ALTERNATIVE PHARMACOLOGY A general term for any agent with presumed therapeutic efficacy that is not currently available in the US; until 1988, any therapeutic agent that was imported (in baggage or by mail) for personal use was subject to seizure by US customs agents or by postal workers, depending on the mode of importation; under pressure, the FDA now allows the importation of non-FDA-approved drugs and other agents for personal use, often for dread diseases, including AIDS and cancer

**overweight** A condition defined as ≥ 75th percentile of body-mass index [weight in kg/(height in m)]$^2$; overweight adults are at increased risk for atherosclerosis, arthritis, cardiovascular disease, diabetes, gallbladder disease, gout, hypertension, and certain malignancies; overweight adolescents are at increased risk for future development of coronary heart disease, stroke, and colorectal cancer (*N Engl J Med 1992; 327:1350oa*). See Morbid obesity, Obesity

**ovolacteal vegetarian** Lacto-ovo vegetarian, see there

**ox balm** Stoneroot, see there, *Collinsonia canadensis*

**ox knee** *Achyranthes bidentata*, see there

***Oxalis acetosella*** Popularly known as wood sorrel, see there

**oxidation** The combination of a molecule with oxygen, which increases the atom's valence with the loss of a hydrogen ion or one or more electrons; oxidation reactions commonly involve the combination with oxygen free radicals, and result in major organ damage that accumulates with time; oxidation reactions are implicated in age-related damage, degenerative phenomena, and cancer, and may be ameliorated with antioxidants including vitamin C, vitamin E, glutathione, and superoxide dismutase. See Antioxidant, Antioxidant therapy

**oxidative therapy** ALTERNATIVE MEDICINE 1. Antioxidant therapy, see there 2. Hydrogen peroxide therapy, see there 3. Ozone therapy, see there

**Oxydonor** HEALTH FRAUD A pseudotherapeutic device invented at the turn of the 20th century by Heracles Sanche, that was claimed to be of benefit for cholera, constipation, hay fever, writer's cramp, and 80 other conditions; it was powered by a high-voltage generator and emitted ozone and a blue light from a glass container, and declared worthless by the American Medical Association. See Equipoise, Health fraud, Quackery

**oxygen therapy** ALTERNATIVE MEDICINE A generic term for any non-'mainstream' use of oxygen as a therapeutic modality, including nonconventional hyperbaric oxygen therapy, hydrogen peroxide (oxidation) therapy, and ozone therapy; unapproved uses for oxygen therapy include arthritis, cancer, multiple sclerosis, and many other conditions; the adminstration of oxygen to athletes is a practice of uncertain efficacy. See Hyperbaric oxygen therapy, Hydrogen peroxide (oxidation) therapy, Ozone therapy

**ozonation** The bubbling of ozone through water as a method of water purification, a process that had been proposed as an alternative to chlorination, which has been linked to an increase in cancer; ozone reacts with bromine in drinking water, forming unstable compounds that produce an array of potential carcinogens; these compounds bind to DNA more easily than does chloroform, a potentially carcinogenic byproduct of chlorination, raising the question of whether ozonation is appropriate for water purification (*Science 1995; 267:1771*); Cf Chlorination

**ozone** The triatomic allotrope of oxygen, which is formed when diatomic oxygen is subjected to an electrical discharge

▶ **TYPES OF OZONE**

• **'GOOD' OZONE** covers the earth's upper atmosphere and blocks the wavelengths of ultraviolet light (UV-B and UV-C) that cause DNA damage; 'good' ozone is being depleted at a rate of 4-5% per decade, and may result in an extra 200 000 deaths in the next 50 years through sun-induced malignancies (*Science 1991; 252:204n&v*); the recent increase in malignant melanomas has been attributed to the destruction of the ozone layer; depletion of 'good' ozone is largely attributed to CFC accumulation in the atmosphere after release from air conditioners, spray cans, and manufacturing plants that produce electronics and plastics; CFCs degrade in the atmosphere, release chlorine, and cause ozone destruction

• **'BAD' OZONE** is a bluish gas with a slightly pungent odor (which at high levels causes tracheobronchitis, pulmonary edema, and hemorrhage) formed in the lower atmosphere through complex photochemical reactions involving volatile organic compounds and nitrogen oxides, internal combustion engines, photocopiers, and laser printers; $O_3$ is used as an oxidizing agent in organic chemical production, as a food disinfectant, and as a bleaching agent; EPA guidelines allow an hourly peak of 0.12 ppm of ozone, which is exceeded in 62 US cities, including Denver, Los Angeles, and New York City

**ozone depletion** $O_3$ is present in 1 ppm in the upper stratosphere; it absorbs virtually all of the UV radiation from the sun; ozone depletion is caused by the release of chloride ions from CFCs (chlorofluorocarbons) produced by industry, which remain free, or react with ozone to form ClO (chlorine monoxide)

**ozone therapy** Ozonation AIDS The administration of ozone per rectum or intravaginally, which was claimed to have antiviral (anti-HIV), activity; it is deemed fraudulent by the FDA (*Am Med News 21 Nov 1994 p13*). See AIDS fraud ALTERNATIVE MEDICINE An unproven therapy that combines 'oxidative' therapy with oxygenation, using ozone ($O_3$), which splits into $O^•$ (which passes through tissues, oxidizing various molecules) and $O_2$, which increases locoregional $O_2$ supply; $O_3$ can be administered parenterally or topically (in a vehicle, eg olive oil or in ozonated water), and is thought to accelerate wound healing, inactivate viruses and bacteria, and increase local temperature; ozone therapy is believed by its advocates to be useful in treating AIDS, allergies, asthma, atherosclerosis, cancer, infections, multiple sclerosis, vascular headaches, and other conditions (*Alternative Medicine, Future Med Pub, 1994*). See Colon therapy, Oxygen therapy; Cf Hydrogen peroxide therapy

Note: Ozone therapy is not an FDA-approved therapeutic modality; it is available in Europe and Mexico

**P30 protein** Onconase®, see there

***pa kua chang*** *Baguazhang*, see there

**PABA** Para aminobenzoic acid, see there

***Pachyma cocos*** Tuckahoe, see there, *Porio cocos*

**Padre Pio** A psychic healer who was subjected to discipline by the Catholic Church. See Healer, Psychic healing

***Paeonia albiflora*** Popularly known as white peony, see there

***Paeonia lactiflora*** White peony, see there, *Paeonia albiflora*

***Paeonia moutan*** Popularly known as tree peony, see there

***Paeonia officinale*** CHINESE MEDICINE see White peony

***Paeonia suffruticosa*** Tree peony, see there, *Paeonia moutan*

**paigle** Cowslip, see there, *Primula vera*

**Painless Parker** DENTAL HISTORY A Canadian-American, née Edgar Randolph Parker (1872-1952), who was formally trained in dentistry in Philadelphia; a flamboyant showman, Parker practiced 'sidewalk dentistry' in an era when dentists were scarce, especially in rural regions, where he sometimes served as an itinerant 'molar mogul'; he advocated preventive dental care and was one of the early users of local anesthetics (*Armstrong, 1991*)

**pale gentian** Gentian, see there, *Gentiana lutea* (other species may be used)

**palm healing** Hand healing, see there

**BJ (Bartlett Joshua) Palmer** The strong-willed son (1881-1961) of DD Palmer, who was instumental in popularizing chiropractic as a health movement. See Chiropractic

**DD (Daniel David) Palmer** A grocer, fishmonger, mesmerist, and spiritualist (1845-1913) from Iowa, who founded chiropractic in 1895. See Chiropractic

**palmistry** Hand interpretation, see there

**palsywort** Cowslip, see there, *Primula vera*

**panax** Ginseng, see there, *Panax ginseng*

***Panax ginseng*** Popularly known as ginseng, see there

***Panax quinquefolius*** Popularly known as American ginseng, see there

***Panax schinseng*** Ginseng, see there, *Panax ginseng*

***panchakarma*** AYURVEDIC MEDICINE An intense detoxification regimen used in ayurvedic medicine to enhance a person's *prana*, the living force of the universe; a *panchakarma* regimen may last one week, and is used once or twice per year to eliminate *ama* (impurities); a *panchakarma* may include a *snehan*–a cleansing herbal oil massage that focuses on specific marma or pressure points, a sauna with herbal oils, which imparts vapors that are inhaled, aromatherapy, herbal tea, and music therapy. See Ayurvedic medicine, *Prana*, *Swedan*

**pangamic acid** 'Vitamin B15' ALTERNATIVE MEDICINE A substance that lacks the properties of a vitamin, samples of which, when subjected to chemical analysis, consist of dimethylglycine hydrochloride, mixed with sodium nitrate; pangamic acid is claimed to prevent cancer, but may itself be carcinogenic, as it is positive by the Ames test; there is no evidence that pangamic acid is an essential human nutrient. See Ames test, Pseudovitamin, Unproven methods for cancer management

**pantothenic acid** Antiachromotrichia factor, anticanites factor, antidermatitis factor, antidermatitis factor of chicks, anti-gray hair factor, chick pellagra factor, liver filtrate factor, vitamin $B_5$, yeast filtrate factor CLINICAL NUTRITION An essential nutrient (vitamin, recommended daily requirements, 100 mg) involved in nutrient metabolism; it is present in dairy products, egg yolks, leafy greens, legumes, liver, and whole grains; it has been used by some alternative health care providers to treat allergies, anxiety, colitis, depression, eczema, fatigue, hay fever, hypoglycemia, urticaria, and to stimulate weakened adrenal glands. See Pseudovitamin

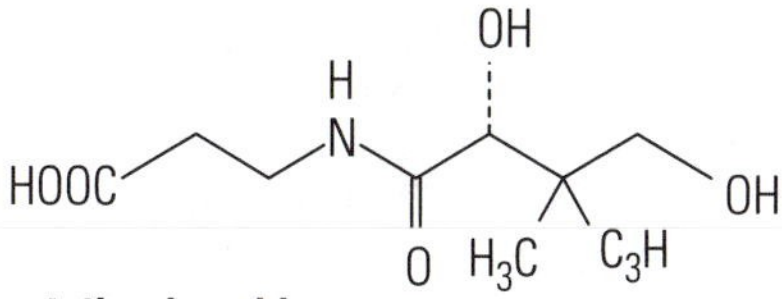

HOOC, H, N, OH, OH, O, $H_3C$, $C_3H$

**pantothenic acid**

***Papaver somniferum*** Opium, see there

**papaya** *Carica papaya* HERBAL MEDICINE A tree-like plant native to the tropics of the Western hemisphere, the unripe fruit of which is 'milked' for the enzymes papain and chymopapain; these enzymes have been prescribed for those with difficulties in digesting protein, are used to lyse post-surgical blood clots, and ruptured vertebral disks, and are used commercially as meat tenderizers. See Herbal medicine

**paper birch** White birch, see there, *Betula alba*

**papoose root** Blue cohosh, see there, *Caulophyllum thalictroides*

**para-amino benzoic acid** PABA, vitamin Bx ALTERNATIVE NUTRITION A provitamin for certain bacteria, which is used to produce folic acid, a sulfonamide antagonist; some alternative health care providers regard PABA as a vitamin, and suggest its use in treating bipolar (manic-depressive) disorder; PABA deficiency does not exist in humans, as it is not a required dietary component. See Pseudovitamin

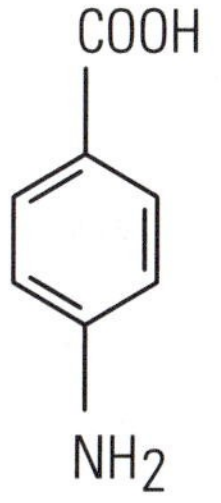

COOH, $NH_2$

**paramedicine** ALTERNATIVE NUTRITION A general term used by the Hungarian Institute of Pharmacy for an agent (eg Beres Drops Plus) that is not known to be effective for a specific disease, which may nonetheless have unspecified supplemental effects (*Moss, 1992*). See Beres Drops Plus

**paranormal** *adjective* Pertaining or relating to phenomena, eg clairvoyance, precognition, telekinesis, telepathy, that are not explained by natural laws and principles of the physical universe. See Parapsychology

**paranormal diagnosis** A general term for a pseudodiagnostic technique that is viewed as being peripheral to fringe medicine. See Fringe medicine, Paranormal therapy

**paranormal therapy** A general term for fringe therapies that are based on no known scientific principle

▶ **TYPES OF PARANORMAL THERAPIES**

- **FAITH** Belief in the healing powers of a higher force or God, which can be tapped when a person is in need; these include those of tribal origins, as well as Christian Science, faith (spiritual) healing, and therapeutic touch
- **DEVICES** Instruments using questionable techniques with dubious effects
- **OTHERS** A gallimaufry of uncertain methods, including past lives therapy, psychic surgery, and shamanism

See Absent healing, Christian Science, Faith healing, Paranormal diagnosis, Parapsychology, Past lives therapy, Psychic surgery, Radionics, Shamanism, Silva mind control, Therapeutic touch

**paraphysical healing** Psychic healing, see there

**parapsychological healing** Psychic healing, see there

**parapsychology** A field that attempts to apply scientific methods to studying 'paranormal' phenomena that are unexplained by natural laws and principles of the physical universe; these phenomena include clairvoyance, precognition, telekinesis, telepathy. See Paranormal

The methods used in parapsychology may be of uncertain validity–Author's note

**parasympathetic dominant** FRINGE MEDICINE A genetically distinct type of person based on an eclectic classification of humans proposed by Nicolas J Gonzales, MD; according to Gonzalez, the ancestors of parasympathetic dominants inhabited the cooler parts of America and Asia, and were primarily meat eaters; he believes that these individuals have an efficient parasympathetic nervous system, and should consume primarily fatty meats, and dairy products (50% of total) in their diet (*Moss, 1992*). See Metabolic typing; Cf Sympathetic dominant

**parasympathetic massage** A bodywork tech-

**parsley** *Petroselium crispum*

nique used to stimulate the parasympathetic nervous system, which is based on the belief that much of the body's tension and disease in general is caused by a prolonged stress (flight-or-fight) response, due to an activated sympathetic nervous system; it is assumed that if the sympathetic nervous system can be down-regulated, the normal 'housekeeping' functions, eg digestion, elimination of wastes, and rebuilding of tissues, can occur more easily, as the circulation would switch from a physiologic 'crisis mode'–in which blood is diverted to the brain, muscles, and heart, to a baseline mode; parasympathetic massage is a hybrid between manual lymphatic drainage and Esalen massage, and is intended to artificially down-regulate the sympathetic nervous system. See Massage therapy

**pareira** *Chondrodendron tormentosum* HERBAL MEDICINE An amazonian vine that is a primary source of a neuromuscular blocking substance, curare, of which the alkaloid tubocurarine is the active component; tubocurarine has been used for strychnine poisoning, tetanus intoxication, to relax muscles in fractures, to treat polio and cerebral palsy, and for seizures. See Herbal medicine

**parenteral nutrition** See Total parenteral nutrition

**pareve** NUTRITION A food that completely lacks animal-derived products, often equated to the term 'non-dairy'. See Vegan; Cf Kosher

***Parietaria diffusa*** Pellitory-of-the-wall, see there, *Parietaria officinale*

***Parietaria officinale*** Popularly known as pellitory-of-the-wall, see there

**parsley** *Petroselium crispum* HERBAL MEDICINE A culinary herb that is rich in vitamins A and C, which is diuretic, expectorant, laxative, spasmolytic, and a digestive tonic; it is used internally for asthma, colds, congestive heart failure, coughs, fever, hypertension, indigestion, irregular menses, and premenstrual syndrome TOXICITY Regular use of parsley requires dietary compensation with potassium, given parsley's potassium-depleting diuretic effect; medicinal levels of parsley should not be used in pregnancy as it stimulates uterine contractions; it should not be given to young children. See Herbal medicine

**parthenolide** PHARMACOGNOSY A natural compound present in feverfew (*Tanacetum parthenium*) that inhibits serotonin and prostaglandins, which may explain feverfew's efficacy in treating migraines

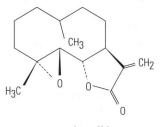

**parthenolide**

**partridgeberry** Wintergreen, see there, *Gaultheria procumbens*

**pasqueflower** *Pulsatilla*, see there, wind flower

***Passiflora incarnata*** Passionflower, see there

**passionflower** *Passiflora incarnata*, apricot vine, maypop, passion vine, purple passionflower, wild passionflower HERBAL MEDICINE A perennial vine that contains alkaloids (eg harmane, harmol, and harmine), flavonoids, and steroids, which is anti-inflammatory and mildly sedative; it has been used for addiction disorders, anxiety, asthma, hyperactivity in children, hypertension, insomnia, neuralgia, seizures in Parkinson's disease, rheumatic pain, stress, whooping cough TOXICITY Passionflower should not be used while driving or operating heavy equipment, given its soporific effect; it should not be used in young children or in pregnancy, as it stimulates uterine contraction. See Herbal medicine

**passionflower** *Passiflora incarnata*

**passion vine** Passionflower, see there, *Passiflora incarnata*

**passive concentration** PSYCHOLOGICAL THERAPY A mental state induced by exercises in body awareness and physical relaxation, which is a component of autogenic training. See Autogenic training

**passive overconsumption** CLINICAL NUTRITION The ingestion of excess calories, due to an increased fat concentration in the food, rather than to an increase in actual volume of food; Olestra, a proprietary artificial fat, is thought to reduce passive overconsumption, as the fat flows undigested through the gastrointestinal tract (*Sci Am Aug 1996, p88*). See Obesity, Olestra

**passive smoking** PUBLIC HEALTH A general term for involuntary 'smoking' by non-smokers who breathe ambient air containing carcinogens inhaled by an "active" smoker

Passive smoking causes an estimated 2500-8400 excess annual cases of smoking-related malignancy (US); physical space separation allows significant reduction in exposure to 'sidestream' or environmental tobacco smoke (ETS) by non-smokers; 'mainstream' smoke is directly inhaled by the smoker; ETS is produced by the smoker, but absorbed more by non-smokers who don't have the benefit of a filter; passive smokers are exposed to dimethylnitrosamine (a potent carcinogen), benzo(a) pyrene, and carbon monoxide (CO), acrolein, arsenic, benzene, cyanide, formaldehyde, nitrosamines, radionuclides and others); levels of nicotine in unventilated areas may exceed industrial threshold limit levels (> 500 μg/mm$^3$); air zones with CO levels of greater than 30 ppm cause a passive smoker to have CO blood levels equivalent to having smoked ≥ 5 cigarettes; prolonged exposure to 30 ppm may cause carboxyhemoglobin levels sufficient to impair visual discrimination and cause psychomotor impairment

**past life regression** PARANORMAL PHENOMENA '*A general term for the use of hypnosis to probe the unconscious mind to retrieve historical memories or information, from childhood or past lives.*' (*Gottschalk Olsen, 1989*). See Bloxham tapes; Cf Freudian psychoanalysis, Past life/lives therapy, Rebirthing therapy

**past life/lives therapy** Progression/regression therapy, regression therapy, transformational therapy PARANORMAL PHENOMENA A therapeutic technique developed in the 1960s and based on the belief that illness may be caused by a person's previous lives burrowing their way into the subconscious; the therapy asserts that once emotional traumas ('psychic intrusions') are brought to the surface*, diseases can be addressed; it is uncertain whether the imprints attributed to a past life actually represent a previous physical experience; possible mechanisms that would explain the past life/lives imprint include fantasy or day dreaming, cryptamnesia-something that was read or seen, which becomes incorporated into one's own déjà vu memory, fraud–conscious or unconscious story-telling, collective unconscious, inherited memory–ie it may have actually occurred, telepathy–acquisition of knowledge or images from other people, or the result of channelling or mediumistic possession (*Gottschalk Olsen, 1989*); past life/lives therapy is believed by its advocates to be useful in treating interpersonal relationships and poor communication, guilt, phobias and compulsions, asthma, and low back pain CONTRAINDICATIONS Schizophrenia, rigid religious background, emotional lability, and overintellectual individuals who tend to focus on the reality and not on the therapeutic opportunity. See Bloxham tapes; Cf Freudian psychoanalysis, Past life regression, Rebirthing therapy

*Much in the way that Freudian psychoanalysts evoke repressed traumas of childhood

**paste** *Gao* CHINESE MEDICINE A general term for a therapeutic preparation consisting of herbs mixed with honey, which may be ingested as a 'spread,' and/or with meals. See Chinese herbal medicine

**patchouli** Agastache, see there, *Agastache rugosa*

**patent medicine** Bottled cure-all, quack remedy HEALTH FRAUD A bottled mixture of herbs and plants, often in a 25 to 50% alcohol base, that was most popular from the 1870s to the 1930s, primarily in the American west; patent medicines were usually *not* patented, but rather proprietary, trademarked, and often had a dreadful taste–at the time, consumers believed that the worse the taste, the more effective the medicine; patent medicines were huckstered as cure-alls for conditions ranging from smallpox to cholera, and sold by mail or in traveling medicine shows; many patent medicines are now believed to have been virtually useless, except as analgesics, which contained alcohol or narcotics. See Frontier prescription, Health fraud, Medicine show, Quackery

The first American patent medicine was Tuscarora Rice, awarded by England in 1715; the more well-known patent medicines included Ayer's Cathartic Pills, Dover's Powder (which contained opium and ipecac), Duffy's Elixir (which contained senna, a bulk laxative), James Fever Powder (which contained antimony), Dr Miles's Compound extract of Tomato (which became today's catsup), Hamlin's Wizard Oil, Lydia E Pinkham's Vegetable Compound (±18% alcohol by weight), Hostetter's Celebrated Stomach Bitters (±44% alcohol), Kickapoo Indian Sagwa, Kickapoo Salve and Dr Townsend's Extract of Sassaparilla (*Armstrong, 1991*)

**pathwork** PARANORMAL PHENOMENA A process of core energetics that is based on material that is believed to have been 'channeled' to Eva Perreikos between 1957 and 1979

**patience dock** Bistort, see there, *Polygonum bistorta*

**patient-oriented medicine** A philosophical stance in which legal issues vis-à-vis the patient's rights, general communication with the patient, and informed consent are viewed from the patient's perspective, rather than from the more traditional physician perspective (*JAMA 1996; 275:1156*). See Alternative medicine

**patterning** A technique for rehabilitating and treating brain-injured children developed by Drs GU Doman and CH Delacato, in which a child performs exercises that are intended to duplicate stages of early childhood development; advocates of patterning claim a 30% response rate in brain-injured children when used in conjunction with optimal nutritional support, and megadoses of vitamins (*Bricklin, 1976*); Cf Alternative medicine

**pau d'arco** *Tebebuia impetiginosa, Lapacho colorado, L morado*, ipes, lapacho, taheebo, trumpet bush, trumpet tree HERBAL MEDICINE A tree native to Central and South America, that is anti-inflammatory and antimicrobial, which has been used for indigestion, infections (bacterial, fungal, parasitic, and viral); anecdotal reports infer that pau d'arco may be useful for AIDS and cancer. See Herbal medicine

**Ivan Petrovich Pavlov** A Russian physiologist (1849-1936) who won the 1904 Nobel Prize for research in gastric physiology. See Behavioral intervention, Pavlovian

**pavlovian** PSYCHOLOGY *adjective* Pertaining or referring to the theories delineated by Pavlov, which is understood to mean conditioned reflexes, in particular, salivation, which occurs after certain stimulation. See Pavlov

**'peak E'** A novel amino acid so designated as it causes a peak (spike) on the paper or 'hard copy' when analyzed by high-performance liquid chromatography; the amino acid was identified in, and held responsible for, the eosinophilic-myalgia syndrome. See Eosinophilia-myalgia syndrome, Tryptophan

**Pealeism** PSYCHOLOGY A self-help philosophy developed in the 1950s by an American cleric, Norman Vincent Peale that is based on positive thinking, prayer to a personal god, and visualization of goals; Pealeism inspired some of the imagery and visualization techniques of healing. See Affirmation, Autosuggestion therapy, Imagery and visualization

**Pearl Index** OBSTETRICS A formula that allows comparison of the efficacy of contraceptive methods, calculated as the pregnancy rate in population divided by 100 years of exposure (see table, page 282). See Breast feeding, Coitus interruptus, Condoms, Morning-after pill, Contraception, Natural family planning, Norplant, Rhythm method, RU 486

**pearl paint** Gromwell, see there, *Lithospermum officinale*

**pectin** ALTERNATIVE PHARMACOLOGY A soluble fiber found in fruits, eg apples, grapefruit, and vegetables; pectin is antidiarrheal, demulcent and used to soothe the mouth and throat, reduce colic and diarrhea, and

**PEARL INDEX** (PREGNANCIES/100 YEARS OF USE)

**PHYSIOLOGIC** 15-30/100 years: Coitus interruptus, natural family planning (rhythm or safe period), eg calendar method, evaluation of cervical mucosa or temperature, breast feeding

**CHEMICAL** 15-20/100 years: Contraceptive sponges

**BARRIER** 2-20/100 years: Intrauterine devices, condoms

**HORMONAL** 1-3/100 years

**SURGICAL** << 1/100 years: Ligation of fallopian tubes; vasectomy

reduces LDL-cholesterol. See Bran, Dietary fiber, LDL-cholesterol, Oat bran, Soluble fiber

**pee-in-the-bed** Dandelion, see there, *Taraxacum officinale*

**peeling effect** NATUROPATHY A general term for a phenomenon seen with the use of Bach's flower remedies, in which the resolution of one emotional crisis allows the manifestation of another. See Bach's flower remedies

**pellagra** Alpine scurvy, chichism, elephantiasis asturiensis, elephantiasis italica, erythema endemicum, Lombardy erysipelas, maidism, mal de la rossa, mal rosso, mayidism, niacin deficiency, niacinamidosis, nicotinic acid deficiency, psilosis pigmentosa, psychoneurosis maidica, Saint Ignatius' itch CLINICAL NUTRITION A deficiency of niacin (nicotinic acid) caused by alcoholism or malnutrition, and characterized by anorexia, glossitis, gastrointestinal disorders, headaches, insomnia, bilateral symmetrical scaly rashes, polyneuropathy, confusion, depression, pseudodementia and psychotic symptoms. See Niacin

**pellitory-of-the-wall** *Parietaria officinale, P diffusa* HERBAL MEDICINE A flowering shrub that contains bitter glycoside, calcium, flavones, mucilage, potassium, sulfur, and tannins; it has been used for kidney and bladder inflammation, kidney stones, and prostatitis. See Herbal medicine

**pembina** Cramp bark, see there, *Viburnum opulus*

***Pen Ts'ao*** CHINESE MEDICINE A textbook on Chinese herbal written by the Emperor Shen-nung (c 2800 BC), which lists 366 herbs, and 1000 herbal formulations. See Chinese herbal medicine, Herbal medicine, *Nei Jing;* Cf *Canon of Medicine, Charak Samhita, The Complete Herbal, De Materia Medica, Natural History, Nei Jing, Philosophy of Natural Therapeutics, Rigveda, Sushrita Samhita, Theatrum Botanicum*

**pendular diagnosis** Radiesthetic diagnosis FRINGE MEDICINE A pseudodiagnostic permutation of radiesthesia, in which a pendulum is held above a patient and believed to change its pattern of oscillation when it is above a diseased organ. See Radiesthesia

**peniscope** A device invented by Bernarr Macfadden for exercising the male genitals, which he recommended to harassed executives (*Armstrong, 1991*). See Macfadden, Physical culture movement

**pennyroyal** *Mentha pulegium* HERBAL MEDICINE An aromatic herb that is used internally for anxiety, bloating, colds, coughs, indigestion, menstrual cramps, and premenstrual syndrome TOXICITY Pennyroyal should not be used in pregnancy as it stimulates uterine contraction; it should not be given to young children; it may cause liver damage. See Botanical toxicity, Herbal medicine

**pennywort** Gutu kola, see there, *Hydrocotyle asiatica*

**Pentecostal healing** PARANORMAL PHENOMENA A form of paranormal therapy in which an individual or group thereof enter a trance-like state, undergo convulsions, and speak in tongues; this form of healing was discouraged in the Catholic Church of the Middle Ages, as it was regarded as akin to possession by Satan. See Faith healing, Psychic healing; Cf Christian Science

**pepper and salt** Shepherd's purse, see there, *Capsella bursa-pastoris*

**peppermint** *Mentha piperita, bo he,* field mint, wild pennyroyal A perennial herb that contains azulene, betaine, carotenoids, choline, flavonoids, menthol, rosmarinic acid, tannins, and volatile oil containing bisabolene, cineole, limonene, menthol, menthone, pulegol, and others; peppermint leaves and stalks are analgesic, antibacterial, antiparasitic, antispasmodic, carminative, diaphoretic, stimulating, a nerve tonic, and sedative CHINESE MEDICINE Peppermint is used in Chinese herbal medicine as an infusion for cough, flatulence, headaches, laryngitis, indigestion, menstrual disorders, and sinusitis. See

Chinese herbal medicine HERBAL MEDICINE Peppermint is used in Western herbal medicine, internally for colic, flatulence, inflammation, and to increase the flow of bile, inhaled as an expectorant and for respiratory tract infections, and topically as a local anesthetic TOXICITY Pure peppermint should not be ingested, as it causes cardiac arrhythmias; peppermint tea should be used ingested with caution in young children and pregnancy, and not at all in those with a history of miscarriage. See Herbal medicine, Menthol, Spearmint

**peppermint** *Mentha piperita*

**peppermint oil** AROMATHERAPY An oil distilled or extracted from peppermint (*Mentha piperita*) that is used in aromatherapy as a mental stimulant, or as a stomachic to relieve gastrointestinal discomfort. See Aromatherapy, Essential oil

**pepperidge bush** Barberry, see there, *Berberis vulgaris*

**peptide T** A short polypeptide present in HIV-1's envelope that was proposed as a possible AIDS therapy, but abandoned before reaching the investigational new drug stage of development. See AIDS therapy

**percussion** Tapotement A massage technique that consists of chopping and drumming by the sides of the hand to 'fleshy' tissues, eg the back, buttocks, and thighs. See Massage therapy

**perforated grass** *Akebia quinata*, see there

**perforated wood** *Akebia quinata*, see there

**performance anxiety** Stage fright PSYCHOLOGY A physiologic 'flight-or-fight' reaction that occurs in an anxious person carrying out an activity in the public eye, eg those in entertainment, public speakers and others; it is associated with tachycardia, increased blood pressure, rate of respiration, and muscle tone. See Flight-or-fight response

**'performance booster'** see Invalid claims of efficacy

**pericardium meridian** Heart constrictor meridian, see there

**Peruvian bark** 1. *China*, see there 2. Cinchona, see there, *Cinchona* species

**pet therapy** PSYCHOLOGY The use of a domestic pet as an adjunct to psychotherapy; pet-facilitated therapy is of use for persons with a marginal role in society, eg children in foster care, the elderly and/or in nursing homes, mentally retarded, physically handicapped, inmates of correctional facilities, for those in mental or physical isolation, or those with a low self-esteem; pet-facilitated psychotherapy may be used for patients who fail to respond to individual psychotherapy, electroshock, drugs, and occupational or recreational therapy; some data suggest that cholesterol and blood pressure are lower in individuals with pets (*Castle-man, 1996*). See Companionship, Most significant other; Cf Social isolation

**pétrissage** MASSAGE A massage technique, in which fascicles of muscles are kneaded, lifted, grasped, squeezed, rolled, and released, with the intent of stimulating locoregional circulation, and relaxing contracted muscles. See Massage therapy

**pewterwort** Horsetail, see there, *Equisetum arvense*

**peyote** *Lophophora williamsii* HERBAL MEDICINE A cactus native to North America, that has over 50 distinct alkaloids; of these, mescaline is the most active and best-known for its mind-altering activities, in particular for causing hallucinations; peyote is an integral part of Native American tribal rituals in the American southwest, but is otherwise illegal. See Herbal medicine

**peyote** *Lophophora williamsii*

**Pfrimmer technique** MASSAGE THERAPY A proprietary form of deep tissue massage developed in the 1940s by a Canadian nurse, TC Pfrimmer; the technique is based on the belief that musculoskeletal malfunction is caused by an interruption in the normal flow of blood and lymph due to fatigue, injury, stress, and buildup of lactic acid, causing induration of muscle fibers and tissue adhesions; anecdotal reports suggest that the technique may be effective for arthritis, poor circulation, fibromyositis, headaches, multiple sclerosis, muscular dystrophy, neuralgia, occupational stress, sciatica, sports injuries, and trauma. See Massage therapy

**phallic-spiritual-warrior center** ALTERNATIVE PSYCHIATRY One of four 'ontological being centers' defined in the construct of organismic psychotherapy, a permutation of Reichian therapy; it is located in the lower back and extremities and mediates perseverance. See Ontological being centers, Organismic psychotherapy, Reichian therapy

**pharmacognosist** HERBAL MEDICINE A person trained in pharmacognosy, who has expert knowledge of the active chemical components of medicinal plants, the means by which new molecules can be identified, and the ways in which various cultures use the plants therapeutically. See Herbal medicine, Pharmacognosy

**pharmacognosy** 1. Herbal medicine, see there 2. The scientific approach to and formal study of the effects and uses of medicinal plants. See Herbal medicine, Pharmacognosist; Cf Traditional herbalism

**phenols** Phenolics A family of simple cyclic compounds present in high concentrations in fruits (grapes and raisins), garlic, onions, and green tea, which may be protective against cardiovascular disease, cancer, and may be antiviral

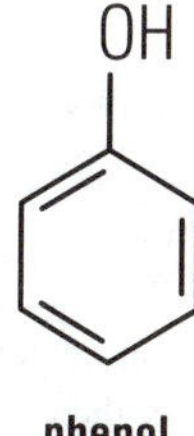


**phenol**

Note: It has been postulated that the decreased cardiovascular disease in wine drinkers is due to wine's phenolic content, which is higher in red wines (seeds, pulp, and skin are added to the milieu) than in white wine (which contains only pulp) (*US New & World Report May 20, 1996, p70*); cardiovascular disease may also be decreased in beer and spirit drinkers, which suggests that the effect is due to the alcohol and not the type of inebrient

**L-,D-phenylalanine** ALTERNATIVE PHARMACOLOGY A 50:50 mixture of *dextro–* and *levo–* forms of the amino acid, phenylalanine, which is present in meats and cheeses; it has been proposed that this form of phenylalanine reverses aging by boosting the internal supply of norepinephrine, and may be useful for fatigue, depression, pain, and other age-related phenomena

**philanthropos** Agrimony, see there, *Agrimonia eupatoria*

***Philosophy of Natural Therapeutics*** A book written in 1919 by H Lindlahr, in which he defined disease and health, how to treat the former, and achieve the latter; his philosophy gave rise to naturopathy. See Disease, Health, Naturopathy, Thompsonianism

**phobia** PSYCHIATRY An irrational fear or an objectively unfounded 'morbid' dread of an element in the environment or particular activity, which is of such intensity, as to evoke anxiety, panic, and adverse physiologic effects, and compel its victim to avoid contact therewith at virtually any social cost

**Phoenix rising yoga therapy** ALTERNATIVE PSYCHIATRY A type of body-oriented psychotherapy rooted in *hatha* yoga, which assumes that negative emotional experiences are encrypted in the unconscious and suppress the body's natural freedom; the technique is believed to restore inner balance by stimulating a person's healing life force. See Hatha yoga, Yoga

***Phoradendron flavescens*** Popularly known as American mistletoe, see there

**phosphate of iron** Ferrum phosphoricum, see Schüssler's tissue salts

**phosphate of lime** Calcarea phosphorica, see Schüssler's tissue salts

**phosphate magnesia** Magnesia phosphorica, see Schüssler's tissue salts

**phosphate potash** HOMEOPATHY 1. *Kali bich*, see there, *Kali dichromicum*, potassium phosphate 2. Kali phosphoricum, see Schüssler's tissue salts

**phosphate of soda** Natrum phosphoricum, see Schüssler's tissue salts

**phosphatidylcholine** Popularly known as lecithin, see there

**phosphorous** A nonmetallic element (atomic number 15, atomic weight 30.97) that is a principal intracellular anion; it has key roles in biochemical synthesis and storage and use of energy in cells through the formation of high-energy phosphate bonds; it is intimately linked to the regulation of calcium levels, carbohydrate, lipid, and acid-base metabolism; it is essential to bone and tooth formation; 85% of the body's phosphorus and phosphates are stored in bone phosphorus is present in dairy products, fish, legumes, meats, nuts, poultry, and whole grains. See *Phosphorus*

***Phosphorus*** HOMEOPATHY A homeopathic remedy formulated from phosphorus; it is used for anemia, circulatory defects, fatigue, gastrointestinal (eg nausea due to food poisoning) and respiratory (eg asthma, bronchitis, pneumonia) tract complaints, burning chest pains, gastritis, hemorrhage, insomnia, menstrual dysfunction, nasal polyps, nosebleeds, and tension. See *Phos* type, Homeopathy

***Phos* type** HOMEOPATHY The *Phos* constitutional type of person is often a 'bubbly' optimistic 'people person,' who gravitates towards the arts and away from formal study; these types like salty, spicy, or sweet foods, cold drinks, cheese, and wine WORSE Dampness, mental and physical exertion FEARS Failure, cancer, death, being alone WEAKEST BODY REGIONS Gastrointestinal and respiratory tracts, liver, circulation, nervous system, left side of body. See Constitutional type, *Phosphorus*, Homeopathy

**photochemotherapy** Phototherapy, see there

**photocurrent deficit** ALTERNATIVE MEDICINE A neologism for a diminution of neural impulses generated by the eye which is believed by some alternative health care practitioners to decrease brain activity and lead to anxiety, depression, fatigue, hyperactivity, insomnia, learning disabilities, loss of concentration and coordination, low self-esteem, mood swings, night blindness, seasonal affective disorder, and others, claims that are difficult to substantiate. See Alternative medicine, Light therapy

**photodynamic therapy** Phototherapy, see there

**phototherapy** 1. Bright light therapy, see there 2. EXPERIMENTAL ONCOLOGY Photochemo-therapy, photodynamic therapy A therapy in which various conditions (eg colorectalcancer, cutaneous T-cell lymphoma, head and neck cancer, Kaposi sarcoma, psoriasis, skin cancer) are treated by light after previous administration of agents (eg hemoporphyrin) that become active after exposure to light *(Moss, 1992)*.

**phrenology** Head-reading, 'bumpology' FRINGE MEDICINE A medical discipline of uncertain validity, that was most popular in the 18th to 19th century; phrenologists believe that the configuration of the skull, and lumps and bumps found thereupon can be used to decipher the intellect, emotions, and instincts being generated in the region of the brain lying below the surface being studied. See Phrenomesmerism

The *Boston Medical and Surgical Journal*, now *The New England Journal of Medicine*, congratulated the *American Phrenological Journal* on its debut: 'It is really an exceptional publication, with which we cannot dispense. It keeps constantly improving the quality of its materials…' *(Armstrong, 1991)*; American phrenology was allied to the temperance movement, vegetarianism, hydrotherapy, natural clothing, and health-related architecture; phrenology fell into disrepute by the early 20th century

**phrenomagnetism** Phrenomesmerism, see there

**phrenomesmerism** Phrenopathy FRINGE MEDICINE The combination of phrenology and mesmerism; according to this pseudoscientific doctrine, there are up to 150 lumps on the head that correspond to cerebral organs, each of which has a characteristic emotional profile. See Mesmerism, Phrenology

**phrenopathy** Phrenomagnetism, see there

**physcultopathy** A term coined by an American bodybuilder and health advocate, Bernarr Macfadden (1868-1955), for the curative aspect of his physical culture philosophy, which promoted consumption of natural foods, exercise, fasting, hydrotherapy, nudism, and abstention from coffee, tea, tobacco, alcohol, and drugs. See Macfadden, Physical culture movement

**physiatry** Physical therapy, see there

**physic root** Culver's root, see there, *Veronicastrum virginicum*

**physical culture movement** A health movement founded by Bernarr Macfadden, was based on his anti-medicine regimen that incorporated rules for diet (primarily lacto-ovo vegetarian), eating (thorough chewing), sleeping (ideally naked), exercise (15 minutes or more each day), breathing (deeply), bathing (once daily), environment (fresh air, avoidance of crowded public transport and buildings), drinking (plenty of water, no alcohol), tobacco use (do not), and sexual activity (only for procreation). See Macfadden

**physical therapy** Physiatry, physiotherapy REHABILITATION MEDICINE The use of mechanical (eg massage, manipulation, exercise, movement, hydrotherapy, traction) and electromagnetic (eg heat and cold, light, and ultrasound) modalities to treat patients who are recuperating from sports injuries, automobile accidents, or who have musculoskeletal disease and reduced joint mobility. See Massage therapy, Rehabilitation medicine

**physiognomy** FRINGE MEDICINE A pseudodiagnostic technique based on the belief that an individual's personality and emotional state can be deciphered by evaluating facial features or lines on the body; if the face is being examined, it is known as face-reading; if the lines of the forehead are being examined, it is known as metoposcopy. See Phrenology

**physiological repatterning** A component of movement therapy, which consists of the appraisal of cognitive-motor functional defects related to suboptimal musculoskeletal use; the therapist addresses perceptual, neurological, and musculoskeletal defects by studying the relationship of the biomechanical structures with the environment and environmental tasks being performed, and employs the appropriate corrective measures. See Laban analysis, Movement therapy

**physiotherapy** NATUROPATHY The use of natural and other forces, eg light, water, heat, cold, ultrasound, electricity, and fresh air to either effect a treatment, or to act as an adjunct to a therapy REHABILITATION MEDICINE Physical therapy, see there

***Physostima venenosum*** Popularly known as Calabar bean, see there

**phytochemical** A chemical of plant origin, eg sulforaphane (from cruciferous vegetables), alicin (garlic and onions), limonene (citrus fruits), isoflavones (beans), ellagic acid (grapes) (*P Talalay, PNAS April 12, 1994*); phytochemicals may be useful for certain diseases, eg in chemoprevention of malignancy, immune stimulation, and so on

**phytochemistry** Plant chemistry

**phytoestrogen** ALTERNATIVE PHARMACOLOGY Any of a number of estrogen-like compounds present in soybeans, flaxseed, and other plants, which may ameliorate some of the signs and symptoms of menopause (*Br Med J 1990; 301:905*)

***Phytolacca americana*** Popularly known as pokeweed, see there

***Phytolacca decandra*** Pokeweed, see there, *Phytolacca americana*

**phytomedicine** Herbal medicine, see there

**phytotherapy** Herbal medicine, see there

**pickpocket** Shepherd's purse, see there, *Capsella bursa-pastoris*

***Picrasma excelsa*** Jamaica quassia, see there

**pigeon diet** Moerman's anticancer diet, see there

**pigeon remedy** Pigeon therapy FRINGE MEDICINE A pseudotherapeutic technique for treating jaundice; a pigeon or dove is placed on a patient's abdomen (the bird and the patient must be of the same sex) and is supposed to absorb the jaundice and die. See Moerman's anticancer diet, Transference treatment

**pigeon therapy** Pigeon remedy, see there

**pigeonberry** Pokeweed, see there, *Phytolacca americana*

**pigeon's grass** Vervain, see there, *Vebena officinalis*

**'pile of bricks'** See Rolfing®

**pill** *Wan* CHINESE MEDICINE A general term for any of a number of therapeutic preparations consisting of ground herbal powder mixed with honey, rolled into a ball, and baked; pills may be mixed with other bases, eg flour paste, beeswax, and fermented dough. See Chinese herbal medicine

***Pilocarpus jaborandi*** Jaborandi, see there

**pimbina** Cramp bark, see there, *Viburnum opulus*

**pineapple** *Ananas comosus* HERBAL MEDICINE A tropical plant, the 'fruit' (it is not a fruit, per se, but rather a complex flowerhead that forms around the stem) of which is anti-inflammatory, thrombolytic, and a digestive tonic; its most active principle is bromelain, an enzyme used commercially as a natural meat tenderizer. See Herbal medicine

***Pimpinella anisum*** Popularly known as anise, see there

***Pinellia ternata*** *P tuberifera, ban hsia, ban xia* CHINESE MEDICINE A tuberous perennial that is antiemetic, antitussive, expectorant, and sedative; it is used for chest pain and cough, insomnia, nausea and vomiting, nocturnal emission, and vertigo. See Chinese herbal medicine

**pineapple** *Ananas comosus*

***Pinellia tuberifera*** *Pinellia ternata*, see there

***Pinites succinifer*** Amber, see there

**pink medicine** FRINGE ONCOLOGY One of two 'anti-cancer' medicines promoted in the 1950s by Harvey Hoxsey, which consists of cascara from prickly ash bark, buckthorn bark, red clover blossoms, burberry root, burdock root, licorice root, pokeweed, and alfalfa; the FDA investigated the Hoxsey 'medicines', and concluded that they were ineffective. See Black medicine, Hoxsey treatment, Unproven methods for cancer management

**pink yarrow** Yarrow, see there

***Piper methysticum*** Popularly known as kava, see there

***Piper nigrum*** Commonly known as black pepper

**pipe tree** Elderberry, see there, *Sambucus nigra*

**piracetam** ALTERNATIVE PHARMACOLOGY A 'smart pill,' agent believed by its prescribers to improve learning, attention span, cognitive and motor skills; in Europe, piracetam has been used for alcoholism, attention deficit disorder, dyslexia, fatigue, recuperation from stokes, and to enhance the immune system; it is believed to be anticoagulant, antioxidant, vasodilatory, reduce lipofuscin deposits, and improve cerebral glucose metabolism; it is not available in the US. See Nervine

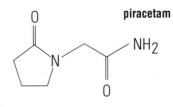

**piracetam**

O
N
$NH_2$
O

**pissabed** Dandelion, see there, *Taraxacum officinale*

**pitch doctor** QUACKERY The principal player in a traveling medicine show of the late 1800s that huckstered patent medicines; most pitch doctors were white, had the mien of circus ringmaster, and usually lacked formal medical education *(Armstrong, 1991)*. See

Frontier prescription, Medicine show, Painless Parker, Patent medicine, Quack, Quackery

***pitta*** Sun force AYURVEDIC MEDICINE The *dosha* that represents fire, a 'transformative' force according to the ayurvedic construct of natural law; *pitta* is linked to digestive and metabolic activity, and control of body temperature; *pitta* energy flows at its peak in the summer. See Ayurvedic medicine, *Dosha*, *Kapha*, *Prakriti*, *Prana*, *Vata*

***pitta* diet** AYURVEDIC MEDICINE A diet believed to be optimal for a person with a '*pitta*' *dosha*, which consists of 'cooling' foods, eg basmati rice, cottage cheese, mint tea, oatmeal, and seed fruits; intake of hot, spicy foods should be avoided. See *Pitta*; Cf *Kapha* diet, *Vata* diet

***pitta* personality** AYURVEDIC MEDICINE A personality profile with a '*pitta*' *dosha*; *pitta* individuals tend to be determined, strong-willed, ambitious, clearheaded, and enthusiastic leaders, who work well under pressure; *pitta* types often have red hair and freckles, and usually have no difficulty in maintaining their weight; *pitta* energy flows at its peak in the summer, when the *pitta* individual is most susceptible to sunburn, poison ivy, and other skin rashes; *pitta* types are also susceptible to gallbladder and liver disease, colitis, conjunctivitis, gastritis, peptic ulcers, and inflammation. See *Dosha*, *Pitta*; Cf *Kapha* personality, *Vata* personality

Note: *Pitta* individuals are irritable, angry, and competitive, and thus similar to the type 'A' personality of Western medicine

**pituitary type** FRINGE MEDICINE An endocrine profile based on a hypothesis advanced by E Abravanel, MD, that each person has a dominant endocrine organ, and each type of person craves and overeats certain foods in an effort to stimulate that organ; pituitary types are supposed to crave dairy products, which are believed to stimulate the pituitary gland; pituitary types have a large head, child-like face, and fat distributed over the entire body; pituitary types are advised to consume more meat, which stimulates the other (nonpituitary) endocrine organs, and drink fenugreek tea. See Body type, Diet

***pizzicilli*** Royal treatment AYURVEDIC MEDICINE A type of *panchakarma* (purification therapy) that was reserved for the royalty of ancient India; *pizzicilli* was intended to promote health and prolong life, and consists of a full body massage by two technicians using herbal oil. See Ayurvedic medicine, *Panchakarma*, *Prana*

**placebo** Sugar pill An inactive material, often in the form of a capsule, pill, or tablet, that is visually identical to a drug being tested; the use of placebo controls is a required component of the FDA's drug approval process, as a pharmaceutical must be proved to be more effective than a placebo; Cf Nocebo

Note: Questions raised about the ethics of certain uses of placebo controls (*N Engl J Med 1994; 331:394sb*) are unlikely to be answered in the near future; when a negative or 'placebo' control is required to evaluate the efficacy of a therapeutic maneuver, a de facto placebo may be used, eg sham plasmapheresis

**placebo effect** The usually beneficial effect that an inactive or inert substance, ie a placebo, has on a patient's clinical course; up to 30% of patients with conditions that have a psychological substrate may report clinical improvement when 'treated' with a placebo; conditions that respond to placebos (eg angina pectoris, arthritis, hypertension and post-operative pain) may also respond to biofeedback; the well-described analgesic effect of placebos may be mediated by endorphins. See Biofeedback, 'Halo' effect, Hawthorne effect, Placebo, Placebo response; Cf 'Nocebo'

**placebo response** Some health care workers believe that as much as two-thirds of a drug's effects are due to the placebo response (*Castleman, 1996*); the placebo response can take many forms including a child's response to mother's kissing 'booboos' and various forms of the therapy administered in a traditional medical context; all appear to increase endorophin levels; placebo responsiveness hinges on four factors: user belief, user anxiety, severity of the problem, and physician enthusiasm. See Mind/body medicine

**plane of existence** Realm of reality, *bardos* PARANORMAL PHENOMENA A nonmaterial 'otherworld' location that cannot be accessed in absence of spiritual medium

**plant alchemy** Spagyrics FRINGE MEDICINE A mystical form of herbal medicine based on astrology and alchemy, which assumes that there are three elements–sulfur, mercury, and salt–that constitute the basis of all matter (*Raso, 1994*); Cf Herbal medicine

**plant protease concentrate** Bomelain, see there

**plantain** 1. *Plantago major*, broad-leafed plantain, *che chien dze*, *che qian zi*, common plantain, *Plantago asiatica*, ribwort, ripple grass, snakeweed A perennial herb, the seeds of which contain alkaloids, glycosides, mucilage, silica, and tannins; plantains are antihypertensive, anti-inflammatory, diuretic, and expectorant CHINESE MEDICINE Plantain is used for dysuria, ocular pain, urinary tract infections, poor vision, and problems of childbirth. See Chinese herbal medicine HERBAL MEDICINE Plantains are used in Western herbal medicine, internally as bulk laxatives, for bronchitis, cystitis, diarrhea, fungal infections, hemorrhoids, hepatitis, neuralgias, urinary tract infections, and topically for cuts, stings, bites, tumors, and varicose veins. See Herbal medicine 2. Psyllium, see there, *Plantago psyllium*

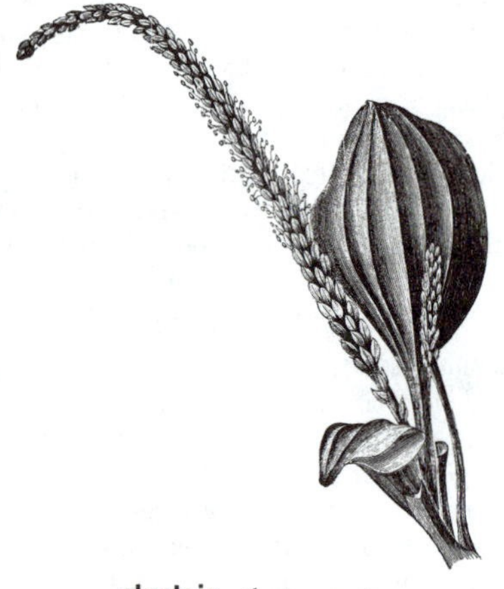

**plantain** *Plantago major*

***Plantago asiatica*** Plantain, see there, *Plantago major*

***Plantago major*** Psyllium, see there, *Plantago psyllium*

***Plantago ovata*** Psyllium, see there, *Plantago psyllium*

***Plantago psyllium*** Popularly known as psyllium, see there

**'plantibodies'** Plant-derived antibodies, first produced in tobacco, which have the advantage of being less immunogenic than mouse antibodies which have been used in research, and are potential therapeutic agents

**plaster of Paris** Calcarea sulphurica, see Schüssler's tissue salts

***Platycodon chinensis*** Balloon flower, see there, formally designated *Platycodon grandiflorum*

***Platycodon grandiflorum*** see Balloon flower

**play therapy** Recreational therapy, see there

**pleurisy root** *Aesclepias tuberosa*, butterfly weed, Canada root, flux root, milkweed, orange swallow-wort, tuber root, white root, windroot HERBAL MEDICINE An annual weed, the root of which contains glycosides (eg asclepiadin), resins, and volatile oil; it is diaphoretic and expectorant, and has been used for respiratory tract infections TOXICITY Fresh roots may cause vomiting, and are toxic in high doses. See Herbal medicine

**plumbagin** FRINGE HERBOLOGY A substance said to be present in the Venus flytrap (*Dionaea muscipula*)* and in a Brazilian plant, *Plumbago scandens*, which is claimed to be effective in treating a number of cancers (*Moss, 1992*). See Carnivora, Unproven methods for cancer management

*The extract of which forms the basis of an uncertain therapy for cancer management, Carnivora

**PLT** Past life/lives therapy, see there

**PNF stretching** Proprioceptor neuromuscular facilitation stretching, see there

**podiatrist** Chiropodist, podologist A person trained in podiatry, who, in the US, has graduated from a 4-year education program in podiatry that follows college or university education; podiatrists are examined and licensed by a state's medical board, carry a title of Doctor of Podiatric Medicine (DPM), and diagnose and treat diseases of the feet by medicine or surgery. See Podiatry

**podiatry** Chiropody, podology The field of health care dedicated to understanding the anatomy, mechanics, and pathology of the foot, and diagnosis and treatment of its diseases. See Podiatrist

**podologist** Podiatrist, see there

**podology** Podiatry, see there

***Podophyllum peltatum*** Popularly known as mayapple, see there

**poetry therapy** ALTERNATIVE PSYCHOLOGY A general term for the use of poetry, and other forms of written expression in a group setting, which enable patients to work together to understand, and hopefully resolve issues and conflicts of mutual interest; the technique was developed in the 1940s by an American pharmacist, E Greifer, and primarily uses 'happy' or uplifting poems; the technique may be of use in Alzheimer's disease, cardiac disease, eating disorders, emotional disorders, mental disorders, mental retardation, schizophrenia, strokes, substance abuse, and other conditions (*Bricklin, 1976*). See Bibliotherapy; Cf Drama therapy, Recreational therapy

Poetry therapy sessions are usually one hour, and include a group discussion of the works that were read

**pogostemon** Agastache, see there, *Agastache rugosa*

**pointwork** A general term for any therapy that stimulates, compresses, or pokes needles into pressure points identified along meridians in a formal health system, eg Chinese (acupressure, acupuncture) or ayurvedic (chakra balancing) medicine. See Co-centering

**poison flag** Blue flag, see there, *Iris versicolor*

**poison nut** *Nux vomica*, see there

**poison tobacco** Henbane, see there, *Hyoscyamus niger*

**poisonous plant** HERBAL MEDICINE A general term for any plant capable evoking a toxic and/or fatal reaction; herbologists must know which plants are poisonous (Table). See Botanical toxicity, Herbal medicine

**poke** Pokeweed, see there, *Phytolacca americana*

**POISONOUS PLANTS**

American mistletoe (*Phoradendron flavescens*)
American yew (*Taxus canadensis*)
Arnica (*Arnica montana*)
Autumn crocus/meadow saffron (*Colchicum autumnale*)
Belladonna (*Atropa belladonna*)
Bird's foot trefoil (*Lotus corniculatus*)
Bittersweet nightshade (*Solanum dulcamara*)
Black locust (*Robinia pseudoacacia*)
Black nightshade (*Solanum americanum*)
Bloodroot (*Sanguinaria canadensis*)
Blue flag (*Iris versicolor*)
Broom (*Cytisus scoparius*)
Calabar bean (*Physostigma venenosum*)
Camphor (*Cinnamomum camphora*)
Castor oil plant (*Ricinus communis*)
Celandine (*Chelidonium majus*)
Chinese lantern (*Physalis alkagengi*)
Coltsfoot (*Tussilago farfara*)
Comfrey (*Symphytum officinale*)
Cotton (*Gossypium hirsutum*)
Daffodil (*Narcissus pseudonarcissus*)
Death camas (*Zigadenus elegans*)
Desert plume (*Stanleya pinnata*)
Ergot (*Claviceps purpurea*)
Figwort (*Scrophularia nodosa*)
Foxglove (*Digitalis purpurea*)
Gelsimium (*Gelsimium sempervirens*)
Goldenseal (*Hydrastis canadensis*)
Green false hellebore (*Viratrum viride*)
Hedge mustard (*Sisymbrium officinale*)
Hellebore (*Veratrum viride*)
Hemp dogbane (*Apocynum cannabinum*)
Henbane (*Hyoscyamus niger*)
Horse chestnut (*Aesculus hippocastanum*)
Ignatia (*Ignatia amara*)
Indian pink (*Spigelia marilandica*)
Indian tobacco (*Lobelia inflata*)*
Jimsonweed (*Datura stramonium*)
Larkspur (*Delphinium ajacis*)
Lily-of-the-valley (*Convallaria majalis*)
Lobelia (*Lobelia inflata*)*
Mandrake (*Podophyllum peltatum*)*
Marsh marigold (*Caltha palustris*)
Mayapple (*Podophyllum peltatum*)*
Mayflower (*Epigaea repens*)
Monkshood (*Aconitum uncinatum*)
Moonseed (*Menispermum canadense*)
Mountain laurel (*Kalmia latifolia*)
Poison nut (*Nux vomica*)
Poison hemlock (*Conium maculatum*)
Pokeweed (*Phytolacca americana*)
Rauvolfia (*Rauvolfia serpentina*)
Red baneberry (*Actaea rubra*)
Rosebay rhododendron (*Rhododendron maximum*)
Rue (*Ruta graveolens*)
Spurge (*Euphorbia* species)
Squill (*Unginea scilla*)
Tall buttercup (*Ranunculus acris*)
Tobacco (*Nicotiana tabacum*)
Tonka beans (*Dipteryx odorata*)
Virgin's bower (*Clematis virginiana*)
Wallflower (*Cheiranthus cheiri*)
White bryony (*Bryonia alba*)
White false hellebore (*Veratrum album*)
White snakeroot (*Eupatorium rugosum*)
Wild cherry (*Prunus virginiana*)
Wild licorice (*Glycyrrhiza lepidota*)
Winter cress (*Barbarea vulgaris*)
Wormseed (*Chenopodium ambrosioides*)
Wormwood (*Artemisia absinthium*)
Yellow jessamine (*Gelsimium sempervirens*)*

*Listed twice, given differences in trivial name

**pokeroot** Pokeweed, see there, *Phytolacca americana*

**pokeweed** *Phytolacca americana, P decandra*, coakum, pigeonberry, poke, pokeroot HERBAL MEDICINE A perennial weed that contains alkaloids, resins, phytolaccic acid, saponins, tannins, and triterpenoids; pokeweed has been used internally to stimulate lymphatic circulation, for rheumatic pain and tonsillitis, and topically for mastitis TOXICITY Abdominal cramps, bradycardia, convulsions, diarrhea, hypotension, nausea, respiratory paralysis, vomiting, coma, and possibly death, due to cardiovascular collapse. See Botanical toxicity

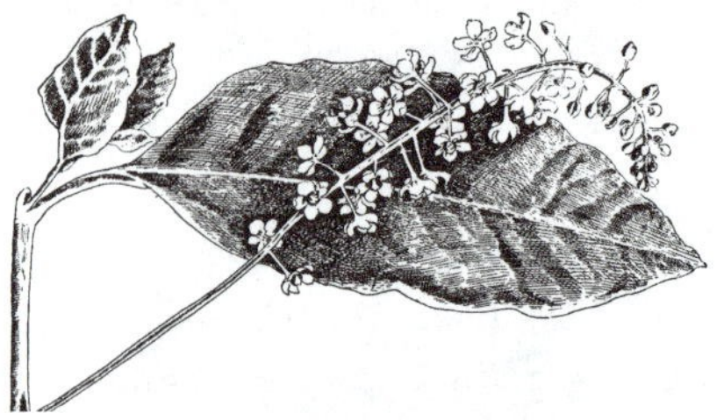

**pokeweed** *Phytolacca americana*

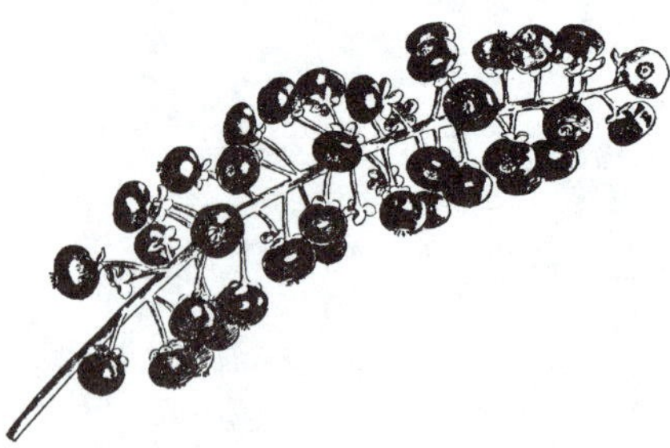

**polarity** Polarity therapy, see there

**polarity balancing** Polarity therapy, see there

**polarity energy balancing system** Polarity therapy, see there

**polarity healing system** Polarity therapy, see there

**polarity squat** POLARITY THERAPY A polarity therapy exercise that consists of squatting while perfectly balanced, which stretches the vertebral column and releases pelvic tension. See Polarity therapy

**polarity system** Polarity therapy, see there

**polarity testing** A general term for the use of magnets to select a homeopathic remedy or nutritional supplement

**polarity therapy** Polarity, polarity balancing, polarity energy balancing system, polarity healing system, polarity system, Polarity Wellness® ALTERNATIVE MEDICINE A system of health care developed in the 1920s by an Austrian-American holistic physician, Randolph Stone, who was chiropractor, osteopath, and naturopath; Stone's system is based on the belief that the life forces controlling a person's physical and emotional well-being can be blocked by poor habits and diet; good health depends on restoring a balance, or polarity of the life forces, by promoting the body's natural self-healing capabilities; each body region is said to have positive (+), or negative (–), or null (0) energy; according to Stone, polarity therapy involves 5 basic elements (ether, air, fire, water, and earth) that affect 5 distinct (but arbitrarily designated) energy centers

▶ **ENERGY CENTERS, POLARITY THERAPY**

- **ETHER CENTER** Voice, ears, throat
- **AIR CENTER** Cardiorespiratory system
- **FIRE CENTER** Eyes, gastrointestinal tract, gallbladder, liver, pancreas, spleen, and sympathetic nervous system
- **WATER CENTER** Pelvic and endocrine secretions, which control the generative and emotional force
- **EARTH CENTER** Rectum and bladder, which eliminate solids and liquids

Four techniques are used to restore polarity: therapeutic touch or bodywork, enhancing awareness, diet (liver flush drink, and 'live foods', eg fruits and vegetables), and stretching exercises. See Bodywork, Humanistic psychology, Liver flush; Cf Massage therapy, Oriental massage, Reiki, Structural integration, Therapeutic touch, Traditional European massage, (contemporary) Western massage *RESOURCE: American Polarity Therapy Association, 2888 Bluff St, Suite 149, Boulder CO 80301 ☎ 1.303.545.2080*

**Polarity Wellness®** Polarity therapy, see there

**polarity yoga** Easy stretching postures A form of polarity therapy developed by an American osteopath, Randolph Stone, that combines elements of *hatha* yoga and martial arts, as a means of improving the body's flow of energy. See Bodywork, Polarity therapy

**polycontrast interface photography** FRINGE MEDICINE A pseudodiagnostic technique developed by Harry Oldfield that integrates features of Kirlian photography and electrocrystal therapy; in PIP, a video camera is attached to a computer, which is designed to interpret the light believed to emanate from an individual and correspond to his aura; the colors generated in PIP are said to translate into illnesses treatable by conventional or alternative methods. See Electrocrystal therapy, Kirlian photography

***Polygala reinii*** Morinda root, see there, *Morindae officinalis*

***Polygala sibirica*** *Polygala tenuifolia*, see there

***Polygala tenuifolia*** *Polygala sibirica, yuan jih, yuan zhi* CHINESE MEDICINE A shrub, the bark of which is analgesic, expectorant, and sedative; it is believed to improve hearing, vision, mental activity, and strengthen muscle and bone, and has been used for coughs, mental sluggishness, depression, nocturnal emission, osteoporosis, urinary tract infections, and vertigo. See Chinese herbal medicine

***Polygonatum biflorum*** Solomon's Seal, see there, *Polygonatum officinale*

***Polygonatum canaliculatum*** *Polygonatum cirrhifolium*, see there

***Polygonatum chinense*** *Polygonatum cirrhifolium*, see there

***Polygonatum cirrhifolium*** Deer bamboo, golden essence, *huang jing*, mountain ginger, *Polygonatum canaliculatum, P chinense, shan sheng jiang* CHINESE MEDICINE A perennial herb, the root of which is demulcent and tonic; it is used to retard aging, build bones, increase semen production, and to treat arthritis, male infertility, malnutrition, and general weakness. See Chinese herbal medicine

***Polygonatum officinale*** Popularly known as Solomon's Seal, see there

***Polygonatum vulgare*** Solomon's Seal, see there, *Polygonatum officinale*

**polygonum** See Chinese cornbind

***Polygonum bistorta*** Popularly known as bistort, see there

***Polygonum multiflorum*** see Chinese cornbind

**polyunsaturated fat** A saturated fatty acid (ie an alkyl chain fatty acid with two or more ethylenic (double) bonds between the carbons in the fatty acid chain. See Fatty acid, Saturated fatty acid; Cf Monounsaturated fatty acid, Unsaturated fatty acid

**pomegranate** *Punica granatum* FRINGE MEDICINE-FLOWER ESSENCE THERAPY A floral essence believed to enhance feminine warmth and creativity, and a sense of nurturing. See Flower essence therapy

***Poncircus trifoliata*** Popularly known as trifoliate orange, see there

**pontine-geniculate-occipital wave** NEUROPHYSIOLOGY An erratic volley of discharges from cholinergic neurons into higher cortical and other regions of the brain that only occurs during dreaming; PGO waves stimulate the motor centers in the brainstem that would otherwise result in motor activity, but are inhibited by spinal cord signals that prevent movement of all muscle groups except for the eyelids; PGO waves also impact on emotional circuits, which explains why dreams are accompanied by strong emotions including anxiety, fear, joy, sadness, guilt, and eroticism. See Dreams

Note: It is possible to enter the cholinergic state without being asleep, as occurs in meditation, and drug-induced or schizophrenia-related hallucinations (*New York Times 16 July 1994; C1*)

**poor man's treacle** Garlic, see there, *Allium sativum*

**poor sleeping hygiene** A general term for prebed habits that are suboptimal, and not conducive to proper rest, which can affect a person's functioning during the workday; sleep disturbances are associated with liquor, tobacco, late night meals or snacks immediately before bedtime, sedentary lifestyle, and daytime napping; insomnia may be related to bereavement, traumatic events and personal tragedies; poor sleep hygiene may respond to regular exercise, abstinence from abuse substances, meditation, and autohypnosis. See Bad habits, Highway hypnosis; Cf Good habits

**The Popcorn Plus Diet** FRINGE NUTRITION A diet formulated by J Herskowitz, MD, the key features of which include the setting of 'reasonable goals' for weight loss, and the ad lib consumption of air-detonated popcorn as a replacement for other calorie-drenched snacks (*The Popcorn Plus Diet, Pharos Books, 1987, New York*)

**poplar buds** Balm of Gilead, see there, *Populus* species

**popular health movement** MEDICAL HISTORY

A transiently popular philosophy that swept the US between the 1830s and 1850s, and sprung from Andrew Jackson's anti-elitism; in brief, it was felt that anyone should have the right to practice medicine (*Armstrong, 1991*). See Graham system

**popular herbalism** Traditional herbalism HERBAL MEDICINE A term referring to a relatively unscientific approach to the administration of herbs and medicinal plants, in which crude and/or poorly quantified extracts are administered by suboptimally trained individuals. See Herbal medicine; Cf Pharmacognosy

For the field of herbal medicine to become fully acceptable to mainstream practitioners, it is imperitive that the herb's purity, potency, quantity and bioavailability is known; if not, the herbalist may overdose or underdose the patient–Author's note

***Populus* spp** Popularly known as balm of Gilead, see there

***Populus tremuloides*** Popularly known as white poplar, see there

***Porio cocos*** Popularly known as tuckahoe, see there

**positioning technique** OSTEOPATHY A technique for determining the position of a painful joint and muscular group at which the pain is at a minimum; positioning serves to relax and relieve the pressure and strain on the musculoskeletal group and reduce muscular spasms. See Osteopathy

**post-hypnotic suggestion** HYPNOSIS The interjection of an 'alien' thought into the mind of a patient undergoing hypnosis, which would compel him to commit an act that he would not normally perform. See Hypnosis, Hypnotherapy

The frequency with which post-hypnotic suggestions are made by hypnotherapists is presumed to be low, but is a popular theme in mass-media entertainment–Author's note

**postural integration** ALTERNATIVE MEDICINE A '...*complete system of bodywork for releasing the blocks and tensions which have accumulated in the body/mind. It works simultaneously with the physical, mental, and emotional aspects of the whole person*...(and includes)...*breathing, postures, movements, positions, thoughts, and feelings*.' (*Kastner, Burroughs, 1993*); the system was developed in the 1970s by Dr JW Painter, and incorporates acupuncture, connective tissue massage, Gestalt therapy, massage therapy, Reichian therapy, Rolfing®, yoga, and zazen; according to Painter's construct of the body, the fascia is not merely a series of coverings of muscles and organs, but rather a single structure that extends from the head to the toes; in the healthy body, the fascia is relaxed and moves without restriction; in the face of poor posture, trauma, repetitive use (occupational) injuries, emotional stress, the fascia becomes indurated; postural integration techniques attempt to smooth and redistribute the disorganized fascia and return the body to a state of harmony. See Bodywork; Cf Postural therapy

**postural therapy** ALTERNATIVE MEDICINE A general term for any therapeutic technique that focuses on correcting the posture as a means of restoring health

**pot** Marijuana, see there, *Cannabis sativa*

**pot marigold** Calendula, see there, *Calendula officinalis*

**potassium** Kalium An alkaline metallic element (atomic number 19; atomic weight 39.09); it is the principal intracellular cation (positive ion) and is critical in the synthesis of new molecules, transferring energy, muscle contraction, transmitting neural impulses, and maintaining blood pressure; potassium-rich foods include bananas, cereals, legumes, potatoes, prunes, and raisins

**potassium bichromate** HOMEOPATHY *Kali bich*, see there, *Kali dichromicum*, potassium dichromate

**potassium dichromate** HOMEOPATHY *Kali bich*, see there, *Kali dichromicum*

**potassium phosphate** HOMEOPATHY *Kali phos*, see there, *Kali phosphoricum*

***Potentilla erecta*** Popularly known as erect cinquefoil, see there

***Potentilla reptans*** Popularly known as five-finger grass, see there

**potentization** Dynamization HOMEOPATHY The process by which homeopathic remedies are prepared; once the raw material is obtained, it is extracted in alcohol–forming a 'mother tincture,' placed in sugar and water, then reduced in concentration (diluted); in the homeopathic formulary, each 10-fold reduction is designated by an additional 'X' (or, in Europe, a D); thus one part of active substance in one million; a less commonly used system is that of the C dilutions, where each dilution corresponds to 1 part in 100, thus a 6C solution is that in which there is one active part in one trillion ($10^{-12}$); the most commonly prescribed homeopathic remedies have potencies of 30X (one part in $10^{-30}$) and 200X (one part in $10^{-200}$)*. See Avogadro limit, Constitutional remedy, Homeopathy, Law of the Infinitesimal dose, Mother tincture, Proving, Remedy, Succussing, Vital force NATUROPATHY The process in which the oils of petals and heads of flowers used in Bach's flower remedies are concentrated. See Bach's flower remedies

It is in the issue of potentization that mainstream biomedical thought has the greatest difficulty in accepting homeopathy as a valid therapeutic system; according to homeopathic principles, remedies with the greatest dilutions have the greatest therapeutic effect, despite the virtual absence of molecules (based on Avogadro's number) in the remedy; this counterintuitive effect has been explained by D Ullman, a homeopath, who believes that the remedy acquires a holographic imprint, or subtle energetic aspect of the primary substance–Author's note

**potentizing principle** see Homeopathic, Law of the infinitesimal dose, Potentization

**poultice** *Fu yao* CHINESE MEDICINE A topical preparation composed of powdered herbs mixed in water placed in cellophane, and taped over the area being treated; herbal poultices are used to relieve pain and repair musculoskeletal injuries, and thus are used for sports injuries. See Chinese herbal medicine HERBAL MEDICINE A moist preparation of crushed fresh herbs applied topically and held in place with gauze

**powder** *San* CHINESE MEDICINE A general term for ground herbs and formulas used in Chinese herbal medicine, to prepare capsules, infusions, liquors, porridges, ointments, pastes, and pills; powders are less concentrated than decoctions, are gentler, and best suited for treating chronic conditions. See Chinese herbal medicine

**power draw** see Healing love (meditation)

**power mushroom** CHINESE MEDICINE A combination of mushrooms (ganoderma–reishi, lentinus–shiitake, silver fungus–white ear, polyporus, and hoelen–poria) used as an immune enhancer, digestive tonic, and diuretic. See Astragalus 8 formula, Astragalus 10 plus, Chinese herbal medicine

***prakriti*** AYURVEDIC MEDICINE The unique pattern of bioforces or *doshas* (*kapha*, *pitta*, and *vata*) that a person has at the time of conception, which corresponds to the Western concept of an individual constitution; there are 7 general patterns of *pakriti*, which reflect the amount of influence that each *dosha* has on a person; a person's *prakriti* is evaluated in part by pulse reading, a system in which 12 positions of the arterial pulse at the wrists are asssessed; the ayurvedic practitioner reads the composition of the 3 *doshas* and determines the balance or imbalance in the patient's various organ functions. See Ayurvedic medicine, *Pranayama*

***prakriti cikitsa*** AYURVEDIC MEDICINE A form of naturopathy based on the 5 elements (air, earth, ether, fire, and water) of the ayurvedic construct. See Ayurvedic medicine

***prana*** AYURVEDIC MEDICINE The primal or vital energy that drives life, as viewed in the construct of ayurveda; *prana* is analogous to *chi* (*qi*), in Chinese medicine and viewed as having the qualities of a 'nutrient' that can be taken into the body; because *prana* is present in the air, breathing exercises are believed to have a central role in promoting health. See Ayurvedic medicine, *Pranayama*, *Chi*, (*qi*), *Prana*. See Vital force

***pranayama*** AYURVEDIC MEDICINE Breathing exercises, in which an individual breathes through alternate nostrils by closing off one nostril, then the other by pressing a finger against it; *pranayama* is believed to enhance the *prana*, the universal life force. See Ayurvedic medicine, *Prana*, *Rasayana*, Vital force

**pranic healing** Bioplasmic healing, radiatory healing AYURVEDIC MEDICINE A therapeutic modality used in ayurvedic medicine, in which the practitioner focuses on an individual's *prana* or etheric (spiritual) body, and diagnoses disease energies, assimilates them into his *chakra*, converts them into healing forces, then transfers the healing energy back to the patient's body; pranic healing is accomplished without physical contact between the practitioner and patient, and thus is similar to therapeutic touch, but more refined, and serves to revitalize the immune system; anecdotal reports suggest that pranic healing may be effective for headaches, gynecologic, low back, and muscle pain; some believe that pranic healing may be used for acute appendicitis and pancreatitis, cancer, deafness, diabetes, drowning, hepatitis, leukemia, sickle cell anemia, sexually-transmitted disease, tuberculosis, and other conditions. See Ayurvedic medicine, *Chi* (*qi*), *Prana*, *Pranayama*, Pranic psychotherapy

**pranic psychotherapy** AYURVEDIC MEDICINE A permutation of pranic healing used to alleviate psychological and emotional problems; according to the ayurvedic construct, trauma and adverse experiences are held in an individual's *prana* or etheric (spiritual) body as negative energy, which can be dissipated and removed by the practitioner without physical contact with the patient; pranic psychotherapy is believed to be effective in treating alcoholism and other addiction disorders, anxiety, compulsive behaviors, depression, grief, hysteria, impotence, phobias, and suicidal ideation. See Ayurvedic medicine, *Chi*, (*qi*), *Prana*, *Pranayama*, Pranic healing; CF Humanistic psychology

**prayer for the sick** Absent healing, metaphysical healing PARANORMAL PHENOMENA A supplication to a higher power by a cleric or individual for the recovery of another from an illness; in the construct of Western medicine, there is no explanation for the occasional 'miraculous' recoveries from (pathologically confirmed) dread diseases (eg cancer) that have been associated with prayer therapy. See Healing shrine, Lourdes, Miraculous cure

**prayer therapy** see Prayer for the sick

**premenstrual dysphoric disorder** The official (*per the American Psychiatric Association–Diagnosis and Statistical Manual, 4th ed-DSM-IV, 1994*) term for premenstrual syndrome (PMS), see there

**premenstrual syndrome** PMS, Premenstrual tension, premenstrual dysphoric disorder (*Term used in DSM-IV*) A cyclical disorder characterized by affective, behavioral, and somatic symptoms that consistently occur during the luteal (2nd) phase of the menstrual cycle, resolve with the onset of menses, and are vaguely linked to the fall in estrogen and progesterone from luteal peaks PATHOGENESIS Uncertain, thought to be linked to serotoninergic dysregulation CLINICAL See Table, premenstrual dysphoric disorder; PMS affects 10 to 30% of menstruating women and is characterized by several days of mental or physical incapacitation of varying intensity, insomnia, headaches, emotional lability (anxiety, depression, irritability, loss of concentration, poor judgement, mood swings and violent tendencies evoked by environmental cues), acne, breast enlargement, fullness or tenderness, abdominal bloating with edema, craving for salty, sweet or 'junk' food TREATMENT Fluoxetine (Prozac) may be use in treating the symptoms of tension, irritability, and dysphoria (*N Engl J Med 1995; 332:1529*), medical or surgical ovariectomy, and anxiolytic drugs may be marginally superior to placebos

Although PMS was assumed to be a progestational endocrine dysfunction, the use of mifepristone, an antiprogestational agent to induce menses and luteolysis, did not affect the severity or duration of a PMS 'attack' (*N Engl J Med 1991; 324:1174, 1208ed*)

**PREMENSTRUAL DYSPHORIC DISORDER** (RESEARCH CRITERIA)

Five or more of below symptoms occurring in a cyclical fashion, at least one of which includes criteria 1 to 4

1. Depressed mood, self-deprecation, hopelessness
2. Anxiety, tension, feeling 'wired'
3. Emotional lability
4. Marked and/or persistent anger, irritability, or interpersonal conflict
5. Decreased interest in usual activities or relationships
6. Difficulty in concentrating
7. Lethargy
8. Change in appetite
9. Change in sleep habits
10. Subjective sense of loss of control
11. Physical symptoms, eg breast tenderness, headaches, arthralgia, myalgia, bloating, weight gain

(modified from DSM-IV)

**premenstrual tension** Premenstrual syndrome, see there

**prenatal technique** Metamorphic technique, see there

**pressed juice** CLINICAL NUTRITION A juice prepared from fresh fruits, which may be ingested as tincture. See Mono therapy

**pressure point therapy** NATUROPATHY A general term for any therapy that massages acupressure points as a means of restoring health. See Acupressure, Head's zones, Polarity therapy,

Reflexology, Shiatsu, Zones of hyperalgesia

**prickly ash** Northern prickly ash, see there, *Zanthoxylum americanum*

**priest's crown** Dandelion, see there, *Taraxa-cum officinale*

**Vincenz Priessnitz** A farmer-turned-healer (1799-1851) from Graefenberg, Austria, whose 'health system' was based on the topical application of cold water compresses and ingestion of gallons of water; until his death, Priessnitz treated many of the upper class at his water-cure establishment for various conditions, including asthma, gout, liver disease, measles, nervous conditions, rheumatic complaints, smallpox, syphilis, and tumors. See Hydrotherapy

**primal therapy** Primal scream therapy PSYCHOLOGY A format of psychotherapy developed by Dr Arthur Janov, who wrote *The Primal Scream* in 1970; primal therapy is based on the belief that many of the psychological problems seen in adult are caused by unresolved conflicts that occurred in the person's childhood; these conflicts, in turn, are due to emotional, physical, or sexual abuse; the patient is encouraged to vent, and express his emotional and mental pain by screaming; methods used to return a person to his mental state of birth include hypnotic age regression, 'psycholytic' methods, simulation of the birthing process, and breathing; once a client emits his primal scream, it is recommended that he undergo 75 3-hour group sessions; primal therapy is believed by some to be effective in treating all mental illness as well as asthma, cancer, claustrophonia, diabetes, hypertension, hysteria, migraines, schizophrenia, sleep disorders, and others. See Humanistic psychology, Hypnotic age regression, Inner shouting, Psycholytic methods for the rebirthing phenomenon, Rebirthing therapy

**primal scream therapy** Primal therapy, see there

**primary care** ALTERNATIVE MEDICINE The first level of an alternative form of health care, which requires that the provider be knowledgeable in at least one formal system of health care, eg acupuncture, and or traditional Chinese medicine, ayurvedic medicine, chiropractic, homeopathy, naturopathy, osteopathy, or other; many alternative therapies are limited in scope, and can only be recommended after a patient is evaluated by a primary care provider, who refers them for a specific adjunctive therapy. See Secondary care

**primary care physician** A mainstream physician who provides care to a patient at the time of first (non-emergency) contact, which usually occurs on an outpatient basis; primary care providers include internists (formerly general practitioners), family practitioners, and pediatricians; in some regions of the US, gynecologists provide primary care to women

**primary control** A term coined by FM Alexander, for the key component of the Alexander technique, in which the vertebral column is brought into its maximum length; according to Alexander technique proponents, achieving primary control–through use of key phrases and gentle manipulation, results in an improvement of the personality. See Alexander technique

**prime minister** Lung, see The Twelve vital organs

**prime psychological addiction** See Enneagram system

***Primula vera*** Popularly known as cowslip, see there

**principle of the maximum mind** RELAXATION A term coined by H Benton, for a type of mental plasticity, which is believed to open the mind to new perceptions of one's self and the world, through the use of imagery to enhance sports and performing arts skills (*Bricklin, 1976*). See Imagery and visualization, Pealeism; Cf Faith factor

**Pritikin diet** CLINICAL NUTRITION A diet that is high in complex carbohydrates (eg whole grains, fruits, and vegetables), which comprise > 90% of caloric intake and low in protein, fat, and cholesterol, with severely restricted caffeine, salt, and sugar; the PD was formulated by Nathan Pritikin after he was diagnosed of coronary artery disease*; the diet reduces the risk of cardiovascular disease, and hypertension, and may be beneficial for arthritis, diabetes, gout, stroke, and other diseases of civilization; a criticism of the diet is its shunning of dairy products and, by extension, calcium;

Pritikin frowned on vitamin supplements, and 'obsessively' eliminated all fats from the diet. See Diet, Ornish regimen

*His total cholesterol at the time (1958) was 7.25 mmol/L (*US: 280 mg/dl*); at the time of his death (due to complications of lymphoma) in 1985, his cholesterol was 2.4 mmol/L (*US: 94 mg/dl*); post-mortem examination revealed mild cardiac hypertrophy and widely patent coronary arteries (*N Engl J Med 1985; 313:52c*); when the Pritikin diet was compared in patients with intermittent claudication of the lower extremities, with a less extreme diet recommended by the American Heart Association, it was not superior; the improvement in cardiovascular function in both groups was attributed to exercise (*Bricklin, 1976, 1983*)

**Pritikin exercise** An exercise program designed by Nathan Pritikin, which is intended to improve cardiovascular function by strengthening the legs (the second heart) through walking, aerobic exercises, weight training, and yoga, after appropriate stretching. See Pritikin diet

**Pritikin lifetime eating plan** Pritikin diet, see there

**proanthocyanidin** ALTERNATIVE PHARMACOLOGY A chemical found in bark and grape seed extracts, which is a more potent antioxidant than vitamins C or E, and has been shown to reduce LDL-cholesterol

**process-oriented psychology** Process psychology, see there

**process psychology** Process-oriented psychology ALTERNATIVE PSYCHOLOGY A form of psychotherapy developed by Arnold Mindell, which is an eclectic synthesis of bodywork, dreamwork, meditation, and spirituality, rooted in a conceptual dreambody

***Progenitor cryptocides*** FRINGE MEDICINE A term for a microbe believed by the late Dr Virginia Wuerthe-Caspe Livingston to reside in all humans which, in a background of a compromised immune system, and facilitated by consumption of non-living foods, causes cancer. See Live foods, Livingston therapy, Unproven methods for cancer management

The existence of this microbe, *Progenitor cryptocides* (Latin, hidden primordial killer) has not been confirmed

**progression/regression therapy** Past lives therapy, see there

**progressive relaxation** ALTERNATIVE MEDICINE A relaxation technique developed in 1909 by E Jacobson at Harvard that is used in mind/body medicine to cope with stress, in which muscle groups are grasped in succession, starting at one end of the body. See Autogenic feedback training, Biofeedback training, Biopsychosocial model, Breath therapy, Flight-or-fight response, Hypnosis, Imagery and visualization, Meditation, Mind/body medicine, Mindfulness Psychoneuroimmunology

**proliferative therapy** Reconstructive therapy, see there

**proprioceptor** NEUROLOGY A general term for a sensory end organ that provides information about the position of the body and its parts in space at a particular moment in time; proprioceptors are present in muscle, tendons, and joint capsules, and include the muscle spindle and the Golgi tendon organ; Cf Cross-fiber friction massage

**proprioceptor neuromuscular facilitation stretching** PNF stretching A stretching technique that reeducates muscles by 'tricking' proprioceptors into allowing increased ranges of motion, by reducing the tensing of the muscles that normally occurs at the preset limits to the range of motion; the technique consists of stretching the muscle to a comfortable limit, followed by having the client tense the muscle during the stretch, which slightly increases the range of motion; PNF stretching increases muscle flexibility, and is of use in sports massage. See Massage

**Prostsafe™** FRINGE MEDICINE A concoction containing zinc, ginseng. *Serenoa serrulata*, certain amino acids, bee pollen, and vitamins A, $B_6$, and E, that is claimed by its vendor (*Whitewing Labs, Granada Hills, CA*) to control prostate-related urinary frequency, and other symptoms seen in men over age 40. Cf Invalid claims of efficacy

**protease inhibitor** ALTERNATIVE PHARMACOLOGY Any of a number of substances that inhibit the activity of proteases that promote the growth of breast, colon and other cancers; these compounds neutralize various carcinogens, and are present in whole grain oats, rice, potatoes, chickpeas, kidney beans, and others foods

**protein diet** Liquid-protein diet, see there

**protein drink** Amino acid drink A type of sports drink commonly produced from whey, a bovine milk product, which is used in the recuperation of fatigued or overly stressed muscles (*New York Times 7 Dec 1994; C6*). See Amino acid therapy, Sports drink

**protein restriction** CLINICAL NUTRITION The reduction of protein consumed in the diet from its normal level (circa 1.3 g/kg/day), a maneuver used in renal failure (*N Engl J Med 1994; 330:877*); extreme protein restriction (very low protein diet, 0.28 g/kg/day) does not significantly slow the progression of renal disease more than moderate protein restriction (low protein diet, eg 0.58 g/kg/day); Cf Caloric restriction

**protein-sparing** CLINICAL NUTRITION Pertaining or relating to minimizing protein catabolism; protein-sparing maneuvers include addition of carbohydrates and fats to a low-protein diet in order to minimize protein breakdown. See Low-protein diet

**proving** HOMEOPATHY The method used in homeopathy to test new substances for therapeutic potential; in a proving, the agent of interest (known as a remedy) is administered to a group of healthy individuals to determine the pattern of symptoms evoked by the remedy; in the second stage of proving, the symptoms evoked by the remedy must be reversed by the remedy. See Homeopathy, Law of similars, Remedy, Vital force

**provocation (test)** Neutralization (test), see there

**Prudden** See Bonnie Prudden, Myotherapy

**prunella** Heal-all, see there, *Prunella vulgaris*

***Prunella vulgaris*** Popularly known as heal-all, see there

***Prunus armeniaca*** Apricot, see there

***Prunus serotina*** Popularly known as wild cherry, see there

***Prunus virginiana*** Wild cherry, see there, *Prunus serotina*

**PSEB**sm A proprietary form of aura balancing, which is an integral component of Reiki plus®, see there

**pseudoallergy** CLINICAL IMMUNOLOGY An adverse, nonimmunologic, anaphylaxis-like reaction of sudden onset, which is associated with food ingestion; pseudoallergies may be due to an anaphylactoid reaction, intolerance, eg psychogenic response, metabolic defect, eg enzymatic deficiency, tyramine reaction), and toxicity, eg tetrodotoxin. See Cheese reaction, Food allergy, Food intolerance

True allergies to foods are hypersensitivity reactions caused by mast cell release of histamines evoked by IgE, in children, most commonly linked to eggs, milk, peanuts, other nuts, fish, soy beans and shrimp

**pseudodiagnosis** FRINGE MEDICINE A diagnosis based on uncertain scientific principles, eg determination of a person's response to containers of colored water, as in aurasomatherapy, or vibrations from a particular organ or tissue, as in biomagnetics

**pseudoprognosis** FRINGE MEDICINE The projection of the future behavior of a particular condition based on uncertain scientific principles, eg the prediction of the behavior of a dread disease through the use of Tarot cards, or horoscopes

**pseudoscience** A field described by Nobel laureate Murray Gell-Mann as '*the dissociation of belief from evidence*'; pseudoscientific thought includes such maneuvers as the recycling of refuted concepts, eg mesmerism, the use of myths as starting points for seeking truth, blind acceptance of an invalid theory, and acceptance of unreliable data that supports a favored hypothesis. See Fringe medicine; Cf Alternative medicine

**pseudovitamin** A substance that does not meet the accepted definition (see below and table) of a required human vitamin. Representation of these substances as vitamins is misleading, as the implication that they have natural curative effects is based on no known scientific principles; US consumers spend an estimated $\$10^9$/year (US) on pseudovitamins

► **PSEUDOVITAMINS, TYPES OF**

- **TRUE VITAMINS**, *but not in humans*
- **SUBSTANCES ONCE DESCRIBED AS VITAMINS**, but not now regarded as such
- **'FACTORS'** in the blood, exotic vegetables and fruits, or minerals that have been termed 'vitamins' by various persons
- **METABOLITES**, including

1. Intermediate metabolites, eg orotic acid ('vitamin $B_{13}$')
2. Substances whose metabolism requires B vitamins (eg choline, inositol, methionine)
3. Substances that are B vitamins for nonvertebrate organisms (para-aminobenzoic acid, a B vitamin for certain bacteria ('vitamin $B_x$') and carnitine, a B vitamin for mealworms ('vitamin $B_t$')

- **PHARMACOLOGIC SUBSTANCES**, which are allegedly capable of favoring certain metabolic processes in humans, but which produce little (if any) objective improvement, eg flavonoids ('vitamin P')

## Pseudovitamins

**Vitamin $B_G$** Obsolete for pantothenic acid

**Vitamin $B_4$** An ill-defined 'factor', of uncertain validity, isolated from yeast or liver, described as alleviating myasthenia in experimental animals; vitamin $B_4$ 'deficiency' responds to a variety of agents, including adenine, arginine, cystine, glycine and thiamin

**Vitamin $B_5$** Obsolete for nicotinic acid (niacin) and nicotinamide

**Vitamin $B_7$**

**Vitamin $B_8$** Adenylic acid (a nucleotide)

**Vitamin $B_{10}$** A growth and feathering promoter in chickens, which corresponds to folic acid and vitamin $B_{12}$

**Vitamin $B_{11}$** A growth and feathering promotor of chickens, similar or identical to Vitamin $B_{10}$ factor

**Vitamin $B_{13}$** Orotic acid, an intermediate in pyrimidine metabolism; it is not a vitamin

**Vitamin $B_{15}$** Pangamate, a pseudovitamin with no known effects

**Vitamin $B_{17}$** Amygdalin, Laetrile A toxic substance claimed to be effective in treating malignancy.

**Vitamin $B_p$** A factor that treats perosis in chickens that respond to a mixture of choline and manganese

**Vitamin $B_t$** A substance promoting insect growth, corresponding to carnitine

**Vitamin $B_w$** Biotin

**Vitamin $B_x$** Para-aminobenzoic acid

**Vitamin $C_2$** Bioflavonoids, substances with activities that partially overlap those of true vitamin C

**Vitamin F** Obsolete for essential fatty acids

**Vitamin $GH_3$** See Gerovital

**Vitamin H** Biotin

**Vitamin $H_3$** See Gerovital

**Vitamin I** $B_7$ 1. Biotin 2. Carnitine (permeability factor)

**Vitamin J** Bioflavonoids

**Vitamin $L_1$** Anthranilic acid, a liver 'factor' in lactation

**Vitamin $L_2$** Adenylthiomethylpentose, a yeast 'factor' involved in lactation

**Vitamin M** Folic acid

**Vitamin N** A preparation from the brain or stomach, which was described as being anticarcinogenic

**Vitamin O** Synonym for supplementary oxygen

**Vitamin P** Synonym for bioflavonoids

**Vitamin $P_4$** Troxerutin

**Vitamin R** A folic acid-related compound that promotes growth in bacteria

**Vitamin S** A streptogenin-related protein that promotes growth in chicks

**Vitamin T** A mixture of amino acids, DNA nucleotides, folacin and vitamin $B_{12}$ that promotes growth and wound-healing in yeasts and insects

**Vitamin U** Methylsulfonium salts of methionine, derived from cabbage juice, claimed to heal peptic ulcers.

**Vitamin V** A tissue 'factor' composed of NAD+ and NADH, which promotes bacterial growth

- **'SNAKE OIL REMEDIES'**, which meet the legal definition of fraud, which include pangamate ('vitamin $B_{15}$'), laetrile ('vitamin $B_{17}$') and gerovital ('vitamin $H_3$')

Cf Vitamins

True vitamins are organic accessory food factors that usually remain in food after removal of the basic elements including carbohydrates, fats, proteins, minerals, water and fiber, and are 1. Necessary in trace amounts (daily intake in milligram to microgram quantities) and 2. Essential as the body either does not produce them or does so in insufficient quantities

***psi*** Extrasensory perception PARANORMAL PHENOMENA The alleged ability to become aware of past, present, or future events without the use of the five senses; *psi*-ability has been attributed to or enhanced by prayer and meditation

***psi* healing** Psychic healing, see there

**psilosis pigmentosa** Pellagra, see there

**psionic medicine** Psionics FRINGE MEDICINE A diagnostic and therapeutic system developed by Dr George Lawrence, in which homeopathic remedies are chosen based on the manner in which a pendulum swings in relationship to a dried spot of a patient's blood; Cf Homeopathy,

**psionics** 1. Psionic medicine, see there 2. Radionics, see there

**psora** HOMEOPATHY A scabies-like skin eruption, which is one of the three miasms in homeopathy; the term miasm was coined by Samuel Hahnemann, for a 'hereditary' condition that may be resistant to homeopathic remedies. See Homeopathy, Miasm

***Psoralea corylifolia*** *Bu gu jih, bu gu zhi* CHINESE MEDICINE An annual herb, the seeds of which stimulate and are tonic, and believed to be aphrodisiacs; it is used for impotence, low back pain, urinary frequency, and to prevent spontaneous abortion. See Chinese herbal medicine

**psyche** Mind, see there

**psychiatric orgone therapy** Reichian therapy, see there

**psychiatrist** A physician specialized in mental disorders, who can prescribe medication, and provide verbal-based psychotherapy. See Psychoanalyst; Cf Psychologist

**psychic dentistry** Miracle in the mouth FRINGE DENTISTRY The alleged healing of dental disease (eg periodontal disease) and/or reconstruction (eg spontaneous production of fillings in carious teeth) by noninterventional maneuvers, including faith healing, laying on of hands, psychic healing and other maneuvers; Cf Alternative dentistry

**psychic diagnosis** Spirit diagnosis PARANORMAL PHENOMENA The rendering of a diagnosis by a untrained person who has been led to the diagnosis by unexplained means; psychic diagnosis was commonly practiced in primitive tribal cultures but is rarely documented in developed nations; psychic diagnosis was meticulously documented with Edgar Cayce (1877-1945), the 'sleeping prophet,' whose high accuracy in diagnosing disease while in a trance defies explanation. See Cayce, Shamanism; Cf Psychic surgery

**'psychic energizer'** A colloquial term for any of a number of antidepressant drugs that elevate mood, increase motivation, and improve the quality of life. See Psychoactive drugs; Cf Nervine

**psychic healer** Paraphysical healer, parapsychological healer, spirit healer, spiritual healer, spiritualist healer PARANORMAL PHENOMENA A person who does not himself possess healing powers, but is a 'channel' for a spirit guide, who provides the information from another plane of existance; Dr L LeShan, an American investigator of the healing phenomenon, has proposed 3 rules for identifying psychic healers who *should not* be trusted: The healer promises results; the healer accepts a patient who is *not* currently under the care of a physician; the healer accepts fees for his services (*Inglis, West, 1983*). See Psychic healing, Spirit guide

**psychic healing** PARANORMAL PHENOMENA 1. Paraphysical healing, parapsychological healing, *psi* healing, psychic therapy, spirit healing, spiritual healing, spiritualist healing A process in which a person undergoes therapy by a psychic healer, who is directed by a spirit guide. See Psychic healing, Spirit guide 2. Psychoneuro-integration, see there

**psychic surgery** HEALTH FRAUD A practice associated with 'spirit healing' in rural areas of the Philippines, in which certain persons allegedly act as mediums for healing forces, allowing them to perform surgery using their fingers and unsterile tools without violating the skin surface; psychic surgery is a form of prestidigitation, in which the tissues allegedly removed correspond to animal parts, eg chicken intestines or minerals, 'kidney stones' which are pebbles or volcanic rocks; the Federal Trade Commission has determined that psychic surgery is pure fakery, and fraud accomplished through sleight-of-hand, tricks, and other devices; '...*American Medical Association's position is clear: it is viewed as quackery*.' (*Kastner, Burroughs, 1993*); despite the fraudulent nature of psychic surgical 'procedures,' there may be a true positive benefit (active placebo) for those who have functional (psychosomatic) disorders, the effect of which is related to the individual's mindset, which may be rooted in shamanism, and a strong belief system; the following individuals are alleged to have practiced psychic surgery: Eleuterio Terte, Tony Agpaoa, ex Orbito, Gerry G Magno, Jose 'Brother Joe' Bugarin, Placido Palatayan (*American Cancer Society-Unproven Methods for Cancer Management; 1989*). See Dry run, Etheric surgery, Health fraud, Unproven methods for cancer management; Cf Psychosurgery PARANORMAL PHENOMENA Some cases of psychic surgery defy explanation, in particular that of Ze Arigo (José de Freitas)*; his methods were subjected to multiple investigations by physicians and health authorities, who found his methods conformed to standards of medical care, and the therapies were effective

*An automobile mechanic who was a clairaudient, and possessed by the spirit of a deceased German physician, Dr Adolf Fritz, who provided an instant diagnosis, advised on drug therapy, and surgery; Arigo performed the surgery with whatever instrument was at hand, without sterilization or anesthesia; the wounds were closed without sutures and healed virtually instantaneously; when Arigo was killed in an automobile accident, Adolf Fritz was channeled through another Brazilian, Dr Edson de Quieroz

**psychic therapy** Psychic healing, see there

**psychoanalysis** See Freudian analysis, Jungian analysis; Cf Psychotherapy

**psychoanalyst** A person who may or may not

be a physician, who is trained in psychoanalysis. See Psychiatrist, Psychologist

**psychobabble** POPULAR PSYCHOLOGY A colloquial term for what experts in human behavior would regard as nebulous, uncertain, or otherwise senseless phraseology; integral to psychobabble are such phrases as to 'be in touch' (with one's 'inner feelings', with one's 'feminine side'), 'letting go', 'losing touch with oneself,' and 'meaningful'; Cf New Age

**psychodrama** A technique developed by JL Moreno (1892-1974) that arose from his observation that people tend to play markedly different roles in their public and private lives

▶ **PSYCHODRAMA TECHNIQUES**

- **MIRRORING**–in which one person's behavior is imitated by another, the 'double,' so that the actor expresses the emotion which the performer feels, but has been unable or unwilling to release
- **ROLE REVERSAL**–one person plays another's role
- **SOLILOQUY**–in which the actors describe their feelings in connection with traumatic life events (*Inglis, West, 1983*)

See Humanistic psychology; Cf Drama therapy

**psychogenic seizure** Hysterical fit, nonepileptic seizure A specific type of seizure regarded as a conversion symptom, which occurs when a person cannot directly express distress; patients are not consciously aware of the conversion symptoms, nor do they intentionally produce them; the seizures may be accompanied by somatic symptoms, which serve several purposes for the patient, eg communication, secondary gain, conflict resolution, expression of hostility, and others; Freud viewed the hysterical fit as a normal response to incestuous sexual abuse, in which the memory of the experience is repressed from conscious awareness CLINICAL Frequent seizures despite therapeutic levels of antiepileptic medication, prolonged duration (more than 5 minutes), wild movements, pelvic thrusting, fluctuating intensity, resolution of symptoms with distraction, nonphysiologic spread of symptoms, crying, bilateral motor activity with preserved consciousness, lack of post-ictal confusion or lethargy PROGNOSIS Good, if female, of higher intelligence, independent lifestyle, no prior psychotherapy, normal EEG; Poor, if accompanied by epilepsy or seizure activity, history of psychiatric disorders, unemployed (*Mayo Clin Proc 1996; 71:493oa*)

**psychogenic syndrome** Any of a number of anxiety-related conversion reactions that are caused by endogenous or exogenous stress; psychogenic syndromes include hysterical reactions, psychogenic chest pain, psychogenic polydipsia, psychogenic purpura, psychophonasthenia and the 'women who fall' syndrome, a conversion reaction to aggressive or erotic impulses. See Psychosomatic disorder; Cf Factitious disorders

**psychological addiction** See Enneagram system

**psychological distress** A general term for the end result of factors (eg psychogenic pain, internal conflicts, and external stress) that prevent a person from self-actualization and connecting with significant others. See Humanistic psychology

**psychological and emotional expression** A component of movement therapy, which consists of the observation of an individual's nonverbal interactions with himself and others. See Laban analysis, Movement therapy

**psychological therapies** PSYCHIATRY A general term for any of a number of modalities used to treat patients with mental disorders

▶ **PSYCHOLOGICAL THERAPIES**

- **BEHAVIORAL THERAPY** A format based on the identification and modification of objective or 'mechanical' components in the patient's environment
- **HUMANISTIC THERAPY** A format in which patient-environment interactions are evaluated; according to A Maslow (*Inglis, West, 1983*), this format overlaps with transpersonal therapy
- **TRANSPERSONAL THERAPY** A format developed by Freud and his followers through psychoanalysis

See Psychotherapy

**psychologist** A non-physician mental health care worker who has either a Master of Arts degree (MA) or a Doctorate in Philosophy (PhD) who, according to the jurisdiction, may prescribe drugs for mental disease. See Psychoanalyst; Cf Psychiatrist

**psycholytic methods for the rebirthing phenomenon** PSYCHOLOGY A technique used in primal (scream) therapy (now in disfavor), in which psychedelic drugs, eg LSD (now in disfavor), are used as a vehicle for returning a client to the trauma of birth. See Primal therapy

**psychometric analysis** FRINGE MEDICINE A

permutation of radiesthesia developed in the early 20th century by Dr Oscar Brunler, based on the belief that all living beings emit waves that can be detected by highly sensitive instruments; in psychometric analysis, the diagnosis is established using a glorified pendulum known as a biometer. See Biometer, Radiesthesia

**psychometry** FRINGE MEDICINE 1. Psychometric analysis, see there 2. Object reading, see there MAINSTREAM PSYCHOLOGY A general term* for any test used to measure a psychological variable, including abilities, intelligence, moods, and personality

*The term psychometric testing is increasingly preferred

**psychoneuro integration** Psychic healing A type of body-mind medicine, in which energy centers are believed to be realigned by integrating various forms of physical energy

**psychoneuroimmunology** The study of the effects of the mental and neurological status on the immune system (*N Engl J Med 1993; 329:1246*); psychoneuroimmunology is an evolving hybrid of several disciplines that studies the complex bidirectional interactions between the nervous and immune systems, where the neuroendocrine system modulates immune function, and nervous and immune interactions influence psychosocial dynamics. See Psychooncology

There are more 30 well-studied overlaps between the 2 systems in terms of shared cells and moderating substances (*J Neurosci Res 1987; 18:1rv*)

**psychoneurosis maidica** Pellagra, see there

**psychooncology** Pyshcosocial oncology ALTERNATIVE ONCOLOGY An evolving field that overlaps psychology and oncology, which formally studies the relationship of personality to malignancy; integral to psychooncology are the elements that affect a person's adaptation to cancer, which occur in sociocultural, medical, and individual contexts; psychooncology attempts to sway the course of advanced and/or metastatic cancer by promoting positive attitude in cancer patients; some 'soft' data suggest that the psyche may enhance the immune defenses (*Lerner, 1994*). See Cancer-prone personality, LeShan therapy, Psychoneuroimmunology; Cf Harvest Moon phenomenon

It is difficult to perform formal studies, given the often anecdotal nature of the data; in one study of patients with metastatic breast cancer, those undergoing psychotherapy lived 19 months longer, and had less anxiety and pain than the control group (*Lancet 1989; 2:888*)

**psychoregression** FRINGE PSYCHOLOGY A permutation of past life/lives therapy developed by Dr Francesca Rosetti, which is based on the belief that a person's present mental problems may be rooted in lives lived hundreds to thousands of years ago; psychoregression is believed to release negative forces allowing the influx of positive healing energy. See Past life/lives therapy

**psychosocial dwarfism** Kaspar Hauser syndrome, deprivation dwarfism SOCIAL MEDICINE A syndrome of largely irreversible hyposomatism personified by Kaspar Hauser, an orphan who was physically and intellectually stunted by abuse and neglect, and abandoned in 1828 at the Haller Gate in Nuremberg (*N Engl J Med 1994; 331:1030br*). See Anaclytic depression, Genie, Social isolation, *The Wild Child*; Cf Companionship

**psychosocial oncology** Psychooncology, see there

**psychosocial support** A general term for any nontherapeutic intervention that helps a person cope with stressors in the home or at work. See Companionship, Most significant other

One study concluded that increased psychosocial support by nurses or social workers for women at high risk (eg decreased income and education, short ≤1.5 m, underweight ≤ 50 kg, previous infant or fetal death) for delivering low-birth-weight infants neither improves maternal health nor decreases the incidence of low-birth-weight infants (*N Engl J Med 1992; 327:1266oa*)

**psychosomatic disorder** PSYCHIATRY A clinical complex* in which 1. An individual has a biological predisposition to a particular condition, which may have genetic, trauma-related, or other predisposing factors, 2. The individual has a vulnerable personality, ie there is a type or degree of stress that the individual coping mechanism's and ego structure cannot manage and 3. The individual must experience a significant psychosocial stress in his susceptible personality area (*Thompson, in Talbott, et al, Textbook of Psychiatry, Am Psychiatr Press, Washington, DC, 1988*). See Factitious disorders, Psychogenic 'syndromes'

*The term used for this constellation of disorders in the DSM-IV is '*psychological factors affecting medical conditions*'; it is unlikely that this term, championed by the American Psychiatric Association will be integrated into the vox populi-Author's note

**psychosomatic medicine** ALTERNATIVE MEDICINE A 'holistic' philosophy of health care, which assumes that an individual's mental state is intimately linked to both the pathogenesis of disease, and ultimately to its treatment (*Science & Medicine Nov/Dec 1994*). See

Alternative medicine, Mind/body medicine, Psychoneuroimmunology

**psychospiritual holistic healing** Psychospiritual therapy, see there

**psychospiritual therapy** Psychospiritual holistic healing MIND/BODY MEDICINE A general term for any eclectic system of body, mind, and spirit integration (natural psychology) that incorporates 'mind' techniques including aura balancing, chakra healing, imagery and visualization (guided imagery), inner child therapy, meditation, philosophical dialog, a positive mental outlook, and other maneuvers. See Behavioral medicine, Mind/body medicine, Psychoneuroimmunology

**psychosurgery** NEUROSURGERY A general term for neurosurgery intended to alleviate psychiatric symptoms, which was first performed in 1890 by G Burckhardt; early psychosurgical procedures included topectomy[1], lobectomy, and leukotomy[2] popularized in the 1940s by W Freeman[3]; tools used in modern psychosurgery result in selective tract destruction and include radioactive $^{90}$Yt implants in the substantia innominata, cryoprobes, coagulation, proton beams and ultrasonic waves; psychosurgery is not commonly performed, as it must be established that a patient is unresponsive to all other therapies and that the condition is chronic, ie greater than three years duration; significant improvement is reported in 60% of carefully selected patients; in 3%, the symptoms worsen after the procedure; the measurable intelligence quotient may increase given the improved ability to concentrate and memorize, while distraction has been cut to a minimum COMPLICATIONS Seen in 1% and include infections, hemorrhage, and seizures; Cf Psychic surgery

[1]Removal of pieces of cerebral cortex, weighing 20 g for pain to 50 g for fulminant schizophrenia [2]Popularized by W Freeman, which consisted of thrusting an icepick-like device through the eye socket and wiggling the handle to rupture myelinated tracts; one author felt that the greatest success was achieved for patients who were older, female, black, and those in simpler occupations; [3]The Freeman procedure's popularity peaked in the late 1940s–its decline coincided with the availability of the first effective psychoactive drugs

**psychosynthesis** Psychosynthesis therapy PSYCHOLOGY A philosophy developed in the early 20th century by an Italian psychiatrist, Roberto Assagioli, who broke with the Freudian school of psychoanalysis; psychosynthesis focuses less on the morbid symptoms of a particular disease, and more on resolving the malfunction of a person who is presumed to be fundamentally healthy; Assagioli viewed a person as having a psychic structure with 3 layers: an unconscious and a conscious self, connected directly with a transpersonal self that interacts with others, known as the collective unconscious; psychosynthesis is a 4-step process that requires thorough self-knowledge, self-control, realization of one's inner self-resulting in the creation of a 'unifying center,' and a final phase (psychosynthesis), in which the personality is reconstructed around the unifying center; Cf Humanistic psychology, Psychoanalysis

**psychosynthesis therapy** Psychosynthesis, see there

**psycho-therapeutic Reiki℠** A proprietary component of Reiki plus®, see there

**psychotherapy** PSYCHIATRY A general term for the treatment of mental (ie emotional, behavioral, personality, and psychiatric) disorders through verbal and nonverbal communication (eg psychoanalysis) with the patient, rather by pharmacologic, surgical, or other physical intervention; the classic format of psychotherapy is based on the Freudian school of psychoanalysis, in which the focus is to bring repressed memories to the conscious mind; once these memories are re-awakened, the patient is encouraged to solve his own problems by discussing the potential solutions with the therapist, whose role is to act as a sounding board; psychotherapy differs from psychoanalysis in that it is more informal and interactive, less intense, and less concerned with repressed mental trauma; psychotherapy begins with a history in order to evaluate the individual's mental 'substrate' including marital and interpersonal relationships, fears, major life events (eg divorce, death, accidents, loss of job), and aspirations; once evaluated, the therapist advises, counsels, and encourages the individual to adjust to his situation. See Psychological therapies

***Psychotria ipecacuanha*** Ipecac, see there, *Cephalis ipecacuanha*

**psyllium** *Plantago psyllium*, *P ovata*, *P major*, fleaseed, fleawort, psyllium plantain HERBAL MEDICINE An annual herb, the seeds of which contain alkaloids, glycosides, mucilage, silica, and tannins; plantains are believed to be antihypertensive, anti-inflammatory, diuretic, and expectorant; psyllium is used internally as a bulk laxative, and for bronchitis, diarrhea, and cystitis, and topically for cuts, stings, insect bites, hemorrhoids, and varicose veins TOXICITY Psyllium powder may evoke an allergic reaction, and unsoaked seeds may cause gastrointestinal discomfort; it should not be used in young children or in pregnancy, as it stimulates uterine contraction. See Herbal medicine

**psyllium plantain** Psyllium, see there, *Plantago psyllium*

**pteroylmonoglutamic acid** Folic acid, see there

**PTZ** HERBAL MEDICINE A proprietary alkaloid extracted from the narcissus plant, which is said to have more anticancer activity than methotrexate; it is not approved for sale in the US *(Moss, 1992)*. See Chinese herbal medicine

***pu gung ying*** Dandelion, see there, *Taraxacum officinale*

***pu huang*** Cattail, see there, *Typha latifolia*

***pu tong an mo*** Chinese massage, see there

***Pueraria lobata*** Popularly known as kutzu vine, see there

**pukeweed** Lobelia, see there, *Lobelia inflata*

***Pulmonaria officinalis*** Popularly known as lungwort, see there

***Pulsatilla*** *Anemone pratensis, A pulsatilla, Pulsatilla nigricans*, meadow anemone, pasqueflower, wind flower HERBAL MEDICINE Pulsatilla is not used in herbal medicine, as the raw material is toxic TOXICITY Abdominal pain, blurred vision, burning of throat and oral cavity, cardiac arrhythmias, chest pain, dyspnea, nausea, paralysis, vomiting, convulsions, and possibly coma. See Botanical toxicity HOMEOPATHY A homeopathic remedy formulated from the meadow anemone native to northern Europe; it is used for mucosal discharges (eg conjunctivitis, runny nose, and sinusitis), as well as for acne, bedwetting, rattling coughs, depression, fever, gastrointestinal complaints, hay fever, frontal headaches, mastitis, menstrual dysfunctions, migraines, nosebleeds, osteoarthritis, otitis, media, rheumatic complaints, sciatica, sinusitis, urinary incontinence, and varicose veins. See Homeopathy, *Pulsatilla* type

***Pulsatilla nigricans*** *Pulsatilla*, see there

***Pulsatilla* type** HOMEOPATHY The *Pulsatilla* constitutional type of person who is indecisive, shy, nonassertive, and likes sweet, rich foods and cold drinks WORSE Heat, premenstrual, standing, evening FEARS Crowds, being alone, loss of self-control, death WEAKEST BODY REGIONS Gastrointestinal tract, bladder, female reproductive organs, veins. See Constitutional type, Homeopathy, *Pulsatilla*

**pulse** A general term for lentils, beans, and peas. See Diet

**pulse diagnosis** ALTERNATIVE MEDICINE A component of Chinese medicine, which is based on the belief that the peripheral pulse is intimately linked to the flow of *chi* through the body; the pulse is measured at 6 different sites (wrist, leg, and neck on both sides), and at three different depths; according to the practitioners of traditional Chinese medicine, the pulse has 28 different qualities, and is described by such adjectives as thick, thin, floating, and others. See Chinese medicine, Twelve pulses

**pulsing magnetic field** EXPERIMENTAL ONCOLOGY A format for delivering chemotherapy, in which a toxic drug (eg mitomycin C) is injected into a solid tumor, followed by the administration of magnetic pulses *(Jpn J Cancer Res 1990; 81:956)*; Cf Magnetic microcapsule

**Pulvermacher** HEALTH FRAUD A 19th century US company which marketed various 'health' devices that delivered 'therapeutic' electricity; the devices were worn outside the clothing for 8 to 12 hours and delivered low-voltage electricity, which was claimed to cure back pain, deafness, dyspepsia, menstrual disorders, renal disease, and many other conditions (*Armstrong, 1991*). See Quackery

**pumpkin** *Curcubita pepo*, field pumpkin HERBAL MEDICINE An annual vine, which is primarily used as a food or a decorative item; the seeds are anthelmintic. See Herbal medicine

**Pure Food & Drug Act** A legislative act passed by the US Congress in 1906 that was catalyzed largely through the efforts of Dr. HW

**pumpkin** *Curcubita pepo*

Wiley,* chief chemist of the US Department of Agriculture; the Act addressed the use of poisonous food preservatives and dyes in foods, unsanitary conditions in meat-packing plants, and exaggerated claims of efficacy made for all-but-useless patent medicines. See Food and Drug Administration, Food Drug & Cosmetic Act, Kefauver-Harris Act, Patent medicine

*His major concerns hinged on the then-extant practice of using toxic chemicals such as boric acid, formaldehyde, and salicylic acid as food preservatives

**pure osteopathy** Classical osteopathy, see there

**pure vegetarian** Vegan, see there

**purgative** Laxative, see there

**purple** FRINGE MEDICINE–COLOR THERAPY The color purple is believed to reduce pain. See Color breathing, Color therapy, Purple metals & chemicals

**purple clover** Red clover, see there, *Trifolium pratense*

**purple coneflower** Echinacea, see there, *Echinacea pupura*

**purple medic** Alfalfa, see there, *Medicago sativa*

**purple metals & chemicals** FRINGE MEDICINE-COLOR THERAPY Purple metals are believed to be of use in reducing pain, and include europium and gadolinium. See Purple, Purple foods, Color breathing, Color therapy

**purple passionflower** Passionflower, see there, *Passiflora incarnata*

**pyramid diet** A diet based on the USDA's food pyramid, which was promulgated in 1992 as a guideline for the proportions of food groups that should be eaten each day; carbohydrates are at the base of the pyramid–6 to 11 portions are recommended daily; this followed by fruits and vegetables–5 to 9 portions/day, dairy products, fish, and meat–4 to 6 portions; at the pyramid's peak are the 'discouraged' foods, which are to be eaten sparingly, including fats, oils, and refined sugars. See Mediterranean pyramid; Cf Five food groups, Four food groups

**pyramid energy** Pyramid power, see there

**pyramid power** Pyramid energy PARANORMAL PHENOMENA The use of a model of an Egyptian pyramid as an instrument for healing, which is based on the belief that the Great Pyramids have the ability to accumulate and conduct living energies; pyramid power is believed by its advocates to be effective in enhancing mental activity, treating burns, wounds, headaches, attention deficit disorder, promoting sleep, and to sharpen razor blades

**pyridoxal** see Vitamin $B_6$

**pyridoxamine** see Vitamin $B_6$

**pyridoxine** see Vitamin $B_6$

**Pythagorean** MEDICAL HISTORY–ALTERNATIVE NUTRITION A lacto-ovo vegetarian of the 19th century, whose abstinence from meat was based on the belief that animals had a right to a complete and natural life; Pythagoreans were named in honor of Pythagoras, the 6th century BC Greek mathematician, who believed meat-eating to be no less than cannibalism (*Armstrong, 1991*). See Lacto-ovo vegetarian

**Q10** Coenzyme Q10, see there

**Qabalah** Cabala, see there

**Qabbalah** Cabala, see there

**qat** Khat, see there, *Catha edulis*

***qi*** see Chi

***qi an mo*** *Qigong* therapy, see there

***qi* healing** *Qigong* therapy, see there

***qi* massage** *Qigong* therapy. see there

***qigong* healing** *Qigong* therapy, see there

***qian cao*** Indian madder, see there, *Rubia cordifolia*

***qian shi*** Foxnut, see there, *Euryale ferox*

***qigong*** *Chi gong, chi gung, chi kung*, Chinese *qigong*, internal *qigong* ALTERNATIVE MEDICINE An ancient Chinese exercise analogous to yoga, which combines movement, meditation, and breath regulation as a means of enhancing the flow of *qi* (*chi,* the vital life energy) along acupuncture meridians; *qigong* has two major components: internal (soft) *qigong*, in which the *qi* (*chi*) is manipulated within one's own body through exercise, and external (hard) *qigong*, in which the *qi* (*chi*) is projected to another person; *qigong* is believed by its advocates to improve circulation, decrease pulse, respiration rate, and oxygen consumption, and enhance immune function; it is believed to be effective in treating hypertension, and gastrointestinal complaints in the form of ulcers and constipation (*Alternative Medicine, Future Med Pub, 1994*). See Traditional Chinese medicine

***qigong* balls** Chinese reflex balls, see there

***qigong* meridian therapy** ALTERNATIVE MEDICINE A proprietary permutation of *qigong* therapy taught at the American Taoist Healing Center in New York. See Alternative medicine, *Qigong*, *Qigong* therapy

***qigong* reaction** PSYCHIATRY An acute self-limited episode of dissociative, paranoid, psychotic, or other symptoms, that follows participation in *qigong*, the 'exercise of vital energy' (*DSM-IV*). See *Qigong*

***qigong* therapy** *Buqi, buqi* therapy, external *qi* healing, external *qigong* healing, *qi* healing, medical *qigong*, *qi an mo*, *qi* healing, *qi* massage, *qigong* healing, *wai qi liao fa, wai qi zhi liao* FRINGE MEDICINE A therapy that assumes that psychokinesis exists and can occur over short distances; physical contact with the patient is minimal or absent. See *Qigong*, *Qigong* therapy

**quack** *adjective* Unproven, see there *noun* Charlatan, montebank A person who impersonates a physician. See Health fraud, Patent medicine, Quackery, Questionable, Unproven methods for cancer management

The word quack arrived in English in the 1500s from 'Quacksalver', for one who hawks or 'quacks' about his miraculous cures or 'salves'; the term was used during the western expansion of the US in the 1800s, when very little or no training was required to open one's own 'surgery'

**'quack buster'** A generic term for any person who investigates alleged health fraud, or claims of efficacy of alternative medicine; the two major quack-busting organizations in the US are the Quackery Action Council and the National Council Against Health Fraud. See Health fraud, Quackery, 'Snake oil' remedy, Unproven methods for cancer management; Cf Alternative medicine

**quack grass** Couch grass, see there, *Agropyron repens*

**quack salad** see Folk cures for cancer

**Quaker buttons** *Nux vomica*, see there

**quackery** False representation of a substance, device or therapeutic system as being beneficial in treating a medical condition (eg 'Snake oil' remedies), diagnosing a disease, or maintaining a state of health; see AIDS fraud, Health fraud, Pseudovitamins, 'Snake oil' remedy, Unproven methods for cancer management; Cf Alternative medicine

Note: The FDA believes it is advisable to avoid: 1. Therapies claiming to cure diseases known to be incurable, or that cure multiple diseases simutaneously 2. Promotions blazoned with superlatives, eg 'foolproof', 'miraculous', 'secret', or which have testimonials only and no scientific evidence, or are administered by practitioners lacking credentials, or with questionable training 3. Experimental treatments that one must pay for, especially if they are extremely costly, administered without a physician's knowledge, or require an interruption of standard therapy (*Am Med News 21 Nov 1994 p13*)

**quadrinity process** Hoffman quadrinity process, see there

**quartz** *Silica*, see there

**Queen Anne's lace** *Daucus carota*, bee's nest, bird's nest, devil's plague, wild carrot HERBAL MEDICINE A biennial, the root of which contains minerals, pectin, and vitamins A, B, and C; the seeds and plant contain daucine, an alkaloid, and volatile oils (daucol, limonene, and pinene); it is antispasmodic, carminative, and diuretic, and has been used internally for gastrointestinal complaints, kidney stones, menstrual dysfunction, urinary tract infections, and gout, and topically for pruritus; the juice is believed to be of use in preventing cancer. See Herbal medicine

**Queen Anne's lace** *Daucus carota*

**queen's delight** *Stillingia sylvatica*, Queen's root, silverleaf, yawroot HERBAL MEDICINE A perennial herb that contains cyanogenic alkaloids, calcium oxylate, resin, and volatile oil; it is diuretic, emetic, expectorant, and laxative; it was once used for syphilis, modern herbalists use it for respiratory tract (laryngitis, and bronchitis) infection and skin conditions. See Herbal medicine

**queen-of-the-meadow** Meadowsweet, see there, *Filipendula ulmaria*

**queen's root** Queen's delight, see there, *Stillingia sylvatica*

**quercetin** The alglucon of quercitrin, or rutin, and other glycosides, which is an antioxidant present in fruits and vegetables including broccoli, Brussels sprouts, cabbage, and oranges, as well as in rinds, barks, clover blossoms, and pollen; it is a capillary protectant (*The Merck Index, 12th ed, Merck & Co, 1996, Whitehouse Station, NJ*)

**quercetin**

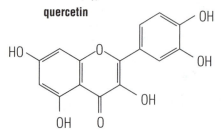

HO OH OH OH OH O O

**questionable** *adjective* FRINGE MEDICINE Unproven A euphemism pertaining or referring to a method or product with one or more of the following features

1. The underlying theory or rationale contradicts accepted scientific beliefs
2. It has no proven efficacy in well-designed studies
3. Its use involves fraud and/or deception
4. It is marketed illegally

Cf Alternative, Fringe, Integrative

**questionable cancer therapy** Unproven method for cancer management, see there

**Quetelet index** CLINICAL NUTRITION A parameter used to determine nutritional status, calculated by the formula

$$QI = \text{Body weight (kg)} / \text{Height (m}^2\text{)}$$

**quick grass** Couch grass, see there, *Agropyron repens*

**quicksilver** 1. *Mercurius solubilis*, see there 2. Mercury, see there

**(Dr Edson de) Quieroz** see Psychic healing

**quina** 1. *China*, see there 2. Cinchona, see there, *Cinchona* species

**quinaquina** 1. *China*, see there 2. Cinchona, see there, *Cinchona* species

**quinine tree** 1. *China*, see there 2. Cinchona, see there, *Cinchona* species

**quinquina** 1. *China*, see there 2. Cinchona, see there, *Cinchona* species

**quivering aspen** White poplar, see there, *Populus tremuloides*

**quiverleaf** White poplar, see there, *Populus tremuloides*

**R.Ac.** Registered Acupuncturist

**Radiac Impedence Device** PARANORMAL PHENOMENA An electrical device marketed by the Association for Research and Enlightment, Virginia Beach, VA, which is claimed to balance a person's mental, emotional and physical energy by drawing his/her aura through one electrode, filtering it, and passing it back into the body through another electrode. See Cayce

**radiance breathwork** ALTERNATIVE MEDICINE A technique developed in the 1970s by a psychologist, Gay Hendricks, that is similar to holotropic breathwork, and believed to facilitate the flow of positive energy. See Bodymind centering, Holotropic breathwork, Radiance movement therapy, Radiance prenatal process

**radiance movement therapy** ALTERNATIVE MEDICINE A technique developed by an American psychologist, Gay Hendricks and his wife, a dance therapist, which is used in conjunction with radiance breathwork; the technique is believed to access the body's innate intelligence and allow old patterns of movement to evolve into new ones. See Bodymind centering, Innate intelligence, Radiance breathwork, Radiance prenatal process

**radiance prenatal process** ALTERNATIVE MEDICINE A permutation of radiance therapy developed by an American psychologist, Gay Hendricks and his wife, that borrows philosophically from rebirthing therapy; in the radiance prenatal process, a male and female practitioner support the client in water, warmed to body temperature and perform bodywork on the head, neck, and shoulders, while the client works through the emotional traumas believed to have occurred during the prenatal period. See Rebirthing therapy

**Radiance Technique®** Real Reiki® FRINGE MEDICINE An ancient Tibetan permutation of reiki, as practiced by members of the American International Reiki Association under B Weber; it is described as '*...a vibrational science of universal energy that allows an individual to access and transmit healing energy through his hands.*' (*Kastner, Burroughs, 1993*); the technique is similar to other forms of 'energy medicine,' including transcendental meditation, yoga, and the science of the mandela; the laying on of hands allows the individual to re-direct universal energy to himself, others, pets, and plants; the technique is used to promote health, heal the individual, enhance personal growth, creativity, and transformation, and release tension and negative energy. See Reiki

**radiatory healing** Pranic healing, see there

**radiesthesia** Medical dowsing, medical radiesthesia FRINGE MEDICINE A healing philosophy developed in 1927 by three French clerics, in which clairvoyancy is used to diagnose and treat disease; central to radiesthesia is the syllogism: All things emit radiation; currents flow through the human hand; the hands can be used to detect emitted radiation; forms of radiesthesia include pendular diagnosis and telediagnosis. See Pendular diagnosis, Telediagnosis

**radiesthetic diagnosis** 1. Pendular diagnosis, see there 2. Radiesthesia, see there

**Radio-Active Appliance** A variation of the Radiac Impedance Device, see there

**radionic photography** UNPROVEN DIAGNOSIS A type of Kirlian photography developed by a Hollywood chiropractor, Ruth Drown, who was convicted of fraud and died in prison. See Drown box, Kirlian photography

**radionics** Psionics UNPROVEN THERAPY A largely abandoned field of medical care, which was based on scientifically uncertain principles proposed by an American neurologist, Dr Albert Abrams, in the early 20th century, that electrons are the basic biological units, and all disease, in particular cancer, but also allergies, arthritis, asthma, dyslexia, hay fever, mental disorders, syphilis, and tuberculosis, represent a disequilibrium in electronic harmony; according to its advocates, radionics allowed the diagnosis and treatment of disease (termed disharmonies or distortions in energy patterns or biocurrents) at a distance, with a device known as an oscilloclast using, for example, a lock of hair, as a link to the patient; more recent radionics devices incorporate pendulums; radionics has fallen into disrepute, and been virtually abandoned; in the US, use of these devices for health care is illegal. See Health fraud, Oscilloclast, Radiothor, Unproven methods for cancer management; Cf Alternative medicine

**Radiothor** MEDICAL HISTORY–HEALTH FRAUD An over-the-counter patent medicine containing radium-226 and radium-228 in water, formulated in 1925 and produced until the early 1930s in the US; radium emits α radiation, which penetrates short distances, but causes considerable damage; Radiothor was self-prescribed, claimed to be an endocrine 'tonic,' and used to treat impotence and chronic conditions including anemia, rheumatic disease, multiple sclerosis, gout and others; the 'mild radium therapy' era collapsed when one of its chief proponents and users died of massive radium intoxication (*JAMA 1990; 264:614*). See Health fraud, Quackery, Radionics, Radium Dial Company

**Radium Dial Company** MEDICAL HISTORY-OCCUPATIONAL MEDICINE A defunct company in Illinois which, in the 1920s, painted clock faces with luminescent radium paint, that was linked to radiation-induced occupational disease*. See Radionics, Radiothor

*The workers, mostly women, often licked the tips of their paint brushes to bring them into a point, making their job easier and, at the same time, ingesting significant doses of radium (a radioactive element in the uranium decay series with a $T_{1/2}$ of 1622 years); over time, many women developed severe osteoporosis and mesenchymal tumors, including malignant fibrous histiocytomas and osteosarcomas

**Radix (neo-Reichian) education** A method developed by C Kelley which is intended to release emotions, which can be used alone, or as an adjunct to bodywork and/or psychotherapy; the method is a synthesis of bioenergetics, Bates' method of vision training, Gestalt therapy, hypnosis, re-evaluation co-counseling, Reichian therapy, and transactional analysis (discussed elsewhere in this work); the method helps the individual cope with emotions that have been repressed within the body armor and other psychological defenses. See Body armor, Gestalt therapy, Reichian therapy

**radon** Radon-222 PUBLIC HEALTH A naturally-occurring radioactive gas in the decay chain of uranium-238 to lead-206 which has a half-life of 3.8 days; radon decays into two solid α particle-emitting daughters; radon exposure is associated with a relative risk of 12.7 for lung cancer in non-smoking uranium miners and an increased risk of childhood malignancy, myeloid leukemia, renal cell carcinoma, melanoma, and prostate cancer. See Radionics, Radium Dial Company

Note: These data have been validated for residential radon exposure in a cohort of 1360 subjects in Sweden; at ≥ 10.8 pCi/L (400 $Bq/m^3$), the relative risk is 1.8; combined radon exposure and smoking exceed an additive and approach a multiplicative effect (*N Engl J Med 1994; 330:159oA*) 13 000 annual excess cases of lung cancer in the US are attributed to radon gas, long-term exposure to 150 $Bq/m^3$ is equivalent to smoking ½ pack of cigarettes/day

**radurization** PUBLIC HEALTH The use of low levels (eg < 1 mrad) of ionizing radiation to retard spoilage, so named as it has the same effects as pasteurization, ie improves shelf life and inactivates bacteria that cause food spoilage. See Food irradiation

**'Raggedy Ann syndrome'** Chronic fatigue syndrome, see there

**ragweed** *Ambrosia artemisiifolia* An herb (illustration, facing page) of the family Compositae, the pollen from which is highly allergenic, and the most common cause of allergic rhinitis DIAGNOSIS Bronchial provocation testing, in which pollen is inhaled through a dosimeter MANAGEMENT Avoidance of pollens by staying indoors; cromolyn, antihistamines, sympathomimetic agents, theophylline, corticosteroids

Note: Dr A Weil has noted that mainstream medicine has proven thus far relatively unsuccessful in treating many chronic illnesses, which would include allergic rhinitis; the above agents are not without side effects; it is possible that the alternative therapeutic options in this work might prove useful in chronic conditions

**rainbow diet** FRINGE NUTRITION A strictly vegetarian diet described by an American physician, Gabriel Cousens, that excludes fast, frozen, junk, or irradiated food; the diet is based on a belief in a universal life force or divine entity; according to Cousens, each food's color corresponds to the color and energy of a specific *chakra,* and serves to energize, cleanse, and reharmonize the appropriate *chakra.* See Diet

**raja yoga** *Ashtanga* yoga, *Astanga* yoga AYURVEDA The self-attainment form of yoga that seeks to maximize personal potential through concentrated meditation, *asanas*, and *pranayama* breathing exercises; *raja* yoga encompasses the philosophies of all schools of yoga. See *Asanas*, Yoga

**rancidity** CLINICAL NUTRITION A state in food marked by the presence of musty, sharp, sour, or other 'off' or unpalatable (rancid) taste or odor, due to oxidation-related deterioration of unsaturated fatty acids and hydrolysis of triglycerides into mono- and diglycerides, glycerol, and free fatty acids. See Browning reaction; Cf Food preservation, Maillard reaction

**rao dzao** Dogwood tree, see there, *Cornus officinalis*

**rasayana** AYURVEDIC MEDICINE Any of a number of health-promoting regimens that a person uses regularly, which may be herbal or behavioral in nature; an herbal *rasayana* is a preparation of 10 to 20 distinct herbs, as well as fruits or minerals, which may be administered in pastes, powders, pills, teas,

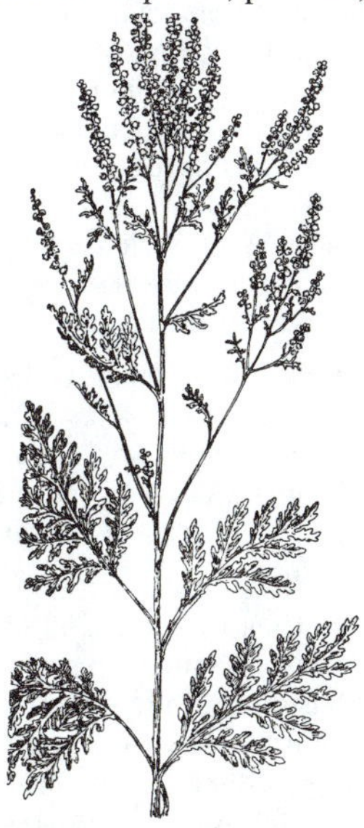

**ragweed** *Ambrosia artemisiifolia*

or tinctures; *rasayanas* are administered to maintain a state of health and harmony, to activate tissue repair, and arrest or reverse the effects of aging; behavioral *rasayanas* include *asanas* (yogic exercises), *pranayama* (breathing exercises), and meditation. See *Asana*, Ayurvedic medicine, *Kapha*; Meditation, *Prakriti*, *Prana*, *Vata*

**raspberry** *Rubus idaeus*, European red raspberry, red raspberry CHINESE MEDICINE see Chinese wild raspberry HERBAL MEDICINE A biennial or perennial shrub, the fruit of which contains sugars, citric and malic acid, pectin, and vitamins A, B, C, and volatile oil; the leaves contain fragarine and tannin; consumed primarily for its fruit, raspberry leaf infusions are believed useful for easing childbirth-related muscle spasms, diarrhea, and morning sickness, and for colds, sore throat, and

**raspberry** *Rubus idaeus*

diarrhea in children. See Herbal medicine

**rattle** ETHNOMEDICINE A device used in Navajo and other Native American tribes to keep the rhythm during healing rituals; the rattle may be covered with animal skin, and decorated with fur, and eagle feathers. See Medicine bundle, Sand painting, Shamanism, Sweat lodge, Vision quest

**rattlebush** Wild indigo, see there, *Baptista tinctoria*

**rattle root** Black cohosh, see there, *Cimicifuga racemosa*

**rauwolfia** *Rauwolfia serpentina, chandrika,* Indian snakeroot, moonshine plant HERBAL MEDICINE A plant native to India, which contains an alkaloid, reserpine; rauvolfia may be consumed in the context of ayurvedic medicine, and is antipyretic and emmenagogic; it has been used for depression, diarrhea, colic in infants, hypertension, and as an antidote to snake poison TOXICITY Abdominal cramps, diarrhea, edema, hypotension, sedation, coma, and possibly death. See Botanical toxicity, Herbal medicine

***Rauvolfia serpentina*** Rauvolfia, see there

**raw food diet** A dietary regimen most commonly prescribed by naturopaths, which is believed by its advocates to promote health and reduce the risk of disease; common to all raw food diets is the consumption of raw fruits and vegetables, preferably in season, which are supplemented with muesli (an uncooked cereal), nuts, lentils, seeds, and sprouts. See Diet, Organic food; Cf Macrobiotic diet

**raw food eater** Frutarian. see there

**raw milk** Unpasteurized milk ALTERNATIVE NUTRITION A product believed by some alternative health care advocates to have a greater nutritional value than pasteurized cow's milk; raw milk is alleged to reduce the incidence of caries, enhance resistance to disease, and contain beneficial enzymes and antibodies; no significant differences have been substantiated; raw milk is associated with bacterial infection by *Campylobac-ter jejuni, Salmonella* species (*S dublin*, uncommon but serious, *S typhimurium*, and *S derby*), *Brucella* spp, *Escherichia coli*, *Listeria monocytogenes, Mycobacterium bovis*, *M tuberculosis, Corynebacterium pseudotuberculosis*, *Staphylococ-cus aureus, Streptococcus* species, *Streptobacillus moniliformis,* and *Yersinia enterocolitica*; raw milk from other ruminants is also susceptible to microbial infections, eg toxoplasmosis (goat's milk), and tick-borne encephalitis (sheep's milk). See Certified milk; Cf Milk, White beverages

**ray methods of healing** Esoteric healing, seven ray methods of healing, seven ray techniques FRINGE MEDICINE A healing system intrinsic to Theosophy, an eclectic religion, in which each of 7 rays or emanations from God corresponds to a personality type or quality of a person's soul; each of the 7 types is believed to indicate a method of exoteric (eg homeopathy) and endoteric (eg pranic healing) therapy (*Raso, 1994*)

**Rayid model** PARANORMAL PHENOMENA-IRIDOLOGY A model of the human iris as a indicator of disease; in contrast to the American and European eye maps used by iridologists, which are based on the belief that subtle changes in the iris reflect physical manifestations of disease, the Rayid constuct claims to identify indicators of psychoemotional and 'soul' development. See Iridology

**R.D.** Registered Dietician

**R.D.A.** Recommended daily allowance, see there

**R.D.T.** Registered Drama Therapist

**Real Reiki®** Radiance technique, see there

**realm of reality** Plane of existence, see there

**rebirthing therapy** ALTERNATIVE PSYCHOLOGY An unconventional form of bodywork and mind/body psychotherapy developed in the 1970s by Leonard Orr, which is based on the belief that the trauma of birth has lifelong consequences to a person's psyche, as the infant passes from the warm, cozy womb to the cold, vast world; in rebirthing therapy, the client is guided through a reenactment of birth with hyperventilation (termed conscious-connected breathing, or vivation) which releases tension believed to have begun at birth; an individual's expression of this repressed trauma is believed by its proponents to facilitate healing of physical, mental, and emotional disease WARNING Hyperventilation induces blackouts, which may have serious long-term consequences for the client, and is often accompanied by a serious headache. See Conscious-connected breathing, Empyrean® rebirthing, Humanistic psychology; Cf Primal therapy

**rebound scurvy** A vitamin C-dependency state that occurs in the fetus of a woman taking megadoses of vitamin C during pregnancy, which is caused by an increase in production of vitamin C metabolizing enzymes. See Vitamin C

**recoil thrust** CHIROPRACTIC One of the two most common techniques used for chiropractic adjustment of the vertebral column; the recoil thrust is a high-velocity, low-force technique performed on the back with the patient lying face-down on a table that can be slightly opened to accommodate the transiently increased pressure and anatomic deviation of the vertebral body. See Chiropractic, Spinal misalignment; Cf Rotational thrust

**recommended daily allowance** CLINICAL NUTRITION A guideline of essential nutrients recommended by the Food and Nutrition Board of the National Research Council, for daily ingestion in an idealized normal person engaged in average activities

▶ **RECOMMENDED DAILY ALLOWANCES**

- **VITAMINS** Vitamin A 1000 µg; vitamin D 5 µg; vitamin E 10 mg; vitamin C 60 mg; thiamin 1.2 mg; riboflavin 1.4 mg; niacin 16 mg; vitamin $B_6$ 2.2 mg; folic acid 400 µg; vitamin $B_{12}$ 3 µg
- **MINERALS** Calcium 800 mg; phosphorus 800 mg; magnesium 350 mg; iodine 150 mg; iron 10 mg; zinc 15 mg

RDAs are increased for increased activity, body growth and size, pregnancy, lactation, and adverse environmental conditions; RDAs are designed for a state of wellness and are poorly applicable in sick, traumatized, and burned patients. See Daily Value, Minerals, Vitamins

Note: A criticism of the RDA is that it was established by the US Food and Nutrition Board in 1941–at a time when sound diets practices were rare, and nutritional deficiencies not uncommon; malnutrition is now rare, as many foods are supplemented with the necessary vitamins and minerals; many nutritionists now prefer the Daily Value standard

**reconstructive therapy** ALTERNATIVE MEDICINE Proliferative therapy The *injection of natural substances* (eg dextrose, glycerine, and phenol) *to stimulate the growth of connective tissue in order to strengthen weak or damaged tendons or ligaments*; reconstructive therapy is reported to be beneficial in treating various musculoskeletal disorders, including bursitis, carpal tunnel syndrome, degenerative joint disease, migraines, tennis elbow, torn ligaments, and cartilage (*Alternative Medicine, Future Med Pub, 1994*). See Alternative medicine MAINSTREAM MEDICINE Reconstructive surgery

**recreational therapy** Play therapy *'Any free, voluntary and expressive activity*...(which may be)...*motor, sensory, or mental, vitalized by the expansive play spirit, sustained by deep-rooted pleasurable attitudes and evoked by whole emotional release* (*JE Davis, Clinical Applications of Recrea-tional Therapy, 1952*); recreational acitivities include hobbies, athletic activities, performance of or listening to the arts, watching films, or listening to lectures. See Art therapy, Dance therapy, Laughter therapy, Music therapy

**red** FRINGE MEDICINE–COLOR THERAPY A color believed to increase circulation and energy, and reduce anxiety; the use of the color red as a therapeutic agent is discouraged if the patient is already 'too red,' eg has a ruddy complexion, red hair, a fever, or is easily excited. See Color breathing, Color therapy, Red foods, Red metals and chemicals

**red arrow** *Gastrodia elata*, see there

**red clover** *Trifolium pratense*, beebread, cow clover, meadow clover, purple clover, trefoil, wild clover FRINGE MEDICINE-FLOWER ESSENCE THERAPY A floral essence believed to provide a sense of calm and presence in emergencies. See Flower essence therapy HERBAL MEDICINE A biennial or perennial herb that contains coumarins, cyano-genic glycosides, flavonoids, phenolic glycosides, and salicylates; it is antispasmodic, expectorant and mildly sedative, and has been used internally for respiratory (bronchitis, cough, whooping cough) complaints, indigestion, and menopausal symptoms, and topically for skin conditions including eczema and psoriasis TOXICITY Red clover has estrogen-like principles, and should not be used in pregnancy or given to young children. See

**red clover** *Trifolium pratense*

Herbal medicine

**red elm** Slippery elm, see there, *Ulmus rubra*

**red eyebright** Eyebright, see there, *Euphrasia officinalis*

**red foods** FRINGE MEDICINE–COLOR THERAPY Red foods are believed to increase circulation and energy and reduce anxiety, and include beets, grapes, liver, radishes, red cabbage, red currants, red wine, tomatoes, watermelon, and whole wheat. See Color breathing, Color therapy, Red, Red metals & chemicals

**red metals & chemicals** FRINGE MEDICINE-COLOR THERAPY Red metals and chemicals are believed to increase circulation and energy and reduce anxiety, and include barium, cadmium, copper, iron, neon, nitrogen, oxygen, potassium, and zinc. See Color breathing, Color therapy, Red, Red foods

**red onion** *Allium cepa*, see there

**red puccoon** Blood root, see there, *Sanginaria canadensis*

**red raspberry** Raspberry, see there, *Rubus idaeus*

**red root** 1. Blood root, see there, *Sanginaria canadensis* 2. Erect cinquefoil, *Potentilla erecta*

**red rot** *Drosera*, see there, *Drosera rotundifolia*

**red sauce** CLINICAL NUTRITION A general term for any low-calorie, vegetable or seafood-based sauce used in preparing fish, meats, pastas, and vegetables; given their low fat content, red sauces are regarded as being healthier than white sauces, which are higher in fat and calories; Cf White sauce

**red seaweed** Agar, see there, *Gelidium cartilagineum*

**red squill** Sea onion, see there, *Urginea maritima*

**red-veined dock** Bitter dock, see there, *Rumex obtusifolius*

**red vine** Indian madder, see there, *Rubia cordifolia*

**reducing factor** Vitamin C, see there

**reefer** Marijuana, see there, *Cannabis sativa*

**refining** FOOD INDUSTRY The processing of a food (eg sugar cane) to extract a component of interest (eg sugar); health and natural food advocates are critical of this process, and believe beet sugar, molasses, and honey to be far superior to refined or 'white' sugar, although the nutritive value of the 'virgin' products in terms of minerals and vitamins is minimal. See Food preservatives; Cf 'Health' food, Organic food

**reflective communication** ALTERNATIVE PSYCHIATRY A general term for a format of client-oriented psychotherapy in which the client is afforded the opportunity to examine his behaviors and interactions with others, while the therapist acts as a verbal 'mirror,' often by restating what the person has just said; in reflective communication, therapist 'interject' is minimal or nonexistent, as it encourages a person to take responsibility for his actions, shows to the client that he can be entrusted with his own destiny, helps him view his circumstances in a different light, and promotes insight into negative behavior patterns. See Humanistic psychology, Natural psychotherapy

**reflex balls** Chinese reflex balls, see there

**reflex point** Cutaneo-organ reflex point. See Reflexology

**reflex zone therapy** Zone therapy, see there

**reflexology** Ingham reflex method of compression massage ALTERNATIVE MEDICINE A form of massage therapy, described by E Ingham and Dr W Fitzgerald, which is based on the belief that there are nerve endings (from 7000 to 72,000) for most organs and body regions in the feet; reflexology consists of manual stimulation with the thumbs and fingers of (cutaneo-organ) reflex points on the feet as well as on the ears, and hands; reflexologists believe that the body is divided into 10 distinct energy zones or energy channels that extend from the head to the feet, and that foot massage* increases the flow of healing energy through any or all of these channels; this energy may be blocked by lumps of crystalline material which reflexologists claim to be able to identify during therapy; anecdotal reports suggest that reflexology may be effective for agoraphobia, arthritis, asthma, athlete's foot, breast disease, bronchitis, cardiovascular disease, claustrophobia, common cold, cramps, cystitis, diabetes, eczema, emphysema, endocrinopathies, gastrointestinal tract problems including constipation and indigestion, headaches, hiccups, hypertension, hypoglycemia, jaundice, low back pain, menstrual disorders, migraines, neck pain, rheumatic disease, psychosomatic disease, renal disease, sciatica, seizures, sexual problems, sinusitis, sleep disorders, stress, strokes, tension, and other conditions. See Acupressure,

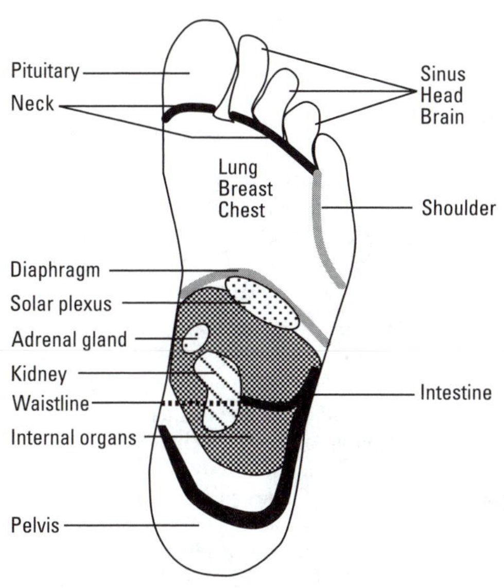


**reflexology regions**

Alternative medicine, Bodywork, Hand massage, Vacuflex Reflexology System; Cf CranioSacral Therapy™, Integrative massage, Massage therapy *Resource: International Institute of Reflexology, PO Box 12642, St Petersburg FL 33733-2642 ☎ 1.813.343.4811*

*Although reflexology massages the feet, its practitioners do not regard the therapy as foot massage per se, as the latter is intended to address the musculoskeletal tissues that are known to be present in the foot, and not energy pathways that are believed by reflexologists to connect with other organs and systems

**reflexotherapy** 1. Reflexology 2. A permutation of homuncular acupuncture that is performed on the feet

**regression therapy** Past life/lives therapy, see there

**regular** MEDICAL HISTORY A term used in the 18th century US for a physician who practiced 'heroic' medicine *(Armstrong, 1991)*. See Heroic medicine

**rehabilitation massage** Medical massage PHYSICAL THERAPY A general term for massage therapy designed for musculoskeletal rehabilitation and/or reduction in pain in individuals who have lost a limb or suffered a cerebrovascular accident. See Massage therapy

**rehabilitation medicine** Physiatry, physiotherapy A field of therapeutics that bridges the gap between conventional and nonconventional medicine; rehabilitation physicians may administer or prescribe mechanical (eg massage, manipulation, exercise, movement, hydrotherapy, traction) and electromagnetic (eg heat and cold, light, and ultrasound) modalities, psychological and pharmacological therapeutic modalities; the patients seen by rehabilitation physicians include those recuperating from sports injuries, automobile and motorcycle accidents and cerebrovascular accidents, amputees, and those with joint disease and reduced mobility. See Massage therapy, Physical therapy, Swedish massage; Cf Physiotherapy

***Rehmannia chinensis*** *Rehmannia glutinosa*, see there

***Rehmannia glutinosa*** *Rehmannia chinensis*, Chinese foxglove, *gan di huang* CHINESE MEDICINE A perennial herb, the root of which is antidiabetic, anti-inflammatory, diuretic, hemostatic, and tonic; it is used to enhance muscle growth and production of bone marrow cells, and semen, and for constipation, diabetes, internal hemorrhage (eg menorrhagia, epistaxis, hematuria), low-grade fevers accompanied by night sweats, irregular menses, low back pain, palpitations, premature graying, loss of hearing and vision, to repair tissue, and may be of use in rheumatoid arthritis TOXICITY Abdominal distension, indigestion. See Chinese herbal medicine

**Wilhelm Reich** An Austrian psychiatrist and biochemist (1897-1957), who was an associate of Freud's; Reich left Nazi Germany and resettled in New York; Reich proposed that the universe is permeated with orgone energy, which is incompletely discharged in those who are sexually repressed; he invented a device that he said restored orgone energy. See Orgone accumulator, Reichian therapy

Reich's devices were deemed fraudulent by the FDA; he died in a federal penitentiary awaiting trial in 1957; mainstream psychiatrists have remained skeptical of Reichian therapy

**Reichian bodywork** Reichian therapy, see there

**Reichian massage** Reichian therapy, see there

**Reichian release therapy** Reichian therapy, see there

**Reichian therapy** Psychiatric orgone therapy, Reichian bodywork, Reichian massage, Reichian release therapy, vegetal therapy ALTERNATIVE PSYCHOLOGY A form of psychotherapy developed by Wilhelm Reich, who believed that the repression of the energy associated with sexual orgasms (orgone energy), results in emotional and psychological defects; Reichian therapy encourages a person to become aware of postural and muscular tension (body armoring) that affects emotions; maneuvers used in Reichian therapy include deep breathing and massage, manipulation of the gag reflex to release body armoring, unmasking of facial expressions, and forced pressure on the chest by the therapist who uses physical movement and postural adjustment to free the tension caused by sexual repression. See Body armor, Orgone accumulator, Reich

**Reiki** Leiki, Reiki healing, Reiki therapy, Usui system of natural healing, Usui *shiki ryoho*, Usui *shiko ryoho* PARANORMAL PHENOMENA An energy healing system based on ancient Tibetan scriptures, which were rediscovered by Professor M Usui in the mid-1800s; Reiki–the name translates from Japanese as '*universal energy of life*; Reiki sessions are performed by practitioners who have been initiated through 'energy attunement' by a Reiki Master, who channels Universal Life Energy to family, friends, and clients; the Reiki practitioner is believed to act as a conduit for cosmic energy, which enters the top of his head and leaves through his hands; Cf Chinese massage, MariEL, Massage therapy, Oriental massage, Polarity therapy, Radiance technique, Reiki plus®, Structural integration, Therapeutic touch, Traditional European massage, (contemporary) Western massage

**Reiki healing** Reiki, see there

**Reiki plus®** PARANORMAL PHENOMENA A proprietary form of Reiki that was developed by a Reiki master, Rev David G Jarrel, who also founded Pyramids of Light, Inc, a nondenominational Christ-conscious church in Tennessee; the healing methods central to Reiki plus® include proprietary forms of aura balancing (PSEB[sm]), release of memories (psycho-therapeutic reiki[sm]), and spinal manipulation (SAT[sm]) (*Raso, 1994*). See Reiki

**Reiki therapy** Reiki, see there

**reishi** *Ganoderma lucidum, ling zhi* An oriental mushroom that has been used in various forms of alternative health care ALTERNATIVE ONCOLOGY Reishi is reported to modulate the immune system through a protein, LZ-8, which is believed to have antitumor activity (*Moss, 1992*). See Unproven methods for cancer management CHINESE MEDICINE Reishi has been used for allergies, asthma, insomnia, nervousness, ulcers, tumors, vertigo, and to stimulate the circulation and immune system, and may be of use in AIDS and cancer. Some data suggest that it may be antihypertensive. See Chinese herbal medicine

**rejuvenating diet** A short-term (30 days or less), primarily vegetarian diet intended to 'detoxify' the body; general rules for a rejuvenating diet include avoidance of overconsumption and salt, drinking water only between meals, use of organic foods, ie without pesticides, preservatives, hormones, antibiotics, or artificial dyes; carbohydrates in the diet consist of raw fruits and vegetables, which may be boiled or steamed, not fried; fats include olive, sesame, and sunflower oils; proteins are from nuts, legumes, whole grains, and low-fat yogurt; the diet is supplemented with vitamins and minerals. See Diet

**Relax-a-Cizor** see Electrical muscle stimulator

**relaxation** 1. The act of not actively acting 2. A generic term for intentional nonactivity, in which a person performs active or passive exercises intended to reduce mental and physical stress. See Relaxation enhancer, Relaxation response, Relaxation technique, Relaxation training

**relaxation enhancer** A generic term for any vehicle used to increase the relaxation response, including reduction or elimination of caffeine, carbohydrates (especially refined sugars), and tobacco, and use of exercise, laughter therapy, and marriage. See Relaxation, Relaxation response, Relaxation technique, Relaxation training

**relaxation response** A term coined in 1975 by Dr Herbert Benson of Harvard Medical School, for the use of 'good breathing techniques,' active muscle relaxation, and meditation as a means of lowering the blood pressure, and reducing internal and external stress. See Meditation, Relaxation, Relaxation enhancer, Relaxation technique, Relaxation training

**relaxation technique** A generic term for any of a number of techniques for relaxing the mind and/or muscles; most relaxation techniques share the need for a quiet environment with few distractions, limiting of attention to an object, phrase, or image, a passive attitude of *letting go*, a comfortable position and loosened clothing; relaxation techniques include autogenic feedback training, biofeedback training, imagery and visualization, meditation, progressive relaxation, relaxation response, sensory deprivation (eg with a flotation tank), systematic desensitization therapy, and yoga, which are discussed elsewhere in this book

**relaxation training** PSYCHOLOGY A generic term for any of a number of techniques (eg hypnosis, electromyograph feedback, relaxing imagery) for relaxing muscles; relaxation training is reportedly successful in reducing the duration, frequency, and the intensity of anticipatory nausea associated with chemo-therapy. See Biofeedback training, Relaxing imagery, Cf Systematic desensitization

**relaxing imagery** PSYCHOLOGY A generic term for a technique in which pleasant scenes and images (eg walking through the woods in spring, ocean surf) are described to an individual, as a means of relaxation and blocking unpleasant sensations, eg nausea; used in conjunction with other forms of relaxation training, relaxing imagery may reduce the duration, frequency, and intensity of the anticipatory nausea commonly associated with chemotherapy. See Biofeedback training, Relaxation training; Cf Systematic desensitizaton

**releasement** Depossession, see there

**religious diet** Ethical diet CLINICAL NUTRITION A generic term for modifications in the diet that are based on religious regulations, some of which may be extremely rigorous

▶ **RELIGIOUS DIET**

- **CATHOLICISM** Proscription of certain foods during Lent, the 40 week days from Ash Wednesday until Easter, a period of fasting and atonement; the ban of meat consumption on Fridays was lifted by Pope John XXIII
- **ISLAM** Proscription of alcohol
- **MORMONS, SEVENTH-DAY ADVENTISTS** Both diets are low in fat, high in complex carbohydrate. Smoking, alcohol, and caffeine are prohibited; these groups have a low incidence of cancer and cardiovascular disease
- **ORTHODOX JUDAISM** The foods must be kosher

See Kosher, Seventh-Day Adventists

**remedy** Homeopathic remedy, see there

**remote diagnosis** PARANORMAL PHENOMENA A general term for any of a number of pseudodiagnostic techniques, including channeling, clairvoyancy, psionic medicine, telediagnosis, and use of the De la Warr box, which are believed to allow a diagnosis to be established without the patient being near the 'diagnostician'. See Absent healing

**remote healing** 1. Prayer for the sick, see there 2. Absent healing, see there

***ren dung*** Japanese honeysuckle, see there, *Lonicera japonica*

***ren shen*** Ginseng, see there, *Panax ginseng*

**repertory** HOMEOPATHY A reference book that lists homeopathic symptoms and the remedies used to treat them; because the details on the modalities, locations, and sensations associated with the symptoms may be 'exhaustive,' repertories may be very large. See Homeopathic symptoms; Cf Materia medica

**repetitive motion injury** Cumulative trauma disorder OCCUPATIONAL MEDICINE A work-related illness caused by overuse of a particular musculoskeletal group to perform a task that is repeated hundreds to thousands of times in an 8-hour shift; repetitive motion injury is the fastest growing health problem in the US, and affects workers in the textile industry, meat-packers, keyboard operators, and others. See Alexander technique, Ortho-bionomy

**rescue remedy** Dr Bach's Emergency Stress Formula, see there

**REST** Restriction of Environmental Stimulation Therapy A technique of relaxation in which a person is placed in either an isolation (dry) chamber, or floatation (wet) tank, as a means of reducing sensory stimulation to a minimum. See Flotation tank, Isolation chamber

**restriction diet** A diet intended to reduce the risk of various diseases

▶ **RESTRICTION DIETS**

- **ATHEROSCLEROSIS** GOAL Reduce weight and cholesterol METHOD Decrease saturated fat and cholesterol; increase bran, fish, garlic, olive oil
- **HYPERTENSION** GOAL Reduce blood pressure METHOD Decrease salt—only ½ of patients respond to salt restriction
- **CANCER** Dietary fat has been linked to cancer of the breast, colon, prostate and ovaries; polyunsaturated fats are a substrate for peroxidative reactions and thus should be

reduced; increased fiber and cruciferous vegetables in the diet are linked to decreased colorectal cancer, an effect thought to be due to decreased contact of the colonic mucosa with carcinogens; alcohol consumption is associated with hepatoma, oropharyngeal and esophageal cancer with very low cholesterol

- **RENAL FAILURE** Low-protein diet slows the progression of renal failure. See Diet

**retinol** Vitamin A, see there

**Revici cancer control** Revici therapy, see there

**Revici method** Revici therapy, see there

**Revici therapy** Lipid therapy, Revici Cancer Control, Revici method FRINGE ONCOLOGY An alternative cancer therapy based on Revici's theory that '*...a disease can be dualistic, with a predominance of one group of lipids* (sterols) *or the opposite* (fatty acids), *one anabolic and constructive, the other catabolic and destructive...*'; according to this framework, the control of disease requires determination of the nature of a biological imbalance and providing the substance that corrects it; the method is said to detect catabolic or anabolic processes by measuring urinary pH; catabolic therapeutic agents include fatty acids, magnesium, selenium and sulfur; anabolic agents include caffeine, iron, lipols, lithium, zinc; the method has no demonstrable efficacy and is based on no known or established scientific principle (*CA-A Journal for Clinicians 1989; 39:119*). See Unproven methods for cancer management

***Rhamnus frangula*** Popularly known as alder buckthorn, see there

***Rhamnus purshiana*** Popularly known as cascara sagrada, see there

***Rhamnus soporifer*** Wild Chinese jujube, see there, *Ziziphus jujuba*

***Rheum officinale*** Popularly known as Chinese rhubarb, see there

***Rheum palmatum*** Chinese rhubarb, see there, *Rheum officinale*

***Rhus tox*** *Rhus toxicodendron*, poison ivy HOMEOPATHY A remedy that has been used for a wide range of skin conditions including blisters, diaper rash, eczema, herpes, and general burning and itching; *Rhus tox* has also been used for arthritis and backaches with stiffness, bursitis, carpal tunnel syndrome, coughs, cramps, dyspareunia, flu, genital herpes, headaches, impetigo, menstrual disorders, eye inflammation, poison ivy, restless legs syndrome, rheumatic complaints, sprains, toothaches, and urticaria. See Homeopathy

**rhythm** ALTERNATIVE MEDICINE–DANCE THERAPY A component of dance therapy that corresponds to repeating patterns of movement, which contain and organize expression of emotional states. See Dance therapy; Cf Synchrony

**rhythm method** Calendar method OBSTETRICS A form of natural family planning, which is the contraceptive method sanctioned by the Roman Catholic Church, in which unprotected intercourse is allowed shortly after a menstrual period or before the onset of the next period; the rhythm method is the least effective form of contraception, resulting in 20 pregnancies/100 women-years; other forms of natural family planning include coitus interruptus, and prolonged breast-feeding. See Breast feeding, Coitus interruptus, Contraception, Natural family planning, Pearl index

**rib raising** OSTEOPATHY Lymphatic pump, see there

**riboflavin** Vitamin $B_2$ A vitamin that is widely present in foods of plant and animal origin, which combines with phosphate to form the enzyme cofactors flavin mononucleotide (FMN) and flavin adenine dinucleotide (FAD); riboflavin is involved in oxidation-reduction reactions in many metabolic pathways, and in energy production in the respiratory chain, which occurs in the mitochondria; riboflavin is present in almonds, dairy products, eggs, enriched flour, leafy greens, organ meats, and soy products. See Riboflavin deficiency, Vitamins

**riboflavin**

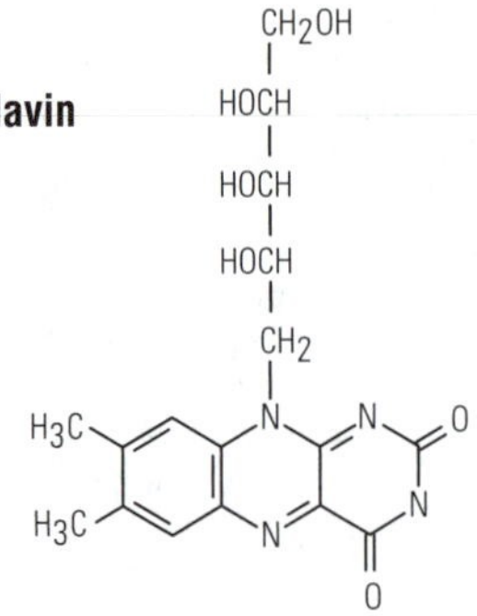

$CH_2OH$
HOCH
HOCH
HOCH
$CH_2$
$H_3C$ N N O
$H_3C$ N N
O

**riboflavin deficiency** A condition caused by a relative lack of riboflavin in the diet; riboflavin deficiency is rare, given its wide distribution in foods, and is almost invariably accompanied by deficiencies of other water-soluble vitamins; it is characterized by hyperemia, erythema, and pain of oral mucosa, stomatitis, glossitis, angular cheilitis, seborrheic dermatitis, normocytic and normochromic anemia, which may be accompanied by pure red cell aplasia in the bone marrow. See Riboflavin

**ribwort** Plantain, see there, *Plantago major*

**RICE** SPORTS MEDICINE An acronym–rest, ice, compression, and elevation, for the maneuvers that constitute first aid for musculoskeletal and joint injuries. See Sports medicine

**rice diet** Kempner rice diet CLINICAL NUTRITION A high-carbohydrate, high-fiber, low-fat, and low-sodium dietary regimen formulated in the 1940s by a German-American physician, W Kempner; the diet consists of unsalted rice, fruit, limited amounts of fruit juices, tea, decaffeinated coffee, and sugar; other grains and vegetables, and non-fat dairy products may be added as the patient progresses; the diet is provided as part of a residential program which, coupled with exercise (eg walking, swimming), is used to treat angina pectoris, congestive heart failure, high cholesterol, diabetes, hypertension, renal failure, obesity, and vascular retinopathy. See Diet

**richweed** Stoneroot, see there, *Collinsonia canadensis*

***Rigveda*** HERBAL MEDICINE An ancient Hindu scripture that describes more than 1000 herbal remedies. See Herbal medicine; Cf *Canon of Medicine, Charak Samhita, The Complete Herbal, De Materia Medica, Natural History, Nei Jing, Pen Ts'ao, Philosophy of Natural Therapeutics, Sushrita Samhita, Theatrum Botanicum*

**ripple grass** Plantain, see there, *Plantago major*

**RISCC rating** CLINICAL NUTRITION Cholesterol-saturated fat index The ratio of saturated fat and cholesterol to calories (RISCC), a parameter used to evaluate a diet's fat content, which is stratified into low– and high-fat diets; the highest RISCC rating in a low-fat diet is 15; the lowest RISCC in a high-fat diet is 22 (*N Engl J Med 1993; 328:1213*); RISCC ratings are calculated by the formula

$$\frac{[1.01 \times \text{saturated fat (g)}] + (0.05 \times \text{cholesterol (mg)})}{\text{kcal}/1000}$$

**R.M.T.** Registered Massage Therapist 2. Registered Music Therapist

**rockberry** Bearberry, see there, *Arctostaphylos uva-ursi*

**rock crystal** *Silica*, see there silica

**rock salt** *Natrum muriaticum*, see there

**rockweed** Bladderwrack, see there, *Fucus vesiculosus*

**Rogers' therapy** Rogerian therapy, see there

**Rogerian therapy** Rogers' therapy, client-centered therapy HUMANISTIC PSYCHOLOGY A form of psychoanalysis developed by Carl Rogers (1902-1987), in which a therapist with an 'unconditioned positive regard' for the client attempts to decrease the negative aspects of a patient's overdependence on others, and increase his level of self-reliance; Rogerian therapy hinges on nurturing the belief that despite negative physical, genetic, and psychosocial influences, the client is ultimately 'in charge' of his life; Rogerian therapy is most useful for patients with anxiety, stress, and emotional problems. See Humanistic psychology; Cf Psychoanalysis, Psychotherapy

**role reversal** see Psychodrama

**Dr Ida Rolf** Dr Elbows An American (1896-1979) biochemist who developed the technique of structural integration, better known as Rolfing®. See Rolfing®

**Rolfing®** Structural integration, structural processing BODYWORK A form of bodywork and deep massage therapy developed by IP Rolf, PhD, who believed that postural and muscular tensions are locked in place by trauma, adhesions, chronic connective tissue tension, and locoregional compromise of movement, resulting in a malalignment of the structural units–termed a 'pile of bricks'; Rolfing® seeks to 'realign' the body by altering the tone of myofascial tissues, facilitating 'structural integration'-resulting in a 'tower of bricks'; Rolfing® is philosophically similar to chiropractic, in that incorrect or poor posture is thought to be detrimental to a person's health, energy, mental, and physical efficiency; like chiropractic, the claims of therapeutic success are anecdotal; a complete Rolfing® consists of 10 sessions that address different zones of the body, and is administered by any of the estimated 800 Rolfers who practice in 27 different countries. See Bodywork, Rolfing movement integration, Structural integration; Cf Alexander technique, Aston patterning, Feldenkreis method, Chiropractic, Hellerwork®, Massage, Ortho-bionomy, Rosen method, Tragerwork® *Resource: The Rolf Institute of Structural Integration, 205 Canyon Blvd, Boulder CO 80302* ☎ *1.800.530.8875*

**Rolfing® movement integration** ALTERNATIVE MEDICINE '...*a movement education for the development of balance, support of action in the gravitational field, and harmonious movement with gravity.*' (*Kastner, Burroughs, 1993*); Rolfing movement integration is based on the concepts formulated by IP Rolf, and evaluates a person's normal patterns of walking, standing, sitting, and various other activities at home, work, and during recreation, and helps a person achieve freer and more balanced movement by releasing specific holding patterns; Rolfing movement can be used alone or in conjunction with Rolfing®. See Rolfing®

**Roman chamomile** *Anthemis nobilis*, common chamomile, English chamomile, romaska, true chamomile HERBAL MEDICINE A perennial weed similar to German chamomile (*Matricaria chamomilla*) in appearance and often used interchangeably therewith. See Chamomile, Herbal medicine

**romaska** Roman chamomile, see there, *Anthemis nobilis*

**root *chakra*** AYURVEDIC MEDICINE The first *chakra*, which governs the survival instinct, is located at the base of the spine, and associated with the color red. See Ayurvedic medicine, *Chakra*

**root of the Holy Ghost** Angelica, see there

**root of life** Kidney, see Twelve vital organs

**rootwork** FRINGE PSYCHIATRY '*A set of cultural interpretations that ascribe illness to hexing, witchcraft, or the evil influence of another person. Symptoms may include generalized anxiety and gastrointestinal complaints (nausea, vomiting, diarrhea), weakness, dizziness*...' and the fear of being poisoned and/or killed; in this context, a 'root' ('spell' or 'hex') must be removed through the work of a 'specialist' or 'root doctor' who can, in turn, place a hex on an enemy; the term rootwork is used in the US South and in the Caribbean; among Latinos, it is known as mal puesto or brujeria (*DSM-IV™, 1994*). See Culture-bound syndrome

***Rosa canina*** Popularly known as dog rose, see there

***Rosa indica*** Multiflowered rose, see there, *Rosa multiflora*

***Rosa multiflora*** Popularly known as multiflowered rose, see there

***Rosamarinus officinalis*** Rosemary, see there

**rose essense** FRINGE MEDICINE—FLOWER ESSENCE THERAPY A floral essence obtained from centifolia, damascena, and gallica variants of the rose; rose essence is believed to most effective in women for postpartum depression, tension, stress, and depression related to the end of a long relationship. See Flower essence therapy

**rose hip** Hipberry HERBAL MEDICINE A berry from the dog rose (*Rosa canina*), which is rich in flavonoids and vitamin C; it is available as tablets and tinctures, and used to make herbal teas for colds and the flu. See Herbal medicine, Wild rose

**rosemary** *Rosmarinus officinalis*, old man HERBAL MEDICINE A perennial herb that contains carnosic acid, camphor, flavonoids, phenolic acids, triterpenic acid, and volatile oils; it is antimicrobial, antiseptic, astringent, car-

**rosemary** *Rosmarinus officinalis*

diotonic, and carminative, and has been used as a gastrointestinal and hepatic tonic, for baldness, colds, colic, coughs, depression, fatigue, gastrointestinal discomfort, gout, headaches, hypertension, laryngitis, painful menses, paralysis, rheumatic complaints, sore throats, stress, tonsillitis, threatened abortion, toothaches, and vertigo; data suggest that rosemary may be antioxidant and anticarcinogenic TOXICITY See Herbal medicine, Rosemary oil—toxicity

**rosemary oil** AROMATHERAPY A volatile oil distilled or extracted from rosemary (*Rosemarinus officinalis*), which contains borneol, camphors, cineol, linalool, verbenol, and others; it is used in aromatherapy to increase a person's energy levels. Rosemary oil should not be used internally, or in pregnancy–it stimulates uterine contraction. See Aromatherapy, Essential oil, Rosemary

**rose noble** Figwort, see there, *Scrophularia nodosa*

**roselle** Hibiscus, see there, *Hibiscus sabdariffa*

**Rosen method** A method of structural integration developed in the 1970s by a German-American, M Rosen, in which neuromuscular tension is viewed as a physical manifestation of repressed emotions; Rosen believes this repression results in holding patterns, which can translate into organic disease; the Rosen method uses gentle touch and verbalization to draw the client's attention to these holding patterns; awareness of the holding patterns is believed to be the key to their resolution or release. See Structural integration; Cf Alexander technique, Aston patterning, Dance therapy, Feldenkreis method, Hellerwork, Massage, Movement therapy, Ortho-bionomy, Rolfing®, Tragerwork

**rosin rose** Saint John's wort, see there, *Hypericum perforatum*

**rotation diet** CLINICAL NUTRITION A diet developed by Dr M Katahn (*The Rotation Diet, WW Norton, New York, 1986*) in which the individual 'rotates' between extreme and less stringent dieting; the diet is based on sound nutritional principles, and consists of a 3 to 4 day period of 600 calories per day for women and 1200 calories per day for men, followed by a 4 day period of 900 calories for women and 1500 calories for men, and finally a 4 day period of 1200 calories for women and 1800 calories a day for men. See Diet, Low-calorie diet

**rotational thrust** CHIROPRACTIC One of the two most common techniques for chiropractic adjustment of the vertebral column; the rotational thrust is a high-velocity, short distance technique performed on the vertebral column with the patient lying with the upper body twisted counter to the pelvis at the extreme range of the normal rotation of the spine. See Chiropractic, Spinal misalignment; Cf Recoil thrust

***rou dou kou*** Nutmeg, see there, *Myristica fragrans*

***rou guo*** Nutmeg, see there, *Myristica fragrans*

***rou qui*** Cinnamon, see there, *Cinnamon cassia*

**round-leaved dock** Bitter dock, see there, *Rumex obtusifolius*

**roughage** NUTRITION A general term for indigestible complex carbohydrates (eg bran and cellulose) of plant origin that form the bulk of the stool; roughage absorbs water, is laxative, and binds bile acids and metabolites; increased dietary roughage is linked to a decreased incidence of diverticulosis and colorectal cancer, and decreased serum cholesterol. See Bran; Cf Slops

**royal jelly** ALTERNATIVE NUTRITION A salivary secretion of worker bees fed to the bee chosen to be the queen of the hive, which causes the designate to grow larger, live longer, and reproduce; royal jelly is claimed to be effective in treating asthma, chronic fatigue, diseases of childhood, Epstein-Barr infection, insomnia, mental disorders, and other conditions; it is also believed to stimulate the immune system, retard aging, and increase mental and physical agility. See Bee pollen, Honey; Cf Mad honey

**royal treatment** *Pizzicilli*, see there

**R.P.T.** Registered Physical Therapist

***rou cong rong*** Broomrape, see there, *Cistanche salsa*

***rou tsung rung*** Broomrape, see there, formally designated *Cistanche salsa*

***ru hsiang*** Mastic tree, see there, *Boswellia carterii*

***ru xiang*** Mastic tree, see there, *Boswellia carterii*

***ruah*** Hebrew, breath of life The spiritual, bioplasmic, or etheric energy field said to surround and penetrate the body. See *Chi, (qi)*, *Prana*, Vital force

**Rubenfeld Synergy Method™** ALTERNATIVE MEDICINE A system of body-oriented psychotherapy developed in the early 1960s by an Israeli-American, I Rubenfeld; the technique is believed to integrate the mind, body, emotions, and spirit through gentle touch, allowing the release of pain and fear; the Rubenfeld Synergy Method incorporates facets of the Alexander technique, aura analysis, dreamwork, Feldenkreis method, Gestalt therapy, humor therapy, hypnosis, kinesis, and therapeutic touch; '*At the heart of every* (Rubenfeld) *session is a four-stage metaprocess. Stages are awareness, experimentation, integration, and reentry. They occur separately and simultaneously on all four interrelated levels of body, mind, emotion, and spirit.*' (*Kastner, Burroughs, 1993; Raso, 1994*). See Structural integration

***Rubia cordifolia*** Popularly known as Indian madder, see there

**rubidium** A rare alkali element (atomic number 37; atomic weight 85.47) FRINGE ONCOLOGY Rubidium is believed to have anticarcinogenic properties and may be used by some fringe oncologists as a high pH therapy for cancer *(Moss, 1992)*. See High pH therapy, Unproven methods for cancer management

***Rubus coreanus*** Popularly known as Chinese wild raspberry, see there

***Rubus idaeus*** Raspberry, see there

***Rubus tokkura*** Chinese wild raspberry, see there, *Rubus coreanus*

**rudbeckia** Echinacea, see there, *Echinacea an-gustifolia, E pallida*, *E pupura*

**rue** *Ruta graveolens*, common rue, countryman's treacle, garden rue, German rue, herb of grace, ruta A perennial herb that contains alkaloids (eg arborinine), coumarins (eg bergapten, psoralen, xanthotoxin), volatile oil with methylnonylketone, cineol, limonene, and others CHINESE MEDICINE In the Chinese pharmacopeia, rue is used primarily to treat snake and insect bites HERBAL MEDICINE In Western herbal medicine, rue is regarded as an antispasmodic, emmenagogue, and vermifuge; it has been used for arrhythmias, intestinal colic, eyestrain, gout, musculoskeletal trauma, rheumatic pain, stress-related headaches, varicose veins, and to evoke menses TOXICITY Cutaneous photosensitivity; it should not be used in pregnancy. See Botanical toxicity, Herbal medicine, Poisonous plants HOMEOPATHY see *Ruta grav*

**ruffled field** FRINGE MEDICINE A term used in the context of therapeutic touch, which refers to zones of congestion in the flow of energy, which the client may perceive as an area of denseness; to unruffle the field, the therapist sweeps his hands over the body several times, an act that is believed to increase and smooth out the energy flow. See Therapeutic touch

**rule of the artery** OSTEOPATHY A tenet advanced by Andrew Taylor Still (1828-1917), the founder of osteopathy, that holds that most, if not all, diseases that respond to osteopathic manipulation, do so because of compromised blood circulation; in years subsequent to Still's early theories, osteopathy has taken a more global view of the pathogenesis of various diseases. See Osteopathy; Cf Rule of the nerve

**rule of the nerve** CHIROPRACTIC A posit advanced by Daniel David Palmer (1845-1913), the founder of chiropractic, that holds that most, if not all, diseases that respond to chiropractic manipulation, do so because of released impingement on the structures (nerves, but also blood and lymphatic vessels) that pass through intervertebral foramina; Cf Rule of the artery

**rum cherry** Wild cherry, see there, *Prunus serotina*

***Rumex obtusifolius*** Popularly known as bitter dock, see there

**runner's 'high'** SPORTS MEDICINE A general term for a state of euphoria experienced by those who run long distances, which is thought to be due to the release of endorphins and enkephalins. See Acupuncture

**running pine** *Lycopodium clavatum*, see there

**Dr Benjamin Rush** MEDICAL HISTORY An American physician (1746-1813) trained at the Royal College of Physicians in Edinburgh, who practiced 'heroic medicine' and is believed to have been instrumental in hastening the demise of his most famous patient, George Washington *(Armstrong, 1991)*.

See Heroic medicine

**Russian bath** NATUROPATHY A type of sweat bath, in which a person is exposed for 10 to 20 minutes to high temperatures and high humidity. See Hydrotherapy; Cf Sauna, Turkish bath

**Russian massage** NATUROPATHY A type of massage used in Russia that is designed to relax (through use of effleurage and friction) and stimulate (through petrissage and vibration); Russian massage, like other massage therapies, is believed to improve circulation, increase muscle elasticity, and reduce edema and pain. See Massage therapy

**ruta** CHINESE MEDICINE, HERBAL MEDICINE Rue, see there, *Ruta graveolens* HOMEOPATHY See *Ruta grav*

***Ruta grav*** *Ruta graveolens* HOMEOPATHY A remedy used for deep, aching pain, in particular of the bones and joints; it is also used for bruising, carpal tunnel syndrome, chest pain, cough, croup, eyestrain, rectal prolapse, tennis elbow, and toothaches. See Homeopathy

***Ruta graveolens*** CHINESE MEDICINE, HERBAL MEDICINE Popularly known as rue, see there HOMEOPATHY See *Ruta grav*

**sabal** Saw palmetto, see there, *Serenoa serrulata*

***Sabal serrulata*** Saw palmetto, see there, *Serenoa serrulata*

**saccharin** The cyclic imine of 2-sulfobenzoic acid, that is > 500 times sweeter than sugar, sold as an artificial sweetener that was temporarily withdrawn from the market*. See Artificial sweeteners; Cf Aspartame, Sweet proteins

*It was shown to cause bladder tumors in rats, if given in 'mega' doses; one pack of Sweet 'n Low® contains 40 mg of saccharin

**saccharin**

O
N
$SO_2$

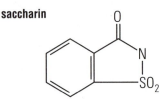

**sacred bark** Cascara sagrada, see there, *Rhamnus purshiana*

**sacred touch** A type of craniosacral therapy, see EmBodyment

**sacro-occipital tchnique** OSTEOPATHY A permutation of craniosacral manipulation, developed by Major B DeJarnette. See Cranial osteopathy, Osteopathy

**SAD** Seasonal affective disorder, see there

**'sad foods'** FRINGE NUTRITION A term coined by Stuart Berger, creator of the *Southampton Diet*, for foods that he believed produced 'negative neurotransmitters' in the brain; 'sad foods' include chickpeas, chocolate, lentils, lobster, sugar, lecithin and choline-rich foods. See Diet, Southampton diet; Cf 'Happy foods'

**safety energy lock** see Jin Shin Jyutsu

**safflower** *Carthamus tinctorius*, *hong hua* CHINESE MEDICINE An herb, the flowers of which are used topically for abscesses, bruises, and burns, and internally as a cardiovascular tonic, for anginal pan, coagulation disorders, and delayed menses. See Chinese herbal medicine

**safflower** *Carthamus tinctorius*

**saffron** *Crocus sativus*, *dzang hung hua*, *fan hung hua*, foreign saffron, Tibetan saffron CHINESE MEDICINE An herb, the flower of which contains crocetin and is used as an antispasmodic, alterative, cardiotonic, and believed be an aphrodisiac; it has been used for anemia, cardiovascular disease (hypertension, palpitations, and tachycardia), delayed menses, obstetrical problems, and muscle spasms. See Chinese herbal medicine HERBAL MEDICINE Saffron is used by Western herbalists much like their Chinese counterparts TOXICITY In extreme excess, saffron has caused death in women who have used it as an abortifacient. See Herbal medicine

**safrole** TOXICOLOGY *m*-Allylpyrocatechin methylene ether A compound present in sassafras (*Sassafras albidum*), camphor, and other volatile oils; once used as a carminative, intestinal tonic, topical antiseptic, and pediculoside, it is hepatotoxic (causes fatty degeneration), carcinogenic, and listed by the FDA as 'unsafe'. See Botanical toxicity, Herbal medicine, Poisonous plants, Sassafras

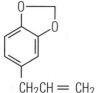

O O $CH_2CH = CH_2$

**safrole**

**sage** *Salvia officinalis*, common sage, garden sage, meadow sage, scarlet sage, true sage HERBAL MEDICINE A perennial evergreen, the leaves of which contain estrogen-like substances, flavonoids, phenolic acids, tannins, and volatile oils (eg borneol, camphor, cineole, pinene, thujone, and others). Sage has a long history of medicinal use and was regarded as a cure-all; it is antibacterial, antispasmodic, carminative, and tonic; it has been used for colds, constipation, indigestion, painful menses, hot flashes, and as a gargle for sore throat and tonsillitis; it is believed to improve memory, relax nerves, and quell 'vicious sexual desires,' and as a poultice for ulcers, sores, and skin eruptions TOXICITY Sage should not be taken during pregnancy or by those with seizures. See Herbal medicine

**sagebrush** *Artemisia tridentata* FRINGE MEDICINE-FLOWER ESSENCE THERAPY A floral essence believed to provide a deep awareness of one's inner self. See Flower essence therapy

**saffron** *Crocus sativus*

**SAHEM** Self-applied health enhancement method, see there

**St Benedict's thistle** Blessed thistle, see there, *Cnicus benedictus*

**sage** *Salvia officinalis*

**St Bernadette** PARANORMAL PHENOMENA A young woman who, in 1858, had multiple visions of the Virgin Mary at Lourdes in southern France, who became a nun; she remained in chronic ill health until she died at age 35. See Healing shrine, Lourdes, Miraculous cure

Bernadette did not exploit her fame; in response to pressure from devout believers in the medical miracles attributed to the spring waters at Lourdes, she was beatified and subsequently canonized

**St Ignatius' itch** Pellagra, see there

**St John's herb** Mugwort, see there, *Artemisia vulgaris*

**St John's neuromuscular therapy** Neuromuscular therapy–St John's method, St John's neuromuscular pain relief BODYWORK A system of bodywork used to treat soft tissue injury, pain, and dysfunction developed in the 1970s by P St John, a former solid waste engineer; the technique is physical therapy-oriented, relies on rehabilitation techniques, and addresses biomechanics, ischemia, trigger points, nerve entrapment and compression, and postural distortion. St John's neuromuscular therapy is intended to achieve a balance between the nervous and musculoskeletal systems, and relieve pain and dysfunction; it is believed to be useful in treating most musculoskeletal pain, including back, neck, and shoulder pain, post-traumatic pain, headaches, migraines, whiplash-related pain, and pain related to poor posture. See Bodywork

**St John's neuromuscular pain relief** St John's neuromuscular therapy, see there

**St John's plant** Mugwort, see there, *Artemisia vulgaris*

**St John's wort** *Hypericum perforatum*, amber touch-and-heal, common St John's wort, goatweed, klamath weed, rosin rose FRINGE MEDICINE—FLOWER ESSENCE THERAPY A floral essence said to provide a sense of consciousness, self-awareness and inner strength. See Flower essence therapy HERBAL MEDICINE A perennial herb that contains flavonoids, glycosides, mucilage, tannins, and volatile oil, which is antibacterial, anti-inflammatory, antimicrobial, astringent, expectorant, and sedative; it has been used internally for arthritis, bed-wetting, bronchitis, colds, mental disorders (anxiety, depression, insomnia, nervousness), menstrual cramps, neuralgia, rheumatic pain, and sciatica, and topically for burns, cuts and wounds; it was used transiently as an herbal therapy for AIDS TOXICITY St John's wort is deemed unsafe by the FDA, given its phototoxicity; it causes hypertension, headaches, nausea, and vomiting; it may interact with amphetamines, amino acids (tryptophan, tyrosine), antiasthmatic inhalants, beer, wine, chocolate, coffee, fava beans, cold and hay fever medication, narcotics, nasal decongestants, and smoked or pickled foods. See Herbal medicine

**Saint John's wort** *Hypericum perforatum*

***Salicornia bigelovii* Torr** GLOBAL NUTRITION A seed crop plant that may be grown in salt water, which was developed from a wild halophyte. S *bigelovii* yields high-quality oil, containing 30% protein and 30% unsaturated fatty acid-rich oil

The crop may be a viable substitute for soybean oil and could be cultivated in 'marginal' regions of the world (*Science 1991; 251:1065*)

***Salisburia adiantifolia*** *Gingko biloba*, see there

***Salix alba*** Popularly known as white willow, see there

**salt glow** Salt rub, see there

**salt rub** Salt glow NATUROPATHY A rigorous massage with sea salts, or Epsom salts, which is believed to improve poor circulation and remove various toxins from the body. See Hydrotherapy

***Salvia officinalis*** Sage, see there

***samadhi* therapy** *Agni dhatu*, see there

**samahdi tank** Isolation tank, see there

***Sambucus nigra*** Popularly known as elderberry, see there

***san*** see Powder–Chinese medicine

***san chi*** *Gynura pinnatifida*, see there

**sand painting** ETHNOMEDICINE A component of Navajo medicine which is intended to address the spiritual cause of illness; the 'sand' consists of ground minerals or vegetables, and is used to construct complex symbolic patterns with culture-specific significance, which may require many hands to complete; the patient is placed in the center, and the sand painting is constructed around him, in order for the painting's healing powers to flow through him; after the ceremony, in which the healer shakes a rattle, chants, and prays, the painting is destroyed. See

Mandela, Medicine bundle, Rattle, Shamanism, Sweat lodge, Vision quest; Cf Mandela

**sand therapy** NATUROPATHY A permutation of whole body heat therapy, in which one is immersed in hot volcanic sand rather than water. Surigahama, Japan is the best known place to 'take the sands'. Sand therapy is believed to improve circulation and relieve pain. See Hydrotherapy, Mud therapy

**sandlewood** *Santalum album, S verum, jen tan, tan hsiang, tan xiang,* true sandlewood FRINGE MEDICINE-FLOWER ESSENCE THERAPY A floral essence that is believed to relieve tension and anxiety, and possibly serve as a sexual stimulant. See Flower essence therapy CHINESE MEDICINE A tree, the resinous wood of which is an antiseptic, carminative, and sedative; it is used to treat bronchitis, dermatitis, poor digestion, sexually-transmitted disease, and urogenital infections. See Chinese herbal medicine

***Sanguinaria*** *Sanguinaria canadensis* HOMEOPATHY A minor homeopathic remedy that is indicated for burning chest pain, and used to treat respiratory tract conditions including asthma and bronchitis, as well as pharyngitis, nasal, and laryngeal polyps. See Homeopathy

***Sanguinaria canadensis*** HERBAL MEDICINE Popularly known as blood root, see there HOMEOPATHY See *Sanguinaria*

**sanguinary** Yarrow, see there, *Achillea millefolium*

***Santalum album*** Sandlewood, see there

***Santalum verum*** Sandlewood, see there, *Santalum album*

***Santureia montana*** Popularly known as winter savory, see there

***sao jou tsao*** Belvedere cypress, see there, *Kochia scoparia*

**sapin** Balsam fir, see there, *Abies balsamea*

***Saponaria officinalis*** Popularly known as soapwort, see there

***Saponaria vaccaria*** Popularly known as cowherd, see there

**saponin** ALTERNATIVE PHARMACOLOGY Any of a number of fat-rich soap-like substances found in a wide range of herbs, sunflower seeds, and soybeans, which inhibit the growth of colon cancer cells in vitro

**sargassam seaweed** *Sargassam pallidum,* seaweed CHINESE MEDICINE A weed harvested from coastal waters, which is a diuretic; it is used for thyroid conditions, hernia-related and testicular pain. Some data suggest that sargassam may lower blood pressure, cholesterol, and have antifungal activity. See Chinese herbal medicine

***Sarothamnus scoparius*** Popularly known as broom, see there

**sashimi** see Sushi

**sassafras** *Sassafras albidum,* ague tree, cinnamonwood, smelling stick HERBAL MEDICINE A deciduous tree, the bark of which was regarded by Native Americans as a blood purifier, as it is antiseptic, diaphoretic, and diuretic; it was used to treat syphilis, abscesses, acne, poison ivy and poison oak, and internally for colic and rheumatic complaints TOXICITY Carcino-genic and hepatotoxic in rats due to safrole; it is listed by the FDA as 'unsafe'. Sassafras oil and raw bark should not be used internally. See Botanical toxicity, Herbal medicine, Safrole

**sassafras** *Sassafras albidum*

***Sassafras albidum*** Sassafras, see there

**SAT**[sm] Spinal attunement technique A proprietary component of Reiki plus®, see there

**satellite point** A type of trigger point, that is a secondary site for muscle pain, which is often located near the site of the original pain. Satellite points can stimulate matrix points. See Bonnie Prudden myotherapy, Trigger point; Cf Matrix point

**satinflower** Chickweed, see there, *Stellaria media*

**sattvic** *adjective* Harmonious, per ayurvedic construct

**saturated fatty acid** NUTRITION An alkyl chain fatty acid that has no double (ethylenic) bonds between carbons; called saturated as the chain is incapable of absorbing more hydrogen; these fatty acids have higher melting points and may be solid at room temperature. Saturated fatty acids, eg stearic acid, are found in animal fats, eg butter, margarine, meat and dairy fats. See Fatty acid; Cf Unsaturated fatty acid

**sauna** HYDROTHERAPY A general term for an activity most popular among Scandinavians; the classic sauna is taken in a small wood-lined room heated to 50ºC (140ºF) or higher, with birch logs, or heating coils; often water is poured on hot stones in the sauna to increase the humidity and stimulate sweating; after the bathers have reached their tolerance, they may rush out of the cabin and throw themselves in icy cold water or roll in the snow. Saunas are used to stimulate the circulation, immune system, nervous system, skin and evoke an increased sense of well-being; the Finns believe saunas to be beneficial for rheumatic complaints, respiratory disease, indigestion, and others. Saunas should not be taken by those with cardiovascular disease or by children. See Hydrotherapy; Cf Russian bath, Sea water therapy, Russian sauna, Turkish bath

**saussurea** Aucklandia, see there, *Aucklandia lappa*

***Saussurea lappa*** Popularly known as costus, see there

**savory food snack** The FDA's term for 'crunchy junk food,' which includes potato chips, tortilla chips, and crackers (*N Engl J Med 1996; 334:984ed*)

**saw palmetto** *Serenoa serrulata*, *S repens*, sabal, *Sabal serrulata* HERBAL MEDICINE An herb, the berries of which contain steroidal saponins, tannins, and fixed and volatile oils; it is diuretic, expectorant, and sedative; it has been used to stimulate the appetite, treat respiratory and urinary tract infections; it has been used for reproductive dysfunction (impotence, prostatitis, loss of libido, infertility in women), for prostatic hypertrophy, and to increase lactation, effects that are attributed to the steroidal saponins. See Herbal medicine

**scabish** Evening primrose, see there, *Oeno-thera biennis*

**scabwort** Elecampane, see there, *Inula helenium*

**scarlet bergamot** Bergamot, *Monarda didyma*

**scarlet sage** Sage, see there, *Salvia officinalis*

**scallion** *Allium ascalonium*, spring onions CHINESE MEDICINE An onion-like plant that is antimicrobial, diaphoretic, a digestive tonic and metabolic stimulant; it is used topically for abscesses and wounds, and internally for abdominal bloating and pain, chills, fever, and nasal congestion. See Chinese herbal medicine

**scented fern** Tansy, see there, *Tanacetum vulgare*

**scentual medicine** Aromatherapy, see there

**Schatz-style yoga** A 20th century permutation of 'low-impact' yoga developed by MP Schatz, MD, which incorporates flowing standing poses into its routine of *asanas*. See Yoga; Cf Ayurvedic medicine

**schiatsu** Shiatsu, see there

***Schisandra chinensis*** *Wu wei dze, wu wei zi* CHINESE MEDICINE A ligneous aromatic vine, the dried berry of which is antidiuretic, antitussive, astringent, demulcent, and tonic; it is believed to have rejuvenative properties, and is used for allergic skin reactions, arrhythmias, palpitations, asthma, coughs, wheezing, dermatitis, headaches, hepatitis, infertility, insomnia, lethargy, neuralgia, nocturnal emissions, sweating, urinary frequency, and vertigo HERBAL MEDICINE *Schisandra* is used by Western herbologists as a tonic to increase the body's resistance to physical and environmental stress TOXICITY Restlessness, insomnia, shortness of breath, and gastritis. See Botanical toxicity, Herbal medicine

***Schizonepeta tenuifolia*** Popularly known as Japanese catnip, see there

**Schüssler's biochemic system of medicine** Biochemic medicine, biochemic system of medicine, tissue salts therapy FRINGE HOMEOPATHY The therapeutic use of Schüssler's tissue salts, which are believed to be useful for abscesses, acidity, acne, addiction disorders, agoraphobia, allergies, anxiety, arthritis, asthma, bipolar

**SCHÜSSLER'S TISSUE SALTS**

| CHEMICAL NAME | FUNCTION | INDICATION |
|---|---|---|
| Calcarea fluorica | Provides tissue elasticity | Strained muscles, hemorrhoids, hernias |
| Calcarea phosphorica | Stimulates hematopoeisis, promotes growth in children, good for bone and teeth | Poor circulation, cachexia, dermatopathies convalescence |
| Calcarea sulfurica | Purifies blood | Dermatopathies |
| Ferrum phosphoricum | Present in red blood cells | Inflammation, minor trauma, common cold, rheumatic disease, respiratory infections |
| Kali muriaticum | Stimulates metabolism | Congestion |
| Kali phosphoricum | Nutrient for nerves, nervous system, muscle, red blood cells | Nervous system disease, insomnia |
| Kali sulphuricum | Promotes epithelial cell growth, destruction of effete cells, oxygen transportation | Asthma, rheumatic fever, rheumatic disease, sinusitis, headaches, indigestion |
| Magnesia phosphorica | Nutrient for nerves, nervous system, muscle, blood, bone, teeth | Nervous system disease, insomnia<br>Neuralgias, spasms, itching |
| Natrum muriaticum | Control of body fluids | Imbalance of electrolytes |
| Natrum phosphoricum | Controls cell acidity | Defects in bile and uric acid metabolism, indigestion |
| Natrum sulphuricum | Stimulates body secretions | Hepatic disease, headaches, asthma, nausea |
| Silicea | Promotes suppuration, a connective tissue component | General weakness, systemic toxicity, malodorous discharges |

(manic-depressive) disorder, blisters, bronchitis, bruxism, candidiasis, chickenpox, common cold, cramps, edema, fever, gastrointestinal problems (eg gastritis and indigestion), gout, hay fever, heartburn, menstrual defects, mineral deficiencies, mood swings, mumps, neurologic complaints, pain, sexual and urogenital problems, and other conditions. See Homeopathy

Note: The understanding of the role of minerals in Schüssler's day was extremely primitive, and the purported function of salts scientifically naive; there is little data in peer-reviewed literature to verify claims of efficacy

**Schüssler's tissue salts** Biochemic tissues salts, cell salts, twelve Schüssler remedies ALTERNATIVE MEDICINE Twelve combinations of salts formulated by a German homeopath, WH Schüssler; the salts can be self-administered and are intended to be taken in low concentrations (one active part in one million), designated as 6X, as in the homeopathic system. See Homeopathy, Homeopathic remedy, Schüssler's biochemic system of medicine

**scientism** A term for 1. The belief that the methods used in the investigation of phenomena in the physical universe can be applied to all areas of research, including the cognitive sciences 2. The use of scientific methods and principles for inappropriate topics (*Nature 1991; 354:118*). See Pseudoscience

**Scientology®** '*An applied religious philosophy...* (which studies)...*the spirit in relationship to itself, universes and other life...*'–L Ron Hubbard (1911-1986), the philosophy's architect, further wrote that '*Scientology...improves health, ability, intelligence, behavior, skill and appearance...*' In a public message, the Church of Scientology states, '*Scientology philosophy and its forerunner, Dianetics®...address only the spirit...the Church...does not wish to accept individuals who desire treatment of physical or mental illness but prefers to refer these to qualified specialists ...*' (*Scientology: The Fundamentals of Thought, Bridge Publications, Los Angeles, 1988*); Cf Christian Science

**scillaren A, B** Compounds isolated from the sea onion (*Urginea maritima*), which are of potential use as cardiotonic agents. See Herbal medicine, Sea onion

**scilliroside** PHARMACOGNOSY A potent emetic agent (figure, page 330) isolated from sea onion (*Urginea* or *Scilla maritima*), which is currently used as a rat poison. See Herbal medicine, Sea onion

**sclerology** FRINGE MEDICINE A pseudodiagnostic technique in which the sclera of the eye is examined as a means of detecting systemic disease; Cf Iridology

**scombroid intoxication** A histamine reaction caused by eating spoiled fish of the

**scilliroside**

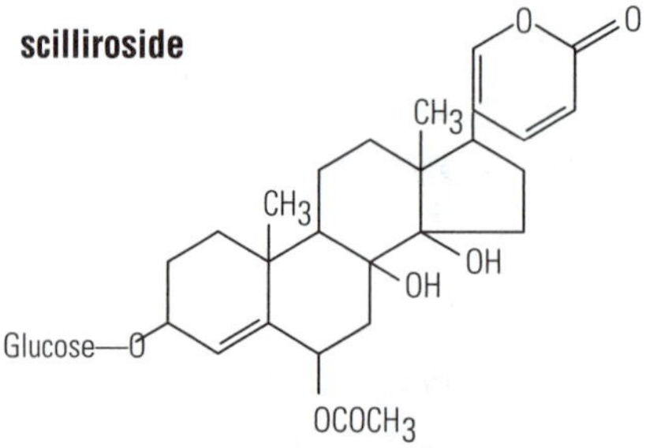

Scomboidea suborder (saury, skipjack, mahi-mahi, dolphin, tuna, bonito, seerfish, butterfly kingfish, mackerel); these fish have free histamine in their muscle that is decarboxylated when infected by *Proteus* spp; if the infection is intense, oral antihistamines or activated charcoal may be needed to ameliorate the systemic effects of histamine (*N Engl J Med 1991; 324:716*). See Fish; Cf Ciguatera poisoning

**Scotch heather** Heather, see there, *Calluna vulgaris*

**Scottish broom** Broom, see there, *Sarothamnus scoparius*

**scouring rush** Horsetail, see there, *Equisetum arvense*

**scrofula plant** Figwort, see there, *Scrophularia nodosa*

***Scrophularia nodosa*** Popularly known as figwort, see there

**scutch** Couch grass, see there, *Agropyron repens*

***Scutellaria lateriflora*** Popularly known as skullcap, see there

**sea onion** *Urginea maritima*, red squill, white squill HERBAL MEDICINE A cabbage-like plant that grows on the sandy soils of the Mediterranean rim and South Africa; of the two variants, red and white squill, the latter is of greater use, as it has less of the poison, scilliroside; the active principles in squill are antitussive, cardiotonic (due to the chemicals scillaren A and B), diuretic, expectorant TOXICITY Scilliroside is a potent emetic, and used as a rat poison. See Herbal medicine, Scilliroside

**sea parsley** Lovage, see there, *Levisticum officinale*

**sea salt rub** see Salt rub

**seasonal affective disorder** Winter 'blues,' winter depression A condition characterized by photolabile depression most prominent in winter. Some SAD patients respond to high-intensity light, which alters their circadian rhythm, a therapy that is most effective in the morning; a light intensity of 10 000 lux viewed at very close range may be required to reset the biological clock. See Bright light therapy; Cf Melancholia, Melancholy

There is female:male ratio of 2:1 for depression; preliminary PET scan data has linked depression to an increase in blood flow through the anterior limbic system, which may ultimately lead to hypoactivity; melatonin is decreased in women in summer and unchanged in men (*Sci Am 1995; 272/6:23*)

**seawater** FRINGE NUTRITION Water taken from the ocean, bottled and marketed as providing critical nutrients; it is claimed that a teaspoon per day is useful in preventing and treating unnamed deficiencies that cause baldness, cancer, cardiovascular disease, mental disorders, and a plethora of other conditions. See Seawater therapy

**seawater therapy** Thalassotherapy ALTERNATIVE MEDICINE A general term for the use of sea water at any temperature (hot, tepid, cold), on any part of the body (soaking, drinking, inhaled in fine mists), with or without mechanical manipulation (massages, jacuzzis, bubbling), and with or without additives (mud, seaweed, oils). Sea water is popularly believed to have health-promoting effects. See Hydrotherapy; Cf Sauna, Turkish bath

**seawrack** Bladderwrack, see there, *Fucus vesiculosus*

**sealwort** Solomon's Seal, see there, *Polygonatum officinale*

**second-hand smoke** Passive smoking, see there

**Second Opinion** FRINGE ONCOLOGY A group of professionals at Memorial Sloan-Kettering Cancer Center (MSKCC) in New York City, who are said to have pressured the hospital's administration to release studies performed at MSKCC on the inconclusive results regarding the efficacy of laetrile (*Pelton, Overholser, 1994*). See Laetrile, Tijuana, Unproven methods for cancer management

**secondary care** ALTERNATIVE MEDICINE The provision of specialized alternative health care *after* a patient has been seen by either a mainstream physician or one trained in an alternative health care system, eg acupuncture, traditional Chinese medicine, ayurvedic medicine, chiropractic, homeopathy, naturopathy, osteopathy, or other system; secondary care may be recommended after a patient is evaluated by a primary care provider, who refers them for a specific adjunctive therapy. See Primary care

**sectarian medicine** Alternative medicine, see there

**sedative** HERBAL MEDICINE Nervine, see there

**sedative music** MUSIC THERAPY Melodic and soothing music used in music therapy, which promotes a sense of serenity. Sedative music has a flowing melody with few major changes in pitch, dynamics, or rhythm, which may be similar to that of the resting heart rate; works regarded as sedative include Pachelbel's 'Canon in D', Mozart's Eine Kleine Nacht Musik, and Bach's 'Air on a G string'. See Music therapy; Cf Stimulative music

**Seder syncope** A vasovagal collapse induced by the horseradish (active ingredient, isothiocyanate) used in the celebration of the Jewish Seder* (*JAMA 1988; 259:1943*). See Black mustard, Horseradish, Spicy food

*A symbolic meal that commemorates the bitterness of Jewish slavery in ancient Egypt, which is partaken during the Jewish high holiday of Passover

**'seeing heart dog'** see Pet therapy

**segmental dysfunction** CHIROPRACTIC A term used in chiropractic for a focal misalignment (subluxation) of the vertebra, which is treated by spinal manipulation, and believed to free 'life forces' and allow the body to heal itself

**seichim** PARANORMAL PHENOMENA An ancient Egyptian healing art, in which life energies are activated and healed through the use of power mantras and imagery and visualization

**seichim reiki** PARANORMAL PHENOMENA An eclectic permutation of seichim combined with reiki, which is said to access other planes of existence with empowering crystals. See Crystal healing, Reiki, Seichim

***seiki-jutsu*** A Japanese technique in which *seiki*—the cosmic healing energy–is believed to be transferred from the therapist's hand to the crown of the client's head

**selenium** A metallic element (atomic number 34; atomic weight 78.96), which is required in trace amounts by certain enzymes, eg glutathione peroxidase; it is present in brewer's yeast, cereals, dairy products, fish, fruits, liver, organ and muscle meats, seafood, vegetables, and whole grains; it interacts with vitamins A, C, and E, serving as an antioxidant. Selenium is believed to be anticarcinogenic, to retard aging, and has been used for arthritis, cataracts, connective tissue disease, dandruff, and age-related loss of vision

***Selenum monnieri*** *Cnidium monnieri*, see there

**self-actualization need** B need, B value, being need, growth need, metaneed ALTERNATIVE PSYCHOLOGY A general term for any higher need of an individual, as viewed by Abraham Maslow, which corresponds to the desire for self-actualization; self-actualization needs include the need for personal growth, truth, justice, meaningfulness, for creative expression, for transcendence of the self, and for peak experiences. See Basic needs

**self-applied health enhancement method** ALTERNATIVE MEDICINE Any of four self-healing methods described by an American acupuncturist, Roger Jahnke; 'SAHEMs' include movement and posture, eg t'ai chi ch'uan, self-massage, acupressure, breathing exercise, and relaxation

**self-heal** Heal-all, see there, *Prunella vulgaris*

**self-healing** Direct healing PARANORMAL PHENOMENA A general term for the use of a person's innate vital forces to heal himself through affirmation, imagery and visualization, and prayer. See Miraculous cure

**self-reflexology** An informal permutation of reflexology, which can be performed by an individual on his hands, feet, ears, or anyplace within the reach of the massaging body part. See Reflexology

**seminal and ovarian kung fu** Healing love (meditation), see there

**senna** *Cassia senna* HERBAL MEDICINE A shrub native to northern and eastern Africa, which contains emodin and anthraquinone glycosides (sennosides A and B); it is primarily used as a laxative TOXICITY In excess, senna may evoke nausea, vomiting, and colic; it should not be used in pregnancy, or in those who are nursing, or have colitis, hemorrhoids, or ulcers; overuse may be associated with the so-called 'lazy bowel syndrome.' See Herbal medicine

**sennoside** MAINSTREAM MEDICINE An anthraquinone glucoside isolated from senna (eg *Cassia senna*) and rhubarb, which is used as a

β–D-glucose-O O OH

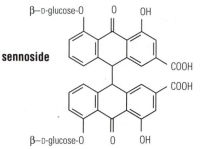

**sennoside**

COOH

COOH

β–D-glucose-O O OH

cathartic

**sensation** HOMEOPATHY A general term for the quality of a symptom, eg a pain can be burning, throbbing, tearing, and so on. See Homeopathic symptom, Homeopathy

**sensitivity group** Encounter group, see there

**sensory deprivation** FRINGE PSYCHOLOGY The elimination of virtually all external auditory, sensory, and visual stimuli, which can be accomplished by immersion in luke-warm water in a flotation tank, or in an isolation chamber; advocates of this form of pseudotherapy believe that it is useful for increasing a person's self-awareness. Sensory deprivation is also used by those who wish to enhance the intensity of meditation. See Flotation, Isolation chamber

**sensory-motor amnesia** A term coined by Dr T Hanna, which refers to muscles that are chronically contracted due to stress and trauma, which have reached a point where they no longer 'remember' how to relax. See Hanna somatic education

**sensory-motor-rhythm feedback** Sensory-motor-rhythm biofeedback, see Biofeedback training

**sensory therapy** ALTERNATIVE PSYCHIATRY A general term for any of the number of techniques that are based on auditory, visual, or other sensory stimulation, and believed to have some therapeutic value; of these, art and music therapies have been well studied, and appear to have a legitimate therapeutic role in patients with mental disorders; color therapy is more peripheral to mainstream medical thought. See Art therapy, Aura, Color therapy, Music therapy

***Sepia*** *Sepia officinalis*, cuttlefish HOMEOPATHY A remedy formulated from the cuttlefish, a soft mollusk native to the Mediterranean Sea; it is used primarily for 'female complaints,' including premenstrual syndrome, physical and emotional changes of pregnancy, prolapsed uterus, and dyspareunia–pain with sexual intercourse. *Sepia* is also used for abdominal bloating, violent coughing, fatty food-related indigestion, genital herpes, hair loss, headaches, itching, increased sweating, 'liver spots' on skin, low back pain, motion sickness, sinusitis, varicose veins, and vertigo. See Constitutional type, Homeopathy, *Sepia* type

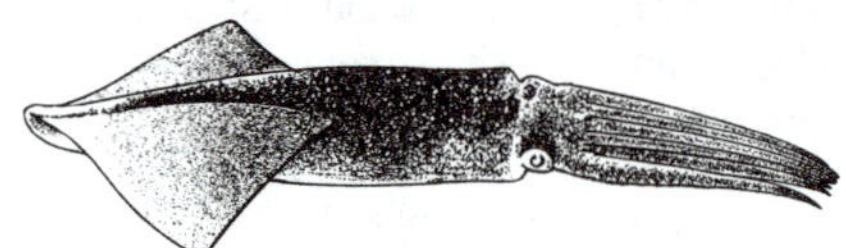

***Sepia*** Cuttlefish

***Sepia* type** HOMEOPATHY Most *Sepia* constitutional types are women; they are annoying in private, charming in public, and always opinionated; they like sweet or sour foods, and alcohol WORSE Humidity, premenstrual, early morning, early evening FEARS Poverty, loss of self-control WEAKEST BODY REGIONS Reproductive organs, skin, veins, left side of the body. See Constitutional type, Homeopathy, *Sepia*

**sequestrant** FOOD INDUSTRY A substance added to certain foods, which binds metals to prevent discoloration and inhibit reactions that result in rancidity. See Food additives

***Serenoa repens*** Saw palmetto, see there, *Serenoa serrulata*

***Serenoa serrulata*** Popularly known as saw palmetto, see there

**serosa** A virtual membrane covered by a single layer of mesothelial cells that lines body cavities including the pericardium, peritoneum, and pleura, and covers the outer surface of the organs (eg heart, intestines, and lungs) present in those cavities

**sesame oil** CHINESE MEDICINE Oil pressed from black sesame (*Sesamum indicum*) seeds, which is used as a laxative, as well as for blurred vision, tinnitus, vertigo, and recuperation from prolonged illness. See Chinese herbal medicine

**set-point hypothesis** A deterministic theory that explains the interplay of appetite and other factors, eg fats and carbohydrates in weight control; according to this hypothesis, the brain is constantly adjusting the metabolism and manipulating an individual's behavior to maintain a target weight; although the set point changes with age, it does so according to a fixed genetic program; while diet and exercise can shift the set point, the target itself is immutable. See Obesity; Cf Glycogen hypothesis, Settling point hypothesis

Note: The set-point hypothesis has been criticized as it does not explain the marked increase in obesity in the general population, nor the differences in weight in the geographically separated Pima Indians; if the SPH is valid, and weight is indeed centrally controlled, the intake of fat would have little impact on weight *(Sci Am Aug 1996, p88)*

**settling-point hypothesis** A theory that seeks to explain how the body controls weight; according to this hypothesis, weight is maintained when the various metabolic feedback loops, which are 'fine-tuned' by the relevant genes, settle into an equilibrium with the environment; the increased obesity seen in the general population is explained by cultural and economic factors (*Sci Am Aug 1996, p88*). See Obesity; Cf Glycogen hypothesis, Set point hypothesis

**setwell** Valerian, see there, *Valeriana officinalis*

**The Seven Moods** CHINESE MEDICINE Those emotional states which, according to construct of traditional Chinese medicine, are thought to affect the *chi* or life energy; the seven moods are anger, anxiety, fear, horror, joy, obsession, and sorrow. See The Six Evils

**714X** FRINGE ONCOLOGY An unproven method for cancer management developed by Gaston Naessens in Montreal, which consists of 3 consecutive 21-day series of intralymphatic injections of nitrogen-rich camphor and organic salts; 714X therapy is based on Naessens' observation that cancer cells require and consume abundant nitrogen, allegedly excreting a substance he calls 'co-carcinogenic K factor,' which paralyzes the immune system; according to Naessens, the nitrogen-rich camphor provides the cancer cells with the required nitrogen, causing them to stop excreting co-carcinogenic K factor, resulting in an up-regulation of immune defenses. See Co-carcinogenic K factor, Unproven methods for cancer management

**seven ray techniques** Ray methods of healing, see there

**Seventh-Day Adventist** A branch of Protestantism founded by Ellen G White (1827-1915), which adheres to certain health-related guidelines. Seventh-Day Adventists abstain from alcohol and tobacco, consume a simple, strictly vegetarian diet, exercise, bathe regularly, and may use prayer instead of physicians, who are consulted when necessary; Adventists operate 73 hospitals, including the Loma Linda University School of Medicine; Cf Christian Science

**sexual *chakra*** AYURVEDIC MEDICINE The second *chakra* which governs the sexual instinct and emotions, is located behind the navel, and is associated with the sex organs and spleen, and the color orange. See Ayurvedic medicine, *Chakra*

**sexual stereotyping** The generalization of a person's abilities and limitations based on tendencies of that person's sex. Sexual stereotypes include the belief that women are more intuitive, men more rational, and others

***sha ren*** Grains of paradise, see there, *Amomum xanthiodes*

**shaman** A 'medicine man' or witch doctor from an aboriginal society, whose healing ability are attributed to trance-like or 'supernatural' states. See Ethnomedicine, Healer, Psychic healing; Cf Neo-shamanism, Quack

**shamanic healing** Shamanism, see there

**shamanic medicine** Shamanism, see there

**shamanic state of consciousness** PARANOR-

MAL PHENOMENA An altered state of consciousness induced by a drumming, chanting, and other rituals, or by ingestion of natural hallucinogens; by entering this altered state, shamans are believed to move at will between ordinary and extraordinary reality, making journeys to other planes of existence or spirit realms. See Shamanism; Cf Harner method, Holotropic Breathwork®, Neo-shamanism

**shamanism** Shamanic healing, shamanic medicine, shamanistic medicine, cultural healing PARANORMAL PHENOMENA An ancient spiritual and medical tradition still practiced in many tribal cultures, which is based on the belief that healing has a spiritual (ie 'other world') dimension; to effect healing, shamans enter altered states of consciousness in order to communicate with other planes of existence, taking a journey to help the patient rediscover his connection to nature and the other plane. Shamanism is steeped in ritual (eg divination, dream interpretation, and prophecy), and tribal psychology (eg through drumming, story-telling, and chanting). See Psychic surgery; Cf Neo-shamanism

**shamanistic medicine** Shamanism, see there

**shameface** Cranesbill, *Geranium maculatum*

**shamrock** Wood sorrel, see there, *Oxalis acetosella*

***shan chi*** *Gynura pinnatifida, see there*

***shan chin*** *Angelica sinensis*, see there

***shan dzao*** Wild Chinese jujube, see there, *Ziziphus jujuba*

***shan jing dze*** Thistle, see there, *Atractylodes chinensis*

***shan ju yu*** Dogwood tree, see there, *Cornus officinalis*

***shan sheng jiang*** *Polygonatum cirrhifolium*, see there

***shan yao*** Chinese yam, see there, *Dioscorea opposita*

***shan zhu yu*** Dogwood tree, see there, *Cornus officinalis*

***shao yao*** White peony, see there, *Paeonia albiflora*

**shark cartilage** FRINGE PHARMACOLOGY A preparation of elastic tissue of shark origin that has been said by some practitioners of alternative health care to be useful in treating various types of malignancy; the alleged active component is an as-yet unidentified anti-angiogenesis factor (*Sci Am 1993; 269/4:24*). Some also believe shark cartilage is useful in treating arthritis, and report an up to 60% response rate in patients with osteoarthritis and rheumatoid arthritis (*Fox, 1996*). See Cartilade®, Cartilage-derived inhibitor, Unproven methods for cancer management

Note: There are no reports in peer-reviewed journals of successful therapy of cancer using shark cartilage; It has been reported that sharks are being harvested in 'alarming' numbers, which may translate into an environmental disaster (*Discover April 1996*)

**shark liver oil** A vitamin A-rich fatty oil that is the key ingredient in a number of over-the-counter antihemorrhoidal agents, eg Preparation H. See Alkylglycerol; Cf Shark cartilage

Note: It is uncertain which of the ingredients in these preparations is responsible for their healing effects; other ingredients include cocoa butter, glycerin, lanolin, and petrolatum

**shave grass** Horsetail, see there, *Equisetum arvense*

***she chuang dze*** *Cnidium monnieri*, see there

***she chuang zi*** *Cnidium monnieri*, see there

**sheep sorrel** *Rumex acetosella* HERBAL MEDICINE A European weed that contains oxalic acid, and is astringent; it is used topically for pruritic (itchy) rashes, eg caused by poison ivy and abrasions, and used internally for constipation, diarrhea, upper gastrointestinal tract ulcers, and hypermenorrhea TOXICITY Nausea, vomiting, headache; excessive ingestion may cause renal failure due to its high content of oxalic acid. See Herbal medicine

**SHEN therapy** ALTERNATIVE MEDICINE A system of energy/bodywork (SHEN = Specific Human Energy Nexus) developed in the 1970s by RR Pavek, for releasing deeply-embedded painful emotions; according to Pavek, the body's life energy flows through the body in a specific direction, and painful emotions can become trapped and disrupt normal functions; he identified a so-called 'autocontractile pain response' as the mechanism by which emotions become trapped and disrupt normal physiologic functions; in SHEN therapy, the practitioner places his paired hands on various sites on the client's body in a specific sequence, allowing the deeply-embedded emotions to '*...flow out of* *the client, the submerged ... feelings of love, joy, and confidence begin to emerge.' (Kastner, Burroughs, 1993).* SHEN therapy is believed to be useful for anxiety, arthritis, chronic gastrointestinal complaints, depression, eating disorders, edema, menstrual complaints, mi-graines, post-traumatic pain, premenstrual syndrome (PMS), and others

***shen tsao*** Ginseng, see there, *Panax ginseng*

***sheng ma*** *Cimicifuga foetida*, see there

**shepherd's purse** *Capsella bursa-pastoris*, caseweed, mother's-heart, pepper-and-salt, pickpocket, shovelweed, witch's pouch HERBAL MEDICINE An annual herb that contains acetylcholine, flavonoids, mustard oil, polypeptides, and saponins; it is antipyretic, diuretic, and hemostatic, and has been used for hypermenorrhea, hematuria, urinary tract infections, epistaxis (nosebleeds), hemorrhoids, and varicose veins. See Herbal medicine

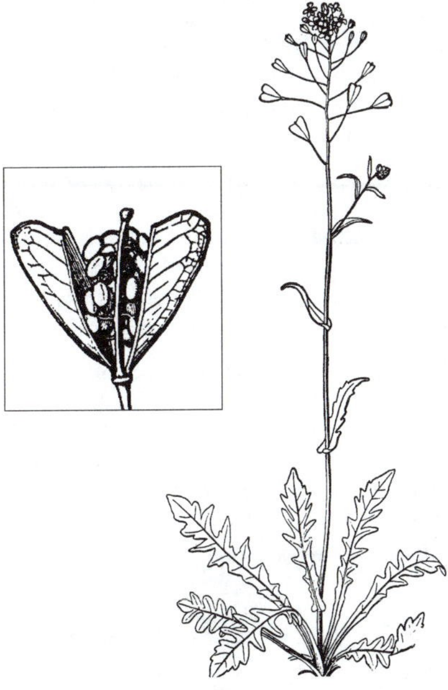

**shepherd's purse** *Capsella bursa-pastoris*

**shiatsu** Schiatsu, shiatsu therapy, shiatzu ALTERNATIVE MEDICINE A type of acupressure used in Japan on the skin surface, which combines components of acupuncture and *amma*; it is more rigorous than standard acupressure, as knuckles, thumbs, hands, elbows, knees, and even feet are used. Shiatsu is intended to increase the flow of *ki* (*qi*); the practitioner rhythmically presses any of 660 neural trigger points (*tsubo*, located on the body's meridians or energy paths, in the regions of the greatest concentrations of vessels and endocrine glands), for periods of 3 to 10 seconds, often using the thumbs, given their capacity to exert greater pressure; the 3 principal forms are shiatsu massage–based on *amma*, acupressure, and Zen shiatsu. Shiatsu is believed to be useful in treating arthritis, chronic pain, migraine, muscle tension, and other conditions. See Acupressure, Amma therapy®, Ki-shiatsu® oriental bodywork

**shiatsu oriental bodywork** Ki-shiatsu® oriental bodywork, see there

**shiatsu therapy** Shiatsu, see there

**shiatzu** Shiatsu, see there

***shih hu*** *Dendrobium nobile*

**shiitake mushroom** *Lentinus edode*, Black Forest mushroom HERBAL MEDICINE A meaty mushroom that contains protein, B vitamins, cortinelin, an antibacterial, and lentinan, a polysaccharide complex that stimulates the immune system, and is thought to be responsible for shiitake's anticarcinogeic properties; it is used for hypertension and to stimulate the immune system in patients with AIDS, cancer, and chronic fatigue syndrome. See Herbal medicine FRINGE ONCOLOGY Shiitake mushrooms have been used to treat cancer, using proprietary extracts, eg PSK and Lentinan. See Lentinan, PSK

**shin tao** Acupressure, see there

**shiny asparagus** *Asparagus lucidus, Asparagus falcatus*, Chinese asparagus, longevity vine, *tien men dung, wan sui teng* CHINESE MEDICINE A deciduous tree, the resin of which is diuretic, stimulant, tonic, and used for angina and chest pain, fatigue, gastritis, hypertension, neurosis, paresthesias, and mental stress. See Chinese herbal medicine

***shirodhara*** AYURVEDIC MEDICINE The pouring of medicated oils on the forehead, a modality used in ayurvedic medicine to eliminate *ama* (physiologic impurities). See Ayurvedic medicine, *Panchakarma*, *Prana*

***shi-un-kou*** JAPANESE HERBAL MEDICINE An herbal formulation containing *Angelica acutiloba*, *Lithospermum erythrorhizon*, and *Macro-tomia euchroma* which, in mice, is reported to inhibit Epstein-Barr virus activation and the induction of skin tumors by certain chemicals, eg phorbol (*Moss, 1992*)

***shivambu kalpa*** Urine therapy, see there

**shoofly** Wild indigo, see there, *Baptista tinctoria*

***sho-saiko-to*** JAPANESE HERBAL MEDICINE An herbal formulation that increases the production of tumor necrosis factor, stabilizes cell membranes, increases the efficiency of the presentation of antigens to the immune system, inhibits Epstein-Barr virus, reduces prostaglandin $E_2$-induced suppression of leukocytes (white cells), and has been used to treat chronic hepatitis (*Moss, 1992*)

**shovelweed** Shepherd's purse, see there, *Capsella bursa-pastoris*

***shu* point** ACUPUNCTURE An acupuncture alarm point located on the back of the body. See Alarm point

**Siberian ginseng** *Eleutherococcus senticosus*, eleuthero HERBAL MEDICINE A plant found in Siberia and China that is similar in effect to Asian (*Panax ginseng*) and American (*P quinquefolius*) ginseng, but is less intense in its activity; like the others, Siberian ginseng is used for colds, depression, fatigue, respiratory complaints, and to stimulate the immune system. See Herbal medicine

**Siberian motherwort** *Leonurus sibericus*, see there

**sick building syndrome** Tight building syndrome PUBLIC HEALTH A condition defined by the World Health Organization as an excess of work-related irritations of the skin and mucous membranes and other symptoms, including headache, fatigue, and difficulty concentrating, reported by workers in modern office buildings; 'sick building' symptoms are 2 to 3-fold more common in those who work in large, energy-efficient office buildings; the clinical manifestations fall into several categories (table); in one-fourth of investigations of such 'outbreaks,' a specific cause is identified, eg bacterial contamination of humidification systems, motor vehicle exhaust, or waste incineration; increased outdoor airflow from 0.85-1.8 $m^3$ (30-64 $ft^3$) does not decrease sick building symptoms (*N Engl J Med 1993; 328:821OA; 329:503c*) CHEMICALS Off-gassed construction materials, eg adhesives, varnishes, volatile organic solvents (*CAP Today March 1992*)

▶ **SICK BUILDING SYNDROME, CLINICAL FEATURES**

- **HYPERSENSITIVITY** Hypersensitivity pneumonitis and allergic alveolitis in response to various microorganisms including water-borne ameba, known as 'humidifier lung'
- **ALLERGIES** Allergic rhinitis and asthma, due to dust mites
- **INFECTIONS** Mini-epidemics, eg Legionnaire's disease, Pontiac fever, by low-level airborne pathogens that thrive in stagnant water and are disseminated through poorly-maintained air conditioning systems
- **MUCOCUTANEOUS IRRITATION** Skin eruptions, due to fiberglass, mineral wool or other particles; contact lens wearers may suffer corneal abrasions
- **MUCOSAL IRRITATION** Dry throat, cough, tightness in chest, sinus congestion and sneezing (formerly due to tobacco smoke), solvents and cleaning materials, eg chlorine, reactions to photochemicals or other toxins, eg in laser printers due to the styrene-butadiene toners (*N Engl J Med 1990; 322:1323c*) and ozone production by photocopiers
- **PSEUDOEPIDEMICS** related to 'mass hysteria'

See Building biology, Environmental disease

**sickle senna** *Cassia tora*, *C mimosoides*, *C sophora*, *jue ming dze*, *jue ming zi* CHINESE MEDICINE An annual herb, the seeds of which are antihypertensive, antipyretic, and laxative; it is used for constipation, poor vision, and inflammation. See Chinese herbal medicine

**siddha** AYURVEDIC MEDICINE A permutation of ayurvedic medicine from the Tamil culture of southern India and Sri Lanka; many of the siddha remedies are basic elements, including copper, gold, mercury, and sulfur. See Ayurvedic medicine

**significant other** Most significant other, see there

***Siler divaricatum*** *Ledebouriella seseloides*, see there

**silica** *Silica*, see there

***Silica*** *Silica terra*, flint, quartz, rock crystal, silica HOMEOPATHY A remedy prepared from quartz, which is used to stimulate the immune system and for abscesses, acne, athlete's foot, breast cysts, earache, fractures, hemorrhoids, infections (eg colds, flu and otitis), insomnia, lymphadenopathy (swollen 'glands'), periodontal disease, poor bone growth, and sweating. See Homeopathy, *Silica* type

***Silica* type** HOMEOPATHY The *Silica* constitutional type of person is said to be conscientious, tenacious, but may lack mental and physical stamina, and be nonassertive. *Silica* types like cold and raw foods WORSE Cold, dampness, immersion in water FEARS Failure, fatigue, sharp objects WEAKEST BODY REGIONS Nervous system, skin, bones. See Constitutional type, Homeopathy, *Silica*

**silicon** A gray-black nonmetallic semiconducting element (atomic number 14; atomic weight 28.09) that occurs in nature as silica and silicates, which is present in whole grains and in organ meats. Silicon is integral to semiconductors and solar batteries, and is essential for normal growth and skeletal development in rats and chickens; a silicon deficiency state is not known to exist in man

**silicone** A polymer composed of a repeating unit $-R_2Si-O-$ in which –R is a simple alkyl group (a hydrocarbon). Silicones can be produced in various forms, eg adhesives, sponges, solid blocks, and gels, and are widely used in medicine given their stability, water repellency, and inert nature; one formerly popular silicone, polydimethylsiloxane was enclosed in plastic bags of various sizes and shapes for use in plastic surgery to impart cosmetically acceptable contours to soft tissues; it was most commonly used in women for breast augmentation, and in men for chin augmentation; the complications of such implants in trained hands are minimal and are confined to rupture of the bags and/or fibrosis. Subcutaneous, often illicit, injection of silicone for breast enlargement without the enclosing bag (which may be self-administered by transsexual males) may be associated with high fever, diffuse arthritis, renal failure, dry cough, hemoptysis, diffuse bilateral pulmonary infiltrates with patchy ill-defined airspace consolidation, acute pneumonitis, hypoxemia, alveolitis (alveolar macrophages with silicone inclusions, neutrophils, eosinophils), decreased pulmonary function and granuloma formation. See Breast implants, Human adjuvant disease

**silky swallowtail** Milkweed, see there, *Asclepia syriaca*

**Silva mind control** Silva method A method of hypnosis and mind control developed in the 1970s by a Mexican-American electronics engineer, José Silva; according to Silva, mind control is dynamic meditation, which is optimized by having the patient think in alpha pattern brain wavelengths; the alpha pattern occurs at 10 cycles per second, and is typical of daydreaming; this contrasts to the deeper 4 to 7 Hz cycle/second theta pattern, sought in yoga and transcendental meditation. Some workers believe that Silva mind control may be dangerous to the emotionally unstable. See Biofeedback training, Hypnosis, Hypnotherapy; Cf Autosuggestion therapy, Mantra, Meditation, Yoga

**Silva method** Silva mind control, see there

**silver birch** White birch, see there, *Betula alba*

**silver fir** Balsam fir, see there, *Abies balsamea*

**silverleaf** Queen's delight, see there, *Stillingia sylvatica*

**silver pine** Balsam fir, see there, *Abies balsamea*

***Silybum marianum*** Popularly known as milk thistle, see there

**silymarin** HERBAL MEDICINE A hepatoprotective flavonoid present in milk thistle (*Silybum marianum*) that has been used for hepatitis and cirrhosis. See Herbal medicine

***similia similibus curantur*** Law of similars, see there

**Beth Ann Simon** A young New York woman, who followed the Zen macrobiotic diet–formulated by George Ohsawa*—to the final stage and died in 1965 of malnutrition and dehydration; her death was a 'signal event' that drew attention to some of the negative aspects of the health food movement. See Kushi, Macrobiotics, Zen macrobiotic diet

*(1893-1966) who formulated the Zen macrobiotic diet, and macrobiotics–a cult-like movement and lifestyle that was popular in the US during the 1960s

**Simonton method** ALTERNATIVE ONCOLOGY A cancer therapy-enhancing method developed by a radiation oncologist, Oscar Carl Simonton, MD, and a psychologist, Stephanie Matthews-Simonton, which is based on the belief that psychological forces can have a significant impact on the pathogenesis of cancer; factors that are believed to increase susceptibility to cancer hinge on the inability to cope with feelings of anger and depression, which may be related to traumatic events

▶ **SIMONTON'S STEPS IN THERAPY**

- **COUNSELING** with a Simonton-trainee, the patient, and family members
- **MUSCLE RELAXATION**
- **VISUALIZING** the disappearance of the malignant cells

Simonton recommends the method only in conjunction with conventional anticancer therapy; it requires a highly motivated patient who is trained in the technique. See Cancer-prone personality, Healing visualization, Imagery and visualization, Psychoneuroimmunology, Unproven methods for cancer management

Note: The consensus of consultants at Memorial Sloan-Kettering Cancer Center and the Mt Sinai Medical Center (both in New York), was that, although in its more positive aspects, the SM may increase patient comfort and ability to deal with cancer, there is no scientific evidence that psychological and psychosomatic factors alter its course (*Am Can Soc, Files on 'Unproven Methods of Cancer Management, Sept 1981*)

***Sinapsis alba*** Popularly known as white mustard, see there

**single remedy** HOMEOPATHY The prescribing of a single homeopathic remedy to treat a condition. Single remedies are commonly used by well-trained and experienced homeopaths to treat constitutional conditions. See Constitutional disease, Homeopathic remedy, Homeopathy

**sinigrin** A glucopyranoside present in horseradish (*Cochlearia armoracia* or *Alliaria officinalis*) which, in the presence of water, converts to mustard oil, and is used as a general tonic.

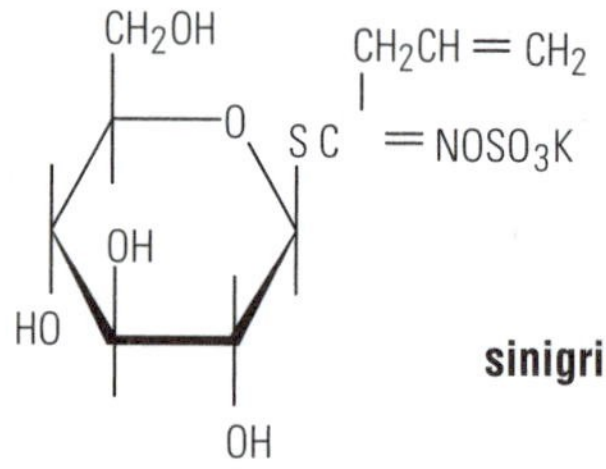


**sinigrin**

See Herbal medicine, Horseradish

**Sister Aimee** see McPherson, Aimee Semple

**'sitter'** ALTERNATIVE PSYCHOLOGY A BRETH* technique practitioner who creates a sacred and supportive environment, in which the client can release the effects of emotional and physical trauma and limiting thought patterns (*Raso, 1994*). See BRETH technique, High touch

*Breath Releasing Energy for Transformation and Healing and/or Happiness

**sitting Zazen** An ancient Zen Buddhist practice, in which an individual sits for hours with the legs crossed in a meditative pose

**sitz bath** NATUROPATHY A technique in which the pelvis and lower abdomen are immersed in water in a seated position (German, *sitz*, seat); in health spas, a common sitz bath is a tub that maintains the water at high temperatures at one end, and at low temperatures at the other end*; the individual switches back and forth several times (ie bottom hot-feet cold, followed by bottom cold-feet hot); less commonly, sitz baths are taken in either cold water (usually less than one minute) or hot water (from 3 to 10 minutes). Sitz baths are believed to be useful for treating gynecologic complaints including pelvic inflammatory disease and dysmenorrhea, as well as prostatitis, constipation,and other gastrointestinal disorders. See Hydrotherapy

*This is known as an alternating or contrast sitz bath

**The Six Evils** The Six Excesses CHINESE MEDICINE Those forces of nature (cold, dampness, dryness, fire, heat, and wind) which, when extreme, or when occurring out of season, can cause disease; according to the construct of traditional Chinese medicine, The Six Evils are external causes of disease; this contrasts with Western thought, which views pathogens, electromechanical, and biochemical forces as primary causes of disease; each of The Six Evils can also be internal, as in internal dampness caused by excessive consumption of various beverages. See Traditional Chinese medicine, Yin, Yang

**The Six Excesses** The Six Evils, see there

**Six Flavor Tea** *Liu wei di huang* CHINESE MEDICINE An herbal tea that is thought to enhance the immune system, and possibly be an adjuvant in cancer therapy. See Chinese herbal medicine, Black tea, Green tea, Tea; Cf Unproven methods for cancer managment

**The Six Healing Sounds** CHINESE MEDICINE A series of vocalizations combined with postures, which are believed to cool and cleanse the corresponding Chinese organ. See Twelve vital organs, Toning

**SKCF** PHARMACOGNOSY A sulfated alkaloid extracted from brown sea algae (*Sargassum*

*kjellmanianum*) that stimulates the immune system and may have antileukemic activity; it is not approved for sale in the US (*Jpn J Exp Med 1984; 54:143*). See Chinese herbal medicine

**Skeffington method** Vision therapy, see there

**Skinner, Burrhus Frederic** An American psychologist (1904–1990) who was the leading exponent of the behaviorism school of psychology, which explains human and animal behavior as a direct response to external stimuli; his pivotal work, *Science and Human Behavior*, was published in 1953. Skinner spent most of his professional life at Harvard. See Behavioral intervention

**skinnerian** PSYCHOLOGY *adjective* Pertaining or referring to the theories delineated by BF Skinner (1904–1990), which is understood to mean conditioned responses to highly controlled environments. Skinner's construct of behavior has fallen somewhat out of favor, as humans, being sentient beings, do not generally respond in a simplistic cause-and-effect manner to environmental cues. See Behavioral intervention, Skinner; Cf Pavlovian

**skullcap** *Scutellaria lateriflora*, blue pimpernel, blue skullcap, helmet flower, hoodwort, mad dog skullcap, mad dogweed, madweed, Virginia skullcap HERBAL MEDICINE A perennial herb that contains flavonoids, glucosides (eg scutellarein), bitter principles, iridoids, tannins, and volatile oil; it is antispasmodic, digestive, sedative, and a nerve tonic, and has been used for anxiety, depression, headaches, insomnia, premenstrual syndrome exacerbated by stress, and withdrawal from substance abuse TOXICITY Skullcap should not be used when driving or when operating heavy machinery as it causes drowsiness; in excess, skullcap may cause convulsions; it was formerly used for rabies and seizures. See Herbal medicine

**sky full of stars** Gutu kola, see there, *Hydrocotyle asiatica*

**sleep** SLEEP DISORDERS Rest resulting from a natural suspension of voluntary bodily functions and consciousness; good sleep hygiene is regarded as a good habit, which enhances the immune system, and is beneficial for common colds, cardiovascular disease, longevity, recuperation from injuries, and increased productivity. See Good habit; Cf Bad habit, Poor sleeping hygiene

**sleep apnea syndrome** Ondine's curse A condition clinically defined by frequent episodes of sleep apnea, hypopnea, and symptoms of functional respiratory impairment; it is potentially life-threatening, and has been associated with daytime hypersomnolence, motor vehicle accidents, and cardiovascular morbidity and mortality in the form of hypertension, stroke, and myocardial infarction; it is more common in the obese and in heavy snorers; 2% of middle-aged females and 4% of middle-aged males meet the criteria for sleep apnea syndrome (*N Engl J Med 1993; 328:1230*) PATHOGENESIS Marked alveolar hypoventilation during sleep (despite normal blood-gas levels while awake) due to a failure of autonomic ventilation, resulting in sleep apnea, cardiac arrhythmias, and hypertension. Sleep apnea primarily affects the severely obese (due to tonsillar hyperplasia, relative micrognathia and central apnea, with loss of the ventilatory drive in the medulla), but may follow bilateral cervical cordotomy used to control intense midline or perineal cancer-related pain (by severing the spinothalamic tract through a ventrolateral incision into the second cervical segment), or may rarely occur in infants; primary hypoventilation is secondary to a loss of central nervous system chemoreceptor response, which affects men aged 20 to 60. See Narcolepsy, REM sleep

Note: Ondine was a mythological water nymph who exhausted her human lovers; according to one victim, '*....all of the things my body once did by itself, it does now only by special command...I have to supervise five senses, two hundred bones, a thousand muscles...a single moment of inattention, and I forget to breathe...he died, they will say, because it was a nuisance to breathe*'—J Giraudoux, *Ondine*, 1939

**sleep deprivation** SLEEP DISORDERS A general term for inadequacy of sleep at the appropriate time. See Poor sleeping hygiene, Sleep disorders, Sleep-onset insomnia

Sleep deprivation has been blamed for the near meltdown of the Three-Mile Island nuclear power plant (1979), the explosion of the space shuttle *Challenger* (1986), and the *Exxon Valdez* oil spill (1989)

**sleep-onset insomnia** The inability to sleep at one's normal time of rest, which may be related to phobias, eg a childhood fear of wetting the bed, or deep-seated fears of dying while asleep. Sleep-onset insomnia may respond to improved sleep hygiene, meditation, autohypnosis, or herbal teas including chamomile, basil, catnip, hops, lemon verbena, and passionflower. See Poor sleep hygiene, Sleep

**the 'sleeping prophet'** Edgar Cayce, see there

**slipped disk** A popular term for any anatomic defect (bulge, degeneration, herniation, prolapse, rupture, or tear) in the intervertebral disk, which may or may not be accompanied by symptoms of nerve impingement including pain and paresthesias

**slippery elm** *Ulmus fulva, Ulmus rubra,* Indian elm, moose elm, red elm, sweet elm HERBAL MEDICINE A deciduous tree that contains mucilage, starch, and tannins. Slippery elm's *inner* bark is emollient and mildly astringent, and has been used internally for coughs, diarrhea, gastrointestinal inflammation, constipation, menstrual and renal dysfunction, and sore throat; it is used topically for burns, wounds, and dry skin TOXICITY Contact dermatitis to powdered bark. See Herbal medicine

**slippery elm** *Ulmus rubra*

**slops** NUTRITION A colloquial term for a bland diet that is easily digested, and based on bread and milk. See Bland diet; Cf Roughage

**SLR factor** Folic acid, see there

**small intestine meridian** Arm greater yang meridian ACUPUNCTURE A meridian that begins at the tip of the little finger, extends up the arm, across the back, up the neck, and ends at the ear. Stimulation of acupoints along the small intestine meridian are used for conditions affecting the face, head, and shoulders. See Acupuncture, (the) Twelve meridians

**smallage** Lovage, see there, *Levisticum officinale*

**smelling stick** Sassafras, see there, *Sassafras albidum*

**smooth strophanthus** *Strophanthus gratus* HERBAL MEDICINE A woody climbing evergreen native to West Africa, used by native herbalists as an anti-inflammatory and antiparasitic, and by native African hunters, due to its content of ouabain, which induces tachycardia; ouabain is used for cardiac arrest and hypotension. See Herbal medicine

**SMR feedback** Sensory-motor-rhythm biofeedback, see Biofeedback training

**snacking** see Nibbling diet

**snake blood** HEALTH FRAUD In Asia, fresh blood from snakes, particularly from venomous snakes, is believed to have various health benefits; it is ingested fresh, and supposed to cure certain diseases, revitalize the mind and body, reverse aging, and serve as an aphrodisiac; the practice is steeped in superstition and results in decimation of snakes and increase in the population of their prey, ie rats and mice (*Butler, 1992*). See Health fraud, Quackery, 'Snake oil'

**'snake oil'** HEALTH FRAUD Any substance that is claimed (without substantive evidence) to be effective in treating a wide variety of medical conditions; in the classic sense, these therapies were sold by 'quacks' in the late 1800s in the Wild West (US), before stringent controls of the pharmaceutical industry, which currently operates under the watchful eye of the FDA; 'snake oil' remedies contained alcohol, herbs, narcotics and various other, often inactive, ingredients; the current generation of 'snake oils' are based on various combinations of multivitamins, pseudovitamins, and amino acids. See FDA, Health fraud, Pseudovitamins, Quackery, Snake blood, Snake oil industry, Unproven methods for cancer management

**'snake oil' industry** HEALTH FRAUD A general term for the purveyors of products (and devices) that are alleged to treat or prevent disease, despite a virtual absence of data to support claims of efficacy or health benefits; the FDA, which reviews all health products, has forced the snake oil industry to operate in more subtle forms than was the norm in the pre-regulatory era; the current generation of 'snake oils' may be marketed using testimonials on their efficacy, and by making false medical claims or scientifically invalid statements about mechanisms of action (*Butler, 1992*). See FDA, Health fraud, Patent medicine, Pseudovitamins, Quackery, Snake blood, Snake oil, Unproven methods of cancer management

**snake root** Bistort, see there, *Polygonum bistorta*

**snake venom** HEALTH FRAUD The venom from poisonous snakes, eg water moccasins, cobras, coral snakes, rattlesnakes, and others, which is allegedly useful for arthritis, multiple sclerosis, and other conditions SIDE EFFECTS Blurred vision, headaches, vertigo, possibly death. See Health fraud, Quackery, Snake blood; Cf 'Snake oil,' Snake oil industry

**snakeweed** 1. Bistort, see there, *Polygonum bistorta* 2. Plantain, see there, *Plantago major*

**snapping hazel** Witch hazel, see there, *Hamamelis virginiana*

**snapping hazelnut** Witch hazel, see there, *Hamamelis virginiana*

**sneezewort** Arnica, see there, *Arnica montana*

**SNMT** Systematic nutritional muscle testing, see there

**snowball tree** Cramp bark, see there, *Vibur-num opulus*

**soap colitis** Chemical colitis, see there

**soapwort** 1. Cowherd, *Saponaria vaccaria* 2. *Saponaria officinalis*, bouncing Bet, bruisewort, lady's washbowl, latherwort, old maid's pink HERBAL MEDICINE A saponin-rich perennial which is diuretic, expectorant and laxative; it is used topically for skin conditions including acne, abscesses, eczema, and psoriasis, or as a skin cleanser TOXICITY Soapwort is a potent emetic and should not be ingested. See Botanical toxicity, Herbal medicine

**soaring crane *qigong*** Crane-style *qigong* ALTERNATIVE MEDICINE A simple and rapid form of *qigong* developed by Zhao Jin-Xiang. See *Qigong*

**social interaction** ALTERNATIVE PSYCHOLOGY The social dialogue that a person has with family, friends, colleagues, acquaintances, and others. See Companionship; Cf Social isolation

**social isolation** ALTERNATIVE PSYCHOLOGY The virtual absence of interaction with others, outside of that required to perform basic life functions including food shopping, transportation, work, and entertainment. Social isolation is common in the disabled, divorced, and elderly, and in those with mental disorders and alcoholism, and is a risk factor for both suicide and deaths from all causes (*Castleman, 1996*). See Anaclitic depression, Nuclear family; Cf Companionship, Extended family, Marriage bonus, Most significant other, Pet therapy, Social interaction

**SOD** Superoxide dismutase

**sodium nitrite** FOOD INDUSTRY A preservative and flavor-enhancing agent added to luncheon (bologna, salami) and other (eg ham and hot dogs) processed meats; heating or decreased pH (as seen in the stomach) causes sodium nitrite to combine with secondary amines forming nitrosamines, which are known to be carcinogens. See Food additives, Nitrates, Nitrites, Nitrosamines

**soft diet** A general term for any dietary regimen that is based on the consumption of soft foods (eg bananas, Jello™, oatmeal, soups, yogurt), and forbids the consumption

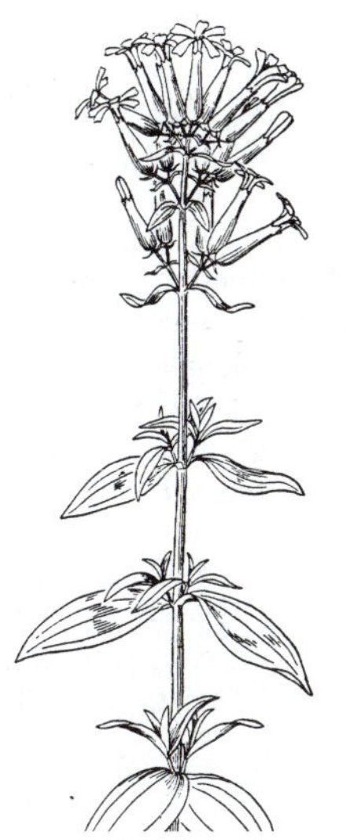

**soapwort** *Saponaria vaccaria*

of hard (eg carrots) or 'chewy' (eg broccoli, jelly beans, steak) foods. Soft diets have been recommended for treating TMJ (temporomandibular joint) syndrome. See Diet, TMJ syndrome; Cf Bland diet

**soft medicine** Alternative medicine, see there

***Solanum dulcamara*** *Dulcamara*, see there

**solar extraction** FRINGE MEDICINE—FLOWER ESSENCE THERAPY The process by which flowers are prepared for use in flower essence therapy; the flowers are collected from their native habitat at the precise moment of flowering, then placed for 2 to 3 hours in the sun in a closed clear glass container filled with distilled water, which allows the flower's oils and other main constituents to enter the water. See Bach flower remedies, Flower essence therapy

**solar plexus *chakra*** AYURVEDIC MEDICINE The third *chakra*, which governs the personal drives, is located below the heart, and associated with the adrenal glands and the color yellow. See Ayurvedic medicine, *Chakra*

***Solidage canadensis*** Popularly known as goldenrod, see there

***Solidage odora*** Popularly known as goldenrod, see there

**soliloquy** see Psychodrama

**Solomon's Seal** *Polygonatum officinale, P biflorum, P vulgare*, sealwort, true Solomon's seal, *yu ju* A perennial herb, the root of which contains allantoin; it is demulcent, nutrient, and tonic CHINESE MEDICINE It is believed by some Asian herbalists to be an aphrodisiac; it is used for anorexia, fractures, gastric ulcers, hypoglycemia, malnutrition, sexual dysfunction, and urinary frequency. See Chinese herbal medicine HERBAL MEDICINE Solomon's seal has been used in Western herbal medicine as an antiemetic and hemostatic, effects which are uncertain; it may be applied topically for wounds and skin ulcers. See Herbal medicine

**soluble fiber** Water-soluble fiber CLINICAL NUTRITION Any of a number of indigestible fibers that are concentrated in certain foods, eg fruits, dried beans, legumes, guar gums, barley, psyllium, and oat cereals. Soluble fiber increases the stool bulk and decreases LDL-cholesterol. See Bran, Dietary fiber, Oat bran

Note: A 5-10 g increase of soluble fiber in the diet translates into ± 5% decrease in serum cholesterol, plasma LDL-cholesterol and apolipoprotein B, and lesser reductions of HDL-cholesterol and apolipoprotein AI (*N Engl J Med 1993; 329:8OA*)

**Soma bodywork** Soma Neuromuscular Integration™, see there

**Soma Neuromuscular Integration™** Soma bodywork ALTERNATIVE MEDICINE A system of deep tissue bodywork, developed in the 1960s and 1970s by Dr BM Williams, in which the client is educated in body awareness; the therapy is believed to improve posture and breathing in asthmatics, reduce stress, and increase the flow of movements. See Bodywork; Cf SomatoEmotional Release™

**somatic dysfunction** Disease OSTEOPATHY A term used by osteopaths for a defect in structure and/or function, which can be diagnosed by identifying tenderness, asymmetry, restricted motion, and tissue texture changes; according to the osteopathic construct, somatic dysfunction occurs when painful stimuli impact on the vertebral column and spinal cord and sensitize them to other stimuli; as a result, the blood supply and neuromuscular transmission in the sensitized segments of the vertebral column and spinal cord are compromised. See Osteopathy, Somatic dysfunction

**Solomon's Seal** *Polygonatum biflorum*

**somatic education** Hanna somatic education, see there

**somatics** Hanna somatic education, see there

**SomatoEmotional Release™** BODYWORK A therapeutic system developed in the 1970s and 1980s by Drs JE Upledger and Z Kami, which is based on the posit that the physical forces absorbed during an injury will either dissipate–in which case the body can heal itself, or be retained–in which case the body will be forced to adapt; the adaptive response consists of surrounding the physical force with a pocket of energy, which Upledger and Kami term an 'energy cyst,' which impedes the healing process, and ultimately itself becomes a cause of disease and dysfunction. See Bodywork, Energy cyst; Cf Soma Neuromuscular Integration™

**son-before-the-father** Colt's foot, see there, *Tussilago farfara*

**sorcerer** PARANORMAL PHENOMENA A shaman in the Middle Ages who sold cures, spells, and hexes. See Shaman, Shamanism; Cf Neo-Shamanism

**sotai** Sotai therapy, sotai treatment BODYWORK A form of bodywork developed in the 1980s by a Japanese physician, Keizo Hashimoto, which is believed to harmonize respiration, digestion, physical and mental activity; in the sotai construct, disease can only be cured by the powers of nature in the form of vital energy; the liver meridian plays a central role in the flow of vital energy; anecdotal reports suggest that sotai may be effective for arthritis, cardiac arrhythmias, cirrhosis, colds, depression, diabetes, dyspnea, edema, fatigue, gastrointestinal complaints including constipation and diarrhea, hangover, hypertension, insomnia, migraines, neuralgias, scoliosis, sinusitis, failing vision, whiplash, and other conditions. See Bodywork

**sotai therapy** Sotai, see there

**sotai treatment** Sotai, see there

**soul** A term defined by Alexander Lowen as '*...the sense or feeling in a person of being part of a larger or universal order*.' (*Raso, 1994*)

**Sound Probe** FRINGE MEDICINE A proprietary device that delivers pulsed sonic waves at three alternating frequencies, which is claimed to destroy any living organism (bacteria, fungi, parasites, viruses) that is not in resonance with the body; it may be used in conjunction with the Light Beam Generator, which is believed to eliminate waste products from tissues (*Alternative Medicine, Future Med Pub, 1994*). See Energy medicine, Light Beam Generator

**sound therapy** ALTERNATIVE MEDICINE The use of sound as a therapeutic modality, which is linked to the release of hormones and other factors–including the so-called harmonic factor. Sound therapy is reported to affect physiologic parameters, including breathing and heart rate, blood pressure, and neuromuscular tone, and may be useful in Alzheimer's disease, in hospice environments for the terminally ill, in childbirth, dentistry, and psychotherapy (*Alternative Medicine, Future Med Pub, 1994*). Some sound therapists use handheld devices to apply the sound waves directly to the body surface, a practice of uncertain efficacy. See Biofeedback training, Cymatics, Harmonic factor, Music therapy, Toning; Cf Dance therapy, Pet therapy, Recreational therapy

**sound wave therapy** 1. Cymatics, see there 2. Sound therapy, see there

**sour trefoil** Wood sorrel, see there, *Oxalis acetosella*

**'South pole energy'** see Imaginetics

**Southampton Diet** ALTERNATIVE NUTRITION A dietary regimen published by an American psychiatrist, Stuart Berger; the centerpiece of the Southampton diet is the division of comestibles into 'happy foods' that produce 'positive neurotransmitters,' and 'sad foods,' which produce 'negative neurotransmitters;' in his first book (*The Southampton Diet, Simon & Schuster, New York, 1981*), Berger regarded whole grains, dairy products, eggs, fish, leafy greens, fruits, and poultry as 'happy foods' that could be eaten ad lib; in his subsequent book (*Dr Berger's Immune Power Diet, New American Library, 1985*), these same foods were regarded among what he then termed the 'sinister 7' foods, which could cause immune damage. See Diet, 'Happy foods,' 'Sad foods'

**Southern jujube** Chinese jujube, see there

**southern pepper** Szechuan pepper, see there, *Zanthoxylum piperitum*

**soy foods** ALTERNATIVE NUTRITION Foodstuffs

(miso, soybeans, soy milk, textured vegetable protein, tempeh, and tofu) produced from soy (*Glycine hispida*) which are widely regarded as 'healthy foods'; they are high in protein and contain isoflavones, eg genistine as well as phytosterols and phytoestrogens, which may protect against cancer, particularly of the breast, as well as the colon and prostate; of all foods, soy is thought to be the most effective in reducing cholesterol, by as much as 25% (*Castleman, 1996*). See Healthy foods, Tofu

**spa** A health resort where one bathes in the water of a particular natural spring. See Health spa, Natural spring

**spagyrics** Plant alchemy, see there

**Spanish fly** 1. Blister beetle 2. *Cantharis*, see there

**Spanish spider** *Tarantula*, see there, *Lycosa tarantula*

**spearmint** *Mentha spicata* A perennial herb used as a carminative and tea; its effect as a medicinal herb is overshadowed by the more well-studied peppermint. See Herbal medicine, Menthol, Peppermint

**Specific Human Energy Nexus therapy** see SHEN therapy

**spell** MAINSTREAM MEDICINE Any period during which an individual is in a particular state, eg spell of hospitalization (hospital stay is widely preferred), spell (bout or period) of sickness PSYCHIATRY A trance-like state in which a person allegedly communicates with dead persons, or various (non-mineral, non-grain) spirits, most often in a culture-specific context, most common among African Americans and those from the southern US; the importance lies in its being misconstrued as a psychotic episode (*DSM-IV*)

**spicy food** NUTRITION A comestible that is marinated in and/or contains chili peppers, mustards with horseradishes, curry or other spices that evoke a desired intraoral sensation that crosses pain with pleasure; when intense, the response to spicy foods may elicit an autonomic nervous system response, including diaphoresis and arrhythmias; the most commonly used 'spicy' condiment is hot pepper containing capsinoids[1]; 'hot' mustards owe their gustatory effects to horseradish, the active ingredient of which is isothiocyanate;[2] it is unclear whether spicy foods are carcinogenic[3]. See Seder syncope, Sushi syncope

[1]Which in mild hot (chili) sauce contains nordihydrocapsaicin and N-nonanoic acid (synthetic vanillylamide); moderate hot sauce contains homodihydrocapsaicin; very hot sauce is high in capsaicin and dihydrocapsaicin, which is effective to dilutions of 1:100 000 [2]A component of wasabe, a mustard used to season Japanese food, and in religious ceremonies [3]Capsaicin is mutagenic by the Ames assay (a bacterial screen for carcinogens) and may cause colon cancer in rats; oxidized capsaicin also binds to and inactivates the 'j' form of cytochrome P-450 enzyme, which is thought to activate certain mutagens, including nitrosamine and polycyclic aromatic hydrocarbons; on the other hand, capsaicin is also an anti-oxidant, and may have anti-carcinogenic properties. Spicy foods have been traditionally denied to ulcer-prone individuals, although jalapeños placed in direct contact with the gastric mucosa cause neither ulcers nor hemorrhage

**spearmint** *Mentha spicata*

**spinal adjustment** CHIROPRACTIC The main type of treatment provided by chiropractors; the most common adjustment techniques used in chiropractic are the high-velocity, low-force recoil thrust and the rotational thrust. See Chiropractic, Recoil thrust, Rotational thrust, Spinal misalignment

**spinal balancing** A type of craniosacral balancing that focuses on the vertebrae (*Raso,*

*1994*). See Chiropractic

**spinal manipulation** Spinal adjustment, see there

**spinal misalignment** CHIROPRACTIC An alteration of the vertebral column that may cause an intervertebral disk to compress a nerve root and produce pain. Spinal misalignments may respond to spinal adjustment. See Chiropractic, Spinal adjustment

**spiramycin** ALTERNATIVE PHARMACOLOGY An antibiotic that is similar to erythromycin, which has been used to treat cryptosporidiosis in patients with AIDS (*Fox, 1996*). See AIDS therapy

**spirit** PARANORMAL PHENOMENA A nonmaterial entity that usually does not exist on the physical plane of existence, but rather in the 'spirit world'; the 'unauthorized' presence (ie trespassing) of a spirit on this plane of existence in a place is termed 'haunting,' and when present in a person is termed 'possession' PHARMACOLOGY A solution containing a volatile substance, usually understood to be alcohol PSYCHOLOGY A term defined by Alexander Lowen as '...*the life force within an organism manifested in the self-expression of the individual*.' (*Raso, 1994*)

**spirit diagnosis** Psychic diagnosis, see there

**spirit guide** PARANORMAL PHENOMENA A spirit (non-material entity) of a doctor, from another plane of existence, who is believed to speak through a psychic (or spiritual) healer on this plane of existence, and provide him with the information needed to treat patients. See Cayce, Plane of existence, Psychic diagnosis, Psychic healer

**spirit healer** Psychic healer, see there

**spirit surgery** Psychic surgery, see there

**spiritual healer** Psychic healer, see there

**spiritual healing** Faith healing, see there

**spiritual psychology** ALTERNATIVE PSYCHOLOGY An eclectic mental health philosophy which has components of anthroposophy, archetypal psychology, and Jungian psychotherapy. Cf Humanistic psychology

**spiritualist healer** Psychic healer, see there

**spiritual healing** Psychic healing, see there

**spirulina** Blue-green algae FRINGE NUTRITION A product obtained from blue-green algae; it is alleged to be a rich source of vitamins A and $B_{12}$, protein, minerals, and neuropeptides, which it is not; it has been promoted as an appetite suppressant and mental and physical stimulant; it has been claimed to be useful in treating alcoholism and other addiction disorders, allergies, Alzheimer's disease, arthritis, depression, diabetes mellitus, fatigue, headaches, herpes, jet lag, mood swings, obesity, warts, and a host of other conditions SIDE EFFECTS Gastrointestinal complaints including bloating and diarrhea, throat irritation and fatigue may occur if there is a high concentration of saxitoxin in the spirulina

**spleen and pancreas meridian** Leg greater yin meridian ACUPUNCTURE A meridian that begins at the great toe, extends up the leg, crosses the front of the body, and ends above the armpit. Stimulation of acupoints along the spleen meridian are used for reproductive, urinary and gastrointestinal tract conditions. See Acupuncture, Meridian, Twelve meridians

**splenopentin** Thymopoietin III FRINGE ONCOLOGY A pentapeptide that is a nonspecific immune stimulant, which increases the number of neutrophils and macrophages; it is believed to be useful for treating the leukopenia of patients whose bone marrow has been partially destroyed by chemotherapy or radiotherapy (*Moss, 1992*). See Unproven methods for cancer management

Research efforts on splenopentin have been undertaken outside of the US–Author's note

**sports drink** Performance drink A generic term for a beverage used to quench thirst in those participating in various sports-related activities, which provides a boost in energy and/or builds muscle mass; water, sugar, salt, and potassium are core constituents common to all SDs

▶ **SPORTS DRINKS, TYPES OF**

- **TRUE ISOTONIC DRINKS** These replace fluid and electrolytes lost during lengthy exercise
- **CARBOHYDRATE DRINKS** These contain glucose polymers and are intended to replenish energy reserves during and after exercise
- **PROTEIN DRINKS** Also known as Amino acid drinks These are commonly made of whey, a bovine milk product, and are

used to help recuperate fatigued or overly stressed muscles (*New York Times 7 Dec 1994; C6*) See Hydrotherapy, Water

**sports massage** ALTERNATIVE MEDICINE A type of contemporary Western massage that addresses the specific needs of an athlete; although sports massages are based on Swedish massage techniques, other techniques are often incorporated, including cross-fiber friction massage, deep compression massage, and trigger point therapy; other physical modalities, eg hydrotherapy, and use of heat and cold temperatures may be required to address acute musculoskeletal injuries. Sports massages may be performed during training, or before or after a sports event, with the intent of enhancing performance, or promoting healing after an injury. See Massage, Traditional European massage; Cf Deep tissue massage, Manual lymph drainage massage, Neuromuscular massage, Swedish/Esalen massage

**spotted alder** Witch hazel, see there, *Hamamelis virginiana*

**spotted thistle** Blessed thistle, see there, *Cnicus benedictus*

**spring fever** A colloquial term for a constellation of mental changes, eg brightened moods, positive attitude, and general joie de vivre, which accompanies the longer, sunnier days of spring. See Heliotherapy; Cf Bright light therapy, Seasonal affective disorder

**spring water** HYDROTHERAPY Water obtained from a natural spring, which may be bottled and sold to the public, or in which a person bathes for alleged therapeutic benefits; if the spring is hot, the waters may be high in certain minerals, eg calcium, magnesium, potassium, sodium, sulfur and others. See Health spa, Hydrotherapy, Mineral water, Natural spring

**sproutarian** A person whose diet consists largely of sprouted seeds, fruits, and raw vegetables. See Diet, Macrobiotics

***srotases*** AYURVEDIC MEDICINE Passageways in the body through which cleansing and elimination of waste products occur. See Ayurvedic medicine

**square stalk** Figwort, see there, *Scrophularia nodosa*

**squawroot** 1. Black cohosh, see there, *Cimicifuga racemosa* 2. Blue cohosh, see there, *Caulophyllum thalictroides* 3. *Cynomorium coccineum*, see there

**squill** *Urginea scilla* HERBAL MEDICINE A perennial herb that contains cardioactive glycosides; it is diuretic and expectorant, but is highly toxic TOXICITY Arrhythmias, convulsions, diarrhea, heart block, nausea, vomiting, and possibly death. See Botanical toxicity

**squill** *Urginea scilla*

**St** Abbreviation for Saint, see there

**stagbush** Black haw, see there, *Viburnum prunifolium*

**stage fright** Performance anxiety. see there

**staghorn moss** *Lycopodium clavatum*, see there

**standardized meal** A generic term for a meal that has specified quantities of carbohydrates, fats, and proteins, which is used to evaluate absorption and digestion. See Diet

**staphage lysate** Lincoln therapy ALTERNATIVE ONCOLOGY An immunostimulant formulated by RE Lincoln, MD, which consists of the supernatant of *Staphylococcus aureus* that has been lysed by bacteriophages. Staphage lysate evokes the production of interferons by activating macrophages; it is uncertain whether the lysate is, as Lincoln claimed, useful in treating respiratory and sinus infections or cancer *(Moss, 1992)*. See Coley's toxin, Unproven methods for cancer management

**Starchamber™** PARANORMAL PHENOMENA A 'visionary tool' claimed to be of use in balancing of the chakras (energy centers); it is purported to filter, focus, and amplify the living energy of any object. See Chakra balancing, Visionary tool; Cf Bio-Chromatic Integration Device

**starflower** Borage, see there, *Borago officinalis*

**star grass** Colicroot, see there, *Aletris farinosa*

**'starlight elixir'** PARANORMAL PHENOMENA A fluid used in cosmic vibrational healing, which according to one producer

'...uses a telescope with silver-coated mirrors. The light of a star is captured by suspending a quartz bottle filled with extremely pure water directly in front of the eyepiece. The telescope has a clock drive that enables the telescope to follow each particular star as it moves and keep it centered within the viewing field...Inert gases are used to eliminate the possibility of negative thought form contamination...' *(Raso, 1994)* see Cosmic vibrational healing

**star tulip** *Calochortus tolmiei* FRINGE MEDICINE-FLOWER ESSENCE THERAPY A floral essence that is believed to provide a sense of inner serenity and inner listening to higher powers. See Flower essence therapy

**starweed** Chickweed, see there, *Stellaria media*

**'starch blocker'** CLINICAL NUTRITION A crude bean-derived amylase inhibitor that was marketed as a means of allowing excess food consumption without gaining weight, a claim not corroborated by well-designed studies; the purified amylase inhibitor may be effective in improving glucose tolerance in diabetes mellitus (*Mayo Clin Proc 1986; 61:442*); Cf Sugar blocker

**starvation** CLINICAL NUTRITION A condition resulting from prolonged global deprivation of food, which occurs in abnormal environmental conditions, eg during war or famine, or in normal society through willful neglect of others, eg children, the handicapped or elderly by parents, family, care-givers or guardians, or by self-neglect in the elderly, mentally feeble, anorectics, or those who irrespective of means, choose to live in apparent poverty; without food and water, the body loses 4-5% of its total weight/day and few survive beyond 10 days; when water is provided, a starving person may survive up to 60 days CLINICAL Hypovitaminoses, malnutrition, decreased subcutaneous fat with thin, dry and hyperpigmented skin stretched over bone prominences, atrophy of organs, marked attenuation of the gastrointestinal tract, with an enlarged concrement-laden gallbladder. See Fasting

**starvation diet** Very-low-calorie diet A potentially dangerous permutation of a 'crash' diet that provides 300-700 kcal/day, which must be supplemented with high quality protein; given the risk of death by intractable cardiac arrhythmias, starvation diets should be limited in duration SIDE EFFECTS Orthostatic hypotension due to loss of sodium and decreased norepinephrine secretion, fatigue, hypothermia and cold intolerance, xeroderma, hair loss, and dysmenorrhea. See Diet

**starvation response** PHYSIOLOGY As caloric intakes decreases, the basal metabolic rate decreases to a minimum to conserve energy; when the calories become available at the end of the diet, the weight rapidly increases. See Diet, On-off dieting, Starvation, Starvation stools, Yo-yo syndrome

**starvation stools** Watery green feces that develop when a person is maintained on a clear-liquid starvation-type diet. See Starvation, Starvation diet, Starvation response

**staunchgrass** Yarrow, see there, *Achillea millefolium*

**steakhouse syndrome** A clinical complex caused by plugging of the lower esophagogastric sphincter with a large, poorly chewed bolus of food, usually meat, often steak, accompanied by intense epigastric pain that resolves spontaneously if the food passes into the stomach PREDISPOSING FACTORS Alcohol imbibition, edentulousness; Cf Cafe coronary, Sushi syncope

**steam decoction** *Yao lu* CHINESE MEDICINE A preparation of traditional Chinese medicinal herbs in which dried herbs are placed in water inside of a tightly sealed receptacle, and steamed, yielding a pure, potent, and rapidly-acting extract termed medicinal dew (*yao lu*). See Decoction

**steam inhalation therapy** Inhalation HERBAL MEDICINE A form of hydrotherapy in which an individual breathes deeply from a pot or kettle filled with a boiling infusion of various herbs. Steam inhalation therapy loosens viscid bronchotracheal mucus, and is believed by its advocates to be useful for various upper respiratory complaints, especially in children. See Hydrotherapy

**Steiner School** See Anthroposophical medicine

**stellaria** Lady's mantle, see there, *Alchemilla vulgaris*

***Stellaria media*** Popularly known as chickweed, see there

**step 1 diet** CARDIOLOGY An abbreviation of a series of 9 dietary recommendations from the Nutrition Committee of the American Heart Association which states that the total fat consumption should be less than 30%

Note: The diet is regarded by some authors as ineffective in preventing cardiovascular disease (*New York Times 25 April 1995, pC1*)

***Sterculia urens*** Karaya tree, see there

***Stevia rebaudia*** Sweet herb, see there

**stevioside** A glycoside present in sweet herb (*Stevia rebaudiana*), a plant native to South America, which is 300-fold sweeter than granulated sugar, which is of interest to diabetologists, as it reduces blood sugar. See Sweet herb; Cf Artificial sweetener

**stickwort** Agrimony, see there, *Agrimonia eupatoria*

**sticky-willie** Cleavers, see there, *Galium aparine*

***Stillingia sylvatica*** Popularly known as queen's delight, see there

**Still, Andrew Taylor** The founder (1828-1917) of osteopathy. See Osteopathy

The amount of formal medical training that Still had is uncertain

**Stillman diet** CLINICAL NUTRITION A low-carbohydrate diet in which 46% of the calories are ingested as protein, 49% as fats, and 5% as carbohydrates. See Diet

**stimulant** HERBAL MEDICINE Nervine, see there

**stimulant laxative** Any of a number of laxatives (eg phenophthalein, sennosides) that is the evacuation of stools by increasing intestinal peristalsis. See Laxative; Cf Bulk-forming laxative, Stool softener

**stimulative music** MUSIC THERAPY Assertive or buoyant music used in music therapy, which may stimulate the rest of the body to join the rhythm, by evoking hand clapping, dancing, and other reactions. Stimulative music may have major changes in pitch, dynamics, or of rhythm, which usually is similar to that of an 'alert' heart, ie 70–90 beats/minute; styles regarded as stimulative include 'Big Band,' Dixie-land, Gospel, and others; Cf Sedative music

**stinging nettle** *Urtica dioica*, common nettle, nettle HERBAL MEDICINE A perennial herb that contains acetylcholine, formic acid, histamine, minerals, vitamins A and C; it is astringent, diuretic, tonic, and administered as an infusion, poultice, or applied topically (the leaves act as a counterirritant); it is used for arthritis, baldness, cystitis, diabetes, diarrhea, eczema, epistaxis, gout, hay fever, hemorrhoids, rheumatic complaints, and tuberculosis; it may be used under the supervision of a physician for congestive heart failure and hypertension TOXICITY Uncooked nettle may cause renal damage; the diuresis-related loss of potassium should be compensated for by increasing potassium intake; it should not be given to young children. See Herbal medicine

**stinking Benjamin** Birthroot, see there, *Trillium erectum*

**stinking Christopher** Figwort, see there, *Scrophularia nodosa*

**stinking nightshade** Henbane, see there, *Hyoscyamus niger*

**stinking Willie** Tansy, see there, *Tanacetum vulgare*

**stinkweed** Jimsonweed, see there, *Datura stramonium*

**stomach meridian** Leg sunlight yang meridian ACUPUNCTURE A meridian that begins at the side of the head, extends down the back, leg and foot to end at the second toe. Stimulation of acupoints along the stomach meridian are used for conditions affecting the head, stomach, and gastrointestinal complaints. See Acupuncture, Meridian, Twelve meridians

**stomachic** HERBAL MEDICINE An herb used to stimulate the secretion of gastric juices. Stomachics include avena (*Geum urbanum*), bitterwood (*Picraena excelsa*), columbo (*Frasera carolinensis*), and sweet flag (*Acorus calamus*) (*Trattler, 1985*). See Herbal medicine

**Stone, Randolph** An American (1890-1981) chiropractor (DC), osteopath (DO), and a naturopath (ND) who developed polarity therapy. See Polarity therapy

**stoneroot** *Collinsonia canadensis*, hardback, horse balm, horseweed, knobroot, knotroot, ox balm, richweed HERBAL MEDICINE A perennial herb that contains alkaloids, saponins, and tannins; it is analgesic, gently astringent, laxative, tonic, and has been used for diarrhea, headaches, hemorrhoids, and varicose veins. See Herbal medicine, Saponin, Tannin

**stoneseed** Gromwell, see there, *Lithospermum officinale*

**stool softener** A type of laxative (eg docusate) that add fluid to stools, softening. See Laxative; Cf Bulk-forming laxative, Stimulant laxative

**'straight' chiropractic** CHIROPRACTIC The method of chiropractic which is most in keeping with the fundamental principles delineated by the DD Palmer, the founder of chiropractic. Straight chiropractic is '...*a primary health care profession* (with) *responsibility and authority... limited to the anatomy of the spine and immediate articulations, the condition of vertebral subluxation, and a scope of practice which encompasses addressing vertebral subluxations, as well as educating patients and advising them about subluxations.*' (*Practice Guidelines for Straight Chiropractic: International Consensus Conference, Chandler AZ, 1992*). Straight chiropractors believe that it is inappropriate to use terminology that has other definitions for other health care professionals, as it lends to confusion, and thus prefer *analysis* to *diagnosis*, *adjustment* to *manipulation*, and eschew the terms *treatment*, *chiropractic medicine*, and *chiropractic physician* (*Collinge, 1996*); approximately 15% of chiropractors are 'straight practitioners'. See Chiropractic, Subluxation-based chiropractic; Cf Mixed chiropractic, Chiropractic malpractice

**strain-counterstrain therapy** BODYWORK A system of soft tissue manipulation developed by an American osteopath, Dr L Jones, which is intended to relieve pain; in strain-counterstrain therapy, the practitioner identifies hypersensitive or painful zones (trigger points) in the muscle and connective tissue which, when stimulated, 'refer' the sensation of pain to another region in the body; once the trigger points are identified, the practitioner moves the body into a position that relieves the referred pain, and maintains the position for 1 to 2 minutes; the body is then placed in its original position and the trigger point pressed; in most cases, the referred pain has disappeared. See Bodywork, Osteopathy

**'strength booster'** See Invalid claims of efficacy

**'strength enhancer'** See Invalid claims of efficacy

***Streptococcus lactis* R factor** Folic acid, see there

**stress management** Stress therapy A general term for the use of any psychological or manipulative maneuvers to reduce physical or emotional stress and tension. Stress management techniques include autogenic training, bio-feedback training, hypnosis, meditation, and progressive muscular relaxation–all are discussed elsewhere in this work. See Stress therapy, Stressor

**stress therapy** Stress management, see there

**stress posture** Any of a number of positional techniques (eg leaning back over a well-cushioned high chair or bending the knees and arching back until a snap or release ie felt), for physical and emotional release, developed by W Reich, which is intended to treat muscle and joint fatigue. See Reich, Reichian therapy

**stress-related disease** PSYCHOLOGY A general term for any medical condition caused by physical or mental stress. Stress-related conditions include bruxism, gastric ulcers, hypertension, insomnia, irritable bowel syndrome, migraines, tachyarrhythmias, tension headaches, and tics. Stress-related diseases may respond to biofeedback training. See Biofeedback training, Stress management, Stress therapy

**stress response** Flight-or-fight response, see there

**stress therapy** ALTERNATIVE PSYCHOLOGY A general term for any therapy intended to minimize emotional (eg art, dance, or other 'distraction') and physical (eg massage, reflexology) tension. Stress therapy is usually coupled to other modalities (eg meditation, psychotherapy, yoga) that help the patient deal more effectively with stressors

**stressor** A general term for any factor that increases a person's mental or physical stress; virtually all stressors can be described as related to environment, housing, or are personal, sexual, social, or related to work. See Stress management

**stretching** A massage technique that consists of pulling a body region or extremity away from its most anatomically neutral position. Stretching may occur with (active stretching) or without (passive stretching) the patient's help. See Massage therapy

**strict vegetarian** Vegan, see there

**stroke** NEUROLOGY A popular term for cerebrovascular accident

**strokes** Kudos PSYCHOLOGY A colloquial term for ego-gratifying verbalizations, eg compliments, bestowed on an individual by others. See Social interaction

**stroker** A colloquial term for a hand healer, see there

**structural bodywork** Awareness-oriented structural therapy, see there

**structural/functional/movement integration** Structural integration, see there

**structural integration** 1. Rolfing®, see there 2. Awareness oriented structural therapy, see there 3. Structural integration, Structural/functional/-movement integration BODYWORK Any of a number of techniques (see cross-references) that are intended to re-organize and 'integrate' '...*the body in relationship to gravity by manipulating soft tissues and/or correcting inappropriate patterns of movement*... (and)...*bring about more balanced use of the body and nervous system*...' (*Collinge, 1996*); central to structural integration therapies is the belief that the fascia is not a series of single units enveloping muscle, but rather an interconnected system that extends from the top of the head to the toes; according to this construct, disease occurs when the fascial system becomes indurated and constricted through the vicissitudes of emotional stress, habitual poor posture, repetitive use syndrome, trauma, and others; anecdotal evidence suggest that structural integration may be effective for allergies, arthritis, flat feet, gastrointestinal complaints, low back pain, sciatica, scoliosis, tennis elbow, TMJ (temporomandibular joint) syndrome, and other conditions. See Alexander technique, Aston patterning, Hellerwork®, Feldenkreis method, Ortho-bionomy, Rolfing®, Rosen method, Tragerwork®; Cf Massage therapy

**structural processing** 1. Rolfing®, see there 2. Awareness oriented structural therapy, see there 3. Structural integration, see there

**strychnine tree** *Strychnos nux-vomica* HERBAL MEDICINE An evergreen, the berries of which evoke muscle spasms, resulting in death; in low amounts, strychnine may be used to increase muscular activity, but can only be administered with extreme caution. See Herbal medicine HOMEOPATHY *Nux vomica*, see there

***Strychnos nux-vomica*** HERBAL MEDICINE Strychnine tree, see there HOMEOPATHY *Nux vomica*, see there

**strychnine tree** *Strychnos nux-vomica*

**stubwort** Wood sorrel, see there, *Oxalis acetosella*

***suan dzao ren*** Wild Chinese jujube, see there, *Ziziphus jujuba*

***suan zao ren*** Wild Chinese jujube, see there, *Ziziphus jujuba*

**subliminal persuasion** Subliminal therapy ALTERNATIVE PSYCHOLOGY A self-help philosophy intended to increase the awareness of subliminal (ie below the level of consciousness) auditory and visual stimuli and use them for behavior modification and as a therapy. Subliminal stimuli in the normal environment include 'white noise' in the form of birds singing, sounds of traffic, and conversation in a crowded room; in subliminal persuasion, positive messages can be 'dubbed' into 'white noise' sound tracks of pounding surf, rustling trees, and others, as a means of deeply penetrating a person's subconscious mind. Subliminal therapy may be successful in addiction (alcohol, drug, tobacco) disorders, pain relief, and stress management

Note: Outside of health care, subliminal messages have been used in businesses to reduce shoplifting and in movie theaters to increase the sales of snack foods

**subliminal therapy** Subliminal persuasion, see there

**'subluxation-based' chiropractic** CHIROPRACTIC A method of chiropractic that follows the fundamental principles delineated by the DD Palmer, the founder of chiropractic; for subluxation-based chiropractors, spinal adjustment is the central focus of their activity, regardless of whether they use ('mixed chiropractic') or do not use ('straight chiropractic') other therapeutic modalities; approximately 80% of chiropractors are subluxation-based practitioners. See Chiropractic, Mixed chiropractic, Straight chiropractic; Cf Medically-oriented chiropractic

**subtle touch massage** A form of massage therapy that '...*infuses touch with inspiration, which reaches into muscle tension to contact and melt away painful emotional holdings*.' (*Gottschalk Olsen, 1989*). See Massage therapy

**succory** Chicory, see there, *Chicorium intybus*

**succotash** CLINICAL NUTRITION A vegetable preparation containing corn (low in lysine, an essential amino acid) and beans (low in tryptophan, another essential amino acid), which in combination, provides adequate dietary protein

Note: Given its complementary nature, succotash is of use in developing nations

**succussing** Shaking HOMEOPATHY The process of shaking, in which homeopathic remedies are potentiated, through dilution with distilled water; each 10-fold reduction in concentrated substance increases its potency by one X. See Homeopathic remedy, Homeopathy, Mother tincture, Potentization

**Sufi healing** ALTERNATIVE MEDICINE A healing system integral to the Christi sect of Islam, based in Iran, which combines hypnosis, prayer chanting, fasting, herbal preparations, an ayurveda-like diet, postures, and the repeating of Arabic phrases

**sugar blocker** ALTERNATIVE NUTRITION A general term for an extract of an Indian plant, *Gymnema sylvestre*, which may reduce the absorption of dietary sugars, resulting in weight loss; although it is uncertain whether sugar blockers result in weight loss, chewing on the bitter leaves of *G sylvestre* may suppress the appetite; Cf Starch blocker

**sugar hypothesis** A term referring to the controversial assertion by many parents and some physicians, that refined sugars, eg sucrose, further stimulates hyperactive children; although physicians may recommend restriction of sugar in a child's diet, '...*it appears that any adverse effect of sugar is by no means as severe or as prevalent as uncontrolled observation and opinion would suggest. ...there is no evidence that sugar alone can turn a child with normal attention into a hyperactive child. The same applies to aspartame, which has also been suspected of causing behavior disorders in some children. Several studies reveal no systemic differences in blood glucose levels after ingestion of sucrose in children with attention deficit-hyperactivity disorder or those reported to be sensitive to sugar*.' (*N Engl J Med 1994; 330:355*). See Diet, Feingold diet

Some data has linked the consumption of sugar on an empty stomach to increased adrenalin, resulting in a decreased ability to concentrate; based on these findings (*S Boulware et al, Pediatrics Feb 1995*), sweet desserts after meals may be preferable to the consumption of sweet snacks between meals (*New York Times 15 March 1995; C11*)

**sugar pill** 1. A colloquial term, most commonly used by mainstream health professionals for a placebo (which often contains lactose), regardless of whether or not it contains sugar 2. A colloquial term used by lay persons for any oral agent used to control diabetes–popularly known as 'sugar'

**sugar substitute** CLINICAL NUTRITION Any of a group of carbohydrates, eg fructose, sorbitol and xylitol, that may be used to replace the usual dietary sugars (glucose and sucrose) in diabetics, as they don't require insulin for certain steps in their metabolism. See Artificial sweetener, Aspartame, Cyclamates

Note: The efficacy of sugar substitutes in reducing serum glucose is suboptimal as the diabetic liver converts a significant portion of fructose and its metabolites into glucose

**suggestive therapeutics** Suggestive therapy, see there

**suggestive therapy** Suggestive therapeutics, suggestive therapy work FRINGE MEDICINE A general term for any of a number of therapeutic philosophies that are based on positive thinking, and may incorporate *psi* healing, self-healing, healing suggestions, spinal adjustments, detoxification diets, and food combining. See Pealeism

**suggestive therapy work** Suggestive therapy, see there

**suggestive therapy zone procedure** Zone testing, see there

**sulfate of lime** Calcarea sulphurica, see Schüssler's tissue salts

**sulphate of potash** Kali suphuricum, see Schüssler's tissue salts

**sulphate of soda** Natrum sulphuricum, see Schüssler's tissue salts

**sulfated polysaccharide** AIDS Any of a family of compounds (eg carrageenan, isolated from red seaweed) that might be used to treat HIV infection. Sulfated polysaccharides are thought to prevent the interaction of epithelial cells and the release of HIV from infected lymphocytes, possibly by coating the cells and virus with a negative charge, making the cells mutually repulsive (*JAMA 1995 273:979*). See AIDS therapy

**sulfides** ALTERNATIVE PHARMACOLOGY Substances found in garlic and cruciferous vegetables that are thought to have anticarcinogenic properties; Cf Sulfites

**sulfites** FOOD INDUSTRY Sulfiting agents (sulfur dioxide, sodium sulfite, sodium or potassium bisulfite or metabisulfite) are food preservatives permitted for use in retarding the spoilage and discoloration of foods including coleslaw, potatoes and avocados served in public places (eg salad bars), or are added to packaged foods (eg canned seafood, grapefruit juice, beer, and wines); although well-tolerated by most people, up to 5% of asthmatics may be sensitive to sulfites (possibly related to low levels of sulfite oxidase), and respond to exposure with nausea, diarrhea, bronchospasm, pruritus, edema, hives, potentially anaphylactic shock and death. Some drugs used for asthma may contain sulfiting agents, potentially exacerbating the problem. See Food allergies, Pseudoallergies

**sulforaphane** Sulphoraphane An isothiocyanate phytochemical present in cruciferous vegetables (eg broccoli), which is thought to be anticarcinogenic. See Cruciferous vegetables

It stimulates the production of phase 2 enzymes that play a role in detoxifying carcinogens; in one rat study, sulforaphane reduced the incidence of mammary tumors induced by dimethylbenzanthracene (DMBA) (*Proc Nat Acad Sci (US) 12 April 1994*)

**sulfur** An element (atomic number 16, atomic weight 32.06), which is a an essential constituent of proteins and biologic compounds. Sulfur oxides are dangerous chemical pollutants derived from combustion of fossil fuels. See *Sulfur*

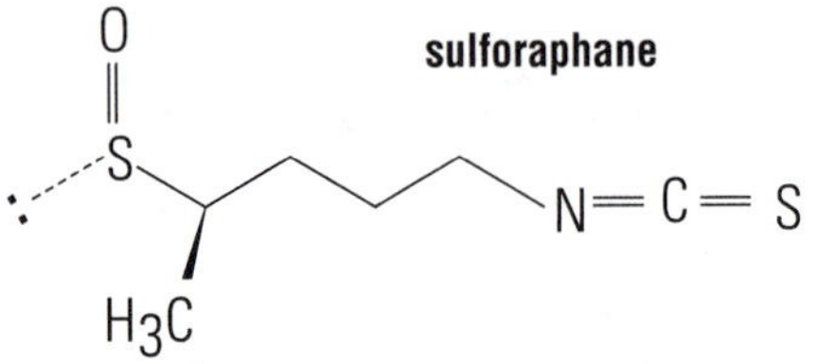

**sulforaphane**

O
S
N=C=S
$H_3C$

***Sulfur*** Brimstone, flowers of sulfur, sulphur HOMEOPATHY A remedy prepared from mineral sulfur, which is used primarily for skin conditions (eg candidiasis, diaper rash, dandruff, and eczema), but is also used for anal fissures, asthma, bursitis, cough with chest pain, depression, fever, headaches, hemorrhoids, indigestion, milk intolerance, low back pain, menstrual dysfunction, migraines, ocular inflammation, and burning vaginal discharges. See Homeopathy, *Sulfur* type

***Sulfur* type** HOMEOPATHY The *Sulfur* constitutional type of person is highly intelligent, creative, often unkempt, generous with time and money, and critical with minor details; they like fatty, sweet, sour, or spicy foods, alcohol, and vegetables WORSE Heat at night, prolonged standing, washing FEARS Failure, heights WEAKEST BODY REGIONS Circulation, mucosal membranes, skin left side of body. See Constitutional type, Homeopathy, Sulfur, *Sulfur*

**sulphur [BRITISH]** Sulfur, see there

**sundew** *Drosera*, see there, *Drosera rotundifolia*

**sunflower essence** *Helianthus annuus* FRINGE

MEDICINE-FLOWER ESSENCE THERAPY A floral essence said to provide a balanced sense of individuality and radiant spirituality. See Flower essence therapy

**sun force** *Pitta*, see there

**sunkfield** Cinquefoil, see there, *Potentilla reptans*

**sunshine treatment** Heliotherapy, see there

***suo yang*** *Cynomorium coccineum*, see there

**supernaturalism** The belief that forces exist outside of the plane of human experience, and these forces may affect the course of human events; Cf Naturalism

**superobesity** Morbid obesity, see there

**superoxide dismutase** An enzyme present in all aerobic organisms that catalyzes the reaction $O_2 \cdot^- + O_2 \cdot^- + 2H^+ = H_2O_2 + O_2$. SOD serves to protect the organism against the havoc caused by oxygen free radicals. See Antioxidant therapy FRINGE MEDICINE Concentrates of superoxide dismutase have been marketed for their claimed ability to reduce aging and degeneration of tissue, and as a therapy for cataracts, arthritis, and other age-related phenomena. See Antioxidant, Antioxi-dant therapy, Free-radical scavenger

**supplement therapy** ALTERNATIVE NUTRITION A general term for the use of vitamin and mineral supplements, usually supplied as multivitamins, to prevent disease. Supplements have been marketed for various purposes; they are claimed to improve the survival or outcome of patients with AIDS, and to be of use in allergies, Alzheimer's disease, arthritis, autism, cancers (bladder, breast, cervical, colon, lung, oral cavity), cardiovascular disease and myocardial infarcts, common cold, depression, fibromyalgia, hypertension (essential or pregnancy-induced), hypercholesterolemia, infertility, memory loss, migraines, osteoporosis, retinitis pigmentosa, tinnitus and many other conditions. See Multivitamin

**support group** SOCIAL MEDICINE A general term for those persons in an individual's 'circle,' upon whom the individual can call in times of personal crisis. Support personnel include children, spouses, siblings, friends, and others, who may help the person through the crisis, often by merely being 'good listeners';

▶ **SUPPORT GROUP BENEFITS**-per Yale surgeon, Bernie Siegel, MD

- Improve the quality of life
- Help patients cope better with stress and pain
- Become more open about 'taboo topics,' eg death, dying

See Companionship, Marriage bonus, Most significant other, Psychoneuroimmunology; Cf Social isolation

Note: While pets may provide companionship, and may, in effect, be a person's 'most significant other,' they cannot participiate in a support group, as their support is passive

**suppository** HERBAL MEDICINE A small cylindrical preparation of herbs in cocoa butter that is inserted vaginally or rectally for direct delivery of an herbal essence to the subjacent mucosa. See Herbal medicine

**suramin** ALTERNATIVE ONCOLOGY A derivative of urea said to be of use as a cancer therapy, based on its ability to block critical enzyme activity and the production of growth factors; it has been used for treating advanced malignancies including leukemia, and cancers of the adrenal cortex, breast, kidney, and prostate; its effect may be enhanced by adding tumor necrosis factor and/or interferon-gamma to the therapeutic regimen (*J Nat Cancer Inst 1992; 84:38*). See Astragalus, Unproven methods for cancer management

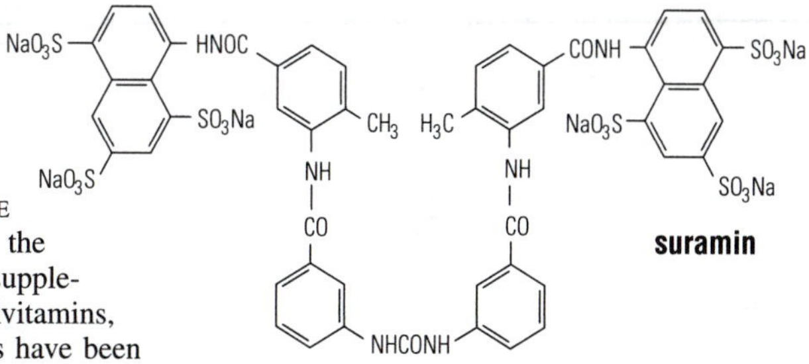

**suramin**

**surukuku** *Lachesis muta*, see there

**sushi** A Japanese raw fish delicacy that may be a vector for parasites, eg *Anasakis*,* which often affect sushi made from mackerel caught in early spring ENDOSCOPY Edema, gastritis, erosion CLINICAL Myalgia, abdominal pain RADIOLOGY Thread-like larvae may be seen in radiocontrast studies

TREATMENT Endoscopic removal

▶ **SUSHI, HOW TO KILL LARVAE (PARASITES)**

- **COOK** 60°C for 10 minutes
- **BLAST-FREEZE** –35°C for 15 hours
- **Freeze** –23°C for 7 days
- **FREEZING FOR 24 HOURS, SALTING, SMOKING, AND PICKLING DO NOT CONSISTENTLY KILL PARASITES.** See Sashimi; Cf Spicy foods

*Most commonly, *A simplex*, subfamily Anisakinae, order Ascaridida, as well as Contracecum, and Phocanema (*Pseudoterranova decipiens*) Notes: 1. Sushi fishes that commonly harbor parasites include ceviche (South American cod), green herring (Netherlands), Pacific pollack, Pacific red snapper and squid 2. Other raw fish dishes of parasitic potential include sashimi, gravlax, pickled herring, lomi lomi and lox (cold-smoked salmon) 3. Other organisms present in sushi include *Dioctophyma renale, Heterophytes, Strongyloides*, trematodes (paragonimiasis, *Nanophyetus salminicola*), *Metagonimus yokogawai*, cestodes (*Diphyllobothrium latum*), and *Vibrio parahemolyticus*

**sushi syncope** A transient condition caused by ingesting a bolus of wasabe, a 'hot' mustard (active ingredient: isothiocyanate) used to flavor sushi. See Horseradish, Seder syncope, Spicy food, Sushi; Cf Hot peppers

The index case had a transient myocardial infarct-like attack with diaphoresis, pallor, confusion, medical and vasomotor collapse (*JAMA 1987; 258:218c*)

***Sushrita Samhita*** AYURVEDIC MEDICINE A medical text written over 2000 years ago by an Indian surgeon that describes plastic surgery, autopsies, mending bones with nails, bloodletting, and manipulation of vital life energy by massaging 'energy points' (*marmas*) similar to those used in acupuncture. See Herbal medicine; Cf *Canon of Medicine*, *Charak Sambita*, *The Complete Herbal*, *De Materia Medica*, *Natural History*, *Nei Jing*, *Pen Ts'ao*, *Philosophy of Natural Therapeutics*, *Rigveda*, *Theatrum Botanicum*

**suterberry** Northern prickly ash, see there, *Zanthoxylum americanum*

**William Garner Sutherland** An American (1873-1954) osteopath who developed cranial osteopathy. See Cranial osteopathy

**swallowtail** Greater celandine, see there, *Cheledonium majus*

**swainsinone** ALTERNATIVE ONCOLOGY An alkaloid derived from *Astralagus oxyphysus* that is reported to inhibit proliferation and metastases in melanoma, an effect that may be related to increased NK (natural killer) cell activity *(Moss, 1992)*. See Astragalus, Unproven methods for cancer management

**Swank diet** FRINGE NUTRITION A diet for treating multiple sclerosis that was developed in the 1940s by an American neurologist, Roy L Swank; the Swank regimen eliminates saturated fats in meats and baked products, lard, butter, palm oil, coconuts, coconut oil, hydrogenated and partially hydrogenated oils, and chocolate; caffeinated beverages, olives, avocados, and sugar are limited; according to Swank's data, patients with multiple sclerosis who followed his diet for 20 or more years had fewer exacerbations of disease, fewer deaths, and less disability; their cholesterol fell by an average of 150 mg/dl, and thus had a lower risk of coronary artery disease. See Diet, MacDougall diet

**sweat lodge** ETHNOMEDICINE; HYDROTHERAPY A Native American permutation of sauna; the lodge consists of a dome-shaped hut made from bent willow branches covered by animal skins; hot rocks are placed inside, on which is poured water, which increases the humidity; once finished, the participants may jump into ice water, roll in the snow or rub sage on themselves to complete the experience. See Hydrotherapy

**sweating bath** See Russian bath, Sauna, Sweat lodge, Turkish bath

***swedan*** AYURVEDIC MEDICINE An ayurvedic cleansing massage that uses sesame oil to warm and penetrate the body. See Ayurvedic massage, Ayurvedic medicine

**Swedish/Esalen massage** ALTERNATIVE MEDICINE A type of massage therapy that is a hybrid of Swedish massage, which is brisk and focuses on kneading the muscles, and Esalen massage, which is slower, rhythmic, and hypnotic, and a form of mind/body medicine. Swedish/Esalen massage is said to relieve muscle tension, increase circulation, and evoke a state of relaxation and sense of well-being. See Massage therapy; Cf Esalen massage, Swedish massage

**Swedish gymnastics** ALTERNATIVE MEDICINE A series of (47) positions and (800) movements that stimulate the circulation, increase muscle tone, and balance the musculoskeletal system, which were described in the 1800s by PH Ling, as a means of stimulating and relaxing the body. See Exercise, Swedish massage

**Swedish massage** ALTERNATIVE MEDICINE A type of massage developed by a Swedish gymnast, Per Hendrik Ling (1776-1839) that manipulates muscles and joints. Swedish massage is designed to invigorate the body by stimulating the circulation, as well as promoting relaxation

▶ **TECHNIQUES, CLASSIC SWEDISH MASSAGE**

- **EFFLEURAGE** Slow, rhythmic, light and heavy pressure strokes from the fingertips, thumbs, knuckles, and palms, which may be combined with aromatherapy
- **FRICTION** Small circular pressure strokes from the fingertips, thumb pads, and palms, with the aim of freeing stiff joints, and enhancing the circulation in tendons and ligaments
- **PERCUSSION** Painless chopping and drumming motions delivered by the sides of the hands to 'fleshy' regions, eg the back, buttocks, and thighs
- **PÉTRISSAGE** Whole fascicles of muscles are grasped, squeezed, rolled and released, with the intent of stimulating the locoregional circulation, and relaxing contracted muscles
- **VIBRATION** Some do not regard vibration as part of the classic Swedish massage. This is a 'soft tissue' technique which entails vibrating movements, usually delivered by an electrical device

See Massage therapy, Physical therapy. Cf Swedish gymnastics, Swedish/Esalen massage

**Swedish Movement Cure** ALTERNATIVE MEDICINE A health care regimen developed in the 19th century by a Swede, PH Ling, which consists of gymnastics, movement therapy, and massage. See Massage therapy, Swedish gymnastics, Swedish massage

**sweet balm** Lemon balm, see there, *Melissa officinalis*

**sweet basil** Basil, see there, *Ocimum basilicum*

**sweet cane** Sweet flag, see there, *Acorus calamus*

**sweet cumin** Anise, see there, *Pimpinella anisum*

**sweet elm** Slippery elm, see there, *Ulmus rubra*

**sweet fennel** Fennel, see there, *Foeniculum vulgare*

**sweet flag** *Acorus calamus*, calamus, flagroot, myrtle flag, sweet cane, sweet grass, sweet root, sweet rush, sweet sedge A perennial herb, the rhizone of which contains mucilage, sesquiterpenes, and volatile oils (azulene, camphor, cineole, eugenol, pinene, and others); it is carminative, spasmolytic, and mildly sedative CHINESE MEDICINE In traditional Chinese medicine, sweet flag has been used for deafness, seizures, and vertigo. See Chinese herbal medicine HERBAL MEDICINE In Western herbal medicine, sweet flag has been used for fever, gastrointestinal complaints (eg dyspepsia and flatulence), menstrual disorders, toothache, and tobacco addiction TOXICITY Aserone, one of sweet flag's volatile oils, is carcinogenic; the FDA has classified the herb as 'unsafe'. See Herbal medicine, Botanical toxicity

**sweet goldenrod** Goldenrod, see there, *Solidago odora*

**sweet grass** Sweet flag, see there, *Acorus calamus*

**sweet herb** *Stevia rebaudiana* HERBAL MEDICINE A perennial herb, native to South America, that contains a glycoside, stevioside, that is 300-fold sweeter than granulated sugar. See Herbal medicine, Stevioside; Cf Artificial sweetener, Cyclamate, Sweet protein

**sweet jujube** Chinese jujube, see there, *Ziziphus vulgaris*

**sweet protein** A protein, eg monellin or thaumatin, that binds specifically to taste receptors, and evokes a sensation of sweetness that is 100 000 times sweeter than sugar on a molar basis. See Monellin, Thaumatin; Cf Artificial sweeteners, Aspartame, Cyclamates, Sweet herb

Note: Breeding plants to increase their sweetness has traditionally been empirical and based on increasing the sugar content, an approach that is often difficult, given the complexity of carbohydrate metabolism and the limited genetic palette of the plants being bred; genetic engineering

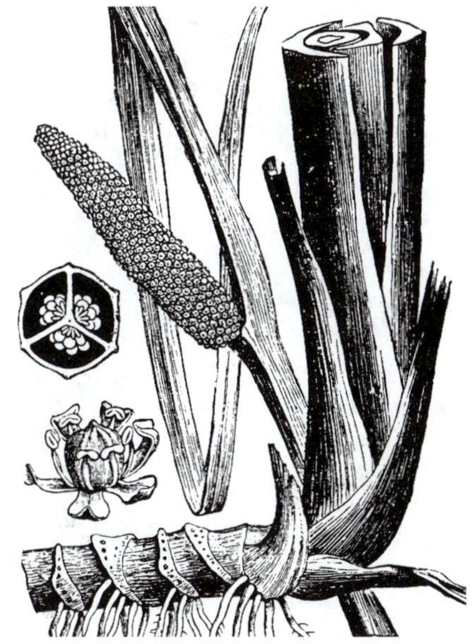

**sweet flag** *Acorus calamus*

of sweet proteins offers an alternative strategy for improving the flavor of edible plant products (*Bio/Technology 1992; 10:561*)

**sweet root** Sweet flag, see there, *Acorus calamus*

**sweet rush** Sweet flag, see there, *Acorus calamus*

**sweet-scented violet** Sweet violet, see there, *Viola odorata*

**sweet sedge** Sweet flag, see there, *Acorus calamus*

**sweet viburnum** Black haw, see there, *Viburnum prunifolium*

**sweet violet** *Viola odorata, V papilionacea*, blue violet, English violet, sweet-scented violet A perennial herb that contains flavonoids, methyl salicylate, odoratine, an alkaloid, saponins, and volatile oil; it is diuretic, expectorant, and mildly sedative CHINESE MEDICINE In traditional Chinese medicine, sweet violet has been used for inflammation and mumps. See Chinese herbal medicine HERBAL MEDICINE In Western herbal medicine, sweet violet is used internally for anxiety, hangovers, headaches, insomnia, sore throat, and respiratory infections, and topically for cracked nipples; it was once believed to be effective for skin cancer TOXICITY Nausea and vomiting. See Herbal medicine

**sweet violet** *Viola odorata*

**sweet weed** Marshmallow, see there, *Althea officinalis*

**sweetwood** Licorice, see there, *Glycyrrhiza glabra*

**sweet woodruff** *Asperula odorata*, waldmeister, woodruff A perennial herb that contains citric acid, coumarin, rubichloric acid, and tannins; it is diuretic and given as a digestive and hepatic tonic TOXICITY Vomiting and vertigo in large doses. See Herbal medicine

***Symphytum officinale*** Popularly known as comfrey, see there

**sweet woodruff** *Asperula odorata*

**sympathetic dominant** FRINGE MEDICINE A distinct type of individual based on an eclectic classification of humans proposed by Nicolas J Gonzales, MD; according to Gonzalez, the ancestors of sympathetic dominants inhabited warmer parts of the world including the tropics and subtropics, and were primarily vegetarians; he believes that these individuals have an efficient sympathetic nervous system, and should consume primarily vegetables (80% of total) in their diet (*Moss, 1992*). See Metabolic typing; Cf Parasympathetic dominant

**symptom-oriented construct** The tenet, held by mainstream medical practice, that an illness is most effectively treated by suppressing its symptoms; this is diametrically opposed to the approach espoused by alternative health care advocates, who ascribe to the belief that the underlying condition represents an 'imbalance' which, once brought into 'alignment,' will result in the disappearance of the symptom

**symptom picture** See Homeopathic symptom

**synchrony** A component of dance therapy which corresponds to movements that occur simultaneously in time and space. Synchronization with others in a dance therapy group is interpreted as social interaction and bonding. See Dance therapy; Cf Synchrony

**synergist** A practitioner of the Rubenfeld synergy method, see there

**synergy** A general term for any eclectic health system that combines breathing and energy techniques, hypnosis, imagery and visualization, and neurolinguistic programming, each discussed elsewhere in this work. See Rubenfeld synergy method

**synthetic coloring principle** Artificial dye, see there

**synthetic dye** Artificial dye, see there

**synthetic flavor** Artificial flavor, see there

***Syringa suspensa*** Weeping golden bell, see there, *Forsythia suspensa*

**syrup** HERBAL MEDICINE A solution of herbs in concentrated sugar, which preserves the concoction, and attenuates potentially bitter tastes, eg onions or garlic; honey is most commonly used; others, eg brown sugar and glycerine may also be used to produce syrups. See Suppository

**systematic desensitization** Exposure therapy PSYCHOLOGY A type of behavioral intervention for managing phobic disorders, in which the therapist has the client focus on his or her worst fear or aversion, while encouraging him or her to relax; the repeated cycling of tension and relaxation ultimately results in desensitization to the stressful stimulus. Systematic desensitization can also be used for anticipatory side effects, eg nausea associated with chemotherapy; a common format of systematic desensitization consists of muscle relaxation, coupled with visualizing each of a hierarchy of anxiety-provoking stimuli, ranging from the least to most unpleasant. See Anticipatory side effects, Aversion therapy, Behavioral therapy, Encounter group therapy, Flooding, Imaging aversion therapy, Relaxing imagery. Cf Relaxation training

**systematic nutritional muscle testing** A simplified permutation of the diagnostic component of applied kinesiology. See Applied kinesiology; Cf Applied Physiology

***Syzygium aromaticum*** Clove tree, see there, *Eugenia aromatica*

**Szechuan pepper** *Zanthoxylum piperitum*, *chuan jiao*, Japanese prickly ash, *nan jiao*, southern pepper CHINESE MEDICINE A deciduous tree, the fruit of which is carminative, diuretic, stimulant, and tonic; it is used for constipation, nocturnal emissions, and urinary frequency. See Chinese herbal medicine

**Albert Szent-Gyorgi** CLINICAL NUTRITION A Cambridge-trained Hungarian who identified vitamin C in 1934, for which he won the Nobel Prize

**table salt** *Natrum muriaticum*, see there

**taheebo** Pau d'arco, see there, *Tebebuia impetiginosa*

***t'ai ji*** *T'ai chi ch'uan*, see there

***t'ai chi ch'uan*** *Ch'ang ch'uan,* Meditation in motion, *tai ji, tai ji chuan, tai ji quan* A health-enhancing system of movements and exercise rooted in ancient Chinese philosophy and martial arts–*t'ai chi ch'uan* translates as '*the supreme ultimate fist*'; the movements are linked to each other in a fluid and continuous stream, likened by some to a slow ballet

▶ ***T'AI CHI CH'UAN*, FIVE ESSENTIAL QUALITIES**

- **SLOWNESS** To develop awareness
- **LIGHTNESS** To help in the fluidity of movement
- **BALANCE** To place the body in a relaxed position
- **TRANQUILITY** To create flowing continuity
- **CLARITY** To cleanse the mind of mental intrusions

The long forms (eg yang and wu) of *t'ai chi ch'uan* have over 100 linked movements, and may require up to 20 minutes each; *t'ai chi ch'uan* may be used to train individuals in dynamic balance, and reduce the risk of falls in the elderly (*JAMA 1995; 273:1341*); it is used in China for chronic diseases and stress, and is believed to be effective for anemia, gastrointestinal complaints, hypertension, rheumatic complaints, and for increasing a sense of well-being and exercise tolerance, and enhancing the immune system *RESOURCE: School of T'ai Chi Ch'uan, 5 E 17th St, 5th Floor, New York, NY 10003 ☎ 1.212.929.1981*

Note: The poetry in *t'ai chi ch'uan* is reflected in the names given to the movements, which include 'grasping the bird's tail,' 'parting the horse's mane,' and 'waving the hands like clouds.'–Author's note

***t'ai ji*** *T'ai chi ch'uan*, see there

***t'ai ji chuan*** *T'ai chi ch'uan*, see there

***t'ai ji quan*** *T'ai chi ch'uan*, see there

**taking the waters** See Health spa

**talking cure** Talking therapy, see there

**talking therapy** Talking cure, verbal therapy PSYCHIATRY A colloquial term for any form of psychotherapy patterned after the Freudian model of psychoanalysis. See Humanistic psychology, Psychoanalysis

***tan hsiang*** Sandlewood, see there, *Santalaum album*

***tan xiang*** Sandlewood, see there, *Santalaum album*

***Tanacetum vulgare*** Popularly known as tansy, see there

***tanden* breathing** A method believed to help a person access his body's *tanden* or *hara*, which is said to be the seat of the body's life energy or *ki*. See *Ki* breathing

***tang*** Decoction–Chinese medicine, see there

**tangerine peel** *Citrus reticulata, chén pi,* Mandarine orange peel CHINESE MEDICINE The aged rind of the mandarin orange, which is used for gastrointestinal complaints including bloating, diarrhea, indigestion, nausea, and vomiting; it may be used for mastitis and hypotension. See Chinese herbal medicine

**tangled vine** Chinese cornbind, see there, *Polygonum multiflorum*

**tannin** HERBAL MEDICINE Any of a family of compounds that react with proteins to produce a leathery coating on animal tissues (hence the term tanning), and give woods their brown, red, and yellow hues; tannins are anti-inflammatory, antimicrobial, and astringent. See Herbal medicine; Cf Flavonoids

**tanning** An activity in which a person lies under a UVA lamp for 15-30 minute periods to achieve a bronzed appearance; occasional cases report of benign[1], premalignant[2], or frankly malignant lesions[3] linked to 'recreational' tanning[4] occasionally appear in the medical literature (*N Engl J Med 1995; 332:1450*). See Tanning device

[1]Eg Keratoacanthoma [2]Eg Actinic keratosis [3]Basal cell and squamous cell carcinomas, and Bowen's disease [4]due to UVA light

**tanning device** PUBLIC HEALTH A bed or booth fitted with ultraviolet (UV) light bulbs that emit UV-A, and lesser amounts of UV-B radiation, homogeneously delivering maximal light in the minimum time

Note: The desire for a 'healthy' tan' has spawned an industry in the US that is serviced by poorly-regulated tanning salons; 58% of subjects in one study reported injury at commercial tanning facilities; 37% were injured at home, with 1. Eye damage–corneal injury 85%, unspecified 13%, and combined corneal and retinal injury 3%, 2. Skin damage–photoaging, 1st- and 2nd-degree burns, and 3. Degeneration of dermal blood vessels and 4. Nonspecific immune dysfunction

**tanning pill** Any of a number of over-the-counter agents (BronzGlo, Darker Tan, Orobronze) containing concentrated canthaxanthin, a beta-carotene-like substance which imparts a 'healthy' red-brown tint to the skin; when ingested in excess, canthaxanthin may evoke headaches, fatigue, weight loss, bruisability, allergic skin reactions, blurred night vision, hepatitis, and irreversible (ie potentially fatal) aplastic anemia (*JAMA 1990; 264:1141*). See Tanning, Ultra-violet light

**tansy** *Tanacetum vulgare, Chrysanthemum vulgare*, scented fern, stinking Willie HERBAL MEDICINE A perennial weed that contains bitter glycosides, citric acid, oxalic acid, terpenoids, and thujone, a volatile oil that is antispasmodic; it has been used as a vermifuge and for scabies, menstrual disorders, and rheumatic pain TOXICITY Thujone is a known central nervous system depressant, and should not be used in pregnancy. See Herbal medicine

**tansy** *Tanacetum vulgare*

**tantsu** Tant(ri shiat)su BODYWORK A component of bodywork tantra, in which an individual is placed on a dry surface, while the practitioner holds the client and squeezes, pulls, and manipulates various body parts. See Bodywork, Bodywork tantra; Cf Watsu

**tantra** AYURVEDIC MEDICINE A yogic method of healing through sexual activity

***tao* rejuvenation-*chi* self-massage** *Chi* self-massage, see there

**Taoist *chi nei tsang*** *Chi nei tsang*, see there

**Taoist five-element nutrition** FRINGE NUTRITION A dietary philosophy based on oriental astrology and the Chinese construct of the universe being composed of five elements–earth, fire, metal, water, and wood; in the Taoist diet, each of the five elements has corresponding foods with certain qualities and functions; it is believed that appropriately chosen food combinations serve to heal and optimize a person's energy levels (*chi*) and health. See Diet

**Taoist healing diet** Taoist five element nutrition, see there

**Taoist healing light technique** *Chi nei tsang*, see there

**Taoist *qigong*** Daoist *chi kung* A healing philosophy that incorporates morality training, and focuses on slowing aging, using *qigong* to develop a person's internal forces. See *Qigong*

**Taoist yoga** *Do-in*, see there

***tao-yinn*** *Do-in,* see there

**tapotement** Percussion, see there

***Tarantula*** *Lycosa tarantula, Tranatula hispanica*, Spanish spider, wolf spider HOMEOPATHY A homeopathic remedy prepared from parts of tarantulas (see illustration, page 360) that has been used for mental and physical hyperactivity, respiratory complaints, headaches, cardiovascular disease and anginal pain. See Homeopathy

***Tarantula hispanica*** *Tarantula*, see there

***Taraxacum officinale*** Popularly known as dandelion, see there

**tarragon** *Artemisia dracunculus*, dragon's mugwort, French tarragon HERBAL MEDICINE A perennial herb (see illustration, page 360) used primarily as a seasoning that contains essential oils; it was formerly used as a diuretic, appetite stimulant, and emmenagogue (data support-

***Tarantula*** *Lycosa tarantula*

ing these effects are weak); tarragon is little used by modern herbologists TOXICITY Tarragon's oil may be carcinogenic. See Herbal medicine

**tarragon** *Artemisia dracunculus*

**TART** OSTEOPATHY A mnemonic–tenderness, asymmetry, restricted motion, and tissue texture changes–for the most common findings in somatic dysfunction. See Osteopathy, Somatic dysfunction

**tartar root** American ginseng, see there, *Panax quinquefolius*

**tartrazine** FD&C Yellow No. 5, see there

**Tasmanian blue gum** Eucalyptus, see there, *Eucalyptus globulus*

**taurine** *adjective* Bull-like *noun* An amino sulfonic acid synthesized from L-cysteine, which is involved in the synthesis of bile acid; it is present in meats and dairy products and believed by some to be useful for hypertension

**tea** ALTERNATIVE NUTRITION An infusion* made from the dried leaves of the tea shrub (*Camellia sinensis*), which is consumed either black (largely preferred among Westerners) or green (preferred by Asians); tea is regarded as a health-promoting food given its content of polyphenols and certain antioxidants, which reduce the risk of cancer; tea may provide symptomatic relief from colds, nasal congestion, and asthma–given its content of caffeine and theophylline, from diarrhea–due to tannins, cardiovascular disease–due to polyphenols, osteoporosis–due to manganese, and tooth decay–due to fluoride. See Black tea, Green tea, Healthy foods; Cf Coffee, Maté

*To be technically correct, teas are hot water extracts of plants which the cognoscenti divide into three types: Beverage teas—which are steeped for 1 to 2 minutes; infusions—which are steeped for 10 to 20 minutes to extract the complete medicinal value; decoctions—which are boiled for 10 to 20 minutes

**teaberry** Wintergreen, see there, *Gaultheria procumbens*

**tea-drinker's disease** Theism A rarely reported condition induced by caffeine* CLINICAL Cerebrovascular congestion, excitement, and/or depression, pallor, cardiac arrhythmia, hallucinations, and insomnia (*JAMA 1887; 7:410*). See Caffeine, Coffee, Green tea

*Black and green teas both have caffeine

**tea pillow** CHINESE MEDICINE An herbal pillow used in traditional Chinese medicine that contains high mountain oolong tea; tea pillows are believed to promote sound sleep, enhance mental activity, and prevent hangovers from alcoholic binges. See Chinese herbal medicine, Herbal pillow

**tea tree oil** HERBAL MEDICINE An oil distilled or extracted from the tea tree (*Melaleuca* spp), which is antimicrobial due to the presence of terpineol; the oil is used topically for abrasions, acne, athlete's foot, bites, cuts, fungal infections and, for dogs, as a flea shampoo TOXICITY Mild skin rashes. See

Aromatherapy, Essential oil, Herbal medicine

**teasel** *Dipsacus sylvestris, hsu duan, jie gu,* mend bones, Venus basin, water thistle, wild thistle, *xu duan*; other species used include *Dipsacus asper* and *D japonicus* CHINESE MEDICINE A perennial plant, the root of which is analgesic, hemostatic, and tonic; it is used for breast tumors, fractures, low back pain, menstrual disorders, postpartum bleeding, sports injuries, increased urinary frequency, and Raynaud's phenomenon. See Chinese herbal medicine HERBAL MEDICINE Teasel was once used in Western herbal medicine as an anti-inflammatory, diaphoretic, diuretic, and digestive tonic, but is rarely used by modern herbologists. See Herbal medicine

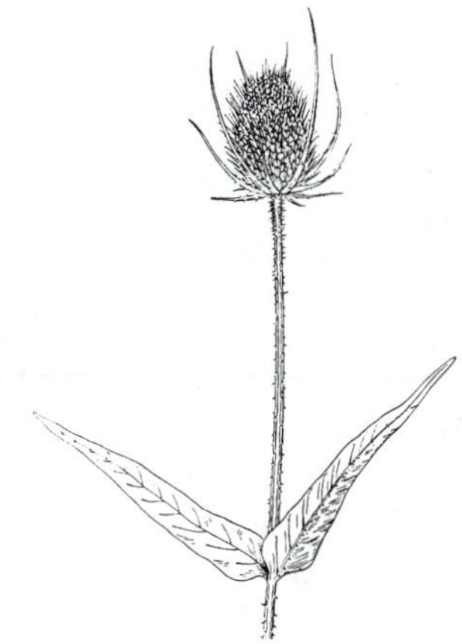

**teasel** *Dipsacus sylvestris*

***Tebebuia impetiginosa*** Pau d'arco, see there, *Tebebuia impetiginosa*

**telecytometry** see Telemedicine

**teleconsultation** The obtention of a medical consultation by either a non-medical consumer, or by a health care professional from a colleague on an electronic network (eg intranet, Internet)

Note: The format and legal issues on teleconsultation are evolving rapidly; it is unclear what (state or other) licenses will be required of a physician who lives in one state and provides legally binding medical opinions in another state (*Am Med News 24 April 1995 p1*)

**telediagnosis** MAINSTREAM MEDICINE A general term for any method of transferring diagnostic data, including consultations and diagnostic images—telecytology, telepathology, and teleradiology PARANORMAL PHENOMENA *Distant biological detection* A general term for any form of diagnosis that is alleged to be established at a distance from a patient, in absence of objective data or images, eg through clairvoyancy, or through the use of a pendulum or other device based on prinicples of uncertain scientific validity

**telekinesis** PARANORMAL PHENOMENA The alleged movement of an object through space without physically apparent cause, a phenomenon that is claimed to be accomplished by thought. See Paranormal, Telepathy

**telepathy** PARANORMAL PHENOMENA The alleged communication of thoughts and/or mental images by means other than those that can measured by physical senses and energy transmission. See Paranormal, Telekinesis

**teletherapeutics** 1. Prayer for the sick, see there 2. Absent healing, see there

**tell-time** Dandelion, see there, *Taraxacum officinale*

**tellurium** FRINGE ONCOLOGY A rare metallic element (atomic number 52; atomic weight 127.60) that may be combined with organic molecules to form organotelluriums, which are thought to have antibacterial properties and, some believe, may have anticarcinogenic effects *(Moss, 1992)*. See Unproven methods for cancer management

**temporomandibular joint dysfunction syndrome** TMJ syndrome, see there

**ten-fingered osteopath** Lesion osteopath OSTEOPATHY A colloquial term for an osteopath who adheres to the original precepts delineated by AT Still, in which all 10 fingers are used to perform hands-on osteopathic manipulation; Cf Three-fingered osteopath

**TENS** Transcutaneous electrical nerve stimulation, see there

**tepid bath** Neutral bath HYDROTHERAPY A bath in which the individual is immersed up to the neck in water that is slightly cooler than the body's normal temperature; tepid baths are believed to useful for anxiety, insomnia, and menstrual disorders. See Hydrotherapy

**terrain therapy** Dosed walking The incremental increase in the distance a person walks and the grade (steepness) of the terrain, a person should walk when he is recuperating from cardiac disease or other health problems;

terrain therapy may be part of the regimen at a health spa

**Teslar Watch** ENERGY MEDICINE A device worn on the wrist and claimed to minimize the effects of deleterious electronic pollution, particularly those of extremely low frequency (1 to 1000 Hz); the devise is said to enhance the immune system, and be useful for allergies, fatigue, and headaches (*Alternative Medicine, Future Med Pub, 1994*). See Energy medicine

**tetramisole** Levamisole, see there

**tetterwort** 1. Blood root, see there, *Sanginaria canadensis* 2. Greater celandine, see there, *Cheledonium majus*

**thalassotherapy** Sea water therapy, see there

**Thai massage** Thailand (medical) massage BODYWORK A form of bodywork intended to redistribute and unblock the impeded flow of energy that may occur at any of the 72,000 energy points along the 10 channels known as *sens*; Thai massage is more related to ayurvedic massage than to the Chinese or Japanese techniques, (for which 12 meridians are recognized); blocks in the flow of energy are linked to poor diet, lack of exercise, emotional stress, and physical injury, which result in pain and organ dysfunction; the Thai massage practitioner unblocks the *sen* points with finger, thumb, wrist, elbow, and foot pressure, in conjunction with passive or active musculoskeletal unit stretching, which may incorporate yoga-like contortions; once the blocked energy is allowed to reflow, the muscle tension decreases, and the malfunctioning organs heal themselves. See Bodywork, Massage therapy

**Thailand (medical) massage** Thai massage, see there

**thaumatin** NUTRITION A 207-amino acid heterodimeric protein produced by the African fruit, katemfe, *Thaumatococcus danielli* Benth which, like monellin, is a sweet protein that binds specifically to taste receptors, eliciting a sensation of sweetness that is 100,000 times sweeter than sugar on a molar basis, given that thaumatin has a greater affinity than dextrose for the sweet taste receptor (*Bio/Technology 1992; 10:561*). See Monellin, Sweet protein; Cf Artificial sweeteners

**THC** Tetrahydrocannabinol(s) Any of a family of compounds present in *Cannabis sativa* var *indica*, the major constituent of which is the $\Delta^1$-3,4-*trans* isomer, also known as $^9\Delta$-THC; (figure) the only FDA-sanctioned use of $^9\Delta$-THC is as an antiemetic, and then only in a highly selected group of patients, given THC's well-known hallucinogenic properties. See Marijuana

**THC**

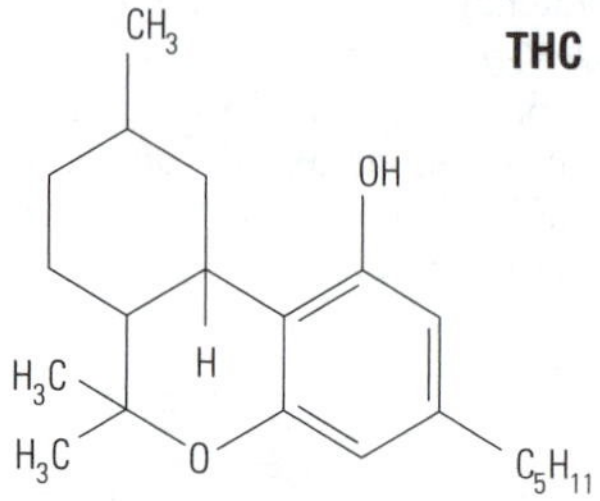

***Theatrum Botanicum*** HERBAL MEDICINE An 1800-page text written in the 1600s by the English herbalist, John Parkinson, which includes details on 3800 plants. See Herbal medicine; Cf *Canon of Medicine, Charak Samhita, The Complete Herbal, De Materia Medica, Natural History, Nei Jing, Pen Ts'ao, Philosophy of Natural Therapeutics, Rigveda, Sushrita Samhita*

**theism** Tea-drinker's disease, see there

**theotherapy** FRINGE PSYCHOLOGY A form of self-healing developed by Peter Lemesurier, in which a person identifies a Greek god or goddess whose personality profile characterizes what he/she wants to become; once identified, the individual attempts to adopt the deity's positive characteristics. See Self-healing

**therapeutic touch** FRINGE MEDICINE A contemporary form of non-oriental (energetic) massage that was developed in the 1970s by an American nurse, Dr Dolores Krieger; therapeutic touch is rooted in the ancient healing arts, and is based on the belief that the human energy field extends beyond the physical boundaries of the skin; in therapeutic touch, the practitioner's hands are held 2 to 4 inches above the patient's body, swept rhythmically over the skin, and attempt to sense local problems and 'treat' them, by acting as a conduit for 'universal energy' to the patient's body; therapeutic touch is said to be taught in 80 universities and practiced by up to 20,000 health professionals in US and elsewhere; is believed by its advocates to increase hemoglobin levels, reduce anxiety, headaches, and postoperative pain, stimulate the immune system, and may increase survival rates of premature infants. See Jin Shin Acutouch®, Laying on of hands, Nonoriental massage, Ruffled field; Cf Massage therapy, Oriental massage, Polarity therapy, Reiki, Structural integration, Touch for Health™

**therapeutic vomiting** AYURVEDIC MEDICINE Emesis used in ayurvedic medicine to remove toxins from the system. See Ayurvedic medicine

**theriac** THERAPEUTIC HISTORY A combination of herbs given by Roman physicians that contained opiates and antispasmodics; theriacs were administered as cure-alls. See Mithridates antidote

**thermic energy of feeding** PHYSIOLOGY A metabolic value that corresponds to the energy cost of feeding, which includes the energy expended in digestion, transportation, and storage of nutrients and metabolic products; the thermic energy of feeding represents approximately 10% of the total energy expenditure (*N Engl J Med 1995; 332:621OA*). See Total energy expenditure

**theta waves** NEUROLOGY 'Deep' brain waves that occur at 4 to 7 cycles/second (Hz), which are normally present in minimal amount in the temporal lobes; they are relatively more common in persons above the age of 60, and are intentionally induced in yoga and transcendental meditation. See Mantra, Meditation, Yoga; Cf Alpha waves, Autosuggestion therapy, Hypnosis, Silva mind control

**thiamin** Aneurine, antiberiberi factor, antiberiberi vitamin, antineuritic factor, antineuritic vitamin, thiamine, vitamin $B_1$ NUTRITION A water-soluble B vitamin that is present in various foods, including grains, yeast, and animal viscera; it is a necessary cofactor in alpha-keto decarboxylation, and links glycolysis with the Krebs cycle (tricarboxylic acid cycle)–the main source of energy in mammals, and is critical in the production of cyclic guanosine monophosphate; thiamin aids in digestion, improves tolerance to pain, is useful against psoriasis, shingles, seborrheic dermatitis, reduces gastric acidity; absence of thiamin results in malnutrition, softened bones, and mental depression. See Thiamin deficiency, Vitamins

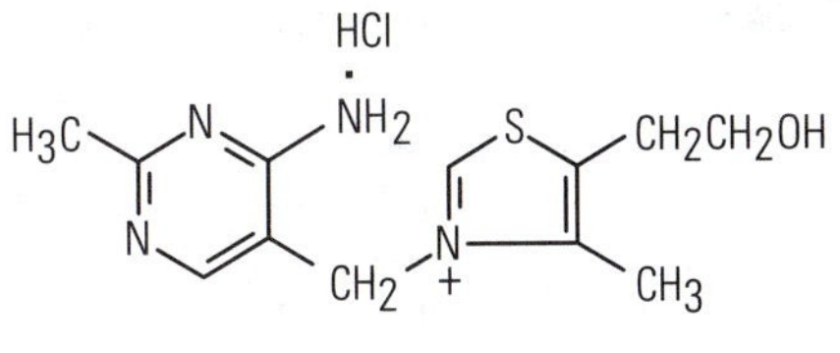

**thiamin**

**thiamin deficiency** A vitamin deficiency caused by a virtual absence of thiamin in the diet, resulting in beri-beri, which has various clinical forms: 'wet' beri-beri causes congestive heart failure; 'dry' beri-beri causes neurologic disease in the form of peripheral neuropathy and Wernicke-Korsakoff syndrome. See Thiamin

**thiamine** Thiamin, see there

**thickener** FOOD INDUSTRY A substance added to certain frozen foods, eg ice cream, that imparts a smooth, thick texture and prevents ice formation. See Food additives

**thioproline** EXPERIMENTAL ONCOLOGY A simple molecule composed of formaldehyde linked to cysteine, that is believed to have carcinoprotective activity, possibly due to the interruption of the cancer's blood supply, inhibition of DNA synthesis by the malignant cells, mopping up of carcinogenic nitrites, and formation of cyclic AMP, which cause the malignant cells to return to a state of metabolic normalcy (*Moss, 1992*). See Unproven methods for cancer management

**third eye *chakra*** AYURVEDIC MEDICINE The sixth *chakra*, which governs the mind, self, and perceptions, is located deep in the brain behind the eyes, and associated with the pituitary gland and the color indigo (deep blue). See Ayurvedic medicine, *Chakra*

**thistle** *Atractylodes chinensis*, *cang zhu*, mountain essence, *shan jing dze*, *tsang shu*; other species used in Chinese herbal medicine include *Atractylodes lancea*, *A lyrata*, *A macrocephala*, *A ovata* CHINESE MEDICINE A perennial plant, the root of which is antiemetic and antidiarrheal; it is used for gastrointestinal complaints, including anorexia, bloating, diarrhea, gastroenteritis, nausea, and vomiting, abdominal and chest pain, diaphoresis, edema, fatigue, joint, muscle, and pregnancy-related pain. See Chinese herbal medicine; Cf Milk thistle

**Thomson, Samuel** MEDICAL HISTORY An uneducated farmer and 'endowed healer' (1769-1843) from New Hampshire, who founded Thomsonianism; Thomson qualified the ancient Greek doctrine of disease being the imbalance of the four 'bodily fluids' (blood, phlegm, yellow bile and black bile) with the modifiers of hot and cold, wet and dry; he concluded that cold was the ultimate pathologic state and sought to cleanse the body, adding to the body's heat with 60 to 65 herbs, in particular lobelia (*Lobelia inflata*), a potent emetic; he advocated vomiting and purging for many conditions. See Thomsonianism

**thomsonianism** MEDICAL HISTORY-NATUROPATHY A health care movement founded by Samuel Thomson that was popular in the US in the early 1800s; the thomsonian movement was an early form of naturopathy;* Thomsonians were at variance with the physicians of the day who, in the pre-germ theory period of medicine, relied on bleeding, blistering, and purging to treat patients. See Alternative medicine, Germ theory, Homeopathy, Hot-cold syndrome, Naturopathy, Thomson; Cf Eclecticism, Graham system

*Thomsonianism celebrated its lack of education as anti-elitist, a reflection of the discontent that was fanned under President Andrew Jackson

**thoracic pump** OSTEOPATHY Lymphatic pump, see there

**thorowax root** Hare's ear, see there, *Bupleurum falcatum*

**thornapple** Jimsonweed, see there, *Datura stramonium*

**thorny burr** Burdock, see there, *Arctium lappa*

**thoroughwort** Boneset, see there, *Eupatorium perfoliatum*

**thousand-leaf** Yarrow, see there, *Achillea millefolium*

**the three-dollar doctor** Henry G Bieler, a physician from Pasadena, California, who advocated a simple, primarily vegetarian diet and fasting; Bieler advised Gloria Swanson, an American actress, who became a convert to the health movement; Bieler remained in obscurity (*Armstrong, 1991*)

**three-fingered osteopath** Broad osteopath OSTEOPATHY A colloquial term for an osteopath who incorporates drugs, surgery, hydrotherapy, and nonosteopathic techniques in his practice of osteopathic medicine; three fingers refers to the fingers needed to write a presciption; Cf Ten-fingered osteopath

**The Three Humors** Those three components which, according to the Tibetan construct of the universe, are present in all living things

▶ **THE THREE HUMORS, TIBETAN MEDICINE**

- **WIND**–linked to respiration and movement
- **BILE**–linked to digestion, skin complexion, and emotion
- **PHLEGM**–linked to joint mobility, skin elasticity, and sleep

See Tibetan medicine; Cf The Four humors

**three-leafed grass** Wood sorrel, see there, *Oxalis acetosella*

**thrifty genotype hypothesis** A hypothesis that ascribes survival advantages to the insulin resistance seen in a state of caloric deprivation that might prove diabetogenic in conditions of caloric adequacy or affluence. See Thrifty phenotype

The increase in obesity and non-insulin-dependent diabetes mellitus among Native Americans as they move to a more affluent lifestyle and diet favor the TGH, while it is challenged by the finding of opposite effects in those with a thrifty phenotype (*N Engl J Med 1994; 331:1226oA*)

**thrifty phenotype** An 'anemic' body type that results from malnutrition during fetal and early postnatal life, which leads to metabolic dysfunction as adults and insulin resistance; Cf Thrifty genotype hypothesis

**throat center *chakra*** AYURVEDIC MEDICINE The fifth *chakra*, which governs intelligence and communication, is located in the neck, and associated with the thyroid gland and the color blue. See Ayurvedic medicine, *Chakra*

**throat pack** NATUROPATHY An alternative therapy for various head and neck complaints that consists of placing warm wet toweling over the neck, which is believed by its advocates to be useful for tonsillitis. See Hydrotherapy

**throatwort** Figwort, see there, *Scrophularia nodosa*

**throwwort** Motherwort, see there, *Leonurus cardiaca*

**thuja** *Thuja occidentalis*, American cedar, arbor vitae, tree of life, white cedar, yellow cedar HERBAL MEDICINE A tree, leaves and twigs of which contain flavonoids, glycosides, mucilage, and volatile oils, primarily thujone, but also borneol, camphor, fenchone, limonene, myrcene, and pinene; thuja is anthelmintic, expectorant, and stimulates smooth muscle–it was used by Native Americans to stimulate menstruation; it has been used topically for skin infections and for rheumatic pain HOMEOPATHY A remedy used for brittle nails, caries, menstrual dysfunction, oily skin, warts 2. *Thuja orientalis,* see there

***Thuja occidentalis*** Popularly known as thuja, see there

***Thuja orientalis*** *Biota orientalis, B chinensis, bo dze ren, bo zi ren* CHINESE MEDICINE A conifer, the seeds of which are anti-inflammatory, astringent, emollient, expectorant, hemostatic, nutritive, sedative, and tonic; *T orientalis* is used topically for burns, and internally for cardiac arrhythmias, bleeding disorders, constipation, diaphoresis, fatigue, infertility, insomnia, malnutrition, and uterine bleeding. See Chinese herbal medicine; Cf *Thuja occidentalis*

**thujone** PHARMACOGNOSY A camphor-like essential oil present in the leaves of cedars (*Thuja occidentalis*) and many other trees; thujone has been used topically TOXICITY Internal ingestion is associated with convulsions. See Thuja, *Thuja orientalis*

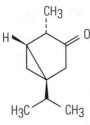

**thumb walk** NATUROPATHY Any of a number of manipulative methods, in which the tip of the thumb adjacent to the nail is used to move slowly (walk) along a particular musculoskeletal group in reflexology. See Massage therapy, Reflexology

**thyme** *Thymus vulgaris,* common thyme, garden thyme HERBAL MEDICINE A perennial herb that contains alcohols (eg linalool), flavonoids, saponins, tannins, and volatile oils including carvecrol, phenol, terpinine, and thymol; primarily a culinary seasoning, thyme is antimicrobial, antiseptic, antispasmodic, antitussive, carminative, diaphoretic, and an expectorant; it is used for colds, upper respiratory tract infections, and topically in liniments for rheumatic pain TOXICITY In excess, thyme can cause gastrointesinal discomfort; it should not be used in pregnancy. See Herbal medicine

**thymic factor** ALTERNATIVE ONCOLOGY Any of a number of polypeptides (eg thymopentin, thymopoietin, and thymosin) produced by the thymus, which orchestrate the maturation and growth of T cells; thymic factors evoked transient interest among experimental oncologists as a possible adjuvant therapy for cancer patients, an interest that has waned in the face of negative results *(Cancer 1985; 56:2771)*. See Unproven methods for cancer management

**thymopoietin III** Splenopentin, see there

***Thymus vulgaris*** Thyme, see there

**thyroid type** FRINGE MEDICINE An endocrine profile based on a hypothesis advanced by E Abravanel, MD, that each person has a dominant endocrine organ, and that each type of person craves and overeats certain foods in an effort to stimulate that organ; thyroid types are said to crave sweets, starches, and caffeine, which are believed to stimulate the thyroid gland; thyroid types may be sluggish and obese, and are advised to eat more meats and dairy products, which stimulate the other endocrine organs, and drink raspberry leaf tea. See Body type, Diet

**Tibetan medicine** *Emchi* A health philosophy that shares features of ayurvedic medicine; in this system, medicine is intimately linked to religious beliefs and incorporates the concepts of good and evil spirits, and fate; in Tibetan medicine, disease is regarded as

**thyme** *Thymus vulgaris*

an imbalance of the 'three humors' present in all living things; the diagnosis in Tibetan medicine is based on the analysis of the pulse, tongue, and urine, and on observation; the therapeutic tools used to restore the balance of the humors include herbs, massage, acupuncture and moxabustion, diets, rituals, and purification methods (*Shealy, 1996*). See The Three humors, Tibetan pulsing; Cf Ayurvedic medicine

**Tibetan pulsing** An ancient oriental healing art, which assumes that bio-electrical energy travels along the skeleton, and blocks in energy flow can be dissolved by stimulating pulse points and through the use of colors associated with specific organs; in Tibetan pulsing, diagnoses are established by eye-reading, and therapy is effected by bodywork. See Bodywork, Tibetan medicine

**Tibetan saffron** See (Tibetan) saffron

**Tibetan yantra yoga** Yantra yoga A Tibetan Buddhist permutation of *hatha* yoga characterized by continuous movement. See Hatha yoga

***tien ma*** *Gastrodia elata*, see there

***tien men dung*** Shiny asparagus, see there, *Asparagus lucidus*

**Tiger Balm** CHINESE MEDICINE A proprietary herbal ointment that is applied topically for various conditions including skin conditions, burns, bruises, and rheumatic complaints. See Chinese herbal medicine, Ointment, Powder-Chinese medicine

**tiger lily** *Lilium tigrinum* FRINGE MEDICINE-FLOWER ESSENCE THERAPY An essence believed to impart a sense of inner peace and cooperation, injecting feminine forces into social situations. See Flower essence therapy HOMEOPATHY *Lilium*, see there

**tiger's soul** Amber, see there

**tiger thistle** *Cirsium japonicum*, *da ji hua*, horse thistle, *ma ji*; other species used include *Cnicus japonicus* and *Cnicus spicatus* CHINESE MEDICINE A perennial herb, which is antihypertensive, hemostatic, and believed to calm the fetus in pregnancy; it is used for burns, colitis, hypertension, internal hemorrhage, morning sickness, and tuberculosis. See Chinese herbal medicine

**Tijuana** A city in northern Mexico that has been a destination for some patients seeking treatment of terminal cancer by unproven methods, which are offered in some clinicas (eg American Biologics Hospital, Bio-Medical Center[1], Centro Hospitalario Internacional del Pacifico[2], Contreras Hospital[3]) of 'alternative oncologists,' many of which are based on some form of 'metabolic therapy' (*Questionable methods of cancer management, Special communication, 13 June 1990, American Cancer Society*). See American Biologics Hospital, 'Metabolic therapy,' Unproven methods for cancer management; Cf Alternative medicine

[1]Where Hoxsey treatment is administered [2]Gerson therapy [3]Laetrile

**timonacic** Thioproline, see there

**tin** A metallic element (atomic number 50; atomic weight 118.69) present in trace amounts in nature; it has been linked to deficiency states in some plants and animals, but has no known physiological rule in humans. See Trace element; Cf Trace mineral

**tincture** HERBAL MEDICINE An alcohol-based (ethanol-brandy, gin, and vodka have been used) extract that contains an herb's essence, which is commonly mixed with water in a 50:50 ratio; tinctures have the advantage over other herbal preparations of a long shelflife. See Herbal medicine, Liniment

**tisane** HERBAL MEDICINE An herbal beverage, in which various parts of the plant are boiled as a tea for their medicinal effects. See Herbal medicine, Herbal tea

**tissue salts** Schüssler's tissue salts, see there

**tissue salts therapy** Schüssler's biochemic system of medicine, see there

**TM** Transcendental meditation, see there

**TM-EX** An organization of former disciples of the transcendental meditation movement, who became disenchanted therewith for various reasons. See Meditation sickness

**TMJ syndrome** Temporomandibular joint-myofascial dysfunction syndrome A complex neuromuscular disorder caused by dental malocclusion, possibly exacerbated by trauma, mental stress, and bruxism CLINICAL Nonspecific unilateral facial pain, masseter muscle spasms TREATMENT No therapy is consistently effective, but may include physical (moist heat) therapy, analgesics, soft diet, and surgery, eg high intracapsular condylectomy. See Soft diet

**tocol** A generic term for a group of 8 naturally occurring fat-soluble compounds with vitamin E activity; the most biologically active tocol is D-α-tocopherol. See Vitamin E

Tocols have a 6-chromanol nucleus bearing two methyl groups and a branched isoprenoid chain

**tocopherol** Vitamin E

**tofu** A cheese-like soy product that has been used as a low-fat meat surrogate. See Soy

**tongue diagnosis** CHINESE MEDICINE A part of the evaluation of patients by an acupuncturist, in which hues, types of coating, moistness, markings, and locations (see figure and key) and other changes are assessed. See Acupuncture, Chinese medicine

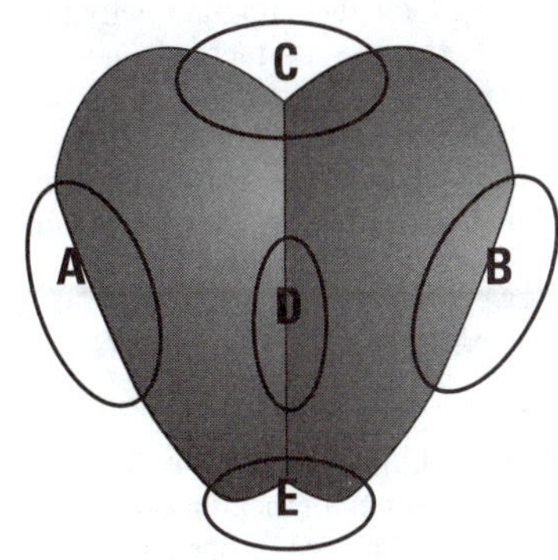


▶ **TONGUE REGIONS, CHINESE MEDICINE**

- **A**–Liver
- **B**–Gallbladder
- **C**–Kidneys
- **D**–Stomach
- **E**–Heart & lung

MAINSTREAM MEDICINE Although intense scrutiny of the tongue is not part of a routine physical examination, certain changes of the tongue may suggest systemic disease

▶ **TONGUE CHANGES, OBJECTIVE–MAINSTREAM**

- **CANDIDIASIS**–Red-rimmed white membranous flecks that are difficult to remove
- **DIPHTHERIA**–Gray-white membrane. Sweet odor
- **SCARLET FEVER**–White coating; reddened laterally
- **TYPHUS**–Gray-white coating; bright red laterally
- **UREMIA**–Bumpy brown coating

**tongue grass** Chickweed, see there, *Stellaria media*

**tongue-retaining device** A device that keeps the tongue in a forward position while a person is asleep, as a means of preventing obstructive sleep apnea (*Bricklin, 1976, 1983*). See Sleep apnea syndrome

**tonic** HERBAL MEDICINE See Nervine NON-WESTERN MEDICINE *noun* A medicinal preparation, usually of herbal origin (eg ginseng) that is used most commonly in traditional Chinese medicine and ayurvedic medicine; tonics are believed to be of use in building vital energy (*qi*); Cf Bitter

**toning** ALTERNATIVE MEDICINE A form of vocal or sound therapy, which consists of producing elongated vowel sounds and allowing them to resonate (eg '*ommmmmmmm*') through the body; toning was developed by Laurel Keyes and is believed by its advocates to reduce stress, balance the mind/body, and improve hearing and speech (*Alternative Medicine, Future Med Pub, 1994*), as well as promote healing, creativity, and vitality; toning is often used in conjunction with meditation and yoga. See Cymatic therapy, Harmonic factor, Meditation, Sound therapy

***toogi-toogi*** Massage, see Massage therapy

**toothache tree** Northern prickly ash, see there, *Zanthoxylum americanum*

**topotecan** ALTERNATIVE PHARMACOLOGY A compound derived from a Chinese tree (*Camptotheca accuminata*) which has potential as a chemotherapeutic agent (*Sci Am 1993; 268/1:142*)

**TOPS** (Take Off Pounds Sensibly) A group therapy diet plan created by Esther Manz in the 1950s. See Diet

**tormentil** Erect cinquefoil, see there, *Potentilla erecta*

**tormentilla** Erect cinquefoil, see there, *Potentilla erecta*

**Touch for Health™** ALTERNATIVE MEDICINE A proprietary form of applied kinesiology developed in the 1970s, by a Britton, B Butler, and an American chiropractor, Dr John F Thie, which is designed for lay people, who learn the technique through a short course; Touch for Health™ incorporates acupressure, sound dietary principles, muscle testing, and massage therapy. See Applied kinesiology; Cf Therapeutic touch

**Touch Research Institute** ALTERNATIVE MEDICINE An academic center created in 1991 by the University of Miami's School of Medicine, for basic and clinical research in the use of human touch as a therapeutic modality; the Institute is directed by T Field, PhD, and staffed by a multidisciplinary team of 40 resident and 30 visiting scientists; its current studies encompass a wide range of conditions, including child and spousal abuse and/or neglect, arthritis, asthma, chronic fatigue syndrome, cocaine babies, depression, diabetes, eating disorders, fibromyalgia syndrome, hypertension, HIV and the immune system, juvenile rheumatoid arthritis, pediatric dermatopathies, pregnancy, sleep disorders, spinal cord injuries, work-related stress, and others. See Office of Alternative medicine

**touch and relaxation technique** ALTERNATIVE MEDICINE A general term for any alternative therapy intended to increase the flow of life forces by manipulating soft tissues and muscles; these techniques include acupressure, Hellerwork, massage therapy, reflexology, Rosen method, Tragerwork, and others, discussed elsewhere in this work. See Relaxation technique

**total energy expenditure** PHYSIOLOGY A metabolic 'unit' that is the sum of a number of energy 'units'

▶ **TOTAL ENERGY EXPENDITURE–TEE**

- **RESTING ENERGY EXPENDITURE** 60% of the TEE
- **THERMIC ENERGY OF FEEDING** 10% of TEE
- **NONRESTING ENERGY EXPENDITURE** 30% of TEE

Maintenance of a reduced or elevated body weight is linked to compensatory changes in energy expenditures that oppose any shift in body weight that differs from the person's usual or baseline weight; these compensatory changes may explain the difficulty that obese subjects have in maintaining lower weights (*N Engl J Med 1995; 332:621OA*)

**'tower of bricks'** see Rolfing®

**toxemia** ALTERNATIVE MEDICINE The accumulation of toxins and metabolic wastes. See Colon therapy

Given the breadth of the definition of toxemia, some mainstream physicians believe that toxemia may be overdiagnosed and/or overtreated by alternative health providers

**'toxic core'** PSYCHIATRY A component or 'factor' hypothesized to increase cardiovascular mortality in type A individuals; 'type As' are angry, cynical, distrustful, and repress marked hostility towards others; clinical data suggest that over time, cardiovascular mortality is 4 to 7-fold greater in subjects with a 'toxic core' personality. See Negative emotions, Type A personality

**toxic emotion** PSYCHIATRY A general term for negative emotions such as stress and anger, which have an adverse effect on a person's mental, and possibly also, physical health

**TPIT** Trigger point injection therapy, see there

**trace element** Any of a group of metal ions present in minimal amounts in the environment, including arsenic, chromium, cobalt, copper, fluorine, iodine, manganese, nickel, selenium, silicon, tin, vanadium, zinc. See Trace mineral

**trace mineral** Any of a group of metal ions present in minimal (milligram or microgram) amounts in biological systems, which are reqired for their optimal activity; trace mineral enzyme co-factors play critical roles in the organization of molecules, membranes and mitochondria, trace minerals include chromium, cobalt, copper, fluorine, iodine, iron, manganese, selenium, silicon, vanadium,* and zinc

*It is unclear whether vanadium is essential; these minerals are maintained in a delicate balance between the Scylla of toxic excess, and the Charybdis of deficiency, which may induce metabolic failure, an event most common in total parenteral nutrition

**traditional Chinese medicine** The ancient Chinese method of health care, which is based on the balance of opposing, yet complementary forces, yin and yang, which are driven by the life force known as *qi*, that flows through the body along pathways known as meridians; traditional Chinese medicine places more emphasis on herbal medicine than on acupuncture, as the former allows a patient to treat himself for minor complaints; the tools used in traditional Chinese medicine are acupuncture, diet, massage, and medicinal herbs, eg astragalus, dong quai, ginseng, and others; traditional Chinese medicine is believed to be most beneficial for allergies, asthma, diabetes, gallbladder disease, gynecologic disorders, headaches, hypertension, systemic lupus erythematosus, and other chronic conditions (*Alternative Medicine, Future Med Pub, 1994*). See Acupuncture, Chinese herbs, Chinese medicine, The Eight Principles, Folk medicine, Herbal medicine, Homeopathy, Naturopathy

Note: A permutation of traditional Chinese medicine developed in communist China as means of integrating the large body of physicians trained in traditional Chinese medicine into the Western-style hospitals

**traditional European massage** MASSAGE THERAPY A generic term for any form of massage therapy that focuses on 'soft tissue' manipulation in the form of effleurage, friction, percussion (tapotement), petrissage, and vibration; the prototypic traditional European massage is the Swedish massage. See Massage therapy, Swedish massage

**traditional healer** Witch doctor ETHNOMEDICINE A person in various primitive societies, who uses long-established methods passed down from one healer to another, often from father to son, to treat a person suffering from various illnesses, many of which have psychological underpinnings; methods used by traditional healers include use of roots, fetish dolls, voodoo dolls, and the smoking out of a possessing spirit or spell (*Proc Roy Soc Med 1967; 60:1055*). See Ethnomedicine, Folk medicine, Healer, Shamanism, Traditional medicine

**traditional herbalism** Popular herbalism, see there

**traditional medicine** 1. A general term for any system of health care that has ancient roots, cultural bonds, trained healers, and a theoretical construct; traditional systems include ayurvedic medicine, ethnomedicine, shamanism, and traditional Chinese medicine 2. Mainstream medicine, see there

**Traditional Usui System of Natural Healing** One of two factions that practice Reiki, see there

**Trager approach** Tragerwork, see there

**Trager bodywork** Tragerwork, see there

**Trager mentastics** Mental gymnastics, mentastics ALTERNATIVE MEDICINE A set of self-guided mental and physical exercises that are 'synopses' of passive, individualized Tragerwork sessions, and used to link the mind and body for optimal performance. See Tragerwork

Tragerwork is a health-enhancing system of movement therapy that consists of dancelike movements intended to evoke sensations of freedom and lightness

**Trager psychophysical integration** Tragerwork, see there

**Tragering** Tragerwork, see there

**Tragerwork®** Trager approach, Trager bodywork, Trager psychophysical integration, Tragering ALTERNATIVE MEDICINE A structural integration system developed by an American physician, Milton Trager, which is intended to enhance the interaction between the body and mind, reawakening a sense of 'playfulness' in the client; Tragerwork releases deleterious 'holding patterns' of muscles through gentle, rocking massage; Tragerwork therapists use their hands and minds to communicate feelings of lightness and freedom (ie 'playfulness') to the client; the aided movement is followed by lessons in mentastics (mental gymnastics) involving dance-like movements, which enhances a sensation of lightness; Tragering is believed to be useful for asthma, autism, depression, emphysema, hypertension, low back pain, migraines, multiple sclerosis, muscular dystrophy, polio, neuromuscular diseases, pain, poor posture, sciatica, sports injuries, and to enhance athletic performance by increasing flexibility, mental control, responsiveness, and conservation of energy in movement. See Hook-up, Structural integration, Trager Mentastics; Cf Alexander technique, Aston patterning, Dance therapy, Feldenkreis method, Hellerwork, Massage therapy, Movement therapy, Ortho-bionomy, Rolfing®, Rosen method *RESOURCE: Trager Institute 33 Millwood, Mill Valley CA 94941 ☎ 1.415.388.2688*

**training** A generic term for deliberate goal-oriented practice, in a mental or physical activity, with the intent of bettering one's performance PHYSIOLOGY Training results in physiologic muscle hypertrophy, especially of the heart, increased skeletal muscle blood supply due to increased capillaries, and change in the proportion of slow- or fast-twitch muscle, depending on the type of training activity

Note: The neurologic changes that result from training are less well defined (*New York Times 11 October 1994; C1*)

**trance logic** ALTERNATIVE PSYCHOLOGY An altered mental state in which a person's normal capacity for critical analysis is suspended, and an increased level of logical inconsistencies are tolerated; trance logic opens a hypnotized individual to suggestion. See Hypnosis, Post-hypnotic suggestion, Trance state

**trance state** ALTERNATIVE PSYCHOLOGY An altered mental state in which the body is still or movements are jerky, the limbs are 'heavy,' the eyelids flicker due to rapid eye movements, the eyeballs roll upwards (as occurs when one is asleep), the eyes tear, the pupils dilate, and speech pattern changes. See Hypnosis

***trans* fatty acid** CLINICAL NUTRITION An unsaturated fatty acid prepared by hydrogenation, which is thought to raise blood cholesterol levels; *trans* fatty acids (TFAs) are not found in nature; minimal TFAs are present in animal fats; TFAs are abundant in margarines, frying fats and shortenings, and are formed when polyunsaturated fat-rich vegetable and marine oils and vegetable shortenings are 'hardened' by partial hydrogenation, producing fats with a firmness and consistency desired by both food manufacturers and consumers; TFAs comprise 6 to 8% of the daily per capita consumption of fat in developed nations; the most abundant TFA is elaidic acid and its isomers, which are 18-carbon molecules with one double bond; increased dietary TFAs result in increased total cholesterol and LDL-cholesterol and decreased HDL-cholesterol, and an increased risk of coronary artery disease (*N Engl J Med 1993; 329:1970c*); Cf *Cis* fatty acid, Fatty acid, Fish, HDL-cholesterol, LDL-cholesterol, Olive oil, Polyunsaturated fatty acid, Tropical oils, Unsaturated fatty acid

*In which the carbon moieties on the two sides of the double bond point in opposite directions

**transactional analysis** PSYCHIATRY A therapeutic modality developed in the 1950s by an American psychiatrist, E Berne, who had trained as a Freudian psychoanalyst; in contrast to the abstract construct of classical psychoanalysis, transactional analysis evaluates the communication that people have with each other, ie their daily transactions; the method is similar to Gestalt therapy, as the intent is to unmask a person's thoughts and emotions, but differs therefrom, as it is more structured, and focuses on the vehicles people use to avoid coming to terms with unpleasant realities; according to Berne's theory, people have 3 different ego states

▶ **BERNE'S EGO STATES**

- **CHILD EGO STATE** Occurs in times of stress; behavior and reactions to life situations are immature and inappropriate
- **ADULT EGO STATE** Stress is addressed in a mature fashion with understanding and use of problem-solving skills
- **PARENT EGO STATE** Situations are dealt with in a quasi-autocratic manner learned from parent figures

The ultimate goal of transactional analysis is to achieve what Berne terms 'social control,' so that situations are addressed as an adult. See Humanistic psychology, Psychoanalysis, Psychotherapy; Cf Gestalt therapy

**transcendental meditation** A form of meditation developed in the 1950s by Maharishi Mahesh Yogi, which consists of silently repeating a mantra for 10 to 20 minute sessions; TM has changed in philosophy from being mystical—and believed to serve as a vehicle for achieving nirvana and the extinction of the ego, to being popular—and believed to enhance mental and physical well-being, personal development, and social advancement. See Meditation; TM-EX

**transcutaneous electrical nerve stimulation** Electrotherapy ACUPUNCTURE See Electrical acupuncture ALTERNATIVE MEDICINE The passing of low-voltage electric currents through gel-coated rubber pads to various sites on the skin surface; anecdotal reports suggest that TENS may be effective for (recuperation from) childbirth or surgery, defects in circulation, lower back pain, sciatica, sports injuries, postpartum stress, urinary incontinence, and weight loss. See Energy medicine REHABILITATION MEDICINE A modality for controlling pain that utilizes low-level electric shocks to the skin; TENS effect is explained by the 'gate' theory of pain and is used to relieve pain of the lower back and neck, 'phantom' limb syndrome, and amputation stump pain. See Electrical acupuncture; Cf Biofeedback training

Note: In low back pain, TENS may be no more effective than a placebo (*N Engl J Med 1990; 322:1627; 323:1423c*)

**transference treatment** FRINGE MEDICINE A general term for any therapy based on the scientifically naive belief that human disease (or sin) can be transferred to animals, plants, or inanimate objects. See Pigeon remedy

**transformational bodywork** BODYWORK An eclectic health-enhancing system that incorporates aura balancing, *chakra* healing, integrative bodywork, and reiki, each discussed elsewhere in this work. See Bodywork

**transformational therapy** Past life/lives therapy, see there

**transpersonal counseling** Transpersonal psychology, see there

**transpersonal psychology** Transpersonal counseling

PSYCHIATRY A general term that encompasses various philosophies about the development of mystical, spiritual, and psychic experiences, which are the springboard for maximizing the human potential; transpersonal psychological therapies are intended to remove a person's 'mask,' which is believed to prevent a person from achieving his maximum personal potential. Some forms of transpersonal psychology (eg Sufism and Buddhism), are primarily religious philosophies; others (eg Jungian psychoanalysis, meditation, prayer, psychosynthesis, and Zen Buddhism), overlap formal and informal healing philosophies. See Psychosynthesis, Zen therapy; Cf Humanistic psychology, Near-death experience, Past life/lives therapy, Rebirthing therapy

**treatment-emergent** *adjective* Pertaining or referring to a symptom that appears only after a therapy has been initiated

**tree of life** 1. Lignum vitae, see there, *Guaiacum officinale* 2. Thuja, see there, *Thuja occidentalis*

**tree peony** *Paeonia moutan, bai liang jin, hua wang,* hundred ounces of gold, king of flowers, *mu dan pi, Paeonia suffruticosa* CHINESE MEDICINE A perennial shrub, the root epidermis of which is antipyretic, antiseptic, antispasmodic, diuretic, and tonic for the circulation; it is used for asthma, fever, headache, infections, internal hemorrhage, menstrual disorders, and muscle spasms. See Chinese herbal medicine

**tree willow** Evening primrose, see there, *Oenothera biennis*

**trefoil** Red clover, see there, *Trifolium pratense*

**trembling aspen** White poplar, see there, *Populus tremuloides*

**tretinoin** (all-*trans*-)retinoic acid A synthetic derivative of vitamin A used for acne, keratinization, and skin inflammation, which is believed to stimulate various cellular functions TOXICITY Skin blistering, crusting, headache, nausea, vomiting, and vertigo. See Vitamin A

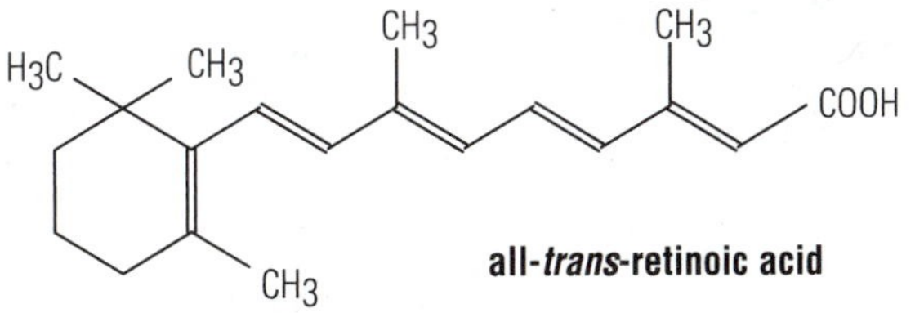

Note: Retinoic acid is the naturally occurring form of the fat soluble vitamin A, which is critical for the transportation of monosaccharides in glycoprotein synthesis, as occurs in the turnover of mucosal epithelia of the oral cavity, respiratory, and urinary tracts. See Retinal, Vitamin A

***Tribulus terrestris*** Caltrop, *ji li dze, ji li zi* CHINESE MEDICINE An annual herb, the fruit of which is alterative, nutritive, and tonic; it strengthens muscles and tendons, facilitates labor, purifies blood, and has been used for anemia, sexual dysfunction, malnutrition, increased urinary frequency, low breast milk production, poor vision, and tinnitus. See Chinese herbal medicine

**triceps skin-fold thickness** A value used to estimate body fat, which is measured on the right arm halfway between the olecranon process of the elbow and the acromial process of the scapula; normal, males 12 mm; females 23 mm; Cf Body-mass index, Mid-arm muscle mass, Obesity

**tridosha** AYURVEDIC MEDICINE The sum of the 3 *doshas*: *kapha*, *pitta*, and *vata* which, according to the ayurvedic construct, orchestrate a person's mental and physiologic functions, including metabolism and mind/body type. See Ayurvedic medicine, *Dosha*; *Kapha*; *Pitta*, *Prakriti*, *Prana*, *Vata*

**trifoliate orange** *Poncircus trifoliata*, also known as *Aegle sepiaria*, citrus shell, *Citrus trifoliata, ji ke, jih shih, zhi shi* CHINESE MEDICINE A deciduous tree, the resinous wood of which is antidiarrheal, diuretic, carminative, and expectorant; it is used for abdominal and chest pain, bloating, cholecystitis, diarrhea, and hemorrhoids. See Chinese herbal medicine

***Trifolium pratense*** Popularly known as red clover, see there

**The 'Trigger Queen'** Dr Jane Travel, so named for her mapping of previously uncharted patterns of referred pain from the trigger points. See Trigger point injection therapy

**trigger point** MASSAGE THERAPY A circumscribed 'knot' of tensed muscles which, when stimulated, triggers a referred pain response in other parts of the body

$H_3C$ $CH_3$ $CH_3$ $CH_3$ $COOH$ $CH_3$

**all-*trans*-retinoic acid**

▶ **TRIGGER POINTS, TYPES OF**

- **MATRIX POINT** The primary site of local and referred pain, which is often located at a distance from the site of the pain

- **Satellite point** A point that is usually located near the site of pain, which can stimulate the matrix points

▶ **Trigger points are related to**

- **Birth**, due to vaginal trauma through use of forceps
- **Accidents**, eg falling on one's coccyx (tailbone)
- **Sports**, eg shin splints
- **Occupational**, eg computer users
- **Disease**, eg Epstein-Barr infection, multiple sclerosis, lupus erythematosus

See Bonnie Prudden myotherapy, Massage therapy

**trigger point injection therapy** A form of pain therapy developed by Dr J Travel, which attenuates muscle spasms by locoregional injection of a procaine-saline solution into painful muscles; Cf Bonnie Prudden myotherapy

**trigger point massage** Neuromuscular massage, see there

***Trigonocephalus lachesis*** *Lachesis muta*, see there

**trigramin** FRINGE ONCOLOGY A cysteine-rich peptide from the venom of the snake *Trimeresurus gramineus*, that inhibits adhesiveness of melanoma cells *(Exp Cell Res 1988; 179:42)*. See Unproven methods for cancer management

**trillium** Birthroot, see there, *Trillium erectum*

***Trillium erectum*** Popularly known as birthroot, see there

***Trillium pendulum*** Birthroot, see there, *Trillium erectum*

**triple burner** Minister of dikes and dredges, triple heater, triple warmer CHINESE MEDICINE An 'organ system,' which is viewed in the construct of traditional Chinese medicine as one of the twelve vital organs; the triple burner regulates the flow of energy through the organs

▶ **Triple warmer, regions of**

- **Upper burner** Extends from the mouth to the gastroesophageal junction; it is responsible for the intake of air, liquids, and solids, and harmonizes the heart and lung energies
- **Middle burner** Extends from the gastroesophageal junction to the pylorus; it coordinates digestion and harmonizes the energies of the stomach, spleen, and pancreas
- **Lower burner** Extends from the pyloric valve and ends at the anus; it is responsible for extracting nutrients from food, and excreting liquids and solids; it harmonizes the activity of the liver, kidney and bladder, large and small intestine, and reproductive activity

See Chinese medicine, Twelve vital organs

**triple burner meridian** Arm lesser yang meridian ACUPUNCTURE A meridian that runs from the side of the hand and arm to the head. Stimulation of acupoints along the triple burner meridian are used for conditions affecting the heart. See Acupuncture, Twelve meridians

**triple heater** Triple burner, see there

**triple warmer** Triple burner, see there

**triticum** Couch grass, see there, *Agropyron repens*

**trophoblastic theory of cancer** Beard's cancer theory A posit proposed by John Beard (1858-1924), a comparitive embryologist at the University of Edinburgh, that trophoblastic cells (those involved in forming the placenta), can become cancerous when they express themselves at the wrong place at the wrong time *(Moss, 1992)*; Beard believed that pancreatic enzymes could be used to treat cancer; the results with these enzymes in his hands proved disappointing; according to supporters of this theory, Beard's enzymes were too crude. See Enzyme therapy, Laetrile, Unproven methods for cancer management

**tropical oils** NUTRITION A family of cooking oils obtained from palm and coconut trees, that differ from other vegetable oils in that, like animal fats, they have a high content of saturated fatty acids, and thus are thought to have significant atherogenic potential. See *Cis* fatty acids, Fish oil, Olive oil, *Trans* fatty acids

***Tropaeolum majus*** Popularly known as nasturtium, see there

**true chamomile** Roman chamomile, see there, *Anthemis nobilis*

**true sage** Sage, see there, *Salvia officinalis*

**true sandlewood** Sandlewood, see there, *Santalaum album*

**'true self'** Authentic self, inner self FRINGE PSYCHOLOGY A term defined in the context of Swami Ajaya's inner self-healing process, as a radiant essence, core energy, and internal healer, which is the source of joy, unconditional love, vitality, wisdom, and other nice things. See Inner self-healing process; Cf 'False self'

**true Solomon's Seal** Solomon's Seal, see there, *Polygonatum officinale*

**true wood sorrel** Wood sorrel, see there, *Oxalis acetosella*

**trumpet bush** Pau d'arco, see there, *Tebebuia impetiginosa*

**trumpet tree** Pau d'arco, see there, *Tebebuia impetiginosa*

**trunk pack** NATUROPATHY A type of hydrotherapy for various complaints, which consists of wrapping a client in warm wet sheets or blankets from the armpits to midthigh, leaving them in place for 3 hours. See Hydrotherapy

**tryptophan** 2-amino-3-(-indolyl)-propionic acid An essential amino acid FRINGE NUTRITION Tryptophan has been promoted for its alleged ability to induce sleep. See Eosinophilic-myalgia syndrome, Peak E

**tryptophan-associated eosinophilic connective-tissue disease** Eosinophilic-myalgia syndrome, see there

***tsang shu*** Thistle, see there, *Atractylodes chinensis*

**tsubo** A general term for any of the energy points that are stimulated in traditional oriental massage therapy. See Massage therapy, Shiatsu

***tu seh dze*** Dodder, see there, *Cuscuta chinensis, Cuscuta japonica*

***tu si zi*** Dodder, see there, *Cuscuta chinensis, Cuscuta japonica*

**tuber root** Pleurisy root, see there, *Aesclepias tuberosa*

**tuber** NUTRITION An enlarged tip of a rhizome or a fleshy outgrowth that stores food; the prototypic edible tuber is the potato

**tuckahoe** *Porio cocos*, China root, Indian bread, *fu ling, Pachyma cocos*, Virginia truffle CHINESE MEDICINE A fungus that grows on the roots of various conifers; it is diuretic, sedative, tonic, and used for anorexia, bloating, cardiac arrhythmias, hypertension, indigestion, insomnia, and oliguria. See Chinese herbal medicine

***tui-na*** *Tui na an mo* CHINESE MEDICINE A permutation (*tui*-to push; *na*-to pull) of acupressure, in which various body parts (fingers, knuckles, thumbs, palms, and elbows) and techniques (grasping, penetrating, pulling, and rubbing) are used to stimulate acupressure points (acupoints), and effect physical and energetic changes; *tui-na* is used to tonify or attenuate energy at acupoints, which are relay stations in meridians and collaterals; *tui-na* acts on the circulatory, gastrointestinal, musculoskeletal, and nervous systems, and has been used for allergies, asthma, arthritis, back pain, colic in infants, menstrual disorders, rheumatic complaints, sore throat, and other conditions. See Acupressure

***tui na an mo*** *Tui na*, see there

**tumor necrosis factor** Either of two molecules (TNF-α and TNF-β) that mediate shock and tumor-related cachexia; TNF-α (cachexin) has sequence homology with other biological response mediators, including lymphotoxin, interferons, interleukin-1, and granulocyte-macrophage-colony-stimulating factor TOXICITY Fever, headache, hypotension, cachexia, chills, fatigue, anorexia and thrombocytopenia ALTERNATIVE ONCOLOGY Some practitioners of alternative forms of health care have proposed that TNF may be of use in stimulating the immune response in patients with immune suppression caused by chemotherapy and radiotherapy *(Moss, 1992)*. See Unproven methods for cancer management

Mainstream oncologists have abandoned TNF as a therapeutic adjunct in view of its toxicity–Author's note

**tumor promoter** Cocarcinogen An often lipid-soluble substance that has no intrinsic carcinogenic potential, but which, when applied repeatedly, is capable of amplifying the cancer-inducing effects of other substances known as initiators; the classic tumor promoter is phorbol ester and its derivatives isolated from *Croton flavens*, which is a potent and specific activator of protein kinase C; certain fats act as 'promoters,' eg linoleic acid-rich corn, safflower, and sunflower oils are promoters; olive oil is not

***tung* tsao** *Akebia quinata*, see there

**Turkish bath** FRINGE MEDICINE A general term for a group bathing establishment, in which two or more individuals sit in a steamy room; Turkish baths are thought to have little, if any, therapeutic effect. Some serve as social clubs. See Hydrotherapy; Cf Sauna, Sea water therapy

**turmeric** *Curcuma longa, huang jiang,* yellow ginger A culinary (the source of curry) and medicinal plant native to India, that contains curcumin and volatile oil CHINESE MEDICINE Turmeric is used in Chinese medicine internally for shoulder and postpartum pain, menstrual dysfunction, and skin infections. See Chinese herbal medicine HERBAL MEDICINE Turmeric is analgesic, anthelmintic, anti-inflammatory, antimicrobial, carminative, and cholegogic, and has been used for anorexia, arthritis, fever, gastrointestinal complaints, hypertension, liver and gallbladder disease, and hematologic complaints, as well as ocular, dermal and other infections. See Curcumin, Herbal medicine

***Tussilago farfara*** Coltsfoot, see there, *Tussilago farfara*

**The Twelve Chinese organs** The Twelve Vital Organs, see there

**The Twelve Meridians** CHINESE MEDICINE The 12 channels for the flow of the vital force (*chi* or *qi*); the meridians are named for each of the 12 vital organs, and extend longitudinally from the hands or feet, ending at the opposite end of the body

▶ **THE TWELVE MERIDIANS**

- **BLADDER MERIDIAN** Extends from the feet to the eye socket
- **GALLBLADDER MERIDIAN** Extends from the fourth toe to the head
- **HEART MERIDIAN** Extends from the little finger to the armpit
- **HEART CONSTRICTOR MERIDIAN** Pericardium meridian Extends from middle fingers to the chest
- **KIDNEYS MERIDIAN** Extends from the soles of the feet to the upper chest
- **LARGE INTESTINE MERIDIAN** Extends from the index finger to the nostrils
- **LIVER MERIDIAN** Extends from the great toe to the base of the thoracic cavity
- **LUNG MERIDIAN** Extends from the ribs to the shoulder, then down to the thumb
- **PERICARDIUM MERIDIAN** See Heart constrictor meridian
- **SMALL INTESTINE MERIDIAN** Extends from the little finger to the head
- **SPLEEN AND PANCREAS MERIDIAN** Extends from the great toe to the top of the thoracic cavity
- **STOMACH 'MERIDIAN'** Extends from the stomach to the lungs
- **TRIPLE BURNER MERIDIAN** Extends from the fourth finger to the head

Each of the above meridians is listed in alphabetical order and discussed at greater length elsewhere in this work. See Acupuncture, Chinese medicine, The Twelve Vital Organs

**The Twelve Pulses** CHINESE MEDICINE A set of 6 functional zones on the right and left wrists (for a total of 12) located over the radial artery; according to the traditional Chinese construct, the radial pulse has a number of qualities that allow the practitioner to evaluate the state of any of the 12 vital organs; the 'deep pulse' of the left hand corresponds to (from the ends of the hands, inward) the heart, liver, and kidney; the 'superficial pulse' of the left hand corresponds to the small intestine, gallbladder, and bladder; the 'deep pulse' of the right hand corresponds to the lung, spleen, and heart constrictor; the 'superficial pulse' of the right hand corresponds to the large intestine, stomach, and triple warmer. See Pulse diagnosis, Traditional Chinese medicine

**twelve Schüssler's remedies** Schüssler's tissue salts, see there

**twelve-step program** ADDICTION DISORDERS A general term for any of a number of programs modeled after the 12-step self-help group programs used for rehabilitating alcoholics; central to all such programs is the belief in a God, transpersonal spiritual form of energy, or superhuman power; 12-step programs have been developed for those with cocaine abuse, emotional lability (Emotions Anonymous), obesity (Overeaters Anonymous), sexual addiction (Sexaholics Anonymous), and others

**The Twelve Vital Organs** CHINESE MEDICINE According to the traditional Chinese medical construct, there are 12 vital organs, each of which has a related energy, either a yin or a yang principle, and a title indicating its relationship to the other organs

▶ **THE TWELVE VITAL ORGANS**

- **HEART** Fire energy, yin organ, King of the Vital Organs
- **SMALL INTESTINE** Fire energy, yang organ, Minister of Reception
- **LIVER** Wood energy, yin organ, chief of staff
- **GALLBLADDER** Wood energy, yang organ, Honorable Minister of the Central Clearing Department
- **SPLEEN AND PANCREAS** Earth energy, yin organ, Minister of the Granary
- **STOMACH** Earth energy, yang organ, Minister of the Mill and the Sea of Nourishment
- **LUNGS** Metal energy, yin organ, Prime Minister
- **LARGE INTESTINE** Metal energy, yang organ, Minister of Transportation
- **KIDNEYS** Water energy, yin organ, Minister of Power (root of life)
- **BLADDER** Water energy, yang organ, Minister of the Reservoir
- **PERICARDIUM**: Fire energy, yin organ II, King's Bodyguard

- **TRIPLE BURNER** Fire energy, yang organ II, Minister of Dikes and Dredges
  see Triple burner

**twentieth century disease** Environmental disease, see there

**twisting** PHYSICAL THERAPY A massage technique in which the skin and soft tissues are wrung between the hands in opposite directions, which stimulates the nerves and promote vasodilation. See Massage therapy

**twitch grass** Couch grass, see there, *Agropyron repens*

**type A personality** PSYCHOLOGY A relatively distinct set of character traits (*JAMA 1959; 169:1286; ibid, 252:1385*), that is commonly observed in individuals who are aggressive, hard-driving, 'workaholics'; 'type As' have been traditionally regarded as being at an increased risk for cardiovascular disease; this risk appears to be related to the presence of a second component, consisting of repressed hostilities towards others, or hopelessly frustrating situations, which induces a 'toxic core' nidus. See 'Toxic core'; Cf Type B personality, Type C personality, Type D personality

**type B personality** PSYCHOLOGY A set of personality traits described in individuals who tend to be relaxed and inclined to do things 'mañana'; Cf Type A personality, Type C personality, Type D personality

**type C personality** PSYCHOLOGY A set of personality traits described in individuals who tend to be quiet and introspective; they are believed, in fact, to be frustrated, swallow their anger, and have an increased risk of cancer; type Cs are the polar opposite of type As; they are nonemotional, nonassertive, and appease others to the point of self-effacement and self-sacrifice; Cf Type A personality, Type B personality, Type D personality

**type 'D' personality** PSYCHOLOGY An anxiety and immunosuppression-prone type D personality; Cf Type A personality, Type B personality, Type C personality

***Typha lattifolia*** see Cattail

***Typha orientalis*** Cattail, *Typha latifolia*

**tyramine hypertension** Cheese disease NUTRITION A complication of monoamine oxidase inhibitors (MAOIs), which are used to treat depression and panic disorders; MAOIs inhibit the metabolism of tyramines and catecholamines; ingestion of tyramine-rich food and/or beverages, eg Chianti wine, cheddar cheese, naturally fermented beer, chicken liver or drugs, eg ephedrine and amphetamines, evokes an acute hypertensive crisis due to the release of tissue catecholamines, which may be accompanied by sweating, tachycardia, or arrhythmia

**ubenimex** Bestatin® ALTERNATIVE ONCOLOGY A peptide isolated from the supernatant (broth) of cultured *Streptomyces olivoreticuli* that inhibits aminopeptidase; ubenimex stimulates the immune system, activates macrophages, increases production and secretion of interleukin–1 and interleukin-2, and stimulates T cells and hematopoiesis; it is said to be effective in treating various cancers including Hodgkin's disease, leukemia, melanoma, and cancers of the bladder, esophagus, head and neck, lung, and stomach. See Unproven methods for cancer management

**ubiquinone** Coenzyme Q10, see there

***Ulmus rubra*** Popularly known as slippery elm, see there

**ultrasound therapy** ALTERNATIVE MEDICINE The use of ultrasonic waves which, when applied locally to joints, are believed to be useful for nonspecific arthritic complaints, including stiffness, arthritis, bursitis, tendinitis, and chronic pain; the effect is attributed to local heat, massage of the locoregional tissues, and to an anti-inflammatory effect; ultrasound may be used in conjunction with acupuncture

**ultraviolet light** Ultraviolet radiation The segment of the electromagnetic spectrum between 200 and 400 nm, including photons emitted during electronic transition states; UV-C (200-290 nm) is damaging to DNA and amino acids, but is blocked by the stratospheric ozone layer, UV-B (290-320 nm) is partially blocked by the ozone layer; UV-A (320 to 400 nm) is the least dangerous but may be hazardous with photosensitizing medications (tetracyclines, thiazides), lupus erythematosus and light sensitivity disorders; UV-A suppresses delayed cutaneous hypersensitivity, causes photoaging and reduces serum carotenoids; the accelerating depletion of the stratospheric ozone is implicated in the increased in incidence of cataract, and malignant melanomas reported in recent decades; UV light may also damage the less sensitive purines, causing spontaneous depurination, leaving a 'naked' deoxyribose residue in the DNA (apurinic sites); repair of UV light-induced DNA damage is defective in some 'chromosomal breakage syndromes,' eg xeroderma pigmentosa and Bloom syndrome. See CFCs, Greenhouse effect, Ozone layer, SOS repair, SPF rating

Note: The mutational effect of UV light is not due to direct DNA damage, but rather occurs during the error-prone process of DNA repair

**umbrella plant** Mayapple, see there, *Podophyllum peltatum*

***unani*** *Unani* medicine ARABIC MEDICINE An Islamic healing philosophy that incorporates major elements of ancient Greek (*unani* is Arabic for Greek) medicine–which assumes four elements (earth, fire, water, and air) and four corresponding humors (phlegm, blood, yellow bile, and black bile, respectively), and minor elements of ayurvedic medicine

**unconventional cancer therapy** Unproven methods for cancer management, see there

**unhealthy foods** A general term for foods that are not regarded as being conducive to maintaining health; unhealthy foods include fats, in particular of animal origin, 'fast foods,' which are often low in fiber and vitamins, 'junk food' (eg potato and corn chips, pretzels, and crackers), which are high in salt and tropical oils, and cream-rich 'white sauces,' which are typical of northern Italian cuisine; Cf Healthy foods

**unhealthy habit** Bad habit, see there

**universal allergy** Environmental disease, see there

**universal reactivity** Environmental disease, see there

**universal reactor syndrome** Environmental disease, see there

**unmasking** Making faces ALTERNATIVE PSYCHOLO-

GY Any of a number of techniques (eg moving parts of the face, 'aping' emotions and opening the eyes widely), that were developed by W Reich for physical and emotional release. See Armoring, Body armor, Reichian therapy

**unpasteurized milk** Raw milk, see there

**unprocessed grains** Whole grains, see there

**unproven** Dubious, nonscientific, not proven, quack, questionable, unscientific *adjective* Pertaining or referring to that which has not been validated by repeatable experiments or other scientifically valid method of determining effect or efficacy

**unproven care** A generic term for any therapy that has no proven* efficacy; unproven therapies have been categorized into those with bioelectromagnetic applications, life-style changes, mind/body control, biological therapies, energy therapies, and ethnomedicine or traditional medicine (see table) (*Am Med News 21 Nov 1994 p13*). See Health fraud, Quackery, Unproven methods for cancer management

*As currently known to the NIH Office of Alternative Medicine; of those therapies listed below, some may reduce the risk for certain diseases, in particular changes in lifestyle and diet–Author's note

**▶ METHODS OF UNPROVEN CARE**

- **BIOELECTROMAGNETIC APPLICATIONS** Electromagnetic fields, electrostimulation and neurostimulation devices, magnetoresonance spectroscopy, blue (and other colored) light treatment, artificial light therapy
- **LIFESTYLE CHANGES** Changes in habits and lifestyle, diet, nutrition, megavitamins, macrobiotics, nutritional supplements
- **MIND/BODY CONTROL** Various forms of external or internal therapy (art, humor, hypnosis, music, prayer), relaxation techniques (biofeedback training, yoga/meditation), and counseling
- **PHARMACOLOGICAL AND BIOLOGICAL TREATMENTS** Antioxidizing agents (eg vitamin A and E), oxidizing agents,* cell treatment, chelation therapy,‡ herbal medicine, naturopathy, metabolic therapy
- **STRUCTURAL AND ENERGETIC THERAPIES** Acupressure, aromatherapy, bodywork, chiropractic, massage therapy, reflexology, shiatsu
- **TRADITIONAL AND ETHNOMEDICINE** Acupuncture, ayurvedic medicine, herbal medicine, homeopathy, Native American medicine, traditional Chinese medicine, folk medicine

*Eg hydrogen peroxide–$H_2O_2$, ozone, both identified by the FDA as fraudulent ‡Other than for accepted medical indications, eg desferroxamine for hemochromatosis (*Am Med News 21 Nov 1994 p13*)

**unproven methods for cancer management** ALTERNATIVE MEDICINE A general term for a wide variety of unorthodox therapies of uncertain benefit that are offered by some self-proclaimed cancer specialists (who may have no or little formal medical training); in a comparison study at similar stages of terminal malignancy between patients treated with conventional and unproven cancer therapies, those receiving conventional therapy had better survival and quality-of-life scores than those receiving an unproven regimen, which consisted of a combination of autogenous immune-enhancing vaccines, bacille Calmette-Guérin (bCG), vegetarian diets and coffee enemas–the difference does not reach statistical significance (*N Engl J Med 1991; 324:1180*); ± $4 billion is spent annually by Americans on unproven cancer therapies; listed on page 378 are various therapies and organizations linked to 'alternative' and 'fringe' oncology

**▶ ORGANIZATIONS THAT ADVOCATE UNPROVEN CANCER THERAPIES (DISCUSSED IN THIS WORK)**

- Cancer Control Society
- Cancer Victims Anonymous
- The Committee for Freedom of Choice in Cancer Therapy
- The Federation of Alternative Cancer Therapies
- The International Association of Cancer Victors & Friends
- The National Health Federation

(*Fact Sheet, American Cancer Society, June 1978*)

**unsaturated fatty acid** NUTRITION An alkyl chain fatty acid with one or more double (ethylenic) bonds between carbons; called unsaturated as the chain is capable of absorbing more hydrogen; these fatty acids have lower melting points and most are liquid at room temperature; unsaturated fatty acids can be monounsaturated, ie have one double bond (eg oleic acid, which are widely distributed in nature) or polyunsaturated, ie has two or more double bonds (eg linolenic acid, which are found in safflower and corn oils). See Fatty acid; Cf Monounsaturated fatty acids, Polyunsaturated fatty acid, Saturated fatty acid

**unscientific** Unproven, see there

**upper body fat obesity** Android obesity, male obesity, 'beer gut' obesity Obesity characterized by increased abdomen-to-thigh skin fold ratio, waist-to-hip circumference ratio, suprailiac-to-thigh skin fold ratio, waist circumference, and thigh skin fold. See Obesity

Note: Increased upper body fat places women at an increased risk for endometrial carcinoma (*JAMA 1991; 266:1808MOA*)

**upper breath** AYURVEDIC MEDICINE Inhalation

**Unproven Substances or Methods for the Diagnosis or Treatment of Cancer**

with associated organizations, entries, individuals, and places discussed in this work

ACPS-R
Alkylglycerol
American Biologics Hospital
Anticoagulant
Antineoplaston
Antistatin
Antitumor B
Arginine
AS-101
Astragalus
Azelaic acid
Beard Anthrone Test
Benzaldehyde
BioStim
Black medicine
Blastolysin
6-Br-AA
Brinase
Bristol diet therapy
Milan Brych
Bryostatin
Lawrence Burton
Butyric acid
CanCell
Cancer fallacy
Cancer myth
Cancer underground
Canthaxanthin
Carnivora
Cartilage-derived inhibitor
Catalyst-altered water
Cell therapy
Cesium
Chelation therapy
*Chlorella pyrenoidosa*
Co-carcinogenic K factor
Coffee enema
Coley's toxin
Colloidal silver protein
Colon therapy
The Committee for Freedom of Choice in Cancer Therapy, Inc
Compound Q
Contreras method
CuDIPS
DHEA
*Dunaliela bardail*
Electric therapy
Epigallocatechin gallate
Essaic
Evers' therapy
Folk cures for cancer
Gamma-linolenic acid
Ge-132
Germanium
GF-1
GFL
Ginseng
Gyoxylide
Golden Book Tea
Greek cancer cure
Green tea
Healing visualization
Health fraud
Health freedom argument
Heat stress detoxification
Hemacytology index
Hematogenic oxidation therapy
Herbal medicine
Herbal tea
High pH therapy
*Hochu-ekki-to*
Hoxsey medicine
Hoxsey tonic
Hoxsey treatment
Hydrazine sulfate
Hydrogen peroxide therapy
Immunoaugmentive therapy
Immunotherapy
Indoles
Ion generator
Iscador®
Isoflavone
Isoprinosine
Issels' whole body therapy
Jason Winters' Products Cancer Tea
*Juzen-taiho-to*
Kelley's cancer theory
Kelley's index of malignancy
Kelley's nutritional-metabolic therapy
Koch treatment
Krebiozen
Krestin
Laetrile
Lapachol
Lentinan
LeShan therapy
Levamisole
Lignan
Limonene
Linseed oil
Lithium
Lycopene
LZ-8
Macrobiotic diet
Magnet therapy
Maitake
MAK-4
MAK-5
Manner cocktail
MAP-30
Maruyama vaccine
MaxEPA
Metabolic therapy
Methylene blue
Mo-ehr
Moerman's anticancer diet molybdenum
Monoclonal antibody
Monoterpenes
MTH-68
Muroctasin
National Health Federation
Nordihydroguaiaretic acid
Onconase
Organotellurium
Orgotein®
Oscilloclast
Pangamic acid
Pau d'arco
Phytochemical
Pink medicine
Plumbagin
Pranic healing
*Progenitor cryptocides*
Psychic surgery
quack
Quackery
Queen Anne's lace
Radionics
Reishi
Revici therapy
Rubidium
Second Opinion
714X
Shark cartilage
*Shi-un-kou*
Shiitake mushroom
Simonton method
Six Flavor Tea
SKCF
Snake oil
Snake oil industry
Splenopentin
Staphage lysate
Sulfides
Sulforaphane
Suramin
Swainsinone
Tellurium
Thioproline
Thymic factor
Tijuana
Tigramin
Trophoblastic theory of cancer
Tumor necrosis factor

| Ubenimex | Viva Natural | Wobe Mugos | Yin cancer |
|---|---|---|---|
| Unproven care | Warburg effect | Yang cancer | Yin & yang cancer |

through the nose, which expands only the upper chest; upper breath is typical of a person untrained in complete breathing; there are three components to the 'Complete breath of yoga,' the upper breath, which is preceded by the deeper abdominal and diaphragm breaths, which are linked in wavelike movements. See Abdominal breath, Complete breath, Diaphragm breath, Yoga

**upper burner** see Triple burner

**urea therapy** Urine therapy, see there

***Urginea maritima*** Popularly known as sea onion, see there

**urine therapy** *Amaroli*, auto-urine therapy, *shivambu kalpa*, urea therapy, uropathy FRINGE MEDICINE The consumptioin of one's own urine as a therapeutic solution, by oral ingestion, injection, instillation in the rectum, or as a topical agent; urine therapy was enthusiastically embraced in the early 20th century by the Britisher JW Armstrong, who believed its consumption was effective for asthma, bladder problems, burns, cancer (*Pelton, Overholser, 1994*), diabetes, fever, gangrene, heart disease, malaria, renal failure, tuberculosis, wounds, and other conditions; because he viewed urine as a panacea, a specific medical diagnosis was unnecessary; urine has been recently extolled (*B Bartlett, M Adelman, The Miracles of Urine Therapy, Margate, FL, Lifestyle Institute, 1987*) as a therapy for AIDS, arthritis, chronic fatigue syndrome, herpes, and leprosy

**uropathy** Urine therapy, see there

***Urtica dioica*** Popularly known as stinging nettle, see there

***Urtica*** *Urtica urens*, dwarf stinging nettle HOMEOPATHY A remedy that may applied topically for allergic reactions, blistering, and eczema, or internally for cystitis, gout, neuralgias, pruritus, rheumatic complaints. See Homeopathy

**usnea** *Usnea* species, larch moss, old man's beard, *niou hsi* HERBAL MEDICINE Any of a family of lichens that contain usnic acid, which is believed to have antibacterial, immune stimulatory and muscle relaxing activity; lichens are used topically for athlete's foot and skin ulcers, as a douche for vaginal infections, and internally for colds, flu, sore throat, and gastrointestinal, respiratory, and urinary tract infections TOXICITY It should not be used in pregnancy, as it stimulates uterine contraction. See Herbal medicine

**Usui, Mikao** A Japanese Christian theologian (1802-1883) who later became a Zen Buddhist monk, and founded Reiki. See Reiki

**Usui *shiki ryoho*** Reiki, see there

**Usui *shiko ryoho*** Reiki, see there

**Usui system of natural healing** Reiki, see there

***uva ursi*** Bearberry, see there, *Arctostaphylos uva-ursi*

**usnic acid**

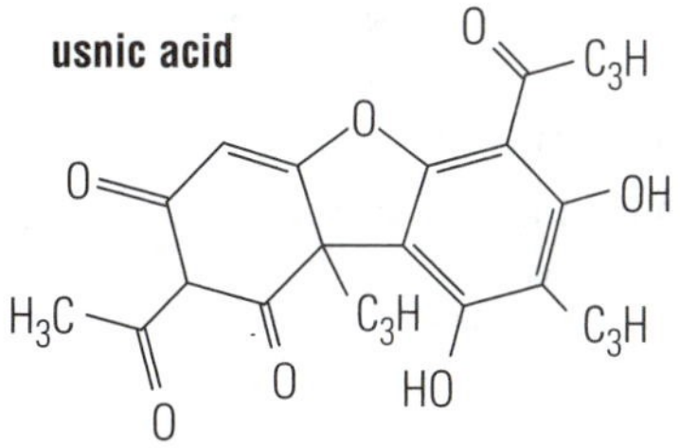

O
$C_3H$
O
O
OH
$H_3C$
$C_3H$
$C_3H$
O
HO
O

**Vacuflex Reflexology System** FRINGE MEDICINE A proprietary system of reflexology developed in the 1970s by a Danish reflexologist, Inge Dougans; the system is based on Dougans' belief that the effects of reflexology are achieved by stimulating energy zones defined by the meridians of oriental medicine, rather than those defined by Fitzgerald, the father of reflexology; the system stimulates all of the reflexology areas simultaneously through the use of a special boot, in which a vaccum is created; after five minutes of suction, the foot is then examined to identify areas of discoloration, which are believed to correspond to areas of illness. Suction pads are then placed on the congested areas, which are believed to stimulate the reflex points into activity. See Reflexology

**vaginal pouch** Female condom, see there

**vahombe** HERBAL MEDICINE A type of aloe from Madagascar which is believed to stimulate the immune system (*Moss, 1992*); Cf Pharmacognosy

**valerian** *Valeriana officinalis*, all-heal, English valerian, garden heliotrope, German valerian, great wild valerian, setwell, vandalroot HERBAL MEDICINE A perennial herb that contains alkaloids, actinidine, choline, glycoside, resins, tannins, valepotriates, valerenic acid, and volatile oils, including limonene; it is antispasmodic, antitussive, and sedative, and may act on the central nervous system; it has been used for anxiety, colic, dandruff, dyspepsia, headaches, hypertension, insomnia, menstrual cramping, nervousness, stress, and tachyarrhythmias TOXOCITY Valerian should not be given to infants and should be used with caution in pregnant women; in excess, it may cause headaches, irritability, and blurred vision. See Herbal medicine

**valerian** *Valeriana officinalis*

***Valeriana officinalis*** Popularly known as valerian, see there

**vanadium** A metallic element (atomic number 23; atomic weight 50.94) present in trace amounts in the environment, which has an uncertain role in humans. Some data suggest that vanadium may lower serum glucose, participate in cholesterol, triglyceride, and bone metabolism, hormone production, and possibly protect against cancer; vanadium is present in fish, liver, nuts, root vegetables, vegetable oils, and whole grains; a vanadium deficiency state is not known to exist in humans

**vandalroot** Valerian, see there, *Valeriana officinalis*

***vata*** Wind force AYURVEDIC MEDICINE The *dosha* that represents the air and ether elements according to the ayurvedic construct; *vata* controls the movements of fluids and cells through the body, as well as the activity of organs, muscles, nerves, and thought. See Ayurvedic medicine, *Dosha*; *Kapha*; *Pitta*, *Prakriti*, *Prana*

***vata* diet** AYURVEDIC MEDICINE A diet believed to be optimal for a person with a '*vata*' *dosha*, which consists of warming foods and spices. Sugar, alcohol, drugs, fats, and cold sweets should be avoided, and the intake of raw foods should be limited. See *Vata*; Cf *Kapha* diet, *Pitta* diet

***vata* personality** AYURVEDIC MEDICINE A personality profile with a '*vata*' *dosha*; *vata* types are active, alert, restless, and romantic; they are often artists or musicians; physically, *vata* individuals may be thin, have curly hair, dry skin, and thick bones; *vata* energy flows at its peak in the fall, the times when the *vata* personality is most susceptible to abdominal discomfort and gas, anxiety, arthritis, nervous conditions, low back pain, neuralgia, paralysis, and sciatica. See *Dosha*, *Vata*; Cf *Kapha* personality, *Pitta* personality

***Vebascum thapsus*** Popularly known as mullein, see there

**vedic healing** Ayurvedic medicine, see there

**vedic medicine** Ayurvedic medicine, see there

**vegan** Pure vegetarian, strict vegetarian NUTRITION A vegetarian who consumes only plant foods (vegetables, fruits, grains, beans, and nuts), but no animal products (meat, fish, dairy products, and eggs); vegans are at risk for vitamin $B_{12}$ deficiency; vegan adolescents may not meet energy requirements during the growth spurt, and become deficient in vitamin $B_6$, riboflavin, calcium, zinc, iron, and trace minerals. See Diet, Pareve, Veganism, Vegetarianism; Cf Lacto-ovo vegetarian

**veganism** CLINICAL NUTRITION The consumption of a vegetarian diet lacking animal proteins (meat, fish, and dairy products); veganism is associated with deficiencies in vitamin $B_{12}$, $B_6$, and riboflavin; the high-fiber vegan diet reduces the absorption of essential cations by chelating calcium, zinc, iron, and trace minerals. See Diet, Kosher, Pareve, Vegan; Cf Vegetarianism

**vegetable juice fast** ALTERNATIVE NUTRITION An 'elimination' fast in which the person ingests only vegetable (eg cabbage, carrot, onion) juice and water, but no solid foods. See Fasting

**vegetal therapy** Reichian therapy, see there

**vegetarianism** CLINICAL NUTRITION The pursuing of a primarily, but not exclusively vegetarian diet (see following classification), which has minimal amounts of animal proteins; the vegetarian diet consists mainly of whole-grain cereals, pulses (lentils, beans, and peas), fresh and dried fruits, nuts, as well as dairy products; the term partial vegetarianism is used for vegetarians who supplement their diet with fish or poultry

▶ **VEGETARIANS, TYPES OF**

- **FRUTARIAN** Raw food eater A person who consumes only fruits, which some also define as vegetables, nuts, and sprouted beans or grains; frutarians eschew the use of fats, oils, sugar, salt, and other flavorings
- **VEGAN** Pure vegetarian, strict vegetarian A person who consumes only plant foods, which includes vegetables, fruits, grains, beans, and nuts
- **LACTO-VEGETARIAN** A vegetarian who consumes the same foods as vegans, as well as dairy products, but no eggs
- **LACTO-OVO-VEGETARIAN** A vegetarian who consumes the same foods as vegans, as well as dairy products, *and* eggs

Famous vegetarians: Micheal Jackson, Steve Jobs, Madonna, Paul McCartney, Mary Pickford, George Bernard Shaw, Upton Sinclair, Cicely Tyson, Richard Wagner

See Diet, Kosher, Pareve; Cf Veganism

**vegetotherapy** A term* coined by W Reich for his form of body-oriented psychotherapy; according to Reich, the resolution of chronic muscle tension required the freeing of life (ie sexual) energies, which he termed orgone. See Armoring, Body armor, Orgone, Orgone accumulator, Reich, Reichian therapy, Unmasking

Note: The root form *vegeto–* in this context refers to a primitive and involuntary level of biological functioning

**vegotherapy** Herbal medicine, see there

**Venus basin** Teasel, see there, *Dipsacus sylvestris*

**Venus syndrome** CLINICAL NUTRITION A colloquial term for a person with a 'bottom heavy' figure, ie who has a relatively thin and well-proportioned torso, and an overly endowed lower half, extending from the waist to the ankles (*Venus syndrome, E Chandris, Doubleday, New York, 1985*)

The name Venus derives from the Venus figurines, which were the first artistic representations of woman, the most well-known of which is the Venus of Willendorf; that Venus was the first of a series of Paleolithic figures fashioned between 30 000 and 20 000 BC

**verbal therapy** 1. Imagineering, see there 2. Talking therapy, see there

***Verbena officinalis*** Vervain, see there

***Verona virginicum*** Culver's root, see there, *Veronicastrum virginicum*

***Veronicastrum virginicum*** Popularly known

as Culver's root, see there

**vervain** *Verbena officinalis*, herb-of-the-cross, pigeon's grass HERBAL MEDICINE A perennial herb that contains alkaloids, bitter principles, glycosides (eg verbenin), tannins, and volatile oil; it is antipyretic, antispasmodic, contraceptive, diuretic, and has been used for headaches, skin infections, and dysentery, suppressing appetite, increasing breast milk, and as a liver and nerve tonic. See Herbal medicine

**vervain** *Verbena officinalis*

**very-low-calorie diet** A potentially dangerous diet that provides 300-700 kcal/day (normal ±2500 kcal/day), which must be supplemented with high-quality protein, given the risk of death due to intractable cardiac arrhythmias; the diet should be limited in duration SIDE EFFECTS Ortho-static hypotension due to loss of sodium and decreased norepinephrine secretion, fatigue, hypothermia, cold intolerance, xeroderma, hair loss, dysmenorrhea. See Diet

**VG26** Jen Chung ACUPUNCTURE An acupuncture point present in humans and in animals, which is believed to be an 'emergency' point–insertion of a needle at VG26 restores the cardiopulmonary function of animals that have suffered circulatory collapse. See Acupuncture, Chinese medicine; Cf Loo Point

**vibration** A 'soft tissue' technique used in massage therapy, which entails vibrating movements, usually delivered by an electrical device. See Massage therapy

**vibrational medicine** Einsteinian medicine ALTERNATIVE MEDICINE A term coined by R Gerber, for any form of alternative health care that attempts to alter factors in a patient that cause disharmony in the flow of vital energy; the goal in vibrational medicine is to move, unblock, or balance life energy over the physical, energetic, and spiritual body; health care formats that have been regarded as vibrational in nature include acupressure, acupuncture, aromatherapy, Bach flower remedies, *chakra* therapy, color therapy, crystal therapy, gem therapy, healing, homeopathy, polarity, psychic surgery, Reiki, reflexology, therapeutic touch, and toning, all discussed elsewhere in this work. See Congestion, Energy balance; Cf Natural healing

***Viburnum opulus*** Popularly known as cramp bark, see there

***Viburnum prunifolium*** Popularly known as black haw, see there

**Vichy** The location (in France) of one of the most well-known therapeutic spas in the world, which has been in operation since the 17th century. See Health spa, Mineral water

**video display terminal** Video display unit, see there

**video display unit** A device containing a cathode ray tube generating a visual display, which emits both extremely low frequency (ELF, 45-60 Hz) and very low frequency (VLF, 15 kHz) electromagnetic fields;15% of the US workforce spends a large part of its day in front of a VDU

▶ **VIDEO DISPLAY UNITS,** POTENTIAL ADVERSE EFFECTS

- **IRRADIATION** Ultraviolet light, ELF, and VLF radiation; potential associations eg cataracts, reproductive disorders, facial dermatitis and epileptic reactions have not reached statistical significance
- **ERGONOMIC EFFECTS** Visual, and musculoskeletal, due to the position required for typing
- **STRESS** The mental stress related to VDU use is thought by some workers to be more a function of the job per se than the VDT itself

VLF fields had been linked by 'soft' data to spontaneous abortions, which is either a statistical canard or due to another factor unrelated to VDUs (*N Engl J Med 1991; 324:728*)

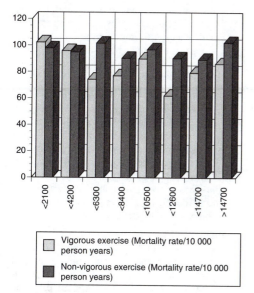

**vigorous exercise** A form of exercise that is intense enough to cause sweating and/or heavy breathing and/or increase of heart rate to near maximum; vigorous exercise is formally defined as that which requires > 6 METs* and includes brisk walking (rate of 6.5-8 km/hour or 4-5 mph) 45 minutes 5x/wk, rollerblading (2-3 hours/wk), running (rate of 9.5-11 km/hour or 6-7 mph), 3 hours/wk, swimming (laps 3 hours/wk), tennis (singles 3 hours/wk), shoveling snow; there is a graded inverse relationship between total physical activity (in particular vigorous exercise) and mortality (*JAMA 1995; 273:1179*). See Exercise, MET; Cf the 'Zone'

*MET is the resting rate of metabolism; numeric prefixes correspond to multiples thereof

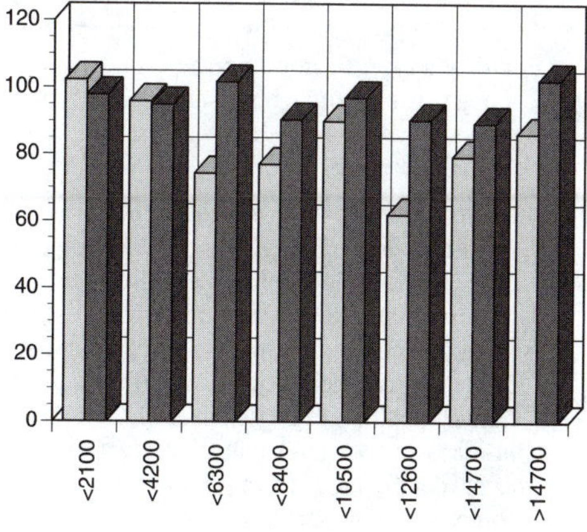


***vikriti*** AYURVEDIC MEDICINE A person's general state of health. See Ayurvedic medicine, *Prakriti*, *Pranayama*

***Vinca rosea*** Madagascar periwinkle, see there, *Catharanthus roseus*

***Viola odorata*** Popularly known as sweet violet, see there

***Viola patrinii*** See Wild Chinese violet

***Viola yesoensis*** Popularly known as wild Chinese violet, see there

**violet** FRINGE MEDICINE–COLOR THERAPY The color violet is believed to cleanse the blood, stimulate healing, improve mental outlook, promote cancer cell destruction by white blood cells, and help balance the body's electrolytes. See Color breathing, Color therapy, Violet metals & chemicals

**violet metals & chemicals** FRINGE MEDICINE–COLOR THERAPY Violet metals and chemicals are believed to cleanse the blood, stimulate healing, improve mental outlook, and promote cancer cell destruction by white blood cells, and include strontium and titanium. See Color breathing, Color therapy, Violet

***virechana*** AYURVEDIC MEDICINE A castor oil purgation used in ayurvedic medicine to eliminate *ama* (physiologic impurities). See Ayurvedic medicine, *Panchakarma*, *Prana*

**Virginia dogwood** Dogwood, see there, *Cornus florida*

**Virginia silk** Milkweed, see there, *Asclepia syriaca*

**Virginia skullcap** Skullcap, see there, *Scutellaria lateriflora*

**Virginia truffle** Tuckahoe, see there, *Porio cocos*

**viroxan** AIDS FRAUD An unsterilized mixture of uncertain nature that was claimed to have anti-HIV activity. See AIDS fraud; Cf AIDS therapy

***vis medicatrix naturae*** *Only nature cures* NATUROPATHY A statement attributed to Hippocrates, which has been quoted by practitioners of alternative medicine, as a justification for any 'hands-off' approach to treating illness

**visceral manipulation** OSTEOPATHY A general term for the stretching, kneading, and gentle poking of deep tissues, eg gallbladder and other internal organs, with the intent of enhancing the flow of fluids and energy and releasing restrictions; visceral manipulation is based on the belief that visceral organs can become distorted from tension and connective tissues dried out, and result in 'sticking' of bodily functions, eg constipation; according to this posit, normal bodily functions can be enhanced by periodic manipulation. See Osteopathy

**vision quest** ETHNOMEDICINE A solitary sojourn into the wilderness undertaken by a boy of the Plains tribes of Native Americans, who goes to pray and commune with nature; the goal of the quest is to have a vision of an animal or other spirit, who will have special significance, and ultimately guide his life. See Medicine bundle, Meditation

**vision therapy** Eye training, orthoptics, Skeffington method, vision training ALTERNATIVE OPHTHALMOLOGY A vision-enhancing method developed in the 1920s by an American optometrist, AM Skeffington; vision therapy uses eye exercises and other techniques to train/retrain the eyes to function as a unit and coordinate the brain's processing of visual information needed for binocular vision; in contrast to the Bates method, vision training not only exercises the extraocular muscles, but also retrains the brain in its processing of visual images; vision therapists are also known as behavioral optometrists; vision therapy is thought to be useful in lazy eye (amblyopia), crossed eyes (strabismus), problems of focusing (vergence and accommodation), oculomotor defects, learning disabilities, athletic performance, and traumatic brain injury (*Castleman, 1996*). See Bates vision training, Eye-robics®

**vision training** Vision therapy, see there

**visionary tool** PARANORMAL PHENOMENA A device, eg Starchamber™ or Bio-Chromatic Integration Device, which is believed to help balance the *chakras* (energy centers). See Bio-Chromatic Integration Device, Chakra balancing, Starchamber™

**visual display terminal** Video display unit, see there

**visual therapy** 1. Vision training, see there 2. See Imagineering

**visualization therapy** Imagery and visualization, see there

**Vita Flex®** FRINGE MEDICINE A permutation of reflexology developed in 1976 by Stanley Burroughs, which is one of 3 arms of his system of natural healing, the others being color therapy and the lemonade diet; according to Burroughs, there are more than 5000 Vita Flex points of control in the body; Burroughs eschewed mainstream medicine, stating, '*Medicine is a form of fiction that feeds on ignorance of the true needs of the body to restore normal health and retain it.*' (*Raso, 1994*). See Color therapy, Lemonade diet

**vital force** HOMEOPATHY The organizing energy responsible for one's health; while the vital force is analogous to *chi* (*qi*) of Chinese medicine and *prana* in ayurvedic medicine, it may be viewed as differing in how it is altered to restore health; in Chinese and ayurvedic medicine the aim is to reverse the forces that result in disharmony, homeopathy provokes the vital force to a higher level of order and harmony, allowing the body to shake off the symptoms and pathogenic influences. Synonyms for the vital force are listed in the accompanying table. See Homeopathy, Proving, Remedy; Cf *Chi*, *Prana*

**vitalistic approach** NATUROPATHY A philosophical stance adopted by some naturopaths, in which the intent of therapy is to detoxify the body and allow the natural healing forces to act in the most optimal fashion (*vis medicatrix naturae*); central to the vitalistic approach is the use of diet, hydrotherapy to improve the blood flow to the gastrointestinal tract, and reduction of stress. See Naturopathy, *Vis medicatrix naturae*; Cf Biochemical approach

**vitalism** PARANORMAL PHENOMENA A philosophical stance, which is unprovable by currently available techniques, that animal functions hinge on a vital force distinct from physically measurable forces; vitalism is the central theme of most forms of alternative health care, which holds that all humans have a soul that continues to exist after death, as a form of energy or vital force. See Paranormal phenomena, Vital force

**vitamin A** The term vitamin A refers to a combination of preformed vitamin A (retinol, retinyl esters, and related compounds) and carotenoids with provitamin activity; vitamin A is a generic term for all β-ionone derivatives that have trans-retinol's biological activity; these fat-soluble molecules are required for monosaccharide transport in glycoprotein synthesis, and for maintaining mucocutaneous epithelia (skin, oral cavity, gastrointestinal, respiratory, and urinary tracts); it is stored in the liver, intestine, kidney, heart, blood vessels, and gonads; after oxidation to retinoic acid, it diffuses into the nucleus, binds to a specific nuclear receptor and interacts with a 'responsive element'[1]; vitamin A is critical for fetal development,

**VITAL FORCE-SYNONYMS**

Air prana
Animal magnetism (mesmerism)
Bio-current
Bioelectric field
Bioenergy
Biomagnetic waves
Bion
Bioplasma
Bioplasmic energy
Breath of life,
*Chi* (Chinese)
Cosmic life energy
Cosmic life force,
Élan vitale
Electrodynamic field
Energy of being
Entelechy, essence
Etheronic force (Cayce)
(the) Force (Hollywood)
Force of life
Force vitale
Innate intelligence (chiropractic)
Inner vital energy
Internal energy
*Ki* (Japanese/Shinto)
Kundalini (Shakti)
L field
Life field
Life force
Life power
M field
*Mana* (Hawaiian)
Morphic field
Morphic resonance
Morphogenetic field
Morphogenic field
Nerve energy
Nerve force
Od
Odic force
Odyle
Ojas*
Orgone
Orgone energy
Orgone field
Paraelectricity
Personal energy
*Prana* (Hindu)
Pneuma
*Psi* field
*Psi* plasma
Psychic energy
Psychic force
Psychotronic energy
*Qi* (Chinese)
Reiki (Usui)
*Ruach* (Hebrew)
*Ruah* (Hebrew)
*Seiki*
Soul (Christianity
Spirit (Christianity)
Spiritual energy
Subtle energy
Superhuman energy
Superhuman power
Tachyon energy
Tachyon field energy
Universal life energy
Universal life force
Universal life force energy
Virtual energy
*Vis formativa* (naturopathy)
Vital cosmic force
Vital curative force
Vital element
Vital energy
Vital energy force
Vital life force
Vital life force energy
Vital life spirit
Vital magnetism
Vital principle
Vital spirit
Vitalistic principle

*In ayurveda, this form of vital energy is that which emanates from vital secretions and reproductive organs; parentheses indicate association with a particular system

differentiation, cell proliferation, and vision[2]; empirical vitamin A therapy in asymptomatic children results in 2-fold decrease in childhood mortality from diarrhea, convulsions and infection-related symptoms. See Retinol, Tretinoin ALTERNATIVE NUTRITION Megadoses of vitamin A have been recommended by some alternative health care practitioners for lowering cholesterol, varicose veins, weakness of bone, teeth and eyes, kidney stone, poor circulation, and have been promoted for curing cancer that has already developed[3]

[1]A DNA sequence that regulates the target genes [2]Vitamin A is critical in the production of rhodopsin [3]There are no currently available data to support this contention–Author's note; it is thought that vitamin A supplements reduce the risk of breast cancer only in those women whose diets are low in vitamin A ab initio; vitamins C and E are not protective against breast cancer (*N Engl J Med 1993; 329:234OA*)

**vitamin A deficiency** A condition characterized by night blindness, keratomalacia, increased urogenital and nasopharyngeal infections, dry eyes. See Vitamin A

**vitamin A embryopathy** Accutane baby syndrome A condition induced by in utero exposure to vitamin A analogs, which may be associated with cardiovascular (ventricular septal, aortic arch and conotruncal) defects, external ear deformity, cleft palate, micrognathia and central nervous malformations. See Category X drugs, Vitamin A, Vitamin A toxicity, Tretinoin

**vitamin A toxicity** A clinical condition that is evoked by the excess ingestion (greater than 20,000 IU for more than 2 weeks) of vitamin A. Symptoms include bone pain, dry skin, gastrointestinal complaints including nausea, vomiting, constipation and diarrhea, poor growth in children, severe headaches, bulging eyes, insomnia, jaundice, menstrual disorders, stress, weight loss; vitamin A toxicity can be fatal. See Vitamin A

**vitamin $B_1$** Thiamin, see there

**vitamin $B_2$** Riboflavin, see there

**vitamin $B_3$** An obsolete term for 1. Nicotinic acid (niacin) and nicotinamide 2. Pantothenic acid

**vitamin $B_4$** An ill-defined 'factor,' of dubious validity, isolated from yeast or liver,

| Nutrient | RDA†/DV‡ | Food sources | Benefit |
|---|---|---|---|
| Vitamin A | 5000 IU*/5000 IU | Apricots, broccoli, cantaloupe, carrots, mangoes, spinach, pumpkin, squash, watermelon | Vision, bone and teeth growth structure and function of skin and mucous membranes |
| B vitamins | | | |
| Thiamin (vitamin $B_1$) | 1.1-1.5 mg/1.5mg | Brown rice, eggs, legumes, oatmeal, oranges, pasta, peanuts, pork, wheat germ | Carbohydrate metabolism Optimizes function of nervous system |
| Riboflavin (vitamin $B_2$) | 1.3-1.7 mg/1.7mg | Asparagus, avocados, broccoli, beef, dairy products, mushrooms, salmon, turkey | Fat, protein, and carbohydrate metabolism, healthy skin |
| Niacin | 15-20 mg/20mg | Asparagus, broccoli, cereals, fish, legumes, meats, peanut butter, poultry, whole grain foods | Carbohydrate, fat, and protein metabolism, nervous system function, oxygen consumption by cells |
| Vitamin $B_6$ | 1.6-2.0 mg/2.0mg | Avocados, bananas, cauliflower, chicken, fish, green peppers, raisins, soybeans, spinach | Protein and carbohydrate metabolism cell growth and function |
| Folate (folic acid) | 0.2-0.4 mg/0.4mg | Asparagus, bananas, broccoli cantaloupe, legumes, mushrooms, poultry, strawberries, tuna, wheat germ | Tissue growth and repair, red blood cell development |
| Vitamin $B_{12}$ | 2.0 mcg/2.0 mcg | Cheese, eggs, fish, shellfish, meat | Tissue growth and repair, red blood cell development nervous system, skin |
| Biotin | 0.3 mg/0.3 mg | Cauliflower, eggs. legumes, nuts, oatmeal, peanut butter, poultry wheat germ | Carbohydrate, fat, and protein metabolism |
| Pantothenic acid | 4-7 mg/10 mg | Avocados, broccoli, eggs, fish, mushrooms, nuts, whole grains | Carbohydrate, fat, and protein metabolism |
| Vitamin C | 60 mg/60 mg | Citrus fruits, broccoli, cabbage, kiwifruit, melons, green peppers raspberries, strawberries, tomatoes | Maintains collagen metabolism in mucous membranes, joints, and blood vessels |
| Vitamin D | 5 mcg/400 IU | Baked goods, cereals, eggs, dairy products, salmon, tuna, and sunlight | Calcium absorption bone and teeth growth |

| | | | |
|---|---|---|---|
| Vitamin E | 10 mg/30 IU | Apples, broccoli, mangos, peanuts, spinach, vegetable oils, whole wheat | Protection of cells from damage |
| Vitamin K | 80 mcg/None | Avocados, broccoli, cabbage, carrots, dairy products, eggs, spinach, tomatoes | Blood clotting |

†Recommended daily allowance ‡Daily value *International Units

described as alleviating myasthenia in experimental animals; the alleged vitamin $B_4$ 'deficiency' responds to a variety of agents, including adenine, arginine, cystine, glycine and thiamine; it is not a vitamin

**vitamin $B_5$** An obsolete term for 1. Nicotinic acid (niacin) and nicotinamide 2. Pantothenic acid

**vitamin $B_6$** Pyridoxine CLINICAL NUTRITION A family of B vitamins (including pyridoxal, pyridoxamine, pyridoxine) that are critical to immune function, neural transmission, metabolism, and red cell synthesis; vitamin $B_6$ is obtained in the diet in avocados, bananas, brown rice, corn, fish, meat, nuts, poultry, and whole grains; pharmacologic doses may be effective for carpal tunnel syndrome, seizures in infants, and in premenstrual syndrome TOXICITY Severe nerve damage, which requires months for recuperation. See Vitamin $B_6$ deficiency

**vitamin $B_6$ deficiency** A rare condition that may occur in malabsortion, diabetes, pregnancy, the elderly, and in those taking oral contraceptives CLINICAL Dermatitis, depression, insomnia, irritability, muscle fatigue, nausea, vomiting. See Vitamin $B_6$

**vitamin $B_6$-dependency syndromes** A group of functional or structural enzyme defects that respond to a massive excess (50-100-fold greater than the minimum daily requirements) of pyridoxine; the vitamin $B_6$-dependency syndromes are heterogeneous in nature, and include vitamin $B_6$-dependent convulsions, vitamin $B_6$-responsive anemia, xanthurenic aciduria, cystathioninuria, homocystinuria and may be due to a defective structure of the apoenzyme, its coenzyme binding site or some aspect of coenzyme synthesis CLINICAL Predominantly neurological disease including mental retardation, psychiatric symptoms, seizures, convulsions, ataxia, spasticity and peripheral neuropathy TREATMENT Neonates respond well to early therapy

**vitamin $B_7$** 1. Biotin, see there 2. Carnitine, see there

**vitamin $B_8$** Adenylic acid (a nucleotide)

**vitamin $B_9$** Folic acid, see there

**vitamin $B_{10}$** A growth and feathering promoter in chickens, considered a pseudovitamin in humans, which corresponds to a mixture of folic acid and vitamin $B_{12}$; it is not a vitamin

**vitamin $B_{11}$** A growth and feathering promotor of chickens, which may be identical to vitamin $B_{10}$. See Pseudovitamin

**vitamin $B_{12}$** Animal protein factor, antianemic factor, antipernicious anemia factor, cow manure factor, cyanocobalamin, erythrocyte maturation factor, extrinsic factor, LLD factor, maturation factor, methylcobalamin, zoopherin CLINICAL NUTRITION A water-soluble vitamin of animal origin, which is required for the synthesis of DNA; vitamin $B_{12}$ is absorbed from the gastrointestinal tract only when it is bound to intrinsic factor, a glycoprotein produced and secreted by the gastic parietal cells; the body stores up to one years' worth of vitamin $B_{12}$ in the liver, kidneys, and heart. States in which there is rapid cell turnover (eg growth spurts in children, malignancy) require increased amounts of vitamin $B_{12}$; vitamin $B_{12}$ is

**INCREASED IN** Chronic myelogenous leukemia, chronic obstructive pulmonary disease, congestive heart failure, hepatocellular disease, obesity, polycythemia vera, renal failure

**DECREASED IN** Atrophic gastritis, drugs (antibiotics, anticonvulsants, antimalarials, antituberculous agents, chemotherapy, contraceptives, diuretics, oral hypoglycemics, sedatives), inflammatory bowel disease (eg Crohn's disease, ulcerative colitis), intrinsic factor deficiency (which causes megaloblastic anemia), malabsorption, malnutrition, parasites (eg *Diphyllobotrium latum*), and veganism*

*A strict vegetarian diet, in which its victim ingests no proteins of animal origin, including meat, fish and dairy products; all vegans are at risk for vitamin $B_{12}$ deficiency; in addition, vegan adolescents may not

meet energy requirements during the growth spurt and may become deficient in vitamin $B_6$ and riboflavin; the high-fiber diet may chelate calcium, zinc and iron, and reduce absorption of essential cations and trace minerals

See Pareve, Vegan, Vegetariansim; Cf Lacto-ovo vegetarian

**vitamin $B_{13}$** Orotic acid; it is not a vitamin

**vitamin $B_{15}$** Pangamate, a pseudovitamin

**vitamin $B_{17}$** 1. Amygdalin, see there 2. Laetrile, see there

**vitamin $B_c$** Folic acid, see there

**vitamin $B_c$ conjugate** Folic acid, see there

**vitamin $B_p$** A factor that treats perosis in chickens, which responds to a mixture of choline and manganese; it is not a vitamin

**vitamin $B_T$** Carnitine, see there

**vitamin $B_\tau$** Carnitine, see there

**vitamin $B_w$** Biotin, see there

**vitamin $B_x$** Para-aminobenzoic acid, see there

**vitamin C** Antiscorbutic factor, antiscorbutic vitamin, ascorbic acid, cevitamic acid, hexuronic acid, reducing factor CLINICAL NUTRITION A vitamin that promotes the growth, formation, and maintenance of bones, and teeth, the repair of tissues and blood vessels, and increases resistance to infections; it is ingested in the diet in citrus fruits, tomatoes, and leafy green vegetables. See Rebound scurvy, Vitamin C deficiency, Vitamin C intoxication

**vitamin C deficiency** Scurvy A condition caused by inadequate consumption of vitamin C, which is characterized by fatigue, bleeding gums, poor wound healing, reduced resistance to colds and infections, and weight loss. See Rebound scurvy, Vitamin C

**vitamin C intoxication** A condition caused by self-prescribed megadoses of vitamin C, which is characterized by diarrhea, dental erosion, uricosuria, kidney stones, interference with vitamin $B_{12}$ absorption, increased iron absorption, reduced copper and selenium absorption, increased estrogens in those receiving exogenous estrogens, rebound scurvy when megadoses are reduced, and possibly death in those with sickle cell anemia (*N Engl J Med 1993; 329:234*). See Rebound scurvy, Vitamin C

**vitamin $C_2$** An obsolete term for bioflavonoids, substances with activities that partially overlap those of vitamin C

**vitamin $D_3$** Cholecalciferol Vitamin D is a mixture of several forms of vitamin D; vitamin $D_3$ is synthesized in the skin on exposure to ultraviolet light; vitamin $D_2$ is derived only from the diet; both vitamins $D_2$ and $D_3$ are metabolized to 25-hydroxy vitamin D in the liver and then to the active 1,25 dihydroxy form in the kidney; vitamin D has a major role in the intestinal absorpton of calcium, bone calcium balance, and renal excretion of calcium, and is measured as part of a 'workup' for hypocalcemia, hypercalcemia and hypophosphatemia TOXICITY Infants given excess vitamin D may develop atherosclerosis, severe mental retardation, facial dysmorphia, kidney damage, recurrent infections, anorexia, failure to thrive, and may die; as with adults ingesting megadoses of vitramin D, the damage is caused by excess calcium absorption. See Vitamin D deficiency, Vitamin D intoxication

**vitamin D deficiency** A condition caused by inadequate intake of vitamin D and characterized by irritability, muscle hyperactivity, diarrhea, and osteoporosis. See Vitamin D

**vitamin D-dependent rickets** Pseudovitamin D resistant rickets An autosomal recessive disorder of bone and calcium metabolism characterized by the signs and symptoms of rickets (hypocalcemia, low-to-normal plasma phosphate, and increased parathyroid hormone)

▶ **VITAMIN D-DEPENDENT RICKETS, TYPES OF**

- **TYPE I** An autosomal recessive condition characterized by defective (25-hydroxy-cholecalciferol 1-$\alpha$-hydroxylase) that converts 25-(OH)- to 1,25-$(OH)_2$ vitamin D; it responds to vitamin 1,25-$(OH)_2D_3$
- **TYPE II** An autosomal recessive condition characterized by alopecia, high plasma levels of vitamin 1,15-$(OH)_2D_3$, end-organ defects of renal tubules, intestinal mucosa and bone; it is refractory to therapy

**vitamin D intoxication** A condition that occurs in those who either self-prescribe megadoses of vitamin D, or consume excess dairy products; it is characterized by anorexia, headaches, muscle weakness, nausea, thirst, and organ damage (heart, liver, kidney) due to calcium deposition. See Vitamin D

**vitamin E** $\alpha$-Tocopherol, antisterility factor, antisterility vitamin A family (see figure) of lipid-soluble antioxidants that stabilizes unsaturated lipids, preventing peroxidative decomposition of membrane lipids and enzyme inactivation, as well as protecting against chemical toxins; vitamin E is a potent antioxidant, carried by low-density lipoprotein, which inhibits smooth muscle proliferation; it is present in soybeans, vegetable oils, nuts and others; pharmacologic doses of vitamin E in the elderly are reported to boost the immune system, increase lymphokine and antibody production, mitogenic response and suppress prostaglandin production. See Vitamin E deficiency, Vitamin E intoxication

*Relative risk ± 0.61 after relevent adjustments *(N Engl J Med 1993; 328:1444OA, 1450OA)* a randomized, double-blinded, placebo-controlled trial involving 34 486 postmenopausal women suggest the intake of vitamin E from food (not from supplements) is inversely related to the risk of death from coronary heart disease; vitamin A and C had no effect *(N Engl J Med 1996; 334:1156OA)* vitamin E supplements may reduce the risk for coronary artery disease, stress, and posibly cancer; it is not protective against breast cancer *(N Engl J Med 1993; 329:234OA)*

**vitamin E deficiency** A condition that may result from chronic fat malabsorption, as occurs in cystic fibrosis, but rarely causes clinical disease in humans CLINICAL Spinocerebellar degeneration, progressive gait ataxia, loss of proprioception, incoordination, dysarthria, ophthalmoplegia, pigmentary retinopathy, generalized muscle weakness, superficial sensory loss, chronic liver disease. See Vitamin E

Note: Vitamin E deficiency was first associated with testicular atrophy in the male rat, leading to its intermittent abuse as a male 'sexual tonic'

**vitamin E intoxication** A condition that may result from chronic excess (often self-prescribed) of vitamin E CLINICAL Gastrointestinal complaints (eg nausea), vertigo, blurred vision, fatigue, oral inflammation, decreased glucose, thyroxine, and wound healing, muscle weakness, increased lipids, cholesterol, and bleeding. See Vitamin E

**vitamin F** An obsolete term for essential fatty acids, which in humans are arachidonic acid, linoleic acid, and linolenic acid. See Linoleic acid, Linolenic acid

**vitamin G** Riboflavin, see there

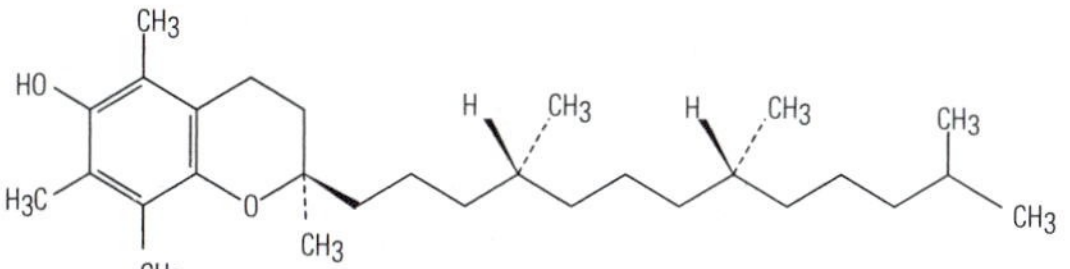

HO, $H_3C$, $CH_3$, $CH_3$, H, $CH_3$, H, $CH_3$, $CH_3$, $CH_3$, $CH_3$, O

**vitamin E**

**vitamin $GH_3$** Gerovital, see there

**vitamin H** Biotin, see there

**'vitamin H'** EMERGENCY MEDICINE A colloquial term for haloperidol, which may be injected in a patient undergoing acute psychiatric decompensation *(the Sciences July/August 1987, p6)*

**vitamin $H_3$** Gerovital, see there

**vitamin I** Carnitine, see there

**vitamin J** Bioflavonoids, see there

**vitamin K** A general term for the fat-soluble vitamins ($K_1$, $K_2$, $K_3$) that are required for the hepatic synthesis of prothrombin and coagulant factors VII, IX, and X) 2-methyl-1,4 naphthoquinone and its derivatives, which have antihemorrhagic activity; vitamin K is present in cheese, green tea, leafy greens, liver, oats, and egg yolks. See Vitamin K deficiency, Vitamin K intoxication

O, O, $(CH_2CH{=}CCH_2)_n$, $CH_3$, $CH_3$

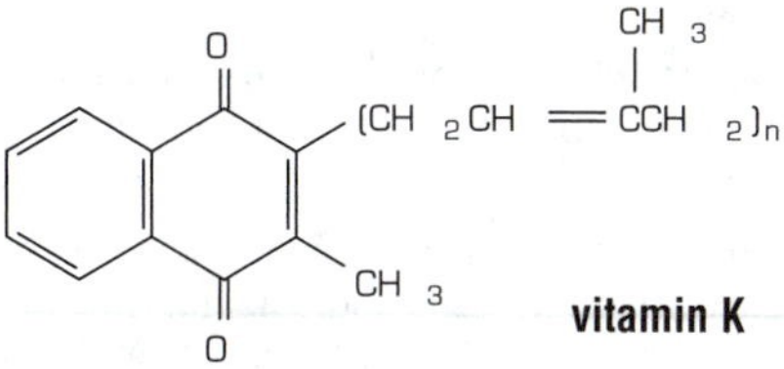

**vitamin K**

**vitamin K-dependent proteins** A group of coagulation factor proenzymes (factors II, VII, IX and X) produced in the liver, which contain multiple residues of γ-carboxyglutamic acid, an amino acid produced by the post-translational action of a vitamin K-dependent γ-carboxylase on certain glutamyl residues

Note: Four other proteins bear γ-carboxyglutamic acid and have been designated proteins C, S, Z and M; while M is poorly characterized, proteins C, S, and Z have amino-terminal homology with prothrombin; VKDPs also have another unusual amino acid, β aspartic acid, currently of unknown function

**vitamin K deficiency** An extremely rare condition, as most vitamin K is produced in the large intestine by bacterial flora; it may occur in infants with inadequate intestinal bacteria and results in clotting defect. See Vitamin K

**vitamin K intoxication** An extremely rare condition that occurs in those who self-prescribe megadoses of vitamin K, resulting in allergic reactions. See

Vitamin K

**The Vitamin King** See Kurt Donsbach

**vitamin $L_1$** Anthranilic acid

**vitamin $L_2$** Adenylthiomethylpentose

**vitamin M** Folic acid, see there

**vitamin N** A preparation from the brain or stomach, which was described as being anticarcinogenic; it is not a vitamin

**vitamin O** 1. Oxygen 2. Any form of supplementary oxygen

**vitamin P** Bioflavonoids, see there

**vitamin PP** Nicotinic acid, see there

**vitamin $P_4$** Troxerutin, a pseudovitamin

**vitamin R** A folic acid-related compound that promotes growth in bacteria; it is not a vitamin

**vitamin S** A streptogenin-related protein that promotes growth in chicks; it is not a vitamin

**vitamin T** A mixture of amino acids, DNA nucleotides, folacin and vitamin $B_{12}$ that promotes growth and wound-healing in yeasts and insects; it is not a vitamin

**vitamin U** A general term for methylsulfonium salts of methionine, derived from cabbage juice, claimed to heal peptic ulceration; it is not a vitamin

**vitamin V** A tissue 'factor' composed of NAD+ and NADH, which promotes bacterial growth; it is not a vitamin

**Viva Natural** FRINGE ONCOLOGY A proprietary seaweed extract that stimulates the immune system, in particular macrophages, which is said to be effective against leukemia and lung cancer *(Moss, 1992)*. See Chinese herbal medicine

**vivation** 1. Conscious-connected breathing, see there 2. Rebirthing therapy, see there

**Viviano method** An eclectic behavior modification technique developed by a New York psychologist, Ann Viviano, which incorporates components of meditation, modern medicine, neuro-linguistic programming, New Age mysticism, quantum physics, and Reiki. See Behavioral intervention

**Vlastimil Brych** see Brych affair

**volatile oil** HERBAL MEDICINE A general term for a type of essential oil produced by plants that volatilizes, ie is aromatic; volatile oils include cineole, limonene, pinene, thymol, and others. See Essential oil, Herbal medicine; Cf Fixed oil

**vomitroot** Lobelia, see there, *Lobelia inflata*

**VX-478** AIDS An inhibitor of HIV-1 protease that may decrease the viral load in those infected with HIV (*Bio/Technology 1995; 13:206*). See AIDS therapy

**W factor** Biotin, see there

***wai qi liao fa*** *Qigong* therapy, see there

***wai qi zhi liao*** *Qigong* therapy, see there

**wake-robin** Birthroot, see there, *Trillium erectum*

**waldmeister** Sweet woodruff, see there, *Asperula odorata*

**wall rose** Multiflowered rose, see there, *Rosa multiflora*

**walking** A health-enhancing low-impact exercise that is encouraged by both conventional and alternative health care practitioners; walking is less traumatic to the musculoskeletal tissues than are the high-impact sports, which include running, jogging, basketball and others; incorporation of a 30 minute-walk/day without an increase in caloric consumption results in a 16-pound weight loss per year; regular walking is beneficial for patients with arthritis, back pain, cardiovascular disease, (non-insulin-dependent) diabetes mellitus, hypertension, osteoporosis, and upper body injuries. See Low-impact exercise, Low-impact sport; Cf High-impact exercise, High-impact sport

**walnut** CLINICAL NUTRITION The ridged edible seed of a deciduous tree of the genus *Juglans;* walnuts are a source of dietary fat* reported to decrease the risk of ischemic heart disease, by decreasing cholesterol, and favorably modifying the lipoprotein profile*. See Nuts

*Other nuts, eg almonds, hazelnuts are thought to have similar effects, although the content of α-linolenic acid in walnuts (6.3g/100g) is much higher (< 0.7g/100g); BIOCHEMISTRY 81% of the total calories from walnuts derive from fat; the polyunsaturated fat:saturated fat ratio is 7.1:1 (one of the highest found in naturally-occurring foods); 12% of walnut fat (7g/100g edible content) is n-3 linolenic acid (*N Engl J Med 1993; 328:603,* for critiques of report's conclusions, *ibid; 329:359c*)

***wan*** Pill–Chinese medicine, see there

***wan sui teng*** Shiny asparagus, see there, *Asparagus lucidus*

***wang bu liu hsing*** Cowherd, see there

***wang bu lio xing*** Cowherd, see there

**Warburg effect** EXPERIMENTAL ONCOLOGY The observation that most malignant cells obtain their energy from anaerobic metabolism. Some practitioners of alternative forms of health care believe the Warburg effect can be exploited by reducing the energy available to malignant cells through use of hydrazine sulfate, and other agents *(Moss, 1992*). See Hydrazine sulfate, Unproven methods for cancer management

**Warriorobics®** A health enhancing system developed by Henry Smith, which combines aerobics, aikido, and *ki* breathing; Cf Aerobics, Martial arts

**water** A colorless liquid composed of hydrogen and oxygen, which is critical to life and most biological reactions ALTERNATIVE NUTRITION Adequate consumption of water (6 to 8 glasses/day) is considered a 'good' habit, although most people do not; proper hydration (ie ingestion of adequate water) is believed to alleviate altitude sickness, common cold, diarrhea (see BRATT diet), muscle soreness, prevent illness, hangover, increase mental faculties, and mental agility. See Hydrotherapy, Mineral water, Spring water

**water balance** A state of equilibrium in which the fluid intake from water and other beverages, and foods equals fluid 'losses' in the urine, gastrointestinal tract, sweat, and other

**walnut** *Juglans* species

secretions. See Water

**waterbed** A bed with a water-filled mattress that has some therapeutic efficacy GASTROENTEROLOGY Waterbed users are reported to be either five times more likely to have reflux esophagitis (*JAMA 1987; 257:2033*), or have no risk for reflux, measured by pH monitors (*Dig Dis Sci 1989; 34:1585*) NEONATOLOGY Oscillating water beds in preterm infants provide compensatory movement stimulation, reducing uncomplicated apnea of prematurity, with increased quiet sleep, decreased crying, fussiness, and enhanced growth; non-oscillating water-beds are used for narcotic-exposed neo-nates*. See Hydrotherapy

*Note: One group of infants born to addicted mothers had significantly higher central nervous system subscores, required less medication to control withdrawal symptoms and had an earlier onset of consistent weight gain (*Am J Dis Child 1988; 142:186*)

**watercress** *Nasturtium officinale*, nasturtum HERBAL MEDICINE A perennial aquatic plant that contains glycosides, minerals, vitamins A, C, E, niacin, and volatile oils; it is diuretic, expectorant, and has been used internally for coughs and bronchitis, diabetes, weakness, and as a poultice for gout and rheumatic disease WARNING Watercress may be a vector for liver flukes, and must be adequately cleaned. See Herbal medicine

**watercress** *Nasturtium officinale*

**water cure** Hydrotherapy, see there

**water cure establishment** Health spa, see there

**water fast** ALTERNATIVE NUTRITION A strict 'elimination' fast in which the person ingests only water. See Fasting

**water filter** PUBLIC HEALTH A device that removes various impurities from the water, including heavy metals, chlorine, microorganisms, and pesticides. See Bottled water

Note: Less than 10% of filters from nearly 600 manufacturers of water filters meet industry standards, and perform as advertised (*Castleman, 1996*)

**water flag** Blue flag, see there, *Iris versicolor*

**water pill** CLINICAL NUTRITION A colloquial term for any drug that evokes diuresis, eg furosemide; water pills have been abused by athletes who attempt to reach a certain weight for combative sports, eg wrestling and boxing

**water plantain** Alisma, see there, *Alisma plantago-aquatica*

**water shamrock** Bogbean, see there, *Menyanthes trifoliata*

**water therapy** ALTERNATIVE MEDICINE A general term for the use of special waters, either externally or internally; external use of therapeutic water–aquatic hydrotherapy, colloqually termed 'taking the waters,' most commonly occurs at a health spa believed to have 'healing' waters, which may be accompanied by exercise, saunas, and massages with therapeutic oils; internal ingestion of therapeutic waters is of uncertain efficacy, as there are no trace minerals or elements in such waters that are not readily available in the usual diet. See Hydrotherapy

**water thistle** Teasel, see there, *Dipsacus syl-vestris*

**water trefoil** Bogbean, see there, *Menyanthes trifoliata*

**watsu** Water shiatsu ALTERNATIVE MEDICINE A component of bodywork tantra, in which the client is placed in warm water to the chest level, while the practitioner rocks and rotates him. See Bodywork tantra; Cf Tantsu

**wax** FOOD INDUSTRY A water-insoluble product used to coat certain vegetables, eg cucumbers, green and red peppers, which may be combined with fungicides to retard spoilage. See Food additives

Note: Given the carcinogenic potential of fungicides, peeling of fruits and vegetables has been recommended by both mainstream and alternative nutritionists

**waxberry** Bayberry, see there, *Myrica cerifera*

**wax dolls** Fumitory, see there, *Fumaria officinalis*

**wax myrtle** Bayberry, see there, *Myrica cerifera*

**wax tree** Japanese wax privet, see there, *Ligustrum japonicum*

**weed** Marijuana, see there, *Cannabis sativa*

**weeping golden bell** *Forsythia suspensa, lian qiao, lien chiao, Syringa suspensa* CHINESE MEDICINE A shrub, the fruit of which is analgesic, anti-inflammatory, antipyretic, diuretic, and has been used for abscesses, allergies, breast tumors, colds, fever, heat rash, and lymphadenitis. See Chinese herbal medicine

**weight cycling** Fluctuation in body weight

**weight-cycling hypothesis** METABOLISM A hypothesis that holds that fluctuations in body weight have negative health consequences, including increased total mortality and mortality from coronary artery disease, independent of obesity body weight trends over time (*N Engl J Med 1991; 324:1839, 1887ed*)

**weight training** A health-promoting exercise, that is useful in any age group, particularly the elderly; weight training increases muscle mass, walking speed, climbing ability, and sense of well-being; it is believed to be beneficial in arthritis, cardiovascular disease, depression, (noninsulin-dependent) diabetes, increasing gastrointestinal transit time, obesity, and osteoporosis

**Weight Watchers®** NUTRITION A proprietary program for weight control based on sound principles of nutrition, ie eating 'healthy foods' and spurning of dietary fads, exercise, and abundant group support ☎ *1.800.651.6000*. See Diet

**Andrew Weil** A Harvard-trained, Tucson, Arizona-based physician who has helped popularize the alternative health care movement through books (*Health and Healing, 1983, 1995 and Natural Health, Natural Healing, 1995, both Houghton Mifflin, New York*), and frequent appearances before the mass media; Cf Chopra

**wellness** ALTERNATIVE MEDICINE A state of well-being; advocates of alternative forms of health 'aggressively' pursue a state of wellness through proper diet, exercise, use of herbal medicines PUBLIC HEALTH A state of well-being. See Health

**Western diet** PUBLIC HEALTH A diet loosely defined as one high in saturated fats, red meats, and 'empty' carbohydrates, and low in fresh fruits and vegetables, whole grains, seafoods, and poultry. See Food pyramid, Mediterranean diet

**Western herbal medicine** See Herbal medicine

**contemporary Western massage** ALTERNATIVE MEDICINE A generic term for any form of massage based on mainstream medical understanding of anatomy and physiology, which uses various forms of manipulation; the Western massage extends beyond the physical aspects of traditional European and Swedish massages, with the intent of balancing the mind and body, and release emotions; contemporary Western massages include Bindegewebsmassage, Bonnie Prudden myotherapy, cross-fiber friction massage, deep tissue massage, Esalen/Swedish massage, manual lymph drainage, myofascial release therapy, neuromuscular massage, and sports massage, discussed elsewhere in this work. See Massage therapy; Cf Bodywork

**Western medicine** Mainstream medicine, see there

**wet rebirthing** See Rebirthing therapy

**wet sheet pack** Body wrap, see there

**wet tank** Floatation tank, see there

**wheat germ** ALTERNATIVE NUTRITION The nucleus of the wheat kernel, which has a high content of octacosanol

Note: Long promoted as a healthy food, there is little data to support the widely held belief that wheat germ increases vigor, stamina, and athletic performance

**wheatgrass diet** CLINICAL NUTRITION The use of wheatgrass juice as a food, medicine, and tonic, a concept first championed in the 1950s by a Ms A Wigmore; its enthusiasts consume wheatgrass juice for anemia, constipation, and detoxification, and apply it topically for bites, burns, and cuts. See Diet

**wheat grass therapy** FRINGE ONCOLOGY Wheat grass is also believed to strengthen the immune defenses against cancer, as wheat grass contains chlorophyll, vitamins, minerals, and phytochemicals; in addition to wheat grass juice, the diet includes sprouted grains, raw vegetables and fruits, nuts and seeds, wheat grass enemas, exercise, imagery and visualization, and stress reduction programs

**whey** The watery fluid separated from a clot of casein and fat in making curds from milk; whey contains most of the lactose and water-soluble minerals found in milk

Note: In cow's milk; the casein:whey ratio may have an effect on an individual's cholesterol levels as an adult (*Science News 1994; 146:137*)

**whippoorwill's shoe** Lady's slipper, see there, *Cypripedium calceolus*

**whirlpool** NATUROPATHY A bath in which the water is moved by small jets over the body as a therapy for arthritic complaints, burns, frostbite, musculoskeletal injuries, skin disease, sports injuries, and to promote relaxation. See Hydrotherapy; Cf Jacuzzi

**whirlpool dermatitis** Hot tub rash, see there

**'white beverage'** CLINICAL NUTRITION A generic term for imitation milks and nondairy milk substitutes (eg soy milk) used in developed nations for children with milk allergies, and in developing countries where animal fats are in short supply. See Breast milk, Raw milk

**white birch** *Betula alba*; *B pendula*; betula, European white birch, paper birch, silver birch HERBAL MEDICINE A tree that contains betulinol, glycosides, flavonoids, saponins, sesquiterpenes, tannins, and volatile oil (eg betulin); it is antipyretic, antirheumatic, antiseptic, diuretic, and has been used topically for eczema and psoriasis, and as a tea to lower cholesterol, stimulate bile flow, and for rheumatic complaints. See Herbal medicine

**white bird's eye** Chickweed, see there, *Stellaria media*

**white bryony** *Bryonia alba* HERBAL MEDICINE White bryony is little used and less justified in traditional herbal medicine given its toxicity; it is a homeopathic remedy that is normally administered in very high dilutions TOXICITY Bronchial irritation, cough, diarrhea, dilated pupils, feathery pulse, gastrointestinal discomfort, headache, hypothermia, jaundice, vertigo, cardiovascular collapse, and possibly death. See Botanical toxicity HOMEOPATHY *Bryonia*, see there

**white cedar** Thuja, see there, *Thuja occidentalis*

**white coat hyperglycemia** A false elevation of glucose levels due to the psychological stress of being examined by 'white coated' health professionals in a clinical setting

**white coat hypertension** Office hypertension A transient increase in blood pressure that occurs in apprehensive patients when faced with the 'white coat' of the physician, especially when the patient is female and the doctor male, possibly resulting in inappropriate anti-hypertensive therapy; this form of pseudohypertension may be prevented by either having a nurse or technician measure the pressure or by measuring the pressure after a physical examination

**Ellen G White** The founder (1827-1915) of the Seventh-day Adventists, who advocated vegetarianism, exercise, cleanliness, abstinence from alcohol, tobacco, and sex; a sickly woman, she recruited John Harvey Kellogg (of breakfast cereal fame) as the chief physician for her first residential health clinic, the Battle Creek Sanatorium; Kellogg and White parted ways in 1907, when he was expelled from White's flock

**white false hellebore** *Veratrum album* HERBAL MEDICINE A weed native to Asia that contains alkaloids, including protoveratrine A and B, that have been used for hypertension; it is also used for arthritis, cholera, gout, muscular dystrophy, rheumatic pain, and skin and other infections. See Herbal medicine

**white birch** *Betula alba*

**white popular** *Populus tremuloides*

**white flour** CLINICAL NUTRITION Wheat that has been milled, removing the outer cellulose layer (bran) and destroying nutrients; the nutrients lost (eg niacin, riboflavin, thiamin, and iron) in milling may be restored by chemically enriching white flour. See Refining, White rice; Cf Bran, Wheat germ, Whole grains

**white horehound** horehound, see there, *Marrubium vulgare*

**white mustard** *Sinapsis alba*, kedlock, yellow mustard HERBAL MEDICINE An annual primarily used as a seasoning, which has been used topically as a plaster for relieving minor pain TOXICITY If left in place for too long a period, mustard plasters may cause vesiculation. See Herbal medicine

**white nut** *Gingko biloba*, see there white nut

**white peony** *Paeonia albiflora*, *bai shao*, Chinese peony, ladle medicine, *Paeonia lactiflora*, *shao yao*; *Paeonia officinale* may also be used CHINESE MEDICINE A perennial herb, the root of which is antipyretic, antiseptic, and hemostatic; it is used for lower abdominal pain, cholecystitis, gastroenteritis, heat rash, menstrual disorders, and poor circulation. See Chinese herbal medicine

**white popular** *Populus tremuloides*, American aspen, mountain aspen, quaking aspen, quiverleaf, trembling aspen HERBAL MEDICINE A deciduous tree (illustration, left) which contains essential oil, glycosides, populin, and tannins; it is analgesic, anti-inflammatory, and antipyretic, and has been used for rheumatic disease. See Herbal medicine

**white rice** CLINICAL NUTRITION Rice that has been milled, which removes the outer cellulose layer (husk) and destroys nutrients, in particular, thiamin, the deficiency of which causes beriberi. See White flour; Cf Whole grains

**white root** Pleurisy root, see there, *Aesclepias tuberosa*

**white sauce** NUTRITION A general term for any high-calorie, cream-based sauce used in preparing fish, meats, pastas, and vegetables; given their high fat content, white sauces are regarded as being less 'healthy' than red sauces, which are lower in fat and calories; Cf Red sauce

**white squill** Sea onion, see there, *Urginea maritima*

**white tantra** AYURVEDIC MEDICINE An early form of *hatha* yoga, which is believed to balance the body's positive and negative energies, through postures (*asanas*), breathing exercises (*pranayama*), and meditation. See Ayurvedic medicine, Hatha yoga

**whitethorn** Hawthorn, see there, *Crataegus monogyna*

**white willow** *Salix alba*, common willow, European willow HERBAL MEDICINE A deciduous tree, the bark of which contains salicylic glycosides and tannins; the bark is analgesic and antipyretic, and has been used internally for digestive complaints, fever, headache, menstrual cramping, muscle, rheumatic, and gout-related pain; it has been used topically for arthritic pain and swelling, burns, and cuts TOXICITY White willow should not be used in children as salicylates are associated with Reye syndrome. See Herbal medicine

**white wood sorrel** Wood sorrel, see there, *Oxalis acetosella*

**whitten tree** Cramp bark, see there, *Viburnum opulus*

**whole body therapy** Issels' whole body therapy, see there

**whole foods diet** CLINICAL NUTRITION A nutritional plan formulated in the 1930s by VG Rocine, a Norwegian-American homeopath, and B Jensen, an American chiropractor, which is based on the belief that whole, pure, and natural foods are needed to maintain health and fight disease. Jensen

**wild cherry** *Prunus serotina*

recommended a diet that was 60% vegetables, 20% fruits, 10% starch, and 10% protein; of the foods consumed, 60% should be raw, and 40% cooked; this 'formula' results in an alkaline:acid ratio of 4:1; while meat is not forbidden in this regimen, it should be of 'high' quality in the form of wild game (which has less fat), and organically-grown livestock; foods that are fired, salted or smoked should be avoided, as should foods that are rancid, or have excess sugar. See Diet

**whole grains** Unprocessed grains ALTERNATIVE NUTRITION A general term for grains (oats, rice, wheat) from which the outer cellulose layer (bran) has not been removed; bran is removed by milling, which results in white flour and white rice, and, in the process, removes dietary fiber, nutrients and, for some, taste

**Whole Person bodywork** A form of bodywork that synthesizes aura balancing and *chakra* healing. See Bodywork

**Wholistic Health Center** An outpatient clinic owned and operated by T and R Sohn in Syosset, New York, which offers training in acupuncture, Amma therapy®, massage, and 'wholistic nursing'. See Amma therapy®

**wild black cherry** Wild cherry, see there, *Prunus serotina*

**wild brier** Dog rose, see there, *Rosa canina*

**wild carrot** Queen Anne's lace, see there, *Daucus carota*

**wild cherry** *Prunus serotina, Prunus virginiana*, chokecherry, common chokecherry, rum cherry, wild black cherry HERBAL MEDICINE A deciduous shrub (illustration, left), the bark of which contains coumarins, cyanogenic glycosides, prussic acid, tannins, and volatile oil; it is antitussive, and an ingredient of cough syrups TOXICITY The pits *and* leaves contain hydrocyanic acid (which metabolizes to cyanide), resulting in dyspnea, incoordination, imbalance, and possibly death. See Herbal medicine

***The Wild Child*** PSYCHOLOGY A film by François Truffaut about a 'wild child' (subsequently named Victor) who is believed to have been raised with little human contact, and was found in a French forest about 150 years ago (*N Engl J Med 1994; 331:1030BR*). See Anaclytic depression, Genie, Psychosocial dwarfism, Social isolation; Cf Companionship

**wild Chinese jujube** *Ziziphus jujuba, Rhamnus soporifer, shan dzao, suan dzao ren, suan zao ren* CHINESE MEDICINE A deciduous shrub, the seeds of which are nutritive, sedative, and tonic; it is used for cardiac arrhythmias, diaphoresis, fatigue, hypertension, insomnia, malnutrition, chronic thirst, and to strengthen bones and tendons. See Chinese herbal medicine

**wild Chinese violet** *Viola yesoensis, dze hua di ding, zi hua di ding*; other species used include *Fumaria officinalis*; *Viola patrinii* CHINESE MEDICINE A highly mucilaginous perennial, which is anti-inflammatory, antipyretic, a snakebite antidote, and used for abscesses and skin infections. See Chinese herbal medicine

**wild clover** Red clover, see there, *Trifolium pratense*

**wild cotton** Milkweed, see there, *Asclepia syriaca*

**wild fennel** Fennel, see there, *Foeniculum vulgare*

**wild fox silk** Dodder, see there, *Cuscuta chinensis, Cuscuta japonica*

**wild geranium** Cranesbill, see there, *Geranium maculatum*

**wild goose breathing exercise** Dayan *Qigong*, see there

**wild hops** *Bryonia*, see there, *Bryonia alba*

**wild indigo** *Baptista tinctoria*, American indigo, baptista, clover broom, horsefly weed, indigo broom, rattlebush, shoofly, yellow indigo HERBAL MEDICINE An annual herb, the root of which contains alkaloids, glycosides, and tannins; it is anti-inflammatory, antiseptic, and has been used topically for minor cuts and pain. See Herbal medicine

**wild lemon** Mayapple, see there, *Podophyllum peltatum*

**wild lettuce** *Lactuca virosa* HERBAL MEDICINE An annual that contains trace alkaloids, bitter latex, iron, triterpenes, and vitamins A, $B_1$, $B_2$, and C; it is antitussive and sedative, and has been used for anxiety, insomnia, and whooping cough TOXICITY Wild lettuce may toxic in large doses. See Herbal medicine

**wild marjoram** Marjoram, see there, *Origanum vulgare*

**wild passionflower** Passionflower, see there, *Passiflora incarnata*

**wild pennyroyal** Peppermint, see there, *Mentha piperita*

**wild rose** *Gelidium cartilagineum*, *Rosa* spp HERBAL MEDICINE A thorny shrub native to the northern hemisphere that has vitamin C-rich fruits popularly known as hips. Syrup made from wild roses are used for sore throat and colds. See Herbal medicine, Rose hips

**wild rosemary** HOMEOPATHY *Ledum*, see there, *Ledum palustre*

**wild succory** Chicory, see there, *Chicorium intybus*

**wild sunflower** Elecampane, see there, *Inula belenium*

**wild rose** *Rosa* spp

**wild thistle** Teasel, see there, *Dipsacus sylvestris*

**wild tobacco** Lobelia, see there, *Lobelia inflata*

**wild yam** *Dioscorea villosa*, colicroot, devil's broom, rheumatism root HERBAL MEDICINE A perennial vine that contains alkaloids (eg dioscorine), phytosterols, steroidal saponins (eg dioscin and tillin, yielding diosgenin), and tannins; it is anti-inflammatory, antispasmodic, cholegogic, diuretic, and has been used for colic, menstrual cramps, morning sickness, threatened abortion, muscle spasms, rheumatic pain, poor circulation, neuralgia, and urinary tract disease. See Herbal medicine

***Wilks* v. *AMA*** CHIROPRACTIC A landmark lawsuit initiated by Chester Wilk and four other chiropractors against the American Medical Association, for unfair business practices on the part of the AMA; in 1981, a jury sided with AMA, but an appeals court overturned the decision on procedural grounds; the decision of the retrial, which was settled in 1987, was based on the principles of the Sherman Antitrust Act, in which the court decided that the AMA had engaged in an illegal boycott against chiropractic, and tried to eliminate their profession; the court's decision was viewed by chiropractics and many other consumers and providers of alternative therapies as an endorsement of chiropractic as a valid profession. Such an endorsement was not and could not be made in the context of civil law (*Butler, 1992*). See Consultation clause; Cf Chiropractic malpractice

**wind grass** *Gastrodia elata*, see there

**wind flower** *Pulsatilla*, see there /

**wind force** *Vata*, see there

**wind root** Pleurisy root, see there, *Aesclepias tuberosa*

**winterbloom** Witch hazel, see there, *Hama-melis virginiana*

**winter 'blues'** Seasonal affective disorder, see there

**winter depression** Seasonal affective disorder, see there

**wintergreen** 1. CHINESE MEDICINE Japanese wax privet, see there, *Ligustrum japonicum* 2. FRINGE MEDICINE-AROMATHERAPY Wintergreen oil is believed to be useful for the common cold, headaches, and chronic pain HERBAL MEDICINE Gaultheria procumbens, boxberry, checkerberry, creeping wintergreen, mountain tea, partridgeberry, teaberry An evergreen shrub, the active principles of which (it is 90% methyl salicylate by weight) are analgesic and anti-inflammatory, and used for muscle and rheumatic pain, and sciatica TOXICITY Oil of wintergreen is poisonous and should not be ingested. See Herbal medicine PHARMACEUTICAL INDUSTRY Any of a number of artificial flavors that are similar to the oil of wintergreen. See Wintergreen

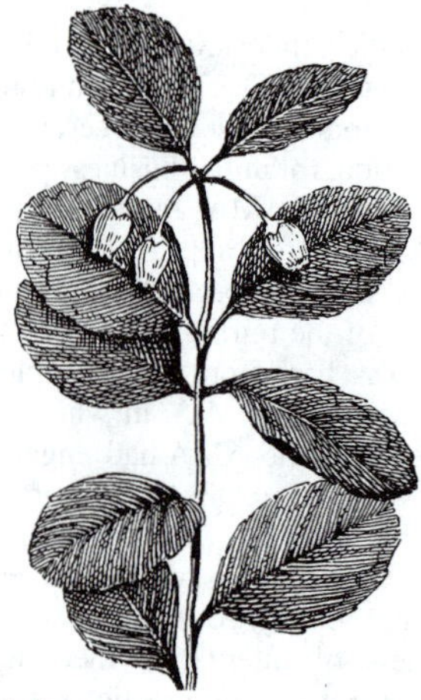

**wintergreen** *Gaultheria procumbens*

**winter savory** *Satureia montana*, mountain savory HERBAL MEDICINE A perennial shrub, the leaves of which contain essential oils (eg carvacrol and cymene), mucilage, phenols, and tannins; it is used primarily as a seasoning, but has been used by herbalists as an antiseptic gargle, appetite stimulant, carminative, and digestive tonic. See Herbal medicine

**winterweed** Chickweed, see there, *Stellaria media*

**winter worm-summer grass** *Cordiceps sinensis, dong chiung-xia cao, dung chiung-hsia tsao* CHINESE MEDICINE A caterpillar fungus* that is antitussive, expectorant, stimulant, and tonic, which strengthens the immune system and retards aging; it is used for anemia, fatigue, immune deficiency states, impotence, low back pain, night sweats, and in recuperation from surgery or chronic disease. See Chinese herbal medicine

*The fungus owes its curious name to the ancient Chinese belief that it was a worm in the winter and a plant in the summer (*Reid, 1995*)

**wise woman healing** Wisewoman ways FRINGE MEDICINE A female-oriented permutation of nature cure, based on a belief in woman's intuition, which is in part guided by the lunar cycle; wise woman healing incorporates herbal medicine, meditation, and various rituals. See Nature cure

**wisewoman ways** Wise woman healing, see there

**witch** PARANORMAL PHENOMENA A shaman in the Middle Ages who sold cures, spells, and hexes. See Shamanism

**witch's bells** Foxglove, see there, *Digitalis purpurea*

**witch doctor** Traditional healer, see there

**witch grass** Couch grass, see there, *Agropyron repens*

**witch hazel** *Hamamelis virginiana*, snapping hazel, snapping hazelnut, spotted alder, winterbloom HERBAL MEDICINE A shrub that contains choline, flavonoids, saponins, tannins, and fixed and volatile oils; it is astringent, and has been used topically for cuts and bruises, sore throat, menstrual cramps, hemorrhoids, and varicose veins. See Herbal medicine HOMEOPATHY See *Hamamelis*

**witch's milk** PEDIATRICS A clear-to-lactescent discharge from the nipples of male and female neonates, which is accompanied by breast hypertrophy, and caused by transpla-

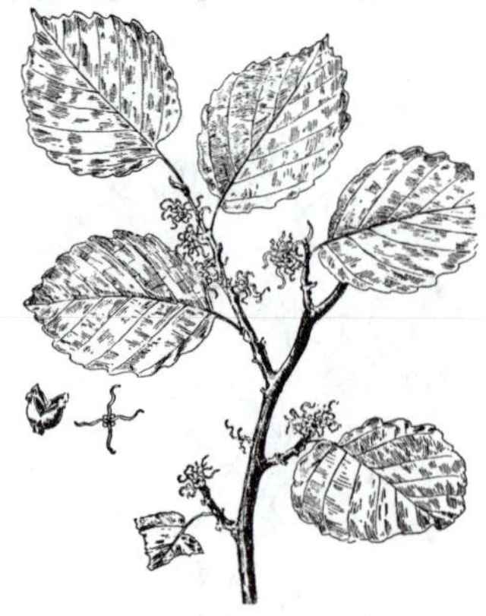

**witch hazel** *Hamamelis virginiana*

cental hormonal effects; it is most common in term infants; Cf Breast milk, Certified milk, Raw milk

**witch's pocket** Shepherd's purse, see there, *Capsella bursa-pastoris*

***Withania somnifera*** Popularly known as ashwaganda, see there

**witherite** *Baryta carbonica*, see there

**witness** Diagnostic witness FRINGE THERAPY A sample, eg a spot of blood or hair, that is believed by the practitioners of radionics to be able to transmit vibrational energies from its owner. See Radionics

**Wobe Mugos** FRINGE ONCOLOGY A proprietary (*Mucos, GmbH, Grünwald, Germany*) concentrate of enzymes obtained from the pancreas, calf thymus, peas, lentils, and papaya, that are believed to be useful for treating cancer (*Moss, 1992*). See Enzyme therapy, Unproven methods for cancer management

**wolf's bane** HERBAL MEDICINE Arnica, see there, *Arnica montana* HOMEOPATHY *Aconite*, see there, *Aconitum napellus*

**wolf's claw** *Lycopodium clavatum*, see there

**wolf spider** *Tarantula*, see there, *Lycosa tarantula*

**'women who fall'** see Factitious 'diseases,' Psychogenic syndromes

**wonder child** see Inner child therapy

**'wonder' drug** A generic term for any therapeutic agent, eg penicillin, tricyclic antidepressants, and others, which rapidly cures or clinically improves the status of a particular condition

**woodbine** Japanese honeysuckle, see there *Lonicera japonica*

**wood cinnamon** Cinnamon, see there, *Cinnamon cassia*

**wood cotton** *Eucommia ulmoides*, see there

**woodruff** Sweet woodruff, see there, *Asperula odorata*

**wood sorrel** *Oxalis acetosella*, shamrock, sour trefoil, stubwort, three-leafed grass, true wood sorrel, white wood sorrel, wood sour HERBAL MEDICINE A perennial herb that contains mucilage, oxalic acid, and vitamin C, which was formerly used as a diuretic TOXICITY Wood sorrel's high oxalic acid content precludes its use in those with renal failure, kidney stones or gout. See Botanical toxicity, Herbal medicine

**wood sour** Wood sorrel, see there, *Oxalis acetosella*

***Woodwardia radicans*** see Fern

**wood sorrel** *Oxalis acetosella*

**woody nightshade** *Dulcamara*, see there, *Solanum dulcamara*

**wormwood** *Artemisia absinthium*, absinthe, absinthium, green ginger, madderwort HERBAL MEDICINE A perennial shrub that contains absinthum (a bitter principle), carotene, tannins, vitamin C, and volatile oils, (eg thujone and chamazulene); wormwood was once used as an anthelmintic, emmenagogue, an appetite stimulant, and and to increase gastric and bile secretions TOXICITY Convul-sions, impotence, muscular weakness, nausea, vomiting, and possibly death; the FDA has labeled wormwood as 'unsafe'. See Botanical toxicity, Herbal medicine

**woundwort** Goldenrod, see there, *Solidago canadensis*

***wu jia pi*** *Eclipta prostata*, see there

***wu wei dze*** *Schisandra chinensis*, see there

***wu wei zi*** *Schisandra chinensis*, see there

**Xanthoxylum americanum** Popularly known as Northern prickly ash, see there

**xi xin** *Asarum sieboldi*, see there

**xiang ru** *Elsholtzia splendens*, see there

**xiao-chai-hu tang** JAPANESE HERBAL MEDICINE An herbal formulation that increases interferon production, which may be of use in stimulating the immune systems of individuals with cancer *(Moss, 1992)*

**xu duan** Teasel, see there, *Dipsacus silvestris*

**xuan fu hua** Elecampene, see there, *Inula helenium*

**yang** One of the two complementary opposite forces of nature in the ancient Chinese construct; yang is believed to have dark, negative, and female qualities. See Chinese medicine, *Fu* organs, Traditional Chinese medicine, Yang food; Cf Yin

**yang cancer** FRINGE MEDICINE A general term for a malignancy believed to have arisen from an excess of yang forces; the concept of yin and/or yang cancers was championed by a Japanese-American, M Kushi, who believed that yang cancers, which include those of the bone, inner areas of the brain, colon, ovary, pancreas, prostate, and rectum, were caused by a life-long excess of yang forces; Kushi believed that yang cancers can be positively influenced by a diet rich in yin foods. See Yang, Yang foods; Cf Yin Cancer, Yin and Yang cancer

**yang food** TRADITIONAL CHINESE MEDICINE A general term for a food believed in the construct of Chinese medicine to have certain polar characteristics; yang foods are grown in a cold and wet environment; they are dry, short, and hard, tend to be sour or salty, and include stems, roots, seeds, meat, poultry, hard cheese, and eggs. See Chinese medicine, Traditional Chinese medicine; Cf Yin food

**yang ru** Chinese wolfberry, see there, *Lycium chinese*

**yantra yoga** Tibetan yantra yoga, see there

**yao jen** Herbal pillow, see there

**yao jiou** Herbal liquor–Chinese medicine, see there

**yao jou** Herbal porridge–Chinese medicine, see there

**yao lu** Steam decoction, see there

**yarrow** *Achillea millefolium*, bloodwort, milfoil, millefoil, nosebleed, sanguinary, staunchgrass, thousand-leaf FRINGE MEDICINE-FLOWER ESSENCE THERAPY A floral essence believed to provide a sense of self-contained inner peace and sensitivity to the needs of others. See Flower essence therapy HERBAL MEDICINE A perennial herb that contains a bitter alkaloid (acheilleine), amino acids, cyanidin, coumarins, flavonoids, saponins, sesquiterpene lactones, sterols, tannins, and volatile oils (primarily azulene, but also borneol, camphor, cineole, thujone, and others); it is anti-inflammatory, antipyretic, antiseptic, antispasmodic, astringent, diaphoretic, diuretic, hemostatic, and vasodilatory; it is used topically for wounds, as a douche for vaginal irritation, and internally for diarrhea, fever, hemorrhoids, hypertension, internal and external bleeding, menstrual cramping, toothaches, to stimulate the appetite, and to induce thrombolysis TOXICITY Ingestion may cause photosensitivity and diarrhea, it should not be used in pregnancy, or in those allergic to ragweed. See Herbal medicine

**yawroot** Queen's delight, see there, *Stillingia sylvatica*

**yeast filtrate factor** Pantothenic acid, see there

**yeast *Lactobacillus casei* factor** Folic acid, see there

**yeast syndrome** Candida hypersensitivity syndrome, see there

**yeh hu sse** Dodder, see there, *Cuscuta chinensis, Cuscuta japonica*

**yellow** FRINGE MEDICINE–COLOR THERAPY A color that combines the energizing effects of red and the tonic properties of green; yellow is believed to stimulate the lymphatic system and cleanse the skin and intestines. See Color breathing, Color therapy, Yellow foods, Yellow metals & chemicals

**yellow cedar** Thuja, see there, *Thuja occidentalis*

**The Yellow Emperor's Classic of Internal Medicine** *Nei Jing*, see there

**yellow fat disease** A vitamin E deficiency syndrome that affects mammals fed excess n-3 polyunsaturated fatty acids, derived from fish. See Fish oil, Vitamin E, Vitamin E deficiency Note: In humans, excess fish-oils cause increased bleeding time, especially after aspirin ingestion, may play a role in cardiac necrosis and in increasing susceptibility to catecholamine-induced stress

**yarrow** *Achillea millefolium*

**yellow flag** *Iris pseudoacorus*, yellow iris, yellow water flag HERBAL MEDICINE A perennial herb, the dried rhizime of which contains alkaloids, salicylates, tannin, and volatile oil; yellow flag was once used as a blood purifier, and for flatulence, headaches, heartburn, colic, and skin complaints TOXICITY Fresh yellow flag root is poisonous, and may cause gastrointestinal pain, nausea, and vomiting. See Herbal medicine

**yellow foods** FRINGE MEDICINE–COLOR THERAPY Foods believed to stimulate the lymphatic system and cleanse the skin and intestines; yellow foods include bananas, banana squash, eggs, most cheeses, corn, yellow sweet potatoes, pineapples, lemons, grapefruits, and butter. See Color breathing, Color therapy, Yellow, Yellow metals & chemicals

**yellow gentian** Gentian, see there, *Gentiana lutea* (other species may be used)

**yellow ginger** Turmeric, see there, *Curcuma longa*

**yellow ginseng** Blue cohosh, see there, *Caulophyllum thalictroides*

**yellow grass** *Dendrobium nobile*

**yellow Indian paint** Goldenseal, see there, *Hydrastis canadensis*

**yellow Indian's shoe** Lady's slipper, see there, *Cypripedium calceolus*

**yellow indigo** Wild indigo, see there, *Baptista tinctoria*

**yellow iris** Yellow flag, see there, *Iris pseudoacorus*

**yellow jasmine** *Gelsemium*, see there, *Gelse-mium sempervirens*, *G sempervitalis*

**yellow jessamine** *Gelsemium*, see there, *Gelsemium sempervirens*, *G sempervitalis*

**yellow lady's slipper** Lady's slipper, see there, *Cypripedium calceolus*

**yellow metals & chemicals** FRINGE MEDICINE-COLOR THERAPY Metals and chemicals (eg magnesium and platinum) that are believed to stimulate the lymphatic system and cleanse the skin and intestines. See Color breathing, Color therapy, Yellow, Yellow foods

**yellow mustard** White mustard, see there, *Sinapsis alba*

**yellow puccoon** Goldenseal, see there, *Hydrastis canadensis*

**yellow root** Goldenseal, see there, *Hydrastis canadensis*

**yellow starwort** Elecampene, see there, *Inula helenium*

**yellow water flag** Yellow flag, see there, *Iris pseudoacorus*

***yen hu suo*** *Cordalis ambigua*

**yerba** *Santa eriodictyon californicum* FRINGE MEDICINE-FLOWER ESSENCE THERAPY A floral essence said to enhance one's emotional 'range'. See Flower essence therapy

***yi mu cao*** *Leonurus sibericus*, see there

***yi mu tsao*** *Leonurus sibericus*, see there

***yi yi ren*** Job's tear, see there, *Coix chinensis*

***yih jih ren*** Cardamom, see there, *Alpina oxyphylla*

***yih zhi ren*** Cardamom, see there, *Alpina oxyphylla*

**yin** One of the two complementary opposite forces of nature according to the ancient Chinese construct; yin is regarded as having bright, positive, and male qualities. See Chinese medicine, Traditional Chinese medicine, Yin food, *Zhen* organs; Cf Yang

**yin-yang**

**yin cancer** Fringe medicine A general term for a malignancy said to have arisen from an excess of yin forces; the concept of yin and/or yang cancers was championed by a Japanese-American, M Kushi, who believed that yin cancers, which include those of the outer areas of the brain, breast, esophagus and upper stomach, mouth and skin, and leukemias, were caused by a life-long excess of yin forces; Kushi believed that yin cancers can be positively influenced by a diet rich in yang foods. See Yin, Yin foods; Cf Yin and yang cancer, Yang cancer

**yin and yang cancer** FRINGE MEDICINE A general term for a malignancy believed to have arisen from a combination of yin and yang forces; the concept of yin and/or yang cancers was championed by a Japanese-American, M Kushi, who believes that these cancers, which include those of liver, lower stomach, lung, spleen, tongue, uterus, and urinary tract were due to life-long combinations of excess yin and yang forces; Cf Yin cancer, Yang cancer

**yin food** TRADITIONAL CHINESE MEDICINE A general term for a food believed in the construct of Chinese medicine is have certain polar characteristics; yin foods are grown in a hot and dry environments, are softer and juicier, tend to be aromatic, and include sugar, sweets, strong spices, alcohol, tea, and coffee. See Chinese medicine, Traditional Chinese medicine; Cf Yang food

***ying hsing*** *Gingko biloba*, see there

***ying xing*** *Gingko biloba*, see there

***yin yang huo*** Horny goat weed, see there,

*Epimedium sagittatum*

***yio*** Ointment–Chinese medicine, see there

**ylang ylang** *Matricaria recutita* FRINGE MEDICINE-FLOWER ESSENCE THERAPY A floral essence from Oriental perfume trees, which is believed to be sedative, balance the emotions, and be of use in shock and pain. See Flower essence therapy

**yoga** Hatha yoga AYURVEDIC MEDICINE A holistic system of health care and maintenance, that is widely practiced throughout the world; the word yoga comes from the Sanskrit word *yug*, for yoke; the purpose of yoga is to join the mind, body, and breath as one unit; if the mind is disturbed, the breath and body are affected; as the body's activity increases, the mind is altered and the rate and depth of the breath changes; yoga attempts to join the 3 units through proper breathing and the assumption of *asanas* (Yogic poses, see below); regular practice of yoga is believed to reduce stress, heart rate, and blood pressure and, some believe, retard aging; yoga is '*...organized into eight "limbs" that provide a complete system of physical, mental, and spiritual health* ...these limbs *...outline specific lifestyle, hygiene, and detoxification regimens, as well as physical and psychological practices that can lead to a more integrated personal development*' (*Alternative Medicine, Future Med Pub, 1994*); central to yoga are the exercises known as yogic postures (*asana*), which are divided into meditative and therapeutic *asanas*, and practiced with breath control; *asanas* is thought to squeeze old blood out of organs and tissues, allowing the influx of fresh blood

▶ **YOGA, FORMS OF**

- ***Adhayatma* yoga** *Adhyata* yoga A form of yoga that seeks the pathway to transcendental wisdom by overcoming identification with the body and mind
- ***Adhyatma* yoga** *Adhayatma* yoga, see there
- ***Ashtanga* yoga** 1. *Raja* yoga, see there 2. A form of yoga based on *raja* yoga, developed by Pathabi Jois, see *Ashtanga* yoga
- ***Astanga* yoga** *Raja* yoga, see there
- ***Bhakti* yoga** A form of yoga that seeks the pathway to a higher power through devotion and love
- ***Hatha* yoga** The 'integrative' form of yoga that seeks the pathway to a higher power by integrating the self (*ha*-sun and *tha*-moon) through relaxation, postures, breathing exercises (*pranayama*), purification practices (*kriyas*), and promoting harmony of the body and mind; *hatha* yoga is the 'gentle' yoga, and is the form best known to Westerners
- ***Japa* yoga** A spiritual form of yoga, in which enlightenment is achieved through the repetition of God's name, as a mantra
- ***Jnana* yoga** *Nana* yoga The intellectual form of yoga that seeks the pathway to transcendental wisdom (*prajna*) through meditation, thought, and understanding of the laws of the universe
- ***Karma* yoga** The service form of yoga that seeks to serve others as a pathway to a higher power
- ***Kriya* yoga** A form of yoga that requires purification practices (*kriyas*), which include the acceptance of pain
- ***Kundalini* yoga** A form of yoga that seeks the pathway to a higher power by activating *kundalini*, the primal force of nature, which resides like a coiled snake at the spine through contemplation and/or *tantra*, a sexual means of evoking *kundalini;* activation of *kundalini* may result in enlightenment, insanity, malignancy, weakness, or death
- ***Laya* yoga** A form of yoga that entails activation of *kundalini*, balancing of *chakras*, and purification practices (*kriyas*)
- ***Mantra* yoga** *Nada* yoga A sensual form of yoga that seeks the pathway to a higher power through mind control and by focusing on vibrations and radiations using sounds (bells, drums and music), which are believed to affect the endocrine system
- ***Nada* yoga** *Mantra* yoga, see there
- ***Nana* yoga** *Jnana* yoga, see there
- ***Raja* yoga** *Ashtanga* yoga, *Astanga* yoga The self-attainment form of yoga, that seeks to maximize personal potential through concentrated meditation, yogic postures (*asanas*), and breathing exercises (*pranayama*); *raja* yoga encompasses the philosophies of all the other schools of yoga

▶ **20TH CENTURY FORMS OF YOGA**

- **Integral yoga** A form of yoga founded by guru Sri Ghose Aurobindo, which synthesizes traditional forms (*bhakti* yoga, *hatha* yoga, *jnana* yoga, *karma* yoga, *raja* yoga and others) of yoga, but eliminates the excesses of some forms, in which the students may pursue physical feats at the expense of spiritual enlightenment
- **Iyengar-style yoga** A form of 'high-impact' yoga developed by BSK Iyengar, which adapts *hatha* yoga, incorporating the brisk performance of certain yogic postures (*asanas*), eg the Sun salutation into quasi-aerobic exercises, known as jumpings
- **Schatz-style yoga** A form of 'low-impact' yoga developed by MP Schatz, MD, which incorporates flowing standing poses into its routine of yogic postures (*asanas*)

In yoga, the intent is to place the mind in a deep trance-like state in which the brain is in a 'theta pattern' of 5 wavelengths/second; the practice of yoga is based on an wide range of training, ranging from self-learning audiocassette courses to rigid adherence to a guru, whose word, especially during the 'hippie years' was viewed as law; anecdotal reports suggest that yoga may be effective for alcoholism, arthritis, asthma, back pain, bronchitis, cancer, childbirth, colds, constipation, depression, diabetes, duodenal ulcers, emphysema, eye strain, fatigue, flatulence, gynecologic disorders (dysmenorrhea, premenstrual syndrome, postmenopausal syndromes), heart disease, hemorrhoids, hypertension, hyperventilation, indigestion, insomnia, mental retardation, migraines, mood swings, neural disease, neuromuscular disease, obesity, pain, panic attacks, prostate disease, rheumatic diseases, sciatica, sexual dysfunction, smoking, stress, varicose veins, (facial) wrinkles, and other conditions. See *Asana*, Autosuggestion therapy, Ayurvedic medicine, Bodywork, Complete breath, Mantra, Meditation, *Pranayama*; Cf Hypnosis, Hypnotherapy, Silva mind control

**yoga pose** Asana, see there

**yoga therapy** AYURVEDIC PSYCHOLOGY A psychotherapeutic component of *hatha* yoga, which addresses past experiences that have clogged the body/mind. See Ayurvedic medicine, Yoga

**yogic pose** *Asana*, see there

**yogurt** Yoghurt NUTRITION A smooth semisolid dairy product produced by fermentating milk with *Lactobacillus acidophilus* and other bacteria that convert lactose into lactic acid, the latter of which causes the milk to thicken; yogurt is widely regarded* as a healthy food; its consumption is associated with a 3-fold decrease in vaginal candidiasis (*Ann Int Med 1992; 116:353*); it is also used for those with lactose intolerance

*Some extreme claims about its efficacy in promoting longevity have been made; yogurt has long had currency among promoters of alternative medicine, and for some has a mystical portent, given its alleged consumption in large quantities by very old individuals living in the mountains of Eastern Europe; the argument that the actual age of these allegedly ancient people remains unconfirmed has done little to weaken the conviction on the part of 'health nuts' that yogurt (and other fermented foods, eg buttermilk, sauerkraut, beer) holds one of the keys to the fountain of youth–Author's note

**yohimbe** HERBAL MEDICINE A plant native to western Africa, which is rarely used in its native form by modern herbologists, given its toxicity TOXICITY Hypertension, insomnia, nausea, palpitations, tremors, vomiting. See Botanical toxicity, Herbal medicine, Yohimbine

**yohimbine** PHARMACOGNOSY An indoalamine alkaloid used to treat impotence which is obtained from the bark of the West African corynan (yohimbe) tree (*Corynanthe johimbe*, and others, eg *Rauwolfia serpentina*); yohimbine may be of use in treating orthostatic hypotension and ischemic vascular disease caused by autonomonic dysfunction in diabetes, narcotic overdose, possibly acting to increase dopamine release, and for psychogenic and organic impotence, possibly increase the inflow to and/or decreasing the outflow of blood from the penis

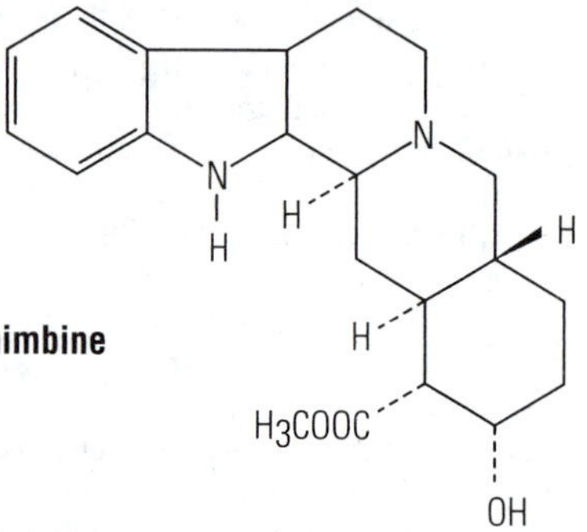

**yohimbine**

**yo-yo dieting** CLINICAL NUTRITION Undesirable dietary cycling in which there is a rapid loss of weight followed by its regain. See Starvation diet

**Yom Kippur effect** Spontaneous premature induction of labor, which occurs in pregnant Jewish women who observe Yom Kippur, the annual 24-hour religious fast of Judaism, in which there is total abstinence from food and water (*JAMA 1983;250:1317cr; JAMA 1983, 250:2469, ibid, 1984; 251:2348c*)

Note: The effect appears to be a relatively universal theme, possibly linked to dehydration, as premature labor is more common in the 'dog days' of summer among women with a different demographic pattern serviced by workers at SUNY-Downstate in Brooklyn (*S LAJINIAN IN SCIENCE NEWS 20 MAY 1995, p315*)

**youthwort** *Drosera*, see there, *Drosera rotundifolia*

***yu ju*** Solomon's Seal, see there, *Polygonatum officinale*

***yu nu*** Dodder, see there, *Cuscuta chinensis, Cuscuta japonica*

***yuan jih*** *Polygala tenuifolia*, see there

***yuan zhi*** *Polygala tenuifolia*, see there

**yuppie disease** Chronic fatigue syndrome, see there

**Zaiela/Dr Salomon** PARANORMAL PHENOMENA A 'multidimensional' entity, in which the body of Ms Ziaela is linked to the soul of a deceased Dr Salomon; in the literature from the Healthspring center Ziaela states, '...*I share the same soul as Dr Salomon* ...(which has)... *taken residence in this body to fulfill my divine purpose on this, the third dimension. I*...*experience myself on the other dimension as a being on an extraterrestrial/angelic craft*.' (*Raso, 1994*). See Body integration

No comment–Author's comment

***zang* organ** CHINESE MEDICINE Any yin organ (heart, lungs, liver, spleen, and kidneys) which, according to the traditional Chinese medical construct, controls the storage of vital substances; Cf *Fu* organs

***Zanthoxylum piperitum*** Popularly known as Szechuan pepper, see there

**zar** ETHNOMEDICINE A 'possessing spirit' that may afflict a person in primitive African cultures, who supposedly speaks through its host's mouth, and places him in a hypnotic trance, evoking distinctly unusual behavior and leaving temporary amnesia; a person may be simultaneously afflicted with multiple zars, who may discuss the host's psychological troubles, and their solutions, each in a different voice; a traditional healer (witch doctor) exorcises the spirit, and the host responds with an intense abreaction accompanied by excitement, collapse, and amnesia for the event (*Proc Roy Soc Med 1967; 60:1055*). See Traditional healer, Zar PSYCHIATRY A term used in north African and in the Middle Eastern societies for being under the influence of spirits, which may evoke various emotions or dissociative episodes that are not regarded as pathological by the person's society (*DSM-IV*). See Culture-bound syndrome

**Zarlen therapy** PARANORMAL PHENOMENA A mental healing technique linked to a New Zealander, Jonathan Sherwood, who in 1984 is believed to have been contacted by a spirit guide, Zarlen; the therapy is claimed to be useful for brain damage, color blindness, dyslexia, varicose veins, and other conditions (*Raso, 1994*)

**zeitgeber** *Zeit*, German, time, *geber*, keeper A factor in the environment that has periodicity and is capable of synchronizing the endogenous circadian rhythm into a 24-hour cycle; without zeitgebers, the free-running human clock is 25.3 hours. See Circadian rhythm, Jet lag, Shift work; Cf REM sleep

**Zen Alexander technique** ALTERNATIVE MEDICINE An eclectic synthesis of the Alexander technique, and Chinese mind/body/spirit methods, which is believed to confer one with synergistic healing abilities. See Alexander technique

**Zen Buddhism** see Zen therapy

**Zen garden therapy** ALTERNATIVE MEDICINE A type of self therapy in which a person creates a Zen garden which, for some, is the epitomy of harmony, and then meditates and contemplates life in general, and himself in particular, in the garden that he created; Zen gardens are believed to relieve stress and tension. See Meditation, Zen therapy

**Zen macrobiotic diet** ALTERNATIVE NUTRITION The original macrobiotic philosophy as formulated by George Ohsawa (1893-1966), in which he divided foods into 7 groups and the dietary regimen into 10 increasingly restrictive stages, starting with a ('normal') diet composed of 30% animal products, 30% vegetables, 15% fruits and salads, 10% grains, 10% soups, and 5% desserts; each stage increased the grain content by 10%, and decreased the non-grain portion of the diet by 10%; by the 6th stage, all animal products were eliminated; fluid intake was restricted at all stages; Ohsawa claimed that the Zen macrobiotic diet was effective for airsickness, baldness, bedwetting, cataracts and other diseases of the eyes, hemophiia, leprosy, polio, schizophrenia, seizures, sexually-transmitted diseases and many other conditions. See Kushi, Macrobiotics, Ohsawa, Simon

The original Zen macrobiotic diet was linked to at least 3 deaths–most notably Beth Ann Simon, who died malnourished and dehydrated, and a number of 'near-misses' due to malnutrition and scurvy, and has been virtually abandoned; the current macrobiotics diet was formulated by Michio Kushi, and is based on many accepted dietary principles

**zen shiatsu** A permutation of acupressure that is more rigorous than standard shiatsu, as it is accompanied by prolonged meditation and strenuous stretching exercises designed to open the meridians. See Acupressure, Shiatsu, Zen Alexander technique

**Zen therapy** ALTERNATIVE MEDICINE A type of therapy that encourages self understanding through prolonged meditation; it is believed by some to be ineffective, and possibly harmful to those who have a history of psychological vulnerability, alienation, emotional lability, and mental disorders. See Meditation, Zen garden therapy

**Zen-touch®** A painless, purportedly powerful, proprietary permutation of shiatsu

**zero balancing** ALTERNATIVE MEDICINE A type of hands-on therapy developed in 1975 by an American physician, F Smith, the purpose of which is to align the body's energy with its physical structure through the use of gentle pressure; according to its advocates, two forms of healing occur after injuries-that of the physical body, and that of its energy field; proper healing requires that the relationship between the two must be brought back to 'zero'; Cf CranioSacral Therapy™, Integrative massage, Massage therapy, Reflexology

***zhi mu*** *Anemarrhena asphodeloides*, see there

***zhi shi*** Trifoliate orange, see there, *Poncircus trifoliata*

***zi hua di ding*** Wild Chinese violet, see there, *Viola yesoensis*

**zinc** A metallic element (atomic number 30; atomic weight 65.39) essential* for growth and development, which is required for more than 200 metalloenzymes including DNA– and RNA-polymerases, carbonic anhydrase, carboxypeptidase, reverse transcriptase, as well as for zinc-finger proteins involved in gene expression; zinc is stored in synaptic vesicles and is a synaptic neuromodulator, acting in the hippocampus to induce depolarizing synaptic potentials (*Nature 1991; 349:521*) ~20% of dietary zinc is absorbed; absorption is enhanced by protein-rich foods (animal proteins, brewer's yeast, legumes, nuts, pumpkin seeds, seafood, whole grains,); ~90% is excreted in feces DISTRIBUTION 50-60% of total is in muscle, 30% in bone (*Clinical Chemistry News August 1993*) LABORATORY 70-150 µg/dL, measured by atomic absorption spectrophotometry TOXIC EXPOSURE Zinc-laden fumes and dusts are generated in the manufacture of alloys, paints, synthetic rubbers, and roofing materials. See Chelatable zinc

*RDA–recomended daily allowance, 5-15 mg/day; normal range 70-120 µg/dL

**zinc deficiency** A condition caused by inadequate dietary ingestion of zinc, and characterized by dermatitis, diarrhea, delayed hypersensitivity response, fatigue, hair loss, loss of taste, difficult pregnancy, retarded growth, hypogonadism, poor wound healing, and in children, stunted growth and sexual development. See Zinc

**zinc intoxication** A condition caused by industrial exposure or by excessive ingestion of zinc supplements, which is characterized by headaches, nausea. vomiting, dehydration, stomachaches, incoordination, and possibly kidney damage. See Zinc

***Zingiber officinale*** Popularly known as ginger, see there

**zinnia** *Zinnia elegans* FRINGE MEDICINE-FLOWER ESSENCE THERAPY A floral essence believed to induce a childlike sense of playfulness. See Aromatherapy, Flower essence therapy

***Ziziphus jujuba*** Popularly known as wild Chinese jujube, see there

***Ziziphus vulgaris*** Chinese jujube, see there

**The Zone** SPORTS MEDICINE A state of maximum physical, mental and psychological performance which is achieved by star athletes for fleeting moments in their careers. See Zone-favorable diet

**Zone-favorable diet** CLINICAL NUTRITION A series of dietary guidelines delineated by Barry Sears (*The Zone, Harper-Collins, New York, 1995*), which he believes can help any person achieve a state of peak performance, known to athletes as 'the Zone'

► **ZONE-FAVORABLE DIET, PRINCIPLES**

- **LIFE-EXTENDING (ANTI-AGING) DIET** A low-calorie, low-fat diet that supplies adequate protein and essential fats, and micronutrients–ie minerals and vitamins; consumption of high-density, high-glycemic cabohydrates, eg breads, grains, pasta, rice, and other starches should be limited, as should be arachidonic acid-rich proteins, eg egg yolks, fatty red meat, and organ meats
- **NEO-PALEOLITHIC DIET** A diet with an optimized protein-to-carbohydrate ratio, which is high in low-density, low-glycemic cabohydrates, eg fruits and high-fiber vegetables, low in high-density, high-glycemic cabohydrates, eg breads, grains, pasta, rice, and other starches, and low amounts of fats, but adequate essential fats
- **HORMONAL RESPONSES**, in particular of insulin and glucagon, which are stimulated by the ingestion of foods
- **EICOSANOIDS**, which have an essential role in human physiology. Sears divides eicosanoids into good ones (prostaglandin $E_1$) and bad eicosanoids (which are derived from arachidonic acid metabolism)

See Diet, Eicosanoids, Life-extending diet, Neo-paleolithic diet, Zone-favorable diet

**Zone of Health** Zone z'drovia, see there

**zones of hyperalgesia** Pressure points, see there

**zona z'drovia** Zone of health An exercise-based health-enhancing program developed in the former Soviet Union, which consists of dance-like movements, accompanied by accordion music. See Music therapy

**zone therapy diagnosis** Zone testing, see there

**zone testing** Concept-therapy adjusting technique, health zone analysis, suggestive therapy zone procedure, zone therapy diagnosis CHIROPRACTIC A format for diagnosing subluxation in chiropractic based on the Concept Therapy® technique. See Chiropractic, Concept Therapy® technique, Subluxation

**zone therapy** Reflex zone therapy, zonotherapy ALTERNATIVE MEDICINE The earliest form of Western (energy-enhancing) pressure point massage, which was developed in 1913 by an American physician, Wm Fitzgerald; the technique is based on the belief that there are 10 energy channels similar to meridians which, when 'blocked,' prevent the flow of neural energy through the body; zone therapy evolved to become reflexology, the form in which it currently exists; other 'energy therapies' include acupressure, reflexology, and shiatsu, discussed elsewhere in this work

**zonotherapy** Zone therapy, see there

**zoopharmacognosy** HERBAL MEDICINE The formal study of plants used by animals in their native habitats, which the animals are believed to use to 'treat' their own illnesses (*Moss, 1992*); Cf Pharmacognosy

**zoopherin** Vitamin $B_{12}$, see there

## Biblioliography

Adams RD, Victor M. Principles of Neurology, 5th ed, McGraw-Hill, NYC, 1993

The American Heritage Dictionary of the English Language, 3rd ed, Houghton-Mifflin, Boston, MA, 1992

Armstrong D, Armstrong EM. The Great American Medicine Show, Prentice Hall, NYC, 1991

Bessette AE, Chapman WK. Plants and Flowers, Dover Publications, Mineola, NY, 1992

Bliss S. The New Holistic Health Handbook, S Greene Press, Lexington, MA, Penguin Books, 1985

Braunwald E. Heart Disease, 4th ed, WB Saunders, Philadelphia, PA, 1992

Bricklin M. Practical Encyclopedia of Natural Healing, Rodale Press, Emmaus, PA1976, 1983

Butler K. Consumers' Guide to Alternative Medicine, Prometheus Books, Amherst, NY, 1992

Carroll D. The Complete Book of Natural Medicines, Summit Books, NY, 1980

Castleman M. Nature's Cures, Rodale Press, Emmaus, PA, 1996

Collinge W. The American Holistic Health Association Complete Guide to Alternative Medicine, Warner Books, NYC, 1996

The Columbia Encyclopedia, 5th ed, Columbia University Press, NYC, 1993

DeVita, VT Jr, Hellman S, Rosenberg SA. Cancer, The Principles and Practice of Oncology, JB Lippincott, Philadelphia, PA, 1993

*Diagnostic and Statistical Manual of Mental Disorders, 4th ed, American Psychiatric Association, Washington, DC, 1994

Dorland's Medical Dictionary, 25th ed, WB Saunders, Philadelphia, PA, 1974

Dorland's Medical Dictionary, 28th ed, WB Saunders, Philadelphia, PA, 1994

Duke M, Acupuncture, Pyramid House, NYC, 1972

Ensminger AH, et al, Food for Health, Pegus Press, Clovis, CA, 1986

Family Guide to Natural Medicine, Readers Digest, Pleasantville, NY, 1993

Fox A, Fox B. Alternative Healing, Career Press, Franklin Lakes, NJ, 1996

Gennaro AR, Ed. Remington's Pharmaceutical Sciences, 18th ed, Mack Publishing Co, Easton, PA, 1990

Gottlieb B, editor. New Choices in Natural Healing, Rodale Press, Emmaus, PA, 1995

Gottlieb B. New Choices in Natural Healing, Rodale Press, Emmaus, PA, 1995

Gottschalk Olsen K. The Encyclopedia of Alternative Health Care, Pocket books, NYC, 1989

Hill A. A Visual Encyclopedia of Unconventional Medicine, Crown, New York, 1979

Inglis B, West R. The Alternative Health Guide, Alfred Knopf, NYC, 1983

International Dictionary of Medicine and Biology, John Wiley & Sons, NYC, 1986

Jacobs J. The Encyclopedia of Alternative Medicine, Carlton Books, Ltd, Rutland VT, 1996

Kastner M, Burroughs H. Alternative Healing, Halcyon Publishing, La Mesa, CA, 1993

Katahn M. The Rotation Diet, WW Norton, NYC, 1986

Lerner M. Choices in Healing, The MIT Press, Cambridge, MA, 1994

Lockie A, Gedde N. The Complete Guide to Homeopathy, Dorling Kindersly, London, 1995

Mabey R. The New Age Herbalist, Gaia Books for Collier Books, NYC, 1988

Martin MC, in DeCherney AJ and Pernoll ML, Eds. Current Obstetrics & Gynecology, 8th, Appleton & Lange, Stamford, CT, 1994

The Medical Advisor: The Complete Guide to Alternative and Conventional Treatments, Time-Life Books, Alexandria, VA, 1996

The Merck Index, 12th ed, Merck & Co, 1996, Whitehouse Station, NJ

Mills S, Finando SJ, Alternatives in Healing, New American Library, NYC, 1988

Moss RW. Cancer Therapy, Equinox Press, NYC, 1992

Mundell E. Herb Bible, Simon and Schuster, NYC, 1992

Nash B. From Acupuncture to Zen, Hunter House, Alameda, CA, 1996

Olshevsky M, Noy S, Zwang M. The Manual of Natural Therapy, Facts on File, NYC, 1989

Pelton R, Overholser L. Alternatives in Cancer Therapy, Fireside of Simon and Schuster, NYC, 1994

Pierpaoli W, Regelson W, Colman C. The Melatonin Miracle, Simon & Schuster, NYC, 1995

Magic and Medicine of Plants, Readers Digest Association, Pleasantville, NY, 1986

Raso J. 'Alternative Healthcare', Prometheus Books, Amherst, NY 1994

Reid D. A Handbook of Chinese Healing Herbs, Shambhala, Boston, 1995

Saltman P, Gurin J, Mothner I. The California Nutrition Book, Little, Brown, and Company, Boston, MA, 1987

Sears B. The Zone, Harper-Collins, New York, 1995

Segen JC. The Dictionary of Modern Medicine, 2nd ed, Appleton & Lange, Stamford, CT, (in press)

Segen JC, Stauffer J. The Patient's Guide to Medical Testing, Facts on FIle, NYC (in press)

Segen JC. Current MedTalk, Appleton & Lange, Stamford, CT, 1995

Shealy CN. The Complete Family Guide to Alternative Medicine, Element Books Ltd, Shaftesbury, Dorset, 1996

Sleisenger MH, Fordtran JS, Eds. Gastrointestinal Disease, 5th ed, WB Saunders, Philadelphia, PA, 1993

Stedman's Medical Dictionary, 26th ed, Williams & Wilkins, Baltimore, MD, 1995

Strohecker J. Alternative Medicine–The Definitive Guide, Burton Goldberg Group, Future Medical Publishing, Puyallup, WA, 1994

Trattler R, Better Health Through Natural Healing, McGraw-Hill, NYC, 1985

Watson D, Dictionary of Mind and Body, André Deutsch Ltd, London, 1995

Weil A. Health and Healing, Houghton-Mifflin, NYC, 1983, 1995

Weil A. Natural Health, Natural Healing, Houghton Mifflin, NYC, 1995

Wilson JD, et al, Ed, Harrison's Principles of Internal Medicine, McGraw-Hill, NYC, 1991

# Sights on the Sixties

A volume in the series *Perspectives on the Sixties*

Edited by *Barbara L. Tischler*